Chapter 1

Comparing and
Defining a Complex World

No human culture is inaccessible to someone who makes the effort to understand, to learn, to inhabit another world.   —*Henry Louis Gates, historian*[1]

In this book we take a comparative approach to the study of Africa,
Asia, Latin America, and the Middle East. How should we refer to this immense collection of countries, people, and cultures composing approximately 80 percent of the
world's population? As you'll see, we are not the first to struggle with what's in a
name. In fact, in this fourth edition of the book, we have changed the title from *Comparative Politics of the "Third World"* to *Comparative Politics of the Global South.*
Some may argue this change was long overdue. This shift in terminology reflects not
only our ongoing discomfort with the "three worlds" terminology, but also a heightened recognition—by scholars, practitioners, citizens, and activists alike—that, despite its drawbacks, the concept of the "global south" is the least offensive and most
value-neutral label (despite some obvious geographic inaccuracies).[2] To understand
a bit of the controversy, let's begin with a short review of some of the terminology and
disputes surrounding characterizations of the majority of the world's population.

There are numerous labels we may employ. One of the most common (and indeed the most provocative) is "third world." Why? The term "third world" (*tiers
monde*) was coined by French demographer Alfred Sauvy. In a 1952 article, Sauvy
borrowed from eighteenth-century writer Emmanuel Joseph Sieyes to compare relatively poor countries of the world to the "third estate" (the people) at the time of the
French Revolution. Sieyes characterized the third estate as ignored, exploited, and
scorned. Sauvy characterized the third world similarly, but pointed out that it, like
the third estate, has the power to overcome its status.[3]

So what's so off-putting, then, about the term "third world"? First and foremost,
it is objectionable for both logical and emotional reasons. WORLD BANK* director

---

*Terms appearing in small capital letters are defined in the Glossary, which begins on p. 515.

Robert Zoellick has declared that there is no longer a third world.[4] Not only do critics of the term disdain the concept as unwieldy and obsolete, but they also fault it as distorting reality in attempting to geopolitically and economically classify a diverse group of countries.

And let's face it, "third world" can be fighting words. The phrase carries a lot of negative baggage. Many people cringe at hearing the term and avoid using it because, at the very least, it sounds condescending and quaintly racist. It is not unusual for "third world" to be flung as an insult. For some, the term suggests backwardness. Third world countries are often thought to play a peripheral role in the world, having no voice and little weight or relevance. That is certainly not the case, as this book will demonstrate.

The geopolitical use of the term "third world" dates back to the COLD WAR, the period of US-Soviet rivalry from approximately 1947 to 1989, reflecting the ideological conflict that dominated international relations. For decades following World War II, the rich, economically advanced, industrialized countries, also known as the "first world," were pitted against the Soviet-led, communist "second world." In this rivalry, each side described what it was doing as self-defense, and both the first and second worlds claimed to be fighting to "save" the planet from the treachery of the other. Much of this battle was over who would control the nonaligned "third world," which served as the theater for many Cold War conflicts and whose countries were treated as pawns in this chess game. Defined simply as the remainder of the planet—being neither first nor second—the concept of the third world has always been unwieldy, often bringing to mind countries that are poor, agricultural, and overpopulated.

Yet consider the stunning diversity that exists among the countries of every region of the world: surely they cannot all be lumped into a single category and characterized as such today. For example, how do we categorize China? It is clearly led by a communist regime (and therefore may be considered second world), but during the Cold War it viewed itself as the leader of the third world. What about Israel or South Africa? Because of the dramatic disparities within these countries, they can be categorized as third world or first, depending on where we look. The same can even be said for the United States. Visit parts of its cities, the rural south, or Appalachia, and you will find the so-called third world. And now, with the Cold War long over, why aren't the former republics of the Soviet Union included in most studies of the third world? Certainly the poorest of them are more third world than first.

The fact is, many countries fall between the cracks when we use the three-worlds typology. Some of the countries labeled third world are oil-rich, while others have been industrializing for so long that even the term "NEWLY INDUSTRIALIZING COUNTRIES" (NICs) is dated (it is still used, but has largely been replaced by "emerging economies"). Therefore, in appreciation of the diversity contained within the third world, perhaps it is useful to subdivide it, to allow for specificity by adding more categories. Under this schema, the emerging countries and a few others that are most appropriately termed "developing countries" are labeled "third world" (e.g., China, India, South Korea, Brazil, Mexico). "Fourth world" countries become those that are not industrializing, but have some resources to sell on the world market (e.g., Ghana, Bolivia, Egypt), or some strategic value that wins them a bit of foreign assistance. The label "less developed country" (LDC) is the best fit in most of these

cases, since it simply describes their situation and implies little in terms of their prospects for DEVELOPMENT. And finally, we have the "fifth world," which Henry Kissinger once callously characterized as "the basket cases of the world." These are the world's poorest countries. Sometimes known as "least–less developed countries" (LLDCs), they are very clearly under-developing. With little to sell on the world market, they are eclipsed by it. The poorest in the world, with the worst ratings for virtually every marker of human development, these countries are marginalized and utterly dependent on what little foreign assistance they receive.

Today it is more common to hear the STATES of these regions variously referred to as "developing countries," "less developed countries," or "under-developed countries." Currently in vogue are also the stripped-down, minimalist terms "low-income countries" (LICs), "high-income countries" (HICs), and even "low- and lower-middle-income countries" (LMICs). These are just a few of the labels used to refer to a huge expanse of territories and peoples, and none are entirely satisfactory. First, our subject—comprising four major world regions—is so vast and so heterogeneous that it is difficult to speak of it as a single entity. Second, each name has its own political implications and each insinuates a political message. For example, although some countries contained within these regions are better off than others, only an optimist would label all of them as "developing countries." Some of the countries we'll be looking at are simply not developing. They are under-developing—losing ground, becoming worse off.[5]

Those who prefer the term "developing countries" tend to support the idea that the capitalist path of free markets will eventually lead to peace and prosperity for all. Capitalism is associated with rising prosperity in some countries such as South Korea and Mexico, but even in these countries the majority of people have yet to share in many of its benefits. However, the relative term "less developed countries" prompts the question: Less developed than whom—or what? The answer, inevitably, is what we arbitrarily label "developed countries": the rich, industrialized states of Western Europe, Canada, and the United States, also known as "the West" (a term that, interestingly enough, includes Japan but excludes most of the countries of the Western Hemisphere).

Although the people who talk about such things often throw about the terms "developed" or "less developed" as a shorthand measure of economic advancement, often such names are resented because they imply that "less developed" countries are somehow lacking in other, broader measures of political, social, or cultural development. Use of the term "developing," or any of these terms for that matter, suggests that countries can be ranked along a continuum. Such terms can be used to imply that the West is best, that the rest of the world is comparatively "backward," and that the most the citizens of the rest of the world can hope for is to "develop" using the West as a model.

In the 2015 annual letter of the Bill and Melinda Gates Foundation, the famed investors turned philanthropists contended that such terminology has outlived its utility—why, for example, should Mozambique and Mexico be grouped together?[6] Critics contend that the terminology is intellectually lazy, outdated, and judgmental. The World Bank got rid of the "developing countries" terminology in 2016, in part to highlight measures of economic success, and in part to point out the importance of differences that exist within countries.[7] Ranking countries more precisely

on income data and other measures, the World Bank grouped Mexico, China, and Brazil each as "upper-middle-income countries," placing India, Pakistan, Bangladesh, and others in the category of "lower-middle-income," while Malawi remains "low-income" (prior to this change, all of these countries were framed as "developing").[8] The World Bank, as it phases out use of "developing" or "developed" world from within its databases, focuses less on general characterization and more on the priority of promoting sustainable development, our focus in Chapter 6.

Geography is the point of reference for some, including those who argue that the West developed only at the expense of the rest of the world. For these analysts, under-development is no natural event or coincidence. Rather, it is the outcome of hundreds of years of active under-development by today's developed countries. Some have captured this dynamic as the all-inclusive "non-Western world." As others have demonstrated, it is probably more honest to speak of "the West and the rest" if we are to use this kind of term, since there are many non-Wests rather than a single non-Western world.[9] At least "the West and the rest" is blatantly straightforward in its Eurocentric center of reference, dismissing 80 percent of the world's population and treating "the rest" as "other." In the same manner that the term "nonwhite" is demeaning, "non-Western" implies that something is missing. Our subject becomes defined only through its relationship to a more central "West."

Resistance to such treatment, and efforts to change situations, are sometimes referred to as the North-South conflict, or the war between the haves and the have-nots of the world. The names "North" and "South" are useful because they are seemingly stripped of the value judgments contained within most of the terms already described. However, they are as imprecise as the term "West," since "North" refers to developed countries, which mostly fall north of the equator, and "South" is another name for less developed countries, which mostly fall south of the equator. Similar to any dichotomy, this terminology invites illusions of superiority and "otherness," homogenizing differences and elevating one's own culture or lifestyle.

So, why has the phraseology of "global south" seemingly come into vogue? Some argue that it has long been the preferred term for what used to be called the third world, even if it must be "used elastically."[10] Used with increasing frequency within the United Nations in the 1970s, "global south" has, in many circles, replaced a three-worlds construct that became increasingly irrelevant after the collapse of the Soviet Union.[11] Even if today the metaphor is used to highlight both the empowerment and shared circumstances of many around the world, its origins, traced to the Brandt Commission reports of the early 1980s, are now viewed as patronizing in their call for the financial support of the "North" for modernization efforts undertaken within the "South."[12] Similar to each of the constructs just discussed, its lines are fuzzy, and we must recognize it for the created construct that it is. To the extent that it helps us grasp some of the common challenges and innovations of people and governments, and how some of these issues are viewed differently than from the vantage point of the developed north, the term "global south" may be useful, albeit imperfect.

Clearly none of the names we use to describe the countries of Africa, Asia, Latin America, and the Middle East are satisfactory, and any generalization is going to be limited. Even the terms "Latin America" and "Middle East" are problematic. Not all of Latin America is "Latin" in the sense of being Spanish- or Portuguese-speaking. Yet we will use this term as shorthand for the entire region south of the US bor-

der, including the Caribbean. And the idea of a region being "Middle East" only makes sense if one's perspective is distinctly European—otherwise, what is it "middle" to? The point is that most of our labels reflect some bias, and none of them are fully satisfactory. These names are all ideologically loaded in one way or another. Because there is no simple, clearly most appropriate identifier available, we will use each and all of them as markers of the varying worldviews presented in this text. Ultimately, we leave it to the reader to sift through the material presented here, consider the debates, and decide which arguments—and therefore which terminologies—are most representative of the world and therefore most useful.

What's to Compare?

In this introduction to the COMPARATIVE STUDIES of Africa, Asia, Latin America, and the Middle East, we take a different spin on the traditional approach in order to discuss much more than politics as it is often narrowly defined. As one of the social sciences, political science has traditionally focused on the study of formal political institutions and behavior. In this book, we choose not to put the spotlight on governments and voting patterns, party politics, and so on. Rather, we turn our attention to all manner of political behavior, which we consider to include just about any aspect of life. Of interest to us is not only how people are governed, but also how they live, how they govern themselves, and what they see as their most urgent concerns.

We employ a political interaction approach. It is an eclectic method that presents ideas from a variety of contemporary thinkers and theories. Our approach is multidisciplinary. We divide our attention among history, politics, society, and economics in order to convey more fully the complexity of human experience.[13] Instead of artificially confining ourselves to one narrow discipline, we recognize that each discipline offers another layer or dimension, which adds immeasurably to our understanding of the "essence" of politics.[14]

Comparative politics, then, is much more than simply a subject of study—it is also a means of study. It employs what is known as the comparative method. Through the use of the comparative method we seek to describe, identify, and explain trends—in some cases, even predict human behavior. Those who adopt this approach, known as comparativists, are interested in identifying relationships and patterns of behavior and interactions between individuals and groups. Focusing on one or more countries, comparativists examine case studies alongside one another. They search for similarities and differences between and among the elements selected for comparison. For example, one might compare patterns of female employment and fertility rates in one country in relation to those patterns in other countries. Using the comparative method, analysts make explicit or implicit comparisons, searching for common and contrasting features. Some do a "most similar systems" analysis, looking for differences between cases that appear to have a great deal in common (e.g., Canada and the United States). Others prefer a "most different" approach, looking for commonalities between cases that appear diametrically opposed in experience (e.g., Bolivia and India).[15] What is particularly exciting about this type of analysis is stumbling upon unexpected parallels between ostensibly different cases. Just as satisfying is beginning to understand the significance and consequences of the differences that exist between cases assumed to have much in common.

Most comparative studies textbooks take one of two roads. Either they offer case studies, which provide loads of intricate detail on a handful of states (often the classics: Mexico, Nigeria, China, and India; curiously, the Middle East is frequently ignored), or they provide a CROSS-NATIONAL ANALYSIS that purports to generalize about much larger expanses of territory. Those who take the cross-national approach are interested in getting at the big picture. Texts that employ it focus on theory and concepts to broaden our scope of understanding beyond a handful of cases. They often end up making fairly sweeping generalizations. The authors of these books may reference any number of countries as illustration, but at the loss of detail and context that come only through the use of case studies.

We provide both cross-national analysis and case studies, because we don't want to lose the strengths of either approach. We present broad themes and concepts, while including attention to the variations that exist in reality. In adopting this hybrid approach, we have set for ourselves a more ambitious task. However, as teachers, we recognize the need for both approaches to be presented. We have worked hard to show how cross-national analysis and case studies can work in tandem, how each complements the other. By looking at similar phenomena in several contexts (i.e., histories, politics, societies, economics, and international relations of the third world, more generally), we can apply our cases and compare them, illustrating the similarities and differences experienced in different settings.

Therefore, in addition to the cross-national analysis that composes the bulk of each chapter, we offer eight case studies, two from each of the major regions of the third world. For each region we include the "classics" offered in virtually every text that applies the case method to the non-Western experience: Mexico, Nigeria, China, and Iran. We offer these cases for the same reasons that so many others see fit to include them. However, we go further. To temper the tendency to view these cases as somehow representative of their regions, and to enhance the basis for comparison, we submit alongside the classics other, less predictable case studies from each region. These additional cases are equally interesting and important in their own regard; they are countries that are rarely (if ever) included as case studies in introductory textbooks: Peru, Zimbabwe, Egypt, and Indonesia. (See the maps and country profiles in Figures 1.2 to 1.9 at the end of this chapter.)

Through detailed case studies, we learn what is distinctive about the many peoples of the world, and get a chance to begin to see the world from a perspective other than our own. We can begin doing comparative analysis by thinking about what makes the people of the world alike and what makes us different. We should ask ourselves how and why such differences exist, and consider the various constraints under which we all operate. We study comparative politics not only to understand the way other people view the world, but also to make better sense of our own understanding of it. We have much to learn from how similar problems are approached by different groups of people. To do this we must consider the variety of factors that serve as context, to get a better idea of why things happen and why events unfold as they do.[16] The better we get at this, the better idea we will have of what to expect in the future. And we will get a better sense of what works and what doesn't work so well—in the cases under examination, but also in other countries. You may be tempted to compare the cases under review with the situation in your country. And that's to be encouraged, since the study of how others approach problems may offer us ideas on how to improve our own lives.

Comparativists argue that drawing from the experience of others is really the only way to understand our own systems. Seeing beyond the experience of developed countries and what is immediately familiar to us expands our minds, allows us to see the wider range of alternatives, and offers new insights into the challenges we face at the local, national, and international levels.

The greatest insight, however, comes with the inclusion of a larger circle of voices—beyond those of the leaders and policymakers. Although you will certainly hear the arguments of leaders in the chapters that follow, you will also hear the voices of those who are not often represented in texts such as this. You will hear stories of domination and the struggle against it. You will hear not only how people have been oppressed, but also how they have liberated themselves.[17] Throughout the following chapters, we have worked to include the standpoints and perspectives of the ostensibly "powerless": the poor, youth, and women. Although these people are often ignored by their governments, including the US government, hearing their voices is a necessity if we are to fully comprehend the complexity of the challenges all of us face. Until these populations are included and encouraged to participate to their fullest potential, development will be distorted and delayed. Throughout this book, in a variety of ways, we will give attention to these groups and their interests within our discussions of history, economics, society, politics, and international relations.

Cross-National Comparison: Recurrent Themes

As mentioned earlier, we believe that any introductory study of the global south should include both the specificity of CASE STUDY as well as the breadth of the cross-national approach. Throughout the chapters that follow, you will find several recurring themes (GLOBALIZATION, human rights, the environment, and disease), which will be approached from a number of angles and will serve as a basis for cross-national comparison. For example, not only is it interesting and important to understand the difference in the experience of AIDS in Zimbabwe as opposed to Iran, it is just as important to understand how religion, poverty, and war may contribute to the spread of the disease. In addition, in trying to understand the challenges of disease in the global south, we should be aware of its impact on development, how ordinary people are attempting to cope with it, and what they (with or without world leaders) are prepared to do to fight it.

In a variety of ways and to varying degrees, globalization, human rights abuse, environmental degradation, the emergence of new and deadly diseases, international migration, and the drug trade are all indicative of a growing world INTERDEPENDENCE. By interdependence we are referring to a relationship of mutual (although not equal) vulnerability and sensitivity that exists between the world's peoples. This shared dependence has grown out of a rapidly expanding web of interactions that tie us closer together. Most Americans understand that what we do as a nation often affects others—for better or worse. On the other hand, it is more of a stretch to get the average American to understand why we should care and why we need to understand what is happening in the world around us—even in far-off "powerless" countries. However, whether we choose to recognize it or not, it is becoming more and more difficult to escape the fact that our relationship with the world is a reciprocal one. What happens on the other side of the planet, even in seemingly less powerful countries, does affect us—whether we like it or not.

Figure 1.1   Global Village of 1,000 People

Imagine that the world is a village of 1,000 people. Who are its inhabitants?

600 Asians
150 Africans
110 Europeans
  90 Latin Americans and residents from across the Caribbean
  50 North Americans

Within this population, a total of 67 have earned a college degree.

The people of the village have considerable difficulty in communicating:

120 speak Mandarin Chinese
  50 speak Spanish
  50 speak English
  30 speak Arabic
  30 speak Hindi
  30 speak Bengali
  30 speak Portuguese
  20 speak Russian
  20 speak Japanese
620 speak other languages

Within this village, 860 are able to read and write (88 percent of males and 79 percent of females); 140 are considered illiterate; 220 own or share a computer; and 750 are cell phone users.

In this village of 1,000 there are

330 Christians
220 Muslims
140 Hindus
  70 Buddhists
120 who do not believe in other religions
120 who are not religious or do not identify themselves as being aligned with a particular faith.

One-third of these 1,000 people in the world village are children, and only 80 are over the age of sixty-five. Half of the children are undernourished. Just under half of the married women in the village have access to and use modern contraceptives. This year 28 babies will be born; 10 people will die, 3 of them from lack of food, 1 from cancer, and 2 of the deaths are of babies born within the year. With the 28 births and 10 deaths, the population of the village next year will be 1,018.

In this 1,000-person community, 200 people receive 75 percent of the income; another 200 receive only 2 percent of the income. Only 70 people own an automobile (although some of the 70 own more than one automobile). Of these 1,000 people, 870 have access to safe drinking water, 650 have access to improved sanitation (160 have no access to toilets), and 780 have access to electricity.

The village has 6 acres of land per person:

     700 acres are cropland
  1,400 acres are pasture
  1,900 acres are woodland
  2,000 acres are desert, tundra, pavement, and wasteland

Of this land, the woodland is declining rapidly; the wasteland is increasing. The other land categories are roughly stable. The village allocates 83 percent of its fertilizer to 40 percent of its cropland—which is owned by the richest and best-fed 270 people. Excess fertilizer running off this land causes pollution in lakes and wells. The remaining 60 percent of the land, with its 17 percent of the fertilizer, produces 28 percent of the food grains and feeds 73 percent of the people. The average grain yield of that land is one-third the harvest achieved by the richer villagers.

In this village of 1,000 people there are

5 soldiers
7 teachers
1 doctor
4 refugees driven from their homes by war or drought

Sources: Adapted from Donella H. Meadows, "If the World Were a Village of One Thousand People," https://populationpress.org, 2014; "100 People: A World Portrait," http://100people.org; and North-South Centre of the Council of Europe, "If the World Were a Village of One Thousand People," http://nscentre.org.

Globalization

The end of the Cold War opened a window of opportunity that has resulted not only in some dramatic political changes, but also in a closer INTEGRATION of the world's economies than ever before. As a result, the world is becoming increasingly inter-connected by a single, global economy. This transformative process is commonly de-scribed as globalization, and it is supported and driven by the full force of capitalism, seemingly unimpeded until now because of the absence of virtually any competing economic ideology. The world has experienced periods of corporate globalization be-fore (the last was associated with European imperialism). What is unique about the current cycle is the unprecedented speed with which globalization has torn down barriers to trade. It has also increased mobility, or cross-border flows of not only trade, but also capital, technology, information—and people. As it has before, tech-nology has driven this wave. The Internet is as symbolic of this era as the Berlin Wall was of the Cold War. Because of their mobility and global reach, MULTINA-TIONAL CORPORATIONS (MNCs) have been key actors (but hardly the only actors) in this globalization. This is a process that has rapidly unfolded and has been under no one's control. In fact, even some of its advocates have maintained that globalization may be out of control.[18]

For those who embrace globalization, its dynamism and power are part of its ap-peal. They consider globalization to be a largely benevolent process. They see it as the surest route to development and prosperity—it is even credited with sowing the seeds of DEMOCRACY worldwide. Because of globalization, no corner of the world remains isolated; new values are being spread that challenge traditional belief systems such as fatalism, elitism, and AUTHORITARIANISM. Poverty is alleviated as trade is increased and jobs are created; as the lines of communication are opened, we learn from and begin to accept one another. Ideally, globalization will help to make us more aware of our common interests, our mutual dependence. Among other things, it has brought people together to form the basis of the international environmental movement; it has enhanced scientific cooperation and raised human rights as a universal concern (which some refer to as "moral globalization" or the "globalization of dissent").[19]

According to its admirers, globalization is spilling over into a variety of areas, creating a "world village" based in cultural and political globalization. As it works to overcome the barriers between us, globalization enhances interdependence. It tightens the web of interrelationships that link the world's peoples. Social media no doubt facilitated the wave of protests, widely known as the Arab Spring, that swept much of North Africa and the Middle East in 2011. Thanks to globalization, this deepening interdependence is fostering a sense of community and sharing over the IDENTITY politics that once divided us by religion, ethnicity, language, and so on. (Although interestingly, some analysts who generally favor globalization argue that being wired for a free flow of information can actually produce hostility and anger. Much of this "shared" information promotes stereotyping and reinforces divisions.)[20]

Some analysts go even so far as to suggest that we are moving toward a "post-cultural" world, increasingly blurring the boundaries marking where one culture ends and another begins. They contend that globalization is not promoting homogenization and that it is not the same thing as Westernization; rather, globalization is promoting eclecticism and advancing our recognition of the world's diversity. So-called tradi-tional cultures aren't so traditional. None of the world's cultures have developed in a

vacuum, unaffected by outside forces. Even those concerned about globalization's impact acknowledge that cultures aren't static. They are always changing—globalization is just hurrying the process along.[21]

In this sense, perhaps it can be said that globalization is producing a more homogeneous world. Then again, antiglobalists maintain that a more homogeneous world means cultural devastation for many. Globalization is a cultural bulldozer. Already the dollar has become the de facto global currency, and English has become the de facto global language. One of the most visible signs of this is the spread of Western consumer culture. While this is something proglobalists generally celebrate, critics despise it as "coca-colonization."[22]

Critics argue that globalization isn't so much about interdependence as it is about furthering dependence. Dependence is a form of international interdependence—except that dependence is marked by an extreme power imbalance. On the left, antiglobalists point out that economic globalization is capitalist globalization, which means that corporations and the rich are being privileged over other social actors. The result isn't anything new. Poverty, the exploitation of the underdog, the erosion of labor and environmental standards, and the abuse of human rights all predate globalization. The difference is that globalization has accelerated and intensified these trends. Antiglobalists on the right embrace capitalism but condemn globalization for the harms they attribute to free trade, multiculturalism, and the loss of sovereignty. For them, globalization has contributed to bad trade deals that have exported jobs to "other" countries. Protectionist measures, even if they devolve into trade wars, are the solution.

Globalization's critics on the right and left condemn it for contributing to income inequality. And even the proponents of globalization acknowledge that it does create winners and losers; globalization brings profits but also problems. They also recognize that globalization is not a uniform process, and that its effects are more evident in some places than in others. Certainly, aspects of globalization such as deregulation or disappearing trade barriers are more obvious in some places than in others (e.g., the creation of trading blocs within Europe and North America). Thus far, globalization is uneven: it appears to have hardly touched the most economically underdeveloped countries in the world, such as those in the Sahel.[23] Yet this is increasingly the exception, and the rapid economic, sociocultural, and political change associated with globalization is the rule worldwide.

Its boosters argue that for better or worse, globalization is inexorable and inevitable; the integration of the world's peoples has gone so far that we can never go back. However, history shows us that even this massive force could be reversed by international events. NATIONALISM and economic downturns have in the past contributed to the end of previous cycles of globalization.[24]

Human Rights

The idea that humans share certain natural, universal, and inherent rights—simply because they are human—dates at least as far back as John Locke's *Two Treatises of Civil Government* (1690). The view that abusers should be held accountable for their wrongs, or that others should interfere with how a government treats its own citizens, has more recent origins. It was not until the systematic murder of millions under Adolf Hitler's Third Reich that the world became willing to challenge two domi-

nant principles of international relations: NONINTERVENTION, or the legal obligation to refrain from involvement in the internal affairs of other states, and sovereignty, the widely shared belief that states are the principal actors in international relations and as such are subject to no higher political authority.[25]

However, the Holocaust served as a catalyst to the development of what is now recognized as an international human rights movement. The Holocaust ostensibly taught us that in some cases the world must intervene against abusers and that state sovereignty must not always be held as sacrosanct. How a government treats its own people does affect the rest of us—and it is being increasingly recognized across the POLITICAL SPECTRUM that the persistent denial of human rights around the world must be reconceptualized as a security issue. If nothing else, respect for human rights is widely recognized as essential to international peace and stability. At least in theory, the international community accepts that it has a moral mandate to prevent the kinds of abuses associated with the genocide in Europe.

Over the first five decades following the Holocaust, the world community set out to develop a variety of international norms to promote human rights and to institutionalize safeguards against the recurrence of atrocities. Prominent in this effort was the creation of the UNIVERSAL DECLARATION OF HUMAN RIGHTS (UDHR) in 1948, which is widely recognized as the most authoritative and comprehensive of all international statements on human rights. Composed of thirty articles addressing a broad range of issues, the UDHR is accepted as setting the standards to which all states should aspire. The UDHR includes attention to what are sometimes known as "first-generation" or "blue" rights: civil and political rights, such as freedom of speech, freedom of religion, freedom from torture or cruel and unusual punishment, the right to DUE PROCESS, the right to SELF-DETERMINATION, and so on. These rights are based on the assumption that the individual should be protected against state actions that are unusual, arbitrary, or excessive. As long as the right to challenge the government's misuse of authority is permitted, other rights (such as freedom from torture) will be safeguarded. First-generation rights are considered by many people to be key to the enjoyment of all other rights. Yet the UDHR also recognizes the importance of "second-generation" or "red" rights: economic, social, and cultural rights, such as access to food, shelter, work, education, and healthcare. This conception of human rights, sometimes known as the "human-needs" approach, considers the aspects of existence necessary to secure the basic development of the person as primary. Proponents of second-generation rights maintain that a government's denial of basic needs is as much a violation of human rights as torture of dissidents.[26]

Although the governments of virtually every country in the world use the language of human rights and claim to believe in the inherent dignity of human beings, for many years the world has been divided over how most appropriately to define human rights. The governments of most developed countries, especially the United States, have traditionally argued that political and civil rights should be prioritized. They contend that these rights, which place an emphasis on liberty, should come first, because the enjoyment of such freedoms will enable the individual to ensure for him- or herself the provision of subsistence or red rights. Yet who cares about freedom of expression and the other blue rights when one's children are dying of hunger? As the former president of Senegal, Leopold Senghor, put it, "Human rights begin

with breakfast." He and others argue that those who seek to exclude red rights have it all wrong, since until people's basic rights, or certain minimal physical needs, are met, there can be no development—let alone enjoyment—of more ambitious rights, such as liberties. (Others point out that for low-income countries, government guarantees of food and housing are actually much more ambitious than the relatively "cost-free" guarantees of freedoms, such as expression and assembly. Nobel laureate Amartya Sen maintains that the right to freedom of speech is a precondition for all other rights, since famine, torture, and other abuses rarely occur in countries with democratic governments and a relatively free press.)[27]

The UDHR, whose drafters included Westerners and non-Westerners, attempts to get around this debate by proclaiming that human rights are indivisible, interdependent, and interrelated, and that all are necessary for the full realization of human potential. Not everyone agrees. According to the proponents of CULTURAL RELATIVISM, including those who support the "Asian values" argument, human rights (or moral claims) should be defined as the product of a particular society's cultural and historical experience. Therefore, according to the cultural relativists, the proponents of UNIVERSALISM are imposing their conception of human rights on others. For cultural relativists, political and civil rights are based in Western Enlightenment values, which have little appeal or relevance in Confucian cultures, wherein higher value is placed on order and discipline. Blue rights also uphold the rights of the individual over those of the community. This idea is unacceptable in many non-Western cultures, which often hold that the rights of the individual should be subordinated to those of the group, since the individual has no meaning apart from the community to which he or she belongs.[28]

Critics of the "Asian values" argument point to the complexity not only of Confucianism, which is not as conservative as many think, but also of Asian cultures themselves, of which there are a great variety and diversity. Asian cultures draw from many different influences, including Buddhism, which emphasizes individual freedoms and tolerance. Millions of non-Westerners, led by people such as Aung San Suu Kyi and Shirin Ebadi, reject arguments that political and civil rights or freedoms (such as freedom from torture) are uniquely Western. Many non-Western traditions view the individual and community as inseparable, and the relationship between the rights of the individual and the rights of the community as one of mutual obligation. While group rights can be used to restrict individuals, they can also exist to protect individual rights.[29]

As you might imagine, this and other debates over how best to define human rights have hamstrung international efforts to promote such rights. However, there is new momentum behind the human rights movement. Just as the Holocaust once spurred a concern with human rights, perhaps it was the specter of ethnic cleansing, its mass killing and systematic rapes, and the "too little, too late" responses in Bosnia and Rwanda, that have propelled this renewed interest. Once again, the human rights movement is developing—and not only toward finding other ways of holding accountable those responsible for such atrocities. The challenges associated with globalization have led to calls for expanding and refining the scope of human rights and including a third generation of "new" human rights. Debate has begun over whether other important values, such as rights to peace, development, and a safe and healthy environment (or "green" rights), qualify as human rights. Are rights to clean drink-

ing water and to live in safety legally enforceable claims, or merely "wishes"? The third generation of rights remains the subject of heated debate. Yet even for the older generations of rights, there remain enormous differences among the governments of the world over how to define human rights, how and when human rights law should apply, and what priority should be given to different categories of rights. While this highly politicized debate continues, it is increasingly common for analysts to return to the argument that is at the core of the Universal Declaration of Human Rights: that the distinction between human rights and human needs is an artificial one. Rather, civil, political, economic, social, and cultural rights are best understood as part of a "seamless web"—indivisible and interdependent.[30] In other words, all the rights discussed here are important because it is difficult to fully enjoy one category of rights without the security offered by the others.

The Environment

Along with globalization and human rights, the health of the planet is another issue of interdependence (and also one that is arguably everyone's business). Environmental issues will turn up in nearly all of the following chapters because the growing body of scientific evidence is becoming more difficult to refute. Development as it is currently being pursued, in both developed and less developed countries, is contributing to a morass of environmental problems that transcend national borders and whose management will require global cooperation. Climate change, rising sea levels, deforestation, desertification, loss of biodiversity, depletion of fisheries and destruction of coral reefs, toxic dumping, water shortages—these are just a few of the problems that will require international solutions.

Take, for example, the issue of deforestation. Even though the rate of global deforestation has slowed since the 1990s, it remains high, with a net loss of approximately 13 million hectares (an area about the size of Costa Rica) lost each year.[31] Put another way, the world has lost the equivalent of 1,000 football fields of forest per hour for the past twenty-five years.[32] However, thanks to local and international efforts, the rate of deforestation has actually decreased (from 16 million hectares destroyed annually in the 1990s). Indonesia and Brazil (which had the highest rates of loss a few years ago) have made particularly impressive efforts to slow the destruction of their forests. But deforestation is still a problem and it is most extensive in South America and Africa, where forests are hot spots for biodiversity (they contain hundreds of species within a single hectare, whereas the average hectare of forest typically contains a handful of species). With a loss of 70 percent of the natural cover protecting them in the past several decades, many of these species have become endangered or extinct. According to the United Nations Environment Programme (UNEP), species are becoming extinct at the fastest rate known in geological history, and this is directly tied to human activities.[33]

Related to deforestation and of similar cataclysmic impact is the threat posed by climate change. According to former UN SECRETARY-GENERAL Ban Ki-moon, it is the major, overriding environmental issue of our time, a growing crisis that will have economic repercussions but also consequences for human health, safety, food production, and security.[34] Others, such as Bill and Melinda Gates, question whether the relative progress we've achieved in recent decades could all be stifled by climate change.[35] Of central concern is the GREENHOUSE EFFECT, which is produced by the emission of what

have come to be known as greenhouse gases: carbon dioxide released by the burning of fossil fuels, as well as naturally occurring methane and nitrogen. Industrialization and economic GROWTH fueled by hydrocarbon-based energy systems (coal, oil, and natural gas) have contributed to the release of these gases, which have reached record highs. These greenhouse gases collect in the upper atmosphere, covering the planet in a blanket of sorts. Incoming heat from the sun penetrates this blanket but is then trapped by it. The effect is likened to a greenhouse, which traps heat indoors. In this sense, the growth of economies based on the consumption of fossil fuels has contributed substantially to global warming over the past fifty years.

While some scientists and politicians argue that global warming is not a human-made event, but naturally occurring and inevitable—part of a long cycle of alternating ice ages and periods of extreme heat—this is the minority view. The majority of the world's scientists agree that we are experiencing a global warming; the main issue under debate is how severe it will be—and how soon it will come. The Intergovernmental Panel on Climate Change (IPCC), the Nobel Peace Prize–winning group of more than 2,000 scientists from a hundred countries, claims to have amassed convincing evidence that climate change is already happening. The first years of the twenty-first century have been the hottest since records have been kept, and concentrations of greenhouse gases have reached unprecedented levels. The planet has warmed by 1.7 degrees Celsius between 1880 (when records were first kept) and 2015, and the heat is accumulating.[36] According to these scientists, there is overwhelming evidence that Earth's climate is undergoing dramatic transformation because of human activities. They call this "anthropogenic warming" and warn that it may continue for decades even if human-made emissions can be curbed.[37] If fossil fuel combustion continues even at twentieth-century levels, virtually every natural system and human economy will be at risk. Higher temperatures will mean rising seas from melting glaciers and ice sheets, more frequent and severe storms, and more intense droughts. These changes will alter every ecosystem on the planet, as pests and diseases will spread to areas where they were previously unknown. There is alarming evidence that we may have reached or surpassed tipping points that could lead to irreversible changes in major ecosystems. Nowhere have scientists observed greater immediate impacts of global warming than the Arctic Ocean, where temperatures have risen as high as 20 degrees Celsius above average, and sea ice has declined 28.5 percent below average—the lowest levels since records were first kept in 1979. No one knows the impact these changes may bring—due to the heat, dramatically higher levels of algae are being produced, impacting the food chain of the region (and beyond).[38] Climate change is exacerbating the misery of already poor areas, creating a vicious cycle in which poverty and environmental degradation coexist and accelerate through globalization.[39]

In a variety of ways, the globalization of the past few decades is just hastening processes that were already well under way. However, because of its speed, globalization is putting unprecedented pressure on the planet's capacities. Displaced rural populations are migrating into cities in search of livelihood, or into forests in search of new resources. This only contributes to the greenhouse effect, not just because the burning of forests releases more carbon dioxide into the atmosphere, but also because the loss of these forests means the loss of "pollution sponges," since forests absorb carbon dioxide and slow global warming. As low-income countries embrace

the developed-country model, pursuing growth at any cost, they will add to these problems. However, as it currently stands, the 20 percent of the world's population living in developed countries consumes 80 percent of the world's resources. In 2006 China surpassed the United States as the largest emitter of greenhouse gases (producing 22 percent of the world's total), but the United States is close behind, producing just under 20 percent of the emissions associated with global warming (India and Russia each contribute about 5 percent).[40] It is less developed countries (those who contribute the lowest levels of carbon dioxide and other gases) that are likely to feel the most severe impact of environmental devastation. Not only are they more vulnerable to many of its effects, but these low- and middle-income countries also are likely to lack access to the technologies that might ameliorate its impact. Over the past few years, a number of creative solutions based on cooperative efforts have been proposed for dealing with the environmental problems that we share. Unfortunately, finger-pointing and recriminations between advanced and emerging economies, and efforts by each to shift the burden of responsibility to the other, suggest that the international leadership (and funding) so desperately needed to address these problems will remain sorely lacking. Even progress achieved with the Paris agreement of 2015, as we discuss in Chapter 17, seems as though it may now be in peril, although the world community is likely closer to a consensus and shared responsibility than perhaps ever before.

Disease and Public Health

Just as environmental degradation is taking an increasing toll on all of us, so is disease. Yet again, it will be the poorest who are hit hardest and have the least capacity to cope with the challenge. Not only is there an income gap between developed and less developed countries, but there is also a health gap. A variety of threats come together to explain why mortality rates remain higher in low-income countries and why life expectancy is still relatively short in so many of them, even if we can note some progress in recent years: undernutrition, infectious diseases, and chronic debilitating diseases—are all associated with poverty. For example, the global mortality rate plummeted by 28 percent between 1990 and 2015, in large part because of efforts to increase maternal and newborn health, as well as to prevent and treat infectious diseases. Between 2005 and 2015, deaths attributed to malaria declined by 40 percent, and maternal mortality declined globally by 30 percent.[41] The challenge, though, is in maintaining these hard-won advances, especially in areas of deep insecurity. Observers note that public health is impacted by factors far beyond the purview of healthcare systems: war, natural disasters, economic downturns, influx of migrants—each can have a dramatic impact on the quality of life and the ability to manage disease in a given environment.[42]

It is well known that cardiovascular diseases are the biggest killers of adults worldwide, yet infectious diseases, such as tuberculosis, malaria, and HIV/AIDS, kill millions every year. HIV is a leading cause of death for women of reproductive age in low- and middle-income countries. The good news is that after four decades of fighting HIV/AIDS, it appears that the epidemic peaked in 1999 and the world has since begun to halt and reverse its spread. Between 2000 and 2015, new HIV infections fell by 35 percent; it is estimated that nearly 8 million lives were saved by awareness campaigns and international efforts to mitigate the impact of the disease.[43]

Of those needing treatment, more people than ever, 18 million, are receiving the medicines that can dramatically prolong and improve quality of life. And it is now possible to virtually eliminate mother-to-child transmission of HIV/AIDS. In many ways, our global investment in prevention and treatment is working. However, approximately 37 million people worldwide are living with HIV/AIDS, and a significant portion of them, 19 million, or close to 40 percent, don't know their status or are denied access to these medicines because of their cost. In 2009, for the first time, global funding for programs to treat and prevent HIV/AIDS flattened. It continued to decline, by 13 percent, between 2014 and 2015. If this trend continues and money dries up, clinics will close, people who need testing and treatment will be turned away, and the fragile progress that the world has made in dealing with this disease will be undermined.[44]

HIV/AIDS is by no means a problem unique to the global south, and the challenges associated with it vary by region. However, most people living with HIV/AIDS reside in lower-income countries (sub-Saharan Africa accounts for most of the global total of new HIV infections, though it is important to note that some regions of Africa, such as western Africa in general, are not as seriously affected as others, such as southern and eastern Africa).[45] Each country and region has its own particular mix of circumstances reflected by patterns of transmission. As we will see in Chapter 6, poverty is a major factor contributing to the spread of the disease.

The global health community faces increasingly complex tasks, as health challenges are compounded by environmental, political, and other weaknesses within the system. For example, the World Health Organization (WHO) reports that nearly one in four global deaths today is attributed to air, water, and soil pollution, or to effects from climate change.[46] As you might expect, environmental risks take an especially harsh toll on young children and older people. Additionally, low- and middle-income countries in Southeast Asia and the Western Pacific face an increased rate of deaths attributable to indoor and outdoor air pollution.[47] WHO data indicate that 92 percent of the world's population lives in places where air pollution exceeds recommended limits; the regions with the highest air pollution are Southeast Asia, the Eastern Mediterranean, and the Western Pacific.[48] Concern is so great that the UN has declared air pollution a public health emergency with "untold effects on future generations." The UN estimates that 3.3 million people around the world die prematurely due to the effects of air pollution every year—mostly in China, India, and Pakistan.[49]

Much of the challenge before us is in preparing to deal with the unknown: when Ebola burst onto the scene in 2014, there were very few scientists who were actively conducting research on responses to the hemorrhagic fever (even though the first case had been diagnosed in 1976). The WHO was slow in its response (waiting nearly eight months after it was clear the disease was resurfacing in large numbers before declaring a public health emergency).[50] The spread of this and other communicable diseases stresses already strained local (and international) systems. This stress extends to the medicines with which we treat such diseases: antibiotic resistance, which according to the UN is responsible for 700,000 deaths each year, is making some diseases untreatable. If this trend continues, such resistance will challenge human health, development, and even security, demanding a coordinated response across the medical, pharmaceutical, manufacturing, and even agricultural communities—especially in densely populated areas where livestock and humans have very close interaction.

The risk is that diseases with known remedies, such as the sexually transmitted disease gonorrhea, are increasingly unresponsive to traditional treatments.[51] As we sit on the cusp of the possible formal eradication of polio (as this book goes to press, Pakistan and Afghanistan are the only two countries reporting naturally occurring polio),[52] such a slide is indeed a haunting possibility.

Conclusion: It Depends on Whom You Ask

Let's put it flatly: there will be no simple answers to many of the questions we have raised here or will raise throughout the chapters that follow. The best we can do is to present you with a wide range of thinking and alternative perspectives on many of the challenges faced to some degree by all of us—but most directly by people living in low- and low-middle-income countries. In this book we will be looking at a series of issues of interdependence, such as the drug trade, migration, and arms transfers, from a number of angles. Before you make up your mind about any of the contending theories we present here, we ask that you judge each on its merits. We firmly believe that reflecting on another's point of view and considering more than one side of any story is the only way to begin to understand the complex social phenomena we now set out to discuss.

Linking Concepts and Cases

The information in this section is provided as a primer for the case studies we will be discussing throughout the rest of the book. Figures 1.2 through 1.9 should serve as a point of reference as you read about the histories, economies, and politics of the eight case studies introduced here. Throughout the book, we will return to the same countries, applying the ideas introduced in the conceptual chapters to the reality of their experiences.

Now It's Your Turn

From a simple examination of the statistical information that follows, what would you expect to be the key issue, or the most pressing problem, each country faces? What can a sketch such as this tell you about life in each of these eight countries? Which ones appear most similar, and in what ways? What are some of the most striking differences between these countries? What other information not included here do you consider deserving of attention? Why?

Notes

1. Henry Louis Gates, "'Authenticity' or the Lesson of Little Tree," *New York Times Review of Books,* November 24, 1991, p. 30.

2. For some examples of the lively terminological debate, see the special 25th anniversary issue of the *Third World Quarterly* 25, no. 1 (2004); the special issue of *The Global South* 5, no. 1 (Spring 2011); Marc Silver, "If You Shouldn't Call It the Third World, What Should You Call It?," National Public Radio, *Goats and Soda,* January 14, 2015, www.npr.org; Dayo Olopade, "The End of the 'Developing World,'" *New York Times,* February 28, 2014.

3. Alfred Sauvy, "Three Worlds, One Planet," *L'Observateur,* August 14, 1952.

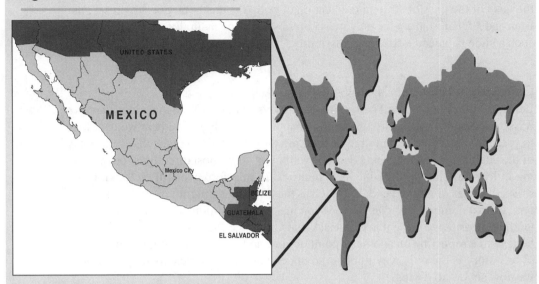

Figure 1.2   Mexico: Profile and Map

Formal name:	United Mexican States
Area, km^2:	1.97 million
Comparative area:	Slightly less than three times the size of Texas
Capital:	Mexico City
Establishment of present state:	September 18, 1810
Population:	123 million (2016)
Age under 15 years:	27%
Population growth rate:	1.2%
Fertility rate (children per woman):	2.3
Infant mortality (per 1,000 births):	12
Life expectancy:	76
HIV prevalence (adult):	0.2%
Ethnic groups:	Mestizo 62%, predominantly Amerindian 21%, Amerindian 7%, other 10%
Literacy rate:	95%
Religions:	Roman Catholic 83%, Protestant 8%, other 9%
GDP per capita (PPP):	$17,500
GDP growth rate:	2.5%
Labor, major sectors:	Services 62%, industrial 23%, agriculture 13%
Population in poverty:	52%
Unemployment rate:	4.4% (with extensive underemployment)
Export commodities:	Manufactured goods, oil and oil products, silver, fruits, vegetables, coffee, cotton
External debt:	$441.6 billion

Source: Central Intelligence Agency (CIA), World Factbook 2016.

Figure 1.3   Peru: Profile and Map

Formal name:	Republic of Peru
Area, km²:	1.28 million
Comparative area:	Almost twice the size of Texas; slightly smaller than Alaska
Capital:	Lima
Establishment of present state:	July 28, 1821
Population:	31 million (2016)
Age under 15 years:	27%
Population growth rate:	1%
Fertility rate (children per woman):	2.2
Infant mortality (per 1,000 births):	19
Life expectancy:	74
HIV prevalence (adult):	0.3%
Ethnic groups:	Amerindian 45%, mestizo 37%, white 15%, other 3%
Literacy rate:	95%
Religions:	Roman Catholic 81%, Evangelical 12.5%, other 3.3%, none 2.9% (2007)
GDP per capita (PPP):	$12,200
GDP growth rate:	3.3%
Labor, major sectors:	Services 57%, agricultural 26%, industrial 17% (2011)
Population in poverty:	26%
Unemployment rate:	5.2% (data for metropolitan Lima; with extensive underemployment)
Export commodities:	Copper, zinc, gold, crude petroleum, petroleum products
External debt:	$68 billion

Source: CIA, *World Factbook 2016.*

Figure 1.4   Nigeria: Profile and Map

Formal name:	Federal Republic of Nigeria
Area, km²:	923,768
Comparative area:	About six times the size of Georgia; slightly more than twice the size of California
Capital:	Abuja
Establishment of present state:	October 1, 1960
Population:	186 million
Age under 15 years:	43%
Population growth rate:	2.4%
Fertility rate (children per woman):	5.1
Infant mortality (per 1,000 births):	71
Life expectancy:	53
HIV prevalence (adult):	3.2% (2014)
Ethnic groups:	(More than 250 groups) Hausa and Fulani 29%, Yoruba 21%, Ibo 18%, Ijaw 10%, Kanuri 4%, Ibibio 3.5%, Tiv 2.5%
Literacy rate:	60%
Religions:	Muslim 50%, Christian 40%, indigenous beliefs 10%
GDP per capita (PPP):	$6,100
GDP growth rate:	2.7%
Labor, major sectors:	Agriculture 70%, services 20%, industrial 10% (1999)
Population in poverty:	70%
Unemployment rate:	24% (2011)
Export commodities:	Petroleum and petroleum products, cocoa, rubber
External debt:	$32 billion

Source: CIA, *World Factbook 2016*.

Figure 1.5 Zimbabwe: Profile and Map

Formal name:	Republic of Zimbabwe
Area, km²:	390,757
Comparative area:	Slightly larger than Montana
Capital:	Harare
Establishment of present state:	April 18, 1980
Population:	15 million
Age under 15 years:	38%
Population growth rate:	2.2%
Fertility rate (children per woman):	4
Infant mortality (per 1,000 births):	26
Life expectancy:	58
HIV prevalence (adult):	15%
Ethnic groups:	African 99.4% (Shona and Ndebele), other 0.4%, unspecified 0.2%
Literacy rate:	87%
Religions:	Protestant 76%, Roman Catholic 8%, other Christian 8%, other 7%
GDP per capita (PPP):	$2,100
GDP growth rate:	1.5%
Labor, major sectors:	Agriculture 66%, services 24%, industrial 10% (1996)
Population in poverty:	72% (2012)
Unemployment rate:	95% (2009)
Export commodities:	Platinum, cotton, tobacco, gold, ferroalloys, textiles/clothing
External debt:	$11 billion

Source: CIA, *World Factbook 2016*.

Figure 1.6   Egypt: Profile and Map

Formal name:	Arab Republic of Egypt
Area, km²:	1 million
Comparative area:	More than eight times the size of Ohio; slightly more than three times the size of New Mexico
Capital:	Cairo
Establishment of present state:	July 23, 1952
Population:	95 million
Age under 15 years:	33%
Population growth rate:	2.5%
Fertility rate (children per woman):	3.5
Infant mortality (per 1,000 births):	20
Life expectancy:	73
HIV prevalence (adult):	0.02%
Ethnic groups:	Egyptian 99.6%, other 0.4% (2006)
Literacy rate:	74%
Religions:	Muslim 90%, Christian 10%
GDP per capita (PPP):	$11,800
GDP growth rate:	4.2%
Labor, major sectors:	Services 47%, agriculture 29%, industrial 24%
Population in poverty:	25%
Unemployment rate:	12.8%
Export commodities:	Crude oil and petroleum products, fruits and vegetables, cotton, textiles, metal products, chemicals, processed food
External debt:	$45 billion

Source: CIA, *World Factbook 2016.*

Figure 1.7   Iran: Profile and Map

Formal name:	Islamic Republic of Iran
Area, km²:	1.65 million
Comparative area:	Almost 2.5 times the size of Texas; slightly smaller than Alaska
Capital:	Tehran
Establishment of present state:	April 1, 1979
Population:	83 million
Age under 15 years:	24%
Population growth rate:	1.2%
Fertility rate (children per woman):	1.8
Infant mortality (per 1,000 births):	37
Life expectancy:	71
HIV prevalence (adult):	0.1%
Ethnic groups:	Persian, Azeri, Kurd, Lur, Baloch, Arab, Turkmen and Turkic tribes
Literacy rate:	87%
Religions:	Shia Muslim 90–95%, Sunni Muslim 5–10%, other 0.3%, unspecified 0.4%
GDP per capita (PPP):	$17,300
GDP growth rate:	0%
Labor, major sectors:	Services 49%, industrial 35%, agriculture 16% (2013)
Population in poverty:	19% (2007)
Unemployment rate:	10.5%
Export commodities:	Petroleum, chemical and petrochemical products, fruits and nuts, carpets, cement, ore
External debt:	$5 billion

Source: CIA, *World Factbook 2016.*

Figure 1.8   China: Profile and Map

Formal name:	People's Republic of China
Area, km²:	9.60 million
Comparative area:	Slightly smaller than the United States
Capital:	Beijing
Establishment of present state:	October 1, 1949
Population:	1.37 billion
Age under 15 years:	17%
Population growth rate:	0.43%
Fertility rate (children per woman):	1.6
Infant mortality (per 1,000 births):	12.2
Life expectancy:	76
HIV prevalence (adult):	0.1% (2012)
Ethnic groups:	Han 92%, Zhuang 1%, other (including Hui, Manchu, Uighur, Miao, Yi, Tibetan, Mongol, Dong, Buyei, Yao, Bai) 7%
Literacy rate:	96%
Religions:	(Officially atheist), Buddhist 18%, Christian 5%, Muslim 2%, folk religion 22%, other 1%, unaffiliated 52%
GDP per capita (PPP):	$14,100
GDP growth rate:	6.9%
Labor, major sectors:	Services 36%, agriculture 34%, industrial 30% (2012)
Population in poverty:	6.1% (2013)
Unemployment rate:	4% (urban; substantial in rural areas)
Export commodities:	Electrical and other machinery, including data processing equipment, apparel, furniture, textiles, integrated circuits
External debt:	$958 billion

Source: CIA, *World Factbook 2016.*

Figure 1.9 Indonesia: Profile and Map

Formal name:	Republic of Indonesia
Area, km²:	1.9 million
Comparative area:	Slightly less than three times the size of Texas
Capital:	Jakarta
Establishment of present state:	August 17, 1945
Population:	258 million
Age under 15 years:	25%
Population growth rate:	0.9%
Fertility rate (children per woman):	2.1
Infant mortality (per 1,000 births):	24
Life expectancy:	73
HIV prevalence (adult):	0.5%
Ethnic groups:	Javanese 40%, Sundanese 16%, Malay 4%, Batak 4%, Madurese 3%, Betawi 3%, Minangkabau 3%, Buginese 3%, Bantenese 2%, Banjarese 2%, Balinese 2%, Acehnese 1%, Dayak 1%, Sasak 1%, Chinese 1%, other 15% (2010)
Literacy rate:	94%
Religions:	Muslim 87%, Christian 7%, Roman Catholic 3%, Hindu 2%, other 1%
GDP per capita (PPP):	$11,100
GDP growth rate:	4.8%
Labor, major sectors:	Services 48%, agriculture 39%, industrial 13% (2012)
Population in poverty:	11% (2014)
Unemployment rate:	6%
Export commodities:	Mineral fuels, boilers, machinery and mechanical parts, electric machinery, iron and steel, foodstuffs
External debt:	$316 billion

Source: CIA, *World Factbook 2016.*

4. Lesley Wroughton, "'Third World' Concepts No Longer Relevant," Reuters, April 14, 2010.

5. Andre Gunder Frank, *Capitalism and Underdevelopment in Latin America* (New York: Monthly Review, 1967); United Nations Conference on Trade and Development (UNCTAD), "The Least Developed Countries Report 2015," http://unctad.org.

6. Bill Gates and Melinda Gates, *Our Big Bet for the Future: 2015 Gates Annual Letter,* Bill and Melinda Gates Foundation, 2015, www.gatesnotes.com.

7. Matthew Lynn, "Why the Title of 'Developing Country' No Longer Exists," *The Telegraph* (London), May 23, 2016, telegraph.co.uk.

8. International Monetary Fund (IMF), "Proposed New Grouping in WEO Country Classifications: Low-Income Developing Countries," Policy Paper, June 3, 2014, www.imf.org; Kiran Kabtta Somvanshi, "World Bank to Change Classification of Countries; India Will Now Be Called Lower-Middle Income," *Economic Times* (India), May 31, 2016, http://economictimes.indiatimes.com.

9. Samuel P. Huntington, *The Clash of Civilizations and the Remaking of World Order* (New York: Simon and Schuster, 1996).

10. Jacqueline Anne Braveboy-Wagner, *Institutions of the Global South* (New York: Routledge, 2009), p. 1.

11. Caroline Levander and Walter Mignolo, "Introduction: The Global South and World Dis/Order," *Global South* 5, no. 1 (Spring 2011), p. 3.

12. Arif Dirlik, "Global South: Predicament and Promise," *Global South* 5, no. 1 (Spring 2011), pp. 13–14.

13. Naomi Chazan, Peter Lewis, and Robert Mortimer, *Politics and Society in Contemporary Africa* (Boulder: Lynne Rienner, 1999).

14. Frank L. Wilson, *Concepts and Issues in Comparative Politics: An Introduction to Comparative Analysis* (Upper Saddle River, NJ: Prentice Hall, 1996).

15. David J. Elkins and Richard E. B. Simeon, "A Cause in Search of Its Effect, or What Does Political Culture Explain?," *Comparative Politics* 11, no. 2 (January 1979).

16. Monte Palmer, *Comparative Politics: Political Economy, Political Culture, and Political Interdependence* (Itasca, IL: Peacock, 1997).

17. Colin Leys, *Underdevelopment in Kenya: The Political Economy of Neo-Colonialism, 1964–1971* (London: Heinemann, 1975).

18. Thomas Friedman, *The Lexus and the Olive Tree* (New York: Farrar, Straus and Giroux, 1999).

19. Howard J. Wiarda and Harvey F. Kline, *An Introduction to Latin American Politics and Development* (Boulder: Westview, 2001); Austin Sarat and Thomas R. Kearns, "The Unsettled Status of Human Rights: An Introduction," in *Human Rights: Concepts, Contests, Contingencies,* ed. Austin Sarat and Thomas R. Kearns (Ann Arbor: University of Michigan Press, 2001); Edward W. Said, *Reflections on Exile* (Cambridge: Harvard University Press, 2001).

20. Thomas L. Friedman, "Global Village Idiocy," *New York Times,* May 12, 2002.

21. Joshua S. Goldstein, *International Relations,* 4th ed. (New York: Longman, 2001).

22. Ibid.; Michael E. Porter, "Attitudes, Values, Beliefs, and the Microeconomics of Prosperity," in *Culture Matters: How Values Shape Human Progress,* ed. Lawrence E. Harrison and Samuel P. Huntington (New York: Basic, 2000).

23. Friedman, *The Lexus and the Olive Tree.*

24. Ibid.

25. Jack Donnelly, *International Human Rights* (Boulder: Westview, 1998).

26. Richard H. Ullman, "Human Rights: Toward International Action," in *Enhancing Global Human Rights,* ed. Jorge I. Domínguez, Nigel S. Rodley, Bryce Wood, and Richard Falk (New York: McGraw-Hill, 1979).

27. Quoted in Michael Ignatieff, *Human Rights as Politics and Idolatry* (Princeton: Princeton University Press, 2001).

28. The UDHR gives equal time to both individual and group rights; it recognizes that protections, privileges, and opportunities not only are for individuals, but also should extend to the family, community, nation, and other groups.

29. Amartya Sen, "Democracy as a Universal Value," *Journal of Democracy* 10, no. 3 (July 1999); Ignatieff, *Human Rights as Politics and Idolatry*.

30. Vojin Dimitrijevic, "Human Rights and Peace," in *Human Rights: New Dimensions and Challenges,* ed. Janusz Symonides (Brookfield, VT: Ashgate, 1998); Ullman, "Human Rights."

31. World Bank, "Forests: Overview," September 26, 2016, www.worldbank.org.

32. Ashley Kirk, "Deforestation: Where Is the World Losing the Most Trees?," *The Telegraph* (London), March 23, 2016, www.telegraph.co.uk.

33. "Deforestation in Decline but Rate Remains Alarming, UN Agency Says," UN News Centre, March 25, 2010, www.un.org; Elizabeth Mygatt, "World's Forests Continue to Shrink," Earth Policy Institute, April 4, 2006, www.earth-policy.org; United Nations Environment Programme (UNEP), "About International Year of Biodiversity," www.unep.org.

34. UNEP, "Climate Change: Introduction," www.unep.org.

35. Gates and Gates, *Our Big Bet for the Future*.

36. Justin Gillis, "Short Answers to Hard Questions About Climate Change," *New York Times,* November 28, 2015.

37. Steve Connor, "Global Warming Fastest for 20,000 Years—and It Is Mankind's Fault?," *The Independent* (London), May 4, 2006; "Intergovernmental Panel on Climate Change," *New York Times,* February 9, 2010; Al Gore, "We Can't Wish Away Climate Change," *New York Times,* February 27, 2010, www.nytimes.com.

38. Carl Zimmer, "Global Warming Alters Arctic Food Chain, Scientists Say, with Unforeseen Results," *New York Times,* November 22, 2016.

39. Lester R. Brown, foreword to *State of the World 2001,* ed. Lester R. Brown and Linda Starke (New York: Norton, 2001); Christopher Flavin, "Rich Planet, Poor Planet," in Brown and Starke, *State of the World 2001;* UNEP, "Climate Change: Introduction."

40. Darren Samuelson, "China: We're No. 1 in Greenhouse Gas Emissions," *Politico,* November 24, 2010, www.politico.com.

41. "The Global Burden of Disease," *The Economist,* October 13, 2016, www.economist.com.

42. Susan Brink, "Global Health Forecast for 2016: Which Diseases Will Rise . . . or Fall?," National Public Radio, *Goats and Soda,* January 4, 2016, www.npr.org.

43. "Funding for HIV and AIDS," Avert, November 2, 2016, www.avert.org; World Health Organization (WHO), "HIV/AIDS Fact Sheet," July 2016, www.who.int.

44. Global Fund, "HIV and AIDS," 2016, www.globalfund.org; "Funding for HIV and AIDS," Avert.

45. "Global HIV and AIDS Statistics," Avert, November 2, 2016, www.avert.org.

46. WHO, "An Estimated 12.6 Million Deaths Each Year Are Attributable to Unhealthy Environments," March 15, 2016, www.who.int.

47. Ibid.

48. WHO, "WHO Releases Country Estimates on Air Pollution Exposure and Health Impact," September 27, 2016, www.who.int.

49. Doug Bolton, "Air Pollution Is Now a Global 'Public Health Emergency,'" *The Independent* (London), January 19, 2016, www.independent.co.uk.

50. Brink, "Global Health Forecast."

51. Maryn McKenna, "How We'll Tackle Diseases That Are Becoming Untreatable," *National Geographic,* September 22, 2016, www.nationalgeographic.com.

52. Brink, "Global Health Forecast."

PART ONE
Historical Legacies

How does one possibly condense thousands of years of the histories of four vast and diverse regions into a few chapters? It is not a simple proposition, but it is a necessary one. For all their differences, there are some experiences generally shared among these regions, and we will draw your attention to some common patterns. In order to make this broad sweep of time more comprehensible, we'll be speaking in generalities. We will illustrate with some specific examples throughout the chapters. However, as much as possible, we have attempted to avoid a long list of names and dates. At the risk of leaving out some exceptions to the rule, we believe that it is important to develop a general sense of the history of these regions. It is only with a sense of the full range of experience that one can go on to understand the complex issues that characterize life in the global south today.

The most renowned historians of our time tell us that there is much still unknown about early human history. Dating back over the past 2 million years or so, much of world history is still incomplete, and (with a few exceptions) this is very much the case for the global south. Unfortunately, this lack of information has provided fertile ground for the development of myths, stereotypes, and distortions—many of which continue to be popular today. As you will see, many of these beliefs—that the peoples of the global south made no contributions, had no achievements, had no history—were used by others to justify enslavement, conquest, and domination. Denials of the contributions of the global south and portrayals of its citizens as pagan, barbaric, warlike, or even childlike in some cases, are widely denounced today. For years, historians have worked diligently to repair the damage done by colonial apologists. A more balanced representation of the past is important work for its own sake. But it is also crucial that these histories be reconstructed because so often colonizers did everything they could to destroy all records of them. A greater understanding of the tremendous variety of human experience may not only help to restore the sense of identity that was taken from colonized peoples—it may also serve as a source of inspiration for indigenous solutions to some of the problems we must face today.

In their zeal to correct for the wrongs of the past, some historians have over-compensated and ended up providing an equally distorted version of history. Some adopted the values of their colonizers and focused only on the "great civilizations" or EMPIRES of Africa, Asia, Latin America, and the Middle East. They ignored the vast array of smaller (but not lesser) forms of social organization. Yet the regions we are studying were inhabited for thousands of years by many different groups of people, with different ways of life. Some lived in relative isolation and some had long histories of contact with other peoples across great distances—well before these territories were "discovered" by white men. In fact, much of the global south was integrated on some level into larger regional and even transcontinental networks of trade.

However, in their efforts to correct negative distortions, some historians provided overly romantic views of these empires, extolling only their virtues and portraying the world as it was before the arrival of Europeans as some sort of golden age of peace and plenty. Most analysts today agree that neither portrayal is accurate. There is fairly wide agreement that each extreme oversimplifies. Because humans populated these societies, it is fair to assume that they were neither all good nor all bad. Most historians currently embrace a more balanced approach that seeks to understand these societies in all their complexity. And that complexity includes attention to the vast diversity of societies that existed in the long stretch of history we refer to as "precolonial"—not just empires or small bands of hunter-gatherers, but also everything in between.

Chapter 2

Precolonial History:
What Once Was, and
Why It Matters

The past reappears because it is a hidden present.   —*Octavio Paz, writer*[1]

One way of conceptualizing the many different ways in which humans organize themselves into groups is to picture a continuum. Large, hierarchical, centralized societies (or EMPIRES) lie at one end of this continuum, and much smaller, more egalitarian, decentralized societies are located at the other end; most societies fall somewhere in between, containing elements of the two more extreme types. Without valuing one form of organization over another, anthropologists often make distinctions between STATE SOCIETIES and STATELESS SOCIETIES. Whereas the great empires have drawn most of the attention of archaeologists and historians, increasingly we are learning about somewhat smaller STATES. Anthropologists tell us that our earliest human ancestors lived in stateless societies. This system of organization has largely disappeared, as its members have been pushed into the most inhospitable environments or absorbed by larger groups. Yet both state and stateless societies could be found in Africa, Asia, Latin America, and the Middle East at the time of European conquest. Consequently, all these systems deserve attention, as no single type can be considered representative of these vast regions.

Stateless Societies

It is the democratic character of stateless societies that observers frequently find most striking. Relatively speaking, in stateless societies power is shared among the members of the group (often but not always both male and female). Also known as ACEPHALOUS SOCIETIES, they have no full-time political leaders, chiefs, presidents, or monarchs. It is not uncommon for elders to guide the affairs of the group. Or a member of the community known for his or her prowess in war or some other talent might serve on a temporary basis to lead communities in a certain function (military, religious, or economic). However, for these groups there is no tradition of a supreme

ruler who governs continuously and beyond their immediate area of settlement. Unlike state systems with their courts, retinues, full-time militaries, and so on, in stateless societies people's day-to-day lives are conducted without interference from "government" as we know it.

Yet no society is truly stateless. Even in these noncentralized societies, there are widely accepted rules that provide a basis for the orderly functioning of the community. Government might appear to be more informal, in that there are no palaces, courthouses, or government buildings of any kind. However, this system is actually highly organized and there are often harsh penalties for violations of the public good. Within stateless societies, a variety of associations (such as all-male or all-female secret societies or age grades) are based on kinship, or family relationships. They exist to settle disputes among members, forge unity, and maintain order. These often-complicated arrangements promote cooperation, and time-honored rules allow families to draw on the labor they need in times of hardship. A web of kinship ties forms the basis for this kind of organization. All members of the extended families who make up the community know that the survival of all is based on this system of mutual aid and obligation.[2]

A strong sense of community pervades stateless societies, and exists among small bands or tribal groups of 20 to 200 people. Stateless societies are renowned for their egalitarianism. Relatively speaking, there are no divides based on CLASS, no rich and poor. Often working as hunter-gatherers who migrate in seasonal cycles, they rarely establish themselves in one place for long, nor do members produce or accumulate wealth above the bare necessities. Whether primarily composed of hunter-gatherers or small farmers, stateless societies are often associated with subsistence economies. However, the extreme hardship such groups live under today is not traditional—they have been pushed to the most inhospitable environmental margins. Life in such societies was not always tenuous. Many hunter-gatherers preferred what they saw as the good life compared to the hard work and risk involved in food production.[3]

Based on their intimate knowledge of the resources available, the members of stateless societies employed a wide range of techniques to support themselves. Going back at least 3,000 years, statelessness is known to have existed among pastoral populations as well as more settled populations practicing slash-and-burn techniques and shifting cultivation. Some groups, such as the Guarani of Brazil, lived off of some combination of these activities. This sense of communalism and egalitarian sharing of resources based on kinship was central to the early success of wet-rice cultivation in Southeast Asia.[4] Stateless societies were identified in the sierras of northern Mexico and in the pampas of South America, as well as in the Amazon Basin.

Small, highly mobile hunter-gatherer populations often lived alongside pastoralists and larger groups of sedentary farmers in symbiotic relationships. There is a great deal of evidence of the interpenetration and complementarity of hunter-gatherer groups by food producers (and vice versa). At times, relations could be described as cooperative, as hunter-gatherer groups like the San, or the !Kung of southern Africa, traded game and other goods such as wild honey for farm products and implements such as nets or other technologies. Trade was also important for forest farmers, such as the Ibo of Nigeria. Through village markets, trading has long been a tradition for women of state and stateless societies in much of western Africa.[5]

However, at other times, relations between these neighbors turned hostile. Conflicts could arise over any number of matters, most notably access to resources. Especially during times of environmental stress, it was not uncommon for settled farmers to come into conflict with pastoralists over land, as herds might destroy a field or farmers might encroach on prime pasture. Like hunter-gatherers, pastoralists did not generally form states, but they did sometimes take them over by conquest. Pastoralists, organized and unified under a strong central regime, were known to raid settled populations. For example, Turkic nomads and other warriors on horses repeatedly swept into India to plunder sedentary societies. Herding populations such as the Masai of eastern Africa had a number of advantages, which enabled them, as well as larger, more centrally organized societies such as the Zulu (southern Africa), to overwhelm their stateless or less centrally organized neighbors. Similarly, the Aztecs started out as a small group of tough nomads who made alliances to conquer sedentary groups. Often, sedentary societies found it necessary to form larger political groupings, to make alliances and take common action in self-defense. They might erect a walled town at the center of their farmlands to serve as a refuge against raids from their neighbors. The need for defense was one of the most common factors behind the development of states.[6]

State Societies

Historians continue to disagree about the causal relationship between population booms and increased food production. It is still a chicken-or-egg question: Does growth in the production of cereals such as rice, millet, and maize contribute to a population boom? Or do population booms necessitate an intensification of agricultural production? Either way, the two factors are clearly associated with the development of state societies. Once production is increased to the point of surplus, time is freed up for some people to work in capacities other than food production, including as full-time political leaders. When this happens, we begin to see more social stratification. There are divisions based on wealth, and clear differences between the rulers and the ruled. A merchant class of traders emerges, markets grow, and trade becomes more regularized. In state societies in all regions, the craftwork produced by an artisan class of weavers, potters, and metal- and woodworkers was highly prized. For example, the Chibcha of Colombia were known for their magnificent gold work, recognized as perhaps the finest in the ancient Americas.[7]

At this intermediate level of social organization, clearly a state society but not an empire, government is described as comprising relatively simple small states or chiefdoms. As states grow larger we see a more centralized political organization and more complex forms of government supported by bureaucracies with increasingly specialized functions such as ambassadors, harbor masters, special judges, treasurers, tax collectors, and so on. Commercial city-states dominated the trade in the Southeast Asian archipelago. Often state societies were absorbed into larger empires in their efforts to monopolize trade. The Swahili city-states of the eastern coast of Africa, such as Pemba, Mombasa, and Zanzibar, were autonomous and loosely linked through commercial ties (until they were all brought under the Omani Empire). Similarly, the city-states of Mesopotamia were eventually integrated into a single, powerful entity to ensure the security of trade routes.[8]

States of this size existed long before the conquest of Latin America, especially in the circum-Caribbean area (Panama, Costa Rica, northern Colombia, Venezuela, Puerto Rico, Jamaica, and Cuba). A paramount chief or king arose (in some cases chosen by election, in other cases because of some exceptional talent or charisma, magical powers, skills as a protector, etc.) and was assisted by councils drawn from the heads of the lineages composing the village. At this level of organization, the chief's rule was not absolute. He was limited by his advisers and required to consult the council, although the power of the council varied by state. Often in state societies in Africa and Southeast Asia, decisions were reached by consensus between a king and a council. After lengthy deliberations, the king would pronounce a final decision representing a compromise of views.[9]

In some cases kings had veto powers and could disregard the consensus of deliberations. Elsewhere, if the council disagreed with the chief's decisions, it could give counter-orders and seek to unseat him. In the Oyo kingdoms of western Africa, a leading minister could command an extremely unpopular king to commit suicide on the basis that the people, the earth, and the gods rejected his rule. There are examples of tyrants in such societies, but generally speaking, rulers still depended on the support of the population. Kings were respected as long as they fulfilled their responsibilities as protectors and providers. There were usually no standing armies to help kings impose their will, and abuses risked reprisals. Therefore, in some states at least, there were traditional checks on the rulers' powers.[10]

Empires

Historians tell us that the differences between chiefdoms and larger, more complex kingdoms or empires are difficult to draw. Certainly empires are distinguished by size of the territories and populations they control. Beyond this, the difference is mostly a matter of degree, as empires are in the simplest sense an expansion and deepening of tendencies found in chiefdoms.[11] The former empires of what is now called the global south greatly resembled more modern empires in terms of size of population or expanse of territory, use of official religions, or conquest of smaller states. Larger kingdoms often developed from these smaller states. Some were very large: historians estimate that the Aztecs controlled a population of nearly 25 million people in the early sixteenth century. Europeans were often surprised at how much the empires they encountered were like the ones at home. In fact, the Aztecs dominated a total area not much smaller than that of Spain. Hernan Cortés wrote that the Aztecs lived much like people in Spain, in terms of harmony and order, and that it was remarkable to see what they had achieved. The Spanish conquerors of Cuzco, the Inca capital, described it as beautiful, with buildings as fine as those in Spain.[12]

The oldest settled communities developed intensive agriculture along rivers, in oases, or in coastal areas. The Nile, the Tigris and Euphrates, the Yellow, and the Niger Rivers were centers of early civilization. The Fertile Crescent of ancient Palestine and Babylon was long accepted as the earliest site for mass cultivation. Yet there are reports of early kingdoms emerging in coastal and delta regions in other regions as well, such as the Niger Bend of western Africa. In several different parts of the world, over thousands of years, people domesticated wild plants or adopted new ones. It is becoming increasingly clear that at various times and places there were

also revolutions in food production—and not all of these crops and methods have a Middle Eastern origin. In the Fertile Crescent, as in other food-producing "homelands" such as China, the Andes, along the Nile, in Amazonia, and in Mesoamerica, it was common that once a mainstay of the diet was perfected, agriculture spread swiftly across the region, in some cases to other continents.[13]

The Egyptian Empire, one of the preeminent powers in the world for over 2,000 years, was based on the soils of the Nile floodplain. It maximized the benefits of the Nile by building canals, dikes, and embankments. Elsewhere as well, empires developed in the most successful areas of food production. Funan, the first empire in Southeast Asia, became rich off the rice from the Mekong Delta. The Chinese Empire began on the Yellow River plain, and is made up of an uninterrupted succession of two dozen dynasties over 4,000 years. Many other empires were also long-lived; Kush, although it influenced and was influenced by Egypt, flourished for over 1,000 years as an original African civilization, and many other empires in the four regions of study survived for hundreds of years. In Latin America, Mesoamerica is often cited as a cradle of civilization. There the Olmecs, Maya, and Aztecs attained remarkable achievements in a variety of pursuits. The desert coasts of Peru and later its highlands became the economic base for the Inca. Food production increased there in part because the indigenous peoples developed irrigation systems that allowed for higher productivity. Moreover, centralized states could compel the cooperation necessary to extend farmlands. These large states could harness the energy of larger populations through the creation of public works programs. Historians argue that the huge projects that contributed to a boom in production required strong and centralized governments and the extension of authority over larger areas.[14]

The production of surpluses meant an increase in the volume and types of goods available for trade. Increased trade not only created the need for greater political organization, but also financed the increasingly complex activities of evolving states. Whereas the trade of some states was land-based, other emerging empires turned to the seas. Commercial kingdoms situated on the coasts or at the edges of the desert were often based almost exclusively on commerce. Their power depended upon a reliable means of transport (navigable waterways or beasts of burden) and their ability to secure routes. For hundreds of years a lucrative overland trade was based on cloth and beads, silks, gold, ivory, and slaves as caravan routes linked Europe, Africa, the Middle East, and Asia. For example, the trans-Saharan trade lasted for over 1,000 years and financed the great empires of Ghana, Mali, and Songhay in western Africa, whose wealth was based on monopoly control and taxation of the gold passing through their domains.[15]

Seafaring states also amassed great riches. For example, Srivijaya, considered to be the only maritime state among the Southeast Asian classical states, was a commercial power taking revenues from passing trade. Its strategic location allowed Srivijaya to dominate maritime activity and patrol the archipelago around the Malacca Strait, one of the most significant links in the world trading system. As the dominant power in the area, Srivijaya controlled piracy, provided harbor facilities for shipbuilding and repair, and offered reprovisioning and warehousing services—all in addition to its business in camphor, bird nests, perfumes, pearls, and peppers and spices, among other goods.[16]

Figure 2.1   Early Non-Western Empires

Determined to maintain control over this strategically important network of sea-lanes, China and Southeast Asia were pioneers in the development of early naval capacities. Their accomplishments in this area were so substantial that China is considered to have been far ahead of any country in the world in the development of the sailing ship and navigational technology until at least the fifteenth century. Shipbuilding and naval activity were especially common in the Southeast Asian archipelago. Some ships were up to 120 meters long and large enough to carry 500 to 1,000 people. In the fifteenth century, China sent treasure fleets with hundreds of ships across the Indian Ocean—decades before Christopher Columbus's three ships made their way to the Americas. There is evidence that Indonesians and possibly the Chinese traveled as far west as Madagascar. Some historians believe Asian sailors may have traveled to the Cape of Good Hope, or even around it, long before Europeans did.[17]

However, as early as the second century B.C.E., Arab middlemen conducted much of the trade between East Africa and Asia. From the seventh century through the twelfth the Muslim trade network was vast, and various Muslim empires functioned as free trade areas. Their central position between East and West gave them a decisive advantage in the various long-distance trades at the center of the world economy for hundreds of years. Through their commercial activities Muslim traders disseminated technological innovations and greatly advanced the areas of navigation, shipbuilding, astronomy, and geography. These coastal merchants visited the Swahili city-states on a sea trade governed by the monsoon winds. Many stayed on and intermarried with African women, forming an ELITE class of merchants on East Africa's coasts.[18]

While a corps of diplomats or ambassadors was key to maintaining stable relations along this trade, an interest in protecting or expanding trade and the accumulation of wealth also contributed to the development of another institution common to the world's empires: full-time militaries. Some kingdoms did not have standing armies. Most soldiers were actually farmers or herders who provided their own weapons and provisions. Other states, such as China by the fourth century B.C.E., had professional armies. In western Africa, Mali was renowned for its disciplined cavalry. It had horses and coats of chain mail long before its neighbors. Some Indian kingdoms, such as the Mauryan, had a cavalry of elephants and chariots. Ghana was said to have had an army of 200,000 men, including 40,000 archers. And the Ottoman militaries became regarded as a state within a state, so powerful that they could make and unmake rulers. Similar corps, such as the Mameluks, ruled Egypt for over 200 years.[19]

Where warfare was endemic, its frequency changed the relative importance of the military, which became the core of some states, such as those of the Zulu and the Assyrians. With superior weapons and horses, some groups gained the military power to conquer neighboring groups and expand in order to collect tribute from subjugated populations or vassal states. As these states grew, they attained larger surpluses by preying on neighboring populations and requiring tribute payments. Warfare between chiefdoms became common, and captives were taken in warfare and enslaved. Stronger groups imposed their wills on weaker groups. The Mongol invasions rearranged politics in India and mainland Southeast Asia. Arab invasions had a similar effect in northern Africa. Tribute could come in the form of material resources or labor. For example, the Akan of western Africa wanted captive labor to

mine gold, the basis of the Asante Empire in the eighteenth century. Slaves composed a large class in most empires; only slightly better off were subjugated peoples paying tribute.[20]

Therefore, one important part of understanding empires is to see them as a collection of different communities over which there is a centralized government. These kingdoms routinely ruled over vast, sprawling, and varied areas. The Inca Empire ran north to south for over 3,200 kilometers. Such large states required effective political and military institutions to integrate conquered people into the system, and exercised executive, judicial, and legislative authority. They set about enforcing laws, organizing armies, and collecting taxes. Some were better administrators than others. Centralized states such as Persia (Iran) were broken into provinces and run by elaborate bureaucracies. The Inca divided their empire into four quarters, each with a lord (usually a close relative of the emperor). Besides tribute collection and organization of public works, the Inca sought to assimilate conquered peoples by encouraging their use of Quechua, the language of the empire. The imperial government required all those living under its rule to accept the official state religion, but allowed people also to continue worshipping their own gods. Similarly, the Persian Empire imposed uniform laws and used a single language for administration, but was tolerant of local cultures.[21]

Still, the relative egalitarianism found among stateless societies appears to have been unknown at the state level. Rather little is known about women in most early societies, and what we do know is mostly about elite women. Men dominated most state systems. This was not always the case; women sometimes played key political, economic, and religious roles in their communities. But there were only three female leaders in 3,000 years of Egyptian history. Hatshepsut, who ruled as pharaoh starting around 1473 B.C.E., at times chose to reinvent herself as male to gain LEGITIMACY. Aztec women inhabited other realms, and worked as doctors, artisans, merchants, and in temple service. In studies of the most famously patriarchal empires (such as those of the Aztecs, Inca, and Zulu—which also tended to be the most militarized), the genders are not described as equal, but as serving complementary functions. Inca noblewomen had access to land, herds, water, and

---

Figure 2.2 Why Wasn't It China That Conquered the World?

With all of its advantages, why wasn't it China that conquered the world? Historians cite internal divisions within China in the fourteenth and fifteenth centuries. A power struggle between two factions in the Chinese court ended with the ascendance of a group who sought to turn inward. This marked a turning point in China's history, as the empire stopped sending out fleets and dismantled its shipyards. It also abandoned other technologies, in effect stepping back from the verge of its own industrial revolution—about 400 years ahead of Europe. Because it was so centralized politically, under this system China effectively retreated from technological innovation and halted it, just as Europe was rising.

Source: Patricia Buckley Ebrey, *The Cambridge Illustrated History of China* (New York: Cambridge University Press, 2010).

other resources through their mothers, and some historians argue that their activities were viewed as of equal importance to those of men. For the Aztecs, death in childbirth for women was considered the equivalent of death in battle for men—and revered with great honor.[22]

Many of the empires of western Africa also reserved an honored place for women. In fact, women's social position and personal liberty often astonished travelers. Women are known to have served as political leaders of Swahili (Zanzibar was once governed by a Muslim Swahili queen) and Mayan city-states. More often, however, women served at lower levels, as the heads of towns and subregions within empires. Among the Yoruba in Nigeria, the iyalode was a female official with jurisdiction over all women, who spoke on women's issues in the king's council. Similarly, among the Aztecs there were female officials charged with overseeing the affairs of women. Women also served in some imperial armies, and there are examples of all-female regiments led by women (such as the Amazons of Dahomey and the Sotho of southern Africa).[23]

Although less commonly found in Latin America, there are examples of empresses and warrior queens in the histories of Asia and Africa. In the Hausa state of Zaria, Queen Amina outfitted her armies with iron helmets and chain mail to successfully wage a series of military campaigns. However, in most cases when women held this kind of power, it was treated as a temporary arrangement. Women served as regents, ruling when the successor to the throne was too young to assume (his) full duties. In matrilineal societies, such as the Asante in Ghana, maternal relations were crucial in determining succession, inheritance, and other matters. Here and elsewhere queen mothers and queen sisters were major power brokers, and often had considerable leverage and influence. An Asante queen mother, Ya Asantewaa, is considered a heroine for leading her kingdom in resistance against British rule in 1900.[24]

The Asante had a relatively large empire. One of the most notable differences between empires and smaller states is that the kinship ties that unite chiefs with commoners in states do not exist in empires. Rather, in empires the ruling group claims separate origins from the MASSES and lives apart from them. A variety of sources tell of the spectacle and luxury of life enjoyed by ELITES in the empires of the global south. Large retinues of ministers, scholars, and courtiers surrounded emperors. Often imperial courts included harems, as royal polygamy was not uncommon. Kings of large states such as Mwene Mutapa (Zimbabwe) distinguished themselves by having 2,000–3,000 royal wives.[25]

Always at the pinnacle of power in this hierarchy was the emperor, who ruled as an absolute monarch. There was little left of the kind of constitutional monarchy described for smaller states, in which a king confers with a council. At the level of empire, the emperor's authority took on a divine status and usually was unquestioned. This far greater centralization of power was supported by a religious IDEOLOGY that had enormous influence over the population. Every empire was linked with a state religion, and based on some mix of THEOCRACY and royal despotism. As the "son of heaven," the Chinese emperor was considered godlike. Egyptian monarchs were regarded as gods on Earth. Rulers often claimed special powers of intercession with God or the gods. As chief religions and philosophies of state, Hinduism and Buddhism helped provide the unity necessary for the first kingdoms of

India to become larger political entities. Similarly, Islam created a unity among rival Arab clans. It was this unity based in religion that contributed to the rapid growth of the Arab Empire, known as the Caliphate. This empire rivaled Rome at its peak, and controlled an area that stretched from the Mediterranean into Central Asia from the seventh to the eleventh century.[26]

Religious ideologies served the state in other ways as well. In all four regions, emperors were believed necessary for performing important rites. For the Inca, the emperor was responsible for defending the order and existence of the universe. For the Aztecs, the emperor was a renowned warrior, and conquest was necessary to the proper worship of the god Huitzilopochtli—the only assurance that the sun would continue to pass through the sky. Across empires in the global south it was also common to find that kings and emperors lived lives of ritual seclusion apart from the population. They were often separated from the public behind a screen and communicated only through intermediaries—all based on the belief that the emperor was too holy for common gaze. For example, the Alafin of Oyo, considered to be the incarnation of a chief god, could only be seen through a veil and could never be seen eating. It was not unusual for emperors to be thought to possess supernatural powers.[27] They were often the only ones allowed to transgress the ordinary rules of social life, such as the taboo against incest.

In deference to emperors' unquestioned power, life at imperial courts around the world was immersed in elaborate ritual and ceremony. We know from various sources that the capitals of these empires were often lavish. These were true cities, serving not only as economic but also as cultural centers and populated by tens of thousands, even millions, of people. For example, the Aztec capital Tenochtitlan and the valley of Mexico were home to nearly 1 million people in the early sixteenth century. Described by Spaniards as an "Indian Venice," the city sat on an oval island connected to the mainland by three causeways and interlaced with numerous canals. Chang'an, the capital of the Tang Dynasty of China, was described as magnificent, and was once probably the largest city in the world, with an estimated population of 2 million. Timbuktu and the other capitals of western African empires were described as awash in gold, dripping in opulence, and capable of serving thousands at banquets. The generosity and hospitality of these courts was commented on by visitors of the time. In the tenth century, the emperor of Ghana was known as the richest monarch in the world. The annual revenue of the Mongol emperor in the seventeenth century was said to be ten times that of his contemporary, Louis XIV. When the Mansa of Mali made his pilgrimage to Mecca in 1324–1325, he impressed the world with his wealth and munificence.[28]

Besides feats of monumental architecture, many empires were renowned for their buildings of remarkable beauty and distinctiveness. Many empires also invested in enormous public works projects. The most famous of these is China's Great Wall, a continuous fortification built along its northern frontier. On a similar scale in China is its Grand Canal, a 1,600-kilometer waterway linking north to south. The massive engineering of water systems, such as the use of dams and irrigation, helped the Chinese, the Funan, the Inca, and others increase food production on limited arable land. The Inca produced a surplus in the highlands through agricultural terracing and irrigation. They maintained control over the empire through an impressive system of

roads and built suspension bridges to render immense gorges passable. For many lowland Asian empires, wet-rice cultivation required sophisticated water management and regulation in order to create the higher volume of production necessary to feed larger populations.[29]

As mentioned earlier, the surplus created by such innovations allowed for state patronage of the arts and religion, which contributed to the development of rich material cultures. Empires were known for their production and vast exchange of goods and services, including luxury items. Various empires had specialists in jewelry making and goldsmithing, feather working, silk weaving, and production of other adornments. Empires from all regions are known for their wall paintings and sculpture, such as the cast-bronze portraits of the kings of Ife and Benin in western Africa. Not only did the Gupta kingdom provide for peace and prosperity by reuniting much of northern India, but its two centuries of rule are also described as a period of cultural brilliance, a creative age for the arts and sciences. In the Middle Ages, Muslim society was the scientific center of the world, and Arabic was synonymous with learning and science for over 500 years.[30]

Arab and other non-Western peoples contributed to the development of technologies in several different fields, such as metallurgy. For example, China used coal as metallurgical fuel and for heating houses 700 years before the West.[31] But such feats were by no means confined to Asia. Although little of the global south is considered industrialized today, a variety of industries once flourished throughout these regions. Weaving, which goes back in Egypt and Nubia for a millennium, was once a primary industry in parts of Africa, Asia, the Middle East, and Latin America. The Chinese are credited with technological achievements such as the invention of water-powered mills, drought-resistant rice strains, gunpowder, and optical lenses. Some historians argue that China was near its own industrial revolution in the thirteenth century, and world history would be much different today if not for the Mongol invasion and later emperors' failures to resume the Song Dynasty's initiatives.[32]

What we today refer to as the global south was the site of a series of accomplishments in the field of mathematics as well. Arab scholars introduced algebra and the use of zero to the West. Egyptians were the first to use the decimal system. The Chinese are known for their use of geometric equations and trigonometry. Several empires prioritized the study of the sciences, particularly astronomy, through which the Maya are said to have made observations and calculations of astounding complexity. This includes the development of a calendar that is more accurate than the common Western systems in making adjustments in the exact length of a solar year.[33]

The Maya are also known for their complex glyphic writing, which has still not been decoded but is widely considered to be the most advanced in the ancient Americas. Although Sumer is believed to be the first civilization to have created cuneiform writing (about 5,000 years ago), the Egyptians developed writing (about 3200 B.C.E.) and the Chinese have preserved script that dates back as far as the second millennium B.C.E. Instead of lettering, the Inca used mnemonic devices, knotted quipu strings, which were used in recordkeeping and accounting.[34] Yet there were also highly artistic and prosperous urban civilizations, such as the Ife of Nigeria, who did not have writing. Oral cultures there and around the world have produced a large body of myths, legends, and poetry, as well as theater, prose, and philosophy. Griots and

other professional historians have transmitted the genealogies and histories of these peoples by memory.[35]

The Assyrians collected their literature in libraries, filled with thousands of stone tablets. The Gupta in India, the Maya, and the Persians are known for their patronage of scholarly activity, including the recording of official histories. In addition to being the center of trade on the Southeast Asian archipelago, Srivijaya was a center of Hindu and Buddhist learning. Correspondingly, Baghdad was such a gathering place for Muslim scholars during the Umayyad Dynasty. Timbuktu, at the time that it was the major hub for the trans-Saharan trade and one of the most celebrated of savanna cities, was also famous for being a city of universities, attracting scholars of international repute. In the third millennium B.C.E. Egypt achieved high intellectual, social, and material standards that compared favorably with most other parts of the world. The Greeks borrowed heavily from the Egyptians in philosophy and the sciences, transmitting to the West many of their accomplishments. Therefore, it is not only the West that has a rich intellectual history. In fact, the West became what it did because of an infusion of knowledge from much of the rest of the world.[36]

For all of their strengths, however, we find a common pattern among empires—authority was inversely related to distance. The larger the area conquered, the more difficult it was to maintain HEGEMONY, or absolute control over the empire. The Songhay Empire in western Africa was almost perpetually engaged against dissidents across its vast frontier, as was the Chinese Empire, which frequently broke down into fiefdoms. Empires tended to overextend themselves and were constantly plagued by problems of administration and succession (one reason Ghana lasted so long is that it stayed relatively small).[37] Whereas smaller groups often unified into larger states under a common cause (such as defense against an external threat), after the shared problem was eliminated these larger units tended to break back down into smaller and more local organizations. This was a cycle that repeated itself in all four regions—Africa, Asia, Latin America, and the Middle East—many times before European conquest.

Yet it is for a variety of reasons (not all of them well understood) that many of the empires described here had long passed from the scene. Their capitals were no longer as dazzling and prosperous by the 1500s, when Europeans began arriving in larger numbers. By the time European powers became intent on expansion, many of these empires were showing signs of distress. They were at risk of DISINTEGRATION from infighting and fragmentation.[38] For example, the Mongol Empire was fragmenting when the Europeans arrived. Indian and foreign rivals defeated the Mongols, so that by the time the West began its invasion the empire was vulnerable and divided into many small successor states that were easily played off each other by the French and British. We see this pattern among empires in all four regions. There were the internecine dynastic struggles of China, the civil wars over succession crises of the Inca and Oyo (Nigeria) states, and slave raiding in Africa, which spread firearms throughout the region and contributed to endless wars between various groups.[39] In all of these places, the once-central leadership was weakened, administrative controls broke down, and outlying tributaries attempted to break free of the empire's grasp.

The potential for revolt in these kingdoms was aggravated by heavy taxation and other stresses. These often became more burdensome as empires struggled to

survive. For example, just before Spanish conquest, the Aztecs greatly stepped up the pressure on conquered groups. They demanded mass human sacrifices to assuage the gods and prevent a predicted cataclysm. Consequently, tributary and minority groups, long resentful of imperial domination, were eager to ally with the invaders. Europeans benefited enormously from this circumstance and employed a strategy of DIVIDE AND CONQUER.[40]

While it is important to remember that Europeans were not invited guests, there are cases in which people didn't immediately recognize the Europeans as invaders and ended up compromising themselves. There are countless stories of how some societies received the European visitors peacefully—even warmly. Many societies active in the Indian Ocean network of trade accepted the Portuguese enclaves as they had other outsiders for as long as anyone could remember. They gave the Europeans a cautious welcome and sought to profit from their presence. The Aztec emperor Moctezuma at first offered generous gifts to encourage his unearthly looking visitors to leave. When that didn't work, Moctezuma warily welcomed Cortés and his men to Tenochtitlan and treated them as guests.[41]

Once the emperor recognized his error, it was too late. The Aztecs, like most of the other military empires of Africa, Asia, Latin America, and the Middle East, were unprepared to counter European penetration. In some cases, people quickly adapted to the new reality and worked hard to reclaim the advantage. However, many groups fought pitched battles against the invaders and some succeeded (at least temporarily). The emperor Menelik drove the Italians out of Ethiopia in the late nineteenth century, and as a result it was one of the few territories never formally colonized. Equipped with European arms his forces had built for themselves through reverse engineering, Samori Touré was able to keep the French out of large parts of western Africa for nearly twenty years. The Inca were able to hold off the Spanish for decades, as resistance was not finally put down until 1572.[42] These are just a few of the examples of indigenous peoples' fierce resistance to European conquest. But in most cases it was too late.

Figure 2.3   The Transatlantic Slave Trade

Unique in terms of the enormity of human devastation it caused, the transatlantic slave trade lasted for nearly 500 years. Although it began on a small scale in the 1400s, by the seventeenth century labor shortages in the Americas had greatly increased the demand for slaves. At its height, thousands of men and women in their most productive years were taken from their communities on an annual basis and sent across the Atlantic on the harrowing trip known as the "Middle Passage." Because so many died along the way, the total number of slaves is still unknown, although most historians estimate that at least 12 million people served as human cargo in this trade.

Source: J. E. Inikori and Stanley Engerman, *The Atlantic Slave Trade* (Durham, NC: Duke University Press, 1992).

Figure 2.4 The Opium Wars

Those states that were not so open or that didn't receive Europe so warmly were also forced into the new order—on Europe's terms. As the Middle Kingdom, China believed itself to be at the center of the universe. Largest in size and population, longest in history, untouchable in cultural achievement, the Chinese Empire was in many ways the premier entity when Europeans started arriving in more significant numbers in the sixteenth century. Yet Europe's appetite for Chinese porcelains, silks, and teas was not reciprocated by Chinese interest in European goods.

As a result, the Europeans (and particularly the British) struggled with their trade deficits until they did find one commodity the Chinese found habit-forming: opium. This narcotic proved to be a boon to the British economy. Although the Chinese government had recognized the devastation caused by opium addiction and outlawed its sale, the British sold the drug through a smuggling network along the coast. When China attempted to destroy the contraband trade, the British fought what were known as the Opium Wars to force open the country to foreign trade. In decline at the time, the Chinese Empire was easily overwhelmed by the British military. The resulting Treaty of Nanjing in 1942 was the first of several "unequal treaties" that established European dominance in China. The Chinese coast was carved up into five ports open to Westerners. In effect, the emperor was forced to grant concessions at gunpoint—truly a low point in the empire's history. At the mercy of foreigners, China faced a century of humiliation.

Sources: Milton W. Meyer, *Asia: A Concise History* (Lanham: Rowman and Littlefield, 1997); David Landes, *The Wealth and Poverty of Nations: Why Some Are So Rich and Some Are So Poor* (New York: Norton, 1998); Rhoads Murphey, "The Historical Context," in *Understanding Contemporary China*, ed. Robert E. Gamer (Boulder: Lynne Rienner, 1999); Edward L. Farmer et al., *Comparative History of Civilizations in Asia* (Reading, MA: Addison-Wesley, 1977).

Notes

1. Octavio Paz, "Critique of the Pyramid," cited in Ana Carrigan, "Chiapas: The First Postmodern Revolution," in *Our Word Is Our Weapon: Selected Writings of Subcomandante Marcos,* ed. Juana Ponce de Leon (New York: Seven Stories, 2001), p. 428.

2. Roland Oliver, *The African Experience* (Boulder: Westview, 1999); Robert W. July, *A History of the African People* (Prospect Heights, IL: Waveland, 1992).

3. Oliver, *The African Experience*.

4. Milton W. Meyer, *Asia: A Concise History* (Lanham: Rowman and Littlefield, 1997).

5. Oliver, *The African Experience*.

6. Benjamin Keen and Keith Haynes, *A History of Latin America* (Boston: Houghton Mifflin, 2000); July, *A History of the African People;* Meyer, *Asia*.

7. Keen and Haynes, *A History of Latin America*.

8. Jane Burbank and Frederick Cooper, *Empires in World History: Power and the Politics of Difference* (Princeton: Princeton University Press, 2010).

9. Magbaily Fyle, *Introduction to the History of African Civilization* (Lanham, MD: University Press of America, 1999); Meyer, *Asia*.

10. Fyle, *Introduction to the History of African Civilization*.

11. Keen and Haynes, *A History of Latin America*.

12. Ibid.; Peter Bakewell, *A History of Latin America* (Malden, MA: Blackwell, 1997).

13. Peter Bellwood, "Early Agriculturalist Population Diasporas? Farming, Languages, and Genes," *Annual Review of Anthropology* 30 (2001).

14. Bakewell, *A History of Latin America;* Meyer, *Asia;* Douglas J. Brewer and Emily Teeter, *Egypt and the Egyptians* (Cambridge: Cambridge University Press, 2007).

15. Fyle, *Introduction to the History of African Civilization*.

16. Meyer, *Asia*.

17. Ibid.; Rhoads Murphey, "The Historical Context," in *Understanding Contemporary China*, ed. Robert E. Gamer (Boulder: Lynne Rienner, 1999).

18. Fyle, *Introduction to the History of African Civilization*.

19. Ibid.; Brewer and Teeter, *Egypt and the Egyptians*.

20. Ibid.; Bernard Lewis, *The Middle East: A Brief History of the Last 2,000 Years* (New York: Scribner, 1997).

21. Matthew W. Waters, *Ancient Persia: A Concise History of the Achaemenid Empire, 550–330 B.C.E.* (New York: Cambridge University Press, 2014); Irene Silverblatt, *Moon, Sun, and Witches* (Princeton: Princeton University Press, 1987).

22. Silverblatt, *Moon, Sun, and Witches;* Susan Migden Socolow, *The Women of Colonial Latin America* (Cambridge: Cambridge University Press, 2000); Brewer and Teeter, *Egypt and the Egyptians*.

23. Sarah Milledge Nelson, *Ancient Queens: Archaeological Explorations* (Walnut Creek, CA: AltaMira Press, 2003).

24. July, *A History of the African People*.

25. Oliver, *The African Experience*.

26. Keen and Haynes, *A History of Latin America;* Brewer and Teeter, *Egypt and the Egyptians;* Murphey, "The Historical Context"; Meyer, *Asia;* Lewis, *The Middle East*.

27. Meyer, *Asia;* Laura Laurencich Minelli, *The Inca World* (Norman: University of Oklahoma Press, 2000); Fyle, *Introduction to the History of African Civilization*.

28. Murphey, "The Historical Context"; Oliver, *The African Experience;* Keen and Haynes, *A History of Latin America*.

29. Ibid.

30. Lewis, *The Middle East;* Meyer, *Asia;* G. Mokhtar, "Conclusion," in *UNESCO General History of Africa: Ancient Civilizations of Africa*, ed. G. Mokhtar (London: Heinemann, 1981).

31. Murphey, "The Historical Context."

32. Ibid.; Meyer, *Asia*.

33. Keen and Haynes, *The History of Latin America;* Meyer, *Asia;* David Landes, *The Wealth and Poverty of Nations: Why Some Are So Rich and Some Are So Poor* (New York: Norton, 1998); Murphey, "The Historical Context"; Edward L. Farmer, et al., *Comparative History of Civilizations in Asia* (Reading, MA: Addison-Wesley, 1977).

34. Minelli, *The Inca World;* David N. Keightley, *The Origins of Chinese Civilization* (Berkeley: University of California Press, 1983); Lewis, *The Middle East*.

35. Oliver, *The African Experience*.

36. Farmer et al., *Comparative History;* Paul Johnson, *The Civilization of Ancient Egypt* (New York: HarperCollins, 1999); Mokhtar, "Conclusion." Fyle, *Introduction to the History of African Civilization*.

37. Ironically, the largest states were often the most fragile, disintegrating much more easily than smaller states (and even stateless nations), which proved to be more cohesive and durable. Stateless societies on the frontier, such as the Chicimecas in northern Mexico and the Araucanians in southern Chile, took the longest to conquer. Small, mobile groups able to live off the land were hard to suppress—until in some cases the Europeans decided that it just wasn't worth it.

38. Oliver, *The African Experience;* Meyer, *Asia;* Minelli, *The Inca World*.

39. Ibid.

40. Maurice Collis, *Cortés and Montezuma* (New York: New Directions, 1999).

41. Ibid.

42. Fyle, *Introduction to the History of African Civilization;* John Hemming, *The Conquest of the Incas* (Boston: Houghton Mifflin Harcourt, 2003).

Chapter 3

How Colonialism Changed Everything

Whatever happens we have got / The maxim gun and they have not.
—*Hilaire Belloc, writer*[1]

In most cases, European conquest of what would become the so-called global south did not come overnight. Rather, colonization was the culmination of processes that had begun hundreds of years earlier. The fifteenth and sixteenth centuries represented a turning point for Europe—and for the global south. Most historians agree that until this time, Europe had little on Africa, Asia, the Middle East, or the Americas. It was just another of the world's regions, with its share of accomplishments and failures. In the fifteenth century few could have dreamed that Europe would dominate the world. How did it all change? How did Europe manage to conquer virtually the entire world? One currently popular view is that Europe simply took advantage of a set of fortuitous circumstances. It was willing to build on the achievements of others (such as gunpowder, the compass, and improvements in shipbuilding) and use its military power to take control of the seas and world trade.[2]

What other kinds of generalizations can we make about colonialism? Several, since the main differences between the colonizers were in degree, but not in kind. There are some interesting comparisons to be made in terms of style, but not in terms of substance.[3] Who were the colonizers, who assumed the role of "MOTHER COUNTRY"? The major colonizers in Latin America were the Spanish and the Portuguese, although the British, French, and Dutch took the Guianas and parts of the Caribbean. Spain dominated the Philippines, Puerto Rico, and Cuba until the United States replaced it after the Spanish-American War. The British took much of Asia, including India, Pakistan, Sri Lanka, Burma, and Malaysia. The French claimed Indochina (including Vietnam, Cambodia, and Laos). In Asia the Portuguese had only a few small holdings, and the Dutch controlled the vast archipelago today known as Indonesia.

The British and French were the dominant colonial powers in Africa, with the French taking much of the northern and western regions of the continent, and the British controlling much of the eastern and southern regions. Other colonial powers

took pieces of the African cake as well, including the Belgians, Germans, Italians, Portuguese, Spanish, and Dutch.

Although several European powers were interested in the area, the British dominated the waters of the Persian Gulf and influenced surrounding territories from the late nineteenth century until the middle of the twentieth. After the fall of the Ottoman Empire at the end of World War I, much of the Middle East was divided as mandates between the French and British. The Russians continued to dominate Central Asia, and they vied with the British for control of Persia until the two agreed to divide it between themselves into spheres of influence.

Not all of the modern global south was formally claimed and occupied by Europeans, but even territories that were never formally colonized fell under heavy European influence. Because China's coast was carved up among five different alien powers and its emperor was rendered a puppet, it is said to have been "semicolonized" after the Opium Wars of the mid-nineteenth century. Similarly, because they were not insulated from trends ongoing elsewhere, Turkey, Thailand, Ethiopia, Liberia, and the handful of states that were never officially colonized share many of the legacies of colonialism.

Just as the players involved vary by country, so do the length and period of colonialism. The Spanish and Portuguese were the earliest colonizers, and Latin America

---

Figure 3.1 How Did Europe Conquer the World?

How did a relative handful of Europeans succeed in conquering these empires? A variety of advantages served the European cause, but the shortest answer is weaponry. Europeans had enormous advantages in military technology throughout the period of conquest. By the seventeenth century, guns were the main weapons favoring Europeans (an early machine gun, the maxim gun, revolutionized violence). Yet weaponry had made all the difference even hundreds of years earlier.

In Latin America in the early sixteenth century, the Spaniards used steel swords, lanes, small firearms, and artillery, as well as steel body armor and helmets against far greater numbers of indigenous soldiers with much less effective weaponry and protection. The Inca and Aztecs were equipped only with clubs and axes of wood or stone, slings, bows and arrows, and quilted armor. Brought in on ships from Europe, horses provided the Spaniards with another tremendous advantage in battle. Horses gave the invaders height in combat (which protected riders by giving them a raised fighting platform) and speed in attack. Foot soldiers could never succeed against

a cavalry in the open. In addition, the Spaniards unleashed massive dogs in combat. As vicious killers they terrorized the population. The invaders benefited from other psychological advantages as well. Aztec priests had been predicting the return of the god Quetzalcoatl, as well as the end of the world. The Aztecs had never before seen men with light-colored eyes and hair, let alone horses (which when mounted by Spaniards appeared to be two-headed animals). Combine these advantages with difference in battle tactics (by Aztec standards, the Spanish didn't fight fairly; the Spanish fought to kill, the Aztecs to take prisoners). Add to that the death toll from the diseases Europeans brought with them, and the effect was the literal decimation of populations—not only in Latin America, but in Africa and Asia as well.

Sources: Peter Bakewell, *A History of Latin America* (Malden, MA: Blackwell, 1997); Jared Diamond, *Guns, Germs, and Steel: The Fate of Human Societies* (New York: Norton, 1997); David Landes, *The Wealth and Power of Nations: Why Some Are So Rich and Some Are So Poor* (New York: Norton, 1998).

was the first region to be colonized. Its era of colonial rule was relatively long, beginning in the early sixteenth century and lasting 300 years or more. Yet independence came relatively early to Latin America; with a few notable exceptions in the Caribbean and Brazil, most of the region became independent in the 1810s and 1820s.

Compared to Latin America's experience, Western colonialism in most of Africa, Asia, and the Middle East was relatively short-lived. After years of encroaching influence, nearly all of Asia was formally colonized after the 1850s but independent less than a hundred years later, in the 1940s and 1950s. Most of Africa was parceled out to the Europeans at the Conference of Berlin in the 1880s and was (formally) self-governing by the end of the 1960s.

The Middle East's experience is somewhat different. Though the Russians had been encroaching on Central Asia since the sixteenth century, most European powers were more cautious about taking on the Ottoman Empire. During the nineteenth century, when Europe was most active in acquiring colonies, most of the Middle East (with the notable exceptions of Persia, Saudi Arabia, and Yemen) was under Ottoman control. Perhaps because of a long history of mutual antagonism between Christians and Muslims, perhaps because Europeans knew relatively little of the land and overestimated the Muslim powers' military strength, European penetration of the Middle East was delayed (or "veiled," as was the case in Egypt, which Britain occupied but over which it had no formal claim). As a result it was the last major area to fall to the West.

However, by the end of World War I, the Ottoman Empire had bottomed out after a long decline. Despite promises of independence to the Arabs, who had risen up against the Ottomans, Ottoman territories (including former German colonies in Africa and the Pacific) were claimed as protectorates (as did Britain in Egypt) or set aside by the League of Nations as mandates, or wards of the international community. The Western-dominated League granted supervision of the mandates to Britain and France. The French acquired Syria and Lebanon. Control over Iraq, Transjordan, and Palestine passed to Britain. Under this system, the Europeans' primary responsibility was to prepare their wards for eventual self-government. However, many analysts characterize the MANDATORY SYSTEM as a fig leaf for colonialism, as the mandates were treated no differently than colonial possessions elsewhere. Still, the period of mandates was relatively brief. Most of these territories declared their independence in the post–World War II period.[4]

Whether it lasted for one generation or for many generations, most students of the non-Western world agree that colonialism was a formative experience. Although they may disagree about how long-lasting its legacy was, the fact remains that, in one form or another, colonialism is the one experience that virtually every non-Western country has shared. Why did the Europeans conquer the world? What were they after? And what impact did their policies have on the colonized? Analysts disagree in terms of the relative weight they assign the different interests that motivated the Europeans, but most agree that it was based in a mix of what Ali Mazrui characterized as "the three Gs"—gold, God, and glory.[5]

Gold

In many ways, colonialism was the culmination of a process that wrecked indigenous economies, ruined local industries, and replaced traditional networks of trade with

a world system in which Europeans dominated and the rest of the world served. Gold, or the economic motive, was a major if not the major drive behind colonialism. By the beginning of the age of imperialism in the fifteenth century, an overland long-distance trade had linked Europe and the non-Western world for over a thousand years. However, it was a technological revolution that would dramatically shift the balance of power—the Europeans' ability to dominate world trade by sea.

From the time of Henry the Navigator, Portugal had led Europe in decades of exploration. Early in the fifteenth century, as the Portuguese began making stops along the coast of Africa, they established plantations in Cape Verde and the Canary Islands. In Africa, the Portuguese were literally seeking gold, but later it was slaving that set in motion a process that would dramatically alter Africa's relationship with Europe. By 1487 the Portuguese had rounded the Cape of Good Hope and entered the bustling Indian Ocean trading network. The newcomers originally sought access to the highly lucrative trade in pepper and spices. They did this by setting up trading posts at strategic bases along the coasts of Africa, Asia, and the Middle East. Over the next hundred years, Portugal practiced a policy of expansionism. Seeking to eliminate the middlemen and gain direct access and control of this trade, Portugal defeated fleets of Egyptians, Arabs, and Persians. Portuguese traders eventually reached as far as China by the early sixteenth century, although the European presence went largely unnoticed by the Chinese emperors until much later.[6]

Meanwhile, seeking another route to the Indies, the Portuguese were joined by the Spanish, who together claimed the Caribbean and much of the Americas as their own. In a papal bull in 1493, Pope Alexander VI randomly determined the line dividing what would become Latin America between the two Iberian powers. This pronouncement formed the basis of the Treaty of Tordesillas in 1494, which formalized their claims. All was decided even before the Portuguese landed in Brazil, but the exclusivity of this relationship would be more or less maintained for another 300 years, until the independence of these territories in the nineteenth century.[7]

The Portuguese weren't as successful at maintaining their interests in Asia. They benefited from a near monopoly in the region for over a hundred years but were later displaced by the Dutch, French, British, and others, who entered the Indian Ocean trade as competitors in the seventeenth century. The employees of chartered companies (such as the Dutch East India Company) were often the first to make contact in these distant territories. Serving as agents of the crown, these companies paved the way for imperialism. Under a royal charter granting him access to much of southern Africa, Cecil Rhodes's British South African Company had the power to conduct warfare and diplomacy and to annex territory on behalf of the British monarch. With enormous resources at their disposal, these companies established empires in Asia and Africa with a variety of economic interests in mind. They later pushed for concessions and enjoyed monopolies in the Middle Eastern mandates—these profits were also repatriated to Europe. With the exception of the early colonies established by the Spanish and Portuguese, Europeans maintained long relationships in these territories prior to outright colonization.

This was the age of MERCANTILISM, the precapitalist stage marked by the accumulation of capital through trade and plunder on a worldwide scale. Under mercantilism, each power sought commercial expansion in order to achieve a surplus in its balance of trade. Colonies were developed to suit the mother country's interest, as

sources of raw materials and guaranteed markets for its manufactured goods. Colonialism was never about free trade. Rather, in the earliest days it was mercantilist, and through to the end it was protectionist. Whether it was the Spanish in the fifteenth century or the French after World War II, this exclusive arrangement served as the umbilical cord linking the mother country to her colonies.

From the earliest days of colonization this arrangement simply meant expropriation without compensation. In Spanish America, mining was the principal source of royal revenue. The crown acquired enormous wealth by hauling treasure off in its galleons, creating monopolies, and taxing all wealth produced in the colonies. Under the *quinto,* one-fifth of all gold, silver, and other precious metals belonged to the crown. Innumerable taxes weighed on the indigenous people, who paid the costs of colonial administration and defense and were expected to produce a surplus for the crown. Such wealth promoted the growth of European industry and subsidized the consolidation of European commercial and military power in Asia and Africa.[8]

With industrialization fully under way in the eighteenth and nineteenth centuries, European economic interests in the non-Western world grew. In order to ensure the quantity and quality of the raw materials they desired, Europeans yearned to eliminate local middlemen and establish their own monopoly control of production and trade. Eager to sell their newly manufactured wares, the colonizers sought guaranteed markets and set about destroying their indigenous competitors. They interfered with preexisting regional and long-distance trades. For example, the Spanish colonies were prohibited from producing any goods produced by Spain. In Africa, Asia, the Middle East, and Latin America, self-sufficient economies were destroyed or transformed and subordinated. India and Egypt, which each produced some of the world's finest cotton yarn and textiles, were flooded by cheap, factory-made British fabrics and effectively eliminated as competitors. Millions of artisans were put out of work, with little choice but to turn to farming. Similarly, the Ottoman Empire's handicrafts manufacturing couldn't compete with industrialized production techniques of the West. Colonized peoples were driven out of the most important sectors of their economies, as industrialists, craftsmen, and merchants.[9]

Europe's industrial revolution also demanded reliable access to cheap raw materials. The colonies were established to serve as feeders to the industrial economies of the colonizer, and the result was the development of economies centered on the export of raw materials. Justified by the principle of COMPARATIVE ADVANTAGE, which holds that efficiency is enhanced by specialization in production, the mother countries decided what their new colonies would produce, based on the colonizers' needs and the particular resources of each territory. Monocultures were created: sugar from Cuba, hides from Argentina, coffee from Kenya, cotton from Egypt. Nigeria and India were unusual in that they exported a handful of different cash crops. The colonies were never to be self-sufficient; instead they were undiversified, vulnerable, and dependent.

To ensure the desired quality and quantity of goods, the mother countries often imposed a system of compulsory crop cultivation. Small farmers were given quotas and obliged by law to produce the assigned cash crops. Those who did not fulfill their quotas could be fined or arrested. In Latin America, Indians were forced to sell their goods at fixed prices usually well below world market value. In addition, they were compelled to buy goods at artificially high prices. Because of the relatively low value of

unprocessed goods versus the high cost of imports, colonialism established a fundamental inequality of exchange. The people of the colonies ended up producing what they didn't consume and consuming what they didn't produce.[10] They were in effect marketing raw goods to the West, to repurchase them in finished form.

For all intents and purposes, the resources of one territory were drained to enrich another. The Europeans opened up mines and plantations. Germans and South Africans stripped Namibia of its once-vast diamond wealth. After the Dutch East India Company took Indonesia, all of Java was set aside and parceled into large plantations to grow export crops such as coffee and pepper. Europeans busied themselves obtaining concessions, such as a sixty-year British monopoly to find and develop petroleum and natural gas in most of Persia. Soon foreigners owned the right to control every aspect of this asset, and Persia was the richest known source of petroleum at the time.[11]

Someone had to produce these commodities, and one of the first concerns of every colonial power was how to meet its labor demands in terms of mining, portage, construction, and cultivation. Slavery, tenancy, and debt peonage existed throughout the colonial period. Although King Leopold of Belgium was unrivaled in the barbarism he used to compel labor in Congo, other colonizers used forced labor as well. Under the Spanish system of *repartimiento* (or the *mita*), all adult male Indians had to spend part of their year laboring in Spanish mines, farms, and public works. Barely disguised slavery, the *mita* was an important source of labor for the Spanish until the end of the colonial period. Similar practices, such as land curtailment, or the large-scale appropriation of territory by Europeans, denied the indigenous people an alternative source of cash income. Once-independent farmers and herders were converted to wage labor. In addition, taxes were imposed at such a rate (and to be paid in the colonizer's currency) that people were left little choice but to seek employment in the colonial economy. Perhaps the most oppressive labor regulations were found in southern Africa, where pass laws and labor contracts created a system of migrant labor that gave employers enormous advantages. To some degree it continues to this day.[12]

Wherever colonialism existed, no matter who was doing the colonizing, the effect on the colonized was much the same. The demands of the colonial economy often resulted not only in an intensification of the exploitation of labor, but also in a great disruption of community and family. Often men and women were forced to leave their families behind to work as migrant laborers. Overall health and nutrition deteriorated as demands for labor grew. Although most people continued to work as farmers, colonial agriculture was much more extensive than anything known before, demanding more energy and resources to produce commodities for sale in markets. Most Africans, for example, were so busy in their cash crop farming that there was little time for the production of staples or to supplement their diets with hunting or fishing as before. Often the result was vulnerability to overwork and disease, which spread rapidly with the dislocations associated with an intensification of production and trade volumes. A variety of colonial policies rendered indigenous populations landless. Under French rule in Vietnam it is estimated that two-thirds of the population were tenant farmers.[13]

In the worst cases, traditional welfare systems were destroyed. The stress and dislocation of colonialism combined with economic hardship contributed to a rise in

social violence and self-destructive behavior, such as opium addiction in southern China and alcoholism in India and southern Africa. In some places populations actually declined, as death rates rose while fertility rates fell. Forced to produce government crops, Indonesians were left dependent on purchasing rice. But the low contract price for the spices they produced meant that entire regions became impoverished. The commercialization of agriculture left peasants vulnerable, and famine occurred with regularity. It is estimated that 15 million people in India died of famine between 1875 and 1900. During the first forty years of colonial rule, overwork and abuse reduced the population of the Belgian Congo by half. Perhaps the most devastating results occurred in the Valley of Mexico, where 90 percent of the population is believed to have died during the first hundred years of colonial rule.[14]

God

Often alongside the conquistadors in Latin America and the traders in Asia and Africa were the missionaries. "God" would be invoked to justify colonialism, and to varying degrees proselytizing was a large part of the colonial effort. Priests came to Latin America on Columbus's second sailing in 1493. The Catholic Church was joined by Protestant missionaries who served as aggressive agents of cultural imperialism as well, to compete for souls in Asia, Africa, and to a lesser extent in the Middle East. Catholic or Protestant, some missionaries saw themselves as protectors of the colonized and were "pronative" in conflicts with the mother country over their treatment. However, these people of God were colonizers as well, collaborators crucial to the administrative success by helping to bring indigenous peoples under control. In a

Figure 3.2 Did Colonialism Benefit Women?

Colonialism is sometimes argued to have improved the status of women, since the missionaries sought to destroy indigenous customs and social practices they saw as barbaric, such as female genital cutting, polygamy, and suttee (the practice of burning widows on the funeral pyres of their husbands). However, throughout the precolonial societies of the non-Western world, women's experience varied by race, class, region, age, and other factors. In some communities non-Western women were much more "liberated" than their Western sisters. Where women had shared political authority or enjoyed economic or sexual autonomy before colonialism, European sexism and colonial policy destroyed such systems and marginalized women. Where patriarchy long predated the arrival of Europeans, colonialism laminated it. Western and non-Western patriarchies joined in an at-

tempt to control women's labor and sexuality, deny them access to education and employment, and deprive them of political power. The colonizers sought to win the allegiance of men by granting them increased authority over women. However, women were not passive victims in this process. In Zimbabwe and elsewhere, some women agitated for a return to the relatively favorable status they had held in their societies before colonialism. In a variety of ways, including the use of so-called WEAPONS OF THE WEAK, they asserted their interests. Often, colonial women (both colonizer and colonized) enjoyed more independence than is usually assumed—despite rigorous efforts to keep them "in their place."

Source: Susan Migden Socolow, *The Women of Colonial Latin America* (Cambridge: Cambridge University Press, 2000).

massive effort, work was fused with conversion. The "heathens" were gathered together so that they could be not only more easily evangelized, but also taught "Christian virtues" of hard work and unquestioning obedience.

More than any other actor, the missionaries were responsible for compelling colonized peoples to recognize their domination by the invading culture. Missionaries assertively challenged all preexisting belief systems. Their churches were often built on holy grounds, on top of razed temples, to drive home their message. The earliest days of conquest and pacification were often times of violence, dramatic social change, and transformation. For many people colonialism meant the destruction of their world, since indigenous religions were assaulted by the persistent imposition of European values. Time and again evangelization was conducted with such zeal, and was so heavy-handed, that it amounted to forced conversion. Christianity was imposed with an intolerance that was new in most regions.

Although there were some significant differences in approach (the Portuguese and Spanish were much more interested in religious conversion than the Dutch, for example), wherever colonialism existed it was based in racism and cultural imperialism. Propounding social Darwinist theories of evolution and survival of the fittest, the Europeans saw themselves as more civilized, cleaner, smarter, and better educated than the people they colonized, who were variously described as devious, lazy, or immoral. The expression of this chauvinism or racism took different forms, depending on the colonizer. For example, whereas the policy of assimilation was based in the French belief in their own cultural superiority, the British were better known for the use of a color bar, based in their sense of racial superiority. However, institutionalized segregation and discrimination was the rule in every colony. Whereas the French were determined that their civilization should be accepted by all living under French rule, the British stressed the differences between themselves and the colonized, and were contemptuous of indigenous peoples' attempts to adopt the English language and culture.

Yet in British colonies and all the others, "white man's burden" was about more than just saving souls. It provided a rationale for domination: the fruits of Western civilization should be shared with the heathen. Again it was missionaries who took it upon themselves to bear this burden. They were given a virtual monopoly over colonial education. Building schools and clinics was an effective way of evangelizing and advancing the colonial effort. Apologists for colonialism often laud these efforts, which did provide formal education and improved healthcare for some. However, these services were grossly inadequate and unevenly distributed. It is estimated that fewer than 10 percent of Zambian children ever saw the inside of a schoolhouse. Secondary schools were rare in colonial Africa until after World War II. Few universities and technical schools were established; not a single university was built in Brazil during the entire colonial period. There was not one university in Indonesia until 1941. Where schools did exist, often it was only whites or the children of "notable natives" who received these benefits.[15]

In other ways as well, the colonial educational systems existed primarily for the benefit of European settlers and administrators. The schools served as instruments of subjugation. They perpetuated racial inequality by indoctrinating the colonized into permanent subservience and sought to convince indigenous people of their inferiority. A few professionals were trained, but mostly the colonized were prepared

to work as soldiers, clerks, and low-level administrators. The curriculum not only was irrelevant to their needs, but also taught colonized people to disown their birthrights, to give up their traditions, dress, customs, religion, language—in some cases even their own names. For example, French language, literature, and history were compulsory in colonial Syrian schools, while Arabic language, literature, and history were ignored. The achievements of non-Westerners were disregarded or denied. European institutions were assumed to be innately superior to anything that might have existed before colonialism. In effect, the children who went through these schools were taught to embrace all that was European. These students, who grew up to be the elites of their countries, ended up alienated from their own cultures. They were taught to assimilate and adore European culture and to look down on their own as decadent and worthless. The result was an identity crisis not easily resolved.[16]

Glory

A third factor commonly observed as motivating European efforts to conquer the world was the search for the glory and prestige that come with recognition as a great power. Nationalistic rivalries for world dominion, in particular the rivalry between the French and the British, compelled the various European powers to claim a share of the cake. Strategic and economic interests combined to raise the stakes in this rivalry. No one wanted to be left out; the colonizers competed fiercely for markets. They also sought control of sea-lanes, access routes, and strategic locations such as the Suez Canal, Cape Town, Aden, Ceylon, and Hong Kong in order to protect their military, logistical, and economic interests. For example, the Suez Canal was considered by the British to be the "lifeline to India," since cutting through it from the Mediterranean to the Red Sea greatly reduced the long journey from Europe around Africa. Not only did this shortcut mean an enormous increase in the volume of trade, but control of India also greatly facilitated the exploitation of China. Therefore, location made Egypt strategically pivotal and the British insisted on maintaining a strong presence there.[17]

Yet other European powers were just as determined to establish their empires. Out of concern that such intense competition might lead to war, the British, French, Germans, Belgians, and others made agreements for the orderly extension of European influence. Through various meetings, they set out rules for the "legal" appropriation of territories. At the Conference of Berlin in the 1880s, the Europeans divided Africa among themselves. The arbitrary lines they assigned as borders are largely the ones that exist today.

Similarly, the Europeans carved twenty-four nations out of the Ottoman Empire with little knowledge or care as to what they were creating. Often the partitions took place on maps that didn't reflect the interior of the territories. Some of the resulting entities were left landlocked; some were left with little base for economic development. Just as devastating in terms of long-term feasibility, the colonizers ignored local factors and drew boundaries between states that cut across religious and ethnic groups.[18] Some groups such as the Kurds became STATELESS NATIONS, spread through Iran, Iraq, and Turkey with no government to call their own. In addition, groups with very different cultures, traditions, and beliefs about government were thrown together to live in MULTINATIONAL STATES. Where divisions are deep, such as

in the Sudan, this has meant real problems for the development of national identities. Fearing dominance by larger groups, minorities often maintain their subnational loyalties. Many religious and ethnic groups in Indonesia, Lebanon, and Nigeria, for example, have little sense of national identity. As a result, state sovereignty is weak. The existence of multinational states and stateless nations has contributed to innumerable territorial challenges over the years. The result has been attempts at SECESSION (Nigeria, East Timor) as well as IRREDENTIST WARS to redraw boundaries (such as those between Israel, Somalia, Iraq, and their neighbors).

In hindsight it is clear that the borders established by the colonizers would pose long-term problems for the global south. However, in the late nineteenth and early twentieth centuries Europe argued that colonialism was for the indigenous peoples' own good.[19] Perhaps to satisfy public concerns back home, the colonizers took the paternalistic position that those with a "higher civilization" should be entrusted with the responsibility of tutoring their "little brown brothers" in Western political and social institutions. Westernization was assumed to be synonymous with modernization, and modernization was identified with progress. Colonized peoples were described as childlike or nonadult. The League of Nations determined that this period of guardianship should continue until the peoples of Africa, Asia, and the Middle East were deemed by its largely European members "to be ready" for self-rule.

The role of benevolent father figure was another aspect of the glory Europe was seeking. This self-aggrandizement was clearest in the mandatory system, when the League of Nations authorized France and Britain to govern the territories of the Ottoman Empire. As stewards responsible for the area's welfare, the period of mandate was to be a "sacred trust." While the mandatory system was supposed to prepare the area for independence as soon as possible and be a benefit to its wards, in fact it was foreign occupation.

Figure 3.3 Israel

After the fall of the Ottoman Empire, a variety of interests motivated the West's desire to create a home for the Jewish people. Yet at about the same time that the British had promised to create a Jewish state, they had also committed themselves to the establishment of a Hashimite kingdom—in much the same area, then known as Palestine. Unclear as to its precise borders and without attention to the rights of the majority Arab Muslims living there, the West helped to found the state of Israel in 1948. Though many people celebrated this accomplishment, for others the creation of Israel was symbolic of the triumph of Western imperialism over the entire Arab world. Only hours after its founding, the inhabitants of the area (Muslim, Jewish, and Christian) began fighting for control over this land, and the fighting continues to this day. It has been particularly fierce over specific sites sacred to all of the inhabitants there, such as Jerusalem. Jews claim the land back to the time of King David as their gift from God. Christians refer to the region as the Holy Land, and for Muslims it is sacred as well. While some Arab leaders accept the existence of Israel as a reality, many Muslims regard the very existence of this state as deeply offensive. Consequently, many Israelis consider their incursions into neighboring areas as necessary for their defense, whereas others in the region regard such moves as expansionist.

Source: Peter Mansfield, *A History of the Middle East* (New York: Penguin, 1991).

How much did the guardians do for their wards? How much tutelage in self-rule occurred during colonialism? What kind of lesson in government was colonialism, exactly? Although some historians get caught up in debates over the significance of style and approach, colonial government was overall rigidly hierarchical, lacking democratic forms of ACCOUNTABILITY, autonomy, or decentralization. Although colonialism's reach was concentrated in the cities and dissipated through the hinterland, its rule was authoritarian, and the primary objective of government was the imposition of order.

To this end the mother countries were abusive. They relied on repression to maintain control. Colonialism created a legacy of military privileges by rewarding soldiers as a special caste with their own set of interests, not subject to civil power.[20] The colonizers created full-time standing armies to crack down on dissent, dissolve political parties, and force nationalist leaders such as Nelson Mandela underground. Others, such as Sukarno, were sent into exile. Justice was arbitrary; the colonizers imprisoned leaders such as Gandhi and Kenyatta and sometimes used appalling force to put down resistance. It was not uncommon for them to collectively punish entire populations. In one of the worst cases, the Germans fought a war of annihilation against the Herero in South West Africa (Namibia), reducing the population by 85 percent. In many places the colonizers became quasi-military authorities, reduced to imposing martial law to maintain control.

Not only was Europe determined to hold on to power, but administration was to be on the cheap, with little or no costs to the mother country. To do this, the colonizers relied on the cooperation of indigenous peoples, and distorted preexisting political systems whenever possible to administer colonial controls. Although there were differences in how much they relied on them, to some degree the British, French, and the others depended on the assistance of "native elites." Known as caciques in Mexico and the Philippines, curacas in the Andes, and mandarins in Indochina, these were indigenous peoples who either were large landholders or had held traditional power prior to colonization. If no local elites were sufficiently accommodating to colonial interests, the Europeans simply appointed what were called in some areas "warrant chiefs," ambitious men with no traditional claim to power but who had proven themselves loyal to the colonizer.[21] Rewarded with privileges such as exemption from taxes or labor service, they served as brokers for the colonial state, charged with overseeing the enforcement of colonial regulations, collecting taxes, and conscripting labor. Under colonialism, corrupt officials often became quite wealthy, administrators embezzled, and offices were bought and sold. In fact, in all four regions it is said that colonialism created a mentality of CORRUPTION. One of its longest-lasting legacies is the notion that government can be manipulated by money, and that political power is the surest route to wealth. Not only was corruption pervasive, but some colonial systems were particularly notorious for their inefficiency and immense bureaucracies.[22]

In effect, then, colonialism destroyed precolonial political systems and delegitimized traditional leaders without providing a viable alternative to authoritarianism. Individual rights and freedoms were subordinated to the mother country's desire to hold on to power. Western ideals such as egalitarianism and self-determination were seldom applied to non-Westerners. The colonial model of government was a small elite maintained in power through reliance on coercion. Despite all its grandiose claims, the colonial state was no democracy. Rather, it was government based on intolerance.

* * *

Government based on intolerance, alienation from one's own culture, and the creation of economic dependency—this was what colonialism meant to the colonized. Gold, God, and glory all had a role to play in the push for empire. Rather than attributing colonialism to any single factor, it is perhaps best to understand European motivation as based in a mix of these three motives. Certainly the impact from political, economic, and cultural imperialism is still felt throughout the former colonies. Although it would go too far to blame all of it on colonialism, much of the instability found in so many former colonies should be understood as the logical consequence of this relationship.

Notes

1. Hilaire Belloc, "The Modern Traveller," cited in Margery Perham II, *Lugard: The Years of Authority, 1899–1945* (London: Collins, 1960), p. 45.

2. David Landes, *The Wealth and Poverty of Nations: Why Some Are So Rich and Some Are So Poor* (New York: Norton, 1998); Jared Diamond, *Guns, Germs, and Steel: The Fate of Human Societies* (New York: Norton, 1997).

3. A. Adu Boahen, "Africa and the Colonial Challenge," in *UNESCO General History of Africa: Africa Under Colonial Domination, 1880–1935,* ed. A. Adu Boahen (London: Heinemann, 1985).

4. Emory C. Bogle, *The Modern Middle East: From Imperialism to Freedom, 1800–1958* (Upper Saddle River, NJ: Prentice Hall, 1996).

5. This terminology was used by Ali Mazrui in his video series *The Africans* no. 4, 1986.

6. Milton W. Meyer, *Asia: A Concise History* (Lanham: Rowman and Littlefield, 1997).

7. Benjamin Keen and Keith Haynes, *A History of Latin America* (Boston: Houghton Mifflin, 2000).

8. Mark A. Burkholder and Lyman L. Johnson, *Colonial Latin America* (New York: Oxford University Press, 1998).

9. Walter Rodney, "The Colonial Economy," in Boahen, *UNESCO General History of Africa.*

10. Ibid.; Bogle, *The Modern Middle East.*

11. Bogle, *The Modern Middle East.*

12. Keen and Haynes, *A History of Latin America.*

13. Meyer, *Asia.*

14. Edward L. Farmer, et al., *Comparative History of Civilizations in Asia* (Reading, MA: Addison-Wesley, 1977).

15. Keen and Haynes, *A History of Latin America.*

16. Boahen, "Africa and the Colonial Challenge"; Farmer et al., *Comparative History of Civilizations in Asia.*

17. Farmer et al., *Comparative History of Civilizations in Asia.*

18. Whereas the colonizers often argued that they had intervened to end anarchy and bring peace to the inhabitants of the territory, in fact the colonizers encouraged fissures and played different groups off each other, to prevent unity and ensure their continued dominance.

19. Not yet democracies themselves until well into the twentieth century, the Spanish and Portuguese certainly never claimed to be promoting self-rule for their colonies in Latin America.

20. Keen and Haynes, *A History of Latin America.*

21. Some traditional authorities refused to cooperate with the Europeans. A Peruvian curaca, Jose Gabriel Condorcanqui, opposed Spanish abuses of the Indians and led the largest colonial rebellion in all of Spanish America. Keen and Haynes, *A History of Latin America.*

22. Peter Bakewell, *A History of Latin America* (Malden, MA: Blackwell, 1997); Boahen, "Africa and the Colonial Challenge"; Keen and Haynes, *A History of Latin America.*

Chapter 4

Independence: In Name Only?

You have tampered with the women. You have struck a rock. You have dislodged a boulder. You will be crushed. The weight is heavy. We need our mothers. We won't give up, even if we're jailed. We are ready for our freedom.
—*Women's freedom song from the 1950s, South Africa*[1]

Colonialism was not only a time of dislocation; it was also a time of unrest. There was always resistance to European domination. However, it grew in intensity and complexity over the years. Especially in the cities, ostensibly nonpolitical associations such as study groups, prayer groups, and even dance clubs provided people the opportunity to congregate and discuss grievances. Such associations became nascent political parties that advocated various forms of resistance. These groups became nationalist movements as they came together for larger demands such as self-determination.

Groups that usually saw themselves as sharing few interests joined together against the mother country (whether Sunnis and Shiites in Iraq or members of different ethnic groups in Ghana and so on) and were relatively successful in setting aside their differences for their common goals. Yet multiethnic, multireligious revolts contained the seeds of possible fragmentation, even self-destruction. Nationalist movements in some countries such as Nigeria were always divided by bitter, regional rivalries. Ideological, ethnic, religious, and other divides simmered just under the surface of many of these movements, yet for a while at least the colonized managed to transcend their differences to unite against the colonizer.[2]

A number of factors combined to promote unity against the colonial powers. In most of Africa, Asia, and the Middle East, the rise and intensification of nationalism corresponded with the period between World War I and World War II. Not only were the colonies expected to sacrifice for the war effort, but the Great Depression hit most of the global south especially hard. An already difficult situation had become intolerable. Asian and African soldiers returning home from the world wars (many of them conscripted) had seen colonial doctrines of white supremacy dramatically

challenged. Nationalist movements were emboldened by the Japanese defeat of Russia in 1905, and the near defeat of the Allies in the Pacific in World War II. Supported by international organizations such as the Pan-African Congress, these servicemen were joined by students, workers, professionals, and others who stridently expressed their revulsion toward occupation. If World War II was a struggle against racism and tyranny, then why should colonized peoples everywhere not be granted self-determination?

Beyond these common questions, nationalist movements varied greatly in terms of ideology, membership, goals, and strategy. They disagreed over whether peaceful change was possible, or if violence was necessary. And there were serious divides over how much change was necessary, if reform would suffice or if REVOLUTION was a must, and over what kind of government and economic system was preferred.

Although sometimes the split within and between nationalist movements was a matter of rival personalities and ideologies, frequently it was generational—the old versus the new elites. The older generation was composed of a relatively privileged class of teachers, religious leaders, and low-level civil servants who resented the restrictions they faced as "nonwhites." Generally social conservatives, they were very class-conscious and tended to distance themselves from the masses. The self-titled "civilized natives" in Africa, for example, were calling for more rights primarily for themselves. These were not radical demands; most old-style elites were not asking for independence. Rather, they were seeking better treatment within the system.[3]

Figure 4.1 The Spanish American Experience

Latin America was the first of our four regions under study to be colonized and the first to win its independence. Nationalism manifested itself there as a sense of "Americanness," which grew rapidly after the 1750s in response to a power vacuum in Spain. Heavily in debt from years of wasteful expenditures, Spain was an absolutist empire decaying from within. When it undertook an assertive program of reforms that had the overall effect of increasing taxes, the colonizer's relationship with its colonies was further strained—and the colonized were already pressed to their limits.

By the end of the eighteenth century, dissatisfaction with the status quo was widespread. Rebellions became more common, and in Mexico, at least, it looked for a while as if self-rule would be won by the masses through social revolution. However, throughout most of Spanish America, Creoles (American-born, of Spanish descent) usurped the more radical nationalist efforts of Indians, mestizos, and people of African descent. An aristocracy with limited access to the highest levels of state and church, they had long resented the favored treatment given to Peninsulars (Spaniards born in Spain), but the Creoles also feared more fundamental social change that might threaten their interests. In the end the American-born elite exploited the crown's weakness and declared their independence. However, Spain didn't give up without a fight. It was only after years of devastating military campaigns that most of the territories colonized by Spain became independent, in the period 1810–1826.

Sources: Jay Kinsbruner, *Independence in Spanish America: Civil Wars, Revolutions, and Underdevelopment* (Albuquerque: University of New Mexico Press, 2000); Benjamin Keen and Keith Haynes, *A History of Latin America* (Boston: Houghton Mifflin, 2000).

Not only were their requests of the colonial government relatively modest, but their tactics were moderate as well. More trusting of the system, the older generation of nationalists played by the rules. During World War I, for example, the Indian National Congress hoped to win favor for its cause by cooperating with the British. These activists undertook letter-writing campaigns and submitted petitions to the colonial powers asking that they end abuses and do more to provide for the welfare of the colonized. Seeking to spur the mother country to take corrective action, they wrote editorials. Some, such as the South African National Native Conference (later known as the African National Congress), used diplomatic means. The Egyptians sent a delegation to London to present their case for self-rule. Elite and commoner alike even went to the colonial courts for redress of their grievances.[4]

On the other hand, the new elite was primarily composed of a later generation of the educated class. Having mostly attended university abroad, the new elites were mobilized by liberal notions of freedom and self-determination. These new elites formed groups such as the Nigerian Youth Movement, which were often more militant and more radical in their aims than the older generation of leaders, whom they frequently disdained as accomplices of colonialism. Many once-cautious and genteel groups that had been known for their moderation, such as the Indian National Congress and the African National Congress, were radicalized by colonial refusals to budge. As a newer generation assumed leadership of these movements, it adopted a harder line.[5]

Well organized under charismatic leaders such as Castro, Nkrumah, Gandhi, Sukarno, Nasser, Ho Chi Minh, and Mandela, the nationalist movements gained in membership and strength. Instead of simply ameliorating colonialism, these new nationalists sought to completely uproot it. Their strategy was much more GRASSROOTS-BASED, including previously excluded groups such as women, workers, and youth.

Figure 4.2 Subversion and Other "Weapons of the Weak"

Although not usually described as "nationalist" resistance per se, people resisted colonial rule for a variety of reasons and in a variety of ways. Tax evasion, desertion, feigning illness, breaking machinery, and other means of subterfuge are known as weapons of the weak. These weapons of the weak are far more common than revolts and wars but are not usually covered in history books. In part, this is because some means of resistance were never recognized as such. Escape, for example, can be a weapon of the weak, such as when mass waves of people took flight across regions during the period of conquest and "pacification" under colonial rule. People sought escape through a variety of other means as well, including alcohol abuse and suicide. Although we generally hear that populations grew under colonialism, in some places birthrates fell because women refused to bring children into this new world of oppression. Abortions and infanticide are believed to have been common in Peru, the Belgian Congo, and elsewhere during the period of colonialism. It is important to recognize that what may appear to be individual, private actions may be linked to larger issues as response to an insufferable situation.

Sources: David Landes, *The Wealth and Poverty of Nations: Why Some Are So Rich and Some Are So Poor* (New York: Norton, 1998); Adam Hochschild, *King Leopold's Ghost* (Boston: Houghton Mifflin, 1998); David M. Davidson, "Negro Slave Control and Resistance in Colonial Mexico," in *People and Issues in Latin American History*, ed. Lewis Hanke and Jane M. Rausch (New York: Markus Wiener, 1993).

Like earlier generations the new elites used the press and international congresses to make their causes known. But whereas the resistance offered by earlier generations was marked by its politeness and civility, this generation of nationalists organized mass campaigns and was much more confrontational toward those they viewed as their oppressors. Demonstrations, strikes, boycotts, and other forms of mass resistance proliferated in Africa, Asia, and the Middle East after World War I, but boomed after World War II. Starting in the 1920s and 1930s, Latin Americans joined broadly based mass parties seeking more radical change as well. At times this nationalism took the form of radical mass mobilization. Demonstrations and strikes turned into countless riots and rebellions—and sometimes even revolutions. In the Aba Women's War, one of the most famous events of this period in Nigeria, market women undressed and marched to Governor's Palace to protest taxes and unfair treatment. In response to the threat to their communities, women also led riots in Mexico and Peru, armed with spears, kitchen knives, and rocks. Men and women turned out into the streets under such circumstances, to let the authorities know that they should listen to their complaints. Often these mass strikes and riots were put down with severe reprisals. In the protests at Amritsar, for example, the British responded savagely, leaving a thousand Indians dead and many more wounded.[6]

Often these movements did attempt to influence the terms of colonialism (or in the case of Latin America, NEOCOLONIALISM). For example, West African farmers sought to alter wage rates and the prices for their crops through cocoa "holdups" of the sale of their produce, refusing to sell until they got a better price. Throughout this period there were many demonstrations of rural and urban discontent. Colonized people everywhere wanted improvement of health and educational facilities, and equality of economic opportunity. Yet the movements led by the new elite generally had larger goals in mind. More willing to use violence if necessary, and more revolutionary in their goals than the old-style elites, these nationalists were seeking some form of national self-determination—autonomy if not independence.[7]

In terms of their vision for the future, many of these groups stressed the positive aspects of indigenous cultures and the need for a cultural renaissance, to revive the traditional order in the face of the foreign assault. Some favored Western constitutional models for change; some advocated peaceful change, practicing techniques of noncooperation such as civil disobedience and passive resistance. Others adopted and adapted Marxist Leninism, in the belief that capitalism would never lead to development and that violent, revolutionary change was the only way independence could be achieved (Algeria, Vietnam, Angola). Others (such as the African National Congress in South Africa and the Muslim Brotherhood in Egypt) used a mix of methods. Again, they disagreed not only about how independence should be achieved, but also about the best blueprint for the future.

For many years the colonizers were able to use the divide between the old and new elites to their advantage. Infighting within and between nationalist movements over goals and strategy no doubt delayed independence. Still, despite the Europeans' best efforts, eventually it became clear that the nationalist movements could not be ignored or written off by the colonizers. The anticolonial struggle was greatly assisted by the fact that after the world wars the imperial powers were weakened, impoverished, and exhausted. Public opinion in Europe had turned against unnecessary expenditures, and most of the remaining colonial powers had lost the will to hold on.

The colonies were reeling as well; the wars had intensified pressures on them not only for troops, but also for forced labor and supplies. After sacrificing for the war effort, living with shortages, price hikes, and wage freezes for years, the Arabs, Indians, Africans, and others expected rewards for their contribution. They wanted concessions from the mother countries and they expected to be granted more participation in running their own affairs. For example, during World War I in return for their cooperation against the Ottomans, the Allies had made promises to the Arabs for immediate self-government. The Arabs were infuriated when it became clear this was not to be.[8] Why freedom for Czechoslovakia and Yugoslavia but not the peoples of Africa, Asia, and the Middle East?

Figure 4.3 Spiritualism and Nationalist Resistance

Just as religion was used to colonize, spirituality was used in resistance. Because of colonial attempts to co-opt or destroy traditional sources of authority, spiritual leaders were frequently the only ones left with legitimacy. Often denigrated by the colonizers as "witch doctors," these priests and mullahs, prophets, spirit mediums, and healers inspired nationalist movements around the world. Some of these movements were moderate and advocated reconciliation and peaceful change. Others predicted the end of the world and a coming cataclysm for whites. In Southeast Asia, Islamic and Buddhist religious revivals mobilized populations. Pan-Islamism fused religion with nationalism, creating a jihadist tradition that spurred resistance to imperial penetration. Separatist and millenarian churches in Latin America and Africa were often based in ancestral traditions. The common theme across the four regions is that these movements sought to recover their identity and defend the cultural dignity of colonized peoples.

Sources: Ali A. Mazrui, "Seek Ye First the Political Kingdom," in *UNESCO General History of Africa: Africa Since 1935,* ed. Ali A. Mazrui (London: Heinemann, 1993); Edward L. Farmer, et al., *Comparative History of Civilizations in Asia* (Reading, MA: Addison-Wesley, 1977).

Figure 4.4 Wars of Liberation

For many countries, the road to independence was one of intense conflict and violence, marked by insurgencies and revolts. Where peaceful means didn't work, where all efforts were met with ruthless suppression, men and women turned to armed struggle. Particularly where there were large numbers of white settlers (e.g., Zimbabwe, Algeria), these conflicts often developed into revolutions and wars of liberation. Contrary to popular perception, both men and women participated in these wars. Women risked their lives to feed and house guerrillas. They performed crucial services, such as moving weapons and information to fighters. In some cases, women carried the rifles, serving as rebel soldiers in El Salvador, Zimbabwe, Algeria, and elsewhere. These women became important symbols and rallying points for their nations. For example, Hawa Ismen Ali, who became known as Somalia's "Joan of Arc," was killed while protesting Italian colonialism in 1948.

Source: Ali A. Mazrui, "Seek Ye First the Political Kingdom," in *UNESCO General History of Africa: Africa Since 1935,* ed. Ali A. Mazrui (London: Heinemann, 1993).

With some notable exceptions, the United States and the Soviet Union generally supported the nationalists' demands. Whether for altruistic or not-so-altruistic reasons, both new superpowers generally adopted an anticolonial stance and pressured Europe to dismantle its empires. Moreover, in much of the diplomatic language of the times — from the Atlantic Charter, which upheld the right to self-determination, to the charter of the newly established UNITED NATIONS — colonial powers were finding it much more difficult to maintain their legitimacy. Increasingly, in the international arena, they were being held accountable for their actions. The UN received complaints from the colonies, and required regular progress reports on how well it was preparing its wards for independence.[9] In effect, a constellation of events, both domestic and international, came together to make the hold of empire less and less tenable. Buoyed by the vacuums created by international events, nationalism throughout the non-Western world was the driving force behind this change. This was as true in the early nineteenth century for Latin America (with the decline of the Iberian powers) as it was by the mid-twentieth century for Africa, Asia, and the Middle East.

The end of colonialism came about at different times and in different ways, but it is fair to say that it mostly came about over the objections of the mother countries. In most colonies, there was little real power-sharing until the very end. The vast majority of colonized peoples were excluded from the rights of citizenship. In much of the global south, all attempts by indigenous peoples to participate in politics were squelched until after World War II. Although the British and French were more likely than the Belgians, the Dutch, or the Portuguese to allow for an independent press and the right to an associational life, overall the "best" of the colonizers hurt democratization more than they nurtured it. Even those most willing to allow some political opening made often-inadequate and superficial reforms. For every concession granted, there were restrictions that continued to limit political participation.

Yet these were the lucky ones. Where the colonizers recognized independence as inevitable, and the forcible retention of empire as impractical and unprofitable, they acted pragmatically. With foresight, they initiated a gradual devolution of power so as to maintain the close ties established under colonialism after independence. While this might have meant problems for the former colonies in terms of continued dependency, a graceful exit by the mother country meant a far greater likelihood that independence would at least begin with some form of democracy.

Others were not so fortunate. For the vast majority of colonized peoples living under Belgian, Dutch, Spanish, or Portuguese rule, there was little preparation for independence or democracy. Even when they left peacefully, as the Belgians and French did from most of their African colonies, they delayed the handover of power until the very end and then left virtually overnight. To punish the colonies for seeking self-determination, the former mother countries cut off aid. There are stories that the French even took the light bulbs with them when they left, and that the Portuguese destroyed water systems. Worse, where strategic interests loomed large or where white settler populations lobbied against independence, the colonizers fought long and bloody wars in a desperate attempt to hold on to power. In countries where class and race conflicts were deepest, independence was achieved with more difficulty and democracy quickly failed. Similarly, where it took a revolution to win liberation, the new government was likely anti-Western, anticapitalist, and based on one-party rule.[10]

Is It "Independence" Only in Name?

However fiercely the colonizers struggled against it, inevitably the period of empire had passed. Although most of Latin America had won its independence more than a hundred years earlier, formal independence in Asia and the Middle East was granted or won in the 1930s, 1940s, and 1950s. The 1960s are the decade most associated with independence in Africa, although several countries were not liberated until later—the last colony to win its freedom was South Africa, in 1994.

For the majority of people living in South Africa and the other former colonies, independence was a time of great optimism and celebration. With the exception of a few elites, most citizens of the global south looked forward to the freedoms associated with self-determination. Freedom was variously defined as everything from the end of forced labor to political autonomy, self-determination, and individual liberty, to the end of colonial monopolies. Finally, it was time for people to control their own resources for their own benefit. Many anticipated a restoration of the dignity taken from them by colonialism, and in these heady days people looked forward to a smooth road ahead. However, too soon it became clear that each newly independent state would have its own problems to face. Above all, the nationalists who had brought their countries to independence faced formidable challenges of organizing new governments that would provide the political stability necessary for economic growth.

Political Development

The architects of these new systems had very different ideas about the best way of organizing government. Consequently, the first experiments in self-rule resulted in a diversity of governmental forms. While some independence governments were established as monarchies (e.g., Iraq, Egypt, Morocco, Saudi Arabia), most became republics. In part, the mode of decolonization explains the range of experience after independence. Although those that won their independence through wars of liberation usually turned to more radical experiments, those that achieved their independence in relative peace often adopted in some form the mother-country model. For example, many of the formerly British colonies experimented with a PARLIAMENTARY SYSTEM. Most of Latin America has spent some time under PRESIDENTIAL SYSTEMS like that of the United States, its highly influential neighbor to the north.

Experience with constitutional government in the newly independent states varied widely. In democracies power often swung back and forth between conservatives and liberals. Over the years we have seen other shifts as well; some constitutions granted a degree of state autonomy through federalism, while others provided for greater centralization in decisionmaking. In Latin America and Africa, most constitutions were short-lived; they were written and rewritten several times. In Mexico, Nigeria, Iran, and many other countries, democratic or not, there has been a constant struggle over how religious or secular government should be. Consequently, for many countries the only thing constant has been change.

For many of the people living in these new states it was their first experimentation with democracy. Others attempted to build on democratic traditions that predated colonialism. The experiment worked better in some places than others; some countries created democracies shortly after independence that continue to exist today

(e.g., India and Botswana). However, such successes were relatively rare. Instead, democracies floundered in most countries just a few years after independence. In many Arab countries, for example, where the idea of popular participation was said to be an alien concept, democratic traditions grew slowly if at all.[11] There and elsewhere power devolved from civilian to military rule, and many other countries as well soon became mired in a variety of despotisms. In part this was due to a REVOLUTION OF RISING EXPECTATIONS. Governments might have been following constitutional and legal procedures, but they were failing to address the needs of their people. Those who had been waiting so long for a decent life soon became disillusioned with the pace of change and frustrated by the inability of their new governments to produce the desired results. As we will see in the following chapters, economic and political instability are closely linked. Across the non-Western world, governments at the helm of countries experiencing economic hardship tend to lose public support. They become weak and vulnerable to upheaval and military takeover. Now as then, people who come to view democracy as only serving the interests of elites frequently end up calling on the military to overthrow constitutional governments to establish stability and carry out speedy reforms.[12]

Whereas the demise of so many of these democratic experiments was disappointing to some, it was widely applauded by large margins in Iraq, Syria, and Egypt. There and elsewhere, dictatorship often had broad appeal, because in many ways "independence" was just a change of masters. These countries' so-called independence did not necessarily mean self-government and did not usually result in radical changes in the lives of the majority. This was most clearly the case in Latin America in the nineteenth century, but was also largely true of Asia, the Middle East, and Africa over a hundred years later. Hierarchies were reproduced, just deracialized (although in Latin America it was mostly a matter of American-born whites replacing the Iberian-born). Democratic constitutions were façades. Political and economic power were concentrated in the hands of a few, linked by class, ethnicity, or religion. When elections were held, they were often blatantly manipulated, and even under civilian rule authoritarianism became entrenched.

Nonetheless, more radical models resulting from revolutions were often no more successful in meeting people's expectations. Interestingly, radicals often justified their rule in the same ways conservatives did. Both left- and right-wing authoritarians maintained that their countries were in crisis, and that they could not afford democracy because it was too disruptive. In some cases it was argued that democracy should be rejected because it was not traditional to indigenous cultures. Elsewhere the justification was that the masses only dimly perceived their own interests. Until they knew what was good for them, they needed to be led by the vanguard, a revolutionary elite that could show them the way.

Dictators used any or all of these arguments to rationalize the emergence of single-party states. Many of the nationalists who led their countries to independence refused to share power through democratic means. On paper or in practice, governments were created in which executives were strong, legislatures and judiciaries weak. Government existed to serve as a rubber stamp for the party and the leader (e.g., Mexico under the Institutional Revolutionary Party [PRI], Egypt under Nasser, China under the Chinese Communist Party [CCP]). Through the creation of cults of personality, leaders monopolized political and economic power.

In Latin America these strongmen were known as CAUDILLOS, and nearly every country in the region had at least one in the early years after independence—and has had since (as we will see in Chapter 13). In Africa, Asia, and the Middle East, in monarchies, and in civilian- and military-ruled republics, these leaders established themselves as "supreme protectors" or "presidents for life." Based on personal not constitutional authority, Sukarno ruled Indonesia for two and a half decades. Ferdinand Marcos clung to power in the Philippines and Mobutu Sésé Seko in Zaire for more than twenty years each. Despite the fact that they were famously corrupt, these leaders portrayed themselves as all-seeing, all-knowing father figures responsible for the welfare of the nation. Much like the monarchs of long ago, their power was based on their charisma, their ability to co-opt populations by doling out favors—and their willingness to use violence to quell dissent.

With few exceptions, under civilian and military rule, in both left-wing and right-wing governments, the size and influence of militaries expanded. Dictators dependent on the use of repression to maintain power tended to overindulge the military in order to maintain its loyalty. As a result, spending on the military ballooned in most countries, further aggravating economic difficulties. Mexico was one of the countries most generous with its military. Military spending under a series of caudillos consumed approximately 60 percent of the national budget in the 1820s, and under Antonio López de Santa Anna in 1854–1855 the military share of the budget was 94 percent.[13] Yet Mexico was unique only in the extent of such excess. Governments around the world (including those of developed countries) have routinely put guns before butter, favoring military spending above healthcare, education, and the like. Although there were some revolutionary military governments that sought to overturn the status quo, most often militaries tended to intervene to protect the interests of conservative landowners and urban elites. However, this relationship on occasion became strained. Growing military contempt for civilians often resulted in coups against democratic and less-than-democratic governments. In many countries, the military's political importance grew as that of civilian authority declined.

Why has authoritarianism been such a persistent feature of politics in all four regions? At times coups were applauded and authoritarians enjoyed widespread popularity, simply because they provided the order that was so widely viewed as necessary to economic growth and progress.[14] Another factor that motivated populations to put security issues above other needs is that very soon after independence many countries had begun falling apart. With their common enemy gone, nationalists turned on each other. Divisions that had run just under the surface during the nationalist period resurfaced to plague many of the newly independent states. With the end of colonialism, the competition for power was naked and constant. Politics quickly became regarded as a ZERO-SUM GAME, in which whatever power one group won came only at the loss of power by another. Although we hear a lot about "tribal" conflicts in the non-Western world, clashes were frequently based on power politics portrayed as based not only in ethnic but also in regional, linguistic, religious, or ideological differences. Across countries in all four regions, these CLEAVAGES have contributed to a process of fragmentation. The result has been civil wars, often involving efforts at secession, and international wars, to redraw boundaries and claim resources. In Nigeria, Guatemala, Indonesia, and elsewhere, when politicians have manipulated religious, ethnic, or other communal divides to win power, it has meant chaos.[15]

Old resentments that may have preceded colonialism but were aggravated by policies of divide and rule were rendered even more deadly by the Cold War. During the period running from the end of World War II until the demise of the Soviet Union in the early 1990s, non-Western countries often found themselves the targets of superpower influence. In the major ideological battle of the twentieth century, the world was divided between the United States and the Soviet Union into spheres of influence. In this struggle the United States favored conservative governments and rebel movements friendly to capitalism and routinely embraced military dictatorships because they were anticommunist. As President Harry Truman famously put it about his counterpart, Anastacio Somoza of Nicaragua, "He's a bastard, but he's our bastard." No more idealistic in its choices, the Soviet Union supported radical, anti-imperialist forces that had come to power (or were seeking to come to power) through revolution. In its own rivalry with China, the communist powers vied with each other to be recognized as the champion of the developing world.

In their effort to divide up what we now refer to as the global south, the superpowers made a series of bilateral treaties and regional alliances, often based on the superpowers' promise of military and economic assistance. The people of Africa, Asia, Latin America, and the Middle East were given an ultimatum by the United States and told that they were either with it or against it. They could not sit on the fence (although India and others objected to such treatment by forming the NON-ALIGNED MOVEMENT [NAM]).

Once the United States and the Soviets had achieved nuclear parity, the fear that direct conflict would result in mutual assured destruction led the superpowers to seek other theaters of war. PROXY WARS were fought in Africa, Asia, Latin America, and the Middle East, with the United States supporting one side and the Soviets the other in various civil and international wars. With both the United States and the Soviets focused on their own battles, the superpowers intervened in domestic politics with little understanding of or interest in local conditions, let alone the issues at stake for their proxies. In Cuba, Afghanistan, and Vietnam, in wars between Somalia and Ethiopia, Israel and its neighbors, and in many other conflicts throughout the non-Western world, the superpowers again and again intervened, hoping to shore up their allies and overthrow governments supported by their adversary. Conflicts in these faraway countries were just a small part of a larger battle that each superpower portrayed as monumental—a war between the forces of good and evil. However, there is an African saying that goes, "When elephants fight, only the grass gets trampled." This was certainly the case for countless civilians caught between the two sides in what were often bloody wars of attrition.

Economic Development

To put it mildly, the political instability exacerbated by the Cold War was hardly conducive to the political or economic development of the non-Western world. Meanwhile, superpower efforts to prop up allies who were doing little or nothing to promote development meant prolonged economic hardship and volatile politics in many non-Western countries. Upon independence these countries had enormous needs but simply not enough resources. New leaders came to power promising to improve standards of living, increase incomes, provide essential services, and build in-

frastructure. Hopes were very high. However, even after formal independence, the economies of most countries were weak and under the direction of foreigners. Because of discriminatory colonial policies, there was a shortage of trained and experienced indigenous professionals, since nationalist leaders had frequently been relegated to a role in the opposition or as revolutionary fighters.

Just as the way in which independence was achieved had an effect on government forms, it also had an effect on the structure of postindependence economies. Countries that were liberated through revolution were much more likely to argue that the main lesson of colonialism was that capitalism didn't work. From their view, private enterprise had contributed to a distorted development, in which wealth was shared among a few. Thus postrevolutionary governments called for a socialist or communist system that would offer protections to the masses by granting a larger role to the state in production and distribution. Yet for a variety of reasons these experiments largely failed to produce the intended results. Isolated from the capitalist world, communist- or socialist-led countries often became just as dependent on the Soviet Union as they had been on their former mother countries.

On the other hand, the majority of countries had won their independence with relatively little bloodshed. They were more likely to be capitalist and to maintain close economic ties with their former mother countries and the West. Often new leaders didn't attempt to transform the status quo. Rather, they sought to open their countries to foreign trade, incorporate them more fully into the international economy, and replace the colonizers as the primary beneficiaries of the system. Most countries became plutocracies, in which rich families joined together to run regions and nations. With a few exceptions, landownership patterns remained largely unchanged. Indigenous elites sometimes replaced foreigners, but existing economic and social structures were largely kept intact.[16]

To the frustration of many, the colonial economic system essentially went on as if there had been no political change at all. With a few important exceptions, most countries continued as producers of raw materials—often exporting the very same commodities assigned to them under colonialism. The performance of these sectors varied; there were occasionally times of prosperity (e.g., Peru's guano boom in the nineteenth century), but for the most part their exports were more vulnerable than finished goods, subject to periodic and dramatic price changes. Cycles of international boom and bust had devastating consequences, even for those countries that had managed to industrialize.

Meanwhile, unless there was strong state intervention guiding these economies, foreign corporations continued to dominate them. This was especially the case in petroleum-producing countries, but to some degree true of all raw materials producers, since most non-Western countries had little control over production levels, pricing, processing, marketing, or the transportation of their goods. Still largely undiversified monocultures, they were dependent not only on foreign investment, but on foreign imports as well. Since these countries were earning too little from their exports to pay for imports of oil, food, medicine, and other consumer items, they soon fell into a pattern of deficit spending. African, Asian, Latin American, and Middle Eastern states became caught up in a cycle of borrowing to pay their debts and spending revenues on debt service rather than the internal improvements that might promote development. Within a few years of independence, many countries were in

default on their debts and vulnerable to the whims of their creditors. Foreign influence, whether through multinational corporations (MNCs) or INTERNATIONAL FINANCIAL INSTITUTIONS (IFIs) and other organizations, eventually became so pervasive that the term neocolonialism was coined to describe the condition of many non-Western states, which were now independent only in name.[17]

Conclusions: From Interdependence to Dependence?

Although we tend to think of the INTERNATIONAL ECONOMIC SYSTEM as a contemporary phenomenon, it existed long before Europeans colonized the world. Empires in Africa, Asia, and the Middle East had prospered in the world marketplace for over 2,000 years. The Americas were linked in a busy regional trade. Although some areas remained isolated, others played an integral part in the evolving international trade. African, Asian, and Middle Eastern craftsmen and merchants once traded on equal par with Europeans, as equal partners in the world economy.[18] It is important to understand that before the age of European empire, Europe was just one part of the international economy. A world economy and system of interdependence predate colonialism.

However, that interdependence was fundamentally changed by European imperial expansion. One major effect of this expansionism was that the economic relationship between the West and much of the world shifted substantially over time—to Europe's favor. Whether it lasted for three decades or three centuries, the mercantilist policies associated with colonialism played a decisive role in Europe's rise to power. Non-economic interests did play a part in motivating this expansionism. But the accumulation of capital created by the transatlantic slave trade, the pillage of foreign lands, and the creation of European monopolies provided the base for Western industrialization and the development of capitalism.

Whereas this early form of globalization meant unprecedented wealth for Europe, for the people to be conquered the European presence was much like an apocalypse. Yes, the history of the world can be described as a series of conquests, and the rise and fall of empires is a recurrent phenomenon in the histories of all regions. This wasn't the first time outsiders had swept through these territories, but it usually involved a relatively marginal disturbance to the underlying continuity of life. The European colonization of Africa, Asia, Latin America, and to a lesser extent the Mid-

Figure 4.5 Attempts at Industrialization

Why not just break out of the raw materials rut? Countries in all four of our regions have attempted to industrialize, to diversify their economic bases, and to lessen their dependence on foreign trade—in most cases through import substitution industrialization (ISI)—that is, by replacing expensive foreign imports with domestically produced consumer items. Some countries (particularly in Asia) have managed to successfully industrialize, mostly due to strong state intervention and protectionism. However, more often these early attempts at industrialization have failed. State-owned enterprises (SOEs) frequently proved to be inefficient, and the infant industries they were trying to launch simply could not compete against more established enterprises in developed countries.

dle East marked a fundamental, long-term change in institutional structures as a whole and a modification of the network of social norms and beliefs that constituted entire cultural systems. It radically altered people's lives. The effect was often devastating as indigenous political systems were undermined or destroyed. Social structures were warped, economies were distorted, and cultures disintegrated.[19]

There are analysts who refute such arguments and characterize the effect of European colonialism on the colonized as essentially benign, or even a positive good. They contend that the colonial experience contributed to the overall well-being of indigenous peoples. Many non-Westerners would remind the defenders of European imperialism that, by and large, colonial rule was established through conquest—it was not something that the colonized ever asked for. It is undeniable that colonial policies resulted in an opening of more international trade routes and an expansion of the volume of trade—but on what basis? The mother countries did introduce new crops and animals, and transfer new tools and techniques to the colonies, but this in no way compensated for the demographic losses and suffering associated with the slave trade and colonialism. The colonizers did bring new ideas and worldviews with them. There was a valuable interchange of ideas, but at what cost—in return for exploitation, pauperization, and humiliation?[20]

Despite all the fanfare, the formal independence of these territories did not fundamentally change the lives of the majority of people living there. Nor did it create the space for the new states' rapid economic development. Rather, colonialism left behind a number of legacies—political, economic, social, and cultural. The former colonizers had put these countries on an unhealthy course from which it has been very difficult to deviate. Much of the global south continues to suffer from neocolonialism in the sense that, since independence, other developed countries have joined the former colonizers to reap the benefits of colonialism without its costs. During the Cold War the global south was clearly allowed only as much "independence" as the superpowers deemed compatible with their interests.[21]

Now as then, during the various incarnations of globalization, the global world has struggled against its dependent status. The West has regularly intervened to overthrow non-Western governments seeking radical structural changes in class relationships and income distribution. Mohammad Mossadeq in Iran, Jacobo Arbenz Guzmán in Guatemala, Patrice Lumumba in the Republic of Congo—these are just a few of a string of leaders who were eliminated because they dared to challenge the status quo. But it is not just radicals who remember and have hard feelings about these foreign interventions. Ordinary people throughout Africa, Asia, Latin America, and the Middle East resent the fact that they are still not treated as equals. Far less than their counterparts in the West, they control their own destinies, plan their own development, manage their own economies, determine their own strategies and priorities, and generally manage their own affairs. Ironically, non-Westerners are uniquely deprived of a fundamental and inalienable right so lauded by the West— the right to liberty.[22]

Whether it lasted for 60 or 300 years, colonialism was not just a historical blip for many people living in the global south. Rather, it was an extremely important part of their experience, a watershed event they still struggle to overcome. Yet in recent years it has become the fashion (even among some living in the global south) to argue that blaming colonialism is an old and tired argument. Those who dwell on its

excesses are increasingly accused of beating a dead horse. Is it high time to get over it and move on? Or is it really that simple?

Notes

1. Julie Frederikse, *South Africa: A Different Kind of War* (Johannesburg: Ravan, 1987), p. 30.

2. Mahmood Mamdani, *Citizen and Subject: Contemporary Africa and the Legacy of Late Colonialism* (Princeton: Princeton University Press, 1996).

3. Ibid.

4. Ibid.; Arthur Goldschmidt Jr., *Modern Egypt: The Formation of a Nation-State* (Boulder: Westview, 2004).

5. Edward L. Farmer, et al., *Comparative History of Civilizations in Asia* (Reading, MA: Addison-Wesley, 1977).

6. Susan Migden Socolow, *The Women of Colonial Latin America* (Cambridge: Cambridge University Press, 2000); Jean Bottaro, *Nationalism and Independence in India* (New York: Cambridge University Press, 2016).

7. Mamdani, *Citizen and Subject*.

8. Emory C. Bogle, *The Modern Middle East: From Imperialism to Freedom, 1800–1958* (Upper Saddle River, NJ: Prentice Hall, 1996).

9. Vrushali Patil, *Negotiating Decolonization in the United Nations* (New York: Routledge, 2008).

10. Mark A. Burkholder and Lyman L. Johnson, *Colonial Latin America* (New York: Oxford University Press, 1998); Bogle, *The Modern Middle East*.

11. Bogle, *The Modern Middle East*.

12. Laith Kubba, "The Awakening of Civil Society," *Journal of Democracy* 11, no. 3 (July 2000).

13. Peter Bakewell, *A History of Latin America* (Malden, MA: Blackwell, 1997).

14. Burkholder and Johnson, *Colonial Latin America;* Benjamin Keen and Keith Haynes, *A History of Latin America* (Boston: Houghton Mifflin, 2000).

15. Bogle, *The Modern Middle East;* J. Isawa Elaigwu, "Nation-Building and Changing Political Structures," in *UNESCO General History of Africa: Africa Since 1935,* ed. Ali A. Mazrui (London: Heinemann, 1993).

16. Burkholder and Johnson, *Colonial Latin America*.

17. David Landes, *The Wealth and Poverty of Nations: Why Some Are So Rich and Some Are So Poor* (New York: Norton, 1998).

18. Ibid.

19. Pádraig Carmody, *Globalization in Africa: Recolonization or Renaissance?* (Boulder: Lynne Rienner, 2010); Farmer et al., *Comparative History of Civilizations in Asia*.

20. Carmody, *Globalization in Africa;* A. Adu Boahen, "Colonialism in Africa: Its Impact and Significance," in *UNESCO General History of Africa: Africa Under Colonial Domination, 1880–1935,* ed. A. Adu Boahen (London: Heinemann, 1985).

21. Carmody, *Globalization in Africa;* Keen and Haynes, *A History of Latin America*.

22. Keen and Haynes, *A History of Latin America*; Boahen, "Colonialism in Africa."

Chapter 5

Linking
Concepts and Cases

The last three chapters have outlined in broad strokes some of the history of what would later become known as the global south. To consider some of the legacies of this past, we invite you to explore the patterns described here in greater detail by taking a look at our case studies. Too many people believe that the so-called third world was always "third world," that life in the non-Western world began only during the period of colonization or that the only "civilization" is Western civilization. As you read about the specific histories of these eight case studies, consider the following questions.

How are the precolonial and colonial experiences of these countries similar? How do they differ? What countries colonized them and in what manner were they colonized? How were these countries integrated into the world system before and after colonialism?

What factors if any aided the European conquest of these territories? How did these countries attempt to free themselves from Western domination, and why were some struggles less peaceful than others? Did the experiences of those countries that became independent through the use of violence differ dramatically from the experiences of those that became independent through peaceful means? Since independence, what kinds of problems have these countries experienced, and how have they approached these problems? Which experiences since independence have been widely shared, and which have differed?

Case Study: Mexico

Well before it was "discovered" by Europeans, the area once called New Spain had developed a variety of civilizations based on maize surpluses and extensive trade networks. Although archaeologists are still piecing together the region's history, it appears that the Olmecs, dating back to 1200 B.C.E., may be the mother civilization to the empires of Mesoamerica. With their distinctive cities, monumental buildings, art, and sculpture, the Olmecs and later the Maya (C.E. 250–900) played an important part in shaping the early history of this region.[1]

The Mexica, relative latecomers to the fertile Valley of Mexico in the thirteenth century, were a minor group who eventually built the Aztec Empire around its city-state, Tenochtitlan. At its height, it is estimated that this powerful, complex civilization ruled a population of 25 million. Much of its wealth was based in conquest, as it subjugated its neighbors and took tribute from them. Built on the belief systems of earlier cultures, the Aztec worldview mixed war and religion. The Aztecs believed that conquest was essential to the proper worship of the Sun God. Perhaps the world's leading practitioners of human sacrifice in terms of volume, the Aztecs saw themselves as staving off the end of the world. To ensure the passage of the sun through the sky, they believed it was necessary to feed the Sun God with life—human blood from ritual killing. To satisfy the Sun God's appetites (in one year just before the Spanish invasion, it is estimated that 20,000 people were sacrificed), they warred on their neighbors, taking captives for sacrifice. As you might imagine, the Aztecs had many enemies.[2]

But when a relatively small expedition of Spaniards arrived in 1519, led by the conquistador Hernan Cortés, the existence of local people willing to ally against the Aztecs was only one factor in favor of the foreign adventurers. Though the stage was already set for a strategy of divide and conquer, just as crucial to the success of the Spanish invasion was a slow and indecisive response by the Aztecs. In part this was because for ten years prior to the arrival of the Europeans, there had been a series of foreboding omens. The emperor and absolute ruler of the Aztecs, Moctezuma II, had expected a coming cataclysm upon the return of the god-king Quetzalcoatl (the feathered serpent). Quetzalcoatl had been known as a white-skinned deity who took the shape of a man. Understandably, then, the emperor was taken aback by Cortés, with his pale complexion, blue eyes, and red hair. Although still suspicious that the newcomers were men and not gods, Moctezuma initially tried to bribe the mysterious visitors to leave by offering them generous gifts of gold. Yet this only confirmed the Spaniards' resolve to march on Tenochtitlan and confiscate all its wealth. With the help of superior weaponry, the invaders were able to overcome their numerical disadvantage and quickly decapitated the empire by taking Moctezuma hostage. Although the Aztecs did rebound and made a last attempt to fight off their attackers, by 1521 they had been devastated by smallpox and were literally starving to death. The empire was destroyed and the rest of central Mexico fell soon thereafter.[3]

Built atop of the ruined Aztec capital, Mexico City became the center of the Viceroyalty of New Spain. The territory it covered was immense; it would eventually run from Panama to California, and include a few Caribbean islands as well as the Philippines. For 300 years, New Spain was the most productive and most populous of the Spanish colonies. Although it was eventually silver that produced the most fabulous wealth for Spain, the Spanish crown also encouraged the establishment of haciendas with the encomienda system, which rewarded the conquistadors with land grants and guarantees of plentiful labor. For the Indians this meant their virtual enslavement, as they were now compelled to provide their colonizers with tribute and free labor, in return for the right to live on their own land. Under their agreement with the crown, the encomenderos were supposed to Christianize and assimilate the Indians into a faithful, Spanish-speaking work force. To help them do this, the Franciscans and other Catholic missionaries arrived early in the sixteenth century and succeeded in making widespread and rapid conversions. However, more

than protecting the new converts, the encomienda system and later colonial policies allowed for their exploitation and abuse.[4]

Eventually it became clear that there simply was not enough labor for the colonial economy to produce the wealth Spain demanded. Living conditions under colonialism were so harsh that the area remained relatively depopulated for some time. To augment the labor force, African slaves were brought in, to share with Indians the lowest rungs of the racist social order. These groups joined mestizos in sporadic rebellions against their mistreatment. However, it was another group—the Creoles, a relatively privileged class—who proved pivotal in Mexico's break from Spain. These second-class citizens within the elite, stigmatized simply because they had been born in the colonies, greatly resented the privileges granted to the immigrant Peninsulars. Moreover, the "Americanos," as they were known, chafed at the fact that the colonial economy was being managed for the benefit of Spain. Instead, the Creoles wanted commercial freedom in order to trade with countries other than Spain, and to become rich without the crown's interference.[5]

For these reasons many Creoles initially supported Father Miguel Hidalgo's social revolution in 1810. However, once it was clear that the changes sought by this movement were so far-reaching as to threaten their interests, the Creoles joined the Peninsulars to put down this and later rebellions seeking radical change. The movement for independence was stalled for nearly a decade until, in 1821, in reaction to liberal reforms in Spain, one elite, led by Agustín de Iturbide, displaced the other. Rallying broader support with talk about popular sovereignty, the Creoles claimed power for themselves. Spain was too weak to do much about it, and Mexico became independent with relatively little bloodshed.[6]

In its first fifty years of independence, Mexico continued to suffer from chronic instability. Between 1821 and 1860 the country went through at least fifty different presidencies, each averaging less than one year, and thirty-five of Mexico's presidents during this period were army officers. Government was changed at gunpoint; it was the age of caudillos, warlords seeking wealth, promising order, and surviving on patronage. Antonio López de Santa Anna was the most notorious of them all—he held the presidency on nine separate occasions. It was also during this period that Mexico suffered its most humiliating experience, enduring several foreign interventions. After a disastrous war with the United States in 1848, Mexico was forced to cede the huge swath of land between Texas and the Pacific (approximately half of Mexico's territory).[7]

For much of the rest of its first hundred years of independence, Mexico was polarized politically, torn apart by the rivalry between liberals and conservatives. In this often-bitter battle, conservatives sought to promote order and defend the Catholic Church, which was by now institutionalized as a wealthy and influential interest group in a firm alliance with elites. On the other hand, liberals were anticlerical and argued that the Church was entirely too powerful—politically and economically—and that reforms were badly needed. The leader of the liberal movement during much of the nineteenth century was Benito Juárez, who as president sought to strip power from both the army and the Church. Conservatives counterattacked and even supported the French, who invaded to collect on Mexico's debt and overthrew the Juárez government in 1864.[8]

The period of French rule under Emperor Maximillian was relatively brief and Juárez was eventually reinstated, but the liberal-conservative divide continued to dominate politics until the rise of the last caudillo, Porfirio Díaz. It can be said that

Díaz, who took the post of president through a coup d'état and remained in power for over thirty years (1876–1911), finally provided Mexico with some stability, if nothing else. Associated with the "modernization" of Mexico, Díaz made generous concessions to foreign investors, sold Indian landholdings to private entrepreneurs, and argued that the repression associated with his rule was for a good cause—to modernize Mexico. Considered a loyal friend of the United States, Díaz ensured that any "progress" for Mexicans made on his watch accrued to himself and his cronies.[9]

One lesson of history is that policies that create such widespread misery tend to invite disorder. Francisco Madero, a liberal seeking democratic change in Mexico, ran for president against Díaz in 1910. However, after his suspicions were confirmed that Díaz would not allow himself to be voted out of power, Madero and his followers resorted to more violent means. From all over the country the people answered his call for the overthrow of Díaz, including Emiliano Zapata from the south and Pancho Villa from the north. This was the beginning of the Mexican Revolution; the movement grew rapidly and Díaz, surprisingly weak, stepped down in 1911.[10]

But it was only the beginning of the first major social revolution of the twentieth century. Madero was now president, but he was more of a parliamentarian than a revolutionary. Because the changes he initiated were deemed too little, too late, he was soon confronted by his former compadres. During the most violent phase of the revolution, the country broke down into a brutal civil war that raged until 1917. It was only after disposing of Zapata and Villa that Venustiano Carranza became president, declaring the revolution a success.[11]

The constitution resulting from this revolution was startlingly radical for the times. It set out a framework for significant changes in Mexico's power relationships. Among other things, the constitution (which remains the foundation of Mexico's government today) places significant restrictions on the Church. Far more progressive than labor laws in the United States at the time, the 1917 constitution established the right to strike, the right to a minimum wage, and the right to a safe workplace. As one might expect after years of foreign domination, the document is intensely nationalistic, and places restrictions on foreign ownership. Most significant, perhaps, the constitution gives the government the right to control Mexico's resources and to redistribute land.[12]

The first years of implementation of the revolution's goals were very slow. In part this was because the government was sidetracked by a civil war in the 1920s when conservative Catholics sought to regain power for the Church. It was also partly due to the fact that the leaders who survived the revolution were not nearly as progressive as its architects. However, by the 1930s, Mexicans had in Lázaro Cárdenas a president determined to reaffirm the revolution's goals. His administration was responsible for distributing 18 million hectares of land, almost twice the amount distributed by all his predecessors combined. Moreover, the Cárdenas government recognized the necessity of providing support services to assist land recipients, whether they lived in the communal system of *ejido*, or on individual family plots.[13]

Although he attempted to steer a middle course, neither too socialist nor too capitalist, Cárdenas was most of all a nationalist, and his attempts to make real the promises of the revolution were perceived by foreign interests—including the United States—as threatening. As late as the 1930s, foreign firms had effectively controlled Mexico's oil reserves. However, invoking the constitutional right of Mexico to con-

trol its subsoil resources, Cárdenas expropriated these properties, compensated the companies, and established PEMEX as a state oil monopoly.[14]

Petroleum was only one vital industry in which the state would play a large role. However, the bulk of the Mexican economy continued to be held privately. From the 1940s to the 1960s, Mexico experienced a "miracle" in terms of economic growth, which was nearly unsurpassed, averaging 6 percent per year. Elites were the primary beneficiaries of the so-called miracle. The Mexican middle class grew, but poverty persisted and the gap between rich and poor actually loomed wider. To address this problem and win the support of the poor, the government created a broad system of social assistance. Although it has never amounted to a significant redistribution of income, since the 1940s Mexico has had one of the most progressive social assistance programs in Latin America.[15]

As indicated by its economic policy, Mexico's politics since 1917 have been more pragmatic than revolutionary. Soon after the revolution, power was centralized under a single party, which took power in 1928 and controlled the government for seventy years. Known since 1945 as the Institutional Revolutionary Party (PRI), its longevity can be attributed to several less-than-democratic factors, including its organization. It gradually took control of the military and organized labor, and then welcomed its rivals into the fold. It operated an immense system of patronage, in effect mobilizing the support of the peasantry and buying the loyalty of those who might threaten it.[16]

Under the PRI, Mexico became known as the "perfect dictatorship" because, unlike many of its neighbors to the south, where coups were the norm, Mexico enjoyed remarkable stability. However, it is important to remember that the PRI government was authoritarian; as we will see in later chapters, it was not above relying on electoral fraud or even physical coercion to retain power.

Still, compared to many other countries such as Chile and Argentina, such behavior was uncharacteristic of Mexico. As the primary force guiding Mexican politics since the revolution, the PRI was pragmatic ideologically. Although there have always been differences within this large and heterogeneous party, a "pendulum effect" ensuring a tendency toward the center worked for decades to hold all the different elements of the PRI together. For many years this was the secret of the PRI's success. Until the 1980s, Mexico was effectively a single-party state; the opposition was small and seldom won elections. However, by the early 1980s this had begun to change, as elements within the PRI recognized that the party's survival was incumbent upon its ability to adapt to a variety of changed realities. The split within the PRI became more apparent as Mexico set out on a long road to POLITICAL LIBERALIZATION. The modest political opening continued gradually and the PRI appeared to reverse course on several occasions, such as when it claimed victory in the highly disputed presidential elections of 1988. However, prodded by CIVIL SOCIETY, the PRI managed its internal divisions to allow in 2000 for the freest and fairest elections in Mexico's history.

Case Study: Peru

Although the first Peruvians are believed to have been semi-nomadic shellfish collectors and fishermen, the earliest known permanent settlements developed with the introduction of maize and the adoption of impressive irrigation systems. The transformation of marginal lands into abundant fields formed the basis of several

pre-Inca civilizations, such as the Moche and the Nazca, known for their sophisticated crafts and ceremonial buildings.[17]

However, it is the civilization of the Inca for which Peru is best known. Its empire was immense, running 4,000 kilometers along the spine of the Andes. Heralded for their material well-being and cultural sophistication, the Inca rivaled or even surpassed other great empires in world history. Although there are still debates as to the origins of the Inca, in a relatively short period of a century they were able to subdue and incorporate nearly 12 million people.[18]

At the helm of power was the emperor, who was considered both man and god. Divinely ordained, he enjoyed absolute power and controlled vast material resources. Systems of mutual assistance and expectations of reciprocity were core values of the Inca. Kin groups were allocated shares of land by the state. In return, individuals were expected to work the land, keeping a third of their produce for themselves and turning over a third to support state functions and a third to serve ecclesiastical needs. Subjects were also expected to perform *mita,* or draft labor, through which they helped construct and maintain public works, including a remarkable system of roads and bridges.[19]

Yet this highly sophisticated, militarized state, defended by tens of thousands of warriors, was unable to stand against 168 Spanish adventurers seeking their fortunes. Clearly, the Spanish had an overwhelming military advantage. Just as crucially, the empire was already factionalized and vulnerable when the foreigners arrived, having just been through a civil war, the result of a succession crisis. The Spanish were able to capitalize on this, using a policy of divide and conquer. Led by the seasoned conquistador Francisco Pizarro, the Spanish ambushed the overconfident Inca and took their ruler, Atahualpa, hostage in 1532. The empire fell soon thereafter.[20]

In the early colonial economy of plunder, Peru became Spain's great treasure house. Lima was constructed as the capital of this seat of Spanish colonial administration, and became known as the Viceroyalty of Peru (1543). Mining overwhelmingly dominated the colonial economy. Little else mattered; as one viceroy famously put it, "If there are no mines, there is no Peru."[21] Silver became the engine for colonial development in Peru, as the demands of the boomtowns created by mining stimulated agricultural production. In addition, Lima became a vibrant center for merchants active in the Atlantic and Pacific trades.[22]

However, because the prosperity of Spain and its settlers was dependent on a reliable source of cheap labor, the indigenous peoples of Peru were pressed into service. Harassed and humiliated by the Spanish, in the early years of colonial rule many Indians were rendered landless and virtually enslaved under the feudal encomienda system. Under a form of extortion known as the *reparto,* Spanish administrators forced Indians to buy European goods at high prices. Distorting the Inca system of *mita,* the Spanish compelled all adult male Indians to spend part of their year laboring in Spanish mines, farms, and public works (without the state providing anything in reciprocity). Because the silver and mercury mines were such notorious death traps and paid little, the *mita* served as a crucial source of labor for the colonial economy.[23]

Such policies had a devastating impact on the indigenous population. The *mita* drained off able-bodied workers, contributing to the social disintegration of indigenous communities. Famine became commonplace, and populations already weakened fell easily to disease. People were demoralized. Abortion, infanticide, and suicide became

common forms of escape. Because of the depopulation of Indian communities, significant numbers of Africans were brought to Peru as slaves to meet the colonial economy's demand for labor.[24] Although they were treated as less than human by the colonial system, Africans, Indians, and mestizos were by no means passive in their acceptance of this situation. The eighteenth century was an especially tumultuous time in Peru, as over a hundred popular uprisings occurred, some of them seriously threatening the established order. The most significant of these insurgencies was the Great Rebellion of 1780–1781. Led by a curaca who adopted the name of the last Inca king, Túpac Amaru, this revolt was based in Inca nationalism and spread rapidly throughout the southern Andes. Determined to contain the well-organized mass movement, the Spanish set out to reconquer the area, terrorizing villages. Six months later this short but vicious civil war was over, with more than 100,000 dead (nearly 10 percent of the entire population).[25]

The Great Rebellion had the effect of unifying Creoles and Peninsulars against the threat to their privileges. By the early nineteenth century, compared to the rest of Spanish America, the Viceroyalty of Peru was a royalist stronghold. And because the colonial ruling class didn't fracture in Peru as it did elsewhere in Spanish America, it took an intervention of foreign armies to bring independence to the country. With General José de San Martín pressing into Peru from the south, and General Simón Bolívar coming in from the north, Peruvian Creoles reluctantly declared independence in 1821. However, it was not until Bolívar undertook his final campaign against Spain in 1824 that his troops, assisted by Indian GUERRILLA forces, finally defeated the royalists. The republic was established and Bolívar set about the difficult task of establishing the first political institutions of independent Peru.[26]

However, Peruvians were divided over what type of government to pursue, and no constitution lasted for long. Although its constitutions contained liberal guarantees of democracy, equality, and respect for human rights, Peru remained a highly stratified society where race and class determined privilege. Power remained dispersed to the countryside as a semifeudal network of Creole landowners controlled vast areas, free from restraint. The 1890–1930 boom in agro-exports accelerated the problem of landlessness for the majority, while the largest haciendas were owned by a group known in Peru as "the forty families." As a result, landholding in Peru remains grossly unequal, and among the most skewed in all of Latin America. During much of the twentieth century, 0.1 percent of farm families controlled 30 percent of the country's land, and more than half of its best soils. This oligarchy, composed of businessmen and landowners, continued for years to dominate Peru. A COMPRADOR class, these elites manipulated politics to serve their own economic interests. For many years this oligarchy was backed by two of the most powerful institutions in the country, the military and the Catholic Church.[27]

In the early years of independence, civilian and military strongmen fought for political power. The country fell into a long period of caudillism. Coups and countercoups were common, particularly in the first thirty years of independence, when there were twenty-four changes of regime. This initial experience established a pattern for Peruvian politics that has persisted, with use of force widely accepted as a means of resolving political conflict.[28]

Just as Peru's politics have swung back and forth between civilian and military rule, its economic fortunes have alternated between boom and bust. After the wars for independence, Peru was in an economic crisis. Silver production had dropped,

military spending was high, and the country suffered from chronic deficits. However, by the mid-nineteenth century, guano, or bird droppings, were to have the same effect on the economy that silver once did. Accumulating over thousands of years on the islands off Peru's coast, guano was rich in nitrogen. Once used by Indians as a fertilizer, guano was rediscovered and exported to Europe in the 1840s. For fifty years the guano boom created great prosperity for the Peruvian oligarchy and the British (who took about half the profits). However, by the 1880s the guano deposits were largely depleted, and Peru was soon unable to pay its bills. Peruvian governments began a tradition of selling off state interests to foreigners, and ended up putting the country's development in the hands of outsiders.

Eventually Peru managed to move away from its dependence on a single export, and began selling a variety of raw materials to Europe such as copper, tin, and rubber. However, because the economy remained focused on production for the international market, not domestic demand, it was more vulnerable to price swings created by forces beyond its control. Adopting a program of export-led growth, Peru continued to experience boom-and-bust cycles. The gap between rich and poor continued to grow. Whenever a government suggested reforms that threatened the interests of traditional elites, the military stepped in.[29]

However, when the military intervened in 1968, "politics as usual" in Peru were dramatically altered. Cuba's Fidel Castro described it "as if a fire had started in the firehouse."[30] The military, which had traditionally repressed all demands for drastic change, initiated a social revolution. At the head of this revolution was General Juan Velasco Alvarado, who as president proclaimed a new economic order that would be based on neither capitalism nor communism. At the heart of this program was a sweeping agrarian reform, to rectify the entrenched imbalance in landownership and severe inequalities intensified by an economic decline and accompanied by a marked growth in population. Military reformers also sought to promote a more autonomous development by nationalizing the assets of the foreign corporations that dominated the Peruvian economy, such as the International Petroleum Corporation.[31]

However ambitious the revolution's goals, very little worked as planned, and by 1975 it was over. The reforms were halted and a new government set out once again to calm the oligarchy's fears, embrace a free market approach, and assure foreign capitalists that they were welcome in Peru. However, the economy did not recover. Rather, world prices continued to decline for the country's exports and its foreign debt ballooned. When Alan García was elected president in 1985, he attempted to turn the country around by rejecting the liberal economic strategies of his predecessors. An economic nationalist, García shocked the international community by announcing he would limit Peru's interest payments on its foreign debt to 10 percent of its export earnings. The INTERNATIONAL MONETARY FUND (IMF) responded by declaring Peru ineligible for new credits. The punishment took its toll; Peru was bankrupt and suddenly the world's basket case.[32]

Meanwhile, Peruvians had become caught up in a brutal civil war provoked by the glaring gap between the affluent coast and the desperately poor sierra. The highly secretive Maoist guerrilla group Shining Path (Sendero Luminoso), called for the creation of an egalitarian utopia. During the 1980s, both Shining Path and the Peruvian military became known worldwide for their use of terror. As the war grew more intense, the rebels seemed unstoppable, taking large portions of the countryside. Civil-

ian governments declared states of emergency, giving the military a free hand in much of the country, and suspended most civil rights. Secret military trials of those suspected of ties to Shining Path landed thousands of innocents in prison. García and his successor, Alberto Fujimori, were both caught in the unenviable position of having to rely on the army against Shining Path. In 1990, after twelve years of uninterrupted civilian rule, Peru's constitution granted excessive powers to the executive, while its democratic institutions were still alarmingly weak.[33] Elected that year, Fujimori immediately took aggressive steps to deal with the economic and political instability rocking Peru. To jump-start the failing economy, he adopted an extreme policy of NEOLIBERALISM and imposed austerity measures advocated by the IMF. In the war against terror, President Fujimori preferred a similarly draconian approach. In return for cooperation in the US war on drugs, he amassed enough military power to turn loose his security forces on the countryside. When questioned about the iron grip he claimed was a necessity, the democratically elected president of Peru carried out an *autogolpe* (self-coup) in 1992, taking for himself the power to rule by decree. With the help of the military, he closed the congress and the judiciary, suspended the constitution, and proclaimed a state of emergency. Initially the public overwhelmingly supported the *autogolpe,* primarily because they were desperate for a solution.[34]

Peruvians later reelected Fujimori president, since he was able to provide some semblance of order. Although Fujimori was eventually credited with destroying the terrorists and stabilizing the economy, over time his support dwindled as the population began to question the necessity of his continued authoritarianism. When Fujimori once again attempted to extend his hold on power, ensuring his reelection through whatever means necessary, Peruvians risked clashing with the military and went out into the streets to demand his resignation. After scandals involving videotapes and a manhunt that now seems almost farcical, Fujimori, one of the few dictators left in the region, did finally step down in 2000, paving the way for Peru to make yet another attempt at democratic government and economic development.[35]

Case Study: Nigeria

The country today known as Nigeria contains hundreds of different ethnic groups, each with its own history. Because of the heterogeneity of these peoples it is impossible to begin to describe all of them here. However, a sketch of the Hausa, Yoruba, and Ibo gives one a sense of the diversity existing in Nigeria. They are the three largest ethnic groups, composing two-thirds of the country's population.

Situated at the edge of the Sahara, the Hausa states of northern Nigeria were kingdoms that rose to prominence based on their location as a major terminus of the trans-Saharan trade. Not only fine craftsmen and rich merchants, their kings taxed goods that traveled through their territory on caravans. A strong cavalry-based military ensured the orderly conduct of business, and offered travelers protection from raiders. From the fourteenth century on, Islamic culture and religion gradually spread through northern Nigeria, primarily through commercial networks. Kano was long a famous center of Islamic learning, although Islam did not become a mass religion among the Hausa until an Islamic revolution in the early nineteenth century. A Fulani preacher, Usman dan Fodio, led devout Muslims displeased with corrupt Hausa kings, excessive taxes, and laxity in the practice of Islam in a JIHAD against their rulers. He brought

together the discontented into a powerful revival movement that incorporated the Hausa states into a vast theocracy, the Sokoto Caliphate. Conversion was brought with war, as the jihad spread Islam into central and southwestern Nigeria.[36]

One of the groups affected by this expansionist policy in the south were the Yoruba. This powerful empire was based on a confederation of ancient Yoruba kingdoms and known for its remarkable bronzes and terracottas. The most influential of these kingdoms, Oyo, was at its height between the sixteenth and eighteenth centuries. A large and prosperous megastate, it controlled the trade routes to Hausaland and had a formidable military, with overwhelming numbers of bowmen and cavalry. The power of Yoruba kings was limited by a constitutional monarchy that required that kings confer with a council. However, by the late eighteenth century the Oyo king had become increasingly despotic, violating the traditional rights of the population to participate in decisionmaking. This contributed to a series of devastating civil wars that lasted for the next century.[37]

As opposed to the more centralized Hausa and Yoruba governments with their kings and hierarchies, the Ibo lived in relatively egalitarian ministates in which political power was decentralized. There was no empire, no expansionist military; in fact, there were no kings, presidents, or full-time political leaders of any kind. Rather, the Ibo lived in stateless societies. If democracy is largely about the right of political participation, then traditional Ibo politics were extremely democratic. Nearly all Ibo were part of the great assemblies that came together to make important decisions for the group. A council of elders and other age- or gender-based associations enforced these decisions. Although the Ibo traditionally lived in the forests of southeastern Nigeria, they were hardly isolated. As forest farmers, the Ibo produced valuable commodities such as kola nuts (important for ceremonial reasons and one of the few stimulants allowed Muslims) to sell in the long-distance trade that crossed the Sahara.[38]

European demand gradually redirected the caravan-based desert trade toward the coast. Nigeria was located in the heart of what became known as the Slave Coast. At the peak of the transatlantic slave trade, 20,000 people each year were taken from this area to be sold as slaves. Throughout much of Nigeria, larger military states such as those of the Hausa and Yoruba raided their neighbors for war captives, who were then passed on to African middlemen and sold to Europeans waiting at trading stations on the coast. Although some Africans became wealthy from this trade, it proved devastating for many others. As the slave trade became less profitable it was replaced by the LEGITIMATE TRADE. A number of European countries were by this time rising industrial powers intent on trading their manufactured goods for cheap raw materials. In Nigeria, British trading houses promoted the production of cash crops such as palm kernel, which could be used as an industrial lubricant and processed into a variety of products, including soap and candles.[39]

French and German merchants were also interested in this territory, which by the late nineteenth century Britain considered to fall within its sphere of influence. In an effort to eliminate foreign competition of all kinds, African leaders were compelled to sign treaties of protection and free trade (in effect bypassing indigenous middlemen and maximizing British profits). The British sent military expeditions to "pacify" those who resisted this encroachment. With conquest still not complete, the British claimed control of the Colony of Lagos and Protectorate of Southern Nigeria (1900) and the Protectorate of Northern Nigeria (1903). The British conquered

these territories separately and they administered them separately, as two very different systems. This policy continued even after the so-called amalgamation of the northern and southern protectorates in 1914.[40]

The architect of this policy was Sir Frederick Lugard, who believed that the north was different from the south and that each should develop autonomously. To overcome shortages of funds and personnel, the British attempted to use a policy known as indirect rule. As opposed to the direct rule associated with the French and which required large numbers of French administrators, indirect rule was much less expensive because it allowed the British to govern through indigenous rulers. It depended on the cooperation of traditional elites, or "native authorities," who served as intermediaries between the British and the indigenous masses and enforced colonial policy.[41]

Perhaps not surprisingly, in many parts of Nigeria the native authorities were hated by their own people and viewed as corrupt collaborators of colonialism. Although people from all classes found ways to indicate their displeasure with foreign rule, ironically it was the Western, Christian missionaries who educated a new elite of African nationalists. Urban and predominantly southern Nigerian teachers, clerks, doctors, and other professionals asserted themselves as agents of social change. They urged other Nigerians to join across ethnic and regional divides to form trade unions, independent churches, newspapers, and various movements that would become the country's first political parties in the 1920s. Leaders of these early political movements, such as Herbert Macaulay (considered by many the father of Nigerian nationalism), often sought reform, not independence. They criticized the colonial government and looked forward to self-rule, but expected the transfer of power to be gradual. On the other hand, radical nationalism experienced an upsurge after the 1930s, as the movement for independence spread beyond Lagos. For example, students organizing the Nigerian Youth Movement were more militant in their demands, calling for mass education, equal economic opportunities, and a transfer of power to Nigerians.[42]

The British reacted in a variety of ways to the nationalist demands. In some cases they resorted to repressive measures, firing on or jailing nationalists. Eventually the British offered some concessions, including a series of constitutional proposals for self-government. After years of negotiations, the transfer of power began in 1948. Suddenly Nigerians were to be prepared for the administration and development of their country. The participants agreed that upon independence they would establish a parliamentary democracy and continue with a capitalist economic system. The British left peacefully, assured that their vital economic interests would be protected.[43]

As the date of independence neared, the nationalists abandoned the unified, pan-Nigerian approach they had adopted against colonial rule. The major ethnic groups formed regionally based political parties caught up in a three-way struggle: the Action Group (largely Yoruba), the Northern People's Congress (representing the Hausa), and the National Congress of Nigeria and the Cameroons (which drew mostly Ibo support). With the British effectively out of the way, now the enemy was other Nigerians. Perceiving politics to be a zero-sum game, there was a polarization of the political process as each group vied for control of the country's resources.[44]

Yet in 1960, when Nigeria finally became independent, most people were still hopeful about the ability of Nigerians to steer the country toward development. The new government was modeled on British parliamentary democracy. The country was to be administered through a federal system, and was initially divided into three regions:

north, west, and east. In the first general elections, in 1964, the Northern People's Congress easily established its dominance, controlling enough seats in parliament to name Tafawa Balewa prime minister of Nigeria's First Republic, its first attempt at civilian rule. When Nigeria became a republic, a Nigerian from the east (Nnamdi Azikiwe) replaced the British queen in the ceremonial role of head of state. Obafemi Awolowo of the Action Group was to lead the loyal opposition.[45]

However, almost immediately, all went wrong. Although technically Nigeria had a multiparty system, in each region one large ethnic group dominated all the smaller ones. Even more problematic, the northern region was given twice the area and population of the other two. Given their long history of distrust, there was little prospect of the eastern and western regions ever joining together effectively against the northern region. Tensions mounted. The 1964 parliamentary elections were widely suspected of fraud, and ethnic minorities complained about their lack of representation. Violence broke out in various parts of the country and the government was too weak to contain it. Politics had become a winner-take-all game in which compromise was extremely difficult. Because the country was in constant crisis during its first six years of independence, no one was surprised by (and many Nigerians welcomed) the country's first coup d'état, led by Ibo officers in 1966.[46]

Yet like the rest of Nigeria the military too has suffered from ethnic, regional, and other divisions. Fear of Ibo dominance contributed to a second coup in 1966, and again northerners controlled the government. The purges and pogrom that followed convinced the Ibo to secede and declare the independent Republic of Biafra. Just seven years after independence, Nigeria was fracturing, consumed by a civil war, the Biafran War, from 1967 to 1970. Determined to maintain the territorial integrity of Nigeria (as well as control over its oil wealth, much of which would have been lost to Biafra), the federal government put up a fierce resistance. The fighting was prolonged, as the federal government could not prevail against the forest fighters. In the end, the government resorted to quarantining eastern Nigeria and cutting off food supplies to the Ibo. By the time the Ibo submitted to such tactics and surrendered, an estimated 1 million people had been starved to death.[47]

Remarkably, the country remained intact, largely because of a government program of reconciliation and reconstruction. Such a policy was greatly facilitated by the sudden windfall produced by the jump in the price of oil in the 1970s. As a member of the Organization of Petroleum Exporting Countries (OPEC), Nigeria enjoyed great prosperity in this period. Overnight it had become one of the wealthiest countries in the world. Unfortunately, since then most of Nigeria's fortune has been stolen or squandered. This was particularly the case during the Second Republic, from 1979 to 1983, when President Shehu Shagari turned politics into a business. The democratic process was subverted as abuse of power occurred on an unprecedented scale. Corruption was so massive and Shagari's government so audacious that fires were set in public buildings to destroy evidence. After a sham vote in which Shagari had himself reelected, the country broke out into open conflict that was only brought to a halt with another coup.

Thus Nigeria settled into a long period of military rule. During most of the 1980s and 1990s, the generals who ruled Nigeria were more authoritarian and kleptocratic than ever, even as the country slipped into a deep economic decline. After years of overspending and misusing funds, it was now a major debtor. The structural adjustment pre-

scribed by the IMF prioritized debt repayment over basic needs. Nigeria's relations with its creditors improved, but the reforms failed to correct the economy's structural ills.[48]

Meanwhile the dictatorship was under foreign and domestic pressure to make political as well as economic reforms. After putting off the transfer of power as long as possible, General Ibrahim Babangida offered up his personal design for a Third Republic. When relatively free and fair elections were finally held in 1993, one of Babangida's handpicked candidates, Moshood Abiola, was elected president. As a Muslim Yoruba, he would be the first civilian president from the predominantly Christian south. However, almost immediately Babangida annulled the result, for reasons that are still unclear. Such actions confirmed Yoruba suspicions that the north would never share power or control over the country's oil revenues. Protests shook the country and Babangida stepped down. Within just a few months, one of Babangida's advisers, General Sani Abacha, had overturned the weak interim government.[49]

Abacha presided over the most predatory dictatorship Nigeria had ever known. Living standards fell to their lowest point in twenty years. Brazenly corrupt and notoriously cruel, Abacha set about crushing all dissent. For asserting himself to be the legitimate president, Abiola was arrested for treason (a capital offense) and imprisoned until his death, of apparently natural causes, in 1998. The government became an international pariah for its use of state terrorism against its own people. It is sometimes said that Nigeria became as quiet as a graveyard—until, in what is widely considered a "coup by God," Sani Abacha was found dead in his own bed under somewhat scandalous circumstances.[50]

Abacha's death was celebrated with dancing in the streets. His sudden departure paved the way for another attempt at a transition to civilian rule. The Fourth Republic began with elections in 1999, with all the same problems of its predecessors. This time, it was up to a former military dictator, Olusegun Obasanjo, to lead the country in correcting these problems before the cycle began yet again.

Case Study: Zimbabwe

There was great cultural, political, and economic diversity among the early people of Zimbabwe. Hunter-gatherers long preceded the Shona, Zimbabwe's largest ethnic group, who arrived in the area around C.E. 300. Among the Shona were several subgroups, some of whom lived in empires, and others who preferred stateless societies. Although they are known to have mined and worked with a variety of minerals, most notably iron ore and gold, cattle-keeping was a more important activity for most Shona, who also worked as farmers. Perhaps the wealthiest empire of southern Africa, Great Zimbabwe was an ancient city famous for its stone buildings and vast walls. For reasons that are still unclear, Great Zimbabwe declined and was abandoned in the fifteenth century. On its heels a larger Shona empire was founded in the north, known as Mwene Mutapa (Great Plunderer). Like Great Zimbabwe, it too had an expansionist policy and took tribute from subjugated populations. Though without the cultural and technological achievements of Great Zimbabwe, Mwene Mutapa was also rich in resources and favored by its river access to the main trading centers on the coast. Long before the Portuguese established trading posts nearby, the Shona had been involved in a regional network of trade that connected southern central Africa to coastal trading cities and the Indian Ocean trade.[51]

Most of Zimbabwe continued to be dominated by various Shona kingdoms until the early nineteenth century, when events in South Africa changed the balance of power dramatically. Various South African ethnic groups, including the Ndebele, fled, seeking shelter from the Zulu military onslaught known as the Mfecane, or Great Crushing. By the 1840s the Ndebele had settled in southwestern Zimbabwe, which became known as Matabeleland. Though unable to defend themselves against the overwhelming might of the Zulu, the highly centralized Ndebele kingdom had a professional army and absorbed the resident Shona-speaking inhabitants. The Ndebele also dominated many Shona groups in eastern Zimbabwe, raiding Mashonaland periodically for cattle, grain, and women.[52]

Another raider of sorts, Cecil John Rhodes was one of the biggest empire builders of the nineteenth century. Having come to South Africa from Britain at age seventeen, Rhodes soon became a self-made millionaire as a founder of DeBeers Diamonds. Interested in money for the power it could buy, Rhodes was a British supremacist and advocate of British imperialism. His interest in Zimbabwe was based on rumors of more gold fields to the north of South Africa's enormous Witwatersrand gold reef. Rhodes sent emissaries to Matabeleland to push for concessions. In 1888 the Ndebele king, Lobengula, was deceived into signing an agreement, known as the Rudd Concession, that basically gave the British mineral rights to the entire territory, placing it within the British sphere of influence.[53]

Soon after winning the concession, Rhodes formed the British South Africa Company, and obtained a royal charter to colonize and administer the area north of the Limpopo River on behalf of Britain. Rhodes recruited a "pioneer column" of settlers to invade and occupy Zimbabwe. Upon arrival in Zimbabwe in 1890, the whites first established themselves in the predominantly Shona east.[54]

Conditions were ripe for conflict. Disappointed with its luck at striking gold, the British South African Company began looking beyond Mashonaland for new areas to mine. Yet not only were the Europeans antagonizing the Shona, but the Ndebele considered the east to be their raiding ground and resented the whites' presence. When the British attempted to establish a boundary requiring the Ndebele to confine their raids to the western side of the "border," a clash between the settlers and the Ndebele was inevitable. After a series of provocative incidents, the two parties were at war. Although the company's forces were greatly outnumbered, the British, with their modern firearms against the Ndebele's spears, swept into the west. Lobengula died during his escape, and with the Ndebele demoralized, Matabeleland was opened to white settlers. The British forced the Ndebele onto dry and infertile reserves and gave Lobengula's cattle to whites. The entire territory was placed under colonial rule in 1895 and became known as Rhodesia. By all appearances, the once-powerful Ndebele were now prostrate, utterly defeated.[55]

So when a series of uprisings broke out in 1895–1896 and spread over Zimbabwe, the British were taken by surprise. Yet for the Ndebele and the Shona, colonialism meant not only political oppression and economic exploitation, but also an assault on their way of life. Aggravating their problems were a series of natural disasters. Many Ndebele and Shona believed that these misfortunes were attributable to the presence of whites on their land. Traditional religious authorities blamed the whites for angering God, and warned that Africans must fight to drive out the whites or they would continue to suffer. Consequently, so many of the indigenous people re-

sponded to the war cry "Chimurenga!" that the whites, even with their military advantages, found the uprisings difficult to put down.[56]

However, with the help of imperial troops, by 1897 the leaders of what is called the First Chimurenga War had been killed or captured. The British colonial office took over responsibility for Rhodesia, although the white settlers largely administered the country to suit their interests. Africans became second-class citizens in their own land, as racist laws enforced a color bar. Blacks were systematically humiliated and exploited. The country was divided into white areas and black areas. White settlers poured in, taking the best land and establishing large farms. Most blacks were left poor and landless, forced to live in the 31 percent of the territory assigned to them—the wastelands known as reserves. Africans were compelled to work in slave-like conditions. To earn money to pay taxes to the colonial state, young men had little choice but to sign contracts requiring them to leave their families behind on the reserves for a year at a time while they worked in white-owned mines or farms. There discrimination was systematic; the disparity in wages between white and black workers was enormous. As late as the 1960s, white mine workers earned twelve times as much as Africans—and white farm workers earned twenty times as much as blacks.[57]

Moreover, the colonial system did everything it could to ensure that African political participation was kept at a minimum. Theoretically, Africans could vote in elections for a legislative council, but because the property and educational qualifications for the franchise were set so high, blacks were legally denied a political voice in this "democracy." This does not mean, however, that blacks had no political voice. Against the overwhelming force of the colonial military, many Africans turned to weapons of the weak, adopting postures of noncooperation or "refusal to understand." When possible, workers simply deserted the most abusive bosses and shared "market intelligence," leaving wayside messages such as signs carved on trees that alerted others to avoid those employers.[58]

Some Africans submitted to colonial rule, but this does not mean that they accepted it. Rather, in order to survive, they chose to cooperate and seek some amelioration in their treatment. Still, self-government was a long-term objective for many. By the 1920s, larger numbers of Ndebele had adopted modern forms of political protest. Led by a new elite known for its moderation, they sought change through constitutional means. Black immigrants to Zimbabwe were frequently the initiators of mass-based protest. South Africans founded the Rhodesian Bantu Voters Association, which brought together Zimbabweans from different regions and ethnic backgrounds, and appealed to ordinary people by focusing on the land issue. Churches such as the millenarian Watch Tower movement mobilized grassroots protest.[59] The first African trade union in the colony, the Industrial and Commercial Workers Union, was formed by a Malawian. In response to desperate conditions, Africans led a number of strikes in the first half of the twentieth century. More often than not, such actions were systematically put down by the state.[60]

In their determination not to give in to African demands, the settlers attempted to tighten their control over Africans. One way of doing this was through repression. Under a state of emergency, government was given power to put people in prison without trial. Political parties were banned; activists were rounded up, detained, and imprisoned. Another strategy was to ally with traditional elites. Many of these elites, who had long worked for the colonial government as Native Authorities,

were valued for their loyalty and the influence they held in their communities. By co-opting these elites and giving them more power than they traditionally held, including more power over women, whites could in effect buy their allegiance and promote a policy of divide and rule, by encouraging tribal consciousness.[61]

A third way of dealing with African nationalism was promoted by white liberals frightened by the Mau Mau killings of British settlers in Kenya. In the 1950s, whites voted in an administration intent upon making Rhodesia appear to be doing something to placate Africans. This government promised land and other reforms (but not "one man, one vote," and franchise qualifications were actually raised). For these reasons, most blacks rejected these "multiracial" reforms as paternalistic delaying tactics.[62]

Nor did the liberal policy sit too well with whites for long. The 1962 elections were the end of the liberal experiment, as for the next two decades white voters put into office right-wing extremists led by the Rhodesian Front. In 1965, without consulting Britain (which still had ultimate responsibility for the colony), Prime Minister Ian Smith cut ties with the mother country. Through the Unilateral Declaration of Independence (UDI), the settlers displayed their disregard of international opinion and declared Rhodesia an independent, white-run state.[63]

Despite African hopes that the British would use force against the UDI government, they were unwilling to intervene. After diplomatic efforts failed, Britain joined the United Nations in imposing economic sanctions on Rhodesia. Sanctions were not a complete failure, but they had little effect, primarily because the United States and other Western countries broke them. Some characterize this policy as racist, and in part it was, because the West viewed the struggle in Rhodesia through a Cold War lens. For Africans the Second Chimurenga War, which began in 1966, was a war for liberation. Yet the white government was able to portray the African opposition as communist, and the conflict in Rhodesia as part of the larger East-West struggle. The two parties that dominated the anticolonial effort, the Zimbabwe African People's Union (ZAPU), led by Joshua Nkomo, and the Zimbabwe African National Union (ZANU), led by Robert Mugabe, eventually joined forces toward the end of the war in what was called the Patriotic Front. Both called for a socialist transformation of society. Even more damning, from a Western perspective, they each received military assistance from the Soviet Union and China, as well as neighboring African countries.[64]

Pressure was building on the white government, and despite Smith's claims that majority rule would come "not in a thousand years," by the early 1970s it was becoming increasingly clear that the white government was losing the war. Desperate to hold on to power, Smith tried to preempt the guerrilla victory by promoting a political coalition. Smith was eventually able to win over Bishop Abel Muzorewa, a conservative who had long been associated with the anticolonial cause. Because Muzorewa could not control the guerrillas and because the Patriotic Front was joined by most of the world in denouncing the new government, the internal settlement was not durable. The guerrillas refused to surrender, international sanctions remained in place, and the war intensified and was virtually won by the guerrillas in 1979.[65]

That year the three parties met in London to negotiate a peace settlement brokered by Britain. The resulting Lancaster House Agreement served as the basis for a new constitution based on majority rule, but with protections for minority rights. It established a parliamentary system with a president acting on the advice of the prime minister and set a date for elections. The parliamentary elections, held in 1980,

were an extraordinary exercise in democracy, as the three bitterly hostile armies put down their weapons to campaign against each other. Voting did largely break down along ethnic lines, and though there were some irregularities, international observers found the process to be free and fair. An estimated 94 percent of the electorate voted and Robert Mugabe, because his party, ZANU (now known as the Zimbabwe African National Union–Patriotic Front [ZANU-PF]), had won an overall majority in parliament, became the first prime minister of independent Zimbabwe.[66]

As prime minister, Mugabe recognized that Zimbabwe needed stability if it were to develop, and that there could be no stability without a policy of reconciliation. Although there were some hard feelings on all sides, Mugabe did create a coalition government, inviting Nkomo and even a few whites to serve as ministers in his cabinet. However, strains resurfaced by the end of the first year, and the country soon fell into a civil war. After years of peacemaking efforts, the two Patriotic Front rivals sat down at the bargaining table. The Unity Accord was reached in 1987 and ZAPU was absorbed into ZANU-PF.[67]

As mentioned earlier, the government's policy of national reconciliation also applied to whites, many of whom had panicked after the Lancaster House accords and planned to leave Zimbabwe. Some did go, but Mugabe worked hard to assure whites that their property rights would be respected. Although an avowed socialist, Mugabe abided by the Lancaster House restrictions on the redistribution of wealth and adopted an economic pragmatism that surprised many. In fact, the mixed economy continued on much as it had before, with the tiny white minority controlling a disproportionate share of the country's resources. For more than twenty years the most crucial issue of all, the land issue, went unresolved. So far, at least, many Zimbabweans have found freedom to offer few material rewards.[68]

Case Study: Egypt

Egypt's history spans three millennia, but going back a mere thousand years or so, to around 7500–5000 B.C.E., most of the occupants of these lands were hunter-gatherers or semi-nomadic herders. As in many other areas of the world, gradually these populations began the shift to agriculture and raising livestock.[69] In Egypt it appears that this adaptation coincided with climatic changes around 5000 B.C.E. As areas of the country grew increasingly arid, people adopted more permanent dwellings along the Nile and plants and animals were domesticated as a survival strategy. The intense competition between farming and herding groups as rivals for resources over time contributed to the emergence of complex, hierarchical societies with chieftain-kings.[70]

It was in the midst of this process, just before 3000 B.C.E., that the two halves of the country were unified into a centralized state that gradually developed into an empire ruled by thirty-one dynasties. This extremely rich agricultural economy, the most productive in the ancient world at its peak, was based in "the Gift of the Nile," which allowed for the production of surpluses of maize and wheat.[71] Over time this economy diversified into manufacturing. The Nile, which is like a major highway running through the valley to the delta and the sea, facilitated the development of Egypt's local and long-distance trade.[72]

For twenty centuries the state's vigorous exploitation of resources sustained rulers and palaces as well as all manner of artistic achievements and monumental

buildings.[73] This system produced large-scale building programs such as the pyramids, which are widely recognized as one of the great administrative feats of history. For example, it took 20,000 men twenty years to construct the Great Pyramid of Khufu, which is composed of 2,500,000 limestone blocks with an average weight of 2.5 tons each. This monumental architecture serves as a testimonial to the power and organization of the state, which is believed to have ruled 3–4 million people at its peak.[74]

Most Egyptians lived as peasants in this highly stratified society. Land was the basis for wealth. All land was controlled by the king (or pharaoh), and allocated by him as a reward for services, and thus was concentrated in the hands of a few.[75] Much of the king's legitimacy was based in the belief that the king was a descendant or the incarnation of the gods. With a dual nature (the divine emanating through his human form), the king was preeminent, an absolute ruler seated at the apex of the political and religious hierarchy.[76]

As elsewhere, class-based inequality coincided and intersected with gender inequality. At times queens ran the country, but they were rarely vested with all the omnipotence of pharaohs. More commonly, as the wives of kings, queens may have had considerable de facto power, but they were not usually considered divine. An exception is Hatshepsut, who ruled a successful and stable regime for fifteen years emphasizing her divine ancestry. She took pains to define her image carefully; in some representations she is presented as female and in others as male, with a beard.[77]

Vested with all-pervasive power, the pharaoh was the king of all lands, the intermediary between the world of men and the gods. His penultimate duty was to protect order by practicing correct behavior and thought, as well as moderation and justice. Failure to uphold these norms—or any loss of control—was traditionally read as a sign that the gods had withdrawn their support from him and that it was time for a change. As a result, the sociopolitical structure over Egypt's thirty-one dynasties should be understood as dynamic, evolving in response to changing local and international events. Droughts and other climatic disasters, along with succession crises, subterfuge, and rivalries, certainly contributed to the fall of more than one dynasty.[78]

Egypt's pharaonic period is also associated with a growing number of military expeditions and a greater opening to the world. Located at the intersection of many trade routes, Egypt became wealthy off the expansion of the long-distance trade in luxury goods.[79] By the final millennium before the common era, Egypt was directing more and more of its energy against foreign enemies and had expanded its empire to include Palestine, Syria, and Nubia. Meanwhile, powerful enemies, attracted by Egypt's strategic importance and extraordinary wealth, had begun to surround the empire. Under this pressure, the empire began to crumble. The central government faltered, rivals began vying for power, and a wave of foreign invasions commenced.[80]

After thousands of years of preeminence, in 535 B.C.E. Egypt dropped in status from empire to the spoils of empire. It was first conquered by the Persians and later the Greeks as Alexander the Great took control of Egypt in 332 B.C.E. The Graeco-Roman period (332 B.C.E. through C.E. 396) lasted for a millennium and marked a seminal event in Egyptian history: the decay of Egypt's cultural core and transformation of the ancient civilization into something new. Perhaps the best way to sum up the significance of these events is this: most accounts of Egyptian history end with Alexander the Great's conquest.[81]

The Egyptians did not passively accept their status as colony; they periodically rose up against corrupt, oppressive, and unjust foreign systems—and they forced the end of more than one foreign occupation.[82] However, for nearly 2,000 years, the country remained a mere province of various larger empires, controlled by Arabs, Europeans (French and British), and the Ottomans. Egyptians found themselves alienated and exploited, second-class citizens in their own land, slaves to foreign rulers.[83]

It was an Albanian soldier serving one of those empires who is said to be the founder of modern Egypt. Ruling the territory from 1805 to 1849, Muhammad Ali, an Ottoman military leader who served as khedive (or viceroy) of Egypt, cut ties to Istanbul and promoted the country's modernization based on a European model. After creating an independent, modern army he transformed Egypt from a provincial Ottoman backwater to an expansionist new state, incorporating parts of neighboring lands.[84] However, after his death his successors were unable to sustain these gains and by the end of the late nineteenth century many of his achievements had been undone. Egypt had fallen heavily into debt and its largest creditor, Britain, had assumed control over the economy and eventually colonized the country.[85]

Clearly, the British occupation of Egypt was driven by economic and strategic interests. The British government shut down Egyptian manufacturers, replacing what was a relatively strong, diversified economy with a monoculture based on cotton (to be sold to British mills). The economy went into shock, stifling inequality grew, and only a tiny minority of landowners and foreigners profited from the cotton economy.[86] Yet, even more essential to British interests was the Suez Canal, a waterway that greatly facilitated transit by connecting the Mediterranean to the Red Sea. The British provided much of the financial backing for its construction and assumed control of what is arguably the most strategic asset in the Middle East.[87]

In a variety of ways (violent and nonviolent), Egyptians resisted British domination. Britain put down the nationalist efforts, sometimes violently, before recognizing Egypt's independence in 1922. Egypt then began a thirty-year liberal experiment with democracy, built around the first comprehensive civic constitution in the Middle East, establishing a constitutional monarchy, the monarch a descendant of Muhammad Ali. It should be noted, however, that there were so many restrictions on this "independence" that for all intents and purposes, the British continued to govern by proxy until 1945, blocking any initiatives or appointments they believed to be contrary to their interests.[88]

After World War II and all the promises of the Atlantic Charter for self-determination, Egyptians were embittered. This "independent country" was still clearly a British dependency.[89] Many Egyptians were disillusioned with parliamentary democracy as a European idea and institution. Some were drawn to Islamic beliefs and values and joined a revolutionary movement, the Society of the Muslim Brothers, which was founded in 1928. Known as the Muslim Brotherhood, the movement rejected political parties, parliaments, and constitutions and instead sought to restore what they considered to be the authentic institutions of Islam as the basis of government. For decades the Brothers led huge rallies against the British presence, but they didn't bring down the government. Rather, it was a group of young, educated, middle-class military officers who changed the system on July 23, 1952, with a swift and bloodless coup. Soon after they dissolved the monarchy and declared Egypt a republic.[90]

One of these officers, Gamal Abdul Nasser, wanted more than just a coup: he wanted a transformation of Egyptian society. The charismatic Nasser, who went on to become the first Egyptian to rule Egypt in over 2,000 years (since Alexander the Great), was a self-declared socialist and POPULIST. Nasser ruled Egypt for sixteen years, giving Egyptians a renewed pride in themselves.[91] Popular because he was anti-imperialist, Nasser reasserted Egypt's standing in the world. He refused to serve as proxy for either side in the Cold War and became a hero in the eyes of many for facing down Britain, France, and Israel in the Suez crisis in 1956. Not only did Nasser nationalize foreign businesses and seek to diversify the economy and reindustrialize it, but he also created a welfare state to raise living standards. He is widely adulated by the masses as the only ruler of Egypt who ever did anything for them. But it was in the later years of Nasser's rule that problems became increasingly apparent. The government had become a police state, autocratic and repressive. The bureaucracy was bloated and mediocre and Nasser's grand projects were wasteful. In sum, the Nasser years failed to transform Egypt; his rule turned out to be more populist coup than revolution.[92]

The power vacuum created by Nasser's death in 1970 was filled by his vice president, Anwar Sadat. In the decade that he ruled practically unopposed, Sadat promised a more liberal regime but proved to be just as dictatorial as his predecessor. But Sadat is best known for breaking with Nasser's policy of nonalignment and opening Egypt to the West by signing the US-brokered Camp David peace accords with Israel. As its reward, Egypt became the second largest recipient of US aid. The peace deal with Israel caused great upset in Egypt, which had fought (and lost) more than one war against its neighbor. Sadat came to be regarded as a puppet and Egypt fell from grace with the Arab world.[93]

Meanwhile, social and economic conditions failed to improve, and many young people, educated and out of work, gravitated toward militant groups inspired by Iran's Islamic Revolution. Sadat was assassinated by a member of such a group on live television in 1981, and Hosni Mubarak, his vice president, a former air force general, was immediately sworn in.[94] Like Nasser and Sadat, Mubarak sought the legitimacy conferred by (less than free and fair) elections. He went on to serve five terms (always winning 90 percent or more of the vote). Also like his predecessors, Mubarak ruled as an absolute power. The "Deep State," the security leviathan institutionalized under Nasser, continued to grow to become far more powerful than any single leader, agency, or branch of the government. Bankrolled by the United States at a rate of $2 billion a year, thanks to Egypt's peace deal with Israel, the Mubarak government was able to hold on to power for decades through co-optation and repression.[95] The tipping point finally came when the United States upped the ante, tying continued US aid to pressure for democracy. It was in the 2005 parliamentary elections that, for the first time, Mubarak allowed the opposition to participate. And when the Muslim Brotherhood, dogged by Egyptian rulers all these years, won 88 of 444 elected seats, it set off an earthquake—with aftershocks that would pose the greatest challenge yet to what had become a near-pharaonic system of government.[96]

Case Study: Iran

Iran, which was known as Persia until 1935, experienced a dramatic transformation from a vast Persian empire (at one point encompassing nearly 45 percent of the

world's population) to an Islamic republic. Grandeur, triumph, invasion, and discord color the historical legacy of this land and people. As a major world empire, Persia and its culture and civilization endured nearly twenty-five centuries of dynastic rule. It was named for the ancient province Parsa, where the first Iranians settled, and at its height ruled over much of the area we now call the Middle East. The survival of Persian cultural and linguistic traditions provides Iranians a nearly continuous cultural tradition up to the present day.

Modern Iranians go out of their way to emphasize their non-Arab, Aryan heritage. One of the clearest manifestations of this is that the dominant language within Iran is Persian, also known as Farsi, rather than Arabic. While the two languages are based in the same alphabet, they have their origins in separate language families (Arabic in Afro-Asiatic, and Farsi in Indo-European). The adoption of Shia Islam (discussed in Chapter 10) also distinguishes Iranians from Turks and Arabs. As evidence of the continuity of some aspects of pre-Islamic culture, the Zoroastrian Norooz is still celebrated today as the first day of the Iranian calendar as well as the first day of spring (March 21).

Inhabitants occupied the region now known as Iran as early as the middle paleolithic times, approximately 100,000 years ago, with sedentary cultures as far back as 18,000 to 14,000 years ago. The Elamites were the original inhabitants of southern portions of the Iranian plateau. Their language is believed to be unique, with no discernible connection to any other linguistic group.[97] The Elamites created a regional civilization, which was highlighted in both Akkadian and Babylonian texts. Iran's abundance of mineral resources was known as early as 9000 B.C.E. and copper metallurgy became common in 5000 B.C.E.

The first dynasty of Iran's pre-Islamic phase was the Achaemenid Dynasty (546–334 B.C.E.), founded by Cyrus the Great, who was known for freeing the Jews from Babylonian captivity. The Achaemenians spoke an Indo-European language and believed in Zoroastrianism, a monotheistic religion that rose in Persia before Christianity. In fact, it is believed that the biblical Three Wise Men who visited the infant Jesus in Nazareth were likely Zoroastrian. A ruler who described his empire as Iranshahr, meaning "land of Aryans," or people who are of pure, noble, and good birth, used the name "Iran" as early as the third century B.C.E.[98] Achaemenid leaders created a hereditary monarchy and empire, which spread throughout the Middle East.

Contemporaneous with the Roman Empire, the Sassanid kings led one of the Persian Empire's grandest dynasties in Mesopotamia and the region now known as Iran. Leadership continued to be hereditary, with a fusion of spiritual and religious power. Sassanid kings imposed Zoroastrianism as the state religion, granting immense powers to members of the clergy. The gradual embrace of Islam began after Persia's wars with the Roman and Byzantine Empires drained the country, increasing discontent within the population. The "golden age" of Islam followed, under rulers known as Abbassids. This 400-year period was marked by tremendous amounts of trade both within the large empire and beyond its borders, widespread public education, scientific developments (especially in medicine and healthcare), and mathematical advances. Although this golden age began to collapse from within—torn apart by internal division and schism—its end was hastened by the European Crusades.

The Mongol invasions of 1258 ended Abbassid rule and divided the Islamic world. A succession of dynasties ruled until 1501, when the Safavid Dynasty—later

known for its militarism and conquest — was seated. Safavid rulers battled with the Ottomans, eventually settling on frontier lines roughly equivalent to the modern Iranian-Turkish border.[99] This was also the dynasty that established Shia Islam as the state religion, in a succession dispute that is discussed in Chapter 10.

A new dynasty of Turkish origin, the Qajars, ruled from 1796 to 1925. Similar to what would follow later in Iran, this dynasty struggled to integrate religious authority with modern rule, all the while attempting to return to the glories of the earlier Persian Empire. It was under the Qajars that Tehran became the capital of Persia. Early nineteenth-century educational reforms began to create elites who challenged Iran's relations with the West, fomenting local protests and rebellion and ultimately leading to the first limits on royal power. In 1902, Qajar Shah Muzaffar al-Din,[100] facing the demands of reformers, designed a constitution (based on the Belgian constitution of 1831) that combined a national assembly (Majles) with a constitutional monarchy. The significance of this was only eclipsed by the discovery of oil in 1908.

The religious-secular debate that colors much of Iran's postrevolutionary history is nothing new. In the constitution of 1906, the government officially enshrined religious influence and recognized some rights of religious minorities (especially Zoroastrians, Christians, and Jews) by granting them the right to elect one representative to the Majles. Yet both legal protections and limits on power were ignored, often at the urging and intervention of imperial powers, especially Britain and Russia, which had divided Persia into spheres of influence as part of their ongoing "Great Game" within the region. (Their influence would continue even after World War II, as Russia continued to occupy the north of the country and Britain controlled most of Iran's oil revenues until nationalization in the early 1950s.) As the constitutional revolution gained fervor, Britain and Russia pressured the Majles to dismiss Morgan Shuster, a US adviser who served as treasurer-general by appointment of the Iranian parliament. Russian forces literally shelled the Majles into submission. As outside influence terminated the hopes of constitutional reformers, the country's independence was essentially nullified.

The Qajar Dynasty gave way to a new era after Reza Khan, a former peasant and military soldier of the Persian Cossack Brigade (commanded by Russia until 1920), staged a coup, dethroned the Qajars, and founded the Pahlavi Dynasty in 1925. In keeping with tradition and alluding to Iran's historical notions of authority, he took the name Reza Shah Pahlavi (Pahlavi was the language of pre-Islamic Iran). He took the Turkish leader Mustafa Kemal Atatürk as his model, promoting secularization and limiting clerical powers. In 1936 he ordered women to unveil, making Iran the first Islamic country to declare veiling illegal (an ironic point to which we will return in Chapter 10). He alienated many groups in Iranian society, but especially the religious clerics. In his modernization plan, Reza Shah attempted to combine retrospective elements of Iran's pre-Islamic civilization with Western technological achievements. He nominally tried to reduce foreign influence, but his desire to modernize meant he was dependent on Western technology, especially since Britain controlled the Anglo-Persian Oil Company, which financed many development projects and had fueled the British fleet in wartime.

External interference in Iranian affairs again became the leading grievance of the people, and ultimately led to the Pahlavi Dynasty's downfall. England viewed Iran as a buffer zone to protect its interests in India and competed with Russia to gain

prominent spheres of influence. At the end of World War I, British and Russian troops (again) partitioned Iran. After the Bolshevik Revolution led to the withdrawal of Russian forces, the British attempted to dictate Iran's transformation into a protectorate. The controversial Anglo-Persian Agreement of 1919 provided British "advisers" to Iran—on Iran's bill—as a way to ensure Iran's stability and ultimately its ability to serve as a buffer state protecting India. The agreement was shady at best: Majles deputies never had any opportunity to comment on it, nor was it presented for discussion at the League of Nations.

Iran was again occupied during World War II, even though its leaders had proclaimed neutrality in the conflict. During the war, the Allied powers accused Reza Shah of being pro-German, forcing him to abdicate, board a British ship, and head toward exile in South Africa, where he died in 1944. Even if the Shah himself did not explicitly support the Germans, there was much public sentiment encouraging him to follow the lead of the Ottoman Empire by entering the war on the side of Germany.[101]

The British and the Russians had considered restoring the Qajar monarchy, but decided instead to continue the Pahlavi Dynasty by transferring power to Reza Shah's son, Mohammed Reza Pahlavi, who ruled from 1941 to 1979. He continued the absolute power he inherited from his father, while deepening Iran's controversial ties to the West, in part to ally the country with the West during the Cold War. During his rule he was significantly challenged by two leaders—both of whom questioned Iran's ties to Western powers. The first was Mohammad Mossadeq, who was considered to be a liberal nationalist. Mossadeq, a Majles deputy educated in Switzerland, became a leading voice in the calls for the nationalization of the oil industry, which England had exclusively controlled. As Mossadeq's popularity increased, the Shah appointed him prime minister in 1953. Yet, even though he was one of the country's leading voices for liberalism, the West vilified the prime minister for leading the changes in Iran's oil dealings. London threatened military force, imposed economic sanctions, and even took Iran to the International Court of Justice in The Hague over oil, to no solution. The final nail in the coffin came when a joint mission between the US Central Intelligence Agency (CIA) and Britain's MI6, in collaboration with the Iranian army, overthrew Mossadeq. As a result of these actions, supported if not encouraged by Pahlavi, the leader lost his domestic legitimacy—already on shaky ground—and was labeled "America's Shah." There was much truth to the charge, as the weakened Shah increasingly relied on Western power games to maintain his own authority as he was vilified at home. Despite objections, the alliance between the Shah and the United States lasted for almost thirty years, as the oil industry was denationalized and the US and British companies raked in the profits.

The second man to challenge the Shah, and ultimately inspire the forces that led to the end of the Pahlavis, was Ayatollah Ruhollah Khomeini, a prominent Shiite fundamentalist cleric. Khomeini's first book, *Secrets Revealed,* published in 1941, defended the Persian constitution of 1906. But after police killed theology students in the holy city of Qum, Khomeini declared war on the Shah, which led to Khomeini's arrest and exile. Khomeini was able to capitalize on the festering resentment within Iran as people grew increasingly discontented in the face of prolonged economic crises, humiliating international domination, and attempts to secularize the state. The regime's attempts to marginalize Khomeini—including articles in the official press accusing him of being an anti-Iranian British spy or a homosexual—

backfired.[102] Khomeini voiced his criticism of the Shah ever louder, increasing his own support. The Shah's response was to expand the power of his repressive secret service, SAVAK, which went to great extremes in arresting perceived enemies of the regime. Increasingly, the Shah lost control over his own government, and in the face of widespread protests and chaos he and his family left the country for good in January 1979. Khomeini came in on the heels of the Shah, declaring the establishment of the Islamic Republic of Iran in April of that year. Rejecting SECULARISM, Khomeini established a Council of Guardians, which institutionalized the role of clerics in interpreting Iranian laws, and ratified himself as the "Supreme Leader" of the state, answering only to God.

Khomeini ruled during an extremely turbulent decade in Iranian life: the country became increasingly isolated from the international community, was devastated by the ten-year war with Iraq, and became fractured along multiple internal divisions that had disappeared during the time of opposition to the corrupt Shah. But people had united around Khomeini and, after his death in June 1989, mourning masses attempting to touch his body caused it to fall from its platform during the funeral march. Defying the Western prediction of the chaos that would follow Khomeini's death, outgoing president Sayyid Ali Khamenei succeeded Khomeini as Supreme Leader in a relatively seamless transition of power. Ali Akbar Hashemi Rafsanjani, the popular speaker of Iran's Majles, was overwhelmingly elected president, and he served in this capacity for two four-year terms, from 1989 to 1997. Rafsanjani was succeeded by the surprise victory of long-shot Ayatollah Mohammad Khatami, the former minister of culture known for his advocacy of relaxed controls over the media. Khatami served two terms and was succeeded by the populist nationalist Mahmoud Ahmadinejad in 2005. Ahmadinejad's eight-year presidency included international scrutiny of Iran's (resumed) nuclear program, a significantly disputed reelection in 2009, and a tense power struggle between himself and Supreme Leader Khamenei (that included an eleven-day walkout by Ahmadinejad). He was followed by former nuclear negotiator Hassan Rouhani, who had been brutally criticized by the Supreme Leader for his actions, and who campaigned as a moderate open to recalibrating relations between Iran and the rest of the world. He faces more than a few challenges with this task.

Case Study: China

It is often said that China is at once over five millennia old and five decades young. This contrast, between one of the world's oldest civilizations and its endurance for more than fifty years as a "People's Republic," captures much of the intrigue that is China today. Ancient China had great influence over its Asian neighbors, especially in the secular rituals derived from Confucian traditions. Today, Chinese civilization is viewed as the world's oldest, charting the relatively continuous existence of human communities for approximately 20,000 years. (Isolated human skeletons have been discovered from much earlier times, contemporaneous with Indonesia's "Java Man.") China's literary tradition is over 3,500 years old, and its written words (known as "characters") can be traced to linguistic precedents dating to approximately 1500 B.C.E.

Similar to many others, Chinese civilization was centered on river systems, especially the Yellow River in the north, where China's earliest recorded history is

found, and the Yangtze River in the central and southern regions. It was a region ruled by over a dozen imperial dynasties, marked by fluctuating periods of stability, chaos, conquest, and cultural progress. The leader of each dynasty exercised authority based on the belief that she or he possessed the "Mandate of Heaven," which can best be understood as receiving the favor of one's spiritual ancestors.

China's first documented dynasty, the Shang, began in approximately 1700 B.C.E. Although Chinese records indicate at least one earlier dynasty, the existence of this community through archaeological records is yet to be proven.[103] Evidence of the Shang Dynasty is found in the so-called oracle bones, discovered only in the late 1800s, which were used to receive guidance from the heavens.

China's first unified dynasty, and indeed the source of the Western name "China," was achieved during the Qin Dynasty, which began in 220 B.C.E. Lasting only fifteen years, this was a remarkable dynasty that completed two wonders of the world. The Qin emperor ordered earlier walls used for fortification and defense to be linked literally into one "Long Wall" (known in the West as the "Great Wall"), providing modern Chinese an incredibly important symbol of the endurance of their culture.[104] The second famed creation of this dynasty was the emperor's elaborate tomb, composed of over 8,000 terracotta soldiers and horses buried to protect their identity. This major capital project of the dynasty required extensive resources, including labor power and coercion, and many of the 750,000 workers who planned and constructed the tomb, located in the ancient capital of Xi'an, were killed so they could not reveal its location. China's greatest dynasty, the Han, lasted for four centuries (206 B.C.E. through C.E. 220), and introduced the world's first wheelbarrow, as well as the widespread use of paper and porcelain. It was during this dynasty, contemporaneous with the Roman Empire, that the famed Silk Road, a 7,000-mile trade route from Xi'an to Rome, increased China's interaction with the rest of the world. China's interaction with the West grew steadily after this dynasty, and by the Ming Dynasty (1368–1644), contacts with the Spaniards, Russians, and Dutch were extensive. It was during this time that the Jesuit Mission of Matthew Ricci was begun, launching China's extensive yet troubled relationship with Western religions.[105]

In the midst of this exploration and grandeur, ordinary Chinese citizens lived a difficult life filled with TOTALITARIAN leaders, extensive tax payments to finance imperial projects, and little freedom in either their work or their personal lives, which were mired in poverty. Advancement in Chinese society throughout most of its past was based on academic credentials achieved through a complex examination system that was based primarily on Confucian texts, affording luxury to an extremely small minority of the population (from which women were expressly excluded).

China's relative isolation and size encouraged a "Middle Kingdom" philosophy in which rulers and ordinary citizens alike viewed themselves at the center of world civilization. This attitude manifested itself in China's tributary system of trade, in which foreign powers were required to give gifts to the emperor to show respect or gain favor (and sometimes protection). Additionally, the Chinese viewed anyone outside of their cultural civilization to be "barbarians," little deserving of equal contact or negotiation. Part of the measure, in Chinese eyes, of whether one was civilized or barbarian was one's allegiance to the teachings of a man who lived approximately 2,500 years ago, Kung Fuzi, known in the West as Confucius. His teachings, which may be viewed more as a way of life than a religious tradition, produced a great degree of cultural

continuity in Chinese civilization, and even though modern leaders have gone to great lengths to eradicate his impact, it continues today. Confucian thought influenced most of East Asia, well beyond the borders of the Middle Kingdom. Some have claimed that he is "every bit as important to East Asian civilization as Jesus was to the West."[106] Confucius was a traditionalist who reflected, in extremely chaotic times, on solutions to his society's problems. He emphasized virtue, tradition, ritual, and the importance of proper relationships. Confucianism emerged as a complex set of doctrines that has been debated and interpreted by leaders for millennia. Confucian thought eventually became required understanding for those who wanted to consider themselves "educated Chinese," and it was officially adopted as the state ideology in the second century B.C.E. The Confucian school certainly was not the only worldview during China's past (the Taoists found these teachings authoritarian and restrictive and the legalists found them too retrospective and lacking in rules), but it certainly was the most important. As a measure of its dominance, the Qing or Manchu Dynasty, China's last, was actually introduced to China by foreigners from the north. The Chinese welcomed them, though, because of their internalization of the Confucian code of conduct and rule.

The Chinese Empire traded extensively with Arabs and Persians for hundreds of years before European contact, under the tributary system discussed earlier. The Chinese never regarded their trading partners as equals, and indeed for much of its history China's power was unrivaled, especially on the seas and in its protectorates and colonies throughout Asia, including Vietnam, Burma, and Korea. China's imperial power began to decline, though, in the 1500s, as its leaders turned increasingly inward and encouraged more isolation from the rest of the world. It was the outcome of this turn of events that led, in many ways, to the eventual European conquest of much of China, beginning in the late 1700s. In their desire to increase access to Asia through a Chinese trading point, the British and others established a structure in which foreign citizens would live in China without being subject to Chinese authority, a system known as EXTRATERRITORIALITY. This was the beginning of the erosion of China's sovereignty, as foreigners began living in the country not bound by Chinese laws, but rather by the laws of their home countries. As its trade deficit with China spiraled higher, England goaded China into a series of battles referred to as the Opium Wars (see Chapter 2). China's loss of Hong Kong (and other regions, including Taiwan, Macau, and Shandong) symbolized the imposition of foreign rule over a grand imperial land, rule that was not relinquished until the end of the twentieth century. (Taiwan, which was ceded to the Japanese in 1895, remains an example of contested sovereignty—discussed in Chapter 12.) On a larger scale, to most Chinese these events symbolized the loss of the famed "Mandate of Heaven" and gave birth to a flurry of potential solutions to the crisis. It was a time when many feared that Chinese civilization would fracture endlessly, exacerbated by localized warlord politics or regional military powers.

Shortly after the collapse of the last dynasty in 1911, Beijing University students staged what became known as the first mass demonstration in China's history, on May 4, 1919, to protest the status of Shandong, administered as a German colony since 1898. The warlord-dominated government in Beijing had entered into a secret agreement with the Japanese during World War I. At the Versailles Peace Conference at the end of the war, many Chinese placed great hope in Woodrow Wilson's rheto-

ric about self-determination, but their hopes were crushed when they learned that Shandong (the coastal province in which Confucius was born, which is also home to one of China's most sacred mountains) was granted to Japan as part of the Versailles settlement. Protests erupted throughout China and within Chinese communities abroad, and China never did sign the Treaty of Versailles, capping another round of betrayal by the West. Out of this environment of distrust and disappointment, two dominant groups led the way to China's future: the Nationalist Party (Kuomintang, or KMT), led by Sun Yat-sen, and the Chinese Communist Party (CCP), eventually led by Mao Zedong (even though he was a minor figure for the first years of the party). Both parties focused on rallying different Chinese groups to their cause, and engaged in bitter battles with each other despite two formal attempts to unite for China's future. The final straw was the Japanese invasion of northern China in 1931, after which the CCP was perceived as the aggressive fighter for Chinese interests and for the needs of ordinary people. Following Japan's defeat in World War II and its expulsion from China, all-out civil war ensued between the KMT and the CCP, with the defeated Nationalists eventually exiling themselves to Taiwan. The People's Republic of China (PRC) was declared on October 1, 1949, although its hold on Chinese territory, and on world opinion, was less than complete, which set the stage for a rough ride especially during its first thirty years.

Mao Zedong, affectionately known as "The Chairman," led China for over two and a half decades, from the beginning of the PRC in 1949 until his death in 1976. His legacy remains mixed: he united the country and made the Chinese people proud of their heritage and achievements, while inflicting incredible civil disarray during his attempt to "continue the revolution" from 1966 to 1976, in the period known as the CULTURAL REVOLUTION (discussed in Chapter 11). Mao was followed by another longtime member of the CCP, Deng Xiaoping, who had been with the party during its rise to power in the 1930s and 1940s. As you will read, Deng dramatically changed the face of China by opening it to the outside world, promoting the development of political and economic institutions, and attempting to move away from the charismatic rule of his predecessor. Deng, who died in 1997, has also left a mixed legacy: while the lives of ordinary Chinese citizens improved dramatically under his watch, the blood of the Tiananmen Square demonstrations of 1989 is also on his hands. Leaders who followed in his footsteps, including Jiang Zemin and Hu Jintao, faced the difficult task of trying to preserve the Communist Party's monopoly on power while attempting to carefully manage China's reemergence as a major regional and global player. This balancing act has consumed current CCP general secretary and president Xi Jinping. Xi, in office since 2012 (and expected to serve until 2022), leads the country as China's imprint on the region and the world magnifies at the same time its population experiences some of the quickest changes in daily life observed anywhere.

Case Study: Indonesia

Modern Indonesia is an identity born of trade routes and colonial experience. Despite regional prominence and rich cultural traditions, there was little sense of commonality among the peoples who lived on the thousands of islands in the South Pacific prior to the early nineteenth century. Throughout this book, you should not be surprised to read about the division and tense unity that exist in modern Indonesia in the

early twenty-first century, as unity was a concept rarely evidenced in the islands of the archipelago.

The region known today as Indonesia was long populated by human beings. You may be familiar with "Java Man," the fossilized bones of a hominid that were discovered in 1891. It is believed that this human, known as *Pithecanthropus erectus,* lived over 750,000 years ago and had the capacity for fire building and language. Subsequent archaeological discoveries confirmed populations extending 35,000–40,000 years ago, including Solo Man, named after a river in central Java, and the later Wajak Man, who lived 12,000–13,000 years ago.

Despite the presence of human communities almost 1 million years ago, the majority of today's Indonesians descended from two ethnic groups who immigrated to the islands from the north. These groups include the Melanesian peoples, who are believed to have inhabited the islands approximately 6,000 years ago, and the Austronesians, who migrated to the Indonesian archipelago from Taiwan at approximately the same time.

The Indonesian archipelago was an active player in the early Malay world, with a handful of states and kingdoms that thrived in trading. Early settlements prospered on the main islands, including Ho-Ling in central Java. Chinese records of this civilization report extensive war exploits, labor surpluses, and entertainment based on shadow plays and drums. By the sixth century, major kingdoms developed on Java and Sumatra, highlighted by the Srivijaya kingdom in southern Sumatra. Considered one of the most powerful kingdoms in Southeast Asia, Srivijaya emerged as the chief state and the only maritime state among the classical states in the region. As a commercial state, it began and ended earlier than others. Srivijaya's rulers controlled the critical Straits of Malacca, the preferred travel route between China and India, and its influence reached to southern Vietnam.[107] The exchange of commercial goods was not the only type of trade in this kingdom: it was also viewed as the center both of Hindu and Buddhist studies.[108]

Not surprisingly, due to its location Srivijaya was famous for its navy, financed largely by taxes collected on foreign ships traversing its path. It eventually controlled a vast territory, including most of Sumatra, present-day Malaysia, and Singapore, yet the authority of the king expanded farther, to Borneo and Sri Lanka. The wealth of this kingdom was memorialized in the story that each day the king would toss a gold bar into the sea to acknowledge it as the source of Srivijaya's prosperity. At the end of his reign, the number of gold bars retrieved from the waters quantified the king's power.[109] Yet because of its export focus, it was a vulnerable state, dependent on the economic situation in India and China.

Even after Srivijaya's decline, Indonesia's prominence in Asian trade continued, and the city port of Malacca rose to prominence in its absence. Asian states (especially China and India) as well as Arab states provided ideal export markets for products abundant on the archipelago, especially spices. The region's abundance of spices, especially cloves, nutmeg, and pepper, were sought by traders around the world. Early Indonesians had established colonies in Madagascar for the transport of spices abroad (especially to the Romans); today, Austronesian languages can still be found there as remnants of this influence.

Increased trade led to heightened cultural interaction between islanders and their mainland Asian neighbors. By the third century, both Hindu and Buddhist traditions

had filtered into the western islands from India. Neither system was adopted writ large; they were both regionally adapted and made to fit earlier customs, especially animism, a tradition based on the reverence for all living things. Islam did not become a major influence until the thirteenth century, and even then it was often combined with native religious traditions, as well as Hinduism and Buddhism. The Portuguese and the Dutch introduced Christianity much later, in the sixteenth and seventeenth centuries. Another cultural artifact of Indonesia's status as the trading center of Southeast Asia was the adoption of the Malay language by dissimilar people: it became the unifying factor facilitating trade between diverse groups. As Islam spread through the archipelago, the use of Malay became even more predominant.

Accounts of Islam's arrival disagree on the century in which it was introduced, some dating it as early as the seventh century, and others contending it was closer to the thirteenth century.[110] Yet experts consistently emphasize the influence of the spice-trading route as a major avenue for the spread of Islam. From the start, Islam was interpreted in diverse ways, with *santri* Muslims closely following traditional Islamic rituals, and *abangans* adapting Islamic traditions to their Hindu beliefs. Aceh was one of the first parts of Indonesia to convert to Islam, and to this day Acehnese are known for their relatively strict interpretations of Islamic traditions and for the strength of their convictions.

European influence in the region began in the fifteenth century. The first Portuguese ships sailed into Malacca in 1509, in search of inexpensive spices to preserve meats. The Portuguese eventually took over Malacca, only to hasten its downfall. Throughout the 1600s, Dutch Protestants established the Dutch East India Company (in search of a monopoly over the spice trade), and gradually increased their territory of control as it fit their economic interests, beginning with the "spice islands" of Maluku and the northwestern coast of Java. They consolidated their rule by expelling other colonial aspirants, including Spain and England (although the English maintained their colonies on Borneo). Even after the collapse of the Dutch East India Company, the Netherlands defeated the English to gain control over their colonies in Southeast Asia by 1816. Despite serious indigenous challenges to their authority, the Dutch prevailed in establishing control.

As Dutch colonial rule over the archipelago increased, and they began to integrate native Indonesians into their administrative structure, the growing sense of discrimination fostered much discontent. A revolution of rising expectations ensued; those native Indonesians who were afforded the opportunity to pursue higher education and serve in colonial officialdom as physicians, engineers, and other professionals chafed at the rigid subordination they faced compared to their European rulers. Although the nationalist movement was just beginning to form, many voices were calling for change, including the Javanese princess Raden Adjeng Kartini, who championed the emancipation of Indonesian women.[111] As discussed earlier, this situation of choosing a select few for opportunities produced extremely difficult identity struggles among those selected.

The nationalist independence movement was launched in the early years of the twentieth century, and was given an added spark by ironic celebrations by the Dutch of their own centennial of liberation from Napoleonic rule—which they commemorated in the midst of occupied Indonesia.[112] It all began to come together under the leadership of a young engineer named Sukarno (following the Javanese custom, he

had one name). Sukarno founded the Indonesian Nationalist Party in 1927. In response to this independence rhetoric, the Dutch exiled Sukarno, Mohammed Hatta, and other nationalist leaders. World War II provided them an opportunity to return, reorganize, and lead their country to independence.

Indonesia's formal colonial era ended with the Japanese occupation of 1942–1945, during which time the Japanese plundered the region's oil fields to support their imperial navy. Ironic in hindsight, many Indonesians initially welcomed the Japanese, believing they would help in their fight for independence, and that the Japanese would not stay long. Instead, the Japanese sent Indonesians to work as forced laborers in Japan's territories. Those Indonesians who had been recruited and trained by the former Dutch colonial powers were again used as pawns during the Japanese occupation, as they became enforcers of the harshest Japanese policies on their neighbors and compatriots. But it was the Japanese defeat at the end of World War II that spurred Indonesia's independence movement into full gear. Prior to that time, Indonesian nationalists Sukarno and Hatta had begun to campaign for independence. Yet the movement was hindered by disagreement, rectified mostly by Sukarno's *pancasila* proposal, which emphasized the five principles (monotheism, national unity, humanitarianism, representative democracy by consensus, and social justice) shared by all Indonesians regardless of ethnic, religious, or political beliefs. These beliefs remain today, enshrined in the preamble to the modern Indonesian constitution.

Indonesia declared its independence in Sukarno's garden the morning of August 17, 1945 (two days after the Japanese surrendered), but struggled with the Netherlands for over four years before the Dutch recognized its independence, only after bloody battles and intense international pressure. Sukarno embarked on a program euphemistically referred to as "guided democracy" for most of his rule, from 1949 to 1965. As a world traveler, Sukarno eloquently espoused the needs of the developing world, especially in the Bandung Conference of Asian and African States in 1955. He was also stridently anti-Western, taking over British and US businesses, expelling Dutch nationals, and withdrawing from the United Nations. A 1965 coup, supposedly masterminded by the Communist Party of Indonesia (PKI), led to much bloodshed. At least 400,000 were killed in fear of communist insurgency in a period that remains one of the country's darkest and least discussed in Indonesia's history.[113]

Out of the ashes of the 1965 coup, the military commander Suharto rose to power. Suharto, who himself had attended a Dutch-run military academy and fought against the Dutch in Indonesia's war of independence, knew well the importance of military strength in maintaining his rule, a principle he applied fiercely throughout his "new order" government, from 1966 to 1998. Although dramatic social improvements were achieved in the first years of his leadership, including declining poverty and increasing literacy rates, Indonesia under his government increasingly became a repressive state, complete with a gulag system used to enforce religious and political oppression. He was forced to resign from power in May 1998, in the face of widespread protests against his handling of the Asian economic crisis and international pressure to resolve the country's economic woes. A caretaker government led by interim president B. J. Habibie, a close associate of Suharto's, was in power for thirteen months before the groundbreaking elections of June 1999, the first free and fair elections to take place in four decades. In this election, the Indonesian Democratic Party–Struggle (PDI-P), led by Megawati Sukarnoputri, scored a resounding

majority once the voting results were finally ratified in August 1999. The Indonesian legislature, the People's Consultative Assembly, in October 1999 met and chose Abdurraham Wahid—who was supported by an unprecedented Islamic alliance—as the state's fourth president.[114] Megawati, a critic of Suharto and daughter of Indonesia's founding father, was named vice president. Wahid, the Muslim cleric who was partially blind and in frail health, led the country for approximately twenty months before he was voted out of office by the legislature in July 2001, capping off a six-month impeachment process. Shortly after Wahid agreed to leave the presidential quarters, Megawati took power in a country dizzied by political upheaval, internal violence, and a reeling economy. Susilo Bambang Yudhoyono, popularly known by the acronym SBY, became the country's first directly elected president in 2004. The retired general brought some stability to the country, serving for two terms, yet his decade in office was marked by indecisiveness and a perceived lack of principle. His successor, Joko "Jokowi" Widodo, seemingly ushered in a new era of Indonesian politics, rising as the first president outside of either the military or political elites. A populist former governor of Jakarta known for walking the streets to converse with ordinary people, the former furniture maker and fan of Metallica and Led Zeppelin has his work cut out for him as he leads this critical Asian state.

Now It's Your Turn

As you move on to more contemporary considerations of these eight countries, keep in mind their diverse and rich histories. In what ways can you see their contemporary experience driven by their past? From the brief overviews provided, what traditions or values do you believe should be revitalized or adapted to serve the peoples of these countries? In what ways do you see legacies of Western domination continuing to play out in these countries?

Notes

1. Lynn V. Foster, *A Brief History of Mexico* (New York: Facts on File, 1997).
2. Maurice Collis, *Cortés and Montezuma* (New York: New Directions, 1999).
3. Peter Bakewell, *A History of Latin America* (Malden, MA: Blackwell, 1997); Benjamin Keen and Keith Haynes, *A History of Latin America* (Boston: Houghton Mifflin, 2000).
4. Ibid.
5. Richard Graham, *Independence in Latin America* (New York: McGraw-Hill, 1994).
6. Ibid.
7. Bakewell, *A History of Latin America;* Keen and Haynes, *A History of Latin America.*
8. Ibid.
9. Ibid.
10. Keen and Haynes, *A History of Latin America.*
11. Ibid.
12. Ibid.
13. Bakewell, *A History of Latin America.*
14. Ibid.
15. Ibid.; Keen and Haynes, *A History of Latin America.*
16. Keen and Haynes, *A History of Latin America.*
17. Bakewell, *A History of Latin America.*
18. Laura Laurencich Minelli, *The Inca World* (Norman: University of Oklahoma Press, 2000).

19. Ibid.

20. Peter Flindell Klaren, *Peru: Society and Nationhood in the Andes* (New York: Oxford University Press, 2000).

21. Ibid., p. 43.

22. Ibid.

23. The Spanish *mita* built on Inca practice, but there were crucial differences. For the Inca, *mita* was part of a larger social contract in which reciprocal benefits linked the community and state. For the Spanish, however, *mita* was purely exploitative, as the state provided no return to the community. Minelli, *The Inca World*.

24. According to Peter Klaren, however, the state did offer some limits on colonial expropriation. For example, indigenous people could appeal to colonial courts for relief, and some became adept at resorting to Spanish legal institutions to defend their interests. But such policies served as safety valves, effectively strengthening the system against radical or revolutionary challenges. Klaren emphasizes that because the system did sometimes rule on behalf of oppressed groups, this in no way vindicates or balances the colonial legacy, which is overwhelmingly negative. Klaren, *Peru*.

25. Ibid.

26. Ibid.; Mark A. Burkholder and Lyman L. Johnson, *Colonial Latin America* (New York: Oxford University Press, 1998); Graham, *Independence in Latin America*.

27. Cynthia McClintock, *Revolutionary Movements in Latin America* (Washington, DC: US Institute of Peace, 1998).

28. Ibid.

29. Keen and Haynes, *A History of Latin America*.

30. Ibid., p. 43.

31. Ibid.

32. Klaren, *Peru*.

33. Ibid.; Washington Office on Latin America, "Deconstructing Democracy: Peru Under Alberto Fujimori," February 2000, www.wola.org.

34. Ibid.

35. Keen and Haynes, *A History of Latin America;* Klaren, *Peru;* Thomas E. Skidmore and Peter H. Smith, *Modern Latin America* (New York: Oxford University Press, 1992).

36. Michael Crowder, *The Story of Nigeria* (London: Faber and Faber, 1978).

37. Robin Law, "The Oyo-Dahomey Wars, 1726–1823: A Military Analysis," in *Warfare and Diplomacy in Precolonial Nigeria,* ed. Toyin Falola and Robin Law (Madison: University of Wisconsin–Madison Press, 1992).

38. Crowder, *The Story of Nigeria*.

39. Ibid.

40. Ibid.

41. Toyin Falola, *The History of Nigeria* (Westport: Greenwood, 1999).

42. Ibid.

43. Ibid.

44. Peter M. Lewis, Pearl T. Robinson, and Barnett R. Rubin, *Stabilizing Nigeria* (New York: Century Foundation, 1998).

45. Ibid.

46. Ibid.

47. Falola, *The History of Nigeria*.

48. Ibid.

49. Karl Maier, *This House Has Fallen: Midnight in Nigeria* (New York: PublicAffairs, 2000).

50. Ibid.

51. D. E. Needham, E. K. Mashingaidze, and Ngwabi Bhebe, *From Iron Age to Independence: A History of Central Africa* (London: Longman, 1985).

52. Ibid.

53. Ian Phimister, *An Economic and Social History of Zimbabwe, 1890–1948* (London: Longman, 1988); A. J. Wills, *An Introduction to the History of Central Africa: Zambia, Malawi, and Zimbabwe* (New York: Oxford University Press, 1985).

54. Ibid.

55. Wills, *An Introduction to the History of Central Africa*.

56. Ibid.

57. Phimister, *An Economic and Social History of Zimbabwe*.

58. Ibid.

59. In the 1920s the Watch Tower prophesied the Second Coming and claimed that a whirlwind would blow whites and nonbelievers away. Ibid.

60. Ibid.

61. Ibid.

62. Needham, Mashingaidze, and Bhebe, *From Iron Age to Independence*.

63. Victor de Waal, *The Politics of Reconciliation: Zimbabwe's First Decade* (Trenton, NJ: Africa World, 1990).

64. Ibid.

65. Ibid.

66. Ibid.

67. Masipula Sithole, "Zimbabwe: In Search of Stable Democracy," in *Democracy in Developing Countries: Africa,* ed. Larry Diamond, Juan Linz, and Seymour Martin Lipset (Boulder: Lynne Rienner, 1988).

68. Ibid.; Needham, Mashingaidze, and Bhebe, *From Iron Age to Independence;* Waal, *The Politics of Reconciliation*.

69. Thomas Schneider, *Ancient Egypt in 10 Questions and Answers* (Ithaca: Cornell University Press, 2013).

70. Charles Freeman, *Egypt, Greece, and Rome: Civilizations of the Ancient Mediterranean* (Oxford: Oxford University Press, 2004).

71. Alan B. Lloyd, *Ancient Egypt: State and Society* (New York: Oxford University Press, 2014); Schneider, *Ancient Egypt in 10 Questions and Answers*.

72. Ibid.

73. Douglas J. Brewer and Emily Teeter, *Egypt and the Egyptians* (Cambridge: Cambridge University Press, 2007).

74. Lloyd, *Ancient Egypt;* Freeman, *Egypt, Greece, and Rome*.

75. Brewer and Teeter, *Egypt and the Egyptians;* Schneider, *Ancient Egypt in 10 Questions and Answers*.

76. Lloyd, *Ancient Egypt*.

77. Ibid.; Freeman, *Egypt, Greece, and Rome*.

78. Schneider, *Ancient Egypt in 10 Questions and Answers;* Brewer and Teeter, *Egypt and the Egyptians;* Freeman, *Egypt, Greece, and Rome*.

79. Tarek Osman, *Egypt on the Brink: From Nasser to Mubarak* (New Haven: Yale University Press, 2010); Schneider, *Ancient Egypt in 10 Questions and Answers*.

80. Brewer and Teeter, *Egypt and the Egyptians;* Freeman, *Egypt, Greece, and Rome*.

81. Brewer and Teeter, *Egypt and the Egyptians;* Lloyd, *Ancient Egypt*.

82. Lloyd, *Ancient Egypt*.

83. Arthur Goldschmidt Jr., *Modern Egypt: The Formation of a Nation-State* (Boulder: Westview, 2004); Osman, *Egypt on the Brink*.

84. Osman, *Egypt on the Brink;* Isa Blumi, *Foundations of Modernity: Human Agency and the Imperial State* (New York: Routledge, 2012).

85. Ibid.; Goldschmidt, *Modern Egypt*.

86. "Egypt: A British Protectorate," *American Journal of International Law* 9, no. 1 (January 1915), pp. 202–204; Thanassis Cambanis, *Once Upon a Revolution: An Egyptian Story* (New York: Simon and Schuster, 2015).

87. Osman, *Egypt on the Brink*.

88. Goldschmidt, *Modern Egypt;* Osman, *Egypt on the Brink*.

89. Afaf Lutfi al-Sayyid Marsot, *A History of Egypt: From the Arab Conquest to the Present* (Cambridge: Cambridge University Press, 2007); Goldschmidt, *Modern Egypt*.

90. Goldschmidt, *Modern Egypt;* Marsot, *A History of Egypt*.

91. Wael Ghonim, *Revolution 2.0: The Power of the People Is Greater Than the People in Power* (New York: Houghton, Mifflin, Harcourt, 2012); Goldschmidt, *Modern Egypt*.

92. Osman, *Egypt on the Brink;* Ghonim, *Revolution 2.0;* Goldschmidt, *Modern Egypt*.

93. Goldschmidt, *Modern Egypt*.

94. Cambanis, *Once Upon a Revolution*.

95. Ibid.; Ghonim, *Revolution 2.0*.

96. Cambanis, *Once Upon a Revolution*.

97. Elton L. Daniel, *The History of Iran* (Westport: Greenwood, 2001).

98. Mike Edwards, "The Adventures of Marco Polo, Part I," *National Geographic,* May 2001; Daniel, *The History of Iran*.

99. Daniel, *The History of Iran*.

100. The title "Shah" reappropriates a pre-Islamic Iranian title for "king."

101. Daniel, *The History of Iran*.

102. Ibid.

103. Lucian W. Pye, *China: An Introduction,* 3rd ed. (Boston: Little, Brown, 1984).

104. Much of the story surrounding the Great Wall is based in legend. While some smaller walls were built prior to the Qin Dynasty, and joined together during the Qin emperor's reign, the bulk of the wall was completed during China's Ming Dynasty (1366–1644), and significantly renovated thereafter. There is evidence to challenge its status as part of China's ancient past. Historian Arthur Waldron has produced extensive research challenging the myth behind the wall, citing, among other points, that even though Marco Polo traveled extensively throughout the region in the thirteenth century, he made no mention of the structure. Similarly, contrary to popular beliefs, the Great Wall cannot be viewed from space, at least not without significant satellite magnification. Yet perceptions of the wall's visibility from space predate space travel by humans—*Ripley's Believe It or Not* made the claim as early as 1930. See David C. Wright, *The History of China* (Westport: Greenwood, 2001).

105. Pye, *China*.

106. Michael Schuman, "Reformers Want to Erase Confucius's Influence in Asia: That's a Mistake," *Washington Post,* May 29, 2015.

107. Barney War, "Teaching Indonesia: A World-Systems Perspective," *Education About Asia* 3, no. 3 (Winter 1998).

108. Milton W. Meyer, *Asia: A Concise History* (Lanham: Rowman and Littlefield, 1997); Björn Schelander and Kirsten Brown, *Exploring Indonesia: Past and Present* (Honolulu: Center for Southeast Asian Studies, 2000).

109. Schelander and Brown, *Exploring Indonesia*.

110. Nina Nurmila, "The Indonesian Muslim Feminist Reinterpretation of Inheritance," in *Islam in Indonesia: Contrasting Images and Interpretations,* ed. Jajat Burhanudin and Kees van Dijk (Amsterdam: Amsterdam University Press, 2013), p. 109.

111. Meyer, *Asia*.

112. Robert Cribb and Colin Brown, *Modern Indonesia: A History Since 1945* (New York: Longman, 1995).

113. Sara Schonhardt, "Indonesia Chips Away at the Enforced Silence Around a Dark History," *New York Times,* January 19, 2012, p. A9.

114. Chris Manning and Peter van Diermen, "Recent Developments and Social Aspects of *Reformasi* and Crisis: An Overview," in *Indonesia in Transition: Social Aspects of Reformasi and Crisis,* ed. Chris Manning and Peter van Diermen (Singapore: Institute of Southeast Asian Studies, 2000).

PART TWO
Economic Realities

Next we will look at the economies of the global south and consider whether the international economic system is contributing to the development or the under-development of much of this world. The following chapters focus on INTER-NATIONAL POLITICAL ECONOMY (IPE), or how economic and political issues interface. As an area of study, IPE's interest in the politics of economics includes a broad array of topics and concerns. In this part of the book we will focus on the gap in wealth and material well-being that exists between high-income countries (HICs) and low-income countries (LICs), as well as disparities that exist within countries. The existence of such often-massive inequality is a major source of friction between rich and poor; it is the source of what is sometimes referred to as the North-South conflict. People belonging to two dominant but diametrically opposed schools of thought, NEOLIBERALISM and STRUCTURALISM, have very different ideas about why this gap exists and how to bridge it. Procapitalist neoliberals are highly optimistic about the ability of the market to work its magic. On the other hand, structuralists characterize capitalism as exploitative. To varying degrees, structuralists are pessimistic about the possibility of authentic development happening under the existing system. As you will see in the following chapters, the two schools of thought offer widely divergent answers for the questions we will consider: Why does the gap between rich and poor countries remain, even if it is narrowing? Why are we observing some of the highest levels of global inequality ever recorded? And why, despite some significant gains in recent decades, do so many of the world's countries continue to suffer from under-development? Is this under-development due to poor decisions made by the countries themselves? Or is it due to the position of these countries in the international economic system, a capitalist system that is dominated by rich countries and the organizations working for them?

Chapter 6

Sustainable Human Development: A Progress Report

I can't afford to eat.
> —*A man screaming as he set himself on fire in Alexandria, Egypt*[1]

Now, we are brave with the IMF. [Our] debt has been paid. We are autonomous. We don't need to beg.
> —*Former Indonesian president Susilo Bambang Yudhoyono,*
> *as he confirmed Jakarta's $1 billion contribution*
> *to the IMF's European bailout reserves*[2]

By late 2016, the world economy appeared to be at a crossroads. On one hand, economists were celebrating the fact that for nearly thirty years globally the percentage of people living in extreme poverty had kept falling. All regions of the world—without exception—reported declines in extreme poverty (the number of people earning $1.90 or less a day). To put this in perspective, in the early 1980s, 44 percent of the world's population lived in extreme poverty. By 2016, that figure was less than 10 percent, and the president of the World Bank categorized the decline in extreme poverty as "the best story in the world today."[3] As you can see in Figure 6.6 later in this chapter, the most significant gains were made in East Asia. Yet trends in the world's advanced economies risk placing these gains in harm's way, especially as stagnation in economically developed countries continues to fuel anti-trade sentiment, restrictions on immigration, and other trends that are known to hamper productivity, growth, and innovation.[4] As one chief economist at the International Monetary Fund (IMF) put it, "taken as a whole, the world economy has moved sideways."[5]

Over the next few years, analysts from the IMF and UN project continued slow growth in advanced economies with a resulting drag on global growth. Slow growth in high-income countries translates into weakness in demand and falling commodity prices, which hurts commodity exporters. The economic prospects are modestly brighter for some regions (much of East and South Asia) than others (Africa, South

America, and West Asia). Consequently, we are not seeing a change in terms of balanced and inclusive growth worldwide. It is important to remember that there are a variety of experiences behind the statistics and important differences within country groups. In advanced and developing economies alike, significant numbers of people remain left behind in the push for progress. Nearly 60 percent of the world's billion extremely poor people live in just five countries.[6] Even though we have fewer people hungry today than a decade ago (as of 2016, 795 million people are chronically hungry, or one in nine people in the world), 98 percent of those unable to meet their basic nutritional needs are found in developing countries.[7] There are concentrated pockets of hunger: for example, two-thirds of Asia struggles with food security with the greatest areas of need found in western Asia. Two-thirds of all maternal deaths in the world are among women who live in sub-Saharan Africa.[8] In the so-called developing world, 66 million schoolchildren go hungry to classes, 23 million of whom are African.[9] And we are witnessing some of the greatest levels of inequality ever seen: the richest 1 percent now have more wealth than the rest of the world combined. Oxfam International reports that in 2015, just 62 individuals had the same wealth as 3.6 billion people—the so-called bottom half of humanity.[10]

As we move further away from the Great Recession (the years of sharp, global economic downturn lasting roughly from the late 2000s through the early 2010s), some patterns emerge. Many developing countries initially experienced faster recoveries than advanced economies, which have suffered through several years of lackluster growth. According to the World Bank, the global growth rate is expected to pick up slowly to 3.0 percent by 2018.[11] Some countries are doing much better than that, but the overall sense is that growth rates will remain below potential across the board, and that significant risks (often closely interconnected) remain. They are amplified by security and political challenges and include sharper than expected slowdowns in major economies (especially China and Brazil) with spillover effects for neighboring countries, falling commodity prices, and natural disasters—especially drought—likely to result in lower agricultural productivity and rising food prices and other inflationary pressures, rising unemployment, deficits, and debt levels. These adverse shocks will pose the greatest challenges for the most vulnerable. Analysts predict a subdued pace of global economic growth for the next few years.[12] But for some time now, observers have noted that most low-income countries (LICs) are now more resilient than they used to be—suggesting that there is much more economic diversity in the global south (and even within regions) than one might expect.

Yet before we go any further with this discussion of how we are all doing, it is important to become familiar with two concepts fundamental to any discussion of international political economy (IPE): growth and development. Both are generally considered to be desirable, and the terms are often used interchangeably to describe economic progress. However, growth and development are actually two very different things. While proponents of NEOLIBERALISM would argue that one needs growth to fund development, structuralists point out that it is certainly possible to have growth without development, as has been the case in many less developed countries. And as the case of Cuba has demonstrated, it is possible to have development without growth, although this is not easy.

Growth refers to an expansion in production, output, and perhaps income. Neoliberals argue that maximized economic efficiency produces growth, which is asso-

ciated with rising profits! A common indicator of growth is gross national income (GNI) per capita, which is obtained by dividing GNI by the size of a population. GNI per capita supposedly gives one an idea of how much income the average citizen earns in a year (see Figure 6.1). There's a world of difference between the $850 Zimbabweans take in versus the $10,690 earned by the average Egyptian. However, keep in mind that income is only one, albeit important, measure of economic well-being, and GNI per capita assumes that income is divided completely equally—a situation that exists nowhere on the planet. In fact, one can assume that in most cases, a few people will earn much more than this figure and the majority will earn far less.

Whereas growth describes an increase in volume or output, DEVELOPMENT is generally understood to mean human development and pertains to issues of distribution. Development is a broad concept that is measured by composite indices such as the Physical Quality of Life Index (PQLI) and the Human Development Index (HDI) (see Figure 6.2). Both indices offer a more detailed picture of the economic well-being of a population. Growth rates alone tell us little about how people are doing. A country's economic growth rate does not reflect how wealthy it is. Similarly, one of the most common measures of inequality is income inequality, but the income redistribution structure of each country, which includes welfare programs, can make a big difference in how severe the gap between rich and poor is. Increasingly analysts studying inequality are interested in inequity of access to opportunity, education, and healthcare. The trend overall is a widening gap between rich and poor in many countries, in both fast- and slow-growing economies. But there are exceptions to this trend, which can have a drag on growth. For example, during its boom early in the first decade of this century, Brazil made some progress in reducing inequality. But because Brazil started out as one of the most unequal countries in the world, it still has far to go.[13]

And Brazil's case is hardly the norm; it is not unusual for citizens of some of the fastest-growing economies to live in some of the worst conditions in the world (e.g., Myanmar in 2015). The years of China averaging 10 percent growth per year are over; the Chinese economy grew 6.9 percent in 2015, the lowest annual growth in a quarter century, and the World Bank estimates that the rate will drop to 6.3 percent by 2018.[14] It is true that a significant number of its citizens have seen their standards of living rise—at a dizzying pace. For example, the average starting salary for migrant laborers in China grew by approximately 80 percent between 2003 and 2009, and the rate of extreme poverty fell from 60 percent in 1990 to 12 percent in 2010.[15] That's a tremendous improvement. Yet even at these growth rates it would take another forty years of constant growth before average Chinese incomes would reach the 2005 income levels in the United States, and China's income per person remains approximately one-third that of Chile's.[16] The scale of China's economic achievements is also vast: government policies have lifted 800 million people out of poverty since the early 1980s. But Beijing's economic model is showing strain.[17] Still, much of this is to be expected: it is known to be more difficult to make the jump from being a middle-income to a high-income country than it is to transition from one that is low-income to one that is middle-income.

As opposed to measures of growth, development indices give us a much clearer idea of people's overall quality of life. Three essential capabilities are commonly associated with development: the abilities to lead a long and healthy life, to be knowledgeable, and to have access to the resources needed for a decent standard of

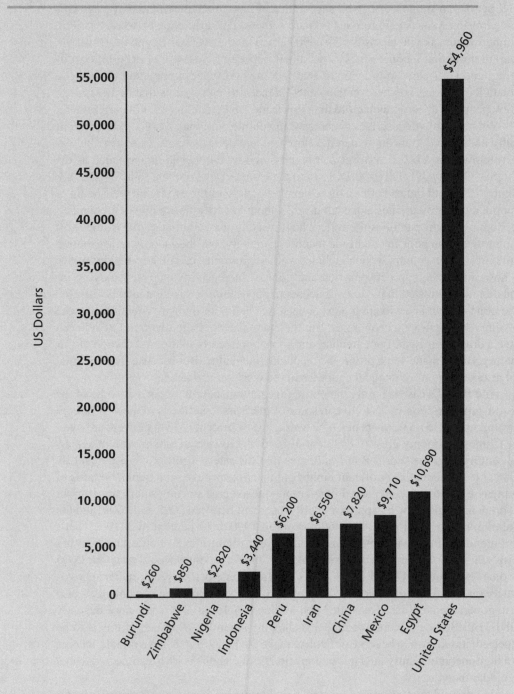

Figure 6.1   GNI per Capita for Rich, Middle-Income, and Poor Countries, 2015

Source: World Bank, *World Development Indicators 2015.*
Note: Data for Iran from 2014 (latest year available).

> ### Figure 6.2   Human Development Index, World Rankings, 2014
>
> | | | | |
> |---|---|---|---|
> | Norway | 1 | China | 90 |
> | Australia | 2 | Botswana | 106 |
> | Germany | 6 | Egypt | 108 |
> | | | | |
> | United States | 8 | Indonesia | 110 |
> | Hong Kong | 12 | Vietnam | 116 |
> | Spain | 26 | India | 130 |
> | | | | |
> | Qatar | 32 | Nigeria | 152 |
> | Saudi Arabia | 39 | Zimbabwe | 155 |
> | United Arab Emirates | 41 | Haiti | 163 |
> | | | | |
> | Portugal | 43 | Rwanda | 163 |
> | Uruguay | 52 | Democratic Republic of Congo | 176 |
> | Kazakhstan | 56 | Niger | 188 |
> | | | | |
> | Iran | 69 | | |
> | Mexico | 74 | | |
> | Peru | 84 | | |
>
> *Source:* United Nations Development Programme (UNDP), *Human Development Report 2015.*

living." Take a look at Figure 6.3. A life expectancy of seventy-seven years for Mexico, because it is comparable to the life expectancies of the citizens of many developed countries, suggests that the standard of living for Mexicans is relatively high. On the other hand, that the average Zimbabwean can expect to live only to fifty-six tells us that something is wrong. The HDI and similar indicators tell us even more— not only in regard to life expectancy, but also about infant and child morbidity and mortality rates and maternal health, as well as access to social services such as healthcare and education (see Figures 6.4 and 6.5). Although there is great variability (within and between LICs) in how well people are dealing with these problems, the difference between LICs and developed countries in dealing with maternal and child mortality can be particularly shocking where progress is slow (or nonexistent). Adolescent pregnancies carry an elevated risk of maternal death and disability. Pregnant girls whose bodies are not fully grown are more likely to develop obstetric fistulas (holes between their bladders and vaginas or rectums and vaginas) as well as other problems; their newborns are more likely to suffer from low birth weight and die in infancy. Although from 1960 to 2014 there was a 50 percent drop in the global adolescent fertility rate, the numbers remain extremely high in several countries, including Niger, Angola, and Mali.[19] In the 1990s, African children were nineteen times more likely to die before reaching their fifth birthday than were children born in high-income countries (HICs), and nearly fourteen times more likely in 2015. Overall, it is heartening that infant and child mortality rates have dropped significantly in developing countries since the 1990s, but in these countries approximately

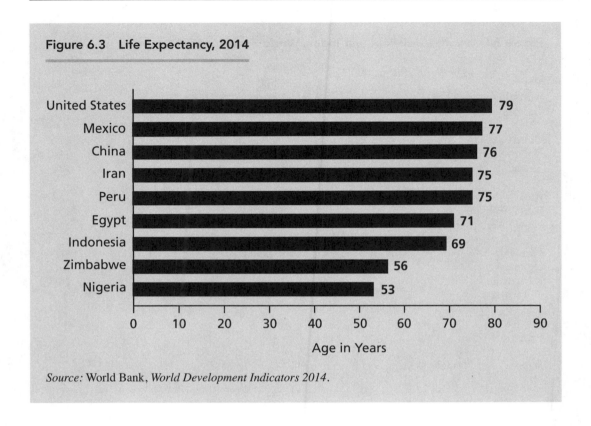

Figure 6.3   Life Expectancy, 2014

Country	Age
United States	79
Mexico	77
China	76
Iran	75
Peru	75
Egypt	71
Indonesia	69
Zimbabwe	56
Nigeria	53

Age in Years

Source: World Bank, *World Development Indicators 2014.*

6 million children under age five died in 2015—more than half of them from preventable or easily and affordably treated illnesses.[20]

Development indices also include attention to other aspects of well-being: caloric intake, access to clean water and sanitation—access even to telephones and computers. For example, the digital divide (in terms of access to computers in the North and South) is high but shrinking overall. There are approximately 3.2 billion Internet users globally, of which 2 billion are from developing countries.[21] This means that more than half of the world's population is not using the Internet (only 21 percent of Europeans are offline, but 75 percent of the populations in African states lack access to the Internet).[22] As we have seen in other areas of life, there is a significant gender gap in access to the Internet as well. The International Telecommunication Union (ITU) reports that, globally, there is a 12 percent difference between the Internet user penetration rate for males and females. The regional gender gap is most pronounced in Africa (23 percent), and smallest in the Americas (2 percent).[23]

The gap in access to high-speed Internet, proven to be so crucial in providing the information necessary to achievement of economic, social, and other goals, remains wide. Approximately 78 percent of the population in Europe and the Americas receive mobile broadband access; throughout Africa, the rate is below 20 percent.[24] A significant divide in smart phone ownership remains, but ownership rates in emerging and developing countries are rising (from 21 percent in 2013 to 37 percent in 2015).[25] There are over 7 billion cell phone subscriptions worldwide (individuals may have more than one account)[26]—subscribers who (besides using them to access and share information)

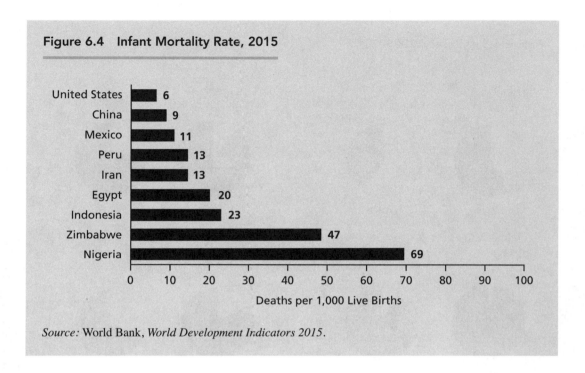

Figure 6.4   Infant Mortality Rate, 2015

Source: World Bank, *World Development Indicators 2015.*

can also utilize these phones in a variety of other ways. For example, people working abroad can use them to access bank accounts and send remittances back home to relatives. Instead of distributing goods or vouchers, aid groups can put money into recipients' cell phone savings accounts. Because the poor rarely have bank accounts, using cell phones for mobile banking or microsavings is a low-cost, safer way to store their money and it is revolutionizing commerce and the provision of services.[27]

Beyond traditional definitions that emphasize access to goods or services, development has more recently been expanded to include considerations of people's range of choice. This dimension of development includes concerns such as political empowerment and participation, HUMAN SECURITY, protection of the environment, and gender equality. In this sense, human development clearly includes but goes beyond material needs. This understanding of development recognizes people's need to be creative and productive, to live in dignity, and to enjoy the sense of belonging to a community. Increasingly, human development is being conceptualized as a development of the people, for the people, and by the people. It must therefore be understood as a process as well as an end, a process in which those targeted for development are participants in deciding how they will pursue it. In other words, human development is ultimately about freedom. It is as much about the process of enlarging people's choices as it is about providing people access to things valuable to their well-being.[28]

The rate of progress in every category of human development varies among and within countries. By some measures, such as a sense of community belonging, it could be argued that, generally speaking, the citizens of the global south are far ahead of those living in the global north. There have been some overall improvements in terms of other, more widely recognized aspects of human development across the

Figure 6.5   Literacy, 2008–2015

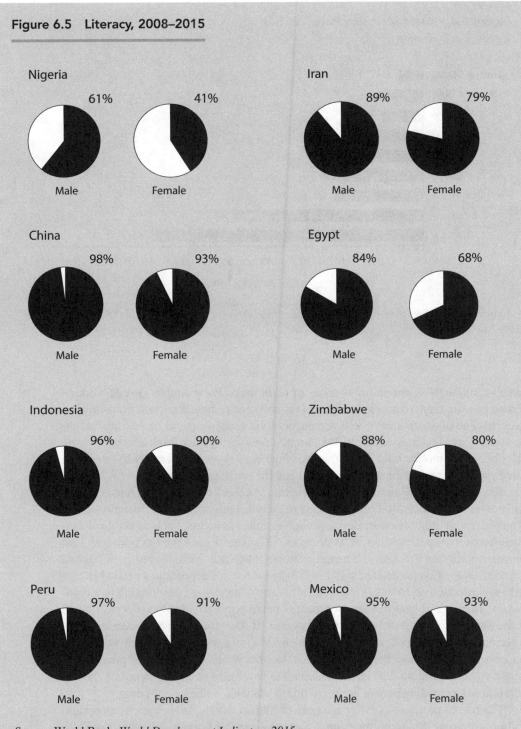

Nigeria

61% Male   41% Female

Iran

89% Male   79% Female

China

98% Male   93% Female

Egypt

84% Male   68% Female

Indonesia

96% Male   90% Female

Zimbabwe

88% Male   80% Female

Peru

97% Male   91% Female

Mexico

95% Male   93% Female

Source: World Bank, *World Development Indicators 2015*.
Note: Literacy is defined as the percentage of the population over age fifteen who can read and write.

world. However, not all have benefited equally from these improvements. Among LICs, some are making faster progress on certain aspects of development (e.g., Peru on infant mortality rates, Egypt on primary-school completion rates for females). For others, progress is much slower (e.g., in Zimbabwe, where because of HIV/AIDS, life expectancy has actually regressed since independence in 1980, though it has improved in recent years after hitting an appalling low of thirty-seven years in 2006). World-wide, more than 2.4 billion people lack access to basic sanitation, including toilets or latrines. Despite progress, the 2015 MILLENNIUM DEVELOPMENT GOAL (MDG) target to halve the proportion of the population without access to improved sanitation facil-ities was missed by almost 700 million people, and in forty-seven countries, less than half of the population has access to a toilet or an improved latrine.[29] On the other hand, the world has made progress in providing more people with access to improved water sources—from 1990 to 2015, the proportion of the world's population using improved drinking water sources increased from 76 percent to 91 percent (although 663 million people worldwide still lack access to clean water).[30]

By comparing the information in Figures 6.1 through 6.6, you can see that growth and development are often very uneven. Between 2010 and 2015, developing countries composed 85 percent of the world's population but accounted for 56 percent of global gross national income. That is up from 36 percent of global GNI in the 1980s.[31] But while we might assume that with time more countries will experience CONVERGENCE— that they will eventually "catch up" economically with developed countries—there is disagreement about whether this will ever happen. In what Fareed Zakaria referred to as "the rise of the rest,"[32] many believed that big, fast-growing emerging markets like the BRICS (Brazil, Russia, India, and China) were on their way toward convergence. Nearly 30 percent of the total increase in world output in 2000–2008 occurred in the BRICS, capturing a great deal of attention (and demand for more decisionmaking power) at international economic and political forums. (Occasionally a few other countries are included with the BRICS: BRICET, comprising the BRICS plus Eastern Europe and Turkey; BRICS, comprising the BRICS plus South Africa; BRICM, comprising the BRICS plus Mexico.)[33] Yet by 2015, many were labeling the BRIC economies "passé," with an "uncertain" economic future, given that average growth rates among them dropped from 7.6 percent in 2010 to less than 4 percent in 2015, with only India (and China, albeit with growth rates the slowest in decades) bucking the trend.[34]

But even for those that aren't members of one of these clubs, not all the news is bad. Some countries in the global south, especially those known as emerging economies, have made impressive progress in improving their citizens' standards of living. Take a look at Figure 6.6. The percentage of people living below the poverty line has declined in all regions of the global south. As discussed earlier, over the past two decades the world has witnessed the largest decrease in ABSOLUTE POVERTY in history; it is estimated that more than 440 million people's incomes grew. This raised them out of the ranks of the extremely poor (the figure was adjusted in 2015 to $1.90 a day). It is estimated that the extreme poverty rate has been cut more than half since 1990. This is a remarkable accomplishment, which analysts attribute to the end of the Cold War along with globalization, new technology, leadership, and luck.[35] But it is important to note that one country—China—accounts for much of this im-provement. This is still, without a doubt, a triumph. Yet these statistics can be de-ceptive; 900 million people remain in extreme poverty, with the overwhelming

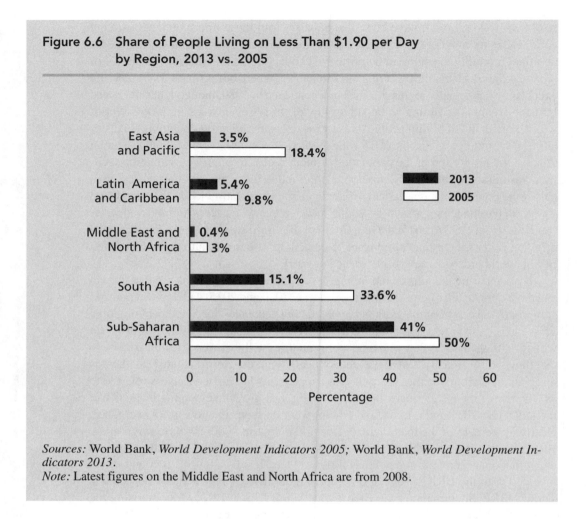

Figure 6.6 Share of People Living on Less Than $1.90 per Day by Region, 2013 vs. 2005

Sources: World Bank, *World Development Indicators 2005;* World Bank, *World Development Indicators 2013.*
Note: Latest figures on the Middle East and North Africa are from 2008.

majority found in Southern Asia and sub-Saharan Africa, and an estimated half of these people are children under the age of eighteen.[36]

Although poverty certainly exists in HICs, most residents of these countries cannot fathom the poverty found in much of the global south. In 2015 it took the average resident of Niger an entire year to earn what the average American earned in a week.[37] It is clear that both relative and absolute poverty remain long-standing problems. With initiatives such as those discussed in Figure 6.7, countries have set goals aimed at ameliorating this situation.

Even within the sweeping category known as the global south, there are major differences in the levels of income and economic development. Taiwan, Singapore, Hong Kong, and Israel, sometimes referred to as advanced economies, are relatively wealthy, on the cusp of being considered economically developed. Of our CASE STUDIES, China, Iran, Peru, and Mexico are upper-middle-income countries. Indonesia, Egypt, and Nigeria are lower-middle-income countries, while Zimbabwe is a low-income country. Although Nigeria is a major oil exporter (upward of 90 percent of its exports are petroleum or petroleum-based products), by many measures it is a

Figure 6.7 Development with a Deadline, Part Two (the 2030 Agenda)

At the start of the new millennium, the leaders of the world's countries and major development organizations agreed on a bold blueprint for action. They set forth an ambitious development agenda and pledged to work toward eight specific goals, known as the Millennium Development Goals (MDGs), aimed at meeting the basic human needs of all people by 2015. As the deadline neared and many successes were hailed (especially in the reduction of extreme poverty, infant mortality, and deaths due to specific diseases), the MDGs were praised for being "concrete, measurable, and time-bound."[a] Even though some targets fell woefully short of their goal (hardly a dent was made in carbon dioxide emissions, for example), former UN Secretary-General Ban Ki-moon called the MDGs "the most successful anti-poverty movement in history."[b]

In 2015, after a three-year negotiating and consultation process, all 193 member states of the United Nations agreed on seventeen new Sustainable Development Goals (SDGs), with the goal to achieve them by the year 2030. As you would expect, the SDGs highlight the need to focus on remaining challenges after the MDGs, which, in hindsight, were too narrowly focused. For example, the MDGs did not emphasize the root causes of poverty, failed to mention human rights, and completely overlooked gender equality.[c] Also, development experts contend that lasting solutions to the vexing problems facing our world need closer partnerships between governments, businesses, and civil society. So, in formulating the seventeen goals to be met in this 2030 agenda (also called the "Global Goals"), the UN embarked on a massive consultation program to assess what should be included, convening a series of "global conversations" (that included door-to-door surveys) alongside the traditional working-group discussions within the UN framework.[d] The emphasis of the SDGs is on ending extreme poverty, fighting inequalities and injustice, and protecting our planet—with every country of the world expected to work to achieve the targets. Yet some point out that the goals—which all together encompass 169 targets to be met over a fifteen-year period—contradict each other at times. For example, in the admirable goal to provide energy to all citizens of the globe (in 2015, more than 1.3 billion people lacked access to any electricity), progress in combating climate change may likely be compromised.[e] Other observers, including the governments of the UK and Japan, believe that the desire to be comprehensive has created an unwieldy catalog of aims that are unlikely to be realized, and that there are real concerns that tracking the implementation of these targets exceeds the capacity of the national statistical bureaucracies in many countries.[f] Can the international community repeat and surpass the successes of the MDGs? The clock is ticking, and the world is watching.

Notes: a. Moisés Naím, "What Comes After the Greatest Anti-Poverty Campaign in History?" *The Atlantic*, January 29, 2014, www.theatlantic.com.

b. United Nations, *Millennium Development Goals Report 2015: Summary* (New York, 2015), p. 2.

c. Liz Ford, "Sustainable Development Goals: All You Need to Know," *The Guardian*, January 19, 2015, www.theguardian.com.

d. Ibid.

e. Charles Kenny, "If Everyone Gets Electricity, Can the Planet Survive?" *The Atlantic*, September 28, 2015, www.theantlantic.com.

f. José Graziano da Silva, "The Challenge of Tracking Progress of UN's Development Goals: Data," *Christian Science Monitor*, November 29, 2016, www.csmonitor.com; Ford, "Sustainable Development Goals."

relatively poor country. Indonesia, Iran, Egypt, and Mexico are also dependent on petroleum exports, but to varying degrees. For example, Mexico's economy, spread across the agricultural, industrial, and service sectors, is much more diversified than Nigeria's. With the proliferation of MAQUILADORAS, or assembly plants, Mexico's economy is increasingly based on the export of manufactured goods, as are the economies of China, Indonesia, and others. At the start of the twenty-first century, the growth of these economies was largely based on the success of this sector.

China is now ranked an upper-middle-income country, with the second largest economy on the planet (behind the United States). It enjoys regular trade surpluses (in 2015 its trade surplus grew by a whopping 55 percent to $595 billion) and absorbs the vast majority of foreign investment going to LICs.[38] If trends continue, China will pass the United States and become the world's largest economy by 2030 (by then India will likely be the fourth largest).[39] On the other hand, the combination of domestic upheaval and international isolation has meant that Zimbabwe missed out on the boom of the mid-2000s. Its growth rate was 1.4 percent in 2016 and it had the world's fastest-shrinking economy until 2009.[40] Peru's economy is heavily dependent on minerals (the prices of which can be quite volatile), and Zimbabwe's foreign exchange is typically earned from the sale of goods such as tobacco and nickel. But the relatively diverse base of their economies makes these countries the envy of more monocultural economies such as Guinea-Bissau, where cashew nut production accounts for 85 percent of all jobs in the country.[41] The economies of all of our case studies are highly export-oriented. Because they are so dependent on sales abroad, they are vulnerable to economic slowdowns in China, the United States, and other developed countries (their biggest customers).

Another measure offering a closer look at poverty, from a different angle, is the Gender-Related Development Index (GDI). Among other things, it tells us that although no country in the world treats its women as well as its men, gender inequality is strongly correlated with poverty. The rising impoverishment of women and their children is sometimes referred to as the "feminization" of poverty. This poverty is manifested in several different ways. According to economist Amartya Sen, by 1990 the comparative neglect of females worldwide in terms of health and nutrition had contributed to more than 100 million "missing" females—most of them in Asia, where a preference for male children is largely still the norm. The numbers have worsened in recent years, in part because of the widespread use of ultrasounds for sex-selective abortions. More recently, the UN Population Fund estimated that there are 117 million "missing" females due to gender-biased sex selection throughout Asia, Eastern Europe, and the Caucasus, and some suggest the number could be as high as 160 million.[42] As a result, the number of boys born (compared to the number of girls) is highly skewed in several countries. The natural sex ratio (in the absence of sex-selective abortion) is 105 boys for every 100 girls. However, the overall ratio within China is currently 106–120 men for every 100 women (with one city reporting 163 boys for every 100 girls), and in India the ratio is 108 to 100.[43] It is estimated that in China men outnumber women by approximately 62 million.[44] A recent report suggests that such imbalances in China are due to its decades-long, repressive (and recently abandoned) one child policy: families simply chose not to register girl children.[45] It remains to be seen whether this is the explanation for the "missing" girls. A gender imbalance may eventually mean that these countries will have surpluses of men; it is expected that by 2030, nearly one-quarter of men in China will be unable to find wives, and demographers predict that such circumstances could lead to social and political instability; skewed sex ratios are known to be associated with increased sex trafficking and bride buying.[46] The governments of these countries are concerned about a looming crisis and are reportedly adopting policies aimed at normalizing the ratio.[47]

There are certainly differences in the status of females between and within countries, depending on class, regional origin, ethnicity, and other factors. However, in

the poorest countries, women and girls are more likely to be illiterate, to earn three-quarters (or less) of a male's wages, to consume fewer calories, to become sick more often, and to die at younger ages than their male counterparts. They are also less likely to own land, despite evidence that women, if they have equalized opportunities, can farm as productively as men, if not more so.[48]

There has been some progress in rectifying these imbalances, largely because development planners now recognize that when women benefit, so do their families and their communities. "Women in development" (WID) has been a catchphrase since the early 1970s. Prior to this time, development planners largely neglected women. If they were included at all, it was mostly for instruction in home economics and family planning. Although WID projects continue to have their problems, the best ones are designed keeping in mind how women contribute to the overall development of their countries. Research in several countries shows that the money women earn is more likely to be spent on their families, whereas men are often more likely to spend it on themselves.

Since the 1960s, larger numbers of women in many but not all countries have entered the paid work force. Female participation in the labor force remained static (at about 25 percent) in Egypt from 1990 to 2014, but it grew tenfold in the past sixty years in China, from 7 percent in 1949 to over 70 percent in 2014.[49] Increasingly, employers worldwide are recruiting women because they are desperate enough to accept the work and pay that men reject. Even controlling for experience and education, women earn 77 percent of what men earn; at the current rate of change, it will take seventy years to close the gender wage gap.[50] Consequently, the feminization of poverty can occur even as more women are entering the FORMAL SECTOR. Women have a higher incidence of poverty than men, and female poverty tends to be more severe than male poverty, despite the fact that around the world, women often work more hours than men. Female poverty is often intergenerational; overworked mothers may find that they must depend on the assistance of their daughters to make ends meet and to help them with childcare responsibilities.

Moreover, if parents are expected to pay school fees, it is less likely that girls will attend school. It is estimated that only 70 percent of children in low-income countries will complete primary school in 2030, revealing an appalling gap in achievement that advocates say "should set off alarm bells" within the international development community.[51] Between 58 and 61 million children of primary-school age do not attend school, a high percentage of whom are girls: at the current rate of progress, it will be 2042 before all children have access to primary school and 2084 before the same goal is met for secondary school.[52] The gaps are largest in low-income and rural areas, and girls from ethnic, religious, or caste minorities are doubly disadvantaged. Yet poverty remains the single greatest barrier to education: in low- and middle-income countries, the poorest have, on average, five fewer years of schooling than the richest.[53]

Thanks to important reforms such as the elimination of school fees, female literacy rates have improved in several regions. Still, two-thirds of the world's more than 770 million people who cannot read or write a simple statement are female—a proportion that has not changed for more than twenty years.[54] As you can see in Figure 6.5, Peru and Mexico aren't part of this club, but in many Latin American countries, girls' enrollment is surpassing that of boys. Many countries have made progress

in promoting gender parity at the primary- and secondary-school levels since 2000. But with entrenched gender barriers, girls continue to face hurdles in obtaining their education, particularly in many southern Asian and African countries, including all of our cases. It is important to remove these barriers because development workers have known for years that the investment in education for females pays off in the long run with healthier children and smaller families.[55]

Many of the girls who leave school do so for a variety of reasons, including early marriage and pregnancy, as well as sexual harassment and the discrimination they face in schools. One of the most common reasons girls leave school is to work. Women are crucial agricultural producers in much of the world, producing the food crops that ensure their families' survival, yet they rarely have equal access to appropriate technologies. Instead, women must rely on manual techniques that are heavily labor-intensive, wasting time and energy. Part of the reason women lack access to tractors, fertilizers, and other inputs is because they lack credit. In Nigeria, Egypt, and elsewhere, women are often unable to obtain credit because they have no independent access to land. Where most of the population is employed in some capacity or another as agriculturists, access to land is the single most important factor in determining well-being. But it is by no means the only one. According to the United Nations, women produce more than 50 percent of the world's food (in sub-Saharan Africa and the Caribbean, the percentage is closer to 80).[56]

In general, rural women are the poorest of the poor, and the gap between their quality of life and that of the rest of the world is not narrowing in the way that it should—if what is being promoted in these countries were truly "development." Gender bias is a large part of why development initiatives have so often failed. Even where there has been impressive growth, we now know that economic growth alone will not eliminate inequality: societies must promote women's rights in order to reduce gender disparities.

When faced with these arguments about the under-development of much of the world, the optimists admit that, yes, the gap between rich and poor is growing wider, but argue that the floor under the poor is rising steadily in much of the world. Analysts disagree about whether the gap between the rich and poor, known as RELATIVE POVERTY, is growing. As mentioned earlier, prior to the recession of the late 2000s, growth was up and absolute poverty was falling. But globalization's effect on inequality is ambiguous.[57] Neoliberals are confident that an unequal concentration of wealth will eventually trickle down. They believe that the concentration of wealth serves as a spur to investment, bringing faster economic growth. They maintain that all states reap benefits from the free trade: the international economic exchange of goods and services. International cooperation is facilitated through the development of trading relationships. This is good for everyone, in that it promotes not only economic stability but also political stability. For the neoliberals, who dominate the governments of developed countries, the boardrooms of MULTINATIONAL CORPORATIONS (MNCs), and the international economic organizations and commercial banks known as international financial institutions (IFIs), growth is everything. Countries cannot reduce poverty and will not develop unless they increase growth rates first.

The best way to increase growth rates, according to neoliberals, is to embrace globalization. In other chapters globalization is discussed more broadly, in terms of its sociocultural and political aspects, or how it has spilled over to affect just about everything: social relations (including class, race, and gender relations), culture, poli-

tics—even climate. In this chapter, we focus on globalization as an economic phenomenon. Globalization should be understood as the spread of capitalism worldwide. It is an all-embracing, multidimensional force based in ECONOMIC LIBERALIZATION, or the adoption of capitalist, market-based reforms.[58] Neoliberals are proponents of this economic liberalization, arguing for open markets and laissez-faire economics. The French term *laissez-faire* translates as "let it be." By this neoliberals mean that government's proper role is to withdraw from economics as much as possible and to "let economics be"—or allow the "invisible hand" of supply and demand to work. Market forces allowed to operate unimpeded by government interference maximize efficiency, according to these analysts.

Consequently, neoliberals regard globalization as a positive force that helps to further integrate the economies of the world into the international marketplace, often referred to as the international economic system. This system is capitalist, and it is supported by a number of very powerful institutions and organizations, most notably the International Monetary Fund (IMF). Both the IMF and its counterpart, the World Bank, were founded in the years after World War II, initially to assist in the reconstruction of Europe. Each of these multilateral institutions has its own mandate, but over the years their roles have changed and today there is some overlap in their functions. Both organizations are dominated by developed countries, since decisions in the INTERNATIONAL GOVERNMENTAL ORGANIZATIONS (IGOs) are made through weighted voting (that is, based on each member country's financial contribution). Structuralists describe this as a system based on "the golden rule" (whoever has the gold makes the rules). Whereas the World Bank's primary mission is to provide development assistance to the world's poorest countries, the IMF serves in a number of capacities, including the promotion of global economic stability. One way the IMF promotes stability is by serving as the lender of last resort to countries in economic crisis. It distributes loans to countries whose economies are failing.

According to the dominant players in this system, further integration into the world economy is exactly what under-developed countries need. LICs should embrace globalization and raise growth rates by trading more in the international marketplace and competing to attract foreign capital. The WORLD TRADE ORGANIZATION (WTO), created to update the GENERAL AGREEMENT ON TARIFFS AND TRADE (GATT), works to promote free trade by providing a forum for discussion of the unresolved issues that cause friction between states. Established in 1995, the WTO has significant influence, since its 164 members account for more than 98 percent of the world's trade.[59] Neoliberals contend that because global capitalism is the best hope for the development of the global south, the WTO provides an invaluable service. The free flow of technology, capital, and ideas is raising living standards higher, faster, and for more people than at any other time in history. For nearly two decades, the integration of economies sparked impressive trade growth: world exports of goods and services nearly tripled between 1990 and 2007, with LICs' share of this trade growing from 17 to 28 percent.[60] Yet due to the lagging impact of the Great Recession, local economic slowdowns, and increased global volatility, world trade experienced sluggish growth in 2015 and 2016, growing 2.8 percent.[61] Exports from developed countries (2.6 percent) lagged behind those from developing countries (3.3 percent), and the WTO forecasts that world trade is likely to grow at roughly the same rate as gross domestic product (GDP) for the short term (rather than twice the rate of GDP,

as it had earlier).[62] While middle- and low-income countries are still being encouraged to make adjustments to liberalize their economies, they recognize, in a very real way, their vulnerability to negative trends from the developed world.

Part of what makes globalization such a fascinating process to study is that it can have positive as well as negative effects. It can contribute to increased cooperation and unity while at the same time creating conditions for fragmentation and conflict. As Thomas Friedman has pointed out, globalization is everything and its opposite. It can be both incredibly empowering and incredibly coercive. Both proponents and critics of globalization agree on its overwhelming force. Neoliberals contend that when it comes to LICs' absorption into the international economy, the question isn't so much "When?" as it is "How?"[63]

Yet structuralists maintain that the majority of LICs already share a common position within the world economy. They are relatively powerless within it. Global south countries as a whole have very little influence in setting the agenda or making decisions for the international economic system. Through its enforcement of the existing rules of trade, the World Trade Organization further marginalizes LICs. Although low-income countries have joined the WTO, in general developed countries are much more enthusiastic about the existence of the WTO than are low-income countries, many of which view the organization as just another way for developed countries to protect their advantageous position within the existing system.

Structuralists also accuse the WTO of selectively dismantling trade barriers in a lopsided liberalization that is skewed in favor of industrialized countries and multinational corporations. In some cases, WTO rules that promote free trade in manufactured goods force LICs to open up their markets to the products of developed countries, while the products of LICs (especially agricultural goods, such as orange juice) often face the highest trade barriers and are effectively shut out of the developed countries' markets.

Ironically, for all their talk about "free trade," it is the subsidies and various protectionist measures of developed countries that have made it hard for much of the global south to earn an honest living through trade. One way that countries boost their own producers while hurting competition is through subsidies, or payments to domestic producers (sometimes small farmers but often large agribusiness corporations). The United States and European Union (EU) spend over $85 billion a year on agricultural subsidies (much more than they spend on aid to poor countries).[64] China spends even more—$165 billion each year—subsidizing agricultural production to support its own domestic producers' agricultural exports, boosting (over)production and driving down world prices for commodities like sugar, wheat, and rice.[65]

From the perspective of many in the global south (and from the structuralists' point of view), if developed countries were to practice the free trade they preach—if the governments of the United States and Europe (as well as China and India) were to cut the billions of dollars per day that they spend on agricultural subsidies—it could dramatically improve the welfare of millions of households. These subsidies suppress world cotton prices by at least 6 percent. Because cotton (also known as "white gold") is so critical to the economies of many of the world's poorest countries, removing just US cotton subsidies would amount to a huge boost for cotton farmers in the developing world, increasing average household income in Burkina Faso, Benin, Chad, and Mali by 2–9 percent. As it is, because HICs' subsidies drive

the world market price for cotton so low, farmers in LICs can't compete; they try to scrape together a living by moving into new areas and overworking the land, causing significant ecological damage.[66]

One recent turn of events did give many structuralists pause (briefly). In what was called a "historic breakthrough" on cotton, Brazil successfully challenged US agricultural subsidies at the WTO in 2009. The WTO found that the US price support program for cotton violated trade agreements. The United States resisted the ruling, but promised to reform its subsidy program and agreed to pay Brazil hundreds of millions of dollars in compensation. At first the WTO decision appeared to reflect a shift in bargaining power. It showed developing countries that they might have a chance at promoting their rights through the enforcement of free trade rules. However, in the end, the United States only replaced its old subsidies with new ones—and very little actually changed.[67]

One way or another, the leaders of LICs are effectively immobilized by the combined influence of the governments, corporations, and international financial institutions of more developed countries. They argue that agents of globalization, such as the International Monetary Fund and the World Trade Organization, wield such power over developing countries that they are in effect being recolonized. Though LICs can bring their complaints to the WTO, they frequently cannot afford costly legal battles. Poor countries can't afford the lawyers and lobbyists that the MNCs and rich countries hire to find loopholes in trade rules and buy the influence they need. In sum, structuralists argue that SOVEREIGNTY is steadily being eroded as governments are forced to give their decisionmaking authority to the IMF, MNCs, and developed countries.

Trade

As you may have guessed by now, structuralists argue trenchantly against the economic orthodoxy, while neoliberals accuse their critics on the left of overstating their case and ask what feasible alternative they offer. This is the case for trade as well. According to neoliberals, the best way to jump-start growth rates is to adopt a strategy of trade liberalization or free trade. They maintain that the wealthiest countries have built their success on trade and (with a few important exceptions) by being open to competition. In fact, neoliberals argue that there is not a single example in modern history of a country successfully developing without trading and integrating with the global economy.[68] On the other hand, they point out, it is no coincidence that until recently at least, it's the poorest countries in the world that have been the least friendly to free trade. The countries that are worst-off have adopted a variety of protectionist policies, artificially "protecting" domestic producers by slapping tariffs on imports. This kind of government interference with trade is notoriously inefficient, argue the neoliberals. Developing countries that have adopted market reforms and opened their economies, such as Hong Kong, Singapore, and Chile, have reaped the largest gains in terms of standards of living. Simply put, open economies grow much faster than closed economies. According to neoliberals, the existence of fast-growing economic powerhouses such as China, Brazil, and India proves that it is possible to thrive in the current economic system.[69]

Neoliberalism's critics (most from the left, but some also from the right) argue that the rich countries are hypocrites when it comes to openness, and that openness

does not guarantee wealth; a country's wealth depends less on ease of trade than it does on what is being traded.[70] Openness involves great risk, and the countries experiencing relative success are few and far between. Not all countries can achieve the success of China, nor should they want to follow the Chinese example, which is hardly the model of an open economy. Structuralists recognize that the impetus toward trade liberalization and embrace of globalization is nothing new. In fact, they argue that the reason why so much of the global south is under-developed today is because of the position it was assigned during colonialism or within the NEW INTERNATIONAL DIVISION OF LABOR (NIDL). What is "new" about the international division of labor today (though it is actually not so new) is that a handful of LICs are moving in to fill the voids in manufacturing that are left as developed countries mature into service-based economies. The textile and steel mills that were once so important to the US, British, and German economies have since moved south, creating the existing division of labor.

One aspect of the NIDL that is actually not so new is the expansion of regional and product specialization, based in the principle of comparative advantage. Seeking to increase efficiency through specialization in production, the colonizers created monocultural economies throughout Africa, Asia, Latin America, and the Middle East. This principle, widely revered by liberals for hundreds of years, is based in the assumption that countries differ in their ability to produce certain goods based on their natural resources, labor, and other factors. In order to maximize wealth, countries should specialize in producing goods for which they have a comparative advantage. Today the vast majority of LICs continue to produce many of the same goods assigned to them during the days of colonialism—unprocessed primary goods for export. This makes good business sense, according to neoliberals. By concentrating on a few goods for export, LIC economies can become more fully integrated into the world economy. With the hard currency they earn from the sale of their raw materials, LICs can pay their debts and import everything else they need (including food, fuel, manufactured goods, etc.). Moreover, if all countries liberalize their economies and open up to trade, it will mean that businesses will have to work harder to be competitive. The result will be improved and less expensive products—a benefit to all.

Neoliberalism's critics on the left argue that it isn't quite that simple. Although many people are giving up and heading for the cities, the majority of the world's population continue to live in rural areas and work as farmers. During colonialism rural communities were disrupted, many subsistence farmers were forced off the land, and small plots were consolidated into large plantations. This is happening again today, as rising world food prices have led to a land rush in which private foreign investors and governments are leasing millions of hectares of arable land owned by African governments and displacing tens of thousands of farmers.[71]

Those so far unaffected by such deals farm plots of various sizes; most are smallholders (working tiny plots of 2 hectares or less) or are landless. The landless often drift around the countryside looking for seasonal work, and are employed as tenant farmers or as migrant laborers on much larger farms or plantations. Smallholders in developed and less developed countries are rapidly being displaced as they find that they can no longer support themselves through farming and are increasingly forced to sell their land to huge agribusinesses. What small farmers had in common is that they once practiced subsistence farming. Farmers ate what they

produced and sold the surplus. However, today the majority of countries have moved away from food production and can no longer be considered subsistence economies. Rather, these are export-based economies, increasingly centered on the production of commodities known as cash crops. Coffee, flowers, sisal, and bananas are just a few examples of cash crops, which are produced for sale abroad (mostly to consumers in developed countries). Mines producing bauxite, copper, and diamonds, and aquaculture and ranches producing salmon and beef, are also sites for the production of cash crops. What many of these commodities have in common is that they are raw materials, or unprocessed goods that will most likely be sent elsewhere for manufacture into finished goods.

Critics of this situation argue that as producers of raw materials, LICs are assigned a disadvantageous position in the world economic system, and not only because most raw materials are vulnerable to sometimes dramatic price fluctuations that make it extremely difficult to plan or budget from year to year. It is a rule of economics that labor adds value. Because raw materials are unprocessed, they will always fetch a lower price than they would once processed into a finished good. The prices of exports by developed countries (mostly finished goods) have risen; meanwhile (with the exception of windfall gains for a few producers due to strong demand for a few commodities such as oil, aluminum, and copper) the prices of "soft" commodities (most of Africa's exports) have been falling, suffering a deterioration in the terms of trade.[72]

The "terms of trade," or the overall relationship between the prices of exported and imported goods, are therefore inherently disadvantageous to LICs' economies. Producers of raw materials must struggle to turn out larger volumes just to earn the hard currency to pay for the higher-priced finished goods they must import. The laws of supply and demand simply work against the LICs. For example, Ghanaian farmers can work harder to produce more cocoa for sale on the world market, but the harder they work the less they will earn, since an oversupply of cocoa will drive down its price. Worse, prices are driven down even further as farmers inadvertently add to the problem of oversupply. They produce even more when prices are down, since it takes a bigger crop to scrape by. Meanwhile, because they do not produce the things that they need, these countries are heavily dependent on imports (but without much income to pay for them). The result is that they import more than they export, contributing to a trade imbalance (which they must finance, often by going into debt). Import dependence, especially within the food and energy sectors, continues to be a very real challenge for many countries in the global south. Thirteen countries were 100 percent dependent on imports for their grain supply in 2013, an increase of 18 percent from 1961.[73] This places states in an extremely vulnerable position—one group of observers contend that Russia's grain export ban in 2010 served as a contributing factor to Egypt's unrest in 2011 that led to the overthrow of a government, as global prices increased and Egypt's state bread subsidy program took a serious hit.[74] In 2016, many Egyptians predicted riots over an increase in the price and shortages of sugar, one of the average citizen's last luxuries (in Egypt one-fifth of the population has diabetes).[75]

There is very little that producers of most raw materials can do about this situation as long as their economies remain centered around the production of cash crops for export. No single country can demand higher prices for its goods, since there are

many other producers competing for the sale. And demand for most raw materials is relatively elastic. Even if producers of any single raw material could form a producer's club or cartel to obtain a stronger bargaining position, consumers could turn to substitutes—they could increase their own domestic production of the good, or simply adjust their consumption of it. It is only because demand for oil is relatively inelastic that the oil producers' cartel, the Organization of Petroleum Exporting Countries (OPEC), has been able to raise oil prices by slowing down production and restricting oil supplies. But even oil exporters are not immune: many countries faced steep declines in revenue and increases in unrest following the slump in oil prices in 2014–2015, especially Saudi Arabia, Venezuela, and Nigeria. Saudi Arabia's income from oil fell by 23 percent in 2015, significant since nearly 85 percent of its export revenue comes from oil. The percentage is even higher in Venezuela, home to the world's largest known oil reserves, where oil exports account for nearly 95 percent of revenue.[76] Although the Nigerian economy is more diverse than that of other oil-exporting states in Africa, 95 percent of the country's foreign exchange is earned from the sale of petroleum and petroleum-based products. This greatly increases these countries' vulnerability to trends far outside their control.[77]

Therefore, even for oil producers, structuralists argue that the world economic system as it currently exists works to reinforce LICs' dependence and leaves them vulnerable to a variety of problems. Having an undiversified economy is like putting all your eggs in one basket. Chinese manufacturers' appetite for commodities such as iron ore, copper, and soybeans helped to raise the price of these goods from 2003 to 2007, but amounted to a "re-primarization" of the economy and made it harder for countries like Peru and Chile to break out of the trap of exporting raw materials and get into the development of value-added manufactured goods and services.[78] When demand remains high, life is good, but then the bottom can fall out. As the Chinese economy began to slow in 2013, the spillover effects hit the rest of the world, especially LICs dependent on exports. The World Bank estimates that China's slowdown alone accounted for about 20 percent of the decrease in import growth in developing countries and countries in transition between 2014 and 2015.[79] So these economies are also vulnerable to swings in world market prices for their goods—as well as to blight, drought, and other causes of crop failure.

Moreover, overreliance on the export of one raw material (or a few) has left countries that were once self-sufficient in the production of food crops, like Nigeria, now dependent on food imports. Even worse, some countries with hungry populations produce food crops for export. Brazil, for example, although trying to ensure that its own population is fed, is tearing down its forests to grow soybeans (a lucrative cash crop) to satisfy Chinese and European demand. Whereas the IMF and donor agencies encourage LIC economies to focus on export-based production as a means of earning revenue, critics maintain that such a focus is unlikely to produce healthy economies that can support their populations.

Most LICs have had little choice but to accept this advice. And although many countries have attempted to diversify their economies, this is easier said than done. The poorer the country, the more likely its economy is centered on five or fewer products.[80] There may be entrenched elites within the country who profit from having the economy structured as it is. Governments that are willing to open up new sectors are limited in the funds available to change things. It takes time and capital to

diversify an economy. Moreover, the skills of local inhabitants are likely to be concentrated in the production of what are now traditional cash crops, and the infrastructure may only tie together existing points of production to points of exit.[81]

Even more debilitating than a monocultural economy is no economy at all. Many of the poorest LICs have little or nothing to sell on the world market. Some governments are so desperate to earn hard currency that they have joined the booming business of refuse disposal. As the citizens of developed countries become more aware of the dangers of pollutants to human health and comfort, they have organized into NIMBY ("not in my backyard") movements. For years, the more affluent communities of developed countries have searched for other places to dispose of their refuse. And for years, poor neighborhoods in these developed countries have become the sites of dumps and landfills. But in response to mounting pressure from NIMBY movements and regulations about waste containment in developed countries, an international trade in refuse removal has emerged. Many LICs that find it difficult making ends meet from the sale of cash crops are now competing to house the garbage and toxic wastes (including e-waste, or electronic waste—such as discarded computers, televisions, and cell phones—which is often hazardous) of developed countries. This practice of wealthy (predominantly white) populations dumping their often-poisonous wastes into poor (predominantly black or brown) communities is known as "environmental racism." The United Nations Environmental Programme (UNEP) estimates that in 2014 alone the improper disposal of e-waste cost $52 billion to the global economy. As a way to skirt international regulations preventing such shipping, thousands of tons of items are falsely declared "secondhand goods" that are illegally exported from developed to developing countries. With continuous upgrades and a growing sense of the disposable nature of these products, one UNEP official stated that "we are facing the onset of an unprecedented tsunami of electronic waste rolling out over the world."[82]

Burgeoning industries such as refuse removal are only the latest examples of how LICs have attempted to cope with their weak position within the international economic system. While some initiatives are best understood simply as coping mechanisms, others have been undertaken with the aim of changing the place of LICs within the system. IMPORT SUBSTITUTION INDUSTRIALIZATION is an example of one such effort. In an attempt to follow the developed-country path to development through industrialization, many LICs have sought to break out of the mold as exporters of unfinished goods and lessen their dependence on imports. However, for a variety of reasons, most notably their inability to break into the markets of developed countries or compete with multinational corporations, this experiment has often failed. Still, most countries of Africa, Latin America, and the Middle East remain locked in their position as producers of cash crops in export-based economies.

Interestingly, until recently it was East Asia that liberals pointed to as evidence that capitalist development worked. The export-driven economies of the FOUR TIGERS—Hong Kong, Singapore, South Korea, and Taiwan, all highly successful emerging markets—were based on the production of light manufactured goods. For decades, growth rates regularly exceeded 5 percent per year. Per capita income increased more rapidly in these economies than anywhere else in the world. Between 1960 and 2009, for example, GNI per capita in South Korea grew almost fifteenfold, far surpassing that of Brazil, China, and India. There were similar gains

in life expectancy and literacy rates, and an overall reduction in poverty, in South Korea and the other industrializing countries. Most impressive, the percentage of South Koreans living under the poverty line during this period was dramatically reduced—from 60 to less than 15 percent.[83]

However, analysts have always disagreed about whether the experience of the Four Tigers could be replicated elsewhere. Since the Asian economic crisis of the late 1990s, more serious questions have been raised about the use of this model. Neoliberals attributed the success of these emerging economies to their openness, embrace of capitalism, and export-oriented approach as well as their well-educated, disciplined, and hardworking labor force. In addition, emerging economies were credited with having an innovative entrepreneurial class, a high rate of savings, and relatively well-developed infrastructures.

Still, these countries were hardly examples of success based on less state involvement in economies. This was not laissez-faire capitalism at work. Under the Asian model of STATE CAPITALISM adopted in the 1950s, governments were heavily involved in nurturing and protecting industries and businesses until they were globally competitive. Although there is some heterogeneity among the East Asian emerging economies, in most cases these states undertook what is called an export offensive. Throughout the region, governments manipulated nationalist interests to promote economic mobilization. Under this policy, the state became a driving force, directing the economy with the aim of improving international competitiveness. The South Korean and Taiwanese governments, and those of other emerging economies, directed economic growth through their allocation of credit to priority sectors. Scarcely a case of the "invisible hand" at work, these governments played an active, catalytic role in guiding investment strategies. They offered incentives and disincentives to prod the economy toward particular exporting industries. Most of these industries were initially light manufacturing and labor-intensive but gradually became higher-tech. These infant industries were nurtured and protected; the state intervened aggressively and employed protectionist practices to ensure that domestic firms could compete with foreigners.[84]

At the same time that these governments were insulating their infant industries from foreign competition, they avidly sought to attract foreign investment. Decades ago, South Korea and Taiwan successfully lured investors by offering tax incentives, keeping unions weak, and eliminating minimum-wage legislation. For many years, these East Asian governments could only be characterized as dictatorships determined to modernize. These authoritarian regimes manipulated nationalist identities to mobilize the population to work and sacrifice for the good of the nation. Governments provided little in terms of social welfare. Air and water pollution soared. Political and civil rights were forsaken for economic growth, and governments used repressive mechanisms to resist popular pressure for change.

It is important to note that incomes in Taiwan, South Korea, and the other emerging economies of Asia have gradually improved, as have quality-of-life indicators and (with the notable exception of China) respect for political and civil liberties. But it is primarily because of this policy of aggressive government intervention in the economy that the emerging markets were able to capture shares on certain goods. For example, today the East Asian economies make up the world's largest source of electronic components (and roughly one in every four laptops in the world is made in

China).[85] They base their success on the partnerships that their governments made with businesses to raise productivity and capture an increasing share of the world market. Although this close relationship has been characterized as "crony capitalism" because it is associated with corrupt practices, it has also resulted in the creation of huge economic conglomerates. These economies were so competitive and their performances so strong that in some cases they dominated the market in certain goods. For two decades now, many of these emerging economies have enjoyed trade surpluses with developed countries. The IMF now characterizes Hong Kong, South Korea, and Taiwan as advanced economies. But it is important to remember that, so far, their experience is the exception, not the rule.

Foreign Investment

Although trends seem to be focused downward, foreign direct investment (FDI) by global corporations continues to be a major part of the development agenda around the world. Yet FDI levels reached their peak in 2007, with 36 percent less investment by MNCs in 2014 compared to the pre-crisis high.[86] In 2015, global flows of FDI increased by 40 percent—the highest level since the Great Recession. Even though the United Nations Conference on Trade and Development (UNCTAD) forecasts a decline of 10–15 percent in 2016 and early 2017, it is counting on a rebound shortly thereafter.[87] These up and down trends point to precisely the concerns that many structuralists highlight.

A global MNC presence is nothing new; since the days of colonialism (and often predating it), multinational corporations have been active throughout the global south. In low-income countries these businesses have dominated the agriculture and mining sectors. Until three decades ago, relatively few of the world's manufactured goods were produced in LICs. However, as mentioned earlier, this has been changing. Some non-Western countries have industrialized, and more and more MNCs are looking to lower the costs of production by creating assembly plants overseas. These corporations are highly influential nongovernmental actors in the process of globalization; their investment decisions often mean the difference between whether a country is increasingly drawn into the global economy, or marginalized by it.[88]

Neoliberals and their critics agree that MNCs are extremely powerful economic entities with an enormous scope and range of activities, including banking, pharmaceuticals, industrial goods, oil, foodstuffs, service—virtually any consumer item or need. Coordinating production on a global scale, they are hardly newcomers to the global economy; their precursors, such as the Dutch East India Company, were at the forefront of colonialism. Now as then, as economic units, the largest MNCs easily dwarf the vast majority of non-Western economies. As of 2015, of the world's 100 largest economic entities, more than half (63 percent) were corporations, not countries.[89] Apple has more cash on hand than two-thirds of the world's countries.[90] The economic power of MNCs is growing rapidly and their power is becoming more concentrated in a few huge firms—Walmart, Apple, and Shell are richer than Russia, Belgium, and Sweden.[91] Analysts have been predicting for years that soon the vast majority of the world's production will be controlled by a handful of MNCs. Such predictions seem to be coming true, as nearly every day one learns of another acquisition, merger, or buyout among these corporate behemoths.

MNCs are headquartered in what we call parent countries. Until recently, the European Union rounded out the top three, but China has joined the United States (the leading single source of FDI) and Japan as the countries parenting the largest number of Global 500 companies.[92] It is in parent countries where decisions are made, and to which profits return. Yet because of their size, some predict that in the not-too-distant future the power of MNCs may overtake that of the NATION-STATE. For decades sociologists have predicted that our primary identity may change as we come to view ourselves more as employees of the company for which we work, than as citizens of the country in which we live. In many ways the power of MNCs already rivals that of the nation-state. While MNCs have been accused of being agents of their national governments, the governments of their parent countries are often put to work for the corporations' interests. US interventions to protect MNCs in Chile, Iran, and Guatemala are just a few examples of political meddling, including the overthrow of LIC governments, when MNCs and developed countries have perceived a government's politics as threatening to the economic status quo.

However, today it is increasingly common to hear that the once-cozy relationship between corporations and their parent countries is over. Multinational because of their international operations, MNCs are truly stateless entities, not obligated to any particular country. For years the United States and other countries have bemoaned their inability to force MNCs to comply with their foreign policies (cooperating with sanctions against Iran, for example).

As you may already be sensing, the role that MNCs play in the development of low-income countries is extremely controversial. However, stripped of all the politics, MNCs are simply for-profit corporations with activities abroad stemming from foreign direct investment. Through their investments these businesses establish subsidiaries or branches in what are known as host countries. In the global south, a high percentage of MNC activity was concentrated in the BRICs (Brazil, Russia, India, and China), which received 21 percent of the FDI in the world in 2014, slightly lower than in 2009. Leading the pack is China. There and elsewhere, these corporations argue that they are just managing the production cycle, cutting costs by subcontracting the work. For example, Apple's iPods are made by smaller enterprises in China and elsewhere.[93]

As for-profit enterprises, MNCs are constantly seeking to improve their profit margins. Two of the easiest ways of accomplishing this are to lower overhead costs and expand markets. That is precisely what these corporations are doing, whether they are investing in LICs or in other developed countries. So much foreign investment goes to China because MNCs want access to the potential spending power of the country's 1.3 billion consumers as much as they want the cheap labor. At the turn of the twenty-first century some workers in China labored for as little as 3 cents per hour.[94] Average wages in China have risen over the past few years—manufacturing wages have increased approximately 12 percent a year since 2001, with a minimum-wage worker earning approximately $270 per month (less than one-fourth of their counterpart in the United States).[95] But pay varies widely. Upset about the rising cost of living, more educated, and aware of their rights, Chinese workers in coastal cities have successfully pressed for higher wages (ranging from $132 to $300 a month). This movement stalled, though, as growth began to grind to a halt. Some localities canceled scheduled increases, holding the minimum wage at earlier levels through 2018, in some cases.[96]

Over the past few years, employer concerns about labor shortages in China (as well as worker demands for higher wages and improved working and living conditions) have led merchandisers such as H&M, Zara, and Walmart to move production to countries such as Bangladesh, Cambodia, and Vietnam, where wages are even lower and workers are thought to be less restive. Many Southeast Asian nations are home to large labor pools with low wages (the average factory worker in China earns $27.50 a day, compared to $8.60 in Indonesia and $6.70 in Vietnam).[97] In Myanmar, for example, clothing exports increased from $700 million in 2011 to $1.7 billion in 2014, and Cambodia's textile and footwear exports now compose 80 percent of its export revenue.[98] These jobs, too, are at risk, especially with the so-called robot revolution that foretells the likely disappearance of low-skilled occupations around the world. While UNCTAD estimates two-thirds of jobs in the global south could be at risk, in some regions the potential losses are even greater. Between 75 and 90 percent of garment and footwear jobs in Cambodia and Vietnam, for example, are at risk due to the introduction of automated assembly lines, known as "sewbots," throughout the industry.[99]

Although some would argue that until these workers are paid a decent wage, they are unlikely to become the consumer market the MNCs so look forward to, neoliberals urge us to take the long view and consider the presence of MNCs around the world generally as a positive force. They contend that foreign investment is an important agent for growth, generating wealth through the ability to invest freely around the world and the efficient use of the world's resources. According to the pro-MNC argument, when these corporations invest abroad by opening factories, mines, or plantations, they accelerate the development of the host country in a number of ways. First, MNCs create jobs, and employees of MNCs frequently earn more than they could elsewhere in the economy. Chinese suppliers to Western multinationals are said to pay more generous wages and offer better conditions because these suppliers are monitored for compliance with labor rules (although this may just be a way for Walmart and Nike to cover themselves, as cheating by their suppliers is said to be pervasive).[100]

But a multinational's presence may mean other benefits for workers. Where Westerners have invested in joint ventures with Chinese firms, workers are said to have more rights, more institutionalized procedures for filing grievances, and so on.[101] Western and non-Western proponents of foreign investment maintain that labor and other activists living in developed countries who call for international standards (such as an international minimum wage) are actually just trying to protect the jobs of workers living in rich countries. Neoliberals argue that activists who are critical of free trade and foreign investment are "the well-intentioned but ill-informed" being led around by "the ill-intentioned but well-informed (protectionist unions and anarchists)."[102] They maintain that consumer boycotts of the goods made in these factories are actually hurting workers in LICs, because such boycotts mean a loss of jobs. They offer examples of assembly-line workers in El Salvador, China, and Vietnam who are horrified that Americans would try to "help" them by putting them out of work. The MNCs are the ones "helping" them, by giving them a chance to earn a wage.

And by offering people the opportunity to work for a wage, MNCs may be assisting in the development of the community as well. The creation of jobs has a spin-off effect for the larger economy, as MNC workers will spend their earnings on rent, food, and so forth, in the local economy. In addition, the wages earned will create

more demand for imported goods, including goods produced by other subsidiaries of the MNC. Furthermore, MNC employees will become skilled workers, familiar with the new technologies the MNC brings with it when it sets up shop. MNC employees and host countries in general are said to benefit from the corporation's presence, in that by simply being there, MNCs alter "traditional" attitudes. They are said to stimulate the spirit of innovation and entrepreneurship, teach important lessons about competitiveness, and create marketing networks that can extend into and benefit the local economy.[103]

On the other hand, critics of globalization and of MNCs in particular contend with virtually every argument the neoliberals put forward. Instead of being the beacons for change, the structuralists and others maintain that these corporations are actually predatory monopolies that compound an already skewed distribution of wealth. MNC activities widen the growing gap between rich and poor—not only between developed and less developed countries, but also within them. A local elite, known as the comprador class, dominates LIC economies and political systems, and makes sweetheart deals with these corporations to exploit their own people. In return for kickbacks, a series of Nigerian political leaders and their cronies have nurtured a very special relationship with Royal Dutch Shell and other oil companies in order to join in on the exploitation of the country's riches for the benefit of a few. Theirs is a reciprocal relationship in which compradors work to maintain a climate conducive to MNC interests, and the corporations in turn use their wealth and political clout to help keep local aristocracies in power. If the relationship falls apart, or the population elects a government less compliant and willing to accede to MNC prerogatives, MNCs have been known to "help create" a government more to their liking (as in the 1953 coup that overthrew the democratically elected government of Iran).

Moreover, critics argue that even ordinary citizens of developed countries are at the mercy of these giants, not only as workers to be displaced in the constant quest for ever-cheaper labor, but also as consumers who are overcharged for goods made for a pittance. Over the past couple of decades, MNCs have sought to reduce the costs of overhead even further by setting up shop in EXPORT PROCESSING ZONES (EPZs) around the world, in countries such as Mauritius and Sri Lanka. Corporations are attracted to EPZs because there they pay only minimal taxes and can operate without being held to the environmental standards they would find at home. Developing as well as developed countries have been accused of taking part in a "race to the bottom," diluting environmental regulations and labor laws in order to attract investment. And it is working: corporations are finding it profitable to relocate for all of these reasons—especially for guarantees of cheap and controllable labor.

Much of the work in MNC assembly plants is labor-intensive and low-skilled. In recent years, EPZ employers have become notorious for hiring females and paying them too little to live on, with the rationalization (true or not) that because females are supported by male breadwinners, their wages are mere "lipstick money" and need be only supplemental. In addition, corporations base their preference for female labor on stereotypical ideas about females being "naturally" patient and better suited for the mind-numbing tedious labor demanded by MNCs. Female workers are assumed to be not only more dexterous (important for sewing operations and in microprocessing computer chips, for example) but also more docile than men, more accepting of male (managerial) authority, and less likely to join unions.

However, another class of workers has joined the labor force—one with nimbler fingers who are even more likely to submit to fatherlike authority. Since 2000, there have been significant declines in child labor (by 78 million people). But the numbers remain daunting: the International Labour Organization (ILO) estimates that there are 168 million children working, 85 million of whom are engaged in hazardous work; most are employed in agriculture (99 million) and INFORMAL SECTORS.[104] The task of ending forced labor and child labor by 2025, highlighted as Target 8.7 of the Sustainable Development Goals (SDGs), is "daunting."[105] Some of the states tolerating the worst child labor practices are India, China, Morocco, and Côte d'Ivoire (known for the slavelike conditions under which children toil for chocolate producers). The most child laborers can be found in Asia and the Pacific (78 million), while the highest per capita incidence of child labor is in sub-Saharan Africa (greater than 21 percent).[106]

In Peru, where a former president (Alejandro Toledo) once worked as a shoeshine boy, the legal minimum age for child workers is fourteen. Still, enforcement is lax, and unknown numbers of children work in the country, particularly in rural areas. Child labor is especially common in the gold-mining regions of the Amazon, since their small size enables eight- and nine-year-olds to work deep in the mines in narrow shafts. Children working instead of going to school is a regular occurrence in Nigeria and elsewhere, particularly in agriculture, and it is likely to continue to grow as long as corporations seek to remain competitive while increasing profits— and as long as consumers demand ever-cheaper goods.

In addition to paying wages that can only be described as exploitative, MNCs are criticized for cutting corners and ignoring abuses, exposing their workers to SWEATSHOP conditions. These corporations have long been associated with abusive practices such as forced overtime and corporal punishment, and "sweatshop belts" run through parts of Asia and Latin America. A fire killed twenty-four garment workers in Bangladesh, where it is not uncommon for factory owners to keep the exits locked (to keep the women at their machines). In China and Mexico, workers often live and toil in compounds behind locked gates and high walls surrounded by barbed wire. Not only is the housing often overcrowded and unsanitary, but the work can be dangerous as well. In 2008, four workers in Turkey producing bed linens for Ikea died due to unsafe working conditions. One died when he fell into the funnel of a coal boiler.[107] In 2013, one of the deadliest industrial accidents in history claimed 1,100 lives in the collapse of a Bangladeshi garment factory that had long been dogged by complaints about the poorly constructed complex and lack of adequate fire exits.[108] In one region near Hong Kong, factory workers producing goods for Dell and Disney on fast-moving assembly lines lose or break 40,000 fingers on the job every year.[109]

In many parts of the world, forced labor and prison labor are routine. Relatively speaking, the lucky ones are those who in effect work as indentured servants, often from 7 A.M. until 11 P.M. seven days a week, with only one day off each month. In factories around the world, workers must stand long hours and handle adhesives and other toxic substances such as lead with their bare hands, in harshly lit, poorly ventilated, and sometimes deafening environments. Though there is variation in practice, it is not uncommon for workers to be subjected to an astonishing array of rules and corporal punishments. There are often strict guidelines limiting bathroom breaks and talking. Punishments for violations can be quite devious. Easily distracted children may be kept at their work by the requirement that they hold a matchbox under their

chins (without using their hands)—under threat of being beaten if they drop it to talk or even look around the room. Women have been subjected to sexual harassment and humiliation, such as compulsory pregnancy testing in *maquiladoras* in Mexico and elsewhere.[110] Such abuses have ended only when brought to light and companies squirm under the pressures of bad public relations.

Moreover, critics of MNCs dispute the claim that host-country populations benefit from exposure to the technologies the corporations bring. Nor do most workers learn a skill: the vast majority remain unskilled or low-skilled and very few local people ever make it to the ranks of management (a position often reserved for nationals of the parent country). Instead of raising productivity by promoting the use of labor-intensive technologies that are relatively cheap, simple to use, and labor-enhancing, the technologies these companies do introduce are often inappropriate and capital-intensive. Such technologies are not well suited to the needs of low-income countries, since they are acquired at a significant cost. Not only are they expensive and sophisticated (requiring fossil fuels, costly imported spare parts, and highly skilled technicians for maintenance), but worse yet, these machines serve as devices of labor replacement. They replace the need for human labor and add to already high unemployment rates.

Another topic of dispute concerns MNCs' claims about the transmission of values such as modernity and entrepreneurship. Many critics are disturbed by such claims because they smack of ethnocentrism. Too often people say "modernity" when they mean "Westernization." By implication then, whatever is non-Western becomes lumped into the category of "backward." Neoliberals assume that this modernity is a universally desired goal, when in fact what most of the world's people want is an escape from their material poverty. People of the global south may want the comforts and choices many Westerners enjoy; this doesn't necessarily mean that they want to become Western. Furthermore, what MNCs are selling isn't modernity—it is the image of modernity. These firms are actually creating dependence by aggressively marketing their products and seeking to alter consumer tastes and attitudes through glossy and often deceptive advertising campaigns.[111]

The classic example of how MNCs prey on the desperation of the poor is the Nestlé baby-formula scandal of the 1970s. In an attempt to create an even more profitable market for its powdered-milk products, Nestlé undertook a massive advertising campaign of misinformation. Targeting countries with appallingly high infant mortality rates, the company designed slick advertisements that strongly suggested that its infant formula was preferable to breast milk. While such claims were patently false on a number of counts, Nestlé was not satisfied with just taking the money of desperate parents. In some countries, it went even further to guarantee itself a market. Ostensibly offered as a welcoming gift, the company went about providing two weeks' worth of baby-formula "samples" to mothers leaving clinics with newborns—without informing them that if they used the formula for two weeks, their breast milk would dry up. The UNITED NATIONS GENERAL ASSEMBLY condemned Nestlé for these actions, but less dramatic forms of abuse by other companies, such as the sale of adulterated baby food, have continued to occur. For example, in 2008 at least six Chinese infants died and 300,000 were sickened because the company making their baby formula had sought to cut costs by lacing it with melamine, an industrial chemical used in plastic that makes the protein content of the formula appear higher than it is.[112]

Under fire for ethical, environmental, and other lapses, many of today's MNCs are fighting negative publicity and working hard to humanize their image by promoting philanthropy and adopting a posture of corporate responsibility. In recent years, several companies have sought to deflect criticisms by hiring monitors to meet with employees to hear complaints and investigate problems. As mentioned earlier, corporations are increasingly subcontracting parts of the production line to smaller firms that work in greater obscurity. When these abuses are exposed, corporations claim that they have limited power or leverage over these independent contractors or that host governments should be blamed for inadequate labor laws. However, as long as the neoliberals' staunch advocacy of deregulation prevails, the most that can be expected from MNCs is voluntary compliance with ethical norms and self-monitoring.

MNCs and neoliberals argue that voluntary codes are good enough, since it just isn't good business to misbehave anymore. In response to a newly recognized aspect of consumer preference, some companies have changed the way they do business and are treating workers better than required by often-weak regional laws. For example, Shell and British Petroleum, though once part of an alliance that lobbied hard against taking the threat of global warming seriously, now advertise with calls for reductions in carbon dioxide emissions. Apple stores boast that the energy supplies in most of their stores are nearly 100 percent renewable. Nike has pressed its suppliers to open their factories to independent inspections, to remove child laborers from its lines, and to provide a better environment for its workers. Walmart has been promoting green initiatives not only looking to become the biggest retailer of organic foods, but also promising to become more energy efficient and to reduce solid waste. There are, of course, economic and environmental incentives at work here: many of these corporations receive subsidies from governments in order to pursue these initiatives, in which they also enter the energy selling business.[113]

In another example of corporations shifting under pressure, although the high price of medicines is still a problem, some pharmaceutical corporations have lowered the prices for some of their drugs in some countries (for example, a common combination of these medicines cost $10,000 per person per year in 2000, whereas the same medicines in 2016 could be had for as little as $100 per person per year). Partly this is a response to the development of cheap generics. Since 2000—when fewer than 1 million people worldwide had access to medicines—there has been a dramatic increase in the number of people receiving HIV/AIDS medicines. There were 18.2 million people on treatment in 2016.[114]

In summary, neoliberals contend that foreign direct investment is a boon for economies. With very few exceptions, multinational corporations abide by the laws of their host countries and if anyone should be blamed for a lack of standards, it is the governments of low- and middle-income countries. But often the only comparative advantage most LICs have is cheap labor and lack of government regulation, including environmental protections—and there are many LICs vying for investment and jobs. But even if these countries were to upgrade their working conditions to the standards of developed countries, they would lose business. So the situation facing LICs is a difficult one. Even among those critics and proponents of MNCs who agree that international minimum standards are necessary to keep people (wherever they live) from being exploited, they have a hard time agreeing on what those standards should be, let alone how to enforce them.

Aid and Debt

Although it played a much larger role during the Cold War, foreign aid of one form or another is still of critical importance to many countries in the global south. The vast majority of foreign assistance is distributed as bilateral aid, commonly defined as the transfer of concessional resources from one government to another. Multilateral aid is the transfer of resources from a group of donors (such as the United Nations or the Organization for Economic Cooperation and Development [OECD]) to a recipient. In either case, aid is very definitely a tool of diplomacy, employed in such a way as to manipulate the behavior of possible recipients. Aid is used as a carrot to encourage or reward loyalty or desirable behavior. Or the withholding of aid can be a stick used to punish those deemed undeserving. In actuality, the majority of US aid does not go to the world's poorest people. In the ongoing "war on terror," as during the Cold War, US foreign aid is largely based on strategic calculation. Since September 11, 2001, the amount the United States spends on foreign aid has increased—particularly for certain developing countries that have clear strategic value, even though the total remains less than 1 percent of GNI, contrary to popular perceptions. As a result, a handful of countries, including Israel, Afghanistan, Egypt, and Iraq, receive the lion's share of all US bilateral assistance, with Israel and Egypt receiving 75 percent of US foreign military assistance.[115] When the United States and Israel signed on to a ten-year, $38 billion aid package in late 2016, it was the largest to date. Keep in mind that this is tied aid. The standard rule is that recipient countries must spend the money on US defense contracts; for the first time ever, Israel was given permission to spend up to 26 percent of its aid within its own defense industry.[116]

Many countries would love such a deal. For years, aid has been welcomed by low-income countries as a spur to development. For a variety of reasons, many countries have become aid-dependent; foreign aid composed 63.3 percent of Tuvalu's GNI in 2014, 44.3 percent of Liberia's, and 35.9 percent of the Central African Republic's.[117] Still, there have always been concerns that much of this aid is being stolen or wasted and not doing much to help countries actually develop.

As with nearly every other topic raised in this chapter, there is a great deal of disagreement about the effectiveness of aid. Both neoliberals and their critics agree that more aid is not necessarily better at promoting development. Nearly everyone, even those who call for increased funding for foreign aid, have problems with the ways in which aid packages have been designed and managed. Neoliberals contend that aid can promote development if it is used as part of a larger package of reforms. Some say that we've wasted too much money on grand solutions and that we need to put the emphasis elsewhere: on piecemeal problem solving and homegrown solutions that are based in local knowledge.[118] Some, such as former UN Secretary-General Kofi Annan, view aid as only one element in a development strategy that can be more effective if it is offered to help recipients run their own economies.[119] Critics on the left argue that aid is too often used to benefit the economic or strategic interests of donor countries, as a tool of capitalism that actually increases dependency and contributes to the further under-development of states. From the right, conservatives argue that foreign aid is too often simply a waste of good money and that development can only come from the efforts of private-sector entrepreneurs and political reformers.

Foreign assistance comes in a variety of forms: loans, cash, food, clothing, medicine, arms, or just about any other commodity. Contrary to popular American belief,

the United States is not a major donor of aid. Most Americans believe that the United States is much more generous, even overly generous, with the aid it offers LICs. Consequently, it is highly unlikely that US politicians will campaign for larger aid budgets. Although the United States does give more in total dollars ($50.1 billion budgeted for 2017), it gives less as a share of its GNI (about 0.2 percent) than any other developed country except Greece, South Korea, and Spain.[120] In other words, on average, each American pays approximately $7–$10 a year in taxes toward foreign aid.[121] Years ago, in 1970, leaders of the world's rich, industrialized countries agreed that this was not enough and set a goal of contributing 0.7 percent of their GNIs to foreign aid.[122] As of 2016, only Norway, Sweden, the Netherlands, Luxembourg, Denmark, and the United Kingdom had met (or surpassed) that goal (Sweden, for example, gives 1.4 percent of its GNI in foreign aid).[123]

Although still well short of their commitments (averaging 0.3 percent of GNI), foreign aid flows from high-income to low-income countries increased 83 percent between 2000 and 2015 (to $131.6 billion total).[124] Yet geographical gaps in distribution seem to be hardening, with so-called donor darlings receiving the lion's share of attention and assistance, leaving the "aid orphans" out in the cold. In recent years, Mozambique and Ethiopia have been consistently tapped as priorities for many bilateral aid agencies, while Madagascar, Guinea, and Nepal have been characterized as "chronic aid orphans" from 2006 to 2012.[125] Clearly, any hope of meeting the UN's target, through its Sustainable Development Goals, of eliminating extreme poverty by 2030 is going to require more coordinated assistance within the development and aid community.

With difficult economic times in the United States, perhaps it is easy to understand why President Barack Obama never made good on his 2008 campaign pledge to double US foreign aid (to $50 billion by 2012).[126] Yet for many years it has been argued that the United States is the principal beneficiary of the vast majority of its foreign aid to other countries, since so much of this aid is "tied" in order to guarantee a market for US goods. For example, the United States might extend a loan to Nigeria to buy tractors. This is a loan that the United States fully expects Nigeria to repay with interest, yet Nigeria has no choice but to use that money to buy US tractors, even if Japanese or French tractors are less expensive, or preferred for some other reason. As a result, tied aid is estimated to reduce the value of development assistance by 15–25 percent.[127]

Aid activists point out that such packages should be recognized for what they are: subsidies of donor economies. Low-income countries argue that development should not be a profit-making enterprise for the rich at the expense of the poor. Britain was an early proponent of this argument, and has begun to untie some of the strings attached to the aid it offers. The United States and other HICs have untied some aid, but given hard economic times at home it is increasingly difficult to persuade their constituents of the need for foreign assistance. Most Americans think that the United States already gives too much aid (for years, polls have shown that most Americans believe that 25 percent of the federal budget goes to foreign aid— when it is actually closer to 1 percent).[128] Regardless of the reality, politicians find it an easy part of the budget to talk about cutting. Those who seek to sustain or increase aid levels find it politically necessary to show that tied aid offers a reciprocal benefit by creating hundreds of thousands of jobs for the citizens of donor countries.

For many years after the end of the Cold War, the vast majority of foreign assistance offered (to most countries) came not in the form of grants or gifts, but as loans. Although most people's definition of "aid" would seem to call for the concessional terms offered by soft loans, with their low interest rates and long repayment periods, a substantial number of these loans are hard loans, bearing high interest rates and short repayment periods. Many of these loans are taken out to service debt (or make the scheduled payment on the debt accrued from past loans).

Therefore, a great deal of the assistance that developed countries offer is in the form of loans meant to pay the interest on an outstanding debt. This only adds to that debt, which may exist for a variety of reasons. In some cases, the West has lent to allies knowing that the resources would wind up in the hands of irresponsible, wasteful, or kleptocratic governments (some consider this to be "odious debt" and argue that creditors should not expect repayment because they made the loans with full knowledge of how the money was to be used). Or LICs lost money in failed (but expensive) attempts at industrialization. In other cases, world recession or unexpected changes in the global economy (such as sudden jumps in the price of oil or food) contributed to deficits that put countries into debt. Most LICs have sunk into debt because they have consistently faced shortfalls in their balance of payments (again, due to their disadvantageous position in the international economy).

Clearly, external factors beyond these countries' control have played a large part in creating the crisis. However, to some extent, each country's debt grows out of its own particular combination of problems. Regardless of the source of the debt, it only became a crisis as far as the IMF and donors were concerned in the early 1980s, when Mexico and other debtors declared their inability to pay and threatened a moratorium (or temporary halt) on servicing their debts. Such threats were widely regarded as amounting to an emergency, since banks had eagerly overextended themselves for years, making loans to LICs without worry as to their creditworthiness. Banks and donors feared that if other countries had joined Mexico in the formation of a debtors' cartel, their collective default could have led to the collapse of the international financial system.

Since the debt crisis of the 1980s, IFIs and donors have recognized how vital it is that the vast majority of debtors be willing and able to pay. Donors are working with international financial institutions and are determined to manage the system to better protect it. There have been a variety of attempts to manage LIC debt over the years. For a variety of reasons, the debt burdens of some LICs have eased, but for others they are still very real. In 1970, total LIC foreign debt was less than $100 billion. It rose to $600 billion by 1980, and to $1.6 trillion by 1990. As of 2015, the total external debt for all low- and middle-income countries was $5.4 trillion (in comparison, the total external debt of the United States in 2016 was $19 trillion).[129] Most of the increase in debt in the 1990s was due to the fact that countries had to take out more loans to service (or pay the interest) on their existing debt. For example, in 2000, Argentina's debt service (as a share of its income) was 69 percent, Turkey's was 29 percent, and Mozambique's was 26 percent.[130] Many American college students can empathize.

When countries are in this position, scraping by, just making the minimum payments on their bills, there is precious little left over to spend on education, healthcare, or other aspects of development. For years, African countries spent much more on debt repayment than on healthcare.[131] They wound up literally choosing between

food and debt, making what has been called "the cruel choice." In 2005, Kenya budgeted as much for its debt payment as it did for water, health, agriculture, roads, and transportation combined.[132] Some analysts contend that the situation amounts to debt slavery, and is as devastating to a population as war. Yet by the mid-2000s, more people (including donors) were beginning to realize that it was time to make the connection between debt relief and development. How could sub-Saharan Africa ever develop when it paid approximately $15 billion each year to HICs and international financial institutions in debt service?[133]

Latin America was the region hit hardest by debt service a decade ago, paying nearly a third of its entire export earnings to the banks. This debt was as debilitating for the countries with the largest total debts (such as Mexico and Brazil) as it was for countries with lower total bills but much smaller economies (such as many countries in Africa) (see Figures 6.8 and 6.9). To put this in some perspective, the World Bank defines countries as "severely indebted" if their debt-to-GNI ratio is over 50 percent. As of 2014, among our cases, only Zimbabwe qualified for this category. It doesn't take an accountant to see that when the debt burden is heavy, at a certain point payment becomes impossible and countries fall into arrears. When this happens, donor response tends to vary, as it frequently hinges on the donors' political interests. Sometimes the response has been stern: the World Bank suspended disbursements to Zimbabwe in 1999 because it was more than six months overdue and tens of millions of dollars behind in servicing its debt. Zimbabwe was even threatened with expulsion from the IMF. Zimbabwe began a staff-monitored program with the IMF in 2009, and in 2015 proposed a plan to clear arrears (continuous since 2001) and resume financing from the IMF. Even though "political fragilities" placed some of this plan in doubt, in late 2016 the IMF announced that Zimbabwe had settled its overdue obligations.[134] Most countries do everything that they can to stay in the IMF's good graces. For example, in order to receive a $12 billion IMF bailout, in 2016 Egypt adopted a series of painful austerity measures. It allowed its currency to devalue by 48 percent against the dollar, raising prices at the same time that it cut government subsidies of energy and foodstuffs.[135]

Although the publics of developed countries largely regard indebted countries as deadbeats that are unwilling or unable to meet their obligations, the major debtors are actually net exporters of capital. In a widely cited example, Nigeria originally borrowed $5 billion, paid $16 billion on that loan, and years later still owed $32 billion more (it was eventually forgiven).[136] Economist Susan George contends that the sums that LICs have paid to service their debts amount to unprecedented financial assistance from the poor to the rich—an amount George estimated to be equivalent to six Marshall Plans (and that was almost two decades ago). She says that we should not worry about the banks going hungry—they've made back the original principal and more through high interest rates.[137] And the banks continue to make tidy profits from the interest earned on this debt.

In Nigeria and elsewhere, many of the governments that accumulated this debt and misappropriated these funds are long gone. However, the citizens of these countries are left holding the bag, responsible for repaying a debt they never asked for, and from which they derived no gain. Eduardo Galeano likens this system to an open artery: LICs are being bled dry. Rather than being healed by the IMF, the veins are kept open for the purpose of drawing more blood—this at a time when

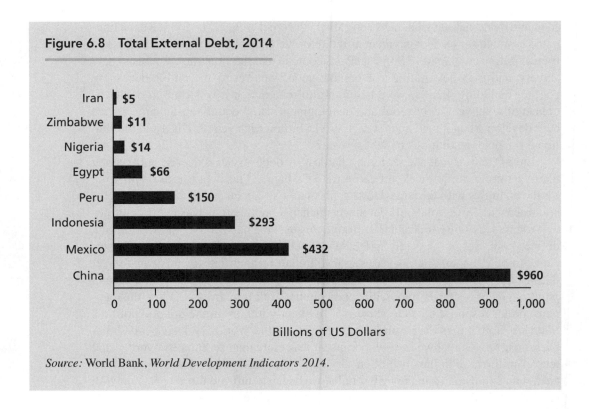

Figure 6.8   Total External Debt, 2014

Iran $5
Zimbabwe $11
Nigeria $14
Egypt $66
Peru $150
Indonesia $293
Mexico $432
China $960

Billions of US Dollars

Source: World Bank, *World Development Indicators 2014.*

the developing world was facing its worst economic crisis since the Great Depression.[138] Even though some progress was made on relieving debt, fears of a domino effect of the Chinese economic slowdown are mounting, coupled with a nearly decade-long borrowing binge among many LICs. For example, foreign loans to these countries tripled between 2008 and 2013, with the World Bank and the IMF expressing concern that more than half of the countries that received relief through earlier plans are at risk of returning to "unsustainable debt levels."[139]

Neoliberals maintain that such characterizations are unfair and point to a variety of efforts over the years that the IMF and donors have devised to pull countries out of debt (which we will describe in the next chapter). Yet their critics argue that what IFIs have been doing is developing strategies to protect themselves so that they will be much less vulnerable to the kind of pressure they experienced in the 1980s—a divide-and-rule strategy that results in debtors having a harder time uniting to confront their creditors because each country has to meet with the IFIs to restructure its debt privately and on an individual basis. The terms of each deal are secret, and in the hope of more preferential treatment, countries know they must go it alone. And this is an offer they cannot resist, since most countries must meet the terms of the IMF or risk being deemed uncreditworthy. For most LICs, a bad rating from the IMF can mean economic suicide. Noncompliance risks isolation and severe punishment: the flow of capital in the form of investment, debt relief, or any other type of assistance dries up. After months of economic crisis stemming from IMF shock therapy in 2001 and 2002, Argentina refused further treatment and defaulted on a $100 billion debt. In 2007,

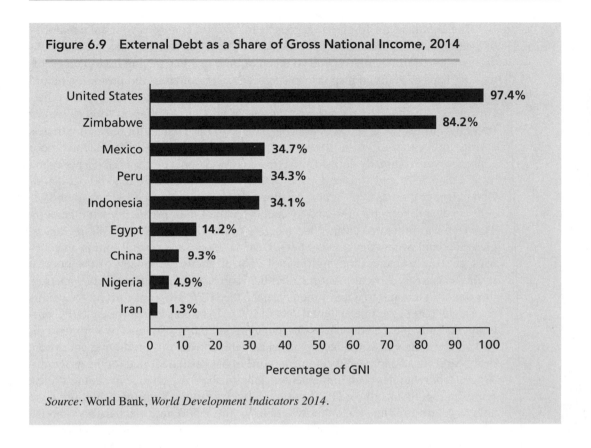

Figure 6.9   External Debt as a Share of Gross National Income, 2014

Percentage of GNI

Source: World Bank, *World Development Indicators 2014.*

Argentina settled outstanding debts, but continued to ban the IMF from conducting a review of the economy, hitting a low point in 2013 when the IMF censured Buenos Aires over its economic accounting. Representatives from the IMF returned to the country, after more than a decade's absence, in September 2016.[140]

On the other hand, countries willing to accept IMF demands are usually offered some form of debt relief, which may involve debt rescheduling or, more rarely, restructuring or forgiveness. Rescheduling of debt defers payment to a later date; it is a temporary reprieve, allowing for an extension of the period of repayment of the loan. Rescheduling is considered crucial for many countries because it makes their debt burden more bearable. As opposed to rescheduling, restructuring is an agreed default on part of a debt, whereas forgiveness means reducing or writing it off. While in the past forgiveness was usually the option of last resort, a global campaign to forgive debt has developed since the late 1990s. This program, put forward by an unusual collection of personalities and religious figures, such as U2's Bono and Reverend Billy Graham, became an international movement, known as Jubilee 2000. It called for forgiveness of debt as part of a biblical mandate (the Book of Leviticus sets down that every fifty years all debts should be canceled, land returned to the dispossessed, and slaves set free). The time of liberation was known as "Jubilee," and its namesake movement pressed during the millennium year for a onetime full debt forgiveness for the world's poorest countries.[141]

The argument for forgiveness goes as follows: in countries where the majority of the population lives on less than one dollar a day, it is not only wrong but also inefficient to require them to spend so much of their revenue paying back their creditors. Perhaps partially in response to such calls, rich countries did promise a record amount of foreign aid in 2005, and some of that aid came in the form of debt relief. However, with a few exceptions (such as tens of billions of dollars of forgiveness for Iraq), the closest the IFIs and donors have come to forgiveness for most countries is a program for HIGHLY INDEBTED POOR COUNTRIES (HIPCs).[142] Highly indebted poor countries were originally defined as having a gross national product (GNP) per capita of less than $675 and "unsustainable" debt (amounting to more than 80 percent of GNP). Under the HIPC program, developed countries promised to expand and accelerate debt relief measures, and to share a token of their prosperity with the poor. This idea was reiterated at the 2005 meeting of the Group of Eight (G8) in Gleneagles, Scotland, where the United States, Canada, Japan, and several European countries pledged to cancel the multilateral debt of about two dozen of the poorest countries (mostly African) that fulfilled the HIPC conditions. Relatively speaking, this does not amount to a lot of money, since the HIPC program currently accounts for a small part of the total external debt of LICs. To be considered for the HIPC program, not only must a country be desperately poor, but it also must be willing to divert all the money it would have paid on its debt to programs promoting education, healthcare, and economic development (none of our cases qualified for the program). Where debt relief has been implemented, it has made a real change in people's lives. For example, thanks to the HIPC program, over 1 million Tanzanian children were able to return to school. Zambia was able to hire 4,500 new teachers and abolish school fees as well as offer free healthcare in rural areas. In Niger, the infant mortality rate dropped from 156 to 81 per 1,000 live births, and the percentage of people with access to potable water climbed from 40 to 69 percent.[143] In virtually every country that has received debt relief, social spending has increased by as much as 75 percent and social indicators have begun to improve.[144]

For countries that qualify for the HIPC program, or for the MULTILATERAL DEBT RELIEF INITIATIVE (MDRI), an enhanced relief program, just one more string is attached: applicants must be willing to faithfully accept all the conditions set for them by the IMF. Only countries that successfully complete key structural reforms are said to have reached the completion point, making them eligible for as much as 100 percent debt reduction. As of 2015, thirty-six countries had been granted reductions of $75 billion on future debt payments, with an estimated $4.1 billion relieved under the MDRI.[145] Jubilee 2000 (now called the Jubilee Debt Campaign) has so far failed to win its demand for full debt cancellation without preconditions. There is some good news: the average debt-to-GDP ratios in many low-income countries have declined since 2000, and most non-Western regions cut the percentage of export revenues that go to service their debt.

On the other hand, since 2008 it is the high-income countries that have accumulated higher levels of debt (Japan's debt in 2013 was more than 200 percent of its GDP, whereas most low- and middle-income-country debt was 30 percent of GDP). As of early 2011, Brazil, China, and India had low debt-to-GDP ratios, and three-fifths of sub-Saharan African countries had what the IMF considers "sustainable" debt positions (thanks largely to debt relief, better debt management, and the ex-

pansion of trade during the boom preceding the Great Recession).[146] In 2015, some of the countries with the highest debt-to-GDP ratios were Japan, Greece, Lebanon, and Italy. In terms of total dollars, the United States has the world's largest external debt, which grew significantly after the 2007–2009 financial crisis. The mounting debt for advanced economies is no doubt concerning, but countries like the United States and Japan have traditionally been considered safer bets in that they can more easily manage debt, in part because they have better credit ratings and can therefore pay lower interest rates (although this is not always the case; in 2010, South Africa's credit rating was better than that of Greece).[147]

However, economists are concerned that the recent positive trends regarding debt in low- and medium-income countries may reverse.[148] Analysts point out that the Group of Eight countries have yet to make good on the commitments they made in 2005, meeting only 60 percent of their total commitments pledged—meaning Africa received approximately $11 billion of the $25 billion increase agreed upon at the Gleneagles meeting.[149] This has hurt sub-Saharan African countries in particular, because the HICs had pledged to double the share of foreign assistance directed toward them specifically. Since the global financial crisis of the late 2000s, there has been a boom in lending, but the amounts of relief pledged by donors and IFIs has been small (compared to the need); there is not enough aid for additional countries to have their debt restructured or forgiven, or to help them achieve sustainable debt. Moreover, most of those countries eligible for the HIPC program are, like Niger, dependent on the sale of one or two raw materials (in Niger's case, uranium), the prices of which have fluctuated widely over the past several years. Consequently, some economists argue that among the countries that have had their debt canceled, the cycle of crises will continue. There is a great deal of talk about debt management, rating countries' risk of debt distress, and limiting debt vulnerabilities through better decisionmaking, but some will eventually fall back into debt unless their position in the world economy fundamentally changes. The Jubilee movement recognizes that debt cancellation must be combined with other, far-reaching change, such as regulating lenders and lessening the dependence on commodity exports.[150] Its members emphasize that forgiveness is only a first step, offering debt-burdened countries the new beginning they desperately need.

Notes

1. Diaa Hadid and Nour Youssef, "Sweet-Toothed Egypt Endures a Sugar Crisis: 'People Are Going to Snap,'" *New York Times,* October 20, 2016, www.nytimes.com.

2. Quoted in Peter Alford, "Fifteen Years After Humiliation, Indonesia Turns the Tables on the IMF," *The Australian,* July 11, 2012, www.theaustralian.com.au.

3. Jose Cuesta, Christoph Lakner, and Mario NeNegre, "Most People, Whether Rich or Poor, Are Totally Wrong About Poverty," *Agenda 2016,* World Economic Forum, November 8, 2016, www.weforum.org; Nicholas Kristof, "The Best News You Don't Know," *New York Times,* September 22, 2016; Matthew Lynn, "Why the Title of 'Developing Country' No Longer Exists," *The Telegraph* (London), May 23, 2016, www.telegraph.co.uk.

4. "IMF Sees Subdued Global Growth, Warns Economic Stagnation Could Fuel Protectionist Calls," *IMF News,* October 4, 2016, www.imf.org.

5. Ibid.

6. United Nations, *Millennium Development Goals Report 2015: Summary* (New York, 2015), p. 2; Maurice Obstfeld, "The World Economy: Moving Sideways," October 4, 2016,

www.blog-imf-direct.imf.org; United Nations, "World Economic Situation and Prospects," Development Policy and Analysis Division, January 2016, www.un.org.

7. World Food Programme, "Hunger Statistics," 2016, www.wfp.org; United Nations, "World Economic Situation and Prospects," p. 69.

8. World Bank, "Inequalities in Women's and Girls' Health Opportunities and Outcomes: A Report from Sub-Saharan Africa," October 2016, www.isglobal.org.

9. World Food Programme, "Hunger Statistics."

10. Deborah Hardoon, Sophia Ayele, and Ricardo Fuentes-Nieva, "An Economy for the 1%," briefing paper, January 18, 2016, p. 2, www.oxfam.org.

11. World Bank, *Global Economic Prospects: Divergence and Risks: June 2016* (Washington, DC, 2016), pp. 3, 5.

12. United Nations, "World Economic Situation and Prospects."

13. Michael B. Sauter, "Countries with the Widest Gap Between the Rich and the Poor," 24/7 Wall St., May 29, 2015, www.247wallst.com; Gemma Corrigan, "Is Brazil Making Progress on Inequality?, *World Economic Forum,* September 7, 2015, www.weforum.org.

14. World Bank, "China," September 14, 2016.

15. Moisés Naím, "What Comes After the Greatest Anti-Poverty Campaign in History?," *The Atlantic,* January 29, 2014, www.theatlantic.com.

16. World Bank, *World Development Indicators 2010;* Central Intelligence Agency (CIA), *World Factbook 2016,* www.cia.gov; Eduardo Porter, "Slowdown in China Bruises Economy in Latin America," *New York Times,* December 16, 2014; Andrew Jacobs, "China's Army of Graduates Faces Grim Prospects, with Few Jobs in Cities," *New York Times,* December 12, 2010; James M. Cypher and James L. Dietz, *The Process of Economic Development* (New York: Routledge, 2009).

17. World Bank, "China Overview," September 14, 2016.

18. United Nations Development Programme (UNDP), *Human Development Report 2000* (New York, 2000).

19. World Bank, "Adolescent Fertility Rate," 2016.

20. World Health Organization (WHO), "Under Five Mortality," 2016.

21. International Telecommunication Union (ITU), "ICT Facts and Figures: The World in 2015" (Geneva, 2015), p. 1.

22. ITU, "ICT Facts and Figures: The World in 2016" (Geneva, 2016), p. 2.

23. Ibid., p. 3.

24. ITU, "ICT Facts and Figures: The World in 2015," p. 3.

25. Jacob Poushter, "Smartphone Ownership and Internet Usage Continues to Climb in Emerging Economies," Pew Research Center: Global Attitudes and Trends, February 22, 2016.

26. ITU, "ICT Facts and Figures: The World in 2015," p. 1.

27. "High-Speed Internet Gap Between Rich and Poor Widening, UN Office Warns," UN News Centre, November 12, 2009; Nicholas D. Kristof, "I've Seen the Future (in Haiti)," *New York Times,* December 5, 2010.

28. UNDP, *Human Development Report 2000.*

29. WHO, "Fact Sheet: Sanitation," November 2016.

30. United Nations, "Sustainable Development Goals, Goal 6: Ensure Access to Water and Sanitation for All," www.un.org.

31. International Monetary Fund (IMF), "IMF Survey: The Global Economy in 2016," January 4, 2016, www.imf.org.

32. Fareed Zakaria, "The Rise of the Rest," *Newsweek,* May 3, 2008.

33. Ugo Panizza, Federico Sturzenegger, and Jermin ZeHelmeyer, "International Government Debt," Discussion Paper no. 199 (Geneva: United Nations Conference on Trade and Development [UNCTAD], June 2010); Cynthia Roberts, "Polity Forum: Challenges or Stakeholders? BRICs and the Liberal World Order," *Polity* 42, December 7, 2009.

34. Itai Zehorai, "The Emerging Economies That Will Shine in 2016," *Forbes,* March 9, 2016; Mark Esposito, Amit Kapoor, and Deepti Mathur, "What Is the State of the BRICS Economies?," World Economic Forum, April 19, 2016, www.weforum.org; Ian Talley, "Brics' New World Order Is Now on Hold," *Wall Street Journal,* January 19, 2016, www.wsj.com.

35. Stephen Radelet, *The Great Surge: The Ascent of the Developing World* (New York: Simon and Schuster, 2015).

36. United Nations, "Sustainable Development Goals, Goal 1: End Poverty in All Its Forms Everywhere," www.un.org; Liz Ford, "Sustainable Development Goals: All You Need to Know," *The Guardian* (London), January 19, 2015, www.theguardian.com; United Nations Children's Fund (UNICEF), "State of the World's Children, 2016," www.unicef.org/swc2016; Alberto D. Cimadamore, Gabriele Koehler, and Thomas Pogge, "Poverty and the Millennium Development Goals: A Critical Look Forward," in *Poverty and the Millennium Development Goals: A Critical Look Forward,* ed. Alberto Cimadamore, Gabriele Koehler, and Thomas Pogge (London: Zed, 2016).

37. CIA, *World Factbook 2016,* www.cia.gov.

38. Aaron Back, "Why China's Hefty Trade Surplus Is Dwarfed by Outflows," *Wall Street Journal,* January 13, 2016, www.wsj.com.

39. David Barboza, "China Passes Japan as Second-Largest Economy," *New York Times,* August 15, 2010.

40. World Bank, "Zimbabwe," 2016, www.data.worldbank.org.

41. Musa Ndow, "Gambia: G/Bissau to Increase Cashew Exports," *All Africa,* April 20, 2015, www.allafrica.com.

42. Amartya K. Sen, "More Than 100 Million Women Are Missing," *New York Review of Books,* December 20, 1990; Ross Douthat, "160 Million and Counting," *New York Times,* June 26, 2011; Mara Hvistendahl, *Unnatural Selection: Choosing Boys over Girls, and the Consequences of a World Full of Men* (New York: PublicAffairs, 2011); Julia Smirnova and Weiyi Cai, "See Where Women Outnumber Men Around the World (and Why)," *Washington Post,* August 19, 2015, www.washingtonpost.com.

43. CIA, *World Factbook 2016;* Smirnova and Cai, "See Where Women Outnumber Men."

44. United Nations, Department of Economic and Social Affairs, *The World's Women 2015: Trends and* Statistics (New York, 2015), p. ix.

45. Simon Denyer, "Researchers May Have 'Found' Many of China's 30 Million Missing Girls," *Washington Post,* November 30, 2016, www.washingtonpost.com.

46. Hvistendahl, *Unnatural Selection;* Kevin Lee, "China's Growing Problem of Too Many Single Men," *Forbes,* May 13, 2011, www.forbes.com; Louisa Lim, "For Chinese Women, Marriage Depends on Right 'Bride Price,'" National Public Radio, *Morning Edition,* April 23, 2013, www.npr.org; Bill Powell, "Gender Imbalance: How China's One Child Law Backfired on Men," *Newsweek,* May 28, 2015, www.newsweek.com.

47. United Nations Population Fund (UNFPA), "New Report Analyzes Skewed Birth Ratios in Vietnam," September 9, 2009, www.unfpa.org; UNFPA, "Asian Son Preference Will Have Severe Social Consequences, New Studies Warn," October 29, 2007, www.unfpa.org.

48. Washington Muzari, "Gender Disparities and the Role of Women in Smallholder Agriculture in Sub-Saharan Africa," *International Journal of Science and Research* 5, no. 1 (January 2016), www.ijsr.net.

49. Rana Foroohar and Susan H. Greenberg, "The Real Emerging Market," *Newsweek,* September 21, 2009; World Bank, "Labor Force Participation Rate," 2015, www.worldbank.org; World Bank, "Labor Force, Female (% of Total Labor Force)," 2016, www.worldbank.org.

50. International Labor Organization (ILO), "Women at Work: Trends 2016," p. 8, www.ilo.org.

51. United Nations Educational, Scientific, and Cultural Organization (UNESCO), *Education for People and Planet: Creating Sustainable Futures for All,* 2016, p. 6, www.unesco.org.

52. Sean Coughlan, "Primary School for All 'Not Until 2042,' Says UNESCO," BBC News, September 6, 2016.

53. UNESCO, *Education for People and Planet.*

54. United Nations, Department of Economic and Social Affairs, *The World's Women 2015,* p. xi; Fatimah Kelleher, "The Literacy Injustice: 493 Million Women Still Can't Read," *The Guardian* (London), September 8, 2014, www.theguardian.com.

55. UN Statistics Division, "The World's Women 2015: Education," www.unstats.un.org; UNESCO, *Education for People and Planet.*

56. Food and Agricultural Organization (FAO), "Women Feed the World," www.fao.org.

57. Moisés Naím, "Globalization," *Foreign Policy* 171 (March–April 2009).

58. Joseph E. Stiglitz, *Globalization and Its Discontents* (New York: Norton, 2007).

59. World Trade Organization (WTO), "What Is the World Trade Organization?," www.wto.org.

60. World Bank, *World Development Indicators 2010*.

61. WTO, "Trade Growth to Remain Subdued in 2016 as Uncertainties Weigh on Global Demand," April 7, 2016.

62. Ibid.

63. Thomas L. Friedman, *The Lexus and the Olive Tree* (New York: Farrar, Straus and Giroux, 1999).

64. Ibid.; Dan Charles, "Farm Subsidies Persist and Grow, Despite Talk of Reform," National Public Radio, *The Salt,* February 1, 2016, www.npr.org.

65. Worldwatch Institute, "Agricultural Subsidies Remain a Staple in the Industrial World," December 7, 2016, www.worldwatch.org.

66. Daniel A. Sumner, "Congress Needs to Cut Ties with the Cotton Lobby," *US News,* January 28, 2016, www.usnews.com; Thomas Lazzeri, "Western Cotton Subsidies Endanger African Farmers," Africa Europe Faith and Justice Network, 2016, www.aefjn.org.

67. Samuel T. Ledermann and William G. Moseley, "The World Trade Organization's Doha Round and Cotton: Continued Peripheral Status or 'Historical Breakthrough' for African Farmers?," *African Geographic Review* 26, no. 1 (April 2012); Sewell Chan, "US and Brazil Reach Agreement on Cotton Dispute," *New York Times,* April 6, 2010; Sumner, "Congress Needs to Cut Ties with the Cotton Lobby."

68. Thomas L. Friedman, "Protesting for Whom?," *New York Times,* April 24, 2001.

69. Daniel Griswold, "The Blessings and Challenges of Globalization," Cato Institute, September 1, 2000, www.cato.org.

70. Jackie Smith and Timothy Patrick Moran, "WTO 101: Myths About the World Trade Organization," in *Annual Editions: Developing World 01–02,* ed. Robert J. Griffiths (Guilford, CT: McGraw-Hill/Dushkin, 2001).

71. Neil MacFarquhar, "African Farmers Displaced As Investors Move In," *New York Times,* December 21, 2010.

72. World Bank, "Sub-Saharan Africa's Growth Will Slow in 2015 amid Falling Commodity Price," *Africa's Pulse* 11 (April 2015); Larry Elliott, "Economics: Poor Nations Ride High on Commodity Boom," *The Guardian* (London), May 10, 2006.

73. "Global Dependence on Food Imports Leaves Countries Vulnerable," Reuters, March 13, 2015, www.reuters.com.

74. Ibid.

75. Hadid and Youssef, "Sweet-Toothed Egypt Endures a Sugar Crisis."

76. "Falling Oil Prices: How Are Countries Being Affected?," BBC News, January 18, 2016.

77. Organization of Petroleum Exporting Countries, "Saudi Arabia: Facts and Figures," 2016, www.opec.org; Omoh Gabriel, "Youth Unemployment in Nigeria up to 50%—McKinsey & Co," *Vanguard,* January 26, 2015.

78. Pádraig Carmody, *Globalization in Africa: Recolonization or Renaissance?* (Boulder: Lynne Rienner, 2010); Alexei Barrionuevo, "A Mine of Riches and an Economic Sinkhole," *New York Times,* September 11, 2010.

79. Carmody, *Globalization in Africa;* United Nations, "World Economic Situation and Prospects," p. 50.

80. World Bank, *World Development Indicators 2010*.

81. Joshua S. Goldstein, *International Relations,* 4th ed. (New York: Longman, 2001).

82. Will Nichols, "Up to 90% of World's Electronic Waste Is Illegally Dumped, Says UN," *The Guardian* (London), May 12, 2015.

83. US Bureau of Labor Statistics, "International Comparisons of GDP per Capita and per Employed Person," Division of International Labor Comparisons, July 28, 2009, www.bls.gov; CIA, *World Factbook 2010*.

84. Andrew Walter and Xiaoke Zhang, "Debating East Asian Capitalism: Issues and Themes," in *East Asian Capitalism: Diversity, Continuity, and Change,* ed. Andrew Walter and Xiaoke Zhang (New York: Oxford University Press, 2012).

85. "A Tightening Grip: The Future of Factory Asia," *The Economist,* March 14, 2015.

86. Michael Gestrin, "Trends in Foreign Direct Investment and Their Implications for Development," in Organization for Economic Cooperation and Development (OECD), *Development Co-operation Report 2016: The Sustainable Development Goals as Business Opportunities* (Paris, 2016), p. 52.

87. UNCTAD, *World Investment Report 2016: Investor Nationality: Policy Challenges* (Geneva, 2016).

88. Parag Khanna, "These 25 Companies Are More Powerful Than Many Countries," *Foreign Policy,* March 15, 2016.

89. Nicholas Freudenberg, "The 100 Largest Governments and Corporations by Revenue," *Corporations and Health Watch,* August 27, 2015, www.corporationsandhealth.org.

90. Khanna, "These 25 Companies."

91. "10 Biggest Corporations Make More Money Than Most Countries in the World Combined," *Global Justice Now,* September 12, 2016, www.globaljustice.org.uk; "Fortune 500," www.fortune.com.

92. "Fortune 500," www.fortune.com.

93. UNCTAD, *World Investment Report 2015: Reforming International Investment Governance* (Geneva, 2015), p. 7.

94. Kathleen Schalch, "Study Finds American Firms Doing Business in China Are Not Improving Conditions for Chinese Workers," National Public Radio, *All Things Considered,* May 5, 2000.

95. "A Tightening Grip," *The Economist.*

96. "China Labor Tests Its Muscle," *New York Times,* July 13, 2010; "The End of Cheap Chinese Labor?," *The Economist,* July 18, 2010; Elias Glenn, "China Looks to Roll Back Worker Friendly Policies as Growth Slows," Reuters, November 29, 2016.

97. "A Tightening Grip," *The Economist.*

98. Ibid.; Adam Minter, "So Long to the Asian Sweatshop," *Bloomberg,* September 4, 2016.

99. Tansy Hoskins, "Robot Factories Could Threaten Jobs of Millions of Garment Workers," *The Guardian* (London), July 16, 2016; Federico Guerrini, "Robots Could Take Away Two Thirds of Jobs in Developing Countries, the UNCTAD Says," *Forbes,* November 18, 2016; Minter, "So Long to the Asian Sweatshop."

100. "Secrets, Lies, and Sweatshops," *Bloomberg Businessweek,* November 27, 2006.

101. Schalch, "Study Finds American Firms Doing Business in China."

102. Friedman, "Protesting for Whom?"

103. Goldstein, *International Relations.*

104. ILO, "End Child Labor in Supply Chains: It's Everyone's Business," June 12, 2016, www.ilo.org.

105. ILO, "Building a Global Alliance Against Child Labour and Forced Labour," November 4, 2015, www.ilo.org.

106. "Update: Child Labor in Decline, but Will Not Make 2016 Goal," *PBS Newshour,* September 25, 2013, www.pbs.org.

107. "Sweatshop Hall of Shame 2010," International Labor Rights Forum, www.laborrights.org; Global Investment Watch, "Ikea, Walmart, Target, and Kohl's Sleeping Easy While Turkish Workers Suffer," May 18, 2009, www.globalinvestmentwatch.com.

108. Rachel Abrams, "Retailers Like H&M and Walmart Fall Short of Pledge to Overseas Workers," *New York Times,* May 31, 2016.

109. David Barboza, "In Chinese Factories, Lost Fingers and Low Pay," *New York Times,* January 15, 2008.

110. "Mexico's Maquiladoras: Abuses Against Women Workers," Human Rights Watch, August 17, 1996, www.hrw.org.

111. Beatrice Newbery, "Labouring Under Illusions," in Griffiths, *Annual Editions: Developing World 01–02.*

112. Aislinn Simpson, "Baby Formula Recall in China After Infant Death," *The Telegraph* (London), September 13, 2008, www.telegraph.co.uk.

113. Marc Gunter, "Walmart Sees Green," *Fortune,* July 26, 2006, www.cnnmoney.com; Diane Cardwell, "Apple Becomes a Green Energy Supplier, with Itself as Customer," *New York Times,* August 23, 2016.

114. Joint United Nations Programme on HIV/AIDS (UNAIDS), "HIV Treatment Now Reaching More Than 6 Million People in Sub-Saharan Africa," July 6, 2012, www.unaids.org; "The Global HIV/AIDS Epidemic," November 29, 2016, www.aids.gov.

115. Nick Thompson, "Seventy-Five Percent of U.S. Foreign Military Financing Goes to 2 Countries," *CNN News,* November 11, 2015.

116. Max Bearack and Lazaro Gamio, "The U.S. Foreign-Aid Budget, Visualized," *Washington Post,* September 26, 2016.

117. World Bank, "Net ODA Received (% of GNI), 2015," http://data.worldbank.org.

118. William Easterly, *The White Man's Burden: Why the West's Efforts to Aid the Rest Have Done So Much Ill and So Little Good* (New York: Penguin, 2007).

119. Kofi A. Annan, "Trade and Aid in a Changed World," *New York Times,* March 19, 2002.

120. OECD, "Net ODA (2015)," www.data.oecd.org.

121. Borgen Project, "U.S. Foreign Aid," www.borgenproject.org.

122. OECD, "The .7% ODA/GNI Target—A History," June 2010, https://www.oecd.org.

123. Mark Anderson, "UK Passes Bill to Honour Pledge of 0.7% Foreign Aid Target," *The Guardian* (London), March 9, 2015; Ryan Wilkinson, "Britain One of Just Six Rich Countries to Meet UN Foreign Aid Target," *The Independent* (London), April 14, 2016, www.independent.co.uk; OECD, "DAC Member Profile: Sweden," 2016, www.oecd.org.

124. OECD and Financing for Development Office, UN-DESA, "Official Development Assistance," August 2016, www.un.org.

125. Frederick Ericsson and Suzanne Steensen, "OECD-DAC Development Brief: Where Do We Stand on the Aid Orphans?," OECD, 2014.

126. "Why Should They Believe Us?," *New York Times,* April 24, 2010.

127. Eckhard Deutscher and Sara Fyson, "Committing to Effective Aid: Why Can't Donors Walk Their Talk?," Development Outreach, World Bank Institute, www.worldbank.org.

128. Sarah C. Sullivan, "Poll: Americans Have Inflated View of Foreign Aid," *PBS Newshour,* December 6, 2010, www.pbs.org; Max Bearack and Lazaro Gamio, "The U.S. Foreign-Aid Budget, Visualized," *Washington Post,* September 26, 2016; Poncie Rutsch, "Guess How Much of Uncle Sam's Money Goes to Foreign Aid? Guess Again!," National Public Radio, *Goats and Soda,* February 10, 2015. Rutsch highlights the annual survey conducted (since 2009) by the Kaiser Family Foundation; every year, the average response to the question about the amount of foreign aid provided by the US government is right around 26 percent, even though the actual amount has remained stable at just under 1 percent.

129. World Bank, *World Development Indicators 2016;* "U.S. Gross External Debt," US Department of the Treasury, www.treasury.gov.

130. World Bank, *World Development Indicators 2010.*

131. Jubilee USA Network, "Debt Slavery Is Foreign Aid in Reverse," www.jubilee.org.

132. Jubilee Debt Campaign, "The Debt Crisis," www.jubileedebtcampaign.org.

133. Jubilee USA Network, "Debt Slavery Is Foreign Aid in Reverse."

134. World Bank, "Zimbabwe: Overview," October 4, 2016; IMF, "Statement by the IMF on Zimbabwe," October 21, 2016.

135. Merritt Kennedy, "IMF Approves $12 Billion Bailout for Egypt After Austerity Measures," National Public Radio, November 11, 2016, www.npr.org; Zahraa Alkhalisi, "Why Egypt Just Let Its Currency Crash by 48%," *CNN Money,* November 3, 2016, www.cnn.com.

136. Jubilee USA Network, "Why Drop the Debt?"; "Ending the Cycle of Debt," *New York Times,* October 1, 2004.

137. Susan George, *Ill Fares the Land: Essays on Food, Hunger, and Power* (Washington, DC: Institute for Policy Studies, 1984).

138. Eduardo Galeano, *Open Veins of Latin America* (New York: Monthly Review, 1973).

139. "Debt Cancellation," www.one.org; "Debt Bubbles 'Popping' in Emerging Economies," Bretton Woods Project, February 9, 2016, brettonwoodsproject.org.

140. "IMF Returns to Argentina," *Deutsche Welle,* September 20, 2016, www.dw.com.

141. Jubilee USA Network, "Debt Slavery Is Foreign Aid in Reverse."

142. "Debt Relief Lifts Aid to Record Highs in 2005—OECD," *New York Times,* April 4, 2006; World Bank, *World Development Indicators 2006.*

143. Emilio Sacerdoti and Philippe Callier, "Debt Relief Yields Results in Niger," *IMF Survey Magazine,* January 25, 2008.

144. "Oxfam Applauds Zambia's Free Health Care," *Ottawa Citizen,* April 1, 2006; Jubilee USA, "Debt, Poverty, and the MDGs," 2007, www.jubileeusa.org.

145. IMF, "Heavily Indebted Poor Countries (HIPC) Initiative and Multilateral Debt Relief Initiative (MDRI) Statistical Update," December 2014, www.imf.org.

146. "Prudence Can Win," *The Economist,* May 30, 2009.

147. Panizza, Sturzenegger, and ZeHelmeyer, "International Government Debt"; "Seeing the World Differently," *The Economist,* June 12, 2010; United Nations, *Millennium Development Goals Report 2010.*

148. World Bank, *World Development Indicators 2010;* Panizza, Sturzenegger, and Ze-Helmeyer, "International Government Debt."

149. "Summit in Sight: The G8 and Africa from Gleneagles to Lough Erne," February 28, 2013, www.one.org; "Why Should They Believe Us?," *New York Times;* United Nations, *Millennium Development Goals Report 2010.*

150. "Debt Sustainability," World Bank, October 9, 2014, www.worldbank.org; Jubilee Debt Campaign, "The New Developing World Debt Crisis," November 2, 2016, www.jubileedebt.org.uk.

Chapter 7

Adjustments, Conditions, and Alternatives

Happy Recession! —*Common greeting among middle-class Nigerians, known for their dark humor*[1]

Poverty is not created by poor people. It is produced by our failure to create institutions to support human capabilities.
  —*Muhammad Yunus, founder of the Grameen Bank of Bangladesh*[2]

As mentioned in Chapter 6, the conditions attached to the program for indebted countries are based in neoliberalism, in a set of ideas known as the Washington Consensus. Although nearly three decades old, the Washington Consensus still sums up the position of the international financial institutions (IFIs) and the donors that dominate them (the United States, Germany, Canada, and Japan): that under-development is due to the domestic failings of the under-developed countries. In other words, it is argued that countries need internal structural reforms to stabilize their economies. Just as the diagnosis of the problem is universal, so is the cure. A fairly uniform prescription is proposed for dealing with any economy's ills: an opening up (or liberalization) of the economy to foreign competition, and the adoption of a series of market-based reforms, including privatization and deregulation, as well as an embrace of globalization. According to the Washington Consensus, economic crises (wherever they occur) should be approached in the same way and treated with a consistent dose of economic liberalization and fiscal austerity, or belt-tightening. The prognosis for low-income countries (LICs) is quite optimistic: if countries will only take their medicine, they will experience healthy growth rates. Healthy growth rates will provide for the growth of a middle class, and then more stable, viable democracies are sure to follow.

It is usually the International Monetary Fund (IMF) that administers the cure. The IMF plays several highly influential roles in the world economy, and these roles have shifted over time. Increasingly, the IMF's focus is on the promotion of global economic

stability (and the prevention and management of financial crises).[3] The IMF promotes stability by serving as the lender of last resort to countries in economic crisis, distributing loans or lines of credit (ideally, concessional loans or credit) to countries whose economies are facing temporary shortfalls. By shortfalls, we are referring to an imbalance in payments, or a situation in which a country is spending more than it is earning. When this occurs, a country is said to be experiencing a deficit, and must find ways to finance or cover this deficit. This is how many countries go into debt: compared to the unpopular alternatives of raising taxes or cutting spending, governments prefer to take out loans to cover the shortfall. When countries run into serious financial trouble, it is often the IMF to which they turn for RESCUE PACKAGES: emergency loans, bailouts, or possibly even debt relief. Again, countries get "rescued" only after they have agreed to the IMF's cure. Obviously, this makes the IMF an extremely powerful institution, with tremendous influence over the decisions of governments.

So what is the cure, exactly? What are the conditions attached to the provision of new loans that are so necessary for the servicing of old debt? The first thing to understand is that there is a regimen associated with the cure, comprising what are known as STRUCTURAL ADJUSTMENT PROGRAMS (SAPs). Also called austerity plans, SAPs are said to allow for more input from the countries they target. According to their proponents, SAPs treat the countries involved more like stakeholders, as participants in the design of the plan, and are somewhat less onerous than they used to be. The old SAPs (which were known as "shock therapy") were designed to be kinder and gentler. They often included fewer conditions and more emphasis on poverty reduction (as opposed to a singular emphasis on growth).

But the IMF's critics contend that the difference between the old and new SAPs is mostly window-dressing—or public relations for the IMF.[4] As before, these programs are premised on the neoliberal consensus that the world should be run like a business. The IMF argues that its goal is debt reduction. That means getting countries to follow what neoliberals would characterize as more sensible economic policies. According to this view, countries need to adopt multiyear plans based in pro-growth policies and ensure that their revenues exceed their expenditures—in order to get out of the red. While there seems to be a steady stream of calls for greater participation from developing countries, there is little actual dialogue taking place. At its core, any adjustment program is based in the adoption of market reforms, which are believed by neoliberals to lay the basis for future growth. What countries need most is to keep their eyes on the bottom line. In general, short-term consumption should be curtailed in order to promote long-term investment.

For all of the talk about local ownership and adapting to local conditions, the new SAPs are still remarkably uniform, based in the idea that debtor countries need to undergo a series of reforms to promote growth, get themselves out of debt, reduce poverty, and foster development. The first order of business is reducing deficits, or attaining a balance of payments. One way to do this is by cutting spending. Although some argue that the prescribed economic reforms aren't quite as draconian now as they were in the past, the governments of debtor countries, after meeting with the IMF, are to return home and cut the "fat" from their budgets, most commonly spending on social welfare programs. Uncharacteristically for the IMF, at the peak of the global economic crisis in 2008, it actually called for a stimulus (or fiscal boost) to prop up a few of the hardest-hit economies, like Tanzania and Mozam-

bique. Other countries, such as China, Malaysia, Vietnam, Brazil, and Chile, also adopted sizable stimulus packages, investing in "make work" programs, investing in infrastructure, and maintaining social spending on poverty alleviation programs (and in some cases even expanding it).

However, after the economic crisis of 2007–2009 subsided, the IMF returned to business as usual.[5] The cuts in social spending associated with deficit reduction are likely to take even more of a toll in LICs than they do in high-income countries (HICs), since in many LICs, private income is so low for so many that public provisioning is crucial. Moreover, cuts in social welfare programs mean reduced government funding for education, healthcare, sanitation, provision of clean water, price controls, and subsidies for food, as well as nutritional supplements for young children and nursing mothers. In China, budget cuts have meant the dismantling of the once hugely popular and widely emulated "barefoot doctor" program. One of the greatest successes of the CULTURAL REVOLUTION, the free rural healthcare provided by the Chinese government greatly improved the quality of life for millions of people. However, since the 1990s there has been a huge reversal in social spending, the safety net has been shredded, as now more Chinese citizens must pay for many healthcare costs out of their own pockets, even though nearly 96 percent of the population has health insurance. Official data show that more than 40 percent of families who were pushed into poverty experienced severe illness that crippled their finances.[6] As a result, access to care, quality of care, and health outcomes vary considerably depending on who you are and where you live. For better-off Chinese, health outcomes have improved tremendously over the years. However, in the case of a catastrophic illness, when the bill for a hospital stay adds up to more than the yearly income of most peasants, a lack of accessible doctors means that families either are pushed further into poverty or simply go without care—often until it is too late.[7]

In addition to the revenues saved by cuts in spending, austerity plans often require governments to increase their income by increasing export earnings. The most common means of doing this is export promotion, which for most countries means an intensification of the production of raw materials for sale on the world market. Working in tandem with this effort at export promotion is the devaluation of one's currency, which a government undertakes by changing its official exchange rate. A currency devaluation is prescribed because it promises to accomplish two goals at once. It should spur increased export earnings, since one's goods will be cheaper (and therefore more competitive) on the world market. At the same time, devaluation means that because the currency is worth less, the cost of imports will rise, putting goods out of the reach of most of the population and therefore conserving scarce hard currency. Again, the idea is to achieve a balance of payments (or even a surplus) where there has been a deficit. According to neoliberals, deep cuts in spending combined with a jump in revenues from export sales will help countries accumulate the hard currency to get out of debt and on the path to prosperity.

Neoliberals counsel that countries need to be patient and forge ahead. The path to prosperity is predicated on the acceptance of some other conditions as well. Here the emphasis is on the adoption of policies that will enhance productivity and encourage capital flows based on foreign investment rather than aid. The way to accomplish these goals, according to the IMF, is to privatize the economy. Privatization means selling off STATE-OWNED ENTERPRISES (SOEs), which are often wasteful and

Figure 7.1   Do Exchange Rates Matter?

When we consider "free" and "state-run" economies (and the multiple variations in between), one example that illustrates the involvement of governments in economic decisions is the value of the country's currency. The relative weight of currencies compared to each other is known as the exchange rate (for example, in December 2016 the US dollar was roughly equivalent to 20.4 Mexican pesos). Although it is certainly not the only one to do so, China is an example of a country that has intervened in the markets to control the value of its currency, known as the yuan or renminbi. For over a decade, the United States encouraged China (and a few other countries as well) to permit their currencies to be traded at more market-oriented rates. Many contended that the Chinese currency was undervalued, which made Chinese exports cheaper and foreign imports (which compete with their products at home) comparatively more expensive. This currency manipulation, it was argued, helped China sell more than it bought abroad, which added to the Chinese trade surplus with the United States.

In an attempt to lend stability to China's emerging economic system, the yuan had long been pegged to the US dollar, a practice that ended only in 2005. After significant pressure from the United States and the International Monetary Fund (IMF), Beijing's leaders decided to allow their currency's value to float, or fluctuate, within a small band of value (permitting the daily exchange rate to increase or decrease by 2 percent). While the loosening of control helped deflect foreign complaints, it also strengthened Beijing's case with the IMF that the yuan be named the fifth currency to be included in the Special Drawing Rights basket of important reserve currencies (a milestone that was reached in late 2016).

While pressure on the Chinese was to *re*value their currency, a common characteristic of structural adjustment programs (SAPs) is the opposite: countries are told to *de*value their currency. One of the most striking examples of this was in late 2016, when Egypt allowed its currency, the Egyptian pound, to fall in value by 48 percent, in order to seal the deal on a $12 billion loan from the IMF. Only a country in crisis would adopt such measures. The immediate effect is pain and panic in the markets as the prices of basic goods suddenly become unaffordable. Governments such as Egypt's are right to worry about a political backlash, but neoliberals counsel that countries must persevere in order to get back into the black, make their exports more competitive, and attract investment.

Source: Zahraa Akhalisi, "Why Egypt Just Let Its Currency Crash by 48 Percent," *CNN Money*, November 3, 2016.

inefficient. Although SOEs were originally created to reduce foreign dominance of LIC economies, neoliberals argue that these government monopolies over the delivery of public services such as water and electricity should be put on the open market and sold to the highest bidder—whether local or foreign. It is not unusual for these state sell-offs to amount to extremely lucrative, high-stakes deals that are less than transparent. Although neoliberals push for privatization because they believe that taking these sectors out of government hands will reduce corruption, it is commonly said that all that privatization does is to privatize corruption. Another problem is that the privatization of utilities has often meant higher prices for water, electricity, and telephone service, but neoliberals argue that private investors have dramatically improved and expanded services, thereby increasing the poor's access to these services.[8]

Others doubt such claims and are concerned particularly about privatization of resources such as water, access to which many consider to be a human right. In one of the most famously contested cases, in Bolivia, citizens fought a "water war" when

the American-owned multinational corporation Bechtel took over the waterworks and nearly doubled the price of water in 2000. After days of nationwide, violent protests and a declaration of martial law, the company was forced to leave the country. The community-run waterworks that succeeded it has not been without its problems, and most analysts now agree that when it comes to water, for example, the private sector has not been the solution.[9] Too often the private sector has been accused of price-gouging, and has not achieved better success than the public sector in extending services. Problems with World Bank–coordinated water privatization projects in Manila, Nagpur, and elsewhere have given anti-privatization activists momentum, as 180 cities in both the developing and developed world have "returned" or "re-municipalized" their water systems, including major Latin American and African cities.[10]

In cooperation with the terms of its IMF reform, Mexico sold off hundreds of state-owned enterprises, including its control over the seaport, railroad, and telecommunication industries. President Enrique Peña Nieto surprised many when he succeeded in pushing through a constitutional amendment to allow for reform of PEMEX, the state-owned oil and gas monopoly—namely, private investment in the oil industry. Such a move previously would have been unthinkable. In 2010 the Egyptian government had to reverse a decision to sell state-owned companies to private investors after widespread protests raised concerns about corruption and insider dealing. India is expecting a huge row over a discussion of just selling shares in (let alone privatizing) its 473 publicly owned companies.[11]

China is feeling some of this pressure, too. As discussed in Chapter 6, much of its growth has been based on state capitalism, or using state-owned companies as the basis of its economy. In 2012, China's state-owned sectors accounted for approximately 18 percent of gross domestic product (GDP) (down from 80 percent in 1978).[12] The country's biggest cell phone operator, China Mobile, is a state-owned company. Although it has closed many of its weaker SOEs, China has been slower to sell off these companies, fearing the creation of social unrest due to mass unemployment. The nonpublic sector in China has developed rapidly in recent years, yet SOEs still employ approximately half of the country's work force. For the first time since the late 1990s, though, analysts noted that SOEs contributed an increased share of the GDP in 2016 (growing to 39 percent), even as many money-losing SOEs increasingly become "zombie-firms," nearly wholly reliant on local government for resources.[13]

It is not uncommon for countries facing similar hardship to experience violent strikes that result in states of emergency. Such strikes and demonstrations in response to the hardship caused by neoliberal economic reform are known as "IMF riots," and they occur on a regular basis around the globe. Rising food prices (some the result of cuts in government subsidies, required by the IMF) led to demonstrations in more than sixty countries in 2007 and 2008. Violence and arrests were associated with the widely publicized 2010 IMF riots in Greece, but also affected India, where a one-day strike protesting a gasoline price hike of 30 cents per gallon shut down much of the country.[14]

Beyond privatization, neoliberals argue that LIC governments must work harder to attract foreign investment of all kinds. They must make themselves attractive to multinational corporations (MNCs) for all the reasons neoliberals have put forward regarding the benefits associated with the presence of MNCs in host countries. Governments

should work aggressively to lure more foreign investment in a variety of ways, including a policy of deregulation (the removal of legal constraints on the operation of businesses, such as eliminating health, safety, and environmental regulations). Neoliberals argue that it also helps if the country has a large pool of laborers who are willing and eager to work with little interference from unions or other activists.

Budget cuts, privatization, deregulation, and openness to foreign investment are just a few of the conditions commonly associated with the IMF's economic reform packages. To fully understand the impact of conditionality, take the case of Indonesia. In 1997, in return for $43 billion in emergency funding, Indonesia agreed to an adjustment that had more than a hundred conditions attached. Among them was the requirement that the government close its clove monopoly and eliminate price subsidies on basic foodstuffs. The upheaval caused by such policies led to the downfall of the long-standing Suharto government (more than one analyst has suggested that this amounted to a coup sponsored by the IMF).[15] In Guinea, still reeling from the Ebola crisis in 2014, the government was spending more on debt than public health.[16]

Back in the early 1990s the IMF and donors added another condition for aid. With the Cold War over, the neoliberals began admonishing LICs to go beyond "getting prices right" and to also work at "getting politics right." Based in the view that democracy is a natural complement to capitalism, donors argued that the hardship blamed on austerity and the IFIs' seeming failure to deliver on promises of growth and development was actually due to failures of government, not the model. As we will discuss in more detail in Chapter 13, the West became convinced that a lack of "good governance" was the problem—not the neoliberal model itself.

When other East Asian countries, which had for so long been upheld as models for economic development, stumbled in the late 1990s, neoliberals blamed the "Asian flu" (a financial crisis in which the markets plunged) on the lack of political liberalization in these countries. For more than a decade, Western donors had ignored rampant corruption in Asia and elsewhere as long as governments embraced neoliberal reforms. However, by the late 1990s, corruption, cronyism, and the "incestuous" relationship between government and business in Asia were deplored as the cause of the region's ills. These countries had gotten prices right, but they had suffered from a lack of regulation, supervision, and TRANSPARENCY—in effect, they hadn't "gotten politics right."[17]

The problem, as identified by neoliberals, was one endemic not only to East Asia but also to much of the global south: political reform had lagged behind economic reform when, from a neoliberal perspective, the success of either reform would be inextricably linked to progress in the other.[18] As a result, political reforms aimed at fighting corruption and promoting democratization became another condition promoted by the Washington Consensus. Interestingly, in recent years many countries have turned to China as a source of loans, because in what is called the Beijing Consensus, China makes it a point not to press such conditions. It attaches other strings (access to markets, support for its policy on Taiwan, etc.), but China certainly isn't going to call on other countries to become more democratic.[19]

Neoliberals maintain that in the long run, perseverance in economic and political liberalization will pay off. It just takes time and patience. They point to a number of countries, such as Mexico and South Korea, that have taken this sometimes-harsh medicine in return for emergency loans, and whose growth rates have since indicated

a recovery. Moreover, Mexico and South Korea underwent extensive political reforms at the same time that they adopted economic reforms. Not that long ago they were authoritarian systems, but both countries today have made substantial progress in their DEMOCRATIC TRANSITIONS and are considered at least partially consolidated.

How "Getting Prices Right" May Be "Getting Development Wrong"

Critics of the neoliberal model don't mince words when they argue that globalization is the new colonialism. Its aims and outcomes are remarkably similar to those of colonialism in that the "development" it promotes is not one that improves the lives of LICs' citizens. Rather, according to the structuralists, free trade and globalization are about ensuring markets for Western goods and retaining developing countries as a source of cheap labor and raw materials. Sure, under SAPs the governments of developing countries are consulted and allowed to have some input in the decisions that affect the lives of their citizens, but the destiny of their citizens is still ultimately left in the hands of their former colonizers. The IMF's economic reforms amount to a financial coup d'état; they undermine the sovereignty of the state and deny people the right to economic self-determination.

Even if the model one day proves effective in promoting economic development, the IMF has been unwilling to reform itself in any significant way that alters the balance of power between high- and low-income countries (or that reflects the changing reality of the global economy). Since 2010, members of the GROUP OF 20 (G-20) called for a redistribution of the IMF's voting power (from rich countries to emerging economies) and for open and meritocratic elections to decide the leaders of the IMF and World Bank. A small shift in voting distribution occurred in late 2015, with China jumping from sixth to third in terms of the weight its vote controls (although the United States retained its veto power). Even though this constitutes the "biggest shake-up" since the establishment of the pillars of the modern world economy in 1944, IMF and World Bank leaders remain American and European, as has been the custom since the bodies were founded in 1944.[20]

Given the existing imbalance of power, the conditions attached by IFIs amount to blackmail, say the structuralists. The restructuring of debt has resulted in a system of international peonage. According to this argument, LICs fell deeply into debt because of their position in the international economic system, and neoliberal economic reforms effectively force them to remain in that position. The donors and the institutions they run appear to be more interested in the business of business than in the business of development. Described as a debt collector for commercial banks, the IMF is so busy making sure countries continue to service their debts that the promise of development as the outcome is a cruel joke. Critics point out that Ghana has been the poster child for IMF reforms in Africa. It began implementing an austerity plan in 1983, and achieved an economic growth rate averaging 5–6 percent from 2004 to 2008 (although this slowed to 3.5 percent in 2015). Ghana was the first country in Africa that Barack Obama chose to visit as president (in 2009), in part because it was considered an African success story. The Ghanaian democracy has had a long relationship with the IMF, meeting its demands, but the country continues to struggle. Even after decades of economic reforms, the poverty rate was above 24 percent as of 2013. In 2015, Ghana's leaders signed a $920 million deal with the IMF requiring the

country to decrease subsidies, decrease public-sector wages, and increase revenue—all moves that increased public dissatisfaction.[21] Thus the economic reforms imposed on countries are often entrenching the very development model that caused their original problem—overreliance on the export of raw materials.

Whereas neoliberals emphasize the positive benefits of globalization and maintain that adjustments are necessary to promote long-term economic health, critics argue that structural adjustment serves the interests of the powerful. Globalization is contributing to a grotesque and dangerous polarization between those who benefit from the system and those who are passive recipients of its effects.[22] The combined effect of the reforms imposed on citizens is devastating. These economic reforms often throw the middle class into poverty, but they take their hardest toll on the poor. There are good reasons why adjustment is known as "shock therapy." Shock waves ripple throughout countries, with multiple consequences. Zambia, for example, benefited from debt reduction, but had to meet the IMF's conditions in order to obtain it. As it edged closer to meeting these conditions, life expectancy dropped, the mortality rate for children under five rose sharply, and three-quarters of the population were living on less than one dollar a day.[23] Even years after Zambia completed its final review for the 2008 loan from the IMF, its economy struggled—the kwacha was Africa's worst-performing currency in 2015, and the economy's reliance on copper exports left the economy fragile and vulnerable.

In the following sections we will briefly describe how the millions who are worse off because of the IMF's reforms are seeking to cope with their effects. According to structuralists, globalization is contributing, both directly and indirectly, to a series of interconnected problems that vividly illustrate the downside of interdependence. Neoliberal reforms have often been promoted by developed countries with little thought to the human and environmental impact on LICs.

The Consequences of Globalization: Migration and Urbanization

In a variety of ways, globalization and structural adjustment are adding to a series of large and growing human migrations. These migrations occur within countries, from rural to urban areas, and between countries, often from under-developed to more economically developed countries. For the poorest, globalization has often made what was once a subsistence living increasingly untenable. With lower prices for their cash crops and no food security in rural areas, people have become desperate. Rural dwellers have always been drawn to the cities (in developed as well as less developed countries) for the opportunities they are believed to hold. Not only do people come hoping for work, but they also come for the chance to improve their lives, through access to education, healthcare, and other government services. For many years, it has been a common practice for governments to try to keep urban populations satisfied and stable by providing subsidies that ensure that the populations surrounding them are fed and the lights are on. As much as there is a pull factor drawing people to the cities, there is also a push factor: the hardship of rural life.

Although millions of immigrants are estimated to have illegally entered developed countries, the majority of LIC migrants do not cross international boundaries, as we discuss in further detail in Chapter 17. Rather, they are setting up residence in São Paulo, Mumbai, Shanghai, and Manila. Today, for the first time in history, more than

half the world's population lives in urban areas. In 2014, approximately 54 percent of the world's population lived in cities, and this is expected to increase to 66 percent by 2050 (in 1800, it is estimated that only 3 percent of the world's population lived in cities).[24] Currently there are 3.9 billion urban residents around the world, and this is expected to grow to 6.34 billion by 2050.[25] Nearly 40 percent of all future urban growth is expected to take place in only three countries: China, India, and Nigeria.[26] The flight from rural areas has had a number of consequences, among them over-urbanization and the rapid creation of megacities—cities with populations of over 10 million. The crush of bodies contributes to overcrowding and a number of health problems. It also raises a number of serious political, economic, and social dilemmas.

The Informal Sector

A variety of factors related to globalization and structural adjustment affect employment rates worldwide. For example, the shutdown of state-owned enterprises associated with structural adjustment often means mass layoffs, adding to unemployment and underemployment rates. Where the unemployment rate is high, as in Zimbabwe, where it is estimated that 95 percent of the population is without work, many of the displaced make their living in the underground economy, also known as the informal sector.[27] Although it is the single largest employer in many LICs, the informal economy is a shadow economy of sorts. It is composed of semilegal or illegal activities transacted under the table, and therefore not included in the calculation of a country's gross domestic product. Given the characteristics of the work, there are no accurate estimates of the numbers of people involved, although analysts agree that worldwide the number of informal-sector workers runs into the millions and is growing much more rapidly compared to the formal economy. In Peru and many Latin American countries, where underemployment is vast, women who have recently migrated from rural areas compose the backbone of this labor force. Latin America's experience is by no means unique; the informal economy provides an important cushion against austerity. It is a central means for survival in Africa, Asia, and the Middle East for men and women alike.[28]

Although informal-sector work is often viewed as independent self-employment, it is also work performed semilegally or illegally for an employer (such as pieceworkers making lace from their homes for subcontractors). In the informal sector there are no explicit, written labor contracts, and no state regulation of wages or working conditions. Much of the informal sector, such as the microenterprises of female petty traders selling the equivalent of fast food along roads and sidewalks, amounts to what are known as male-dependent enterprises: they replicate in the public sphere the work that is often traditionally undertaken within the reproductive realm. This is true of the other major sources of work for women in the informal sector, such as domestic labor and as sex workers. As you might imagine, much of this work is highly dependent on disposable income, and during times of austerity these sectors are hit especially hard.[29]

Violence Against Women

The rapid economic change associated with globalization has created opportunities for some women, but it has exposed them to a rising backlash. This backlash

is expressed in a number of ways, including dramatic growth in the range, incidence, and intensity of gender violence. According to the United Nations, just over one in three females worldwide are targeted for attack simply because they are female.[30] Where populations are undergoing rapid change and economic hardship, newly autonomous women become an easily identified threat. Women are often caught between neo-liberal policies that propel them into the work force and a traditionalist backlash that seeks to drive them back into their homes. In many parts of the world, men experience what some analysts call status inconsistency, or anxiety associated with changes in gender relations, the structure of the family, and the position of women. As Valentine Moghadam argues, the World Bank wants women to have fewer babies, work outside the home, and earn enough to feed their families, but isn't doing much when things get ugly and women are scapegoated. Globalization is related to a backlash of sorts, one manifested in a rising incidence of violence against females. For example, in Peru, where seven in ten women have experienced some form of gender violence, sexual harassment is too common, a way of putting women "back in their place," and women are blamed for provoking their mistreatment. The legal system participates in this abuse, as an estimated 90 percent of sexual assault reports are never investigated.[31]

Where there is mass unemployment, women's entry into the labor force is sometimes viewed with hostility by men, who see women as displacing them. In cases around the world, women are finding themselves more often to be the targets of individual attacks as well as attacks by conservative social movements. Women are blamed not only for taking jobs from men, but also for the loss of traditional cultures (another by-product of globalization). Often considered the keepers of tradition, their growing visibility and perceived competition with men in the labor market anger and terrify traditional elements, both male and female. The autonomy that comes with work outside the home is often believed to make women immodest, decadent, cultural traitors. Conservatives uphold tradition as providing a secure base in a scary world and argue for a world in which men and women know and accept their proper place. They acclaim virtues of traditional womanhood, and the proper dress and behavior of women become paramount. Those who accept this role as wife and mother are honored and exalted; those who resist are deemed traitors who must be punished. As a result, working women are held morally accountable and subjected to a broad variety of assaults and affronts, both public and private. For example, in Afghanistan, female candidates for election have received death threats, and young Afghan schoolgirls have been sprayed in the face with acid for daring to seek an education.[32] As we mention in Chapter 13, around the world (in low- as well as high-income countries) women who are perceived as resisting social norms face retaliation. The result has been a variety of "cleanup campaigns," which include mass arrests of women, punishment for violations of dress codes, a rise in honor killings, as well as sexual harassment and other forms of discrimination against females.[33] Sexual assault (or merely its threat) is another way of "putting women back in their place."

Although we usually think of mass rape as a weapon of war, it is also utilized in other types of conflict. For example, during demonstrations and political celebrations at Egypt's Tahrir Square, women were singled out by regime supporters in more than a hundred mob sexual attacks in 2012 and 2013. In what is called "the circle of hell," women were beaten, forced to the ground, stripped, and raped by large groups of men,

some of whom recorded the attacks with their cell phones.[34] Similar public sexual assaults have occurred in Myanmar, the Democratic Republic of Congo, South Sudan, Kosovo, and elsewhere, where such attacks can be compared to lynchings.

The Environment

The assault on the environment is another negative consequence of globalization. Urged on by the IMF, the World Bank, and other donors, many industrializing countries have followed the path of the industrialized world: for years they placed a higher premium on growth than on environmental protection. The results are staggering: in Mexico City, an estimated 80 percent of the year is tagged a "bad air day," as a warning to residents. Reportedly, some residents' noses are so badly damaged from inhaling toxic particles that they are losing their sense of smell and, at its worst, birds fall dead from the sky.[35] Yet in other ways as well, the results of a policy of "growth at any price" are long-term and devastating. China's economic boom, based on the use of coal and fuel-inefficient technologies, has created pollution problems of unparalleled magnitude. Until recently, HICs were the biggest polluters and consumers of the world's resources, but now China and India are among the top four producers of greenhouse gas emissions (China is the top producer, followed by the United States, Russia, and India). According to the World Health Organization (WHO), a staggering 98 percent of cities with populations above 100,000 in low- and middle-income countries fail to meet WHO air quality standards (within HICs, it is 56 percent).[36]

However, the blind pursuit of growth at all costs is the approach taken by industrializing countries and the exporters of raw materials as well. Globalization and structural reforms that encourage export promotion result in intensified pressures on the land and other resources. Neoliberal economic reforms have accelerated deforestation and desertification as countries are incentivized to open up untouched areas. The top debtors of the global south are all among the top ten deforesters: Brazil, India, Indonesia, and the Democratic Republic of Congo, to name just a few. Hardly anyone would argue that debt is the exclusive cause of deforestation and the other problems described here. However, the landless of these countries have few alternatives but to push into the forests for their subsistence needs.[37] In the drive to increase sales on the world market, land is needed and new mines and plantations are opened to satisfy the growing demand for resources. For example, the Indonesian central government has attempted to move away from this approach and adopted laws to reduce deforestation. But corrupt officials and companies continued to collaborate to put economic growth ahead of all else, and as of 2016, Indonesia had the highest rate of deforestation in the world.[38]

Poor management of the environment is costly in monetary terms as well. The British Petroleum oil spill in the Gulf of Mexico is said to be puny compared to what Nigeria has experienced every year without end.[39] Haiti is now almost completely deforested; without trees (or their roots) holding the soil together, hurricanes and earthquakes create landslides, eroding the topsoil and devastating agriculture, which exacerbates the country's already wrenching poverty.[40] In regard to climate change, experts expect that Africa, Asia, and Latin America will suffer disproportionately, with the most deaths and livelihood disruptions. The United Nations estimates that many of the 40 million people uprooted around the world in 2010 were climate

change refugees and that their numbers could reach staggering proportions, ranging from a conservative estimate of 50 million to possibly even 200 million by 2050.[41]

As the world focuses on the global threat that environmental disasters pose, the IMF, World Bank, and other donor agencies have come under increasing pressure to be more environmentally responsive, and have allocated larger staffs to address the issue. Environmental targets fare prominently in the Sustainable Development Goals (SDGs), for example. There is more funding for environmental projects, and environmental impact statements for development projects are now mandatory.[42]

But for every important gain in promoting a green initiative, there is another project that appears oblivious to the ecological havoc it causes. For example, the World Bank is continuing to invest in fossil fuel plants in India and China rather than pursuing the development of renewable forms of energy. Hydropower is considered a relatively clean energy source. Huge and expensive dams are built to irrigate plantations owned by agribusiness and to electrify cities, but they damage fragile ecosystems and often result in the loss of irreplaceable archaeological treasures. The 50,000 large dams around the world have forced the resettlement of hundreds of millions of people, often creating what are known as "development refugees."[43] These are all examples of how "development," as it is currently being pursued, can be problematic.[44]

Disease and Public Health

The massive population movements associated with globalization have a number of effects, including the spread of disease. And any number of dangers to human health can be aggravated by the changes associated with structural adjustment. Shifting rainfall patterns linked to global warming, and the movement of populations into previously forested areas, have been linked to the spread of new diseases like the Zika virus as well as others long present, such as yellow fever. For example, the dramatic, global increase in the incidence of dengue fever in recent decades is due not only to explosive outbreaks of the disease, but also to its spread into new areas. Half of the world's population is now at risk of this disease, which is spread by mosquitoes. But children are particularly vulnerable to dengue, which is considered a leading cause of serious illness and death in several Asian and Latin American countries.[45]

As mentioned, economic hardship has added not only to political instability but also to pressures on the environment. In a vicious circle, these are diseases of poverty and causes of poverty.[46] Economic and environmental pressures are contributing to the emergence of resistant strains of malaria, as well as to the surfacing of new diseases such as the West Nile virus and Ebola. Austerity has contributed to rapid urbanization, which means that health workers must deal with a host of public health nightmares—just as the budget cuts often necessitated by austerity have left them profoundly ill-equipped to deal with these problems. Total healthcare spending per capita in Madagascar in 2014 was $15. In Myanmar it was $20. Of our case studies, Mexico, at $677 per capita, had the highest healthcare expenditure in 2014, while China spent $420, Peru spent $359, and Zimbabwe allotted $58.[47]

Plus, the meager sanitation systems that may or may not have served city populations a decade or two ago simply cannot handle the massive influx of people now fleeing the poverty of rural areas. Budget cuts mean that the public health sector is

drained: it is not uncommon for clinics and hospitals in the poorest countries to lack not only electricity and running water, but also sterile equipment and protective gear. Under such circumstances the healthcare system itself becomes a vehicle for the transmission and spread of disease. The situation described here is very similar in regard to education, which has often taken cuts due to austerity. While everyone recognizes that uned-ucated and unhealthy populations are highly correlated with poverty and a major impediment to development, in a variety of ways it could be argued that structural adjustment is ensuring much of the world's continued under-development.

Is Globalization Entirely to Blame?

Although the single-minded pursuit of the neoliberal paradigm has unleashed an array of problems, manifested in various forms of social disintegration and economic dysfunctionality, there is no one cause for all of the troubles described in this chapter. While the spread of disease, destruction of rainforests, massive human migrations, and violence against women are based in social and economic institutions and systems of relationships that predate globalization, these processes are argued by some to be accelerated by the adoption of the neoliberal reforms that provide the momentum for globalization. Perhaps it is an overstatement to suggest that such tragedies are due to structural adjustment, but growing evidence suggests that the variety of problems identified here are associated with growing economic hardship. Structuralists assert that in many ways—economically, socially, culturally, politically, ecologically—the neoliberal approach has been a disaster for the world's poor. It is not working, it has cured nothing, and the international financial institutions have had plenty of time to impose their plans.[48]

Neoliberals reject such assertions. When presented with these arguments, they point out that many countries in the global south now deserve the name "emerging economies." They counter that if their way appears to be failing in some countries, then this failure is due to irrational or inefficient domestic policies, not to the irretrievably inequitable position of these countries in the world economy. The problem is poverty. It isn't globalization that is contributing to disease, emigration, and the like—it is the poverty that results from a lack of integration into the world economic system. It is the countries that are most integrated into the international system (the BRICs, for example—Brazil, Russia, India, China) that (until a few years ago anyway, in Brazil's case) are the fastest-growing and have the best shot at development. It should be pointed out, however, that the BRICs have to varying degrees accepted neoliberal reforms. The Chinese state is still heavily interventionist, for example. Brazil, under former president Luiz Inácio Lula da Silva, combined some of the macroeconomic reforms of the Washington Consensus with enhanced spending on social services, pursuing what some call the Brasilia Consensus. This approach, which views social welfare as being just as important as structural reform, has improved the lives of many Brazilians.[49]

There is still much work to do in terms of income inequality and poverty reduction in Brazil and in all the BRICs, but impressive numbers of people are entering the middle class in these countries. Per capita income in Brazil, China, and India is still relatively low, but it has grown significantly in just a decade or so, and these countries have made progress in alleviating poverty. In 1981, for example,

84 percent of Chinese lived below the poverty line. By 2005, only 16 percent did. During this same period, Brazil cut its poverty rate from 17 to 8 percent and India from 60 to 42 percent (admittedly, the percentage of the poor in India is still very high, but a nearly 20 percent decline is significant).[50] On the other hand, according to the neoliberals, if other countries aren't achieving these results, it is because they have undertaken needed economic reforms too slowly or halfheartedly. They warn that economic liberalization is like riding a bicycle: you either move forward, or you fall off. It is this hesitancy, or lack of full cooperation, that explains why so few have yet to see improvement in their standards of living.

Neoliberals go on to contend that many of these problems are rooted in individual behaviors: people choose to work for the wages they are offered, they make the decision to have unsafe sex, they deplete the forests in search of firewood. Therefore, it is individuals and their choices—not structures—that should be blamed. However, others contend that more often than not, each of these so-called choices should be understood as a coping mechanism. For most of the world's population, the behaviors condemned are not so much about choice as they are about survival.

The Neoliberals Make an Adjustment

For all of their arguments, it has been hard for the neoliberals to avoid acknowledging the IMF riots—the dislocation and hardship associated with their economic reforms. The near-collapse of East Asian economies in the late 1990s and the Great Recession a decade later forced a broader reassessment of the reform model by even its most ardent advocates. Under criticism from the right and left, the IMF and other international financial institutions maintained that they have made some needed reforms of their own. In an effort to salvage the neoliberal approach by softening some of its hardest edges, the World Bank became the leading player charged with helping (some) countries construct safety nets to carry them through the period of adjustment. It and the IMF appeared to have heard their critics, declaring that there was no single recipe for economic success. In an interesting turnabout, the IMF took the position that every country was different and a one-size-fits-all solution would be unlikely to suit the particular needs of each. According to the IMF today, with the shift to extended-credit facilities, countries can now play a greater role in defining the terms of their adjustment and setting their path for reform. Such a modification would mark quite a departure from the old IMF, in which decisions were made by donor countries, for aid recipients.[51]

In 2014, IMF director Christine Lagarde declared that structural adjustment was before her time and that the IMF didn't do that anymore. It was claimed that the "new, cuddly IMF" had changed its lending practices.[52] Perhaps this signifies the transformation to what is called a "beefier but gentler" approach based on partnering with countries in order to make the system work better. Does this mean that the nearly seven-decade-old international financial system—and foundation of the Washington Consensus—has truly undergone a conversion? Given more than two decades of IMF reform and relatively few success stories, is there a crisis of legitimacy now for the neoliberal model and its prescription? The answer, according to neoliberals, is a resounding no. The lesson learned is not that the Washington Consensus is wrong, but that it is incomplete. It is probably safe to assume that the Washington

Consensus isn't declining; rather it is evolving, adapting, shifting in response to perceived needs.[53] The new, more flexible IMF has retooled its conditionality: conditions continue to be necessary, but countries are allowed more of a voice in helping to identify what those conditions should be. Part of this voice will come through voting reform, or allowing developing countries more of a role in decisionmaking in the IMF and World Bank. This idea has been on the table for several years. As of late 2016, there had been some redistribution, but only 6 percent of the IMF's voting power had been shifted from high-income countries to emerging market and developing economies (most notably Brazil, Russia, India, and China).[54]

According to the IMF, these reforms are historic; these countries were given more voting power in order to reflect their relative size and growing clout in the international economy. Those with the most clout—the United States (which has 17 percent of the IMF vote) and Europe (23 percent)—maintain that they support this reform in the hope that it will restore the institution's legitimacy and encourage these emerging powers to feel more invested in the current system. For now, at least, the poorest countries of the world—those most dependent on the IMF—continue to have a very small role in the discussion.[55]

The IMF's very disparate group of critics have differed over how seriously they take the talk about reform. Some neoliberals have even split with the IMF over the question of its proper role. They insist that the organization is already doing too much, that it needs to get out of the antipoverty business. These more conservative analysts maintain that the IMF's rescue packages are a mistake, because they give countries (and lenders) the idea that they will always be bailed out. As a result, governments and investors are never forced to recognize the consequences of their mistakes. They will continue to be reckless with their lending and this will only mean future crises.

On the other hand, others reject such an analysis. Their issue is that the IMF is offering nothing new; countries resent the reforms forced onto them as a precondition to assistance, and argue that it still treats them like children. The BRICs have at times taken the lead in facing down Western demands (sometimes using neoliberal institutions such as the World Trade Organization [WTO] to do so). But there is tremendous diversity between and within the large number of countries comprising the global south. Those who experienced enormous hardship in association with the IMF's reforms are deeply distrustful of it and other international financial institutions. All states object when IFI intrusion veers toward violations of sovereignty. Three decades of neoliberalism have resulted in increased social inequality and a great deal of frustration in the poorest countries, and there is a great desire to find another way. Although few alternatives appear promising, there is no doubt that those who are left behind very much want change.

Structuralists insist that they see through all this talk about change. They claim that for neoliberals, there is still only one road to development. But some analysts view the neoliberal mea culpa and subsequent reforms as having some potential, particularly if this means that countries might be able to travel the road at different speeds, or even at their own pace. There is some public support for this idea within all four of our regions. In Latin America, for example, public opinion polls suggest that most people favor the market economy and see their countries as progressing.[56] But many support leaders such as Brazil's former president Lula, who demanded that the IMF no longer urge LIC governments to adopt policies promoting trade

liberalization that the rich developed countries themselves have yet to undertake. As mentioned earlier in this chapter, it is common for IMF reforms to force LICs to open their economies to foreign trade while developed countries continue to subsidize and protect their domestic producers from LIC competition with subsidies and tariffs. LICs argue that they would have a much better shot at benefiting from free trade if everyone played by its rules. Whatever the case, it appears that in its effort at "getting politics right," the IMF may need to take some of its own medicine. Perhaps it, too, should have to work harder at good governance—become more democratic, more transparent, and more accountable to the public, as well as to all of its 189 member states.[57]

What's the Alternative?

Both proponents and critics of globalization argue that it is faceless, emerging everywhere at once. Like the view that promotes and seeks to perpetuate it, based in neoliberalism, globalization's overwhelming dominance verges on the hegemonic. By hegemonic, we mean that something is so dominant, so powerful, that there are no apparent rivals. When it comes to globalization and the neoliberal approach to development, low-income countries are told again and again to remember TINA—"there is no alternative." Yet critics of the orthodoxy struggle to provide other choices; they demand a counterhegemonic approach that includes considerations of justice. These analysts seek to put development on an equal par with growth, if not ahead of it. Instead of "getting prices right" or "getting politics right," they argue for "getting institutions right for development."

Over the years a variety of alternative paths to development have been proposed—some reformist, some more revolutionary—but few of them have met with much success. Many of these proposals urge the creation of indigenous models and self-reliance, such as Tanzania's Afro-socialist *ujamma*. Others, such as China's Great Leap Forward, centered on a rejection of the capitalist world system and instead proposed autarchy. Still others, such as the NEW INTERNATIONAL ECONOMIC ORDER (NIEO), attempted to reform the international economic system to make it fairer. The proposals of the NIEO were wide-ranging and comprehensive and have periodically been resurrected for consideration. However, thus far, even the most moderate reforms have failed, mostly because LICs have so little power with which to renegotiate the terms of their incorporation into the world economic system.

Today, a variety of activists concerned about the continued under-development of much of the world are facing the same fundamental problems that earlier generations did in their calls for a restructured world order or the creation of a counterhegemonic approach. Although there is plenty of disagreement among the critics of corporate-led globalization (or "globalization from above"), they generally agree on the need for "globalization from below," or a GRASSROOTS-BASED APPROACH that prioritizes sustainable human development and security. In short, sustainability considerations (not only sustainable development but also sustainable consumption) are based in the belief that the welfare of present generations should not be pursued at the expense of future generations. In its broadest sense, even the World Bank and World Trade Organization have embraced the term "sustainability," calling it one of their principal objectives. Yet critics argue that sustainability means much more, and

that it directly runs counter to neoliberal values that place a premium on greed, the profit motive, and consumerism.

Human security, on the other hand, is based in an entirely different set of values, such as cooperation, compassion, economic democracy, and decentralization. It speaks to individual and collective perceptions of present and potential threats to physical and psychological well-being. "Human security" is a relatively new term that takes understandings of security beyond issues of armaments and territorial security. Analysts who support the counterhegemonic approach maintain that security against direct violence is just one form of human security, and have extended the concept to include the security of people, not just nations. Human security is defined as the absence of structural violence such as poverty and other forms of economic, social, and environmental degradation.[58]

Efforts to promote human security center on the eradication of extreme poverty and take a holistic approach. This definition of development views it as a process and an end, the result of a complex set of interactions between political, economic, social, environmental, and cultural factors. For example, one aspect of human security is the promotion of gender equality, which seeks to end discrimination against females in all areas of life. Such initiatives are proactive as well, focused on creating choices and opportunities for women and ending all forms of violence against them. Human security is also promoted through projects that target investments to benefit low-income groups. One example is agrarian reform, which includes land redistribution, the building of infrastructure such as rural roads and clinics, as well as increasing access to credit and appropriate technologies. In order to get the maximum benefit from such policies, all aspects of the reform (including land titles) need to be made available to women (and men). Other "pro-poor" economic growth policies invest in physical and human capital and expand employment opportunities by upgrading skills in traditional and untraditional occupations, so that businesses and other enterprises can be more competitive.[59]

One area of intense disagreement within the counterhegemonic approach centers on the question of whether it might be possible to promote human security through globalization. Some (such as Dot Keet) call for "deglobalization," a move away from the dominant economic system and toward large-scale change that would require, among other things, reconceptualizing our understanding of progress.[60] On the other hand, reformists like Joseph Stiglitz argue for a "reglobalization" (a re-do, so to speak). They aren't fighting globalization as much as they are resisting its worst features. They believe that, if properly managed, a fairer globalization can be created. Stiglitz advocates Keynesian reforms that allow for more state management of economies (rather than leaving it to the market forces that set off the Great Recession and have left too many mired in poverty for too long). Public management of the economy was the approach that President Franklin Delano Roosevelt used to lead the United States out of the Great Depression. According to this idea, the state stimulates the economy through deficit spending. Investments in infrastructure, industry, and other projects are undertaken to generate employment and create conditions for stability and growth.[61] You may recognize this as the line of attack that the Obama administration credited for keeping our recent recession from becoming a depression.

This approach has been used elsewhere as well. The high-income countries that have been the most successful in eradicating poverty (the Scandinavian countries)

have not left it to the market to sort out—rather, their governments have actively intervened with antipoverty measures. Similarly, many developing countries, including Brazil and Mexico, have reduced income inequality by promoting pro-poor stimulus programs such as CONDITIONAL CASH TRANSFERS (CCTs). Under CCT programs in Mexico, the government invests in human capital by providing stipends to poor families who take their kids for medical checkups and ensure that they stay in school. When designed effectively and implemented transparently, such social assistance programs have proven to be enormously successful at promoting short- and long-term development goals.[62]

According to Stiglitz, these are ideas that can benefit both LICs and HICs.[63] Although they disagree about how to get there, those who promote reglobalization and deglobalization agree that it is time for a post–Washington Consensus. They are joined by labor and human rights activists, environmentalists, consumer advocates, and others who are prioritizing equity and working to replace the corporate view of economic liberalization with a more democratic, fully participatory model. Such a model would press donors to honor their pledges in regard to aid and hold MNCs accountable for their misdeeds. It would allow countries to escape externally imposed conditionality and redefine their own (homegrown) development directions, tailored to local conditions.[64]

Those who believe the question is not whether we globalize, but how we globalize, are seeking to adapt or manage globalization. Groups such as Oxfam and the Jubilee movement are offering credible alternatives for the way we think about debt relief, labor standards, and other issues. As a whole, those who seek to adapt globalization are defining a goal. They want people to have more choices and more control over their own lives, and to expand the possibilities for self-determination. A one-size-fits-all approach to development is counterproductive. Instead, countries are like patients; they have different ailments and will require different treatments.[65]

Most of these activists generally acknowledge that there are some benefits of globalization, but they want to blunt its negative impacts. The majority agree that integration into the world system is inevitable and possibly even desirable, but they call for stricter labor and environmental regulations to minimize the system's exploitative potential. They may not be able to reduce conditionality, but they can reshape it. In other words, the reformists favor engagement with the global system on terms and conditions carefully selected and coordinated by a state committed to social interests and accountable to its citizens. They seek to rewrite the rules of globalization, to make it work for people and not just profits. Such ideals are summed up by the slogan "Another world is possible."[66]

In addition, the advocates of a post–Washington Consensus argue that local people should be encouraged to evolve development solutions that are self-governing and culturally appropriate, in conformity with their own norms and practices. They contend that projects should begin on a small scale. Community successes can then be scaled up to regional and even national levels, but remain reflective of local ways of life and prioritize social responsibility. They suggest that in some cases the end result may be a hybrid, a fusion of two or more approaches that may even still include aspects of the neoliberal model. For example, they recognize the necessity of a free market, but argue for a more flexible one in which governments set their own path and pace for reform. Some offer China as a model for the flexible approach. Its gradual installation of eco-

nomic reforms, including the creation of rural industry to employ displaced farmers, hasn't been without hardship (inequality continues to be a major problem), but it has resulted in high, consistent growth for over twenty-five years.[67]

Other initiatives include a variety of successful grassroots-based projects that exist throughout the global south. Whether they come in the form of cooperatives, microenterprises, or the like, grassroots-based projects are the purest expression of the idea of "development of the people, for the people, by the people." Advocates of this approach insist that participation that includes the poor and previously excluded groups is key to human security. Sustainable development is a people-centered development. Examples of success stories in terms of participatory, sustainable development include the not-for-profit, local public water management utility operated with citizen oversight in Porto Alegre, Brazil. Similarly, youth groups in Nepal and Bangladesh have coordinated villagers to install public toilets or latrines that benefit all.[68] This approach values local knowledge and wisdom as the basis for an authentic development. While the government can play an enabling role, providing people with the opportunity and environment for self-development, a just and sustainable development is based in ownership and inclusiveness—it is a people's movement, not a foreign-funded initiative.[69]

Such a line of attack demands a fundamental shift away from the majority of development thinking, which takes a highly centralized TOP-DOWN APPROACH. We shouldn't be treating targeted populations as victims to be "saved." This only winds up patronizing and ultimately alienating the very people whom agencies are trying to assist. Instead, a participatory, grassroots approach is decentralized and BOTTOM-UP: it views the targeted population as a rich source of information, as the real experts on the environment in which they live, as conveyors of a culture that has sustained them for thousands of years. Economist Nancy Birdsall is an advocate of this approach, which is based in the idea that donors should trust local people and give them more control over aid spending, because it is the people who live there who know what they need and the best way to deliver results. She calls for cash-on-delivery aid, in which aid donors and recipients draw up a contract that recipients design and implement. Together they come up with a solution to an agreed-upon problem and donors pay agreed-upon sums only after specific outcomes are achieved (such as reducing HIV transmission or maternal mortality rates).[70]

Democratically determined development is manifested in a variety of forms. Among other things, it focuses on long-term goals of practical relevance while also setting immediate targets that are achievable in the near term.[71] It may involve land reform, a focus on small farmers and the production of staple foods, enhancement of the role of women as agents of change, satisfaction of critical needs, investment in human capital, or any variety of self-help programs.[72] The Grameen Bank, founded in Bangladesh in 1976 by economist Muhammad Yunus (recipient of the 2006 Nobel Peace Prize), is a powerful example of how a seemingly novel, indigenous-based, bottom-up approach can effectively alleviate poverty. The opposite of a trickle-down approach, the Grameen Bank offers microcredit, or small, microenterprise loans (the average is $395) to the landless, poor, and others without collateral. The vast majority of the landless and poor targeted for assistance by the Grameen Bank are women (97 percent), whose only other choice would be to turn to moneylenders or loan sharks.[73] But these microcreditors do much more

than provide credit to those without collateral. They foster entrepreneurship and emphasize self-employment over wage labor. Loans are not extended for immediate consumption needs, but as seed money to encourage the startup of small businesses. For example, a woman might borrow just enough money to buy thread and start an embroidery business, or open a small kiosk or lunch stand. Or, where telephones are a luxury, she might buy a cell phone and charge for its use.[74]

Critics argue that programs such as these and many initiatives associated with the Millennium Development Goals fail to address the structural causes of poverty, but such programs can make a real and immediate difference in people's lives. On the other hand, a comprehensive approach that combines grassroots-based programs focusing on individuals with larger-scale efforts aimed at changing the playing field may hold the most promise of all. But the larger-scale efforts have proven to be more problematic. For example, many of the analysts promoting a reglobalization or deglobalization doubt the benefits to LICs of entering into free trade agreements with HICs. Too often such agreements have undermined labor rights, proven environmentally costly, and wound up leaving the developing country more dependent on its rich partner. They argue that we need to reorient globalization to give poor countries the space they need to restructure their economies and promote new industries while addressing concerns over inequality and distributive justice.[75]

With a view to making change on a larger scale, many countries have attempted to emulate the success of the European Union (EU) and promote regional integration. As we discuss in greater depth in Chapter 17, many of the more successful efforts at integration began as initiatives to reduce barriers and promote preferential trade arrangements between partners. Building on their successes, they later developed into political and security alliances as well. Regional trade accords have proliferated since 1995; the WTO counts more than 500 created since 1948. Every part of the world has undertaken a number of attempts to build strength in numbers and harness its economic energies in order to create economies of scale and to lessen dependency on developed countries.[76] In this effort to gain strength from numbers, these experiments have varied widely in their ability to create growth or development, let alone produce any leverage within the international economic system for developing countries. If globalization is indeed the only game in town, the countries of the global south must try to strengthen their position by diversifying their trading relationships.

The rise of giant economies such as China, India, and Brazil has provided many countries with a way to do just this. As with the Association of Southeast Asian Nations (ASEAN), the BRICs (Brazil, Russia, India, China) have significantly increased their economic linkages to their neighbors in recent years, and are expanding their reach. The most prominent example is again China, whose primary interest in the rest of the global south is as a market for its manufactured goods, as a source of natural resources for its industry, and as a source of lucrative investment. However, China is beginning to disappoint as an alternative to the West. Because of asymmetries in its relationships with other countries, China's activities in Asia and Africa in particular (but also the Middle East and Latin America significantly) are increasingly resented and characterized as a new colonialism.[77]

Such asymmetries are not limited to but have long plagued intraregional trade blocs, leading to tensions, disputes, and (in more than one case) the demise of these unions. Unless special and differential terms are accorded to members to make up

for disparities in power, the existence of regional hegemons is likely to mean that the benefits of even South-South integration will not be shared by all.

Conclusions: Must We Accept TINA?

In this chapter we have discussed some of the challenges experienced by the global south that are at least partially attributed to globalization and the adoption of the Washington Consensus. As we have seen, a variety of "post–Washington Consensus" development paradigms have been adopted, sometimes in combination with other alternatives. Some are radical and others reformist; some focus on individuals as agents of change while others promote international cooperation. Yet repeatedly we are reminded by neoliberals that "there is no alternative." Neoliberalism remains hegemonic, so much so that adherents do not even self-identify as neoliberals because "the ideology is almost a given in establishment policymaking circles."[78] Even critics of globalization agree that it can seem unstoppable. Most debtor economies are expected to conform to the rules and accept the adjustments pressed upon them by their creditors. With very few exceptions, low- and middle-income countries are operating within the constraints of a global capitalist system.

As we have seen, even within the IMF, there is a growing recognition of the need for further adjustments, recognizing especially the role that open borders and austerity have on increasing inequality. Within an IMF publication, scholars highlight that while "there is much to cheer in the neoliberal agenda . . . there are aspects of the neoliberal agenda that have not delivered as expected."[79] They especially indict the free borders granted to MNCs (for exposing economies to undue volatility) as well as austerity plans that combine to increase inequality, setting up, in their words, an "adverse feedback loop" that imperils growth and development alike.[80]

It is important to recognize that while they are not powerless, the political leaders of non-Western countries are limited in their capacity to make decisions. To some degree, of course, this is true for the leaders of relatively rich countries as well. With a total national debt of nearly $20 trillion as of December 2016, the United States has several times the combined debt of all of the developing world.[81] However, because of the advantageous position of the United States within the international economic system, and because it is a leading member of the international economic organizations calling the shots, even the world's largest debtor is not held accountable to the rules in the same way that less powerful debtors are.

It's true that the world's largest debtor isn't held accountable to the rules in the same way that less powerful debtors are. But in an interesting twist, the countries that usually play the role of neoliberal enforcer have jumped ship and are now playing the role of anti-establishment renegade seeking to overthrow the established order. The turning point was the 2008 recession, but by 2016 enough of these leaders were rising to power to make it feel at least like an upheaval.

But these aren't exactly the structuralists you've been reading about. In recent years the status quo has become unacceptable in much of the global north, where no one was paying attention to the many people who feel left behind by globalization. Within the global north there is a divide between those who, as Dani Rodrik put it, "can take advantage of the global economy and those who don't have the resources and skills to do so."[82] Precarious global markets, disappointing recoveries for some, painful

austerity for others—all this has produced an angry, seething populism, a backlash that blames globalization and political dysfunction for no jobs or low-paying jobs.[83] What we have is a global populist insurrection of sorts against the establishment and it has resulted in political shocks in more than one country. Brexit was a sign of what was coming, and President Trump is just one of a rising chorus of voices from both ends of the political spectrum to offer a rebuke to the neoliberal orthodoxy.

One thing that Bernie Sanders and Donald Trump tapped into was the desire to turn away from neoliberalism (and with it free trade). Instead, they called for a reining in of the excesses of globalization, an economic nationalism based on protectionism, tariffs, and standing up to corporations that have put their quarterly earnings above all else.[84] But from there neoliberalism's critics from the left and right diverge. Renegades on the right throughout the global north are calling for what sounds a lot like the state capitalism used by authoritarians in East Asia decades ago. Through aggressive state intervention they promise to create a government that revives dying sectors of the economy and bring back jobs for those who have been dispossessed. Their blueprint for action takes the opposite of a laissez-faire approach. Instead, the state should set out to reclaim its autonomy and the sovereignty lost to globalization and become a driving force in the economy, playing an active role guiding investment strategies, offering tax breaks, and keeping unions weak, wages low, and regulations minimal to lure investment.

After years of hearing that there is no alternative to neoliberalism, it turns out that we only had to look to the past to see the option that was there all along. Previous cycles of rising globalization have always been followed by retreat. The push led by Trump and others has turned what has been the accepted wisdom on its head, at least for now. We will have to wait and see how far the world goes down this road. But if this trend does result in a deglobalization, it certainly won't be the first time. And as it did the last time, such policies may lead to trade wars or worse.[85] Sure, it may not come to this. In the meantime, many people in the global south must be watching all this with some bemusement, at the very least, at how the global north is reacting to a taste of its own medicine.

Notes

1. Chimamanda Ngozi Adichie, "Chimamanda Ngozi Adichie: Nigeria's Failed Promises," *New York Times,* October 18, 2016.

2. "Breaking the Poverty Cycle," *Asiaweek* 26, no. 40 (October 13, 2000).

3. Sam Perlo-Freeman, Olawale Ismail, and Carina Solmirano, "Military Expenditure," *SIPRI Yearbook 2010,* Stockholm International Peace Research Institute, November 23, 2010, www.sipri.org.

4. Ross P. Buckley, "Improve the Living Standards in Poor Countries: Reform the IMF," *Emory Law Review* 24, no. 1 (April 1, 2010); "Mission: Possible," *The Economist,* April 11, 2009.

5. "Austerity Alarm," *The Economist,* July 3, 2010; "Counting Their Blessings," *The Economist,* January 2, 2010.

6. "China Healthcare Costs Forcing Patients into Crippling Debt," Reuters, July 10, 2016; World Bank, "Report Recommends Deeper Healthcare Reforms in China," July 22, 2016.

7. Organization for Economic Cooperation and Development (OECD), "Economic Survey of China, 2010: Improving the Health Care System," February 2, 2010, www.oecd.org; Elisabeth Rosenthal, "Without 'Barefoot Doctors' China's Rural Families Suffer," *New York Times,* March 14, 2001.

8. Nancy Birdsall, "Managing Inequality in the Developing World," in *Annual Editions: Developing World 01–02,* ed. Robert J. Griffiths (Guilford, CT: McGraw-Hill/Dushkin, 2001).

9. Tom Evans, "'Water Justice' Advocate: Don't Privatize," January 8, 2010, www .cnn.com; Juan Forero, "Who Will Bring Water to the Bolivian Poor?," *New York Times,* December 15, 2005.

10. John Vidal, "Water Privatization: A Worldwide Failure?," *The Guardian* (London), January 30, 2015.

11. Kelly Morrison, "The End of an Era," Council on Hemispheric Affairs, June 19, 2014, www.coha.org; Michael Slackman, "Egypt Concedes to Resistance on Privatization 'Push,'" *New York Times,* June 27, 2010; Vikas Bajaj, "As India Sells Assets, Political Tensions Rise," *New York Times,* February 24, 2010.

12. Barbara Wang and Harold Chee, "China's Public Sector: A Different Way of Working," *The Guardian* (London), January 3, 2012.

13. Laura He, "Analysts Raise Red Flag as China's State Sector Reverses Nearly 20 Years of Declines in the Share of the Economy," *South China Morning Post,* November 28, 2016.

14. "Whatever Happened to the Food Crisis?," *The Economist,* July 4, 2009; Heather Timmons and Hari Kumar, "Protests over Fuel Costs Idle Much of India," *New York Times,* July 5, 2010.

15. Steve H. Hanke, "Regime Change?," *Forbes,* June 5, 2006, www.forbes.com.

16. "Zambia: The Hard Road to HIPC Completion," *Africa News,* January 6, 2005; Jubilee USA, "A Silent War," www.jubileeusa.org; Jubilee USA, "Ebola Debt Relief Victory," www.jubileeusa.org.

17. "The IMF and Good Governance—Address by Michel Camdessus," International Monetary Fund, January 21, 1998, www.imf.org; Daron Acemoglu and James Robinson, *Why Nations Fail: The Origins of Power, Prosperity, and Poverty* (New York: Crown, 2013).

18. Acemoglu and Robinson, *Why Nations Fail.* This is ironic, since one of the least-liberalized countries in the region, the People's Republic of China, was also the emerging economy least affected by the Asian crisis. In a remarkable exception to neoliberal rules, China has not been subjected to an austerity plan, but it has soaked up the largest amount of the world's foreign investment.

19. "The Beijing Consensus Is to Keep Quiet," *The Economist,* May 6, 2010.

20. "IMF Reforms Clear Last Hurdle with US Adoption," BBC News, December 19, 2015; Sewell Chan, "Perils Remain Despite Recovery's Pace, IMF Head Says," *New York Times,* April 25, 2010; "Mission: Possible," *The Economist;* Center for Global Development, "London Summit Q & A with Nancy Birdsall," March 30, 2009, www.cgdev.org.

21. David White, "Stuck in Poverty After 40 Years of Aid," *Financial Times,* November 25, 2004; "Ghana," CIA, *World Factbook 2016.*

22. United Nations Development Programme (UNDP), *Human Development Report 1999,* www.undp.org.

23. "Zambia: The Hard Road to HIPC Completion," *Africa News,* January 6, 2005.

24. Kanishk Tharoor, "The Rise and Fall of Great World Cities: 5,700 Years of Urbanisation—Mapped," *The Guardian* (London), June 27, 2016; UN Habitat, "World Habitat Day: Background Paper," July 2014, www.unhabitat.org.

25. Mark Swilling, "The Curse of Urban Sprawl: How Cities Grow, and Why This Has to Change," *The Guardian* (London), July 12, 2016.

26. Ibid.

27. "Zimbabwe," CIA, *World Factbook 2016.*

28. Valentine M. Moghadam, *Globalizing Women* (Baltimore: Johns Hopkins University Press, 2005).

29. Ibid.

30. UN Women, "Facts and Figures: Ending Violence Against Women," February 2016, www.unwomen.org; UNDP, "Living Up to Commitments," in *UNDP Annual Report 2009,* May 2009, www.undp.com. UN Women (2016) also reports that national studies indicate that up to 70 percent of women have experienced physical and/or sexual violence from an intimate partner in their lifetime.

31. Moghadam, *Globalizing Women;* Gabriela Wiener, "The Day Peruvian Women Rebelled," *New York Times,* August 23, 2016.

32. Virginia M. Moncrieff, "Afghanistan Election: Woman Candidate Braves Retaliation with Presidential Run," *Huffington Post,* June 23, 2009.

33. Valentine M. Moghadam, *Gender and National Identity* (London: Zed, 1994).

34. Patrick Kingsley, "80 Sexual Assaults in One Day: The Other Story of Tahrir Square," *The Guardian* (London), July 5, 2013.

35. Monica Campbell, "Why Mexico City's Bad Air Can't Be Ignored—or Fixed," *PRI: The World,* May 12, 2016; Mica Rosenberg, "Mexico City Smog Hurting People's Sense of Smell," Reuters, June 4, 2008.

36. World Health Organization (WHO), "Air Pollution Levels Rising in Many of the World's Poorest Cities," May 12, 2016, www.who.int.

37. World Bank, "Deforestation," 2015; Sakshi Rai, "On the Frontline: Landless and Displaced—the Future of Indigenous Tribes in India?," *Discover Society,* October 4, 2016.

38. Sarah Porter, "Can Indonesia's Forest Fires Be Put Out for Good?," BBC News, March 14, 2016.

39. John Vidal, "Nigeria's Agony Dwarfs the Gulf Oil Spill: The US and Europe Ignore It," *The Guardian* (London), May 30, 2010.

40. Joshua E. Keating, "The World's Ongoing Ecological Disasters," *Foreign Policy,* July 16, 2010, www.foreignpolicy.com.

41. Graciela Chichilinisky, "Financial Innovations and Carbon Markets," *UN Chronicle* 66, no. 3 (January 8, 2009); Coral Davenport and Campbell Robertson, "Resetting the First American 'Climate Refugees,'" *New York Times,* May 3, 2016; Bradley C. Parks and J. Timmons Roberts, "Inequality and the Global Climate Regime: Breaking the North-South Impasse," *Cambridge Review of International Affairs* 21, no. 4 (December 2008). The estimates vary widely because of disputes about measurement. For more discussion about the challenges of estimation and some of the controversies related to these figures, see Hannah Barnes, "How Many Climate Refugees Will There Be?," BBC News, September 2, 2013.

42. "Embedding the Environment in Sustainable Development Goals," United Nations Environment Programme, 2013, www.sustainabledevelopment.un.org.

43. Peter Bossard, "The Forgotten Downstream Victims of Large Dams," *Huffington Post,* June 18, 2010; David Stoez, Charles Guzzetta, and Mark Lusk, *International Development* (Boston: Allyn and Bacon, 1999).

44. Maria Cheng and Christina Okello, "Tons of Bushmeat Smuggled into Paris, Study Finds," *Huffington Post,* June 17, 2010; Biosynergy Institute, "The Bushmeat Project," 2004, www.bushmeat.net; Sharon Begley, "Is That an Alligator in Your Suitcase?," *Newsweek,* June 18, 2010.

45. WHO, "Dengue and Severe Dengue," July 2016, www.who.int.

46. United Nations, "Progress Towards the Millennium Development Goals, 1990–2005," www.unstats.un.org.

47. World Bank, "Health Expenditure per Capita," 2014.

48. Susan George, *The Debt Boomerang: How Third World Debt Harms Us All* (Boulder: Westview, 1992).

49. Roberto Fendt, "The Brasilia Consensus: A New Model for Development?," Center for International Private Enterprise (CIPE), September 27, 2004, www.cipe.org.

50. "The Gloves Go On," *The Economist,* November 28, 2009.

51. Alexander Kentikelenis, Thomas Stubbs, and Lawrence King, "Did the IMF Actually Ease Up on Structural Adjustment? Here's What the Data Say," *Washington Post,* June 2, 2016.

52. Ibid.

53. "Interview with IMF Managing Director Rodrigo de Rato," *People's Daily Online,* July 9, 2004.

54. International Monetary Fund (IMF), "Quota Reform," in *Annual Report 2016*.

55. Ibid.; Steven R. Weisman, "IMF Votes to Enhance Power of China and Others," *New York Times,* September 19, 2009; IMF, "Factsheet: IMF Quotas," March 11, 2010,

www.imf.org; "IMF Board Approves Far Reaching Governance Reform," *IMF Survey Magazine,* November 5, 2010.

56. "A Slow Maturing of Democracy," *The Economist,* December 12, 2009.

57. Joseph Kahn, "International Lenders' New Image: A Human Face," *New York Times,* September 26, 2000.

58. Jorge Nef, *Human Security and Mutual Vulnerability* (Ottawa: International Development and Research Centre, 1999).

59. UNDP, "A Decade to Eradicate Poverty," in *Annual Editions: Developing World 01–02,* ed. Robert J. Griffiths (Guilford, CT: McGraw-Hill/Dushkin, 2001); John Tessitore and Susan Woolfson, eds., *A Global Agenda: Issues Before the Fifty-Fourth General Assembly of the United Nations* (Lanham: Rowman and Littlefield, 1999).

60. Dot Keet, "Alternatives to Neoliberal Globalization," Transnational Institute, October 2010.

61. Joseph Stiglitz, *Making Globalization Work* (London: Penguin, 2006).

62. World Bank, "Social Safety Nets: Lessons from Rich and Poor Countries," April 24, 2009, www.worldbank.org.

63. Stiglitz, *Making Globalization Work.*

64. Julius E. Nyang'oro and Timothy M. Shaw, "The African State in the Global Economic Context," in *The African State at a Critical Juncture: Between Disintegration and Reconfiguration,* ed. Julius E. Nyang'oro and Timothy M. Shaw (Boulder: Lynne Rienner, 1998); Theodore H. Cohn, *Global Political Economy: Theory and Practice* (New York: Longman, 2000).

65. Michael Hardt and Antonio Negri, "What the Protesters in Genoa Want," *New York Times,* July 20, 2001; Thomas L. Friedman, "Evolutionaries," *New York Times,* July 20, 2001.

66. Nyang'oro and Shaw, "The African State in the Global Economic Context"; Daniel Kauffmann, "Aid Effectiveness and Governance: The Good, the Bad, and the Ugly," Development Outreach, World Bank Institute, February 2009, www.worldbank.org; "Meanwhile, in Another World," *The Economist,* February 9, 2002.

67. Meredith Woo-Cumings, "Introduction: Chalmers Johnson and the Politics of Nationalism and Development," in *The Developmental State,* ed. Meredith Woo-Cumings (Ithaca: Cornell University Press, 1999); Jorge Castañeda, *Utopia Unarmed* (New York: Knopf, 1993).

68. Elisabeth Malkin, "At World Forum, Support Erodes for Private Management of Water," *New York Times,* March 20, 2005.

69. Adebayo Adedeji, "Popular Participation, Democracy, and Development: Is There a Dialectical Linkage?," in *Nigeria: Renewal from the Roots? The Struggle for Democratic Development,* ed. Adebayo Adedji, Onigu Otite, Kunle Amuwo, et al. (London: Zed, 1997); Judith A. Teichman, *The Politics of Inclusive Development: Policy, State Capacity, and Coalition Building* (New York: Palgrave Macmillan, 2016).

70. "More Is More?," *The Economist,* June 12, 2010.

71. United Nations Development Fund for Women (UNIFEM), "Making the MDGs Work for All: Gender-Responsive Rights-Based Approaches to the MDGs," November 2008, www.unifem-eseasia.org.

72. Adedeji, "Popular Participation, Democracy, and Development."

73. Celia W. Dugger, "Peace Prize to Pioneer of Loans to Poor No Bank Would Touch," *New York Times,* October 14, 2006; Grameen Bank, "Banking for the Poor: Grameen Bank at a Glance," October 2010, www.grameen-info.org.

74. Grameen Bank, "Banking for the Poor."

75. Julio Boltvinik and Araceli Damián, "Irrelevance of the MDGs and a Real Solution to Poverty: Universal Citizen's Income," in *Poverty and the Millennium Development Goals: A Critical Look Forward,* ed. Alberto Cimadamore, Gabriele Koehler, and Thomas Pogge (London: Zed, 2016); Dani Rodrik, "Put Globalization to Work for Democracies," *New York Times,* September 18, 2016, www.nytimes.com.

76. World Trade Organization (WTO), "Regional Trade Agreements: Facts and Figures," 2016, www.wto.org.

77. Khadija Sharife, "China's New Colonialism," *Foreign Policy,* September 25, 2009.

78. Jon Stone, "Neoliberalism Is Increasing Inequality and Stunting Economic Growth, IMF Says," *The Independent* (London), May 27, 2016, www.independent.co.uk.

79. Jonathan D. Ostry, Prakash Loungani, and Davide Furceri, "Neoliberalism Oversold?," *Finance and Development* 53, no. 2 (2016), p. 38.

80. Ibid., p. 40.

81. David Ransom, "The Dictatorship of Debt," *New Internationalist,* no. 312 (May 1999), www.oneworld.net; US National Debt Clock, accessed December 11, 2016, www .usdebtclock.org.

82. Dani Rodrik, "Put Globalization to Work for Democracies."

83. Alissa J. Rubin, "New Wave of Popular Fury Could Hit Europe in 2017," *New York Times,* December 6, 2016.

84. Gardiner Harris, "In Europe, Obama Warns Against Nationalism," *New York Times,* November 16, 2016.

85. Ruchir Sharma, "When Borders Close," *New York Times,* November 12, 2016.

Chapter 8

Linking
Concepts and Cases

As we turn now to a discussion of how our eight case studies are faring in the international economic system, think about the impact of the Great Recession on each. Identify some of the various ways in which these countries are coping with the economic pressures on them.

How are our cases doing in terms of growth and development? Have there been any significant changes in their economic fortunes since this book was published? Which countries do you consider to be better-off? Which are performing the worst? Why have some countries been more successful in their adoption of neoliberalism than others? How do you define "success"? How do you see the struggle between growth and development playing out in these countries? How did these countries fare in their progress in achieving the Millennium Development Goals? In which countries has the pursuit of economic growth meant environmental devastation? How dependent is each of these countries on the export of raw materials? How diversified are their economies? Is it appropriate to characterize all (or any) of these countries as "developing," or "under-developing"? Why?

Case Study: Mexico

Mexico today is in many ways considered by the West to be a model of economic reform. However, twenty years earlier the country was at the epicenter of a debt crisis. Its economic problems can be traced at least as far back as the 1970s, when it was one of the world's largest oil producers. Oil prices had reached an all-time high and governments of the Institutional Revolutionary Party (PRI) borrowed large sums and spent lavishly. Unfortunately for Mexico, oil prices dropped by the early 1980s and the country was left with one of the largest debts in the world—$80 billion. The government had borrowed far beyond its means, was being charged exorbitant interest rates, and could not keep up with its payments.[1]

After Mexico rocked the international financial system by threatening to default on its debt, the country was compelled to adopt a series of austerity plans throughout the 1980s. However, Mexico's economic problems continued and its debt piled

up. By late 1994, in order to win US support for Mexico's membership in the North American Free Trade Agreement (NAFTA), Mexico agreed to the terms of another round of economic reforms. Mexico had little choice but to faithfully meet the conditions outlined by the International Monetary Fund (IMF). These included a series of measures, including a 40 percent devaluation of the peso, that went into effect literally overnight. The combined effect of the reforms proved a shock to the system. Growth rates plunged into the negative digits. Inflation and interest rates soared. The effect was like that of a financial neutron bomb: it destroyed the population, leaving only the real estate standing.[2]

The gravity of this crisis spurred the IMF to provide Mexico with a $40 billion emergency bailout package—at the time the largest rescue ever. This intervention prevented Mexico from defaulting on its debt and enabled it to continue on with its economic reform. Growth rates have been up and down since then, with two steep declines but growth rates averaging 2 percent.[3] Much of this growth has been due to the country's membership in NAFTA, a free trade zone between the United States, Canada, and Mexico. Because goods produced in Mexico can be exported duty-free to either of its NAFTA partners, and because of Mexico's low wages and lax enforcement of environmental regulations, multinational corporations eagerly set up shop in the country. Since the passage of NAFTA trade between the United States and Mexico has taken off, growing from $104 billion in 1994 to $583 billion in 2015.[4]

As the country made the transition to a manufacturing economy the numbers of *maquiladoras* in Mexico have mushroomed and created millions of jobs, but with devastating results for rivers, which are now rank with industrial by-products and raw sewage. Many Mexicans farming on small plots have had a hard time holding on after NAFTA eliminated tariffs and opened up Mexico to competition against US and Canadian agribusinesses, which could now sell their cheaper foodstuffs in Mexico duty-free. Yet by other measures NAFTA has been a boon for the Mexican economy, which is the second largest in Latin America.[5] There is so much back-and-forth between the US and Mexican supply chains that 40 percent of the content of the products the US imports from Mexico actually comes from the United States. In other words, it may say "made in Mexico," but these goods are made in both the United States and Mexico.[6] Moreover, because many of these companies are American-owned, much of the profit goes north.[7]

In terms of development, more needs to be done to close income gaps; democracy has not had much effect on lessening inequality in Mexico.[8] The richest 1 percent own almost half the country's wealth, and almost half the population lives below the poverty line. Extreme poverty has dropped, but just barely. As a result, Mexico has the highest income inequality of all Organization for Economic Cooperation and Development (OECD) countries.[9]

On the other hand, Mexico is on track to achieve its Millennium Development Goals by 2020. This is partly due to its model conditional cash-transfer program now known as Prospera. Nearly 25 percent of the population benefits from this program, which incentivizes healthcare, nutrition, and school attendance (including a onetime payment for those graduating from high school).[10]

Because Mexico's market is already one of the most open in Latin America, the country's experience illustrates both the benefits and the risks of globalization. The Great Recession, which began in the United States in 2007, hit Mexico harder than

any other Latin American country. Economic contraction in its neighbor to the north dramatically affected demand for Mexican goods.[11] It should come as no surprise (given that 80 percent of the country's exports go to the United States) that analysts make their forecasts for Mexico based on the status of its major trading partner to the north, and its recovery was (and is) largely dependent on that of its northern neighbor. As of 2016, Mexico was suffering from slow growth, at 2.5 percent annually.[12]

President Enrique Peña Nieto believes that the answer to these financial woes is a more vigorous application of neoliberal principles. But so far at least, the "Aztec Kitten" has not transformed into an "Aztec Tiger," replicating the success of Asian economies.[13] Mexico's economy is stagnating, suffering from a slow growth compared to India and China. There are a variety of reasons for this, including slumping oil prices, which haven't helped this oil producer. Yes, there are more Mexican millionaires than ever and the middle class has grown and amounts to nearly half the population. But most people aren't seeing benefits of Peña Nieto's economic reforms and public confidence is down, particularly because so little appears to have been done about corruption and other forms of crime, which take a toll on growth and development.[14] In Mexico, which once prided itself on having the lowest unemployment rates in Latin America, over 20 percent of the population is unemployed or underemployed. Over half of the Mexican population works in the informal sector. And the wage convergence promised to come with NAFTA has yet to appear. US autoworkers earn five times more than their counterparts in Mexico, who make on average $5 an hour. Still, this is much better than the minimum wage in Mexico, which is $4 a day. Adding to the pain is the fact that the peso had depreciated to record lows against the dollar. This means higher prices for imports when 42 percent of Mexicans were already having a hard time making ends meet on their salaries. Donald Trump's election introduced even more uncertainty. Since November 2016 the peso has plummeted and analysts have cut their growth forecasts for Mexico.[15] So it can't be surprising that when asked to rate their satisfaction with their lives on a scale of 0 to 10, most Mexicans gave it a 6.2, a D.[16] As you can imagine, they're likely feeling rueful when hearing claims that their country is a model for economic reform.

Case Study: Peru

Since independence, Peru has struggled through fifty-year cycles of debt, dependence, and default.[17] In the nineteenth century its economy was based on the export of raw materials such as guano and nitrates, and it has been dependent on the sale of agricultural goods and mineral products for much of the past hundred years. Here is a country where the gap between rich and poor is only recently beginning to show signs of closing. As discussed in Chapter 5, a tiny elite of landowners and merchants has long controlled the country's wealth.

In the 1970s, prices for Peru's exports plummeted while its expenditures rose, and the country fell deeply into debt. Peru was in crisis. By the 1980s its creditors were demanding that the country pay half of all the hard currency it earned each year to service its debt of $16 billion. Unable to keep up with its payments, Peru fell $1 billion into arrears. In what has been described as a "brave but dumb" strategy, then-president Alan García declared a moratorium on servicing its debt, limiting payments to 10 percent of its export earnings. The international financial community

responded by making Peru ineligible for credit. Peru became a pariah—desperate for cash, forced to dramatically cut imports, and living day to day. Economic trends in Peru in the 1980s were among the worst in Latin America—and the region as a whole was struggling with what is often called the "lost decade."[18]

By the end of García's term many Peruvians were frantic for another approach. Although as a presidential candidate Alberto Fujimori had campaigned against IMF reforms, after his inauguration he promised that he could get results from an ambitious program of neoliberalism. With the backing of business elites, the new president undertook one of the most radical privatizations in Latin America and opened Peru to foreign investment. The displacement of workers associated with the sale of state-owned enterprises, combined with drastic cuts in social spending, was likened to a form of shock therapy (so named for the invasive psychiatric procedure in which the patient is nearly killed in order to be saved). This policy became known in Peru as "Fujishock."

In this case the patient reacted by going into a deep recession. The sudden lack of government services, including sanitation and potable water, paved the way for a reappearance of cholera, a poverty-related disease that had been unknown in Peru since the 1800s. Some parts of Peru had never before known such economic distress. Yet because Fujimori was willing to push through the reforms, Peru was able to resuscitate its relationship with the IMF and obtain debt relief. By the mid-1990s foreign investment was up and the country was registering impressive growth rates. Most important for Peruvians, inflation was brought down to the lowest levels in forty years. Despite the hardship associated with Fujishock, the end to hyperinflation bought the president enormous goodwill.[19]

Yet events beyond Fujimori's control soon brought that brief period of recovery to a close. Growth remained stagnant until Fujimori was forced to step down in 2000. Washington applauded as his successors continued with neoliberal reforms, but their policies were met with violent protests. Since the transition to democracy Peru has entered into a number of free trade agreements, including one with the United States.[20] It was on board with the Trans-Pacific Partnership, the enormous, controversial trade deal involving a dozen countries that Barack Obama supported and Donald Trump promised to halt, and appears open to going on with a similar deal, without US participation.[21]

For the past decade and a half, in macroeconomic terms, the Peruvian economy appeared to be one of the most vibrant in the region, often characterized as thriving. Growth rates in Peru ranged from 0.6 to a whopping 9 percent per year during the 2000s, based largely on a growing Asian (especially Chinese) demand and higher prices for its minerals. The global financial crisis did take a toll, but growth rebounded to a high of 8.5 percent by 2010.[22] The services sector (telecommunications and financial services) has recently surpassed mining as the main contributor to the country's gross domestic product (GDP), with nearly 60 percent of GDP stemming from this sector. As of early 2017, Peru was being rocked by a huge corruption scandal involving previous administrations, which was also hitting much of the rest of Latin America. This turmoil hurt most forecasts for the economy, but Peru had cut its debt to almost half of what it had been twenty years earlier. Compared to Brazil and Mexico, Peru isn't considered to have a lot of debt. For several years Peru's has been considered one of the strongest, most stable economies in Latin America.[23]

Remarkably, generally stable, healthy growth since the Great Recession has translated into some improvements in the lives of more Peruvians. Gross national income (GNI) per capita grew steadily from $1,900 in 2001 to $6,370 in 2014, before dipping slightly in 2015.[24] The percentage of the Peruvian population earning less than $2 a day has been cut from 58 percent to about 22 percent over the past decade (2004–2014).[25] Much more still needs to be done to extend the benefits of this growth to a greater proportion of the population and to reduce poverty.[26]

Growth without development can be a problem, as it can impact investment. Peruvian governments have looked to open the Peruvian Amazon to business, to develop "idle land" in order to develop the country and create jobs, by boldly granting new oil and gas concessions to large (many of them foreign) corporations in territories long claimed by indigenous communities (and thus closed to such production).[27] The government's promotion of extractive projects, mining, as well as oil and gas has resulted in a series of socio-environmental conflicts in Peru. For example, at least three demonstrators were killed in protests against a Chinese-owned mining project in 2015.[28] We see in Peru that neoliberal economic policy has been criticized as not only destructive to the environment, but also as racist, awakening what some see as a sustained, unprecedented wave of indigenous social activism.

As a result, Peru is ranked by investors as "medium risk." There are riskier places, but social unrest always poses a challenge—regardless of any government's openness to investment.[29] Peru's 2016 presidential election was largely a contest between two candidates both set on continuing the neoliberal model as a means of attracting investment and reinvigorating the economy. Pedro Pablo Kuczynski (known as PPK), an investment banker who previously worked for the World Bank and IMF, and who won the election, campaigned for tax exemptions for corporations and is popular with business. But this right-of-center technocrat seems to recognize the need to promote development as well as growth—to improve public health including access to drinking water and sanitation and to reduce corruption.[30] Yet it remains to be seen whether PPK can get the cooperation from the opposition-controlled parliament to follow through on those promises. This leaves Peru in a curious situation. Much is made of Peru having the strongest economy in Latin America, but Peruvians, living in a democracy, still can't count on basic needs like water.

Case Study: Nigeria

As the world's sixth largest exporter of oil, Nigeria would seem to be the envy of much of the world. However, Nigeria is also one of the world's poorest countries. Seventy percent of the population lives below the official poverty line.[31] Oil didn't guarantee Mexico's development, and it is often said to be a curse for Nigeria.

Part of the problem is that one Nigerian government after another has stolen a large portion of the hundreds of billions of dollars in revenue generated by oil. And what hasn't been stolen has often been misspent. Windfalls from the days when oil prices were high were wasted on "white elephants." Worse, Nigeria is known as being "fantastically corrupt."[32]

But before all the blame goes to corrupt or incompetent policymakers, a word needs to be said about the role of multinational corporations (MNCs) in Nigeria, especially Shell Oil, the region's biggest operator, which carries on with little or no

government oversight.[33] The Niger Delta, site of most of the country's onshore petroleum and natural gas reserves, is an environmental basket case. Although it has received almost no attention from the international media, it is estimated that 13 million barrels of oil have been spilled in Nigeria's wetlands, which is equivalent to an *Exxon Valdez* disaster every year for the past fifty years. The large oil companies have rarely if ever cleaned up. These companies resist taking responsibility for the devastation, however, blaming most of the spills from pipelines on oil pirates, pipeline sabotage, and illegal refining.[34] It is true that oil theft by cartels is a big business as well. Meanwhile, the Niger Delta remains one of the country's poorest areas. Little of the wealth created by the extraction of oil has been returned to its residents.[35]

But this poverty is hardly restricted to the country's southeast. Nigeria's rank on almost any level of human development is especially tragic given the country's tremendous potential. Its vast resources could provide a diversified economic base; its huge population could create an economy of scale. Particularly since the decline in oil prices since 2014, President Muhammadu Buhari has talked enthusiastically about his plan to diversify, investing in mining and agriculture. But there's no getting around the fact that Nigeria is a classic monocultural economy. Approximately 90 percent of its foreign exchange is earned from the sale of petroleum and petroleum-based products. Worse, the industry fails to serve or employ many Nigerians (it is estimated that youth unemployment is as high as 50 percent).[36] Ironically, because of the state of disrepair of its refineries, Nigeria actually has to import nearly 70 percent of its fuel needs; power outages that go on for days and long lines at gas stations are routine.[37]

Back in 1999 Nigerian citizens turned out at the polls hoping that after years of dictatorship a civilian-run government might be able to straighten out the country's economic mess. By the time he took office, Olusegun Obasanjo found the treasury empty and the country in arrears in repayment of a nearly $30 billion debt that exceeded 75 percent of the country's GDP. Obasanjo came into office desperate for debt relief.[38]

To stay in good stead with the IMF and other donors, Obasanjo and his successors all pledged themselves to be neoliberal reformers. They have attempted to raise revenues by increasing Nigeria's output of oil and by attracting foreign investment. They accepted austerity plans that (among other things) meant cutting government subsidies of food, which resulted in higher prices for basics.[39] And because it accepted the IMF's conditions, Nigeria was able to make a deal with the UK, France, and other creditors in 2005 to reduce its debt by $30 billion.[40]

Although some of the money saved by the debt relief was to go toward meeting basic human needs, Nigeria had mixed results in meeting the challenges of the Millennium Development Goals. It met its goals on maternal mortality and made progress on reducing diseases such as polio and HIV/AIDS and increasing enrollment in basic education, but it has not done much to increase the proportion of women in wage employment or in parliament, and it has largely failed to meet its goals in providing sanitation or dealing with the environmental challenges associated with climate change.[41] Life expectancy has lengthened only a bit, from forty-seven to fifty-three years. Infant mortality has been reduced more substantially (but is still high) at 72 deaths per 1,000 live births (compared to 5 infant deaths per 1,000 live births in the United States).[42] President Buhari, who inherited a virtually empty treasury, is having to borrow money just to pay the salaries of doctors, teachers, and civil servants.[43]

Moreover, after nearly two decades of civilian rule, severe inequality persists. From 2011 to 2014 economic growth rates remained relatively strong and steady (mostly due to high oil prices as well as demand for oil), averaging 4–6 percent annually. But even when business was good, income inequality persisted, and there was very little trickle down. As of early 2017, although there has been some growth in agricultural and other sectors, business is not good: oil prices globally are at the lowest point in two decades (a nearly 70 percent decline since 2014). Not only is Nigeria suffering due to the drastic decline in oil revenues, but the naira declined in value by over 50 percent during this same period, and foreign investment is the lowest since the financial crisis. All this, plus continued instability in the oil-producing regions, has contributed to the country's slip into a full-on recession in 2016. This was the first recession Nigeria had experienced since the return to democracy. Projected growth for 2017 was near zero, at 0.8 percent.[44]

What does a recession mean for the average Nigerian? Inflation has risen dramatically—to the highest rates in several years. This alone means devastation, as people already living in or on the edge of poverty are feeling the pain and simply can't obtain basic needs. Where the insurgent terrorist group Boko Haram has devastated food production, there is a looming humanitarian disaster that is killing hundreds every day.[45] It is worst in the northeast, but across the country supermarket shelves are sparse, fuel is rationed, prices are gouged. As one economist put it, it's like the country has been hit by a macro-hurricane.[46]

Not that long ago, foreign investors were bullish on newly democratic Nigeria. For years Nigeria and South Africa have run neck and neck, but in 2016 South Africa clearly surpassed Nigeria as the largest economy in Africa. With the opening of shale reserves and fracking, this oil giant's economic prospects simply aren't what they used to be. Africa's most populous country is left asking, "What's next?" Few Nigerians can answer that question, but they will tell you that they had expected more from democracy.

Case Study: Zimbabwe

With what was once its comparatively diverse base, Zimbabwe's economy should be better off than that of many other African countries. At independence it was relatively more industrialized than much of Africa, with its sugar refineries and textile industry. It sold tobacco, gold, and other minerals on the world market. A couple of decades ago it was able not only to feed its population, but also to export its surplus foodstuffs. Back then, under President Robert Mugabe and the government of the Zimbabwe African National Union–Patriotic Front (ZANU-PF), a liberation movement turned political party, Zimbabwe was making significant strides in human development with an antipoverty campaign as a priority. The new government invested heavily in schools and healthcare, undoing the years of neglect that had been policy under white minority rule. Such programs succeeded in attaining for Zimbabweans one of the highest literacy rates on the continent.[47]

However, deep in debt for many of the reasons mentioned in previous chapters, the Mugabe government had little choice but to accept the terms of a structural adjustment program (SAP) in 1991. Because of the budget cuts required by the IMF, the government's "Growth with Equity" program was reversed and the country was

losing the impressive gains it had made in terms of infant and child mortality and literacy rates. In much of Zimbabwe the SAP came to stand for "Suffering for African
People."[48] When the government decided to back away from structural reform after
1998, the international financial institutions (IFIs) withdrew their lines of credit, and
growth rates hovered around zero.

For years, things only got worse, with plenty of blame to go around. Growth
rates in 2008 were negative 18 percent and 80 percent of the population was living
below the poverty line.[49] People found that they could not afford basic necessities as
inflation grew from 22 percent in 1995 to 80 percent in 2000 to 500 billion percent
in 2008 (the highest rate on the planet).[50] The Zimbabwean dollar became worthless
(a 100 trillion Zimbabwean dollar note equaled about 35 cents US). With nothing
there for them, a full quarter of the population left the country. Those left behind
were eating one meal a day or less.[51] And famine was something that many Zimbabweans had thought was a thing of the past.

The Mugabe government blamed several years of drought and the IFIs for the
country's economic shambles. The World Bank and Western donors blamed the Mugabe government's corruption and mismanagement for the country's woes. Analysts
such as Richard Bourne contend that ZANU's stance and all that follows can be explained by Zimbabwe's history.[52] In 1999, Mugabe struck out on his own. He appealed to the 70 percent of the population who live in rural areas, resurrecting the
long-neglected issue of land reform (which dated back to the days of Rhodesia's
own apartheid) and seizing white-owned farms.[53]

Thousands of poor black farmers were supposed to get the lands, but they got
small plots; the best lands went to high-ranking officials. The effect on the economy
was clear. By 2006, harvests were half of what they were when the 2000 land reform
began.[54] Not only did the confiscation of large farms mean the loss of jobs for hundreds of thousands of farm laborers, but business confidence was in tatters, investors
were scared off, and tourism ground to a halt. In sum, the 2000s amounted to a head-
long fall into the abyss. Zimbabwe became a pariah for international lenders that
lasted fifteen years.[55] Its GDP growth rate hit a record low of negative 17.7 percent
in 2008.[56] As a snapshot of how bad it was for the average Zimbabwean, by 2006 life
expectancy had dropped from sixty-one years two decades earlier to thirty-seven—
the shortest in the world.[57]

Since hitting this nadir, there are signs that land reform was not a total disaster.
Some ordinary people have benefited from the program. They were able to access land
and they have become productive farmers.[58] In recent years the ZANU government
began negotiations to normalize relations with creditors. By 2015 Zimbabwe's debt ratios were high; its external debt burden was heavy, estimated at $7.1 billion (or 51 per-
cent of its GDP) and most of its debt (79 percent) was in arrears. After years of resisting
structural reforms, Zimbabwe gave in. It agreed to cut the size of the public work force
(which accounts for 97 percent of government expenditures) in return for help with
clearing $1.8 billion of its debt. However, further assistance, such as opening a new
credit line for Zimbabwe, is contingent on further political and economic reforms. As
of early 2017 the Mugabe government had not so far been willing to make the cuts the
IFIs say are necessary to get out of this cycle of debt distress.[59]

However, the thawing of relations between Zimbabwe and its creditors has
produced some positive results. GDP growth rates did climb above zero, to 1.5

percent growth, in 2015. This is definitely an improvement, but it is not the turn-around the country needs. Another sign that things were improving is that life expectancy has increased to fifty-nine years (sixty-two for women), but again this is still very low compared to the rest of the world.[60] Zimbabwe's Human Development Index (HDI) score has improved slightly but remains low (in 2014 it ranked 155th out of 188 countries).[61]

Perhaps one could argue that Zimbabweans have seen worse, but the country is in crisis and life is extremely difficult for most people. It's hard to imagine, but the unemployment rate in 2016 was over 90 percent, and 90 percent of the jobs to be had were in the informal sector. As a result, most people rely on remittances from relatives abroad to stay afloat.[62] Chronic cash shortages (we mean literally: the ATMs often run out of currency) are the norm. One might not have expected this in one of the world's poorest countries, but Zimbabwe is one of the first going to a cashless economy—in the cities, everyone uses plastic (in the countryside, bartering is making a comeback).[63]

Worsening the situation, an El Niño–induced drought affected all of southern Africa in 2016. The situation is critical in Zimbabwe; it is estimated that 4.5 million people (and perhaps as much as a quarter of the population) are facing food shortages due to poor harvests. The water shortage is so severe that in some areas, people must walk for miles to get water.[64] Meanwhile, the government found a way to celebrate President Mugabe's ninety-second birthday, reportedly at a cost of $800,000.[65] Clearly, the government has got its priorities askew, and this fact dims any glimmers of hope for the economy.

Case Study: Egypt

President Abdel Fattah el-Sisi may face many of the same economic challenges his predecessors did, but it looks like he has not learned from their mistakes. Like them, he is grappling with a variety of intersecting problems: a resource-poor country, a bloated and inefficient bureaucracy, a huge budget gap and rapid population growth, along with endemic unemployment and underemployment. All this . . . not to mention an emphasis on growth over development, resulting in subpar educational and healthcare systems. Like his predecessors, he is relying on state-led growth and mega-projects to solve the country's problems.[66]

After years of more growth than development under Mubarak and a crisis during the turmoil associated with his ouster, by some measures Egypt's economy has marked some progress. Prior to the 1990s, Egypt was considered impoverished. Today it is considered a lower-middle-income country, but the number of people living in poverty (officially defined as those earning less than $500 a year) rose from 21 percent in 2009 to 28 percent in 2015—amounting to nearly a third of the population.[67] Still, Egypt falls somewhere in the middle in terms of human development, having made significant strides in child mortality, life expectancy, school enrollment, and literacy rates over the past thirty years. However, the country has made less progress in other areas; the World Bank illustrates this with its characterization of Egypt's economic growth over this period as "moderate and uneven."[68] Income and other benefits have failed to trickle down. Unemployment is high; it has hovered around 13 percent for the last several years.[69] Many people, especially the young, among whom the jobless rate is more like 34 percent, have nowhere to turn but to

informal sector jobs, which account for 48–70 percent of employment.[70] This is especially problematic given that nearly half the population is under twenty-five.[71]

Meanwhile, the state (under Mubarak and Sisi) has simply disengaged from its social obligations. Egypt has experienced shortages of essential goods; the welfare system, pensions, and key subsidies have all been cut; the education and healthcare systems have crumbled.[72] The main sources of foreign currency have long been remittances from workers abroad, Suez Canal fees, tourism, and oil. The slow European recovery and low oil prices have meant declining foreign investment as well as reduced remittances sent home by Egyptian workers abroad. Tourism, upon which much of the economy is dependent, has certainly taken a hit (especially since the terrorist attack on a Russian passenger plane in 2015) as the number of foreign visitors has been cut in half since before the 2011 uprising.[73]

After bottoming out in the aftermath of the uprising, the economy started to recover in 2014, reaching 4.2 percent growth in 2016. But a combination of unfavorable domestic and external factors will continue to undermine growth.[74] Government spending continues to far outpace revenue. Egypt's economy simply does not produce and sell enough goods and services to keep up with its debt. As a result, Egypt's debt-to-GDP ratio is high—it was 90 percent in 2015.[75] And the debt is a heavy burden on Egypt: nearly one-third of government expenditures goes to servicing this debt.[76]

Desperate to receive a $12 billion bailout from the IMF, the Sisi government has adopted some neoliberal reforms. Under pressure it made the unprecedented decision in 2016 to devalue the Egyptian pound by 48 percent before allowing it to float. And Sisi has cut subsidies for fuel, so these reforms will likely spillover into higher transport and food prices. But inflation was already high—at 14.6 percent, almost double from the year before—and analysts agreed that things were likely to get worse for Egyptians before they get better. In part this is because the government lacks a credible plan to promote the development that would create equitable growth.[77] Analysts agree that far-reaching structural reforms are needed to transform Egypt's economy into a dynamic system that can reduce poverty, create productive employment opportunities, and maintain social and political stability.[78] Instead, it is pursuing a largely state-driven, military-led strategy centered on megaprojects such as the $8.5 billion expansion of the Suez Canal development project. Meanwhile, corruption continues to be rampant; the only difference between today and the Mubarak years is that now the military has come from behind the curtain to show itself as a leading economic actor.[79]

The Sisi government's acceptance of austerity and reliance on reactionary policies have created uncertainty within Egypt's population, raising the question of how much longer such decisionmaking can stave off more "days of rage" in the streets and economic collapse. The government's historical pattern of enacting an austerity measure—testing the public's response and amending its policies accordingly—has often resulted in simply putting off painful but necessary reforms. But that strategy cannot last forever; the IMF for now, at least, appears to be calling the shots.[80] President Sisi, mindful of the fate of his predecessors, has been careful to calibrate reforms so as not to provoke massive protests.[81] In what has become an all-too-familiar tale in Egypt, the strongman finds himself on a tightrope, facing countervailing winds. He must choose his steps carefully, or lose the fragile stability upon which his rule rests.

Case Study: Iran

Leaders of the Islamic Republic of Iran have long struggled with many issues related to political economy. The current economic system combines central planning, state ownership of key industries, village farming, and small-scale private industries. Iranian leaders have long tried to balance economic well-being, self-sufficiency, and the role of the postrevolutionary government in providing for the Iranian people. The founder of the Islamic state and first Supreme Leader, Ayatollah Ruhollah Khomeini, famously promised, "We will build real estate, make water and power free, and make buses free." This revolutionary pledge, among others, has yet to be realized.[82]

Iran's financial problems have intensified in recent decades—impacted by both domestic mismanagement and external sanctions (the bulk of which were only lifted in early 2016). Iran has faced sanctions for human rights abuses as well as both its nuclear and its missile programs. These sanctions have exacted a huge cost: US Treasury secretary Jacob Lew stated that Iran had lost more than $160 billion in oil revenue since 2012. He also contended that, between 2012 and 2014, the Iranian GDP shrank by 9 percent and that its economy was 15–20 percent smaller than it would have been if sanctions hadn't been expanded in 2012.[83] While many of the most crushing international sanctions related to Iran's uranium enrichment program were due to be lifted after verification by the International Atomic Energy Agency (IAEA), sanctions related to its sponsorship of international terrorism and domestic human rights abuses remain intact, as does the US trade embargo.

Not surprisingly, then, one of the central issues facing Iran is its economic dependence on Western countries, especially through the preeminence of oil in Iran's political economy. Sometimes referred to as "black gold," oil has dominated all aspects of life in Iran since its discovery in the early 1900s—Iran possesses massive amounts of both oil and natural gas, with the fourth largest proven oil reserves and second largest proven natural gas reserves. Yet it remains the last major economy that is not explicitly integrated into the global economy.[84] Iran is the largest economy that is outside of the World Trade Organization; even though it submitted its application in 1996, it only became an observer state in 2005, and the accession process is likely to be rocky at best. For many years, Iran's identity in the world economic system was as a provider of cheap oil and a consumer of Western goods and services. Economic self-sufficiency was a goal elucidated by the post-1979 leadership, largely in vain. Despite these concerns, which prompted attempts to diversify, Iran continues to be plagued by export dependence and the fluctuations that accompany it. At times this has worked in Iran's favor, such as in the early 1970s and mid-1990s, but at other times, when oil prices are low, this reliance has caused problems, including after the oil price crash of 2015, just before the country was due to emerge from sanctions. Profits from oil keep the government afloat—receipts from oil and gas exports constitute 70 percent of the government's fiscal budget.[85] With an oversupplied market, Iran remains subjected to volatility that is largely beyond its influence.

Iran's economy was hobbled by its war with Iraq in the 1980s, and by the painful economic reconstruction that followed. Natural disasters (the country is very prone to earthquakes, with small tremors almost daily), combined with the high numbers of refugees fleeing to Iran from Afghanistan, Iraq, and Syria, have stretched the economy to its limits. Additionally, attempts to produce growth through rapid industrialization and

virtually unlimited urbanization have wreaked havoc on the Iranian natural environment, which is only belatedly receiving attention.

As an Islamic state, Iran has attempted to integrate the teachings of the Quran into all aspects of life, including the financial sector. In fact, Iran is viewed as one of the "pioneers of Islamic finance," with a system operating SHARIA-compliant products since 1983 (even if Iran's Islamic banking is grounded in Shia, rather than Sunni, jurisprudence).[86] Iran is the only country besides Sudan where the entire financial industry is obliged to be consistent with the principles of *sharia* law,[87] although other countries, including Turkey, Malaysia, Afghanistan, Pakistan, and Kuwait, offer Islamic banks as an option to conventional, interest-bearing banks. Banking assets in Iran total more than those of Saudi Arabia, Malaysia, and the United Arab Emirates (UAE) combined.[88] Yet a combination of a high number of nonperforming loans and derision due to competing interpretations of *sharia* by Shiites and Sunnis limits the strength of Iran's banking structures.

One persistent economic challenge within Iran has been unemployment, especially among the youth. Attempts to privatize nationally owned companies and corporations threaten to further increase unemployment, and plans to decrease state subsidies on critical items, including basic foods (flour, sugar, eggs), medical goods, gasoline, and utilities, are met with fear and sometimes violence. Poverty remains endemic for nearly a fifth of the population. While women are increasingly integrated into the work force, they tend to have the strongest presence in fields such as education and healthcare, and their employment can be curtailed by the wishes of their husbands.

The economy has been the focus of recent presidential elections. Economic woes played right into leader Mahmoud Ahmadinejad's hand (2005–2013), and his populist appeals nearly broke the Iranian banking system. Ahmadinejad managed the economy so poorly (despite a boom in world oil prices) that fifty prominent Iranian economists attacked him in an open letter.[89] President Hassan Rouhani focused his 2013 campaign around his platform of economic revitalization and the importance of reversing the Islamic Republic's economic and diplomatic isolation. It has been clear that the president's embrace of a more globally engaged Iran is not always welcomed by the Supreme Leader, who has called for a revitalization of Iran's "resistance economy" that is focused on self-sufficiency over interdependence. Rouhani's legacy (and potential for reelection in 2017) will be largely tied to the extent that ordinary people perceive benefits from the nuclear accord.

On the surface, the economy should be one of the greatest strengths of the Islamic Republic of Iran, given its relatively diverse economic structure and significant reserves of natural resources, in addition to its highly educated, urban youth population. Yet economic malaise has been the norm. The discussion over the real impact of lifting of sanctions after the 2015 nuclear accord points both to the uncertainty of Iran's economic future as well as to the degree to which economics is dependent upon political—and religious—barriers within the Islamic state.

Case Study: China

It is perhaps ironic that a state that once prided itself on autarky and self-sufficiency (in the 1950s and 1960s) is now one of the most interconnected economies in the world. When China hosted the Group of 20 (G-20) ministerial meetings in 2016,

this was interpreted as a sign of the global acceptance of Beijing as the world's second largest economy. Yet it's been a bumpy few years, and increasingly it is becoming clear that the so-called China miracle may be nearing its end. While analysts have always found the official data from Beijing suspect, we are increasingly questioning how much we reliably know about the Chinese economy, including both its vitality and its weaknesses. While no future development could ever erase the significant achievement of lifting more than 800 million people out of poverty between 1978 and 2015,[90] there is great uncertainty about the future of this economic giant and its impact regionally and around the globe.

China's leaders have adopted multiple economic models, some disastrous and some successful. In the late 1950s, Mao Zedong launched the so-called Great Leap Forward as a way to economically modernize the country and catch up with the West. Through intense agricultural and industrial programs that included encouraging farmers to construct "backyard burners" in their fields in order to melt down pots and pans to make steel, Mao proclaimed that the Chinese people could surpass Western production totals in less than fifteen years. The results were devastating: as many as 20 million people are believed to have died of starvation and terror because of the misguided agricultural and ideological policies of the period—and recent archival research estimates this total could be as high as 45 million.[91] The man to follow Mao, Deng Xiaoping, took economic growth and prosperity as his primary goal. Touting such non-Marxist phrases as "to get rich is glorious" and "it is all right for some to get rich first," Deng launched a new economic revolution of sorts in the 1980s—it is his policies that prepped the People's Republic for its reemergence at the onset of the twenty-first century. Ordinary people could start up their own companies and trade their agricultural products with local governments, and even foreign firms such as Atlanta-based Coca-Cola were invited to produce, market, and sell their products on the mainland.

The Chinese economic situation today is sprinkled with many contrasts. On the one hand, China has surpassed the United States in terms of the numbers of billionaires in the country (594 in China; 535 in the United States).[92] This includes the largest number of female self-made billionaires in the world, including the world's richest self-made billionaire woman, Zhou Qunfei.[93] Chinese banks were once prototypes of the most cumbersome bureaucratic practices around, but today four of the world's five largest banks (by capital) are Chinese, even though profits are starting to dip and they remain laden with bad debts.[94] The country is awash with entrepreneurial startups, especially in consumer goods and real estate, and increasingly in services and technology. Yet inflation continues to present huge challenges to many, and unemployment threatens to derail much of the newfound wealth of the early 2000s. The government reports the official unemployment rate at 4 percent, yet when underemployment is taken into account, the rate is closer to 13 percent.[95] Structural changes make this impact even larger. The minister for human resources and social security estimates that approximately 1.8 million workers could lose their jobs in the steel and coal industries alone.[96]

Perhaps the most concerning impact of these economic difficulties, most certainly from Beijing's view, is the possibility of unrest in response to economic difficulties. The widening gap between rich and poor is producing a possible cauldron for social unrest over increasing food and housing prices, and, at least as early as

2010, the Chinese Communist Party (CCP) has endorsed an "inclusive growth" model that highlights the need to balance development across different geographic regions as well as the different sectors of society, even if it hurts overall growth (as may be already happening). Strikes and work stoppages are increasingly common, even if the state-controlled media are limited in their appetite for covering these events. In what has been dubbed the "wage contagion" by the *New York Times,* workers at Honda plants in the south forced closures in order to negotiate higher wages and better working conditions.[97] As word of the strikes spread, Tianjin plants faced paralyzed production as well. Widely publicized suicides at Taiwanese-owned Foxconn plants (the world's largest manufacturer of electronics) brought attention to abhorrent conditions and worker strife in the enormous gated compounds that have been used to lure rural workers to cities.

Most analysts, Chinese and Western alike, argue that in order for China to continue its economic gains of the past two decades, the government will need to stimulate its own domestic consumption of products rather than remaining reliant on exports. The Chinese economy has grown by exporting inexpensive items around the world (exports make up approximately one-third of the country's GDP), but manufacturers are already relocating to Vietnam, Cambodia, and elsewhere in response to the increased wages in China. Demographically, China faces a dwindling labor supply of sixteen- to twenty-four-year-olds, the age bracket that once packed factories and fueled the country's export-driven success. Beijing is taking efforts to spark domestic consumption, including increasing pensions and unemployment checks and providing subsidies for major investments such as education, homes, and durable goods. There are some signs that the campaigns are working: in 2009 the number of automobiles sold in China surpassed the number sold in the United States for the first time ever. It's unclear how far this trend may go: as a culture, the Chinese remain frugal (credit cards remain a rarity, for example).

After China emerged from the global financial crisis arguably better than any other country, many spoke of an emerging "Beijing Consensus" to rival the neoliberal, laissez-faire orthodoxy of the Washington Consensus. This potential model incorporates state-ordained economic progress, propped up by low wages and subsidies and undervalued currency, with restrictions on civil liberties—clearly the antithesis of the Washington Consensus, which maintains its hegemonic status. Through its establishment of the Asian Infrastructure Investment Bank (AIIB) to rival the World Bank and the Asian Development Bank, to the continued promotion of the "One Belt, One Road" free trade zone throughout Eurasia and East Africa, Beijing's leaders are making it clear that they are comfortable asserting their economic strength beyond their borders.

Chinese leaders are in a bind. They can no longer entertain thoughts of self-sufficiency. In fact, projections of China's future growth patterns fare prominently in World Bank estimates of global economic health.[98] They can also no longer call for a "developing country" exemption to major world policies, as they have attempted to do in the past. Now that, within the IMF, the yuan holds special drawing rights as one of the five major world currencies, the time has come for Beijing to step up to the mantle of the major world economy that it always aspired to be. Yet with this newfound status comes responsibilities and vulnerabilities that Beijing's leaders may not welcome.

Case Study: Indonesia

From the late 1980s until the late 1990s, Indonesia was hailed as one of the successful "Little Tigers" of Southeast Asia. Although there was a period when it seemed the tiger would fall, Indonesia, the largest economy in Southeast Asia, is now viewed as one of the best-performing emerging market economies.

Indonesia, one of the most diverse countries in the world, has long been searching for a viable economic model that fits the needs and resources of its people. Even after its hard-fought political independence from the Dutch, the Indonesian economy continued its dependence on primary crops introduced by the Netherlands (namely, pepper, coffee, rubber, and sugar). Under the so-called Guided Economy of 1959–1965, Sukarno nationalized all plantations—a move that led to widespread stagnation and capital flight. The president and his economic cronies concentrated on prestige projects, paying scant attention to day-to-day management of financial matters. Inflation and poverty were widespread after the government defaulted on its foreign debt and foreign assistance ended. Indonesia's second president, Suharto, attempted to turn the economy around, especially by mending ties with other countries. As a staunch anticommunist (who came to power under the guise of overthrowing a communist plot in 1965), Suharto received much aid from Western countries. His model of economic development was a familiar one in Asia: promote industrial and business growth under the tutelage of government sponsorship and support, with political control to limit unionization and dissent.

After Indonesia's oil boom, Suharto began to shy away from the so-called Berkeley Mafia free market advice of the 1960s (Indonesia's own version of the Washington Consensus). Throughout the 1970s the president pursued increasingly restrictive trade and investment policies, favoring the steel, shipbuilding, and aircraft industries. The oil collapse in 1985 and 1986 wreaked havoc throughout the country as prices fell below $10 per barrel; in response, returning to "Mafia" advice, Indonesia increased its exports of textiles, clothing, footwear, and wood. This system was marred with corruption: contracts were traded for regime support, and the families of high-profile politicians did famously well. The Suharto family, believed to have amassed a family fortune totaling $15–$35 billion, held a monopoly over the control of some spices, including cloves, and other prosperous domestic industries, such as the processing of citrus fruit. Because of back-scratching financial arrangements, few cautioned against (or even noticed) trends in poor loans, increases in short-term external debt, and other ill-conceived projects, including Suharto's children's scheme to build a "national car," which was later abandoned.[99]

All gains came to a screeching halt as the crisis of 1997 hit—no Asian country fared worse than Indonesia. The economy contracted nearly 14 percent in 1998. Inflation topped 65 percent and the national currency lost 70 percent of its value, producing what the World Bank referred to as one of the most dramatic reversals of fortune ever. In January 1998, Indonesia's rupiah was labeled the world's worst-performing currency. After the crisis, many Indonesians looked to the Chinese model of state-supported economic growth, the so-called Beijing Consensus, as an apt replacement for the neoliberal Washington Consensus, which many blame for the extreme economic crises of this period.[100]

After nearly a decade of political instability, President Susilo Bambang Yudhoyono (SBY, the first directly elected president, who served from 2004 to 2014) attempted

to promote growth and employment while at the same time addressing the challenges of poverty. He is credited with prudent management of the economy and success in boosting average incomes. Indonesia emerged from the Great Recession in a relatively strong position, thanks to increased domestic consumption, strong investment, and exports. One part of this success can be tied to Indonesia's wealth of natural resources, including oil. After suspending its membership in the Organization of Petroleum Exporting Countries (OPEC) in 2009, it rejoined in late 2015 as the only Asian member of the cartel, as well as the only member that is a net importer of petroleum (Indonesia has been a net importer of oil since 2004). Indonesia has cornered the market for palm oil (a major source of revenue during its colonial period as well), which is a common ingredient in many processed foods; and it is the world's leading exporter of tin. Indonesia is also the world's fourth largest coal producer, and the world's largest gold mine and third largest copper mine are both found in Papua, Indonesia's largest province.[101] SBY's successor, Joko Widodo (popularly known as Jokowi), inherited a strong but struggling economy. The vulnerabilities of relying on export commodities emerged in sharp focus as the Chinese economy started to put on the brakes. Jokowi's humble background has influenced his populist approach to politics and economics both: his family was evicted from their illegally built shacks three times while growing up, and he began working jobs to support his family at the age of twelve. One journalist referred to his background as "Indonesia's version of Abraham Lincoln's log cabin in the woods."[102] Jokowi faces many economic challenges now as well: Indonesia struggles with a tremendous infrastructure gap, made more acute as it pursues some of the most rapid urbanization in the world: only 48 percent of households have access to safe water (compared to 50 percent a decade earlier), and only 2 percent of city dwellers utilize centralized sanitation systems (sewage treatment structures are found in only eleven of Indonesia's ninety-eight cities).[103] While there was initially market panic in Indonesia after the election of Donald Trump (mostly due to his protectionist stances and concerns increased fiscal spending in the United States would hurt Indonesian exports), officials reiterated the fundamental strengths of the Indonesian economy. In late 2016, its economic growth rate was over 5 percent, higher than most of its regional peers.[104]

In subsequent chapters we will discuss Indonesia's regional discord. Although much of this strife is highlighted by cultural and religious differences, there are clear economic components to Indonesia's regional battles as well: the restive areas of Aceh and northern Sulawesi have long been economically oriented to the outside world, and when economic constriction hits, these regions tend to fare the worst. The problems aren't always human-made. Aceh was nearly leveled following the 2004 tsunami in the Indian Ocean—some coastal villages were nearly decimated, and the Asian Development Bank estimates that 44 percent of the people in Aceh lost their livelihoods. Additionally, disparities in economic well-being between Indonesia's myriad ethnic groups are more pronounced compared to the relatively prosperous ethnic Chinese community—a group that is consistently targeted for attack when the economic situation sours. As we see in so many other situations, a debilitating economic environment tends to exacerbate other conflicts into crisis.

Similar to many of our country case studies, Indonesia was rocked by the demands of lending institutions to make dramatic changes. IMF conditions for the $45 million aid package in 1998 included a requirement to redirect funds away from as-

sistance programs and social spending, and sparked a fury of unrest throughout the country. Initial runs on banks led to street riots and the economy shrank by 13.5 percent. Demonstrations against Suharto, who was viewed as impotent in the face of outsider demands, eventually toppled the longtime president. In the post-Suharto period, Indonesia has experienced some debt forgiveness (including a $3 billion restructuring plan following the 2004 tsunami), and a gradual restoration of assistance programs. Indonesia faced tremendous struggles making its debt payments throughout the middle to late 1990s, yet achieved significant progress by 2009, when it became the only country in the G-20 to reduce its public debt-to-GDP ratio.[105] Corruption and poor governance, though, have curtailed monies from multilateral institutions (especially the World Bank and the Asian Development Bank) as well as from individual governments, and millions of Indonesians remain under the poverty line. Yet the tables were turned in 2012 when Indonesian leaders confirmed a $1 billion contribution to the IMF's European bailout reserves—money drawn from precisely the same foreign exchange reserves that leaders had amassed in case they faced more demands from the IMF.[106] And in 2016 the World Bank characterized Indonesia as "a confident middle income country," having made enormous gains in poverty reduction (from 57 percent in 1999 to 11 percent in 2015), even in the face of slowing growth rates.[107] If this course continues, the Sumatran Tiger may once again demonstrate its prowess.

Now It's Your Turn

Perhaps as the neoliberals tell us, the experience of a handful of countries should be a lesson to all the rest. However, after two decades of sacrifice and deteriorating conditions for the majority, is it right for developed countries to continue to insist that the neoliberal model is the only feasible path to development? Are neoliberals correct about TINA—is there really no alternative?

Should the leaders of less developed countries simply press for a more flexible approach to further integration into the international economic system as it currently exists? Will the managers of the system (Western donors and the international organizations they control) allow alternative paths to be forged? Or can a combination of strategies that utilize indigenous experience and culture create a system more beneficial for all? What does "independence" mean in a globalized world economy?

Notes

1. James Nelson Goodsell, "Mexico's New President Takes Office—with $80 Billion Debt," *Christian Science Monitor,* December 1, 1982.

2. Alejandro Nadal, "The Microeconomic Impact of IMF Structural Adjustment Policies in Mexico," in *The All-Too-Visible Hand: A Five Country Look at the Long and Destructive Reach of the IMF* (Washington, DC: Friends of the Earth, April 1999).

3. World Bank, "GDP Growth: Annual Percentage," 2016 http://data.worldbank.org.

4. Ioan Grillo, "Forget Trump's Wall: For Mexico, the Election Is About Nafta," *New York Times,* September 23, 2016.

5. D. E. Campbell, "A Saint for Lost Souls," *Foreign Policy* 179 (May–June 2010); Elisabeth Malkin, "Nafta's Promise, Unfulfilled," *New York Times,* March 24, 2009; James McBride and Mohammed Aly Sergie, "NAFTA's Economic Impact," Council on Foreign Relations, January 24, 2017.

6. Shannon K. O'Neill, "Six Markets to Watch: Mexico," *Foreign Affairs,* January–February 2014.

7. Malkin, "Nafta's Promise, Unfulfilled"; Office of the United States Trade Representative, "Mexico," 2016; Grillo, "Forget Trump's Wall."

8. World Bank, "Poverty and Equity," 2016 http://data.worldbank.org.

9. Brianna Lee, "Mexico's Economy: President Peña Nieto Promised Sweeping Reforms, but Corruption Accusations Have Stalled Growth," *International Business Times,* September 2, 2015; Brianna Lee, "Mexico's Economy: Rising Poverty, Inequality Undermine Peña Nieto's Economic Agenda," *International Business Times,* September 3, 2015.

10. World Bank, "A Model from Mexico for the World," November 19, 2014 www.worldbank.org.

11. World Bank, "GDP Growth."

12. Office of the United States Trade Representative "Mexico"; World Bank, "GDP Growth."

13. Pamela K. Starr, "Mexico's Problematic Reforms," *Current History,* February 2014.

14. O'Neill, "Six Markets to Watch"; Joshua Partlow and Gabriela Martinez, "Mexico's Economy Was Supposed to Soar," *Washington Post,* August 8, 2015; "67% Increase in Mexican Multi-Millionaires Under Peña Nieto," *TeleSur,* June 9, 2016.

15. Elisabeth Malkin, "Pessimism Pervades Mexico as Economic Promises Fall Short," *New York Times,* September 1, 2015; Grillo, "Forget Trump's Wall."

16. McBride and Sergie, "NAFTA's Economic Impact"; "Mexico: How's Life?" in *OECD Better Life Index 2015.*

17. Cynthia McClintock, *Revolutionary Movements in Latin America* (Washington, DC: US Institute of Peace, 1998).

18. Susan George, *The Debt Boomerang: How Third World Debt Harms Us All* (Boulder: Westview, 1992); McClintock, *Revolutionary Movements in Latin America.*

19. George, *The Debt Boomerang.*

20. Simon Romero, "Peru's Leader Uses Second Chance to Rewrite Legacy," *New York Times,* October 2, 2006; Robert Plummer, "Peru Still Wary of García's Past," BBC News, June 5, 2006.

21. "Peru," Observatory of Economic Complexity, 2016; Gaspar E. Nolte and Mariano J. Beillard, "The U.S.-Peru TPA Five Years of Spectacular Growth," USDA Foreign Agricultural Service, February 10, 2014; Colin Post, "What Did Peru Get Out of the Trans-Pacific Partnership?," *Peru Reports,* November 12, 2015; "Peru Says TPP Can Be Replaced with New Trade Deal, sans U.S.," Reuters, November 11, 2016.

22. World Bank, "GDP Growth"; Nathaniel Parish Flannery, "Political Risk Outlook: How Will Peru's Economy Perform in 2016?," *Forbes,* January 19, 2016.

23. "Playing for Time," *The Economist,* July 18, 2009; "Peru: Free Traders," *The Economist,* July 1, 2006; Toni Johnson, "Peru's Mineral Wealth and Woes," Council on Foreign Relations, February 10, 2010; "Peru Economic Outlook," *Focus Economics,* February 14, 2017; Maureen Taft-Morales, "Peru in Brief: Political and Economic Conditions and Relations with the United States," Congressional Research Service, June 7, 2013; Nicholas Casey and Andrea Zarate, "Corruption Scandals with Brazilian Roots Cascade Across Latin America," *New York Times,* February 13, 2017.

24. World Bank, "Peru," 2016.

25. Ibid.

26. "Peru Economic Outlook," *Focus Economics;* World Bank, "Peru."

27. World Bank, "Peru Brief," April 28, 2010; Johnson, "Peru's Mineral Wealth and Woes."

28. Flannery, "Political Risk Outlook."

29. Ibid.

30. Taft-Morales, "Peru in Brief"; "Peru Economic Outlook," *Focus Economics;* Flannery, "Political Risk Outlook."

31. Daniel Workman, "Crude Oil Exports by Country," World's Top Exports, www.worldstopexports.com, August 14, 2016; CIA, "Peru," *World Factbook 2016.*

32. "Is Nigeria 'Fantastically Corrupt,' as Cameron Claims?," BBC News, May 11, 2016.

33. "How Nigeria Is Fighting Corruption," *The Economist,* July 26, 2016.

34. Adam Wernick, "Shell Oil Faces a Lawsuit in the UK over Oil Spills in Nigeria," *Public Radio International,* March 27, 2016; Stanley Reed, "Shell and Nigerian Partner Are Sued in Britain over Spills," *New York Times,* March 2, 2016; "Shell to Pay $83.5M for Nigeria Oil Spill," Al Jazeera, January 7, 2015.

35. "Crude Oil Disruptions in Nigeria Increase as a Result of Militant Attacks," US Energy Information Administration, August 18, 2016; "The Economist Explains How Nigeria Is Fighting Corruption," *The Economist,* July 26, 2016.

36. Omoh Gabriel, "Youth Unemployment in Nigeria up to 50%—McKinsey & Co," *Vanguard,* January 26, 2015.

37. Elisha Bala-Gbogbo, "Nigeria Says Companies to Give $200 Million for Fuel Imports," *Bloomberg,* April 7, 2016.

38. Douglas Farah, "Nigerian Leader Pushes for Debt Relief," *Washington Post,* October 30, 1999.

39. Jean Herskovits, "Politics in Nigeria Have 'Ground to a Halt,'" Council on Foreign Relations, March 25, 2009.

40. "Nigeria Settles Paris Club Debt," BBC News, April 21, 2006.

41. Office of the Senior Special Assistant to the President on Millennium Development Goals (MDGs), "Nigeria 2015: Millennium Development Goals—End-Point Report," 2015.

42. CIA, "Nigeria," *World Factbook 2016;* World Bank, "Poverty Headcount Ratio at $3.10 a Day (2011 PPP) (% of Population)," 2016.

43. "Nigeria's Economy: More Pain, Little Gain," *The Economist,* July 28, 2001; Thabile Manala, "Nigeria on a Borrowing Binge," CNBC Africa, May 13, 2015.

44. Trading Economics, "Nigeria GDP Growth Rate, 2013–2016," 2016; "Nigeria Economic Outlook," *Focus Economics,* August 23, 2016; Henry Umoru and Joseph Erunke, "Nigeria's Economy in Bad Shape," *Vanguard,* July 20, 2016.

45. Phoebe Greenwood, "UN Accused of Failing as North-East Nigeria at Risk of Famine," *The Guardian* (London), July 14, 2016.

46. IMF, "World Economic Outlook"; CIA, "Nigeria," *World Factbook 2016;* Dawn Kissi, "Nigeria Goes from Powerhouse to Pariah as 'Hurricane' Hits Economy," CNBC News, May 8, 2016.

47. "Zimbabwe," CIA, *World Factbook 2006.*

48. Julius E. Nyang'oro and Timothy M. Shaw, "The African State in the Global Economic Context," in *The African State at a Critical Juncture: Between Disintegration and Reconfiguration,* ed. Julius E. Nyang'oro and Timothy M. Shaw (Boulder: Lynne Rienner, 1998); Robert I. Rotberg, "Africa's Mess, Mugabe's Mayhem," *Foreign Affairs,* September–October 2000.

49. Michael Wines, "Zimbabwe's Leaders Want to Delay Presidential Vote," *New York Times,* September 25, 2006; CIA, *World Factbook 2006.*

50. Greg Mills and Jeffrey Herbst, "Bring Zimbabwe in from the Cold," *New York Times,* May 28, 2009; Celia W. Dugger, "Zimbabwe Health Care, Paid with Peanuts," *New York Times,* December 19, 2010.

51. Angus Shaw, "Zimbabwe Government Wary of Annan Intervention in Political, Economic Stalemate," Associated Press, May 26, 2004; Celia W. Dugger, "Opposition Party to Join Zimbabwe's Government," *New York Times,* January 31, 2009; Jeffrey Moyo and Norimitsu Onishi, "With Little Choice, Zimbabweans Hurtle to a Cashless Economy," *New York Times,* November 4, 2016.

52. Richard Bourne, *Catastrophe: What Went Wrong in Zimbabwe?* (London: Zed, 2011).

53. Rachel L. Swarns, "Zimbabwe Starts Arresting White Farmers Defying Eviction," *New York Times,* August 17, 2002; "From Breadbasket to Basket Case," *The Economist,* June 29, 2002.

54. Daniel Pepper, "Zimbabwe's Army Takes Over Black Farms," *Christian Science Monitor,* June 5, 2006; "World," *Christian Science Monitor,* April 24, 2006; Norimitsu Onishi, "'No One Is Safe': Zimbabwe Threatens to Take Foes' Farms," *New York Times,* August 28, 2016.

55. Donald G. McNeil Jr., "Zimbabwe: Report Shows Health Care System Declining After Years of Authoritarian Rule," *New York Times,* October 12, 2009; Mills and Herbst, "Bring Zimbabwe in from the Cold."

56. Trading Economics, "Zimbabwe GDP Annual Growth Rate."

57. "Zimbabweans Have 'Shortest Lives,'" BBC News, April 8, 2006.

58. Joseph Hanlon, Jeannette Manjengwa, and Teresa Smart, *Zimbabwe Takes Back Its Land* (Boulder: Lynne Rienner, 2012).

59. Piers Pigou, "Zimbabwe Deep in Limbo," International Crisis Group, March 6, 2016; Chido Munyati, "Why US Reengagement Is Critical to Zimbabwe's Debt Arrears Clearance Strategy," *Foreign Policy Journal,* March 4, 2016; Moyo and Onishi, "With Little Choice"; Onishi, "'No One Is Safe.'"

60. World Health Organization (WHO), "Zimbabwe," 2016; United Nations Development Programme (UNDP), "Zimbabwe: Human Development Report 2015."

61. "HIV and AIDS in Zimbabwe," *Avert,* July 22, 2016.

62. Pigou, "Zimbabwe Deep in Limbo"; "Zimbabwe Pastor Evan Mawarire 'Charged with Inciting Violence,'" BBC News, July 12, 2016.

63. Jeffrey Moyo and Norimitsu Onishi, "A Cashless Economy in Zimbabwe? With Little Cash, There's Little Choice," *New York Times,* November 3, 2016.

64. Andrew Mambondiyani, "Parched Zimbabwe Faces Dire Water Shortages as New Dry Season Nears," Reuters, August 25, 2016; Hopewell Chin'ono and Norimitsu Onishi, "In Zimbabwe, Mugabe's Birthday Is Rife with Political Jockeying," *New York Times,* February 29, 2016.

65. Jeffrey Moyo and Norimitsu Onishi, "Protesters Fume as Zimbabwe Vice President Runs Up a Hotel Bill," *New York Times,* July 27, 2016; "Letter from Africa: Zimbabwe's Flag Fury," BBC News; Chin'ono and Onishi, "In Zimbabwe, Mugabe's Birthday."

66. Julia Goldman, "Egypt's Economy Stuck in the 'Doldrums,'" Atlantic Council, June 16, 2016; "Thinking Big," *The Economist,* March 21, 2015.

67. UNDP, "About Egypt," 2016.

68. UNDP, "Egypt: Human Development Report 2015"; World Bank, "Egypt: Overview," 2016.

69. "Egypt Economic Outlook," *Focus Economics,* October 4, 2016.

70. Mohamed Samir, "Are Egypt's Economic Reforms Enough to Solve the Informal Economy Problem?," *Daily News* (Cairo), July 6, 2016.

71. Zachary Laub, "Interview: Washington's Egypt Dilemma," Council on Foreign Relations, June 23, 2015.

72. Tarek Osman, *Egypt on the Brink: From Nasser to Mubarak* (New Haven: Yale University Press, 2010).

73. UNDP, "Egypt: Human Development Report 2015"; Mustansir Barma, "Struggles for Egypt's Tourism Sector," Carnegie Endowment for International Peace, December 17, 2015.

74. "Egypt Economic Outlook," *Focus Economics.*

75. CIA, "Egypt," *World Factbook 2016.*

76. "Egypt Economic Outlook," *Focus Economics.*

77. "Egypt Averts Economic Collapse, for Now," *New York Times,* November 5, 2016; Nour Youssef and Diaa Hadid, "'We Don't Owe Anyone': Egypt Jousts with Its Chief Benefactor, Saudi Arabia," *New York Times,* November 1, 2016; Michael Wahid Hanna, "Getting over Egypt: Time to Rethink Relations," *Foreign Affairs,* November–December 2015; Emad El-Din Shahin, "Egypt's Revolution Turned on Its Head," *Current History,* December 2015.

78. World Bank, "Egypt: Overview."

79. Laub, "Interview: Washington's Egypt Dilemma"; Abigail Hauslohner, "Egypt's Military Expands Its Power over the Economy," *Washington Post,* March 17, 2014.

80. "A Dollar Crisis Threatens Egypt's Economy," *Stratfor,* March 10, 2016.

81. Declan Walsh, "Where's My Mercedes? Egypt's Financial Crisis Hits the Rich," *New York Times,* March 10, 2016.

82. Quoted in Robert F. Worth, "Iran's Plan to Phase Out Subsidies Brings Frenzied Debate," *New York Times,* December 2, 2009.

83. "Remarks of Treasury Secretary Jacob J. Lew to the Washington Institute," April 29, 2015, www.washingtoninstitute.org.

84. Cyrus Amir-Mokri and Hamid Biglari, "A Windfall for Iran? The End of Sanctions and the Iranian Economy," *Foreign Affairs,* November–December 2015.

85. Jahangir Amuzegar, "Iran's Economy in Turmoil," *International Economic Bulletin,* March 2010 (Carnegie Endowment for International Peace). Amuzegar is a former minister of commerce and minister of finance who has represented Iran and other member states on the IMF's Executive Board.

86. Jacopo Dettoni, "Iran and the Islamic Finance Crown," *The Diplomat,* June 16, 2015, www.diplomat.com.

87. Ibid.

88. Golnar Motevalli, "World's Largest Islamic Banking System Sees Hope in Iran Accord," *Bloomberg,* April 6, 2015.

89. See International Crisis Group, "Iran: Ahmadi-Nejad's Tumultuous Presidency," Middle East Briefing no. 21, February 6, 2007, p. 8, www.crisisgroup.org.

90. World Bank, "World Bank Country Report: China," September 14, 2016, www.worldbank.org.

91. Frank Dikötter, *Mao's Great Famine: The History of China's Most Devastating Catastrophe, 1958–1962* (New York: Walker, 2010).

92. "China Tops US in Numbers of Billionaires,'" BBC News, October 13, 2016.

93. David Barboza, "How a Chinese Billionaire Built Her Fortune," *New York Times,* July 30, 2015.

94. The government continues to own a majority stake in the five major banks, and the CCP continues to appoint top leaders. "World's Biggest Banks," BBC News, July 2, 2016.

95. Michael Schuman, "Is China Stealing Jobs? It May Be Losing Them Instead," *New York Times,* July 22, 2016.

96. Ibid.

97. David Barboza and Hiroko Tabuchi, "Labor Strife Signals Shift in China," *New York Times,* June 9, 2010.

98. David M. Lampton, "What If China Fails? We'd Better Hope It Doesn't!," *Wilson Quarterly* (Autumn 2010), p. 62.

99. William E. James, "Lessons from Development of the Indonesian Economy," *Education About Asia* 5, no. 1 (Spring 2000).

100. Andrew Higgins, "Some in Indonesia Praise, Seek to Replicate China's Fight Against the United States," *Washington Post,* March 29, 2010.

101. "Spicing Up Growth," *The Economist,* May 9, 2015.

102. Michael Bachelard, "Joko Widodo: Man with a Mission," *Sydney Morning Herald,* June 14, 2014.

103. World Bank, "Indonesia's Urban Story," June 14, 2016, www.worldbank.org.

104. Prima Wirayani, "Indonesian Markets Panic over Trump's Policies," *Jakarta Post,* November 12, 2016, www.thejakartapost.com.

105. Thomas Rumbaugh and Laura Lipscomb, "Indonesia's Economy: Strong with Room for Improvements," *IMF Survey Magazine,* September 17, 2010.

106. Peter Alford, "Fifteen Years After Humiliation, Indonesia Turns the Tables on the IMF," *The Australian,* July 11, 2012, www.theaustralian.com.au.

107. World Bank, "Indonesia: Overview," April 5, 2016, www.worldbank.org.

PART THREE
Politics and Political Change

Ideas are among the most powerful forces we possess. All people hold opinions and viewpoints about the world around them. Should income be equally distributed? Should political leaders provide moral and religious guidance? How should citizens respond to perceived corruption and abuse of power? Thoughts about authority, society, gender relations, economic resources, the environment, and other priorities help shape the general perspectives that people hold about their role in the world. Ideas about the way things should be often impel people into action, sometimes in violent ways. This will be the subject of the chapters that follow.

In this part of the book we will also consider the impact of ideas and their translation into action in terms of the "waves" of democratization, which hit much of the world toward the end of the Cold War. (The "first wave" of democratic transitions is commonly identified with the expansion of democracy in the United States and Western Europe [1820s–1926]. The "second wave" [1945–1962] is associated with independence and the experimentation with democracy in much of Asia and Africa. The "third wave" began in the 1970s and stretched through the late 1990s, impacting states in Europe, sub-Saharan Africa, Asia, and Latin America.) Since the so-called Arab Spring, which began in 2011, the push for renewed political transitions has grown strong. As we will see, the result for governments around the world has been a crisis of sorts. We will explore the various ways in which different governments have handled this crisis. In doing this we will consider, implicitly at least, the chances for democracy throughout the global south, the odds of which vary by country. While several countries do not appear to be headed in the direction of Western-style democracy at all, there are some well-established democracies in the global south. On the other hand, some fragile democracies have already broken down. Many countries are at varying stages in the process of reform. Others just appear to be making this transition, as their democratization is more "virtual" than real. In more than a few cases political liberalization has been precluded by instability, due to fundamental problems such as disagreements concerning whether the state should continue to exist intact. In most but not all cases, carefully crafted negotiations, pacts, and other

agreements have at least temporarily resolved some problems. But even when contested sovereignty is not an issue, both democratic and nondemocratic governments struggle to grapple with other demands. Any new democracy faces a host of challenges. In the chapters that follow, we will discuss these challenges and assess the nature of political transitions in the global south.

Chapter 9

Civil Society
Takes on the State

I am the free and the fearless. I am secrets that never die. I am the voice of those who will not bow.　　*—Lyrics popularized by Tunisian singer-songwriter*
Emei Mathlouthi during the Tunisian protests
at the beginning of the Arab Spring, 2011[1]

Sometimes decades pass and nothing happens; and then sometimes weeks pass and decades happen.　　*—Attributed to Vladimir Lenin*

In this chapter we explore a range of perspectives held by ordinary citizens, activists, and leaders. These viewpoints derive from many sources, including history (both ancient and recent), practical experiences of daily life and policy, and leadership cues and demands. Additionally, worldviews are framed by a combination of more seemingly subtle influences, as varied as the educational systems, entertainment opportunities and institutions, and basic information sources that are made available to the public. We examine belief systems that both unite and divide people, and focus on ideas as sources of conflict and cooperation. Passion is a major part of the story. Yet our emphasis goes beyond simply the beliefs that people hold: we examine the forums in which these views are expressed, the ways that other groups attempt to curtail people's ability to express opinions, and how crafty activists subvert limits on expression.

Ideas merge theoretical, often-fuzzy concepts of the way the world "should be" with the necessarily concrete actions that people take on a day-to-day basis to try to implement their visions. The sheer multiplicity of ideas invites controversy: When one person's or group's ideas conflict with those of others, how can these differences be reconciled? Why do some people's ideas seem to count, at least in the public realm, more than those of others, and how is this negotiated (or not)? We often think of leaders as holding a monopoly on creating the ideas that "count," but this is certainly not always the case. When groups of people begin to identify with a value or idea system

different from that of their leaders, they may organize and challenge the status quo. Sometimes they succeed, and sometimes their efforts result in painful failure.

Ideologies

Ideas that are free-floating, unattached to a more general perspective or value system, are not very likely to have tremendous impact. Yet when connections between sets of values and perspectives are recognized as interconnected, and when these views impel people to action, they literally have a force that may change the world.

When people share similar ideas linked to programs for action, we refer to this idea set as an ideology, literally the "science of ideas" (although such beliefs are hardly described with scientific precision). At their most fundamental level, ideologies are sets of ideas that describe the world or current state of affairs, help people understand their role within society, and arouse people to take an action, either to preserve or to change the existing situation. Ideologies consist of loosely connected systems of ideas: few traditions propose a strict laundry list of beliefs one must hold in order to subscribe to a given ideology. Rather, people notice common tendencies in beliefs, and often unite together with others who share similar perspectives.

Ideologies attempt to simplify complex problems and point toward potential solutions. They tend to be the foundation of most policies and actions, even if they are not identified as such. Most of the major systems of ideas that have been at the forefront of the global south were formulated in response to experiences with colonialism and dependence, especially the economic struggle to survive. Leaders and ordinary citizens alike turn to ideologies to help them cope with civil unrest, crushing poverty, and international humiliation. Ideologies often provide deceptively clearcut answers to complicated realities, especially during times of instability. Frequently, groups of people who share an ideological worldview get together to form a political party as a way to implement the ideas that they feel are important. Political parties serve as mechanisms to recruit like-minded members to lobby and govern. While political parties appear and disappear, and quite often adopt varying and misleading names, political ideologies endure.

Common in discussions about ideologies are the terms "conservative" and "liberal." These concepts represent two major schools of ideological thought. They are relative terms, meaning that what is seen as conservative in one country or social situation might not be so seen in another. Liberalism, which developed throughout European societies in the early 1800s, is often considered the first coherent political ideology. Liberals emphasize the freedom of the individual, limits on governmental interference, and the equality of all human beings. The idea that all people possess inalienable rights to life, liberty, and the pursuit of property, for example, is a classical liberal idea derived from the writings of John Locke. Liberals hold optimistic beliefs about what individuals and groups can achieve, and they often fight for progressive (forward-moving) changes.

Because of liberalism's high value on freedom, this ideology had a tremendous impact on the wars of liberation discussed in Chapter 4. If all people are created equal, as liberalism contends, then individuals should be able to rule themselves, rather than having decisions made for them by colonial leaders in a faraway land. Liberal beliefs encouraged the fight for self-governing peoples who had been sub-

jugated to foreign rule, some for centuries. This movement was particularly pronounced in the post–World War II environment. The outcome of many of these wars of national liberation, however, was the perpetuation of political control and limits on freedom. Liberalism also has influenced the desire by some ethnic groups to pursue their own homeland, often distinct from the government in which they live. We discuss these ethnonationalists in Chapter 12. Yet the desire for cultural representation and self-expression does not always lead to the fight for a new state. Owing to the influence of liberalism, some ethnic groups have staked a claim to greater public expression of their culture and ways of life, achieving rights to use their native language, educate their children about their history and culture in public schools, and demand greater representation in public life.

Liberal ideas have also been responsible for many revolutions throughout the world, especially popular movements to overthrow monarchies, dynasties, and other forms of hereditary rule that precluded individuals from power. Some liberal revolutions attempted to redistribute land and economic resources that had been taken away from people. One example is found in President Benito Juarez's La Reforma program in Mexico in the mid-1800s, which stripped the Catholic Church of much of its property and power and formally granted civil rights to indigenous peoples. Juarez's liberal program was also popular for its staunch resistance to French invaders. Other liberal movements fought to bring voting rights and other participatory freedoms to groups, including women, minorities, and youth. Liberal proponents today in the global south attempt to advance greater respect for human rights and individual freedoms, and they often lead the vocal charge toward democratic institutions. Fundamentally, liberals agree that the power of government needs to be limited, although they disagree over the fine lines of state involvement, especially in the realm of economics.

If liberals agree that governmental power should be limited and that individuals should have a say in decisions that are made about their lives, there is disagreement about matters of degree. Debates about the role of government in people's lives have led to two major types of liberals. One group, often called positive liberals, arguing that government ought to shoulder some level of responsibility for people's lives, calls for diminishing the inequality among groups, fostering greater participation, and in general promoting the well-being of citizens. Positive liberals are often the strongest supporters of welfare-state policies, including childcare, healthcare, education, unemployment insurance, and pensions. People often assume that welfare policies are designed only for the needy in society, but actually many welfare programs, including public education and public pensions, are distributed to all citizens, irrespective of need, and are present in most states of the world. In contrast, negative liberals believe that there should be minimal government involvement in the economy, arguing that the market, regulated by the forces of supply and demand, should be allowed to operate freely. This group argues that government involvement often has the unintended consequence of limiting individual freedom by creating patterns of dependence and perpetuating cycles of poverty. These debates can become quite heated. Yet in the global south, the degree of governmental assistance is often framed not by ideological but rather by economic concerns.

Ideas rarely exist in a vacuum. They often are formulated, expressed, and modified in response to other views of the world. This explains the development of the

other major school of thought, conservatism. Conservatives are known for attempting to preserve the status quo, and sometimes for encouraging a return to values and traditions of the past. As conservatism began to develop, it challenged each of the major premises of the liberal way of viewing the world.

Traditional conservatives emphasize an organic view of society, in which the needs of the whole society, the so-called social fabric, are more important than individual freedom. In contrast to the liberals' emphasis on the equality of all people, conservatives emphasize that every person is born with natural inequalities, thereby contradicting the liberal notion of the fundamental equality of all people. Conservatives emphasize the talents and skills that some people have at birth that others do not. They advocate a slower approach to change, highlighting the utility of existing institutions and patterns of behavior and reviling the dangerous passions and actions of revolutionaries. They lament the liberals' pace of rapid change, and believe that revolutions tend to bring about more harm than good, because they damage key traditions and hierarchical structures that serve as the basis for social traditions and identity. Many conservatives prefer familiar patterns of relations, rather than the uncertainty that comes from progressive change. It is from this belief that we tend to associate conservatives with the status quo; in fact, the label "conservativism" derives from the Latin word *conservare,* which means "to save or preserve." Conservative parties and groups today, while they often support democratic institutions, urge caution in the pace of transitions and cast a wary eye toward liberal causes.

One modern manifestation of conservative ideas is found in religious fundamentalism, including Christian and Islamic variants, the adherents of which promote the value of religious institutions and authority, often placing great emphasis on traditional family structures and gender roles. Much of the debate surrounding fundamentalists and their detractors relates to the adaptations of religious institutions to the modern world. Adherents to fundamental traditions often promote a stricter, sometimes-literal interpretation of religious texts, whether they be the Torah, Bible, or Quran. Islamist movements, also discussed in this chapter, have often been motivated by the perceived encroachment of Westernization, concomitant with the rise of individualism and secularism, which are viewed as threatening to traditional lifestyles. After the Soviet withdrawal from Afghanistan in 1989, civil war ensued. One group that emerged from the ashes was the Taliban, an Islamist political group that ruled the country from 1996 until late 2001, and reemerged as an insurgent movement in 2004. This antimodern group promotes a rigidly conservative approach to Islamic religious beliefs that includes strict gender segregation based on a belief that men and women are fundamentally unequal. The Taliban's actions are couched in the refutation of Western, secular standards of behavior. The resurgence of the Taliban throughout Afghanistan has been disastrous for all Afghanis (as well as many Pakistanis), but especially for women. The world has witnessed several grim images that testify to this fact—for example, one Afghani woman was mutilated, her ears and nose sliced off, because she fled an abusive marriage; another, a pregnant widow, received 200 lashes and then was shot to death because she was accused of adultery. When top Taliban spokesmen deny complicity, they hardly convince critics; for example, in the case of the pregnant widow, a Taliban spokesman argued that she should not have been shot to death, but stoned instead.[2] Honor killings, public executions, and other forms of punishment are promoted by extremist leaders, with aggrieved citizens

Figure 9.1   Do All Muslims Agree?

In the early decades of the twenty-first century, followers of the Muslim faith are second in number only to Christians. While estimates vary, most agree that Muslims compose nearly 25 percent of the world's population, and that Islam is the fastest-growing faith tradition in the world. With so many adherents, it is logical to assume that there are varying levels of agreement and disagreement among the Muslim faithful. The biggest source of lasting division originated in a succession struggle launched after the prophet Muhammad's death in 632. Today, the majority of Muslims, approximately 90 percent, characterize themselves as Sunni Muslims. The name *Sunni* derives from *Sunna,* meaning "the tradition of the prophet Muhammad." The primary schism is with Shia Islam; the name *Shia* means "Party of Ali."

Upon Muhammad's death in 632, his cousin and son-in-law, Ali, claimed to be the leader of all Muslims. But most believers followed Abu Bakr, who was reputed to be the first outside of Muhammad's family to convert to Islam. Abu Bakr became the first of the four caliphs, or successors, in the Sunni tradition. Twenty-three years after Muhammad's death, Ali was named the caliph. His rise to leadership was controversial and not recognized by many; Syria's leader, among others, refused to recognize Ali, who ruled from Kufah, Iraq, facing much dissention.

A series of succession crises, including the murder and torture of disputed leaders, led to the creation of Shia Islam, the first major schism within Islam. Sunnis today continue to outnumber Shiites (followers of Shia Islam), although Iran, Iraq, Azerbaijan, and Bahrain are majority-Shiite states. The Shiites replaced the caliphate with imams, claiming that their leadership was hereditary from Muhammad. After the schism, Shiites were persecuted and acted in secret, during which time they devised their own teachings on the implementation of the word of Muhammad. One change was the designation of an authoritative figure to interpret divine will, rather than placing the onus on the community of believers, as Sunnis taught.[a] The Shiites believe that imams, as religious leaders, possess knowledge of which the masses are incapable. This view complicated the challenges of rival suc-

cessors, since imams were viewed as infallible leaders. Although most Turks are Sunnis, the Shiite minority in Turkey are known as Alvis.

The major Shia sect is the "Twelvers," named for the twelve imams following Muhammad. Twelver Shia Islam is the state religion in Iran. Developed in the sixteenth century, this sect highlights the twelve legitimate imams, beginning with Ali and ending with the twelfth or "hidden" imam, who went into concealment in 941 but who will reappear some day in the future to finish the triumph of Shia Islam. Between the sixteenth and eighteenth centuries, Twelver Shia Islam merged with Persian tradition, forging a tight bond with the development of Iranian identity and nationalism.[b]

The Iraq War had a lasting impact on Shiite communities, even though Shiites, like their Sunni counterparts, remain a greatly diverse and amorphous sect who are not united under a single leader. As Vali Nasr, author of *The Shia Revival* argues, "The Middle East that will emerge from the crucible of the Iraq war may not be more democratic, but it will definitely be more Shiite."[c] Despite the sectarian bloodshed that marked much of the Iraq War and the conflicts that have followed, the two major sects of Muslim believers have lived mostly in peace throughout the centuries.

In the eighth century, the mystical movement of Sufism developed, in protest to the formalism of Islam. The title comes from the Arabic word *suf,* meaning "wool." Many Sufis wore coarse woolen clothes, imitating the Christians from Syria. Although both Sunni and Shiite fundamentalists reject it, Sufism has appeal among those who are frustrated with the power-seeking ulamas, or clerics, who view Islam as a religious experience rather than a call to political action.[d]

Notes: a. Sandra Mackey, *The Iranians: Persia, Islam, and the Soul of a Nation* (New York: Penguin, 1996).

b. Ibid.

c. Vali Nar, "When the Shiites Rise," *Foreign Affairs* 85, no. 4 (July–August 2006), p. 59.

d. Mackey, *The Iranians*.

watching and even getting in on the action. Multiple concerns remain, including whether or not groups even loosely affiliated with the Taliban may become the face of law in the region.

Christian fundamentalists express hostility toward individualism and secularism, objecting to the liberal separation of church and state that made religious values and practices a private rather than a public matter. Conservative evangelical Christians have been very active in many parts of the global south, including Latin America (especially Guatemala and Brazil), Africa (including South Africa and Zimbabwe), and some Asian states (notably the Philippines). While there is great variation among followers, in general evangelical Christian churches advocate conservative sexual and gender mores, economic discipline, as well as a greater role for some newer church institutions. In Brazil, for example, evangelical leaders in government have publicly contested the role of the Catholic Church in society. In Guatemala, fundamentalist Protestant groups rally in opposition to unions and against LIBERATION THEOLOGY, a left-leaning perspective on Catholicism discussed later in this chapter. Many of the fundamentalist traditions in Africa trace their origins to anticolonial movements. Pentecostals make up approximately 12 percent of Africa's population, constituting somewhat of a Pentacostal "boom," according to the Pew Research Center.[3] Disparate groups of fundamentalist Christians in Africa, believed to number in the tens of millions, have joined together in opposition to abortion, feminism, and the rights of homosexuals.[4]

Conservatism and liberalism are only two of many traditions of like-minded ideas. The other major world ideologies that have affected social, political, and economic life include socialism, communism, fascism, and anarchism. Each of these ideological systems developed in response to liberal views of the world, and promotes its own ideas about the value of individualism, governmental involvement in the economy, and the structure of society. It is important to understand the basic definitions of each of these distinct ideologies. But it is also necessary to keep in mind that the underlying components of any ideological system are manipulated, changed, and adapted by people to fit their particular circumstances and to match their goals. Nonetheless, an understanding of the common characteristics of these views provides an important starting place for this inquiry of the role of ideology in the non-Western world.

Socialism is an ideological tradition that has had tremendous impact throughout the entire world, either in its application or in its opposition. Because of the centrality of economic matters, socialism, in multiple variants, has been a particularly important ideology in the global south. Historically, socialism was critical of private property and the uneven distribution of wealth. It is an idea that significantly predates one of its most famous adherents, Karl Marx, who adapted early socialist ideals and melded them onto a revolutionary framework. Marxist socialists argued that fundamentally there are two types of people in the world, making up the dominant CLASSES of society. First are the few who own property and therefore exert much influence in economic, political, and social affairs. They are known as the BOURGEOISIE. Yet the bourgeoisie could not exist without the masses, who in a Marxist framework are forced to work at the mercy of the powerful, and labor tirelessly without proper compensation or protection against abuse. This second class, which always outnumbers the first, is known as the PROLETARIAT. Writing in the midst of the European industrial revolution of the late 1800s, Marx argued that once the workers

of the world were made aware of their uneven plight caused by the powerful property owners, inevitably they would rise up in anger and overthrow their oppressors. Marx predicted that after the revolution, which was likely to be violent, proletarians would rule in their self-interest, attempting to eliminate the bourgeoisie. During this stage of initial socialism, economic inequalities would persist, but they would be eradicated in the final stage of the revolution, when communism would be achieved.

While Marx's ideas may seem particularly appropriate for individuals living and working in the countries of the global south, it was really only after the innovations of another revolutionary activist that his ideas were applied in the effort to promote wide-scale change. In imperial Russia, the activist later known as Vladimir Lenin, hardly a paragon of the industrial battlefield that Marx predicted would bring his revolutions to life, took up the ideas articulated by Marx and his collaborator, Friedrich Engels, and from them crafted a plan to implement a Marxist revolution by a group of elites, a highly disciplined VANGUARD PARTY. This Leninist party would not wait around for electoral victories that Lenin believed would never come. Rather, it would seize state power and implement a Marxist revolution from above. Revolutionary hopefuls throughout the developing world found a solution in Lenin's model, which ran counter to Marx's initial focus on worker-led mass revolutions. Lenin's ideas on the connection between imperialism and capitalism seemed especially relevant to many at a time when capitalism was rapidly becoming a global movement. Lenin taught that richer capitalist countries used the poorer countries of the world to finance their own growth and prosperity. Capitalism, by definition, would promote uneven development, as the rich countries would get richer on the backs of cheaper labor in the non-Western world, which was becoming increasingly dependent on trade with the imperialist powers. These ideas strongly resonated with citizens in the global south who recognized that they were being exploited, especially in countries with formal imperialist governing structures. Communist movements, following the Leninist model, were integral in independence movements in Vietnam, Indonesia, Angola, Mozambique, and Guinea-Bissau.

Even though Karl Marx believed that communist revolutions would be conducted in the advanced, industrialized countries of Europe and North America, his ideas were most vigorously applied to countries in the global south. In fact, some would argue that the perceived failures of communism since 1989 were predictable from the beginning: a Marxist revolution simply was not tailored to a non-Western, nonindustrial country. Yet even today, the world's largest communist party, with approximately 87 million members, can be found in the People's Republic of China (PRC), a country that retains a large proportion of its citizens engaged in agriculture. Chairman Mao Zedong's application of Marxist communism in a nonindustrialized setting spawned similar revolutionary movements in other countries, including in Peru through Sendero Luminoso (Shining Path). In countries where full-fledged Marxist-Leninist revolutions have been undertaken, however, the leadership has never moved beyond the stage of initial socialism, during which time a single party can rule, theoretically, in the name of achieving final communism. It is because of this connection, some would say deviation, of Marxist socialism that many people associate socialism with one-party rule. This correlation, however, is not wholly accurate.

Democratic forms of socialism have also influenced SOCIAL MOVEMENTS in the countries we are studying. Fabian socialists argue that the original goal of socialists

has been distorted by their revolutionary application by Marx and his adherents. They argue that democratic, peaceful means are the only viable way to promote the socialist cause. These democratic socialists attempt to promote greater equality (especially economic equality) among citizens, and advocate a strong role for government in promoting the needs of society. Democratic socialism was especially influential during the African wars of independence of the 1970s, when leaders encouraged governments to be proactive in citizens' lives, especially in the areas of literacy and education. From the mid-1960s until the recession of the 1970s, President Julius Nyerere of Tanzania, for example, promoted a socialist model of economic development under the *ujamma* model, a Kiswahili word that means, roughly, "familyhood" or "pulling together." Nyerere not only collectivized agriculture and factories, but also, under the leadership of a single party, mandated major investments in primary schools and social services. In general, socialist leaders are critical of unbridled capitalism, pointing to often-disastrous effects of the market on the environment, family and social relations, and culture. They tend to be the people leading the charge against international economic institutions such as the World Bank and the International Monetary Fund (IMF), although they are certainly not alone in their critiques. Socialism in the non-Western world, though, emphasizes nationalism and local traditions, rather than the international and universal working-class identity promoted by initial socialist activists.

If liberalism emphasized people as individuals, conservatives urged a focus on society and its traditions, and socialists viewed the world in the framework of classes. In response to each of these ideologies, another combination of ideas—fascism—found fault with each of the preceding characterizations of the world. Similar to the other ideologies, its basis was found in historical tradition, including linguistic interpretations of history, so-called scientific understandings of race and racial identity, and an elitist prescription for political power and governance. Ideas that would form the core of fascism existed long before the ideology was named. Fascism emphasizes that which unites people as a way of segregating individuals into homogeneous groups in order to promote unity and strength. Because of its opposition to most of the systems of ideas that developed before it, and because of its negative proscriptions on life in general, it may be argued that it is easier to understand what fascists are against than what they are for.[5]

Fascists believe that the class focus of socialism is too divisive, especially because it emphasizes status as either a worker or an owner over a person's national heritage. The term "fascism," first coined in Italy, comes from the Latin word *fasces*, alluding to a set of reeds tightly bound together. Fascist leaders emphasize the importance of race and nationality, promoting in many cases a racially pure community of individuals who work together without division. Fascism also teaches that it is necessary to have a strong leader who will provide guidance and direction to the masses, and that the all-powerful leader understands the needs and the interests of the people better than they themselves do. In this sense, fascism is clearly an elitist ideology, which openly concentrates the majority of the power among a small minority of seemingly qualified individuals.

Fascists emphasize the fundamental inequality of humans and promote a clear hierarchy, often based on biological conceptions of race, of "superior" and "lesser" peoples. While fascists are not the only group to deny the universal equality of all

people, they go further, openly advocating the use of violence for handling contradictions that exist between people. While the most destructive fascist dictatorships were promoted in the European countries of Italy (under Benito Mussolini) and Germany (under Adolf Hitler), fascist authoritarian movements have also been strong in the global south as well, especially in Chile under Augusto Pinochet. Fascism is an authoritarian ideology of exclusion, and regimes that adhere to it promote division and hierarchy, violating the fundamental human rights of those deemed inferior and preventing individual liberties for all except the few deemed worthy of holding power. Fascists deny the desirability of a multicultural society, arguing to violent extremes that multiple ethnic groups cannot coexist within a single society. This ideology calls for a strong government that organizes and leads the masses, as well as a developed propaganda system that educates and motivates them into action.

In recent years, groups adhering to neofascist beliefs have gained prominence in many parts of the world, especially in economically troubled regions where immigrants, refugees, migrant workers, and other groups seen as outsiders can be scapegoated for a wide range of social and economic problems. Neofascist violence is aimed at particular ethnic communities. Neo-Nazi attacks in Germany, for example, have targeted the immigrant Turkish, African, and Vietnamese populations with firebombs and other violent attacks. Similar to their ideological predecessors, these activists condone the use of violence and segregation in order to promote the cause of their own, self-defined group.

Ideologies develop as a way to capture the relationship between leaders in government and ordinary citizens. Anarchists challenge the desirability of hierarchical power structures, emphasizing voluntary cooperation and free association over power and control. Anarchism is difficult to characterize as a single school of thought, as its adherents' beliefs straddle those of almost all groups along the ideological spectrum. Noam Chomsky defines anarchism as a "historical tendency" or a "tendency of thought and action" rather than an ideology per se.[6] Anarchists are often known for their acts of disobedience. They share a concern about the concentration of power, whether governmental power over ordinary citizens, patriarchal power of men over women, or global corporate power exercised by business conglomerates. Most anarchists promote the values of democratic participation, decentralization, and opposition to bureaucracy. While some anarchist groups condone the use of violence to further their cause, this is a point of disagreement among those adhering to this ideological perspective.

Anarchist movements have been especially popular among youth. In Mexico, for example, anarchists are especially focused on environmental causes, railing against capitalism and supporting animal liberation. Conscientious objectors of required military service have also aligned with antimilitarist anarchist youth groups. Anarchists claim that no one should have authority or control over another. In this they often challenge basic rules of behavior. Puerto Rican feminist and labor activist Luisa Capetillo is perhaps Latin America's best-known anarchist; she gained notoriety by becoming the first woman to wear pants in public in Puerto Rico. Through her work to encourage labor unionization in Puerto Rico, she worked to redefine women's freedom. The 1994 Zapatista uprising in Mexico and student strikes there have been particularly influenced by anarchism, challenging especially the power of government over minority ethnic groups. This movement, which has been viciously repressed by authorities, has awoken indigenous activists across Latin America and in

other regions as well. The Zapatistas, who long ago dismissed Mexican elections as corrupt, have made an about-face and plan to put forward an independent, indigenous, female candidate to run for president in 2018.[7]

Because of their disdain for governing structures, anarchist movements tend to reach across borders and geographic limitations to embrace a global audience. The environmental movement Earth First! confronts government and corporate behavior, especially its disregard for ecological concerns and its anthropocentric, or human-centered, bias. Additionally, diverse movements against transnational corporations and seemingly supranational organizations such as the World Trade Organization (WTO), the IMF, and the Group of 20 (G-20) have mobilized activists of all stripes to challenge the authority and actions of large bureaucracies. Protests organized to disrupt such meetings unite environmentalists, farmers, students, intellectuals, feminists, and union activists. Although not all of the participants are necessarily anarchists, the focus on the negative aspects of global capitalism goes right to the core beliefs of anarchism. Many terrorist groups, discussed in Chapter 11, base their actions in the ideology of anarchism as well.

While it is clear that a variety of often-competing ideological systems exist in our world at the beginning of the twenty-first century, true understanding of the power of these worldviews can only be found in comparison. To examine systems of ideas, it is helpful to visually align beliefs on the political spectrum. We commonly use the terminology of "left, right, and center" to place beliefs in comparison with each other. The terminology we use comes from seating arrangements in the National Assembly of France during the revolution of the late 1700s. Moderates sat in the center, those who favored democracy and rapid change congregated on the left side (or wing), and those who supported the monarch and the Catholic Church, arguing against change, sat on the right. We continue to use this linear system today to compare belief systems, although it is helpful only as a general guideline. People and groups cannot be placed on the spectrum with clear precision (few of us hold completely consistent views and opinions), and all discussions about the spectrum in a particular country or society must be understood as relative to particular circumstances.

To aid the comparison of beliefs, ideas are placed along the political spectrum according to views on the importance and desired direction of change, the role of government in the economy, and the perceived value of religious institutions. To the left of center, beliefs focus on the positive value of change (especially forward-moving developments), a larger role of government in economic matters, including the promotion of greater equality, and a smaller public role for religious institutions in the lives of people. To the right of center, church and religious institutions serve a more important role in both government and society. Advocates of right-wing ideologies are more suspicious of change, and prefer that government be less involved in economic affairs generally. To the right of center, people tend to emphasize the decline of society and advocate a reevaluation of social, political, and economic structures, and often a return to values of an earlier period. Because anarchist beliefs usually complement other ideological traditions, and because of the great variety of perspectives embodied within anarchism, it is difficult to clearly place it on one side of the spectrum or the other. As the language of this explanation suggests, there are few absolutes in the characterization of ideologies, but these general patterns capture the most important ideas. Keep in mind that an understanding of the dominant ide-

ological leanings in a particular society or governing administration will provide only limited information about the policies of the regime. For example, although we have highlighted the role of government involvement as a point distinguishing some ideological traditions, state interventionist economic programs have been used both by regimes characterized as rightist (Juan Perón's Argentina) as well as by those characterized as leftist (Salvador Allende's Chile).

How and why do people develop particular opinions and views? We are all products of a lifelong process generally referred to as socialization, through which individuals acquire their beliefs and values. Some of this socialization is accidental. Other aspects of socialization are deliberate attempts to pass on values and belief systems from generation to generation. Beliefs about government, politics, economics, and the role of the military are all influenced by some of our earliest life experiences. Educational and religious institutions, the media, peer groups, and family each influence the development of beliefs. While much of the process of acquiring attitudes about society is implicit and somewhat taken for granted, such as family relationships between women and men, governments and social groups may also explicitly influence people's sense of values, especially as they relate to the governing system. Institutions of the media are often overlooked as sources of socialization, yet news organizations, television programs, and official social media can be important sources of information about civic and political life.

The media both inform and persuade. Recognizing the power implicit in controlling access to information, many governments exercise some level of control over communications media, often through a monopoly over news and publishing outlets. Sometimes two versions of media are produced, an official version for public consumption, which downplays the tensions existing in society, and a version meant only for viewing by government leaders, which expresses a more accurate account of pressures and hot spots. Government regulation of the media, which makes the expression of unofficial opinions problematic and even dangerous, often forces dissident groups to publish their opposition views underground, in the so-called gray media or second channel.[8] These unofficial communication avenues, which straddle the permissible and the forbidden, have been especially lucrative in environments where entrepreneurship and risk-taking are encouraged. In China, for example, simply stamping a book "for internal consumption only" means that there will be a huge market on the side for bootlegged copies. Arguments over media control also fare prominently in Iran, where, despite the proliferation of media sources, both print and electronic, boundaries are enforced by the powerful Council of Guardians. Editors who challenge the boundary of the permissible have been shut down, jailed, and even flogged.

The proliferation of the Internet, including blogs, social-networking sites, and online petitions, has provided new ways to communicate while at the same time inviting novel means by which a government can spy on its population. China introduced its "Great Firewall" in 2003 to block access to seemingly sensitive websites and information, especially references to dissident movements and views. Iran has some of the most sophisticated means of controlling and censoring information on the Internet, including the ability to monitor individual communication using "deep-packet inspection," which permits central authorities to infiltrate all online traffic.[9] In 2011, after Facebook posts sharing images of police brutality drew people into the

streets in protest, the Hosni Mubarak government tried to cut off all Internet access in Egypt. In his reminder to the people that they were not free, Egypt went officially offline, but the protests only gained momentum and eventually overthrew the government. Four years later, a successor was conducting his own, unprecedented crackdown on freedom of expression, accusing the news media of insulting public officials, spreading false news, or belonging to the outlawed Muslim Brotherhood. In 2015 the government was detaining more journalists than at any time since 1991.[10]

In the face of such repression, cyber-duels ensue, and crafty Netizens find ways around limits. In China, users can use a virtual private network (VPN) to circumvent censorship by way of a secure connection through a different country, browsing the Web as if they were in that country. When Tehran blocked text messaging on the day of the 2009 presidential election, people turned to Twitter (and simple word of mouth) instead.[11] Internet censorship is conducted by countries all around the world, Western and non-Western alike, as content is inspected to assist in fighting TERRORISM, child pornography, human trafficking, and other illegal activities. The NONGOVERNMENTAL ORGANIZATION (NGO) Reporters Without Borders reports a "decline on all fronts" of media freedom in 2015, stating that "media freedom is in retreat on all five continents."[12]

Looking at the world around us, we observe similarities and differences among groups of people. It is often difficult to articulate the source of differences, when they exist. Much of it is related to the processes of socialization. When we compare political attitudes across multiple societies, people commonly speak of a POLITICAL CULTURE that exists among a defined group of people, such as "Mexican political culture" or "Egyptian political culture." This concept was developed to capture the commonly shared understandings and basic assumptions that people in a common experience tend to exhibit.

To say that a group of people shares a particular political culture does not mean that they agree on all of the important issues of politics and governance. Rather, it means that they are likely to share a common perspective about their public surroundings, including their political leaders, governmental structure, and the enduring symbols and values of public life.[13] Political culture includes citizens' general feelings toward government, including their desire (or lack thereof) to participate in political issues. It also captures a sense of people's understanding of the decision-making process, including attitudes about its merits. Understanding that people have social, political, and economic experiences different from our own helps us avoid assumptions that the way relationships and institutions operate in one setting is the way that they exist elsewhere. The concept of political culture helps us recognize the long-term impact of social, historical, and economic circumstances.

A classic study on political culture attempted to use these ideas to compare cultures throughout the world. The Civic Culture study of the 1950s and early 1960s, based on survey research, was conducted by a group of leading US political scientists.[14] It identified three dominant types of political culture. First, Gabriel Almond and Sidney Verba classified a "participant culture," in which most people exhibit pride toward their country's political system, feel that they should participate in it, and have a sense that their participation makes a difference. They also generally understand the way the system works. Second, the study identified a "subject culture," in which people tend to discount their ability to participate in and change politics;

Figure 9.2 "Antisocial" Media

The Internet provides some novel opportunities for social organization and the expression of citizen voice. Yet many of the same characteristics that make these technologies useful can make them dangerous as well: the forum is quick, rife with information that its users provide (including sensitive contact information and personal details); it crosses national borders, making the legal terrain more complicated; and the (at least temporary) anonymity it can provide makes accountability more difficult to establish. In some societies, "Internet mobbing" and "virtual lynchings" have arisen, sometimes with grim consequences. *The Economist* quipped that "antisocial" media are developing, providing opportunities to target individuals for revenge or retribution.[a] Lists of targeted teenagers appeared on Facebook in southern Colombia, with three of the sixty-nine people named on the hit list killed within less than two weeks (police originally viewed the lists as a hoax, even though just a month earlier, a university student in Bogotá was imprisoned for allegedly creating a Facebook page calling for the assassination of the Colombian president's son). In China, a woman was dubbed the "stiletto kitten killer" for crushing a kitten's skull with her high heels, and a nationwide hunt began. She was tracked down five days after her personal contact information was posted on QQ, China's wildly popular, free instant-messaging service.[b] Chinese Internet forums, dubbed "human-flesh search engines," are creating a "cyberposse" of sorts[c]—eager Netizens hunt down presumed violators of an unwritten moral code, forcing individuals to take cover to attempt to evade the branders of local justice. *Un*civil society has met the information age.

Notes: a. "Antisocial Media," *The Economist*, August 25, 2010.

b. Richard Spencer, "Just Who Is the Glamorous Kitten Killer of Hangzhou?," *The Telegraph* (London), March 4, 2006.

c. Tom Downey, "China's Cyberposse," *New York Times*, March 3, 2010.

rather, they view themselves as obedient subordinates of the government. People in these societies tend to be aware of the operations of the political system, but overall are cautious about participating in it. Finally, the study identified a "parochial culture," in which people tend to identify almost exclusively with their immediate locality, feeling that national political issues have very little to do with them. In such cultures, people tend to speak little about political affairs, because in their viewpoint such matters rarely touch their lives.

What did Almond and Verba conclude about political culture from this study? The only one of our cases that was included in this original study was Mexico, which was characterized as the prototypical parochial culture. While recognizing that each country contains people with a mix of views, the leaders of the study generalized about each society as a whole. This was a pivotal attempt to make broad statements about many countries at once, in a comparative framework.

Yet there are serious limitations to such an approach. For one, it invites the potential for discriminatory assumptions or even establishing a hierarchy of favored characteristics. It was clear by the way the findings were presented that a participatory, aware, and active population should be the ultimate goal for each society. Yet there was little recognition that the standards for the study were based on Western traditions and cultures, which promote civic duty and activism as a virtue. The Civic Culture study and others that have followed in its footsteps are indicative of the wide-eyed optimism of many Americans in the late 1950s and 1960s. The implicit

hope was that Western-style democracies were going to flourish around the world, and that there was a single model of the so-called developed, democratic state. In fact, the guiding assumption of the Civic Culture study was that the participant culture is a precondition to stable democracy.

In addition to being ethnocentric, this approach tended to emphasize the changes that were not taking place, presumably because people did not exhibit characteristics found in other Western cultures, rather than the realm of the possible, or what could take place. Also, such an aggregated view of single political cultures oversimplifies complex societies. The assumptions of national culture make grandiose claims that are difficult to substantiate. For example, in a state like Nigeria, with over 250 different ethnic groups, does it really make sense to talk of a singular "Nigerian" political culture? There is also a problem of translation: concepts such as EFFICACY, duty, and participation do not always translate very clearly, and people have differing images in their minds as to the precise meaning of these terms. Political culture is useful to explain differences among groups, but it is less helpful when used to explain so-called national traits, as David Elkins and E. B. Simeon identified.[15] While it is clear that culture is important, it is less clear how to measure it. At best, the concept of political culture is useful for understanding general orientations, but it is important that we not make assumptions much beyond this.

Identities

When individuals make assessments about the world around them, they make decisions based on a self-perception of who they are, or their identity. Increasingly, we understand that people's self-perception influences their behavior and attitudes. It affects whom we define as potential collaborators or competitors, and it impacts the outcomes we seek. The traditional ideologies discussed earlier are largely devoid of an explicit awareness of self-identity: they aim to provide an outlook based on larger issues often irrespective of individual attributes. Yet a growing trend in social thought and action revolves around identity issues that fundamentally get at the question of who we are. They tend to be very personal ideologies that encourage people to fight for recognition of the joint needs and preferences of particular groups, often those that have been denied expression in the past. Identities are extremely complex concepts. For one thing, we each have multiple individual characteristics: one individual may embody the identities of friend, daughter, Asian, worker. We choose to emphasize a particular trait based on the context in which we are involved. For example, at a sporting event, people are usually defined as either athletes or spectators. At an international sporting event, it becomes even more complex, with the characteristic of national identity becoming important. Yet at other gatherings, such as some religious meetings, one's categorization as a female or male, or as a believer or nonbeliever, can be the defining characteristic.

Individual and group identities are quite closely related; in addition to describing themselves individually, people group with others. This involves the development of a collective, or shared, identity. Groups of ordinary people mobilize around a common self-definition, usually as a way to achieve a common goal. Additionally, leaders attempt to rally their citizens around an identity related to their own power. Officials who are defensive about their own ability to maintain power are particularly adept at

rallying people around a shared sense of belonging, often making promises to varied groups as a way to lock in their support. Zimbabwe's Robert Mugabe provides a good example, with his promises of land and "Africa for Africans." Such populist attempts can be particularly strong in countries undergoing dislocation or change. The Peronists in Argentina exemplified populism by forming coalitions of the urban poor and parts of the organized working and middle classes, promising greater economic equality and independence (especially economic) from foreign countries. The 1979 Iranian Revolution was a populist movement that rallied the common people against the West, personified in opposition to the Shah. Even long after his election in mid-2005, Iranian president Mahmoud Ahmadinejad seemed to deliver campaign-style speeches across the country, dressing plainly, speaking simply, and promising a better life for his audience while railing against corruption and the wealthy, including the powerful clerics.[16] Populist movements are fundamentally about identity and pride: they attempt to rally groups to action in the name of the self-described "people": they may be left or right in orientation, but their motivation is nearly the same. The difficulty with populism on its own, however, is that "the people" rarely fit into one category. Populism is usually combined with other movements. Nationalist movements, for example, have been common bedfellows for populist leaders.

For over 200 years, the idea of nationalism has been used to promote the interests and needs of a particular nation, or group of people. Usually, nations are identified as sharing a common history, culture, language, ethnicity, or religion, although the actual components of national identity can vary widely. Nationalist movements have been a potent uniting (and dividing) force throughout many of the countries that we are studying. The initial struggle faced by many of these countries was to establish a common identity after the colonial period. National identities were therefore defined more in opposition to the colonial rulers than in composition of shared characteristics. The concept of "Indonesia," for example, was an entirely novel identity for the disparate ethnic groups who had operated a vast trading network from the islands of Java and Sumatra for centuries. Yet especially between the two world wars, the notion of a single, independent Indonesia was created and promoted, mostly by students and young professionals, in opposition to Dutch rule. It is an identity still waiting to be wholly crafted and accepted by all who live under the government of the republic.

Throughout the global south, indigenous nationalist movements developed as a way to honor unique local traditions and ethnic identities. After a sense of identity was mobilized against the occupying powers, nationalist movements sometimes turned to violence as a means of expelling foreign influence, as in Vietnam, Algeria, Indonesia, Zimbabwe, Mozambique, and Angola. Some nationalist leaders propelled their movements with socialist ideology, such as Ho Chi Minh in the Vietnamese struggle against France and later the United States. Other nationalist leaders turned to socialist policies to help reconstruct their countries after achieving independence, including Algeria, India, Egypt, Mozambique, and Angola. In its opposition to capitalism, socialism presented a means for national self-sufficiency and economic independence.[17]

Today, nationalist movements of identity are on the rise, but they certainly are not new—as discussed in our study of wars of national liberation in Chapter 4. We identify two types of nationalist mobilization: one calls for independence from larger political units that attempt to incorporate multiple national groups, and the other tries to bring attention to their identity in the face of global homogenization. Most of the

countries that we are studying are richly multinational, made up of people with diverse linguistic, religious, historical, and cultural traditions. For some, this has not been an issue of great division, either because the leadership suppresses such discussion (as in the case of Tibetan identity in China), or because the groups themselves fail to see a need to challenge the status quo. For others, the expression of diverse national identities can be dangerous business. For example, the Kurdish people, many of whom identify as a nation with a common language and culture, have increasingly challenged their incorporation within the political entity of Turkey. Turkish leaders have defined the "Kurdish question" as a terrorist threat, and have until recently outlawed any independent expression of Kurdish identity, including their native language. The arrest of Kurdish leader Abdullah Öcalan lessened separatist tensions somewhat, but the potential for aggression, in both separatist action and state response, remains. We will return to the question of the role of violence in irredentist movements in Chapter 11.

In addition, with increasing economic interdependence and trade, the rise of globalization motivates some national groups to emphasize their unique characteristics in the face of commercial and cultural homogeneity. While there are many positive aspects of a global economy and the conveniences it brings, many believe that it inhibits indigenous cultures and traditions in the name of modernity. In response to the perceived growth of Western values and goods, many groups increase their expression of microidentities. Some of this has been in response to global corporate developments. For example, there was much resistance in China when Seattle-based Starbucks opened a coffee shop in the cherished Palace Museum, the former residence of the emperors and empresses known outside China as the Forbidden City. Many Islamic groups decry the pervasiveness of Western standards in areas of fashion, gender relations, and entertainment. One scholar, Benjamin Barber, has named the tension "Jihad vs. McWorld."[18] Since September 11, 2001, though, Barber and others have quickly cautioned us not to make the easy and inaccurate assumptions that the world can so neatly be characterized in a binary fashion, grouping people in tight categories as either in favor of Western-style modernization, or not. Rather, the image that Barber attempted to convey in the provocative title of his study is more accurately viewed as a means of capturing the diverse opposition that has formed to the proliferation of mass markets, technology, and Western-dominated popular culture.[19] For many groups on the receiving end of this new culture, it forces a reevaluation of their fundamental identity.

People also emphasize their class identity, which is based on their status within the economic structure. For example, people who consider themselves "working class" tend to identify with others who receive hourly wages for their labor. Although the origins of class awareness are largely Marxist, people who speak of a class identity are not necessarily Marxist revolutionaries. Income is unevenly distributed in every society. Guillermo O'Donnell and others have argued that a middle class, who are without the extremist tendencies of either wealth or dire poverty, is critical in transitions to democracy, as we discuss in Chapter 14. But especially in societies where there is a sharp divide between the rich and the poor, such as Peru, identity as a member of the working class or the upper class is extremely important, a lesson that feminist mobilizers took some time to learn. Class identity has been an often-cited rallying cry to stand in opposition to the status quo.

Figure 9.3   Tibet and the Tibetan People

Located in southwestern China, Tibet is a great example of a region in which people exercise multiple identities. Living on the world's highest plateau, the Tibetan people have fought against conquest by many peoples, including the Mongols, the imperial Chinese, and the British. Shortly after the declaration of the People's Republic of China in 1949, troops of the Chinese Communist Party marched into Tibet, attempting to enlarge their rule over the important border region. Suppression of the Tibetan uprising was fierce: thousands of Tibetans were killed and hundreds of sacred monasteries were destroyed. While the Chinese Communist Party was nominally successful at establishing its rule, many, including the main spiritual leader of the Tibetan people, the Dalai Lama, fled to India in 1959, where the government-in-exile remains today.

Buddhism was declared the official religion of Tibet in the eighth century. Yet Tibetan Buddhists are not all unified in their expression of religious tenets or doctrine—in fact, a fierce rivalry has long existed between two groups, the "Yellow Hat" sect (known as the Gelugpa) and the "Black Hat" sect (the Kagyupa). Until the 1600s the Black Hats, led by the Karmapa Lama, dominated Tibetan affairs, but for the past four centuries the Yellow Hats, under the leadership of the Dalai Lama, have persevered. The current Dalai Lama, believed to be the fourteenth reincarnation of the spiritual leader, received the Nobel Peace Prize in 1989 for his advocacy of peace and environmental concerns. Not all Tibetan Buddhists, though, share his passion for nonviolence.

Residents of Tibet today include native inhabitants of the region, as well as Chinese migrants from other regions of the country—including many of the Han Chinese majority, who moved to Tibet in search of economic opportunities promoted by the government in Beijing. Many native residents of the territory fear they are losing their indigenous culture, religious traditions, and way of life, which are challenged not only by Han migration to the region but also by the modernizing ways of young Tibetan residents. Changes are likely to accelerate now that the world's highest railway route has opened between Beijing and Lhasa (a forty-eight-hour trek).

Another source of identity that is often masked by the dominance of the government is a regional identity. This shared identity among residents of a particular region, such as a north-south distinction, or the type of region, such as urban or rural, is heightened when governments pursue economic reforms that promote regional disparities. For example, regions in Mexico may be differentiated by the prevalence of export industrialization in the north, leading to relative prosperity as compared to destitution in the south, where the economy is more dependent on domestic sales. Northern Nigeria, which is predominantly Muslim, has since independence dominated political power and decisionmaking, but most of the oil is found in the southern, predominantly Christian and animist parts of the country. Indonesia is another country with pronounced regional differences, compounded by linguistic and religious differences that are geographically concentrated. The westernmost province of Aceh, deemed the most "Islamic" of any region in the state, is sometimes called "the front porch of Mecca" because it points toward Saudi Arabia. It also has great natural wealth in its possession of liquefied natural gas, which distinguishes it from other provinces.

In many countries of the global south, a majority of the population lives in the countryside, often making their living off of the land. Contrary to popular belief, rural dwellers are not necessarily conservative in their political views, nor are they passive recipients of the status quo. In some cases, peasants may be the forerunners to progressive change. For example, one scholar counters popular belief by

demonstrating that voter turnout in African rural areas tends to be higher than in the cities.[20] Peasants around the world are known as crafty political entrepreneurs who know how to work the system to their maximum advantage. Throughout the global south, we see rural residents rallying for their rights, whether it is protesting the loss of land to the state, advocating for education and safe drinking water, or standing up to corruption, among other issues. But the picture is complex, and clientelism, or the maintenance of PATRON-CLIENT RELATIONSHIPS that reinforce the status quo, can persist in rural areas. Mexico's Institutional Revolutionary Party (PRI) relied on rural support for years, and rural dwellers fearful of change have been a crucial base of support for the Mugabe regime in Zimbabwe.

Throughout the world, religious affiliations also serve as an important sense of identity. It is not surprising that one's basic values and assumptions about human beings, morality, and justice color opinions on issues of politics, economics, and culture. In the United States, a separation of church and state tends to be promoted, meaning that religion is often viewed as a personal matter, and that religious beliefs should not become too closely involved in matters of politics and governance, although the dividing line is often challenged. The separation of church and state is a contested concept in many regions and within many spiritual traditions of the world. In fact, in some of the countries that we are studying, a greater fusion of religion and politics is desired not only by the political elites, but by some ordinary citizens as well. The declining rate of affiliation with formal church organizations in the United States (as well as Western Europe) does not mimic trends found in the global south, as rates of formal religious identity continue to increase, due in part to religious conversions, but even more so to powerful demographic trends. Data from Pew suggest that by 2050, the number of Muslims will be nearly equal to the number of Christians around the world, comprising approximately one-third of the world's population.[21] Yet restrictions on religious expression (by the government as well as social actors) in many of the most populous countries of the world, including China, Egypt, Indonesia, and Pakistan, are also becoming increasingly common.[22]

When contemplating religious issues and their importance in politics and governance, many think of the Middle East, the birthplace of the world's three major monotheistic religions: Islam, Judaism, and Christianity. While religious issues are indeed important in this region, religious values and beliefs are difficult to separate from events in other parts of the world as well. Two predominantly Muslim countries present an interesting paradox. In Turkey, where the population is 99 percent Muslim, until very recently the government has fiercely upheld secularism, established at the beginning of the modern republic in 1923 (current President Recep Tayyip Erdogan appears to promote the more open expression of religious identity, rattling many). The Islamic Republic of Iran, however, established by the revolution in 1979, is a formal theocracy. For example, Iran's highest institution of authority, the Council of Guardians, bases its decisions on the sacred Muslim text, the Quran, rather than on the country's 1979 constitution. Attempts to develop political and religious pluralism face fierce opposition from religious clerics, who hold much of the power within the country.

Another source of the controversy is related to the connection between those who use Islam as a source for their political ideology and those who undertake violence in the name of Islam. Most Muslims view *jihad,* often translated from the Ara-

Figure 9.4   Are All Arabs Muslim? Are All Muslims Arab?

Despite the fact that the terms are often used interchangeably, there are important differences in meaning between "Arabs" and "Muslims." Generally, Arabs are viewed as a community defined either linguistically (countries in which the dominant language is Arabic, which is a member of the Semitic family of languages), politically (citizens of a country that is a member of the Arab League, an organization of twenty-two states headquartered in Cairo, Egypt), or genealogically (families who trace their ancestry to the Arabian Peninsula or Syrian desert). Any categorization has exceptions—Somalia, for example, is a non-Arab country that is a member of the Arab League, and many people who speak Arabic do not consider themselves to be Arab.

Arabs identify with many different religious traditions. The majority of Arabs are Muslim, but there are also Arab Christians (concentrated in Lebanon, Egypt, Palestine, Jordan, Sudan, and Syria), and Arab Jews (in Morocco and Tunisia). Not all Muslim-majority states are Arab: the Islamic Republic of Iran is Persian, not Arab.

Muslims are adherents of Islam. Muslims come from many different ethnic groups, and are connected by their belief in Islam. Less than a quarter of the world's Muslims are Arab—the world's most populous Muslim countries are in Asia: Indonesia, Pakistan, Bangladesh, and India.

bic as "struggle," as an individual struggle to overcome temptations and submit to the will of God, or Allah (the term *Islam* means "submission to God"). It is true that some, a minority within the faith, view jihad as struggle against enemies of Islam. These individuals and the groups they support may accurately be characterized as advocates of militant Islam, just as we have discussed regarding adherents of more aggressive forms of other traditions. And extremists who claim that their faith inspires violent acts usually lose the support of others in their faith community, as al-Qaeda experienced in most Muslim circles after 9/11.

As we have discussed, the labeling of any action or group is fraught with difficulty, especially from the perspective of the people being discussed. This controversy has become particularly acute as analysts try to characterize so-called political Islam. Many terms have been coined to capture the ideology and political program that some derive from their Islamic faith, with "Islamism" becoming a commonly used term by both advocates and detractors alike.[23] As we find with almost any label, as much is obscured as is understood—not all politically active Christians see the world through the same lens, for example, so why should it be assumed that all Muslims do? Because of these terminological debates, trying to characterize the numbers is difficult.

The intellectual roots of Islamism as an ideology can be traced to Sayyid Abul Ala Maududi, an Indian journalist who fought in the anti-imperial struggle and then moved to Pakistan to build a more pure Islamic state, later founding the Islamist party Jamaat-e-Islami (JEI) in 1941 to counter the secularism and Westernization of Pakistan. He emphasized personal transformation and the grounding of all human activity in faith. Another source of Islamist views was Sayyid Qutb, an Egyptian civil servant who, after graduate study in the United States, rejected Western values as corrupt and immoral. Returning to Egypt, he vocally criticized what he perceived to be his government's replication of Western decadence. Qutb eventually became a leader of the oldest Islamist party, Egypt's Muslim Brotherhood. His outspokenness as an

activist ways landed him in jail (where he refined his ideas), and ultimately he was hanged by the Egyptian government.

More recently, some Islamists have been emboldened by what they perceive as the corrupt, hegemonic ways of Western governments, most notoriously the United States. They took great exception when, following the Gulf War in 1991, Saudi Arabia agreed to the stationing of US troops inside of the land that is home to Mecca and Medina, the two most sacred sites of Islam. (Even though US troops were formally withdrawn in 2003, small US military contingents, including a drone base, remain.)[24] Islamists hold views in varying levels and degrees, some arguing that the greatest threat to peace is internal (e.g., believers who are not faithful), and others targeting external threats (e.g., the United States). Cartoons depicting the prophet Muhammad insult Muslims (whether Islamist or not) around the world to varying degrees, and contribute to the sense that, as a faith community, Muslims remain poorly understood by many non-Muslims. Pew data reflect a lack of factual knowledge about Islam by many Americans, with nearly half stating that they do not personally know a Muslim. A global 2011 survey cited in the Pew report also highlighted negative views (including greedy, fanatic, violent, and immoral) that Muslims and non-Muslim Westerners have of each other.[25]

The role of formal Catholic Church institutions has been a keen issue in Mexican politics since as far back as the mid-1800s. Mexicans have fought two civil wars to decide the Church's role. The country is overwhelmingly Roman Catholic but fiercely anticlerical. The 1917 revolution sought to limit the Church's involvement in politics. Religious schools were closed, and church property was seized. Priests were prohibited from voting or wearing the collar in public. But the election of the socially conservative National Action Party (PAN) in 2000 emboldened the Church and reignited a number of controversies.

In some countries, governments construct a specific doctrine to explain the role of religion in politics and society. Political and military leaders in Indonesia, for example, long promoted the importance of the *pancasila,* literally the "five principles." These pillars of Indonesian life are monotheism, national unity, humanitarianism, representative democracy by consensus, and social justice. Sukarno, the first president of Indonesia, created the *pancasila* creed as a way to unite the diverse peoples of Indonesia. Although the meaning of the *pancasila* doctrine is debated today, it remains an important symbol of leaders' aspirations to create unity out of diversity.

Another example of the importance of religious identity in the global south comes from a Christian tradition. Liberation theology is a movement that started within the Catholic Church, and it has had an especially powerful impact in Latin America. In Brazil alone—the world's most populous Roman Catholic state—there are more than 80,000 lay communities organized around this philosophy.[26] It is by definition an action-oriented ideology that calls on its followers to promote social justice, focusing especially on the most economically poor members of society. As a system of thought, it is intriguing because of its combination of Marxist revolutionary ideas (which are explicitly hostile toward organized religions) with Christian teachings. While its origins were within Roman Catholicism, it is increasingly becoming an ecumenical movement, including other Christian churches and institutions. And although many of its leaders received training in European religious institutions, liberation theology is increasingly becoming an indigenous intellectual

and ideological movement, with native theologians addressing the social ills plaguing the less developed world.

In 1971, Peruvian theologian Gustavo Gutiérrez published *A Theology of Liberation,* considered by many to be the definitive statement.[27] In it he stressed social praxis (practice), with a commitment to critical reflection and a renewed dedication on the part of the universal church to the disenfranchised poor and destitute. Gutiérrez argued that too many Christians, especially Catholics, focus on the orthodoxy (correct teachings) rather than on the orthopraxis (correct practice) of a Christian life. Liberation theology maintains that people need to move beyond doctrine to focus on the economic, political, and social issues that affect ordinary people on a daily basis. Advocates of this approach contend that poverty is caused by structures (such as the international economic system) rather than individual, idiosyncratic characteristics, including laziness, bad luck, or other sources of blame. Therefore, the "liberation" of the poor is more than an act of individual charity; it is a demand for a new social and economic order in order to promote the universal humanity of all peoples. Second is the idea of collective sin, articulated by Brazilian theologian Leonardo Boff, who argued that people who support unjust regimes, even if they do not personally exploit the poor, are collectively responsible for the result.[28] Boff's statements implicated not only leaders and citizens in the Western, developed world, but citizens of poorer countries as well. Liberation theology has impacted many of the countries we are studying here. A 2000 pastoral letter in Mexico, for example, criticized political and economic systems as "poverty-generating structures," and called on people to fight to build a more just society. The South African Council of Churches applied the principles of liberation theology, through black theology, to end apartheid. Several ecumenical organizations, including the Zimbabwean Catholic Bishops Conference and the Zimbabwe Council of Churches, played important roles in the struggle against white minority rule, and continue to condemn human rights abuses. They argue that poverty is due to oppressive structures and call for activism, primarily through the development of base Christian communities that work to educate, evangelize, and empower the economically poor. Movements inspired by liberation theology have met with harsh repression by governments (backed by military force) and institutional churches as well, especially in El Salvador and Guatemala. This has provoked an increase in violence by adherents.

Mobilization around issues of gender has been particularly strong throughout the non-Western world, especially since 1975, when the United Nations held its first international women's conference, in Mexico City. Similar to other groups, women have mobilized in response to repression, exclusion, and other crises, both on their own behalf and in the interest of others, especially children. There is no single brand of feminism, but rather many different viewpoints commonly united around the desire to advance the voice of women in today's world. Some view feminism as a solely Western idea, unaware of the rich history of feminism throughout the global south.[29]

Feminism is a complex worldview that includes many perspectives, and there are vigorous debates about what defines a "feminist." One school of thought distinguishes feminists who work primarily for civil equality that recognizes the fundamental equality between women and men. Such groups, often called liberal feminists, have been at the forefront of suffrage movements as well as civil rights movements that fight for gains in equality before the law. This view is contrasted

with another school of thought that emphasizes the differences that exist between women and men. Commonly known as radical feminists, they argue that liberal feminists fail to recognize the unspoken assumption that women should perform the same as men. In contrast, radical feminists fight for the equal recognition of women's standards as well as men's; they argue that women's ways need to be recognized for their inherent contributions as well. It is a question of standards and assumptions; while radical feminists agree that men and women are equal, they contend that stopping there fails to challenge the continued dominance of a male-centric society.

Feminists have actively challenged notions of "correct" female (and by association male) behavior that are rooted in custom and tradition. In a related fashion, many women openly confront the notion that politics is the exclusive domain of men. Mexico, for example, has a long feminist history. Some analysts argue that it is Mexico, not the United States, that has been the cradle for feminism in the Western Hemisphere. Sor Juana Inéz de la Cruz, who lived in the 1600s, is said to be the first feminist of the Americas. In large numbers, Mexican women joined the revolutionary armies of Pancho Villa and Emiliano Zapata. Benita Galeana led the first land takeovers by squatters during the Great Depression. She was arrested sixty times and lost her eyesight while on a hunger strike fighting for women's suffrage. Since the 1980s, *maquiladora* workers have claimed an unusual degree of freedom for themselves, despite the low pay and sexual harassment they continue to face in the factories. Mexican feminists today are fighting for reproductive rights, for better working conditions, and to have violence against women (especially sexual assault and wife battery) taken more seriously. However, in Mexico and in Latin America as a whole, women have not fully harnessed their potential as a political force compared to other interest groups such as labor movements and church groups.

Similar to other sets of activists, groups working to further women's causes disagree about the point of focus for their actions. Some groups accuse others of reinforcing gender distinctions by focusing on issues of family, motherhood, and children, replicating traditional political roles. Engaging in so-called motherist activism (discussed later), groups in Latin America, for example, were challenged by radical feminist leaders because their work focused on practical interests, such as providing meals to deprived children, rather than on more "strategic" issues, including sexual freedom and domestic violence.[30] Yet the mothers' groups, in their emphasis on seemingly practical needs, rallied tens of thousands of activists against military regimes, revealing that the emperor had no clothes. Some argue that women are uniquely placed to fight for the interests of their children, and indeed women have potently harnessed this connection to challenge state norms and policies.

Another debate centers on the relationship between culture and feminism. This has definitely been a theme of contention and division among Latin American, African, and Islamic feminists. Women who work within the system, or within the structure of prevailing religious norms, are accused by others of replicating traditional views that subordinate women, rather than challenging the status quo.

Non-Western variants of feminism have argued that "practical" concerns, including providing meals and healthcare to families, can be just as feminist as the political concerns of other feminists, such as demanding access to political decisionmaking. Adherents to the latter focus, which is considered to be more "strategic" than practical, claim to be working for larger structural changes that would ulti-

mately transform gender relations. But non-Western women do not hold a monopoly on this desire: in Latin America, for example, feminism was central to the effort to delegitimize military rule and re-create civil society.[31] Yet other feminist groups, in the face of the same struggles, adopted an explicitly human rights character to their activism. Economic crises and the imposition of austerity programs impelled women to organize and demand relief, filling in the gaps of what government could not (or would not) provide. Maybe some viewed this as practical and too "traditional," but to the women who were organizing, it was feminism at its best.

To be successful, people plan their strategies within existing contexts—sometimes this means radically challenging the system, and other times it means reforming it along the edges. Patriarchy and social conservatism are so pervasive, for example, that many women in northern Nigeria believe that reform within Islamic law is the only hope for promoting gender equality. The issue of modest clothing associated with some interpretations of Islamic customs captures some of this controversy. Many Westerners associate the traditional headscarf or veil with women's oppression and submission to male authority. Yet for many Muslim women, the decision to wear a headscarf is a conscious choice; the wearing of a veil, or *purdah* (literally, "curtain"), provides them an avenue of expression and even opposition. For some, veiling literally creates a wall

---

Figure 9.5 LGBT Rights in the Global South

One of the most personal aspects of identity can also be the most dangerous. Advocates for the rights of lesbian, gay, bisexual, and transgender (LGBT) individuals point out that throughout many countries of the global south, individuals lack the basic freedom to express gender identity or sexual orientation. As of 2016, seventy-six countries around the world have laws that criminalize or harass people on the basis of their sexual orientation or identity, including states in which the death penalty can be applied for cases of consensual homosexual conduct (Iran, Mauritania, Saudi Arabia, Sudan, and Yemen, as well as parts of Nigeria and Somalia).[a] Uganda's record is particularly severe, where legislation has been passed—with overwhelming popular support—to eradicate homosexuality from the country; the sponsor of the bill, who has connections to a largely discredited group of US evangelicals, minced no words as he stated his goal: "to kill every last gay person."[b]

The record on rights is not all negative, however. Argentina, for example, legalized same-sex marriage in mid-2010, becoming the first Latin American state to do so. In Mexico, the Supreme Court ruled that marriages registered in Mexico City, where same-sex unions are legal, must be recognized throughout the country, providing the potential for nationwide marriage rights.[c] Even though there is no legal prohibition on discrimination against gay couples in China, more individuals are openly expressing their orientation, even as government censorship and intimidation continue. Researchers have found that the social stigma toward homosexuality in China is grounded less in religious principles than it is in the mandate to marry and continue the family line.[d]

Notes: a. United Nations High Commissioner for Refugees (UNHCR), "Discrimination and Violence Against Individuals Based on Their Sexual Orientation and Gender Identity," May 4, 2015.

b. Interview with Jeff Sharlet, "Finding the Root of Anti-Gay Sentiment in Uganda," NPR, August 25, 2010; Jeffrey Gettleman, "Americans' Role Seen in Uganda Anti-Gay Push," *New York Times*, January 3, 2010.

c. David Agren, "Mexican States Ordered to Honor Gay Marriages," *New York Times*, August 10, 2010.

d. Tania Branigan, "Beijing's 'Happy Couples' Launch Campaign for Same-Sex Marriages," *The Guardian* (London), February 25, 2009.

that allows women to move through the male world of school and work; it allows a quiet insubordination. For others, it is liberating to be listened to, rather than looked at. In Tunisia, where donning a religious veil was forbidden until after the Arab Spring revolution of 2011, selecting the *niqab,* a full Muslim veil that leaves only the eyes showing, was a welcome expression of religious devotion.[32] In Turkey, the Islamic veil is a source of fierce controversy; secular feminists are against it and religious women march for their freedom to wear it. Covering was only legal in public spaces—including civil service and government jobs—after 2013, although it is still not allowed on the job at military or judicial positions. Some women have refashioned traditional styles into a modern fashion of headscarf, granting them expression and individuality. In this sense, women have reappropriated Islamic admonitions for modest dress as a means of heightening their presence and voice.

Clearly, not all women are feminists. In fact, some ardently oppose mobilization and action in the name of equality or women's causes. Some groups, self-proclaimed antifeminists, reject the importance of feminist issues and often agree with gender segregation and clearly defined family roles. They often advocate a culturally conservative position, reaffirming the notion of a predetermined place for women at home, rearing the family, rather than in the marketplace or other public domains of men. Key issues of antifeminists include opposition to abortion and women's employment outside the home.

Each of these approaches, and the actions they inspire, arouse debate about cultural values and standards. Are there universal norms, applicable to all people irrespective of culture, level of development, or social system, or is there merit in an approach referred to as cultural relativism, in which standards are dependent on relative circumstances?

Elites, Masses, and Legitimacy

It has been implicit in our discussion to this point that power is distributed unequally. Usually in public life, some people hold power and other people are influenced by it. In this chapter, we have emphasized that all people possess ideas about the world around them. It is obvious that in many areas of life, the ideas of some matter more than the ideas of others. In every society around the world, people can be divided into two categories, either the elites (possessing power and influence) or the masses (lacking power and influence relative to the elites). There are always more of the latter. Even though the so-called elites may exercise more influence and authority in economics, politics, culture, or other areas, they are not able to maintain this status indefinitely.

An important term that conveys one of the most fundamental political relationships between elites and masses is legitimacy, sometimes viewed simply as "rightfulness."[33] All leaders, no matter their level, need to be concerned about their legitimacy. It can be viewed as a sense that an individual or group who has power, holds such power properly. Individuals or groups can possess power or influence, but if the people over whom they have influence do not view them as legitimate, their power and influence will likely be short-lived.

Sociologist Max Weber identified three primary sources of legitimacy: tradition, charisma, and legality. Traditional legitimacy is based on cultural precedents established for recognizing authority and power. A tribal chief, for example, bases his

legitimacy on this source. Hereditary monarchies, in which some people receive their influence because of membership in particular families, are other sources of traditional legitimacy. The "Mandate of Heaven," possessed by members of the Chinese imperial leadership, is another example of legitimacy that is traditional in nature. Charismatic sources of legitimacy are based on personal attributes that command attention, respect, and often obedience. Charisma is both something that people are said to exhibit, as well as something given to them in the eyes of ordinary people. For example, Ayatollah Ruhollah Khomeini, the former religious leader of the Iranian Revolution, was viewed as a mythical hero to many. Before the 1979 revolution, while he was living in exile (mostly in Turkey, Iraq, and France), people in Iran insisted that they could see his face in the moon.[34] The third source of legitimacy, according to Weber, is legality: establishing seemingly impersonal rules and procedures to determine the recipients of leadership and authority. In this example, elections and laws transfer a sense of legitimacy to individuals and groups.

Legitimacy is what makes political systems last. It transforms raw power into a sense of authority. Without legitimacy, rulers' mandates are enforced out of a sense of fear, rather than a sense of duty or obligation.[35] A lack of legitimacy can cause a government to crumble. In some cultural traditions, there would be signs from the ancestors or the spirits that a leader had lost his or her legitimacy. In imperial China, for example, natural disasters were perceived to be signs that the emperor had lost the legitimacy to rule. In many modern democracies today, legitimacy is based on the popular mandate. Although elections are increasingly being viewed as the legitimizing tool of modern leaders, this has not always been the case, nor do many leaders maintain their legitimacy based on legal means alone.

Do powerful elites really need to be concerned about their legitimacy? They do. It is difficult to survive on coercion alone, and leaders need authority in order to accomplish the day-to-day tasks of governing. Coercion and the violence it entails are costly, not only in a crude financial sense, but in terms of morale as well. Certainly, some authoritarian leaders have made extensive use of threats and coercion as a means of maintaining their power. But it is extremely difficult (although not impossible) to maintain power in this manner for long. Leaders in all areas of public life need to develop connections with the masses, and must be able to foster a sense that they are legitimately empowered to make decisions. When citizens no longer believe that the leadership has legitimacy, they are often impelled to act. Ordinary citizens, even in the face of dire constraints on their behavior and threats of coercive responses from leaders, attempt to challenge circumstances that they feel are unjust and illegitimate. While some of these attempts face anguishing defeats, others are successful at challenging the state of affairs and bringing about desired change.

Leaders maintain their legitimacy in a variety of different ways. Ideology plays a key role, as members of the elite attempt to craft views and actions to their liking. The manipulation of ideologies by leaders is particularly acute in totalitarian systems, in which the government has control over most aspects of people's lives. The use of important symbols, such as buildings, images, linguistic phrases, and historical heroes, is another means by which leaders attempt to promote and increase their legitimacy. In societies that have experienced revolutions, or have had a recent history of revered leaders, paying homage to and noting a lineage from these leaders can be a powerful source of legitimacy, especially in uncertain times. On the fiftieth anniversary

of the founding of the People's Republic of China, for example, then-president Jiang Zemin, who was also general secretary of the Chinese Communist Party (CCP), ordered large pictures of himself to be carried on high behind the traditional posters of Mao Zedong and Deng Xiaoping. This rather blatant attempt to demonstrate the source of his authority is not unlike other public relations campaigns in which leaders engage. In examining legitimacy in the non-Western world, one must be careful to avoid connections between legitimacy, stability, and popular consent. Just because a pronounced sense of legitimacy may seem to be present in a particular country does not mean that citizens agree with all (or even most) of the actions that their government takes.

Leaders may also promote their legitimacy by providing material gains to the population. Indonesia's former president Suharto based much of his legitimacy, especially in the later years of his rule, on promises to the people that their economic lives would improve. When the futility of this promise was painfully realized in the spring of 1998, however, his legitimacy plummeted, and he was forced from office. This example provides another lesson about the importance of stability. When leaders are successful at maintaining it, for the most part life is stable. When they fail, it can often lead to popular mobilization or other forms of participation, a topic to which we now turn our attention.

Ideas in Action

If they are not acted upon, ideas remain a possibility, rather than an expression of will. In the remainder of this chapter, we examine the next step: when individuals and groups decide to take action based upon their beliefs. We examine forms of political participation, which we define simply as efforts by ordinary people to influence the actions of their leaders.[36] Sometimes activists work within the bounds of legal activity, although they often attempt to change or break the conventional rules. While in some systems, especially totalitarian regimes, citizens are forced to participate in governmentally sponsored demonstrations, rallies, or protests, for our purposes we only examine participation that is voluntary. Fundamentally, political participation is about communicating preferences to the people who have power and influence (elites).

Certainly, not everybody, even in the most developed democracies, participates. One important characteristic that participants tend to exhibit is a sense of efficacy, which is a sense that one's participation can make a difference. If you believe that by writing a letter to an elected official you are likely to influence her or his point of view, you have a strong sense of efficacy. On the other hand, if you do not vote because you are of the mind that it does not make a difference, you have a low sense of efficacy. Often a sense of efficacy also correlates with level of education, as well as socioeconomic security. It takes time to be active and engaged in public life, and few people can afford to take time off from work or be away from family in order to speak at a neighborhood assembly or picket against an unjust action.

How do people participate in their political, social, and economic world? We often think of voting in elections as the primary means of political participation, but in fact this is just one of four primary ways that people can participate in public life: (1) explicit communication, both spoken and written; (2) regime action, including voting and joining political parties or legal organizations; (3) mobilizational action,

including demonstrating in social movements or rallies or participating in boycotts or other forms of group resistance; and (4) inaction, by refusing to vote or obey authority, or utilizing the so-called weapons of the weak. These categories are not necessarily mutually exclusive. In fact, individuals and groups who feel dissatisfied with one type of action, such as normal constituent communication, often decide to pursue another strategy, such as joining a protest.

Spoken and Written Communication

Many citizens decide to communicate with their public leaders, often using simple means such as social media, online petitions, telephone calls, letters to officials or to the media, speeches, and public signs. Most officials establish some form of channel to foster communication between themselves and their constituents. Some leaders embrace this digital diplomacy, or even "Twiplomacy," more than others: the entire governments of Chile and Mexico are on Twitter—but no world leader comes close to Donald Trump's level of digital presence.[37] Argentine president Mauricio Macri is branded the master of Snapchat, and the longtime autocratic leader of Cambodia, Hun Sen, also turns to Facebook to craft his popular image.[38] Citizens' use of social media, as we have seen, is skyrocketing, even in authoritarian contexts in which such communication outlets are formally banned.

Letters to the media can be an extremely useful way to communicate dissatisfaction with a leader or policy. Even in the most totalitarian systems, government-controlled newspapers—print and online—are designated as receiving points for citizen letters and complaints. Even if the letters themselves are not published in the "official" media, they are often collected and distributed for the leadership to read. Petitions, often put forward by groups of people, provide another open channel, although not without risk.

Regime Action

The second major category of participation is regime action, or participation that is overtly designed to support the functioning of the larger political, social, or economic system. This is the type of participation with which most people are likely familiar. In many countries, democratic and nondemocratic alike, citizens are called on to elect representatives to make decisions in their name. The difference in nondemocratic systems, though, is that there is little if any choice of candidates, or the candidates who are elected fail to exercise power or influence. Citizens are also called on to vote in a referendum, a direct vote in which the entire electorate is asked to accept or reject a proposal. Examples of referendums in the global south include the 2011 constitutional referendum in Egypt, the 2016 constitutional referendum in Thailand, and the 2016 referendum in Colombia in which citizens narrowly defeated the landmark peace agreement with FARC rebels.

Political parties stand out as one of the most common vehicles of participation. They develop as groups of similarly minded individuals organized so that they can influence policy decisions. Parties help individuals identify with issues in public life, and they organize people into action. They also promote a common identity among participants, in some cases helping to bridge ethnic or cultural divides. In democratic and nondemocratic systems alike, political parties form so that the elites can appeal to ordinary citizens. In some countries, until very recently a single party dominated

public life, and citizens have had few choices but to belong to the ruling party. In others, a meaningful PARTY SYSTEM has developed in which competing groups of people openly vie for attention and power. Parties often rename themselves, craft new coalitions (with other parties as well as constituent groups), and shift power balances, all in the attempt to maintain dynamic links between elites and masses.

Maurice Duverger classified three main types of political parties, based on their style of organization and operation.[39] The first is the CADRE PARTY, in which PERSONALIST REGIMES, often based on friendships and favors, together with factional groupings comprising people with similar approaches who try to stick together, dominate the relatively small group of elites involved in political matters. Often in systems where cadre parties prevail, the right to vote is limited, meaning that political parties do not face the need to justify their ideological positions or policies beyond the groups already possessing power or influence. A second type is the MASS PARTY, which attempts to reach out beyond the walls of power to appeal to less politically engaged individuals and groups. Mass parties have open membership, but their leaders often target specific segments of the population to whom they plan to pitch their ideological appeal: factory workers, intellectuals, peasants, or other groups. In order to maintain their interest and support, mass parties develop local branch offices that provide services and information to their likely constituents. Duverger's third type is the DEVOTEE PARTY, which is dominated by a charismatic leader and a small elite united in forging a revolutionary path. The Chinese Communist Party during Mao's leadership is an exemplar of such an elitist party, even if its rhetoric attempted to cater to a mass audience.

How important are political parties within the global south? In single-party states, such as the PRC, they are the primary venue through which the elites exercise their power. In transforming states, such as Egypt and Indonesia, the nascent political party system is dominated by personalities and crowded with minute factions. In other countries, including Peru, traditional parties have become virtually extinct. Many leaders sense they are better off without a party than with one. In states where personal relations continue to dominate politics, elections tend to be centered on candidates rather than parties. These systems are marked by extreme electoral volatility, and can easily open the door for populist antisystem candidates who have few qualms about dissolving democratic institutions once they capture the seats of power.

Another type of institution that facilitates the participation of ordinary citizens is the employment organization or union. Independent unions attempt to provide a collective voice to workers. They attempt to promote workers' rights and interests, including sick leave, access to healthcare, and the right to strike, which is restricted in many areas of the world. Unions played an important role in civil rights movements in South Korea and South Africa. In some countries, unions work closely with elites; left-leaning political parties tend to develop strong ties with labor and trade unions. Unions may also serve as the launching pad for oppositional movements and parties. The Movement for Democratic Change (MDC) in Zimbabwe, for example, which has posed the greatest challenge that the ruling Zimbabwe African National Union–Patriotic Front (ZANU-PF) has ever faced, grew out of labor unions. In other countries, governments attempt to co-opt independent expression through the establishment of official, state-sponsored unions. If Chinese workers attempt to organize independently of the CCP-run federation of trade unions, they face almost certain jail time, or are sent to camps for "reha-

bilitation through labor." The famous big-box stores in China are the only location in the world where Walmart employees may form a union—one that is under the firm supervision of the Communist Party organization (local offices are usually directed by someone from company management).[40] In fact, independent unionization is dangerous business throughout the global south.

In countries reliant on exports, including Nicaragua, El Salvador, Guatemala, Mexico, and Honduras, trade unionists face many restrictions on their ability to strike. Labor repression is also common in many African countries, where arrests for union activities are common. Throughout the Middle East, independent trade unions are virtually nonexistent. In this region, the situation is particularly bleak for foreign workers, who make up approximately two-thirds of the labor force in many countries. In most countries in the region, foreign workers are not permitted to join or form any type of workers' union.

Union organizing can also be found among the youth. Children's labor unions, whose origins are found in the New York newsboy strikes against Joseph Pulitzer and William Hearst at the turn of the twentieth century, are vying for a stronger voice in national and international debates about child labor. According to the International Labour Organization (ILO), there are more than 168 million children workers worldwide,[41] although it is important to point out that this is a decline from more than 215 million nearly a decade earlier.[42] Labor organizing for youth can be tough, yet Brazilian street children formed the first modern children's labor union, in 1985.[43] Similar groups can be found throughout Africa, Southeast Asia, and India. Children's labor unions are becoming increasingly organized (some now hold international meetings), and they are united in the voice that child labor should not be abolished, but rather reformed.

Mobilizational Action

The third category of participation is mobilizational action, which includes social movements and other forms of collective action by aggrieved groups of people. By definition, this form of participation involves more than one person. People around the world understand the strength that can be found in numbers. When a group of like-minded individuals forms to influence the turn of events around them, they are said to have formed a social movement. We often think of participants in social movements as attempting to change the status quo and bring about a new state of affairs, but in fact many participants in social movements are fighting instead to maintain the current state of life. Social movements form when there are grievances, because people sense either that they are being unfairly singled out or that they are not doing as well as other groups (RELATIVE DEPRIVATION), because they feel that promises, either implicit or explicit, have not been kept (rising expectations), or because they perceive a threat of some sort. There is also a sense that "time is ripe" for change, providing an opportunity structure for action. There are seemingly favorable times for groups of people to engage in collective action, often because of a political or economic transition, unexpected access to power, divisions among leaders, or a decreased likelihood of repression.[44] Changes in the international environment and movements with "spillover effects" also inspire action. Savvy activists develop expectations of the likelihood of repression, and act accordingly.

Social movements can be defined by an issue, such as civil rights or environmental protection, by a core group, such as women's movements or students' movements, or

by a common target, such as antiglobalization protests or antimilitary demonstrations. One of the most common characteristics of social movements is that they often begin with a narrowly defined issue, and then rather quickly blossom to include other complaints and interests, broadening their appeal to a greater number of groups. Rarely are social movements confined to a single issue, and alliances between sets of activists are common. A group of students begins a protest ostensibly about economic corruption. Then they are joined by unemployed workers angered by layoffs, and state employees frustrated at the inattention of their government-controlled union. The widespread protests then attract others who are at odds with the regime, including mothers who are confined to the home because of factory cutbacks, migrant peasants who cannot find work for more than a week at a time, and high school dropouts wanting to get in on the action. This situation was part of the story of the widespread demonstrations in China in the spring of 1989.

University students wanting to pay homage to a fallen leader sparked the movement. After other groups joined the students in Beijing and 300 other cities, and after the international media picked up on the unlikely protests, a prodemocracy movement formed. As participants multiplied, the task of the protest organizers increased exponentially. Disagreements about tactics increased, such as whether protesters should stage a hunger strike, whether they should openly confront the regime by blocking Tiananmen Square during an international summit, and whether they should negotiate with other protesting groups. We now know, thanks to extensive documentation and interviews with exiled protest leaders, that a serious factional split developed early on in the movement. Disagreement among movement leaders is common after a protest gets off the ground.

Participants in social movements often disagree about the scope of their protest actions. Do they want to provide a wake-up call to the regime and then return to life as usual, or do they want to bring regime leaders to their knees, attempting to cripple the economic and diplomatic base of the state? Some protesters view dialogue (especially with governments) as "selling out," while others view it as a strategic tactic. Some activists want to forge alliances with other organized social groups, uniting in their common cause of increasing regime TRANSPARENCY and accountability. Movements to extend political freedom and promote environmental protection are often linked, either in formal coalitions or because activists cross lines. Concern for the survival of indigenous peoples is often linked to environmental concerns, as in Nigeria with the Movement for the Survival of the Ogoni People (MOSOP), and in Mexico with the Zapatistas. In China, many of the same activists who supported the movements in 1989 have been among the harshest critics of the Three Gorges Dam and other similar megaprojects.

Economic concerns have been a major mobilizing force throughout the global south. For many years, people unable to cope with AUSTERITY PLANS (discussed in Chapter 7) have protested against structural adjustment programs, most visibly in what has come to be known as an "IMF riot." These riots, which often involve looting and burning, are a form of protest that has broken out in India, Jamaica, Egypt, Indonesia, Greece, and Argentina as people find that they can no longer manage with such devastating hardship. Less dramatic but sometimes more deadly versions of IMF riots take the form of mass demonstrations, such as those in Bolivia motivated by fatigue over fifteen years of structural adjustment.

In addition to achieving a desired goal, social movements are important because they provide a sense of identity and belonging to participants. In her studies of Peruvian women's movements, Maruja Barrig argues that by participating in democratically organized programs such as communal kitchens and milk distribution programs, women develop a sense of solidarity and model behavior that could be extended into other areas of life.[45] To better understand the organization and impact of social movements, we examine two subtypes: women's movements and youth mobilization.

People often think of women's movements as being involved in suffrage, or the right to vote. Women's mobilization, though, has gone well beyond the vote, and women activists have refused to be held back by the absence of the right to vote. For example, even though Mexico had some of the most vibrant and developed women's networks throughout Latin America as early as the 1930s, it was among the last countries in the Southern Hemisphere to grant women suffrage.[46] Women's movements, especially in the global south, have been particularly strong at demonstrating that personal issues are indeed political issues. As discussed in Chapter 7, neo-liberalism has contributed to crises and poverty, and women have been channeled disproportionately into low-paid and transitory work. This has led many women to seek participation in community-based and neighborhood organizations to survive as they struggle to fill the gaps created when the state cuts services. Already struggling to support a family, these women face a huge burden without social services to rely on. Yet it sometimes seems that the most burdened and desperate people can mobilize to accomplish huge tasks. For example, women spearheaded the Madres de Plaza de Mayo movement in Argentina, which brought attention to the "disappeared" husbands and sons of the participants, ignited human rights protests, and launched similar movements throughout Latin America. Another example of motherist activism can be found in China following the crackdown on the students in Tiananmen Square. Ding Zilin, whose son was killed on the last evening of the demonstrations as he attempted to vacate the square, and other mothers have staged an international movement to publicize the plight of their children and the brutality of the Chinese government. Although mothers go to the front lines for defense of family and morality, often they are subjected to STATE-SPONSORED TERRORISM, sexual abuse, and humiliation. They face similar discrimination within other participatory channels, including parties and unions that co-opt women into auxiliary chapters. Whether in traditional parties or social movements, women must prove themselves against visible and invisible obstacles. Women in many countries form their own organizations because their demands for equality and justice are viewed as divisive or frivolous.

Women throughout Latin America, especially in Peru and Chile, have established communal dining programs to pool resources and feed the economically poor. During the mid-1980s, one of the largest social movements in Latin America was the Vaso de Leche, or Municipal Milk, program. Based in Lima, Peru, its participants distributed at least a single serving of milk a day to millions of children. While the military concentrated on progressive and radical rural reform, popular social programs initiated by women attempted to incorporate new groups into public affairs, especially the urban lower class and peasants. Their mobilization was especially critical because of the disastrous economic crises that battered the region throughout the 1980s. In the end, though, they maintained some reliance on government, especially at local levels, for funding. They also received support through international

donations, mostly from the United States. These activities are important not only for the services they provided to needy people, but also for the linkages they established between women's groups. They help many women feel a sense of belonging and empowerment, which helps promote active involvement in public affairs that otherwise seem "off limits." The challenge they face for more long-term impact, though, is to be able to organize when not in the face of crisis.

Additionally, college and university students tend to be at the forefront of protests and social movements. Why? Students tend to be skeptical of the norms of government and society, yet optimistic about their ability to make a difference. Many Latin American youth argue that their role is to offer sorely needed answers for the new situations their countries are facing. The traditional model of the party is exhausted; the youth need new organizations capable of responding to demands for a new, more participatory, and flexible political culture. Students tend to be risk-takers, willing to sacrifice time, money, and sometimes their lives in order to make a point. Some have noted a correlation between presence of major universities and presence of social movements, especially in capital cities (Tehran, Mexico City, Beijing). University campuses also can be ideal locales for communication networks. The national university of Peru, San Cristóbal de Huamanga, for example, served as the launching pad for one of the most violent movements in Latin America, Sendero Luminoso. Some student movements to unseat leaders have been successful, such as in Indonesia in 1998 and Iran in 1979, while others have been painfully unsuccessful, notably in Mexico in 1968 and China in 1989.

University students also have a history of political activism in Iran. In November 1979, in the early days of the Islamic Revolution, students were one of the groups leading the seizure of the US embassy in Tehran when fifty-two American hostages were captured. Twenty years later, in July 1999, student-led demonstrations for press reform broke out at Tehran University, spreading to eighteen cities. Sensing an open opportunity caused by widened rifts between Iran's conservative Supreme Leader, Ayatollah Sayyid Ali Khamenei, and the popularly elected but lower-ranking president Mohammad Khatami, students staged five successive days of protest for democratic reform and press freedom. Students mobilized after the legislature passed a restrictive press law and after conservative leaders ordered the closure of a popular left-leaning Islamic newspaper, *Salam*.

In response, police forces raided the university dorms while students were sleeping, pushing some from multistory windows. In response, even more students joined the protest, using updated twists of slogans from the 1979 revolution. The chant "Independence, Freedom, Islamic Republic," was altered to "Independence, Freedom, Iranian Republic." Most accounts claim that the police killed one student, and approximately twenty more were seriously injured. In addition, nearly a thousand students were arrested for participating in the unrest, and at least four people were sentenced to death, in secret trials, for inciting violence. In July 2000 a military court acquitted the Tehran police chief blamed for leading the charge to violence the year before, inciting a muted but audible outcry from many in Iran and abroad.

During the summer of 2009, a daring movement played out throughout Iran and the global blogosphere as millions of Iranians took to the streets to demonstrate against the announced results of a presidential election that had been ceded to the incumbent, Mahmoud Ahmadinejad. Protesters from many walks of life challenged

the legitimacy of his reelection in a poll that saw 85 percent turnout among eligible voters. In what has been called the "Twitter Revolution," activists engaged in unprecedented use of information communication technologies to gather protesters, adopt last-minute strategies in response to government repression, and spread brutally explicit evidence of the government crackdown—around the world. The most haunting image of the movement was that of Neda Agha-Soltan, a young woman who was shot to death during the protests. A witness captured the image on his mobile phone, which was eventually transferred to YouTube (outside of Iran), after which the clip of the dying woman went viral. The day after the election, the state shut down the Internet entirely for half an hour while the authorities struggled to gain control—possibly allowing the Revolutionary Guards to draft Internet-savvy youth to help organize attacks on Twitter and other websites, which led to a "battle for control of the web . . . between governments and individuals."[47] The regime responded with blunt force. One eighty-year-old woman lamented, "They have killed so many of the young and the well intentioned. Even the shah did not kill like this."[48]

Weapons of the Weak

The final type of participation is powerful in its ability to cause disruption through inaction or (on the surface) seemingly inconsequential acts of individual resistance. If the traditional spaces to which people can turn are denied (unions, political parties, media, protest channels), they learn to turn elsewhere to express their sentiments, especially their grievances. Anthropologist James C. Scott identified weapons of the weak as a way to categorize concealed, disguised, individual resistance. These actions, which he viewed as part of a larger category of everyday forms of resistance, include seemingly small acts such as concealing a pig from state officials or falsifying income records. They may not garner the same amount of attention as a revolt in the national capital, but they can be extremely effective tools against injustice nonetheless. People pursue less obvious and less explicitly confrontational forms of resistance when open challenge to authority is too risky. In varied contexts, Scott and others draw our attention to these forms of resistance pursued by dominated groups, such as women, peasants, or other disenfranchised individuals. As discussed in Chapter 4, some of these tactics were common forms of resistance in struggles for national liberation.

Some analysts have sought to explain why women and other repressed groups in some parts of the world appear to be aloof from politics and less likely to participate in democratic struggles. They argue that in many cases women's political power and participation have declined since the precolonial period. Women's initial response to being politically marginalized during colonialism was resistance. However, this resistance often proved ineffective and was followed by a disengagement from formal politics or withdrawal into a consciously apolitical stance. Instead, women have come to favor private, extralegal channels and institutions including families, secret societies, spirit cults or prayer groups, and traditional women's associations. Additionally, women tend to be more active in regard to socioeconomic issues at the local rather than the national level.

But part of the reason why some groups appear complacent to outsiders is that observers fail to recognize acts of resistance that do not utilize more conventionally recognized channels of protest. Many actors employ weapons of the weak in the face of power, accomplishing in subtle acts what might never be achieved in more traditional

routes. Individuals feign support for a cause, while subtly putting a cog in the wheel to block it. Actors can drag their feet, pretend compliance, and organize others to break rules through acts of civil disobedience. As Célestin Monga argues, outsiders often lament the absence of civic participation in African societies because they overlook the long tradition of indigenous activism, what he terms the "anthropology of anger."[49] People get angry when systematically oppressed, and they develop ways of escaping repression. They pretend to accept the rules imposed by authoritarian groups, and are constantly adjusting to escape domination and circumvent coercive strictures. Such participation is grassroots-based and highly creative. Activists subvert the rules by not confronting power directly. These informal methods of participation and protest may be what truly pushes change.

Subversive music is a common form of political expression. For example, one of Africa's most famous Afrobeat musicians, Fela Anikulapo-Kuti, considered music a weapon. While praise-singing is a tradition associated with greats such as King Sunny Adé, Fela invented a new art: abuse-singing. In the late 1970s, Fela took on then-president Olusegun Obasanjo, the military dictator of Nigeria, arguing that Afrobeat was the only music through which people could say what they felt and tell the government what they thought. Fela was beaten and jailed. His seventy-eight-year-old mother was thrown from a second-story window and later died of her injuries. He is followed in these pursuits by his son, Femi Kuti, whose Afrobeat songs attack corrupt politicians and warn about AIDS. Punk bands in China, which emerged on the scene after rock bands were significantly censored for their connections to protest movements, draw small crowds, which helps them evade censors and the police. They perform their most anti-establishment lyrics—including tributes to the Tiananmen mothers and others associated with the movements in 1989—in broken English. In this way, they reach their audience and express their disillusionment, without being hauled away.[50]

Another highly influential political forum for dealing with real-life issues such as corruption, drug trafficking, AIDS, and sexism is the telenovela, or soap opera, a favorite form of entertainment for millions in Latin America. The telenovela is much more influential than the newspaper in Mexico; it is said that writers are using this art form the way Thomas Paine used the pamphlet. As dictatorships have been retired, a flourishing independent medium is taking advantage of the political openness to tackle once-taboo subjects.

Weapons of the weak are seemingly invisible and unthreatening, yet they convey a strong message about the grievances and power of dominated people. Mass abstention can be another discreet weapon of last resort. In expectation of massively fraudulent elections in Peru, the main opposition party encouraged people to stay away from the polls, to spoil the ballots, or to write "no to fraud" on them. Mexican voters employed a similar strategy by writing "null and void" on their ballots. Dissidents might slip an encrypted missive into a newspaper article, the true meaning of which becomes clear when the last word of each sentence is read vertically up and down the column. In the middle of a photograph portraying an abundant harvest, "down with dictatorship" is subtly carved in the wheat. By the time these tricks are discovered, it is too late for authorities to pull thousands of magazines or newspapers from the shelves. Another example is found among the women of Iran, who boldly challenge traditional Islamic customs of modesty by turning to a Facebook

page ("Stealthy Freedoms of Iranian Women") and posting photos of themselves flaunting their hair in public (without hijab). Resisting the "morality police," these women frame their actions, which include posing at major tourist attractions, or letting a scarf slip while driving on the highway, as "small acts of rebellion." Sometimes, a male family member joins in the picture, as a sign of approval and as an attempt to ward off criticism.[51] While these actions may not seem forceful, or overtly political, each is an expression of voice and power in its own right.

Some find their situation so egregious that they perceive their only option to be that of "exit."[52] Increasingly, analysts recognize suicide as an explicit political choice by individuals who feel they have no other option. Women who feel trapped in arranged marriages, or torn between the modern world of the city and their desire to return to more traditional patterns in their rural homes, gain a sense of control over their fate through suicide that they cannot find in life. While suicide is usually conducted in private, these cases are often unique in their public display. A spate of highly public suicides at factories in China served as a wake-up call to the conditions within some of these factories, including at Foxconn, the world's biggest contract electronics supplier, which is a supplier to Apple, Dell, and Hewlett-Packard, among others. Interpretations of these so-called weapons of the weak, which also included employees simply walking off the factory floor, vary, including sociologists' claims that they were signs of a generation rejecting the regimentation of their predecessors who served as the "cheap labor army" responsible for China's economic reemergence.[53] The spark that ignited the Arab Spring—when Mohammad Bouazizi, a vegetable salesman in Tunisia, set himself on fire after a policewoman confiscated his unlicensed cart, slapped him, and spat in his face—demonstrates how one act can serve as a contagion across great distances. His protest and painful death (he lay in the hospital for nearly ten days before he died), sparked protests that toppled the government of Tunisian president Zine el Abidine Ben Ali, spreading to much of the Arab world.

The management of information is another classic form of everyday resistance. For example, rumor is especially popular and effective in Africa, where oral traditions are highly valued. Rumor has been described as a potent brew of what is not known in the here and now, linked to what may or may not be known by those able to manipulate the supernatural. Rumors are hypotheses; in places where there is no authoritative news or information source, rumors don't just titillate, they are currency.[54] In the last days of Mobutu Sésé Seko's reign in Zaire, rumors about prophecies of his impending doom greatly undermined what was left of the regime's credibility and contributed to its ultimate demise.

Conclusions: Civil or Uncivil Society?

To what can such varied forms of citizen participation and activism lead? Some speak of the potential emergence of a civil society in which citizens are able to enjoy some level of autonomy, or independence, from the government, and a multiplicity of voluntary associations are permitted to form. The belief is that if citizens are able to seek membership in independent associations, absent of government control or influence, this promotes an actively engaged citizenry who adopt a moral sense of obligation to participate in civic causes. With a multiplicity of groups and voluntary associations, people have an increased opportunity to express themselves as well as

encounter competing viewpoints and perspectives. This leads many to connect civil society with democracy. This straightforward connection is misleading.

In many regions of the world, the development of an independent merchant class is viewed as part of a nascent civil society. If people have an area in their life over which the government has no influence or control, this is said to foster an independent, civic identity above political divisions. For example, after the 1985 Mexico City earthquake, the urban poor worked through neighborhood organizations to force the government and World Bank to alter their recovery plans. Similar civic action groups have formed to fight crime and corruption in Mexico and South Africa. The combination of high crime rates and distrust of police competence contributed to the phenomenal growth of one South African vigilante group that has morphed into a private security business, Mapogo a Mathamaga, which is infamous for its use of corporal punishment. This form of mob justice is very popular; Mapogo has branches throughout the country and boasts of thousands of members and that 85 percent of those who display the group's stickers on their premises and property never experience any criminal activity.[55]

High literacy rates and access to independent media promote an independent sense of society, as citizens can educate themselves about alternative ideas and approaches to issues. The Internet revolution, spawned by changes in communication technology, also has the potential to change people's sense of self, state, and society. These changes are important not only for the options they make available for citizens, but also for the increase in accountability they can foster. Some view the development of an increasing space for civil society as a potential birthing ground for democracy, because it promotes the existence of diverse competing groups and encourages citizens to take an interest in and participate in government.

Yet citizens with access to information and freedom to organize will not automatically be more benign or democratic. Given the increased space for organization and mobilization, it is just as likely for antidemocratic groups to form. This is especially, although not exclusively, the case in regimes with a recent history of political and social violence in which individuals were socialized into accepting coercion and repression as a regular mode of behavior. The existence of competing groups is not a silver bullet against repression. Leigh Payne referred to the proliferation of "uncivil movements," paramilitary groups, death squads, and the like, that promote exclusion and violence as a means of competing and gaining power within a democratic system.[56] Such groups are common in a variety of countries, with or without past experiences of authoritarianism. They gain influence through the use of threats, legitimating myths, and coalition formation, and no system is immune. Exclusionary movements are capable of securing their demands within the democratic system, so they face no pressing need to overthrow it. But these groups provide an insidious threat to an inclusionary democratic society. They use democratic language, institutions, and strategies toward their own uncivil ends. They can transform themselves into political parties with undemocratic goals. The Oodua People's Congress in Nigeria, a Yoruba militia that once played a big part in the prodemocracy movement, transformed its message into a hard-line ethnic supremacist agenda. Given the elitist, antipeasant rhetoric common among student demonstration leaders in China, many wonder whether the 1989 movements, had they been successful, would have resulted in a more or a less democratic outcome than exists today.

The presence of these "uncivil" groups and behaviors highlights the value-laden approach to the civil society debate. David Rieff argues that many have used the concept of a civil society, correlated with increased tolerance, expression, and diversity, to welcome groups we approve of.[57] Yet if civil society merely refers to groups who are able to operate independent of the reach of the state, their ideology about mode of action or inclusion of minority groups has nothing to do with it. In this estimation, war criminals fall into the same category as human rights leaders. The US National Rifle Association, which the United Nations has refused to admit as a legitimate nongovernmental organization, is as much an agent of civil society as is the International Campaign to Ban Landmines, which has received considerable international financial and emotional support. Rieff, Payne, and others cause us to question the mere proliferation of organizations as a desirable consequence linked to the weakening of political power. As Alison Brysk reminds us, constituents participating in free and competitive elections have returned authoritarian leaders to power in many countries—and not only in the global south.[58] It is possible that, in some circumstances, citizens can be the individuals and groups who most repress other citizens.

Notes

1. Quoted in "The Arab Winter," *The Economist,* January 9, 2016.

2. Quill Lawrence, "Brutality Against Women Stirs Fear in Afghanistan," National Public Radio, August 20, 2010.

3. "Overview: Pentecostalism in Africa," Pew Research Center, October 5, 2006, www.pewforum.org.

4. David Martin, "The People's Church: The Global Evangelical Upsurge and Its Political Consequences," *Christianity Today,* January–February 2000.

5. Roger Eatwell, *Fascism: A History* (New York: Penguin, 1997).

6. Noam Chomsky, *On Anarchism* (New York: New Press, 2013).

7. "Zapatistas to Present Indigenous Presidential Candidate in 2018," *Telesur,* October 15, 2016, www.telesurtv.net.

8. Orville Schell, "Letter from China," *New Yorker,* July 1994, reprinted in *The China Reader: The Reform Era,* ed. Orville Schell and David Shambaugh (New York: Vintage, 1999).

9. Christopher Rohads and Loretta Chao, "Iran's Web Spying Aided by Western Technology," *Wall Street Journal,* June 22, 2009.

10. Brian Stelter and Brad Stone, "Web Pries Lid of Iranian Censorship," *New York Times,* June 22, 2009; Andy Greenberg, "Mubarak's Digital Dilemma: Why Egypt's Internet Controls Failed," *Forbes,* February 2, 2011; Noam Cohen, "Egyptians Were Unplugged, and Uncowed," *New York Times,* February 20, 2011; "Egypt: Head of Press Syndicate Detained in Unprecedented Crackdown on Media Freedom," *Amnesty International,* May 30, 2016, www.amnesty.org.

11. Stelter and Stone, "Web Pries Lid of Iranian Censorship."

12. "World Press Freedom Index 2015: Decline on All Fronts," Reporters Without Borders, February 12, 2015, www.rsf.org.

13. This definition is based on the classic perspective on political culture that was developed in the 1950s and 1960s. Its most common source is Sidney Verba, "Comparative Political Culture," in *Political Culture and Political Development,* ed. Sidney Verba and Lucian Pye (Princeton: Princeton University Press, 1965).

14. Gabriel A. Almond and Sidney Verba, ed., *Civic Culture: Political Attitudes and Democracy in Five Nations* (Princeton: Princeton University Press, 1963).

15. David J. Elkins and E. B. Simeon, "A Cause in Search of Its Effect, or What Does Political Culture Explain?," *Comparative Politics* (January 1979).

16. "World Takes Notice of Iran's Ahmadinejad," National Public Radio, *All Things Considered,* February 13, 2006.

17. Roberta Garner, *Contemporary Movements and Ideologies* (New York: McGraw-Hill, 1996).

18. Benjamin R. Barber, *Jihad vs. McWorld* (New York: Times Books, 1995).

19. See Benjamin R. Barber, "Beyond Jihad vs. McWorld," *The Nation,* January 21, 2002.

20. Célestin Monga, *The Anthropology of Anger: Civil Society and Democracy in Africa,* trans. Linda L. Fleck and Célestin Monga (Boulder: Lynne Rienner, 1996).

21. Sarah Pulliam Bailey, "The World Is Becoming More Religious—Not Less," *Washington Post,* April 24, 2015.

22. Angelina E. Theodorou, "Religious Restrictions Among the World's Most Populous Countries," *Fact Tank,* June 28, 2016, www.pewresearch.org.

23. Martin Kramer, "Coming to Terms: Fundamentalists or Islamists?," *Middle East Quarterly* (Spring 2003), pp. 65–77.

24. Robert F. Worth, Mark Mazzetti, and Scott Shane, "Drone Strikes' Risks to Get Rare Moment in the Public Eye," *New York Times,* February 3, 2013.

25. Michael Lipka, "Muslims and Islam: Key Findings in the U.S. and Around the World," *Fact Tank,* July 22, 2016, www.pewresearch.org.

26. Larry Rohter, "As Pope Heads to Brazil, a Rival Theology Persists," *New York Times,* May 7, 2007.

27. Gustavo Gutíerrez, *A Theology of Liberation: History, Politics, and Salvation* (Maryknoll, NY: Orbis, 1971). Other key events in the development of liberation theology included the 1968–1969 Second General Conference on Latin American Bishops, in Medellín, Colombia, which met to discuss the implications of the Second Vatican Council (also known as Vatican II) for Latin America; the 1967 publication of "A Letter to the Peoples of the Third World"; and the 1979 meeting of the Council of Latin American Bishops, in Puebla, Mexico.

28. While some of these ideas were and continue to be extremely popular at the grassroots levels in many countries, the institutional Catholic Church has responded with harsh criticism. Leonardo Boff, for example, was required to spend a year in "obedient silence" from 1985 to 1986 because of opposition from Rome toward some of his writings. He was eventually forced out of the priesthood for mixing politics and religion too much.

29. There have been many books and edited collections that focus on non-Western views of feminism. For a sampling, see Kumari Jayawardena, *Feminism and Nationalism in the Third World* (London: Zed, 1986); Guida West and Rhoda Lois Blumberg, eds., *Women and Social Protest* (New York: Oxford University Press, 1990); Jane Jaquette, ed., *The Women's Movement in Latin America: Participation and Democracy* (Boulder: Westview, 1994); Leslie Bethell, ed., *Ideas and Ideologies in Twentieth-Century Latin America* (Cambridge: Cambridge University Press, 1996).

30. Jaquette, *Women's Movement in Latin America.*

31. Jane Jaquette, "Introduction: From Transition to Participation: Women's Movements and Democratic Politics," in Jaquette, *Women's Movement in Latin America.*

32. "Tunisia: Can Niqab and Bikinis Live Side by Side?," BBC News, March 27, 2013.

33. Andrew Heywood, *Political Ideas and Concepts: An Introduction* (New York: St. Martin's, 1994).

34. Bager Moin, *Khomeini: Life of the Ayatollah* (New York: St. Martin's, 2000).

35. Heywood, *Political Ideas and Concepts.*

36. This definition is based on the pioneering work on this subject conducted by Sidney Verba, Victor H. Nie, and Jae-on Kim, *Participation and Political Equality: A Seven-Nation Comparison* (New York: Cambridge University Press, 1978).

37. Mattias Lüfkens, "Tweet Me to Your Leader: How the World's Big Shots Use Social Media," *The Atlantic,* October 19, 2012, www.theatlantic.com.

38. Denise Hruby, "Meet the True Kings and Queens of Facebook and Snapchat," *BBC Capital,* May 20, 2016.

39. Maurice Duverger, *Political Parties: Their Organization and Activity in the Modern State* (New York: Wiley, 1963).

40. Harold Meyerson, "Wal-Mart Loves Unions (in China)," *Washington Post,* December 1, 2004, p. A25; "Wal-Mart Establishes First Trade Union in China," *Xinhua,* July 29, 2006; Matthew Kirdahy, "Wal-Mart Strikes Pay Deal with Chinese Union," *Forbes,* July 25, 2008.

41. International Labour Organization (ILO), "World Report on Child Labor: Paving the Way to Decent Work for Young People," press release, June 10, 2015.

42. ILO, "ILO Calls for Zero Tolerance of Violence Against Children in the Workplace," press release, November 20, 2006.

43. Sarah Bachman, "Underage Unions: Child Laborers Speak Up," *Mother Jones,* November–December 2000.

44. Sidney Tarrow, *Power in Movement: Social Movements and Contentious Politics* (New York: Cambridge University Press, 1998); William A. Gamson, "The Social Psychology of Collective Action," in *Frontiers in Social Movement Theory,* ed. Aldon D. Morris and Carol McClurg Mueller (New Haven: Yale University Press, 1992).

45. Maruja Barrig, "The Difficult Equilibrium Between Bread and Roses: Women's Organizations and Democracy in Peru," in Jaquette, *Women's Movement in Latin America.*

46. Ibid.

47. Jon Leyne, "How Iran's Political Battle Is Fought in Cyberspace," BBC News, February 11, 2010.

48. Will Yong and Michael Slackman, "Across Iran, Anger Lies Behind Face of Calm," *New York Times,* June 11, 2010.

49. Monga, *The Anthropology of Anger.*

50. Julien Girault, "Anarchy in the People's Republic of China, According to Chinese Punks," *Japan Times,* October 12, 2014, www.japantimes.co.jp.

51. Fernaz Fassihi, "Iranian Women Find New Platform for Personal Freedom Push," *Wall Street Journal,* May 13, 2014, www.blogs.wsj.com.

52. See Albert O. Hirschman, *Exit, Voice, and Loyalty: Responses to Decline in Firms, Organizations, and States* (Cambridge: Harvard University Press, 1970).

53. David Barboza, "After Suicides, Scrutiny of China's Grim Factories," *New York Times,* June 7, 2010, p. A3.

54. Stephen Ellis, "Tuning In to Pavement Radio," *African Affairs* 88, no. 352 (July 1989).

55. Evidence Wa Ka Ngobeni, "Vigilante Group Sweeps Suburbs," *Daily Mail and Guardian* (Johannesburg), January 25, 2000; "Mapogo a Mathamaga," www.mapogo.co.za.

56. Leigh A. Payne, *Uncivil Movements: The Armed Right Wing and Democracy in Latin America* (Baltimore: Johns Hopkins University Press, 2000).

57. David Rieff, "The False Dawn of Civil Society," *The Nation,* February 22, 1999.

58. Alison Brysk, "Democratizing Civil Society in Latin America," *Journal of Democracy* 11, no. 3 (July 2000).

Chapter 10

Linking
Concepts and Cases

Now that you have a sense of the variety of views and actions that are taken in the global south, we present you with evidence from our eight case studies so that you can explore these ideas further. As you look at issues of voice and participation in these countries, try to observe patterns of similarity and difference between and among them. What is the impact of history on the development of political culture? To what do you attribute differences in the frequency and volatility of expression? In which of these cases can you see generational-based clashes, and what is their source? Which countries have more mobilized civil societies, and which cases appear to be less vibrant? Why do you think this may be so?

Case Study: Mexico

Fifty years ago, poet Octavio Paz described Mexico as trapped in a labyrinth—with a political culture of cynicism and suspicion deeply rooted in the country's history.[1] Part of the explanation for this is that for decades under the Institutional Revolutionary Party (PRI), the Mexican government actively sought to preempt all meaningful citizen participation. Through its use of CORPORATISM, the government attempted to incorporate or co-opt all potentially influential groups in society. But Mexicans (perhaps simplistically identified as "parochial" in classic civic culture studies) agitated for change and exercised their democratic rights in a variety of ways. Thanks to the efforts of citizen groups Mexico made the transition to democracy nearly two decades ago. But civil society is still fighting to change old ways and let Mexico's leaders know that it should be society that dictates and the government that obeys.

It was in 2000 when, for the first time in over seventy years, Mexicans voted, in free and fair elections, into power a party other than the PRI. That election ushered into government the National Action Party (PAN), the party of Presidents Vicente Fox (2000–2006) and Felipe Calderón (2006–2012). The PAN is a conservative pro-business party long opposed to the PRI. It has a religious agenda (as opposed to the two other main parties, which tend to be secular) and is socially conservative. It is most

popular in Mexico's northern states and very much believes that globalization is the best way to promote economic growth, along with free market, neoliberal reforms. However, as we discuss in later chapters, after twelve years in power it struggled to deal with a range of political and economic challenges and its popularity flagged. By the 2012 elections, many Mexicans were feeling that the PAN was equally corrupt to the PRI—and incapable of leading Mexico out of the economic and security crises it faces.[2]

People are disenchanted with the largest parties. There are several other new but growing smaller parties, and starting in 2018, for the first time independent candidates will be able to run for office.[3] But the other major party in Mexico, one that has so far largely played the role of outsider, is the leftist Party of Democratic Revolution (PRD), which was formed when its leaders split from the PRI to demand democratic rule. Although as of yet it has not held the presidency (the PRD's candidate, Andrés Manuel López Obrador [known as "AMLO"] strenuously claimed that he was the rightful winner in the very close 2006 race—according to the official count, he lost by less than 1 percent—and threatened to shut the country down), PRD candidates have won other offices at all levels of government and the party continues to be influential as a voice of the opposition. A social democratic party, it has long promised to renegotiate the North American Free Trade Agreement (NAFTA), subsidize farmers, and spend more on welfare programs. Most PRD supporters are from central and southern Mexico—the poorest regions of the country, those most marginalized by globalization. AMLO represented the party again in the 2012 contest, losing this time more decisively, by more than 6 percent.[4]

So, after a dozen years in time-out, the PRI—which was never really sitting out—roared back into the presidency with Enrique Peña Nieto's win in 2012. Currently the PRI is considered center-left, although its ideology has fluctuated over time in what is described as the "pendulum effect." Immediately following its loss in the 2000 elections, the PRI went into a tailspin and some analysts predicted that the party was dead. Yet since 2000 it has for the most part been the largest party in both houses of congress—and even when it was losing presidential elections the PRI continued to be influential because it branded itself as a party that can make deals and govern.[5] In fact, in his first days in office, President Peña Nieto announced a "Pact for Mexico," a tri-partisan alliance to get things done. The PRI president brought in the PAN and even coaxed the PRD into work on a wide range of agreed-upon reforms. Several of these proposals successfully made their way through the usually fractious legislature and Peña Nieto has signed them into law—although implementing them is another thing.[6]

Meanwhile, in its efforts to hold its political representatives accountable, Mexican civil society has remained active. For example, it has always been a weapon of the weak, but in 2009, citizens frustrated by their lack of choices on the ballot undertook a *voto nulo* ("vote null and void") campaign. This initiative, which has continued through subsequent elections, is unique for the speed with which it swept the Internet, urging voters to *voto nulo* instead of voting for any of the candidates for office that year. The activists' argument was that voting for nothing was better than continuing with the politicians who were currently running the country. It is estimated that in 2009, 2012, and 2015 approximately 5 percent of voters rejected the establishment and canceled their ballots (60 percent in some areas). Because the *nulo* vote crosses party lines, it isn't believed to have affected the outcome of

the elections (analysts say that would only happen if 10 percent or more of the vote were to go *nulo*), but it does send an important message. Instead of staying home and not voting, people are coming out to show their annoyance with the dysfunction of the political system.[7]

Mexican citizens are upset by the recession, the lack of security in the country, and their sense that corruption is as bad as ever.[8] Mexicans are demanding that their government continue evolving, moving toward finally realizing the core ideals of the Mexican Revolution. Mexicans have been galvanized to action because, even in this democracy, institutional channels are still not responding to people's needs.[9] For example, because corruption is recognized as the root of most of Mexico's problems, there's the "3 out of 3" initiative, which imposes public disclosure rules for all public servants and requires government officials (and their close relatives) to prove they are paying taxes and reveal their assets and any potential conflicts of interest. If it passes, it would be one of the world's most far-reaching rules to combat corruption. This initiative, which is the result of a grassroots effort and has the support of business, amounts to a historic event in terms of civil society mobilization.[10] Yet civil society in Mexico seeks to engage the state in other, less legalistic ways as well. In some places schools have been closed for months due to strikes and teachers and students have clashed (sometimes violently) with the government over its attempts to change the education system, which some see as the government's effort to deny them of their rights.[11] As with the *nulo* campaign, most in this movement are practicing civil disobedience precisely because they believe in democracy. And they will use whatever tactics are necessary to demand that the system work for them.

Case Study: Peru

It is often said that Peruvians, traditionally identified as having a strong civil society and a weak state, value decisive leadership over institutional checks and balances. Some analysts suggest that this tendency to favor authoritarians goes back to the days of the Inca Empire and centralized rule. Such traditions continued under colonialism—as did militarism, which has been a constant in Peru.[12]

There is a long tradition of military intervention in Peruvian politics; most of the country's nearly 200-year history has been spent under military rule. During much of the 1990s, large numbers of Peruvians supported President Alberto Fujimori's growing authoritarianism as a necessity in the country's wars against terrorism and inflation. However, by the end of the decade this justification no longer rang true for most people. Peruvians became increasingly divided over what they valued more highly—security or freedom. Although Fujimori still had his supporters, Peruvians were becoming impatient with his excesses. They resisted Fujimori's efforts to overturn the constitution and destroy the integrity of the electoral process. Because of the groundswell of activism that brought Fujimori down, observers argued that the 2001 elections showed that it could no longer be said that civil society in Peru was weak or antidemocratic.[13]

In fact, parties may be weak and fragmented, but Peruvians have proved willing to take their politics to the street.[14] It was primarily an urban, middle-class civil society that rallied to prevent *continuismo,* the open-ended continuation in office desired by Fujimori. Fifteen years later, tens of thousands turned out in 2016 to

protest against Fujimori's daughter's possible election to the presidency, chanting "Fujimori Never Again."[15]

Peruvians have turned out to protest a variety of issues, but some of the most vocal groups, including farmers, miners, and indigenous people, have mobilized around the use of resources.[16] Historically, indigenous movements in Peru have been weaker than in neighboring countries. However, in recent years they have emerged bigger and more powerful than ever. In response to economic liberalization, over fifty native groups, comprising as many as 300,000 people, have forged broad coalitions that cut across class and the urban-rural divide to challenge the extractive economy. Utilizing noninstitutionalized forms of collective action, they are proving capable of disrupting politics-as-usual and face down presidents intent on pushing economic growth by opening up lands (as much as 72 percent) of the Amazon that have traditionally been respected as off-limits.[17]

More visible and better organized than they have been in the past, communicating across the jungle to isolated communities via radio, Amazonian indigenous groups have turned out in the thousands, successfully calling general strikes and closing down roads and rivers to traffic for weeks at a time. They have even threatened to cut off the supply of oil and natural gas to the capital. These activists insist that the land is theirs and that if the government opens it up to mining, oil, and natural gas companies, a variety of problems will follow, including destruction of the environment and loss of a way of life. From their point of view, this is a life-or-death struggle and they have dug in for a protracted fight—and it is the most serious challenge to state authority that recent governments have had to fight.[18]

Some presidents have taken a harder stance than others, but the state's response has been that economic interests need to come first. It has argued that those who seek to keep the Amazon for themselves are selfish and are sitting on resources that the state owns the right to by law—untouched resources that could be used to modernize and develop the entire country.[19] In 2009, after sixty-five days of civil disobedience against an oil project in the Amazon, the government suspended civil liberties, criminalized peaceful social protest, and sent the police in to stop the demonstrations. Tensions flared, and in what is known as the Bagua massacre, a violent altercation broke out between police and protesters in which thirty-three died and hundreds were injured.[20] President Alan García defended his actions, characterizing the activists as "wild," "savage," and "terrorists." Such amped-up rhetoric is concerning to some, who fear that the government may be giving security forces and vested interests who oppose the protesters carte blanche to resort to extreme measures. This looks to be well under way; Peru is believed to be one of the deadliest countries in the world to be an environmentalist or land defender. Between 2002 and 2014, at least fifty-seven people were murdered in Peru for these forms of activism—most of them since 2010.[21]

Meanwhile, Peruvian governments continue to put economics ahead of environmental interests and open lands to exploitation. And people continue to turn out in protest. The uprising of 2009 did mark a turning point in that for the first time it drew attention to the mistreatment of the Amazonian people and made possible a long-elusive alliance between Amazonian and Andean indigenous peoples (who also know racism, marginalization, and the negative impact of extractive industries). There is plenty of reason for these groups to work together, and if they do, analysts agree that a united indigenous social movement in Peru will be a force that

can demand territorial and cultural autonomy, if not the suspension of the neoliberal approach to development.[22]

Case Study: Nigeria

Often described as a "conglomerate society," Nigeria is composed of more than 250 different ethnic groups whose divisions are complicated by regional, religious, and linguistic identities. For most of the years since independence in 1960, political power, both civilian and military, had been largely under the control of northern Muslims, who dominated the military and resented the southern domination of commerce that dates back to colonialism. Until 1999, only northern Muslims had served as president (elected or not) and many southerners felt that they had never had a government that represented their interests.[23]

Since the transition to democracy in 1999, several political parties have been hastily formed, but few of them have much of an ideological base. Rather, many Nigerian politicians continue a tradition of manipulating identity to achieve political power. Fearing loss to a rival, they mobilize populations by asserting their cultural distinctiveness. In this oil-rich country, where political power translates into access to economic resources, politics is viewed as a winner-take-all gamble. Politicians from all regions have propagated myths of irreconcilable differences, while working hard to blur the glaring disparity between rich and poor. This explains why elections in Nigeria, as in many other countries, are fought as mortal combat.[24]

It is often said that Nigeria's political leaders fear being usurped by each other more than by a popular revolt. Through backroom deals, identity politics have certainly been at play in all the elections since the return to civilian rule in 1999 (when, for the first time in Nigeria's history, a Yoruba Christian from the southwest won the elections and was inaugurated president). Something that had the potential to touch off instability is actually an arrangement worked out years earlier to promote stability: a "power shift" or "rotation" guaranteeing that presidential candidates from the major regions get a turn (or two) at the presidency.[25] Here's the deal: back in 2007, as the retirement of the first democratically elected president (Olusegun Obasanjo) neared, Nigeria's power brokers agreed that after two terms of the southwesterner's presidency, it was time for someone different. To strengthen the democracy's legitimacy and send a signal that no single group would monopolize power, they decided that the next president would be a Muslim northerner—although those from the south and southeast were pointing out that they had never had a turn. Analysts agreed that because of the advantages of incumbency (money and the backing of political godfathers), whoever won the ruling People's Democratic Party's (PDP) nomination would have a very real edge in the 2007 election. Although there were several contenders (all northern), Umaru Yar'Adua, a conservative Muslim governor from the northern state of Katsina, became the PDP nominee.[26]

Yar'Adua won the election (under dubious circumstances) in April 2007. More important, Nigeria witnessed the first civilian-to-civilian transfer of power in its history. However, this crowning achievement was followed by crisis. In 2010, Yar'Adua died rather suddenly of health problems and the vice president, Goodluck Jonathan (a PDP Christian from the southeast) was inaugurated as president. However, even before he could take the oath of office, questions swirled regarding Jonathan's right to

rule. Many northerners from his own party began agitating for new elections, since according to the practice of rotation, it was still a northern Muslim's turn at the presidency. Jonathan tamped down tensions by promising simply to serve out Yar'Adua's term, and not run in the next scheduled elections. However, in the end, he changed his mind and became the PDP nominee, despite those who insisted on continuing the rotation (and bringing in a northerner) and those who wanted to do away with the system. Many observers worried that reneging on the deal could be destabilizing and dangerous for the democracy. Others welcomed the prospect of a PDP split, arguing that Nigeria had become in effect a one-party state and it was time to reboot.[27]

The PDP did not split at that point and Jonathan won the 2011 elections against Muhammadu Buhari, a former dictator who had for several years been looking to make a comeback, having also run (and lost) in 2003 and 2007. In those elections, no other party had a chance of beating the PDP, and Nigeria looked like it had become a dominant party democracy. But in what some argue was a good thing for the democracy, the party did divide for the rematch of the two candidates in the 2015 elections.[28]

One sign that change was finally coming was when former President Obasanjo quit the PDP to publicly come out for Buhari, as did many other high-profile PDP defectors who were unhappy with Jonathan's upset of the rotation system and his performance as president. Buhari, who for a time was advised by former Obama campaign manager David Axelrod, was the candidate of the All Progressives Congress (APC). A relatively new party, it was founded in 2012 as an alternative to the PDP. It is to the left of that party, and calls itself social democratic. With Buhari as its leader, the APC merged a number of parties from different parts of the country. Buhari campaigned on a staunch anticorruption platform, and was able to beat the incumbent, Goodluck Jonathan. The APC won a majority of seats in Nigeria's senate and house of representatives.[29]

The 2015 election marked a turning point for the country. It was the first PDP loss since the return to democracy and the first time in Nigerian history that an incumbent seeking reelection ever had to turn over power to his opponent. After a less than friendly contest, some were worried that Jonathan and his supporters might not follow through with the alternation in power. But Jonathan stepped aside graciously, leaving office on a high note. Meanwhile, instead of one dominant party replacing another, the rising APC, which is a big-tent party, including a variety of personalities and interests, has already shown signs of disarray. Meanwhile, the PDP is hardly washed up; it appears on the mend and eager to resume its dominant position, but it is no longer the only game in town. And even the temporary unseating of the dominant party and its political machine is welcomed by those seeking to hasten Nigeria's democratic CONSOLIDATION.[30]

Case Study: Zimbabwe

Although it appears to go quiet from time to time, Zimbabwe has a flourishing rural and urban civil society. Its urban civil society had largely come together to challenge the Zimbabwe African National Union–Patriotic Front (ZANU-PF) and the monopoly on power it has held for nearly four decades. The grievances that contributed to the opposition's rise had been festering for years. Economic hardship has turned many people who didn't normally think of themselves as political into ac-

tivists. At the turn of the twenty-first century, almost all Zimbabweans disapproved of the government's handling of the economy, and three-quarters of those surveyed wanted President Robert Mugabe to resign.[31] A new party, the Movement for Democratic Change (MDC), capitalized on this sentiment with its election slogan "Change Everything, Everything Changes." With a focus on political and civil rights, this liberal party called for ending government corruption and increasing transparency, reducing poverty, and strengthening the RULE OF LAW. It has since been joined by a variety of others, converging on Mugabe from all directions.

The multiracial MDC enjoys a remarkably broad base of support. Although the party grew out of Zimbabwe's trade unions, which are very male-dominant, it included a feminist plank in its campaign.[32] The MDC's core supporters are the young urban dwellers (the so-called Born Frees) who were either children at independence or born soon after. Mugabe's appeals to black nationalism fall flat with much of this younger generation, who are too young to remember the humiliation and suffering that blacks experienced under white rule. Although members of ZANU-PF have spoken ominously about a "Rwandan solution" for the country's whites, it is undeniable that the membership of the MDC is multiracial.[33] Interestingly, voting is based not so much on ethnicity as on an urban-rural split (the MDC is popular in predominantly Ndebele Matabeleland, whereas ZANU-PF has never been well liked there).

What has happened in Zimbabwe is a good example to the world of what happens when crucial questions are left unresolved for decades. For many activists, land has sacred and cultural value as well as productive potential. The effort to reclaim the land is for them not just a development issue but also a restitution and justice issue.[34] While some analysts accuse Mugabe of having cynically used land reform to hang on to power, it is important not to forget the very real needs asserted by this social struggle and to recognize that the anger stems from past injustices and deprivation. The reconciliation model promoted by the West has not resulted in justice or reparation. From the point of view of many rural people in Zimbabwe, the neoliberal, laissez-faire approach to land reform had to be challenged.[35]

Because the opposition had been supported by the West, the government portrayed it as the lackey of white farmers and Britain. Although the MDC once threatened to take President Mugabe down in much the same way that Yugoslavian dictator Slobodan Milosevic was finally ousted, until early 2007 Mugabe hadn't had to face the angry crowds. Perhaps this is because Zimbabweans were remembering the lessons of China's Tiananmen Square more than those of Yugoslavia. The MDC's Morgan Tsvangirai once said that he wouldn't call the massive street protests he once threatened for fear of a bloodbath. It very nearly came to that in 2008, when Mugabe came closer than ever to losing power in a runoff election, as hundreds of MDC supporters were beaten, arrested, and murdered. To stop the bloodshed, Tsvangirai dropped out of the race and tried to bring the crisis to a "soft landing" by entering into a coalition government in order to promote power-sharing, stabilize the country, and avoid catastrophe.[36]

For his part, it appears that Mugabe only entered into this unity government to co-opt or demobilize his opposition. There were irregularities, but the 2013 elections were relatively peaceful (compared to those in 2008) and although Tsvangirai rejected the outcome, international observers from the African Union (AU) and Southern African Development Community (SADC) recognized the results of the

2013 presidential and parliamentary elections as "generally credible." Mugabe won with 61 percent of the vote, ahead of Prime Minister Tsvangirai's 34 percent. Mugabe's ZANU-PF continued to hold two-thirds dominance of parliament, with 158 of 210 seats to the MDC's 50, which is enough to amend the constitution.[37]

What this shows is that Mugabe has certainly succeeded in frustrating his opponents and has outlasted them. There was a lull in large-scale protests after the 2008 elections, in part due to splits in the MDC and a lower public profile for the opposition. There was not another major demonstration until early 2016, when things began to change. In the biggest turnouts in nearly a decade, a sea of red appeared in major cities as thousands of MDC supporters, wearing the color of the party, protested economic conditions. Since then, protests have proliferated, often with nearly twenty opposition groups (including former vice president Joyce Mujuru and Morgan Tsvangirai) to participate in what they called "mega demonstrations."[38] These mass, weekly protests were accompanied by the biggest stay-away (or strike) since 2005, organized via social media. For example, a Twitter campaign under the hashtag ThisFlag urged Zimbabweans to reown their flag and call the government out for blaming the country's problems on the West. Given Mugabe's hold on security forces, the opposition has chosen not to encourage a popular uprising; rather, they have only gone as far as to call for a "dignified exit"—not an overthrow of Mugabe.[39] This movement, led by Evan Mawarire, a charismatic young pastor and social media star, galvanized the nation with his calls for nonviolent protest against the state. These efforts, however, have been met with violence as police fired tear gas and water cannons at the crowds. After being arrested and charged with inciting violence, Mawarire and his family fled the country. With a crackdown on social media it appeared that energies were flagging and the new movement was having a hard time maintaining momentum, which is a common problem faced by similar groups worldwide.[40] Moreover, as the government has pointed out, campaigns on Twitter have little to no effect on the rural populations that are not online, and who have consistently turned out for Mugabe. But the war hero Mujuru also enjoys some grassroots popularity in the countryside. So, what is new, and perhaps a game-changer in the 2018 vote, is that broad opposition coalitions have the best chance of forcing transitions in authoritarian systems such as Zimbabwe's.[41] That's assuming that it is somehow a free and fair election. But if they can stick together, this broadly based opposition has the best chance so far of ending Mugabe's nearly forty-year rule.

Case Study: Egypt

Egypt's national identity is based in its greatest claim to exceptionalism: a history that spans millennia. Central to Egyptian political culture is the ancient concept of *maat*, which defines acceptable behavior as recognizing one's place in society, respecting authority, and acknowledging and respecting the will of God—as opposed to being excitable, argumentative, and insistent in demands. Clearly, such a system places a premium on obedience and conformity.[42] The old religions (and new) closely tie the subject to the state, and political obedience has long been considered an important part of the individual's religious duty. Therefore, *maat* explains much of the abiding authoritarianism found in Egyptian political culture.[43]

Given that the culture puts a premium on obedience to authority, it can't be surprising to hear that the Egyptian people are said to be easy to govern. But this worldview does not prescribe blind obedience to the ruler. The king too was answerable to *maat*; he did not stand above the order but was a part of it. When the incompetence of elites exhausted people's patience, uprisings against rulers who fail to maintain *maat* were deemed necessary to restore balance.[44]

It is easy to see how this pattern unfolded in recent years. For decades under Hosni Mubarak and his predecessors, Egyptians had fulfilled their part of the bargain with the state. Citizens had been taught to "walk next to the wall," to keep their heads down and not to get involved in politics. They raised their kids to fear politics and the state, to choose safety over activism.[45] Some obeyed authority because it was habit or they were cynical about the possibilities for change. In addition, many Egyptians' political competence is said to be low, the average person's factual knowledge of politics limited.[46] So, depending on the individual, there were a variety of reasons for Egyptians not to tangle with the state.

But Mubarak's failures in regard to *maat* were legion by 2011, and recognition of this fact culminated in the massive, unprecedented mobilizations at Tahrir Square. Because the ruler was unable to maintain the social contract, the nature of his relationship with the governed changed unequivocally. And in a change without precedent in Egypt, people felt entitled to decide who ruled them and pushed out three regimes in three years (first President Mubarak, then an interim military administration, and finally President Mohammad Morsi). Egypt's revolution fueled uprisings across the Arab world and shook authoritarian regimes in China and Russia.[47]

What was particularly shocking was that compared to its neighbors, Egypt has never seemed vulnerable to falling apart. But there are divides over identity and ideology in Egypt, which is widely characterized as radically polarized ideologically. Within civil society we see traditions of both secular nationalism and religious radicalism. Consequently, Egyptians disagree vehemently over central questions regarding the best form of government, the role that religion should play in public life, the role of the military in politics, and the status of women. On these questions there is little consensus-seeking or attempt at negotiation—and dictators made the most of it, playing groups off each other. As a result, Egypt is said to have a fragmented political culture.[48]

This fragmentation has been aggravated by the state and private media, which played a game of divide and rule and served their own interests. Under Mubarak citizens had virtually no opportunity for critical engagement or debate. It wasn't until "liberation technology" (the Internet and new media) that people were able to circumvent control by elites and make use of unconventional means of public expression and participation.[49] On the other hand, new media have facilitated the spread of misinformation and hate speech. As elsewhere, social media, which are designed to favor posts over dialogue, have intensified polarization and undermined the democratic transition in Egypt.[50]

Perhaps no other political movement in Egypt is more polarizing than the Muslim Brotherhood, the one opposition party the various dictatorships feared (and continue to fear) most.[51] Even though it has spent most of history banned with its members persecuted, the Brotherhood has proven to be the best-organized and most enduring opposition group Egypt has ever known. Founded in 1928, this mainstream Islamist group became known for its religious activism and simple message: "Islam

is the solution."[52] Over the years the Brotherhood became known for its members' self-discipline and for its violent and nonviolent tactics: it could turn out huge crowds in demonstrations and provide the schools and clinics that the government didn't. It could also inspire the most brazen terrorist acts, most notably the 1981 assassination of President Anwar Sadat.[53]

However, starting in the 1980s—while still banned—the Brotherhood shifted away from the use of violence to engage in democratic politics by running candidates as independents. Eventually it was successful, winning a sizable number of parliamentary seats in 2005 and 2011–2012, as well as the presidency in 2012. But the Brotherhood had significantly less success in the actual operation of government. President Morsi was ousted from power and the group was outlawed again in 2013. Still, today the Brotherhood has the support of hundreds of thousands (perhaps millions) of Muslims—not only in Egypt, but also throughout the world.[54] The only question is how it will proceed now that it has won power and lost it.

Having overthrown Morsi's elected government, President Abdel Fattah el-Sisi is trying to replace Islamism with another perennial favorite, ultranationalism, and to distract citizens by blaming scapegoats and stoking fears of foreign plots.[55] He is counting on Egyptians' deep love of the military and comfort with authoritarianism—and that their fear of sliding into civil war like their neighbors will keep Egyptians walking next to the wall. As of 2017 his approach appeared to have worked: in large part the only Egyptians not walking next to the wall are more or less divided into two partisan camps—those who want a religious dictatorship and those who want a military dictatorship.[56] This leaves things looking pretty dim to those who were rooting for those young Tahrir protesters, secular and Islamist liberals alike, who once stood for democracy.

Case Study: Iran

Iranian civil society has, since the revolution of 1979, reflected (and sometimes magnified) the structural tensions created by the dual system within the Islamic Republic: the coexistence of competitive elections for parliamentary and executive leaders, alongside a Supreme Leader, appointed for life, at the helm of the system. Yet as one set of analysts put it, given the "highly securitized setting" within which Iranian civil society operates, it is quite paradoxical that it has "managed not just to survive, but in some ways even to thrive."[57] Iran is known to encompass a broad political spectrum of ideas, often in conflict with each other.

Mobilized by the revolution, but then quickly shuttered, civil society within Iran in recent decades has vacillated under the presidencies of attempted reformists (Presidents Ali Akbar Hashemi Rafsanjani, Mohammad Khatami, and Hassan Rouhani) and a populist conservative (Mahmoud Ahmadinejad). Yet given the theocratic structure of the Iranian regime, stability has been maintained by the Supreme Leader, who in the end possesses the ultimate final say on nearly all public (and many private) matters, even if the stature and influence of Ayatollah Sayyid Ali Khamenei (who also served as president from 1981 to 1989) have been shrinking in recent years.[58]

A significant split between many religious teachers and scholars and the Supreme Leader became public during the disputed 2009 presidential election, as Khamenei lost the support of many clerics, both for his vocal support of Ah-

madinejad, even in the face of substantiated voter fraud behind his reelection, and especially because of the Supreme Leader's support for repression against democracy and human rights activists. Constitutionally, the Supreme Leader serves as an impartial arbiter between factions, a tenet that many believe was violated in 2009, as Khamenei became a "truly despised" leader of a minority faction within Iran, especially after he called Ahmadinejad's 2009 victory a "divine assessment" that could not be challenged.[59] Tensions even threatened to bring down the institutional structure of the Supreme Leader, as some religious leaders—including many who had been active in the foundation of the Islamic Republic in 1979—emphasized the human fallibility of any individual who would assume this post.[60] It is striking to note that these challenges to Khamenei came from religious leaders and seminarians. As there is more talk about Khamenei's successor (he has been Supreme Leader since 1989, and is both aging [born in 1939] and ill), some are even circulating the possibility of crafting a "leadership council" rather than a Supreme Leader, much to the chagrin of some conservative clerics.[61]

Iranian civil society is fueled by an internal struggle between groups who want to forge a uniquely Islamist path to a modern state and society, and those who envision a modern Iran less hostile to secular demands and more open to Western traditions.[62] One observer even claims that Iranian society is "a culture at war with itself."[63] The integration of religious values and rules with everyday life has long been a struggle among the elite of Iran, especially following the colonial influences of Russia and England. After the Islamic Revolution of 1979 established Iran as a theocracy, this debate was muted. Ayatollah Ruhollah Khomeini often declared that "politics and religion are one" and that Iran's theocracy is "God's government." The implication of this conception puts dissenters in a dangerous space: opposition to the government is de facto opposition to God.

Since the election of centrist Hassan Rouhani in 2013, civil society has been provided more latitude, but the human rights situation has become more problematic. Rouhani, who has served as a lawmaker, academic, and diplomat within the Islamic Republic, favors increased civil liberties and freedoms of expression, yet lacks the unfettered ability to implement many of these changes. So, even though nongovernmental organizations (NGOs) have greater legal protections, UN studies have concluded that the overall human rights situation has worsened since his election, with a surge in the number of executions, as well as the jailing of journalists and activists.[64]

Conservatives today take issue with the accusation that they are trying to go backward. They state that they, too, are interested in reform, just not Western-style reform. In their view, changes in Iran must fit within the context of "Islamic-style" democracy, in which clerics still hold political power befitting an Islamic and not a liberal republic. In the eyes of conservatives, liberalism is too risky, and is seen as a genuine threat to the status quo. There are many within Iran—including some religious clerics—who are pushing discussion about the ways in which an active faith life can thrive in a more open society.

Of the many groups pushing for greater change in Iranian politics and society, women and youth stand out. Women were prominent during Iran's constitutional revolution of 1906–1911, and they are once again returning to the public forefront. Since 1997, women have submitted their names as presidential candidates to the Council of Guardians, challenging the orthodox interpretation of Article 115 of the

Iranian constitution, which states that "the president should be elected from among spiritual and political men" (the language may be interpreted as either "men" or "personalities"). To date, no women have been approved as candidates, but there have been some named as cabinet ministers, and Rouhani tapped a woman, Masoumeh Ebtekar, to serve as one of the country's twelve vice presidents. More than half of university students are women, and curtains no longer divide male and female students within classrooms. Yet this advancement has created both opportunities and dilemmas—it is problematic, for example, for women with degrees to find husbands with the same level of education, and married women still require their husband's permission in order to work outside the home.[65] Until recently, women were barred from men's sporting events (Ahmadinejad made an exception—without consulting the clerics—because of loud demands by female soccer fans).[66] As we observe elsewhere, Iranian women are not a solid ideological bloc; some women promote gender segregation and the withdrawal from UN bodies and agreements that are deemed too feminist or un-Islamic.

Some point to a potential "marriage crisis" in the Islamic Republic, as many couples find marriage, with the resulting change in housing status, too expensive or less desirable, and, to the consternation of many religious leaders, are pushing back the average marriage age. (Real estate prices—especially in major cities—have skyrocketed in recent years.) The potential change in sexual mores is viewed as a threat to the spiritual core of the country—the head of Iran's National Youth Organization presaged, "The sexual bomb we face is more dangerous than the bombs and missiles of the enemy."[67] The government's proposal—"semi-independent marriage" in which young couples legally marry but continue living apart in their parents' homes—was rapidly condemned and dropped after especially vocal outcries from women, who saw the scheme as providing the sexual bounty of marriage without social or security status for themselves.[68] In what may—at least partially—be interpreted as a form of passive resistance against the state, Iran is experiencing a sexual revolution that runs counter to the conservative trends evident in much of the rest of the region, experiencing declining birth rates, skyrocketing divorce, and a visible increase in both female and male sex workers.[69] The mullahs are not amused.

One of Iran's most prominent women is Shirin Ebadi, a lawyer who champions the cases of women and children and who was jailed for violating Iranian publishing standards by writing about human rights in the Islamic Republic. In 2003 she became the first Iranian and the first Muslim woman to receive the Nobel Peace Prize, much to the consternation of then-president Khatami. Since the disputed 2009 elections (during which time she was an outspoken critic of Ahmadinejad and Khamenei), authorities have confiscated her Nobel Prize medal from her safety-deposit box, arrested her sister, and framed her husband for adultery (forcing him to publicly renounce her as a puppet of the West). Not surprisingly, she has lived in exile since 2009.

Younger citizens, especially university students, have a long history of activism in Iranian politics. Their role is significant, as more than 50 percent of the Iranian population is under thirty-five years of age. College students supported former president Khatami's reform movement, staging boycotts and protests at great risk. This is the segment of the population most adept at using smart phones and the most recent advances in information communication technologies, and they use them to angle their case. Youth were the backbone of the Green Movement in 2009, and they continue to take to

the streets to demand change, incurring the wrath of the administration and its security apparatus. They are likely to continue to demand a voice in the increasingly crowded public arena of the Islamic Republic of Iran and may likely form the backbone of Iran's sometimes wary, yet always resilient, civil society.

Case Study: China

For all of the economic liberties that we highlighted in the earlier case study, when it comes to civil society and freedom of expression, China is moving in the other direction. The expression of ideas—especially political—within modern China is limited by the continued dominance of the Chinese Communist Party (CCP). Even though alternative parties exist—they constitute the so-called loyal nonopposition—decisions within China today need the approval of CCP officials. China continues to abide by the Leninist principle of mandating a singular, elitist, unchallenged party. Those attempting to form groups or engage in behavior that can be perceived as formal opposition have been imprisoned for charges including "subverting state power," "divulging state secrets," and "inciting subversion." Perhaps the most well-known Chinese dissident who has been imprisoned for his views is Liu Xiaobo, a former literature professor and activist who has been in and out of detention and labor camps since 1989 and who, despite receiving the 2010 Nobel Peace Prize, is largely unknown within China due to the state-controlled media (and continues to serve his time as a political prisoner).

Despite the known risks, there is a strong tradition of dissent and disagreement within China, dating back to the first student demonstrations against the government in the May 4th Movement of 1919. Ironically, some of the same leaders who gathered in Beijing to denounce the Chinese government then were responsible for violently ending student demonstrations in the nation's capital in 1989. Those demonstrations in Tiananmen Square attracted global attention as university students and citizens from all walks of life protested against inflation, corruption, and the absence of political reform. As the world's television cameras captured the dynamic events taking place in Beijing and other Chinese cities, the government prepared to send tanks to crush the movement, which it ultimately did on the nights of June 3 and 4, 1989.

In addition to explicitly political demonstrations and protests against corruption and the abuse of constitutionally guaranteed rights, increasingly Chinese citizens organize around other collective identities, especially rural farmers and activists of varying religious affiliations. With great frequency, Chinese peasants wage protests against illegal levies and fees in the countryside, uneven implementation of the planned-birth policy, and official corruption, among other matters. This is part of a larger pattern of both increased participation from citizens as well as surprising acknowledgment from regime officials. It is believed that there are approximately 130,000 "mass incidents" (riots and other disturbances) each year, which would average out to nearly 400 every day.[70] Because of the coverage of crackdowns against major dissidents, many assume that protests in China are risky, rare endeavors: officials demonstrate few qualms about heavy-handed suppression. But the risks don't seem to quell the desire to speak out against perceived injustices.[71]

Also, in defiance of state limits on religion, Chinese citizens seek membership in underground Christian churches and other spiritual associations. It's a sensitive

topic, but one academic survey conducted by researchers at Shanghai's East China Normal University reported that 31 percent of Chinese self-identify as religious, or approximately 300 million people, challenging the long-stated estimate of 100 million. This figure includes 40 million Christians (although most missionary organizations put the total at 60–80 million), and 200 million believers in traditional Chinese religions.[72] The latitude for religious choice and expression has been front and center in disputes between China and Vatican City (the two states lack formal diplomatic ties—although there has been some movement toward normalization by Pope Francis), as Beijing asserts its right to appoint and supervise the behavior of Chinese Catholics and the Holy See refuses to acknowledge most CCP-appointed priests and bishops. The tenacity of the dispute points to the broad numbers of Chinese, both in cosmopolitan urban settings as well as in rural communities alike, who seek spiritual communities for expression.

While newspapers and magazines continue to operate under the official sponsorship of the CCP, most observers note a qualitative change in the types of stories covered by the media, as well as the increasing investigatory powers of newspaper and magazine journalists. There are even cases of the central government's using state-run media to rein in corrupt local officials, such as after a rash of lead-poisoning broke out in children who lived near a smelting company in the central province of Shaanxi. Widespread Internet access is also creating a wealth of options for Chinese citizens; as if the government monitors targeted individuals, even reading their draft e-mails, Chinese Netizens have shown a voracious appetite for social media.[73] Even Facebook, which has been blocked in China since 2009, is moving toward a "probable" relaunch within the PRC—after it (quietly) developed software to suppress posts by geographic area.[74] Despite the proliferation of virtual private network (VPN) access in order to circumvent regime censorship, Internet service is regularly blocked to regions during and following disturbances—in the western region of Xinjiang, for example, service was not restored until ten months after the ethnic rioting that convulsed the capital, Urumqi. On the day the Internet was restored, many residents took the day off school or work and flocked to Internet cafes to catch up on messages and return to online gaming—imitations of *World of Warcraft* are by far the most popular.[75] The Internet is the prime source of entertainment for Chinese youth who are bored and frustrated by state-run television and the limits on foreign programs.[76]

The effects of development on gender in China have been very uneven. Communist leaders inherited a dismal record of attention to women in 1949, and although the situation has improved greatly (baby girls, for example, are no longer forced to have their toes broken to create a small foot through binding), women in China today continue to face many struggles. Traditional attitudes toward girls have been reinforced by the one-child-per-couple policies implemented since the 1980s. Economically, one of the most disturbing trends affecting the mobility of women is the feminization of agriculture, as women are left behind in impoverished rural areas while the men in the family go to the cities in search of more lucrative employment. Recognizing this and other seemingly unintended consequences of the population-control policy, the Chinese government has loosened the plan in recent years, permitting two children per couple in major urban areas. Such exceptions had already been permitted in the Chinese countryside, where families with a firstborn girl were permitted to have a second child. Additionally, conspicuous wealth makes some of

the penalties irrelevant for families who are unlikely to turn to government-provided social services in the first place, while travel to Hong Kong allows couples to side-step some of the restrictions.

If we measure civil society in terms of independent organizations, there are challenges: most organizational life is corporatist, and groups need permission from local authorities to form and gather. An area that has been swelling with grassroots participation in recent years has been environmental activism—there are well over 10,000 formally registered environmental NGOs in China today. China's first legal nonprofit group was Friends of Nature, an environmental organization founded in 1994. An executive with a group that helps domestic nonprofits in China stated, "Civil society is now a phrase people in China are beginning to understand."[77] Environmental groups have more autonomy than other potential groups, in part because of the severity of environmental problems in China, and in part because Beijing's leaders have recognized the inherent connection between environmental degradation and sustainability of economic growth. Large projects that have received the sanction and funding of Beijing, such as massive dam and water-diversion projects, remain off-limits.[78] Under the leadership of Xi Jinping, whom many analysts contend is the strongest leader since Mao Zedong, NGOs operate under a much more careful eye, and a particular pall was cast when a registration law for foreign NGOs was passed in 2016.[79] Despite these limits, though, Chinese citizens continue to find ways to express their opinions and find their voice.

Case Study: Indonesia

Indonesia is a country rich in diversity (which should not be surprising, given its geography of more than 17,000 islands). Rather than viewing linguistic, cultural, and religious diversity as strengths, however, Indonesian leaders and to some extent ordinary citizens, have, at times, viewed them as threats. Especially during the thirty-two-year reign of General Suharto, Indonesia's second president, any identity that contradicted national unity was squelched. The two biggest offenders were expression of religious division and communism. In fact, until recently, any printed materials containing Chinese characters could be confiscated, on the suspicion that they might promote communist infiltration. In this environment, citizens tended toward compliance rather than confrontation. Yet months of protest, ignited by the Asian financial crisis, led to Suharto's dramatic resignation in 1998. Throughout the streets of Indonesia's major cities, Indonesia's second president was vilified for his corrupt, heavy-handed rule. After they were successful in toppling the president, however, diverse groups of demonstrators faced a dilemma familiar to other activists protesting authoritarian rule: since organized opposition had been illegal for so long, there were few available networks through which opposition groups could communicate and mobilize. Today, while members of civil society have many more freedoms to associate and spread their message, civil society remains fragmented and often weak.

During Suharto's "New Order" (1966–1998), the only viable electoral force—not technically a political party at the time—was Golkar, a federation of functional associations and trade unions that served as an umbrella for anticommunist associations and a government-fabricated identity. Opposition parties existed and ran candidates in the People's Consultative Assembly, but their acceptance was always at the

discretion of government leaders: Golkar was the dominant legislative power from 1973 to 1999, promoting anti-communism and secular policies and dominated by the armed forces. Government employees were open to charges of disloyalty for joining any party that might challenge Golkar—the source of their bread and butter.[80] Truly competitive political parties were not permitted until 1999, and Golkar remains as a viable force. Having served in the opposition previously, Golkar switched allegiance during its annual party meetings in mid-2016, throwing its support behind President Joko "Jokowi" Widodo.

Indonesian civil society includes a variety of semiautonomous groups, although they remain fragmented and often have a close connection to core political elite. Citizens are actively engaged in political discussions, especially online. Some analysts have even called Indonesia the "social media capital of the world," as one of the most Twitter- and Facebook-friendly countries on the planet.[81] Despite a relatively low Internet penetration rate (approximately 30 percent),[82] Indonesia's young population and the rabid popularity of social media in urban areas account for these high numbers. Indonesia's Internet users are known to be very critical of government and society, and they play an outsized role in elections, with campaign staff members using WhatsApp groups to communicate. Paid posters strategically submit Tweets so that drivers snarled in rush-hour traffic are likely to read and repost their ideas. After (then-candidate) Donald Trump pledged to consider a ban on Muslims entering the United States, an online petition urging President Jokowi to ban the billionaire and his businesses from the country received more than 45,000 signatures.[83] In many ways, current President Jokowi owes his rise to social media: his staff developed and distributed a wildly popular adaptation of "Angry Birds," with the candidate throwing exploding tomatoes at corrupt officials.[84] His campaign also was involved in releasing a remake of the popular One Direction song ("What Makes You Beautiful"), highlighting the traffic, corruption, and flooding problems that people hoped Jokowi could fix.[85]

It surprises many to learn that Indonesia is the world's largest Muslim-majority state (approximately 87 percent of citizens identify as Muslim, primarily Sunni), and that there are almost as many Muslims living in Indonesia as in the entire Arabic-speaking world. Although religious expression is more common today than it was even a decade ago, Indonesia's political institutions are secular, designed to help mediate potential fissures along religious lines. Muslims have long been the standard-bearers of independent organizations in Indonesia; even during the Suharto years, groups of organized Muslims—some with membership rolls in the tens of millions—challenged the regime.[86] Yet in recent years, observers have noted an atmosphere of declining civil liberties, and especially declining religious tolerance. The highly publicized and contentious trial of Jakarta governor Basuki Tjahaja Purnama, commonly known by his nickname, Ahok, brought these tensions—and, in the mind of some observers, Indonesia's commitment to maintaining a secular state—to the surface. Ahok, the first non-Muslim governor of Jakarta since 1965 and a Christian of Chinese descent, was an extremely popular political independent known for improving public transportation and cracking down on corruption. He stands accused of insulting Islam by challenging some of his contenders in the governor's campaign (including a former president's son) who quoted a Quranic verse challenging whether Muslims should live under the leadership of non-Muslims. Although Ahok has repeatedly apologized for any misunderstanding, he denies blasphemy (a

charge that could imprison him for five years). Jakarta endured months of marches, mostly calling for Ahok's downfall, in a case that is widely viewed as a litmus test for Indonesia's continued religious tolerance.[87]

Religious-based cleavages in Indonesia are not new. Formerly, the most serious religious-based conflict had been within Islam, between parties with varying adherence to Islamic law. Violence between Indonesia's Christians, who make up the second largest group of religious believers (but still constitute less than 10 percent of the population), and Muslims, has been less commonplace, although activist-representatives of many faiths have been calling on the government to uphold the secular constitution and guarantee the right to freely practice religion. Since its foundation, Indonesia has guarded its secular principles as necessary for accommodating the diversity across the archipelago. During the Ahok trial, for example, Indonesia's largest Islamic group, Nahdlatul Ulama, explicitly enjoined its members not to take part in the anti-Ahok rallies.[88]

Since the landmark 2005 peace agreement that granted Aceh unprecedented autonomy within the republic (the province of Aceh is seen as the birthplace of Islam in Indonesia), formal Islamic courts organized on the principles of Islamic religious law, or *sharia,* have been established throughout the province, which is long known for its orthodox views. Since their implementation in 2006, the *sharia* courts have received mixed reviews, with flogging—even of non-Muslims—becoming more frequent.[89] Some women's groups have reported increased harassment of women (including the arrest of three women who gathered in a hotel corridor after a United Nations–sponsored seminar on women's rights) as well as detainment of foreign aid workers, both male and female, for meeting with a person of the opposite sex in ways considered inappropriate by the *sharia* police. Others praise the changes, viewing *sharia* courts as proof of the province's autonomy and as demonstrating that it is possible to be both Muslim and modern.[90]

Indonesian identity is an extremely sensitive topic, and debates over inclusion in this category continue to rage with great ferocity. One region that has faced simmering discontent and discord is West Papua, Indonesia's least-populous province, which prior to 2007 was known as West Irian Jaya. Activists in this heavily militarized region have been subject to much abuse at the hands of the Indonesian military in attempting to respond to separatist demands by some Papuans, whose physical appearance, more Melanesian than Asian, is distinct from that of other Indonesians. Individuals have been imprisoned for treason after displaying the outlawed Papuan flag, the Morning Star. Similar to many conflicts in Indonesia, the challenges in Papua follow the pattern of coinciding cleavages: in addition to differences in ethnicity and socioeconomic opportunities, a significant religious cleavage exists. Locals are mostly Christian or animist, and clash with the newer, predominantly Muslim residents of the region, whose migration to the island has been encouraged by Jakarta. Movement toward a UN-sponsored referendum, modeled after the one held in Timor-Leste in 1999, picked up in 2016, although Jakarta is likely to continue its stiff opposition to such a move (and, to date, independence activists lack the support of the major regional strongholds, Australia and New Zealand).[91]

Indonesia's population is diverse and dynamic, and in recent years has engaged in both civil and uncivil activism. As with our other case studies, Indonesia continues to grapple with contending meanings of citizenship, nationality, and voice.

Now It's Your Turn

Why do you think people turn to political ideologies to achieve their causes? How can ordinary citizens and leaders alike be manipulated by ideologies? Why do you think youth are attracted to particular movements? After reading about some of the forms of activism and expression discussed in this chapter, do you view any actions, such as wearing an Islamic headscarf, differently than you did before? Why or why not? What are some of the seemingly unusual ways in which people are making their concerns known? Why do they choose these methods? How do economic, political, and cultural factors contribute to activism (or lack thereof)?

Notes

1. Octavio Paz, "Latin America and Democracy," in *Democracy and Dictatorship in Latin America: A Special Publication Devoted Entirely to the Voice and Opinions of Writers from Latin America,* ed. Octavio Paz, Jorge Edwards, Carlos Franqui, et al. (New York: Foundation for the Independent Study of Social Ideas, 1982).

2. Katherine E. Bliss, "Party Politics in Mexico's Midterm Elections," *Hemisphere Focus* (Center for Strategic and International Studies) 17, no. 3 (July 9, 2009).

3. Tim Johnson, "In Foul Mood, Mexican Voters Ponder How to Send Message in Sunday Elections," *McClatchyDC,* June 5, 2015.

4. James C. McKinley Jr., "Mexico Faces Its Own Red-Blue Standoff," *New York Times,* July 9, 2006.

5. Ibid.; "Mexico's Midterm Elections and the Future of Democracy," Wilson Center, July 10, 2009.

6. "Mexico's New Government: With a Little Help from My Friends," *The Economist,* December 8, 2012.

7. "Mexico's New Political Reality: New Electoral Processes and Bodies," Canning House, London, 2016, www.canninghouse.org.

8. Marc Lacey, "Disgruntled Mexicans Plan an Election Message to Politicians: We Prefer Nobody," *New York Times,* June 21, 2009; Malcolm Bleith, "Mexico's Blast from the Past," *Newsweek,* July 2, 2009.

9. "As You Were," *The Economist,* July 5, 2010; "Taking It to the Streets," *Houston Chronicle,* November 4, 2006.

10. Kirk Semple, "Grass-Roots Anticorruption Drive Puts Heat on Mexican Lawmakers," *New York Times,* May 28, 2016.

11. Azam Ahmed and Kirk Semple, "Clashes Draw Support for Teachers' Protest in Mexico," *New York Times,* June 26, 2016.

12. Francisco Durand, "The New Right and Political Change in Peru," in *The Right and Democracy in Latin America,* ed. Douglas A. Chalmers, Maria do Carmo Campello de Souza, and Atilio A. Borón (New York: Praeger, 1992); Ernesto García Calderón, "Peru's Decade of Living Dangerously," *Journal of Democracy* 12, no. 2 (April 2001).

13. Durand, "The New Right and Political Change in Peru."

14. Moises Arce, "The Persistence of the Two Perus," *Current History,* February 2014.

15. Dan Collyns, "Thousands Protest Against Presidential Bid by Daughter of Corrupt Former Peru Leader," *The Guardian* (London), April 6, 2016.

16. Alex Emery, "Peru's Farmers Fight Police over Southern Copper Mine," *Bloomberg Businessweek,* April 15, 2010.

17. Arce, "The Persistence of the Two Perus"; Kristina Aiello, "Peru's 'Cold War' Against Indigenous Peoples," North American Congress on Latin America (NACLA), July 15, 2009, https://nacla.org/node/5995.

18. Simon Romero, "Protesters Gird for Long Fight over Opening Peru's Amazon," *New York Times,* July 11, 2009.

19. Gerardo Rénique, "Law of the Jungle in Peru: Indigenous Amazonian Uprising Against Neoliberalism," *Socialism and Democracy* 23, no. 3 (November 2009).

20. "Blood in the Jungle," *The Economist,* June 13, 2009; Stephanie Boyd, "The Ticking Time Bomb," *New Internationalist* 427 (November 2009); "To the Barricades," *The Economist,* December 6, 2008; "Documentary About Peru's Bagua Massacre Wins Award in Madrid," *Telesur,* May 7, 2016.

21. Juan Carlos Riveros, "Climate Justice for the Indigenous People of Peru," World Wildlife Fund, December 15, 2014; Marisol de la Cadena, "Indigenous Cosmopolitics in the Andes," *Cultural Anthropology* 25, no. 2 (May 2010); Romero, "Protesters Gird for Long Fight"; Andrew C. Revkin, "Peru Prepares to Host Climate Talks as Its Indigenous Forest Defenders Die," *New York Times,* November 17, 2014.

22. Laura Fano Morrisey, "The Rise of Ethnic Politics: Indigenous Movements in the Andean Region," *Development* 52, no. 4 (2009); Rénique, "Law of the Jungle in Peru."

23. Funso Afolayan, "Nigeria: A Political Entity and a Society," in *Dilemmas of Democracy in Nigeria,* ed. Paul A. Beckett and Crawford Young (Rochester, NY: University of Rochester Press, 1997).

24. Ibid.

25. "The Candidates to Be Nigeria's Leader," BBC News, December 4, 2006.

26. "Profile: Umaru Yar'Adua," BBC News, December 17, 2006.

27. Ernest Aryeetey, "Can Nigeria Fail?," Brookings Institution, Washington, DC, June 24, 2010; Peter M. Lewis, "Nigeria: Cycles of Crisis, Sources of Resilience," in *Coping with Crisis in African States,* ed. Peter M. Lewis and John W. Harbeson (Boulder: Lynne Rienner, 2016).

28. Chris Stein, "Nigeria's Ruling All Progressives Congress Dealt Setback," *VOA,* June 10, 2015.

29. Ibid.; Nicholas Ibekwe, "Nigeria: How Progressive Is the APC?," *New African,* February 10, 2015.

30. Brandon Kendhammer, "Nigeria's New Democratic Dawn?," *Current History,* May 2015.

31. "Zimbabwe's Tighter Belts, and Shorter Tempers," *The Economist,* October 28, 2000.

32. Not all women are MDC supporters. Older, rural women with less formal education are some of ZANU-PF's staunchest supporters, and many of them fear the uncertainty that would come with a new government.

33. Douglas Rogers, "Zimbabwe's Accidental Triumph," *New York Times,* April 15, 2010.

34. Sam Moyo, "The Land Occupation Movement and Democratization in Zimbabwe: Contradictions of Neoliberalism," *Millennium* 30, no. 2 (2001); Douglas Rogers, "Zimbabwe's Accidental Triumph," *New York Times,* April 15, 2010.

35. Ibid.; Joseph Hanlon, Jeannette Manjengwa, and Teresa Smart, *Zimbabwe Takes Back Its Land* (Boulder: Lynne Rienner, 2012).

36. Greg Mills and Jeffrey Herbst, "Bring Zimbabwe in from the Cold," *New York Times,* May 28, 2009.

37. Michael Bratton, *Power Politics in Zimbabwe* (Boulder: Lynne Rienner, 2014); Columbus S. Mavhunga and Faith Karimi, "Mugabe Declared Winner of Presidency in Zimbabwe," *CNN News,* August 3, 2013.

38. "Zimbabwe Anti-Mugabe Protest: Police Fire Tear Gas," BBC News, August 26, 2016.

39. "Zimbabwe Holds Largest Anti-Mugabe Protest in Years," Agence France-Presse, April 14, 2016.

40. Letter from Africa: Zimbabwe's Flag Fury," BBC News, June 1, 2016; Jeffrey Moyo and Norimitsu Onishi, "Mugabe Mocked the Internet, Then Discovered Threat in Online Pastor," *New York Times,* October 3, 2016.

41. Andrew Mambondiyani, "Parched Zimbabwe Faces Dire Water Shortages as New Dry Season Nears," Reuters, August 25, 2016; Jeffrey Moyo and Norimitsu Onishi, "Police in Zimbabwe Hit Protesters with Batons, Tear Gas, and Water Cannons," *New York Times,* August 26, 2016; Alexander Noyes, "To Beat Mugabe, Zimbabwe Needs a United Opposition," *New York Times,* November 26, 2015.

42. Alan B. Lloyd, *Ancient Egypt: State and Society* (New York: Oxford University Press, 2014).

43. Thomas Schneider, *Ancient Egypt in 10 Questions and Answers* (Ithaca: Cornell University Press, 2013).

44. Arthur Goldschmidt Jr., *Modern Egypt: The Formation of a Nation-State* (Boulder: Westview, 2004).

45. Ashraf Khalil, *Liberation Square: Inside the Egyptian Revolution and the Rebirth of a Nation* (New York: St. Martin's, 2011); Wael Ghonim, *Revolution 2.0: The Power of the People Is Greater Than the People in Power* (New York: Houghton, Mifflin, Harcourt, 2012).

46. Jakob Erle, Jakob Mathias Wichmann, and Alexander Kjaerum, "Political Culture in Egypt: The Political Values and Norms of the Voters," Danish Egyptian Dialogue Institute, 2012.

47. Thanassis Cambanis, *Once Upon a Revolution: An Egyptian Story* (New York: Simon and Schuster, 2015).

48. Hanan Badr, "Public Sphere, New Media, and Political Culture in Post-Revolutionary Egypt," in *Media Culture in Transformation: Political Communication, Social Networking, and Transition in Egypt,* ed. Hanan Badr (Bonn: Max Weber Stiftung, 2016).

49. Marc Lynch, "The Rise and Fall of the New Arab Public Sphere," *Current History,* December 2015; Badr, "Public Sphere, New Media, and Political Culture."

50. Lynch, "The Rise and Fall of the New Arab Public Sphere"; Thomas L. Friedman, "Social Media: Destroyer or Creator?," *New York Times,* February 3, 2016.

51. Ghonim, *Revolution 2.0.*

52. Cambanis, *Once Upon a Revolution;* Tarek Osman, *Egypt on the Brink: From Nasser to Mubarak* (New Haven: Yale University Press, 2010).

53. Osman, *Egypt on the Brink.*

54. Cambanis, *Once Upon a Revolution;* Goldschmidt, *Modern Egypt.*

55. Mona Eltahawy, "Sisi's War on Reporters," *New York Times,* November 23, 2015.

56. Michael J. Totten, "The Muslim Brotherhood Takes Off Its Mask," *World Affairs,* May 21, 2015.

57. Paulo Rivetti and Mohsen Moheimany, "Upgrading Civil Society in Iran: Dynamics of Adaptation," Middle East Institute, September 17, 2015, www.mei.edu.

58. Muhammad Sahimi, "Iran's Incredible Shrinking Ayatollah," *National Interest,* May 8, 2016, www.nationalinterest.org.

59. Ibid.; Scott Peterson, "After 8 Defiant Years, Ahmadinejad Leaves Iran Isolated and Cash-Strapped," *Christian Science Monitor,* August 2, 2013.

60. "Future Perfect," *Newsweek,* November 18, 2009.

61. Former president Akbar Hashemi Rafsanjani was most closely associated with this proposal, which he contended was being discussed by a group of clerics within the Assembly of Experts, the constitutional body that appoints the supreme leader. See Muhammad Sahimi, "Who Will Succeed Ayatollah Khamenei?," *Huffington Post,* January 4, 2016, www.huffingtonpost.com.

62. In her book *Honeymoon in Tehran: Two Years of Love and Danger in Iran* (New York: Random, 2009), Azadeh Moaveni highlights this divide between religious militants and those preferring a more private interpretation of their faith.

63. Reza Afshari, "A Historic Moment in Iran," *Human Rights Quarterly* 31, no. 4 (November 2009), p. 840.

64. Monavar Khalaj, "Iran's Rouhani Softens Stance on NGOs," *Financial Times,* August 28, 2015, www.ft.com.

65. David Blair, "Iran's Big Woman Problem: All of the Things Iranian Women Aren't Allowed to Do," *The Telegraph* (London), September 21, 2015.

66. Amir Daftari, "Iran Split over Female Soccer Fans," *CNN News,* May 1, 2006.

67. Azadeh Moaveni, "Will Iran's 'Marriage Crisis' Bring Down Ahmadinejad?," *Time,* June 9, 2009.

68. Ibid.

69. Afshin Shahi, "Erotic Republic," *Foreign Policy,* May 29, 2013, www.foreignpolicy.com.

70. Tyler Headly and Cole Tanigawa-Lau, "Measuring Chinese Discontent: What Local Unrest Tells Us," *Foreign Affairs,* March 10, 2016; Willy Lam, former China editor of the Hong Kong–based *South China Morning Post,* in Weiliang Nie, "Chinese Learn to Leap the 'Great Firewall,'" BBC News, March 19, 2010.

71. Chris Hogg, "Protest Not Unusual in China," BBC News, July 7, 2009.

72. Wu Jiao, "Religious Believers Thrice the Estimate," *China Daily,* February 7, 2007.

73. "The Party, the People, and the Power of Cyber-Talk," *The Economist,* April 29, 2006, p. 27.

74. Mike Isaac, "Facebook Said to Create Censorship Tool to Get Back into China," *New York Times,* November 22, 2016.

75. Edward Wong, "After a 10-Month Ban, Western China Is Online," *New York Times,* May 15, 2010, p. A5.

76. David Barboza, "For Chinese, Web Is the Way to Entertainment," *New York Times,* April 19, 2010, p. B1.

77. Jan Pierini, executive director of Beijing's PeopleLink, interviewed in Christina Larson, "China's Emerging Environmental Movement," *Yale Environment 360,* June 3, 2008.

78. Ibid.

79. Edward Wong, "Clampdown in China Restricts 7,000 Foreign Organizations," *New York Times,* April 28, 2016.

80. Robert Cribb and Colin Brown, *Modern Indonesia: A History Since 1945* (New York: Longman, 1995).

81. Karishma Vaswani, "Indonesia's Love Affair with Social Media," BBC News, February 16, 2012; Tony Starr, "Indonesia's Social Media Savvy Moves It onto the Movember Map," *PRI's The World,* November 5, 2013, www.pri.org; Sam Bollier, "Voting in the 'World's Social Media Capital,'" Al Jazeera, July 2, 2014.

82. "Internet Users in Indonesia Reach 73 Million," *Jakarta Post,* March 10, 2015.

83. Franklin Nangoy and Randy Fabi, "Trump Already a Tainted Name in Indonesia After Muslim Ban Remarks," Reuters, March 8, 2016.

84. Bollier, "Voting in the 'World's Social Media Capital.'"

85. Ibid.

86. Annette Clear, "Politics: From Endurance to Evolution," in *Indonesia: The Great Transition,* ed. John Bresnan (New York: Rowman and Littlefield, 2005), pp. 143–144.

87. Kikue Hamayotsu, "Indonesia in 2014: The Year of Electing the 'People's President,'" *Asian Survey* 55, no. 1 (January–February 2015), pp. 174–183; "Indonesia Blasphemy Case: Emotional Scenes as Ahok Trial Begins," BBC News, December 13, 2016; "Jokowi Blames 'Political Actors' for Violence at Indonesia Rally," *Bloomberg,* November 4, 2016; Yenni Kwok, "The Blasphemy Trial of Jakarta's Governor Puts Indonesian Secularism in a Shockingly Poor Light," *Time,* December 12, 2016.

88. "Indonesia Blasphemy Case," BBC News.

89. "Aceh Flogs 13 Young People for Breaking Its Strict Islamic Laws," Agence France-Presse, October 17, 2016.

90. Karishma Vaswani, "On Patrol with Aceh's Sharia Police," BBC News, February 2, 2010.

91. Helen Davidson, "West Papua: UN Must Supervise Vote on Independence, Says Coalition," *The Guardian* (London), May 3, 2016.

Chapter 11

Militaries, Militias, Guerrillas, and Terrorists

It's like setting a wolf loose amongst a flock of sheep.
—Former Iranian Basij militia member,
reflecting on the militia's response to internal unrest[1]

If you watch the headlines, it is not difficult to walk away with the im-pression that the world is falling apart, that violence lurks around nearly every corner, and that things have never been this bad. Horror sells, and, as the saying goes, "If it bleeds, it leads." We don't expect journalists to report the daily absence of conflict, terrorist attacks, or brutalities. Yet over the long-term, rates of homicide, war, genocide, and terrorism are all trending downward, and these acts of violence are a fraction of what they were in the 1960s, 1970s, and even the 1980s.[2] However, in large part due to the ongoing conflict in Syria, there is concern that some of these trends may be shifting, and it is clear that violence remains a significant force in our world today.

On September 11, 2001, Americans faced violence in a way that most in this country had never experienced. When planes were crashed into the towers of the World Trade Center in New York City, the Pentagon just outside Washington, D.C., and a field in rural Pennsylvania, the power of organized violence jolted the country's sense of security in a way most had also never experienced. As the United States and the world struggled to understand the reasons for these actions, we contemplated a force that has long been employed by individuals and groups. In Chapter 9 we discussed people's option of "voice," focusing on ideologies and participation. In this chapter we investigate participation that engages the use of violence. We examine a variety of means of violent expression, highlighting the individuals and groups behind the actions and emphasizing the role of governments and militaries, terrorists and revolutionaries. The World Bank now estimates that violence is becoming the primary cause of poverty in the world, pointing to the development of a "violence trap" that may become even more significant than the well-known "poverty trap" some countries experience.[3]

Some view violence as the breakdown of politics, but we encourage you to view it instead as a tool used by actors to accomplish their goals. Violence is a powerful weapon, used by terrorists, governments, guerrillas, militaries, militias, and activists canvassing the whole gamut of ideological persuasion. While many commonly view the use of violence as a means of gaining territory, such tactics are also often used to exact responses including fear, intimidation, surrender, and subjugation, as we will see in this chapter. The psychological force of violence (or the threat thereof) is perhaps the greatest source of its potency.

Violence can take many forms, and its perpetrators justify it in a variety of ways. Behind violent acts are myriad motivations, aspirations, and justifications—all open to competing interpretations. As students of the global south, we attempt to classify types of actions taken by ordinary people and political elites alike, but these labels are often reductionist (overly simplified) and may imply judgment. Take one form of violence with which we have all become more familiar in recent years: terrorism. As analysts, we can come up with a clear-cut definition of what we mean by the term—it involves purposeful acts against innocent civilians in order to provoke fear and insecurity. Clearly, some individuals and groups engage in these acts in ways consistent with this view, and they take action without apology—priding themselves as among the world's most renowned terrorists. Yet there are other times when the term is used as a political label to characterize a seemingly unjustifiable action by a group of people. In discussions of this topic, watch carefully the labels that are tossed around; tagging a group as "terrorist" can often fulfill a political agenda to delegitimize a group's perspective. Classifying acts of political deviance is a subjective enterprise.

Terrorist violence is used in many different types of conflict and by many activists of all stripes. Here we will observe terrorism at work, including during warfare, revolutions, and times of peace. The designation of terrorist acts can sometimes be a puzzle; dependent upon one's perspective, the task of defining what exactly "terrorism" is has befuddled many social scientists. As linguist, activist, and political commentator Noam Chomsky has often contended, the difference between terrorism and heroism is often based on perception more than reality.[4] Sometimes the fiery debate has taken on the language of "freedom fighters" versus "terrorists"—it should not be surprising that groups of people using violence believe that the ends justify the means.

Rather than trying to argue for or against a particular definition, we highlight key components: terrorism is a deliberate organized act, with the goal of inspiring fear. Usually, innocents are victimized, although the definition of who is "innocent" can be manipulated. Terrorists have shown devastating flexibility in both their targets and their tactics, which include bombings, kidnappings, hijackings, and the threats of such actions. They want to gain an audience—attention, even negative attention, is what they seek—in order to publicize their causes. They seek to alter opinion and policy. Contrary to popular belief, they're not all after land or material resources. Rather, they sometimes fight bigger, more seemingly abstract issues, such as globalization. Since attention is what these groups are after, the proliferation of nonstop news reports on television, radio, and the Internet has become an accessible platform. Terror tactics evolve based on the response of societies and governments. In a scenario that seems almost quaint by today's standards, planes used to be commandeered by hijackers to go to Cuba. Nowadays groups are creating weapons of

mass destruction out of airplanes. Why? The flexibility of terrorism requires relatively few people to pull it off, and in the twenty-first century it is easier to acquire adequate materials to invoke terror. Maybe the world has become jaded and it takes more to get our attention—which is precisely what advocates of terror and other forms of violence desire.

As we discuss various manifestations of violent expression, watch for the use of threats by perpetrators and for the use of labels by victims, and try to understand the motivations behind competing sides of the issues.

Conflict and War

Why do people, especially in groups, turn to aggressive acts of defiance? There have been many theories to explain when and why people turn to violent means.[5] To some, resorting to violence is a way of dealing with their dissatisfaction over a state of affairs. When facing frustration and unmet expectations, it is argued, people are likely to turn to aggression. Conflict is also likely in societies that experience great change, whether political, economic, or cultural. This can be especially true if that change is uneven, as the fits and starts of life often are. Promises of dramatic improvement are often unfulfilled, leaving some, particularly those who believe they made the most sacrifice in the name of the cause, feeling betrayed. People who believe they have limited options to make their voices heard try to challenge each aspect of security and comfort.

Another explanation, known as the RESOURCE MOBILIZATION approach, emphasizes agents' ability to put together effective leadership and political opportunities for expression. In this view, collective action is taken when the time is right and when the necessary connections between resources and people can be crafted. Because of the power of human agency, though, no single approach can be used to help explain the rise of violent action.

Significant differences, also known as cleavages, can almost always be found in societies and groups of people. These are based on a variety of factors, including the myriad identities discussed in Chapter 9, as well as perceptions of well-being and fair treatment. Yet these differences are not always viewed as relevant, and they may remain latent for long periods of time. What sparks the change? In other words, what are some of the factors that make cleavages important enough for people to act on, even in violent ways?

One of the issues that alters a situation from low to high priority is the perceived extent of differentiation between and among groups. Many argue that the perception of stark differences between the rich and the poor in a given region or society can often be a source of violence. In the literature on social movements and mobilization, this view is referred to as relative deprivation. It is one thing if everyone is poor, but if some people are poor and others are very rich by comparison, the likelihood for action is much greater. If there is a strongly held perception that the difference between those who have benefited from a particular policy or program is great, a sense of indignity may impel people to act. As we saw in Chapter 7, the general state of the economy is an important factor that influences individuals' and groups' perception of their well-being and their decisions about action or inaction. In times of economic hardship, especially if policies are perceived as unevenly harming some groups of people, we have observed that some groups will turn to crime,

violence, and other disruptive forms of behavior. China, for example, has witnessed increases in crime, secret societies, triads, and gangs, accompanied by a rise in unauthorized gun ownership, although official statistics are not collected. Attacks on young schoolchildren are especially shocking. This has become a problem in the western reaches of the country, which have benefited less from China's economic boom than southern and coastal regions.

Expectations about changes in lifestyle are also important. If people have little reason to hope for anything from society or government, they often remain passive and largely inactive. But if they are given reason to anticipate more, especially through sacrifice, their hopes increase. Expectations sometimes end up going dangerously unfulfilled. Sometimes there is an ASPIRATION GAP between what one expects and what one can actually achieve or acquire. Exposure to international media that portray a variety of lifestyles and norms, increased interaction with other members of society who live in different circumstances, and especially elite cues about this way of life can all help create circumstances that widen this chasm. A related idea is the revolution of rising expectations, which people experience as they begin to believe in the possibility and likelihood of positive change, for either themselves or their families. People naturally develop expectations about their future life. For example, many students attend college with the expectation that they will be able to get a good job to support themselves after graduation. Expectations often have a way of increasing in scope, and it is common for people to believe that with hard work and effort, life will get better. If this cycle is broken, and quality of life decreases rather than improves, it can be followed by frustration and disappointment.

Yet the motivation for action is not always as it appears, and people sometimes use unexpected public forums such as sports events and funerals to vent their frustration. Soccer matches have long been fertile ground for the expression of discontent. In what was dubbed the "Soccer War," 6,000 people were killed and 12,000 were injured during the 1969 World Cup qualifying game between El Salvador and Honduras. Frustrated by the perceived lack of fairness of referees during a match in the Democratic Republic of Congo (DRC) after the Congolese lost a World Cup qualifying match to the Italians, fans took to the streets, attacking Chinese businesses because they misperceived that the referee was Chinese (he was from Japan). Chanting "Chinese go home," many used the event to protest Chinese investment in the copper-mining industry throughout the DRC.[6] Funerals have also been known to spark protests and sometimes riots, especially if mourners seek retribution because they perceive that their loved one was targeted.

Others, led by political scientist Arend Lijphart, have assigned importance to the patterns of division existing within society, distinguishing between coinciding and crosscutting cleavages.[7] These expressions are used to characterize whether or not the significant conflicts and areas of difference in society are diffused among varying groups, or are concentrated among particular sectors of society. For example, if the economically poor in a given country also tend to be the religious minority, employees in the service sector of the economy, and predominantly women, this would be an example of coinciding cleavages. In all aspects of differentiation, a particular group of people seems to be getting the short end of the stick. Coinciding cleavages are more volatile, as all of the conflicts are stacked up into tidy groups and it is clear who does not agree with whom. In contrast, crosscutting lines of division help diffuse the con-

flict: the significant points of difference are spread among multiple groups in society, keeping any one group from perceiving any tremendous amount of injustice. Although real life never conforms to neatly crafted categories, Nigeria is often cited as an example of coinciding cleavages, where differences in religion, ethnicity, and region line up. Yet not all Yoruba are Christian, and of course the regions are not entirely homogeneous. Some Ibo, for example, live in the north. Another example can be found in Mexico, since the south is much poorer, less industrial, and more Amerindian than the rest of Mexico. Again it is an imperfect categorization, since the southern region of Chiapas contains some divisions between Indians who are Protestant and those who are Catholic. The point remains, though: more pronounced divisions can invite greater potential for conflict along these lines. They certainly invite an "us versus them" distinction that can significantly hinder consensus building.

Another factor that influences the potential for violent action relates to the availability of meaningful avenues of expression. Protests and riots are sometimes designed to be turbulent from the outset, but other times they turn violent when participants feel they are being ignored or that it is only through destructive action that their voices will be heard. Yet violence is not always an act of desperation. Ironically, some groups have engaged in violent tactics just as they were about to achieve their goals.[8]

In our discussion of the relevance of differences, we have concentrated mostly on groups smaller than governments and states. We now turn to a discussion of types of war, which is usually one of the first categories of violent conflict that comes to mind. Since the eighteenth century, war has been defined as violence between states or between organized groups, with the explicit goals of gaining territory, seeking revenge, or conquering recalcitrant groups of people. The twentieth century has been called the "century of war" because of the dominance of hostile conflict—three times as many people died in war during this century than during all of the prior nineteen centuries combined.[9] Wars produce scarred soldiers, lonely widows, traumatized victims of torture and rape, and political prisoners. Increasingly, the casualties of war are civilians rather than combatants.

There are many different types of wars, and an increasing variety of conflicts are now categorized as such, or as warlike situations, including "nonconventional" wars such as the war on terrorism. Some of the main types of warfare include interstate, civil, guerrilla, and proxy wars, as well as wars of liberation waged by ethnonationalists, as also discussed in Chapter 4.

Interstate and Separatist Wars

Interstate wars are the most conventional type of modern warfare, even if today they are no longer in the majority. Wars between states mostly involve traditional militaries, and commonly occur over border disputes, contested landholdings, and perceived threats to security. The legacies of colonialism have often been the source of wars in the global south, with conflicts over borders that fail to recognize significant historical, ethnic, and cultural continuities, and the creation of MULTINATIONAL STATES and stateless peoples. China, for example, has fought border wars with India (1962) and the Soviet Union (1969–1978), and has invaded Vietnam (1979).

One extremely volatile border situation can be found between two South Asian giants, Pakistan and India, in the region called Kashmir. It has been a point of conflict since the departure of the British in 1947; in two full-scale wars and other outbreaks

of violence, tens of thousands of people have died on what is viewed as the highest battlefield on the planet. A United Nations cease-fire in 1949 provided both India and Pakistan a portion of the Kashmir region, which is rich in resources and historical connections, but this compromise barely held—and it is rarely viewed as little more than a temporary solution. The territory controlled by New Delhi, India's only Muslim-majority state, is referred to as Jammu Kashmir, while the Pakistani-controlled territory, also predominantly Muslim, is named Azad (Free) Kashmir. In addition, China, since Pakistan ceded a small tract of land to it in the 1950s, has occupied the northernmost part of the territory (Aksai Chin), even building a road linking Tibet and Xinjiang. Part of the reason for the enduring conflict in the region is that inhabitants themselves are not united in their desire for the future, a common dilemma in border wars. Plans to hold elections in 1995—with the hope of resolving the dispute—were abandoned after an attack on a Muslim mosque. Nuclear tests by both Pakistan and India in 1998 escalated tensions even further, and an attack on the Indian parliament in December 2001 again brought these two Asian states to the brink of war. Multiple peace talks have taken place to attempt to resolve the Kashmir conflict, although there has been dispute about who can legitimately represent the multiple sides involved, and violence (both by protesters and by paramilitary forces sent in to quell them) accompanies any effort to resolve the seven-decade-long dispute.

One of the most devastating interstate wars in the global south was the eight-year war between two Middle Eastern giants, Iran and Iraq. Claiming over 500,000 lives, it was one of the longest wars in the recent history of the Middle East.[10] Although the conflict began when Saddam Hussein ordered Iraqi forces to invade Iran during a perceived time of weakness for the young Islamic Republic, its origins can be found in historical, territorial, and ideological differences. Even though Iraq initially welcomed the Islamic Revolution of February 1979, it broke relations with the Iranian regime in October of that year, branding it "non-Islamic" for inciting Shiite communities throughout the Gulf to rebel against their regimes.[11] Hussein and many Iraqis feared that the Islamic Revolution would embolden Iran to challenge contested waterway claims and the Gulf region in general. At one point during the war, Iran demanded Hussein's ouster as a precondition for peace talks, flaming internal opposition within Iraq. Iraq's capture of Kharg Island, Iran's principal Gulf oil terminal, in December 1985, quieted anti-Hussein movements within the country.

The war was one of the most brutal in the region, as Iran launched so-called human-wave attacks in which hundreds of thousands of civilians, including boys as young as nine years old, were sent to their death in assaults on Iraqi artillery positions. (This has been a strategy used by combatants with large populations, such as China in the Korean War and by both sides of the Ethiopia-Eritrea conflict.) Religiously motivated troops joined the war in their attempt to seek martyrdom; some were even given symbolic keys to a paradise that was promised to martyrs. Iraq responded with mustard and nerve gas agents. Iraq was surprised that Tehran didn't crumble during the initial attacks, and by 1982 began to seek peace. Iran refused these initiatives and attacked across the border, significantly weakening the Iranian military and leading to a long standoff with Iraq. After a prolonged war of attrition, a UN-brokered cease-fire was accepted in 1988. The only border-crossing between Iran and Iraq was reopened in 1999 to allow Iranian pilgrims to visit Shia holy sites in Iraq.

Wars are also fought over contested definitions of states—questioning what amount of territory should be included within internationally recognized borders. In Chapter 9 we introduced the notion of the nation-state and the existence of areas of tensions in some, although by no means all, multinational states. The preservation of borders and territorial integrity is an ESSENTIAL FUNCTION of states. Yet the modern state has "deterritorialized" many national groups, sometimes because of the artificial demarcation of boundaries, often at the hands of imperial powers. Groups challenge their incorporation into a particular state for a variety of reasons, often relating to issues such as religious expression, ethnic disputes, or pressures relating to natural resources. Of course, few of these issues stand alone. Some indigenous groups, such as the Dayaks and Igorots in Southeast Asia, seek to maintain a traditional, nonindustrial, nonurban life that conflicts with national economic development plans of many states. Other groups take issue not with the industrial or economic goals of the government, but rather want to have their own homeland or government. This phenomenon is also known as secession. For most, the goal is either to achieve national liberation from political occupation or to create a new political state. For others, the struggle is for humane treatment, more autonomy, and the right to the free expression of their cultural traditions. Sometimes—though not always—this can lead to violent conflict, either in the suppression of the movement (such as China's response to the expression of an independent Tibetan identity), or in the expression of the need for a new identity. The Sikh community in Punjab, India, seeks a homeland called Khalistan, the "Land of the Pure." To date, India has been hostile to calls for this homeland, which geographically stands at the strategic intersection of India, the People's Republic of China (PRC), and Pakistan.

The results of separatist conflict can be disastrous, including displacement, ethnic cleansing, and genocide. The global south is riddled with the tragedies of such conflict, including the murder of Armenians by Turks (1915), of Kurds by the Iraqis (1984–1991), of Hutu and Tutsi in Burundi (1993–1998), of Tutsi and moderate Hutu in Rwanda (1994), of Hmong by Laotians and the Chinese (1975–1979), and of Africans by Arabs in Darfur (since 2003). Muslim rebel groups have been campaigning for self-determination in the south of the Philippines, a predominantly Christian state, for more than three decades. One group of Malaysian Muslims, the Moro National Liberation Front (MNLF), fought for the establishment of some degree of self-rule within the autonomous region in Muslim Mindanao, which was established in 1996 (followers of Islam are called Moros or Moors in Spanish). A more famous group of armed Muslims in the Philippines is the Abu Sayyaf Group (ASG), known for kidnapping foreigners and Christian Filipinos, for which it has received large ransom payments. Formed in 1991, it is a splinter group of the MNLF and is rumored to have ties with al-Qaeda. The primary goal of the ASG is to create an "Iranian-style" Islamic state on Mindanao and the Sulu Islands. Yet some caution against viewing these conflicts as rooted in "ancient tribal" or even distinctly religious rivalries.[12] Such conflict, rather, has been stoked by modern power plays or by rivalries that were introduced by external, often colonial powers. It remains true that more groups of people are actively fighting today for new forms of political independence and expression than in decades or centuries past.

Indonesia has also faced much secessionist conflict following independence from the Dutch. The state leadership vigorously pushed nationalist assimilation policies

Figure 11.1   The Kurds

Another important example of separatist conflict can be found in the diverse Kurdish population, who are considered the largest group of stateless people (approximately 30 million) in the Middle East. At least one-fifth of the Kurds live in Turkey, with significant populations also found in Iran, Iraq, Syria, Lebanon, Armenia, and Azerbaijan. Facing widespread persecution since the late 1980s, many Kurds have immigrated to Germany (where they have faced much neo-Nazi violence) and the Netherlands. Contrary to popular perception, the Kurds are not a single, homogeneous group. Kurdish people speak several different, often mutually indecipherable languages and espouse different forms of Islam (although most are Sunni Muslims). Even in a similar fight for autonomy and the creation of an independent Kurdistan (not to be confused with the Iranian province of Kurdistan), rivalries dominate, and thousands of Kurds have died at the hands of other Kurds.

Turkey is the Kurds' main path to the West. Yet depending on the mood in Ankara, one can be sent to jail for broadcasting in Kurdish, running a political campaign on the basis of ethnicity, or too openly advocating a sense of Kurdish pride, which is viewed as a separatist act by some, a terrorist act by others. Since 1984, war between the Turkish government and some Kurds has claimed at least 40,000 lives and driven several million Kurds from their homes. Common interpretations of Turkish law hold the promotion of "hatred between ethnic groups" to include any mention of Kurdish identity. Approximately 1.4 million Kurds live in Iran's remote northwestern province of Kurdistan; about twice that many live elsewhere in Iran. As Sunni Muslims, many Iranian Kurds face oppression from the Shiite regime in Tehran, and Iran's Kurdish Nationalist Movement has been driven into Iraq. Even though Kurds in Iran enjoy relative autonomy, protests since Mahmoud Ahmadinejad's presidency have turned more urgent, especially after five Iranian Kurds were hanged in Tehran, accused of belonging to a political party viewed by the Iranian government as a terrorist organization.[a]

The Kurdish problem has been particularly acute in Iraq. Following the 1991 Gulf War, most Iraqi Kurds (approximately 2.5 million) moved into a semiautonomous northern district, protected by a no-fly zone enforced by the United States and Great Britain. Violence against them, though, began long before the Gulf War. US intelligence estimates that from 1987 to 1988, Saddam Hussein's government used chemical agents to gas to death 50,000–100,000 Kurds.[b] The development of an autonomous Kurdistan in Iraq has helped spur Kurdish pride in other areas of the Middle East. As a community, Kurds have a huge stake to play in the debates over Iraq's future—they are viewed by some as the "kingmakers" of the troubled state.[c]

Notes: a. Kawe Qoraishy, "Iran's Kurdish Question," *Foreign Policy,* May 17, 2010.

b. Barbara Crossette, "Iraq Is Forcing Kurds from Their Homes, the UN Reports," *New York Times,* December 11, 2000.

c. Ranj Alaaldin, "Kurds Are Iraq's Kingmakers," *The Guardian* (London), October 18, 2010.

that emboldened resistance. Aceh, a northwestern province on the island of Sumatra with a population of 4 million, has been home to the longest-running and most violent separatist conflict in Indonesia. The Acehnese are considered to be more orthodox Islamic than residents in other regions of Indonesia—after receiving some degree of autonomy, Aceh's leaders opened the first provincial *sharia* court in 2003, although there already had been local religious courts to handle family matters.[13] The region is also a major oil and gas producer, and there is a sense of bitterness felt by many Acehnese that Jakarta skims off much of the revenue of the region.[14] The area has been rife with conflict, with murder of innocents by both the Free Aceh (Aceh Merdeka) guerrillas and the Indonesian security forces alike, and the proliferation of gangs operating under the guise of the Free Aceh movement. Following the 2004

tsunami in the Indian Ocean (Aceh was the land closest to the epicenter of the underwater earthquake), new life was breathed into the peace negotiations that had been ongoing since 2000 and a formal peace agreement between Free Aceh and the Indonesian government was signed in 2005. This accord led to legislation granting considerable autonomy to Aceh province, and elections in 2006, direct elections for provincial and district leaders, were held in Aceh as the Free Aceh movement attempted to morph from an armed insurgency into a political movement.

Civil Wars

Although interstate conflicts are obviously important, an increasing number of battles in the world today are internal. Even some of the major cross-border wars, including those between India and Pakistan, and Eritrea and Ethiopia, trace much of their origins to civil conflict. The global south has been beleaguered by civil wars, including conflicts in Algeria, Angola, Cambodia, Chad, China, Côte d'Ivoire, Laos, Nicaragua, Nigeria, the Philippines, Rwanda, Somalia, Sudan, Syria, Uganda, Yemen, and Zimbabwe—to name just a few. Civil wars, which occur within a single country, are known to be among the most brutal and damaging types of conflict, inflicting particularly heavy tolls on civilian populations. Families are often separated in civil wars, either by the outcome of the war or along lines of allegiance. Because of the brutality involved, ill will and the scars of war often continue after the official conflict has ended. Sometimes the estrangement can last for decades or longer.

Civil wars are fought for a variety of reasons. Some researchers are challenging the assumption that the existence of multiple ethnic groups makes a country more prone to civil war. In their study of 127 civil wars from 1945 to 1999, James D. Fearon and David D. Laitin found that irrespective of the ethnic mix, the probability of civil war declines as countries get richer.[15] If these findings hold true, they turn the table on past explanations of conflict and suggest that efforts to promote good government, economic development, and capacity building, including policing, could be successful strategies in war-torn countries. These findings also remove the aura of inevitability that tends to cloud some views of conflict.

Often, battles rage over which leader or group should rule a country. Such was the nature of the Chinese civil war from 1945 to 1949, which ended with Nationalist Party (Kuomintang, or KMT) forces fleeing to the island of Taiwan and the Chinese Communist Party (CCP) proclaiming the People's Republic of China. Other civil wars are fought between rival leaders or groups. Colombia is a country that was torn apart by civil wars throughout much of the nineteenth century, waged between rival Liberal and Conservative Party leaders, guerrillas, drug traffickers, and other entrenched interests. The war in Colombia was launched in the mid-twentieth century by a conflict now referred to as La Violencia. This war initially started out as a street riot in Bogotá, following the assassination of a Liberal Party leader and candidate for president. It worsened as Colombia's problems have mounted; there has been continued elite conflict over the future direction of the country, the deepening and professionalization of the drug trade and the concomitant development of a police force that rivals the military in many ways, and the development of paramilitary groups throughout the country. A war that began between two rival political parties has devolved into an ideological struggle including more than one group of Marxist-Leninist guerrillas, the military, narcotraffickers, and

militias, with significant regional and international involvement. Five decades on, Colombia endured the longest-running insurgency in Latin America, resulting in the world's largest population of internally displaced people (6.9 million, closely followed by Syria with 6.6 million—and counting). Exhausted, the government and the Revolutionary Armed Forces of Colombia (FARC) finally struck a peace deal in 2016. Yet to the surprise of many observers, a narrow majority of citizens voted down the peace agreement in a plebiscite, objecting to the leniency with which the accord treated the rebels. Colombia's president, Juan Manuel Santos (who was awarded the 2016 Nobel Peace Prize for his efforts), refused to give up on the deal. He renegotiated it to win additional concessions from the FARC and sent it to the Colombian congress, which approved the deal. As of early 2017 it is just a matter of whether this still-polarized country could see it through.[16]

From 1967 to 1970 a civil war was fought in Nigeria in which more than 1 million people died. The declaration of war was the culmination of a series of events, most immediately a pogrom directed against Ibos in the north. Led by Odumegwu Ojukwu, the Ibo sought to create "Biafra," an independent and sovereign state carved out of their traditional home in Nigeria's southeast. However, for a variety of reasons, including concern over the loss of the substantial oil revenues coming from the region, the north and west combined forces to resist secession by all conceivable means. Biafra became Africa's most internationalized war in the 1960s as the countries of the world lined up on one side or the other. When the much larger and better-equipped federal army found that it could not prevail against the Ibo forest fighters, it resorted to a policy aimed at starving the Ibo into submission. The blockade had devastating consequences, particularly on women and children. Although they eventually lost the war, the Ibo won international sympathy, as the Biafra conflict was considered by many to be a genocide led by the largely Islamic north against the Christian southeast.[17]

Guerrilla Warfare

The term *guerrilla,* deriving from the Spanish word for "little war," refers to troops operating independently of state militaries, and often in opposition to them, following a relatively loose set of methods designed to deceive enemy forces and overcome deficiencies in equipment, force size, and location. In their attempt to damage the legitimacy of a government, guerrilla forces target civilian populations for recruitment. Women soldiers have participated in this form of combat more than other types of warfare.[18] Additionally, there is often an extensive effort, through propaganda, terror, and policies, to win the support and fighting power of peasant populations. Guerrilla groups are known for setting up successful pilot projects, including schools and clinics, to provide services to groups often ignored by the state and to win their support.

In guerrilla warfare, conventional rules of engagement, especially concerning noncombatants, are largely ignored. Policies, both psychological and concrete, are designed to exhaust and demoralize the enemy while recruiting civilians through either fear or persuasion. Battles tend to center around long, protracted campaigns, often from a rural base. Guerrilla tactics are mobile, necessitated by their smaller troop sizes, and often rely on the element of surprise. Revolutionaries who perceive the unorthodox methods of fighting to be their only shot at victory often use guerrilla warfare. Examples include the Chinese civil war and revolution, Fidel Castro's

Figure 11.2 Taiwan: "Renegade Province" or Independent State?

The controversy surrounding the status of Taiwan, just off the southeastern coast of China, demonstrates that in some ways the Chinese civil war of the 1940s still rages. After the Chinese Communists defeated the Chinese Nationalists in the fall of 1949, Chiang Kaishek and his supporters completed their transfer to Taiwan, much to the chagrin of the indigenous population. (An uprising in 1947, prior to the complete arrival by the Nationalists, is believed to have claimed over 20,000 lives.) From their base in Taipei, the Nationalists pledged to "retake" mainland China, up until the death of Generalissimo Chiang in 1975. Major combat was averted largely by the positioning of the US Seventh Fleet in the Taiwan Straits, which separate the two lands. Owing to anticommunist sentiment in the 1950s and 1960s, most of the world, with the exception of France and later Great Britain, refused to recognize the newly minted Communist Party regime as the legitimate government of China—they recognized the Nationalist regime on Taiwan instead. This continued until the early 1970s, when Taiwan left the United Nations and most countries of the world completed normalization of relations with the People's Republic of China.

Both groups involved in the dispute purported to support "one China," but both the Nationalists and the Chinese Communist Party viewed themselves as the legitimate government of all Chinese people. (Taiwan maintains formal diplomatic ties with just over twenty small states and lacks formal representation in the United Nations.) Recent Taiwanese leaders, including the first directly elected president, Lee Teng-hui, and the two presidents from the proindependence Democratic Progressive Party, Chen Shuibian and Tsai Ing-wen, have challenged the traditional interpretation of "one China," in careful but very intentional ways, much to the consternation of Beijing. Even during the strongest periods of cross-Strait disagreement, however, trade links between China and Taiwan flourish: China is Taipei's top export market. From the perspective of Beijing, Taiwan's eventual reunification with the motherland remains a top priority, as then president-elect Donald Trump found out after he accepted a "congratulatory phone call" from Taiwan's Tsai—the first direct communication between the executives of the United States and Taiwan since 1979.

Sources: David A. Graham, "So, Why Can't You Call Taiwan?," *The Atlantic,* December 2, 2016; Evan Osnos, "The Real Risk Behind Trump's Taiwan Call," *The New Yorker,* December 3, 2016.

1959 revolution in Cuba, and Ho Chi Minh's battles against the Japanese, French, and later US troops in Vietnam.

The modern Chinese state was founded largely upon the principles of guerrilla violence. Mao Zedong, the leader of China's 1949 revolution and one of the modern world's leading revolutionaries, was a man of contradictions. He was a poet and librarian, which is how he first encountered Marxist and Leninist theories about revolution. Mao came of age in a China that was on the brink of collapse, worn down by the imperial wars of the late 1800s, the infighting of the warlord period following the collapse of the Qing Dynasty, as well as the economic misery and political uncertainties that follow the end of an empire. Although Mao was a relatively insignificant participant in the founding of the Chinese Communist Party in Shanghai in 1921, he grew to lead it throughout the revolutionary war with KMT forces, and was the man who proclaimed the beginning of the PRC in Tiananmen Square on October 1, 1949. Throughout the revolutionary war and in wars that followed the establishment of the PRC, Mao advocated a type of warfare known as "people's war," which combined guerrilla tactics with Mao's emphasis on China's "human factors,"

highlighting the importance of the masses and the need to motivate and organize them. Mao often stated that "if our hearts are pure, we will fight with the strength of 10,000 men." The so-called people's war of 1927 to 1949 combined elements of social revolution with a war for national sovereignty. From its base in China's northern rural areas, the CCP successfully employed guerrilla tactics to conquer cities, win the support of the population, and reign victorious.

Proxy Wars

Another type of conflict, sometimes referred to as "warfare by substitutes," involves surrogate fighters who are recruited to fight battles that other, often more powerful groups do not want to get involved in directly. Such proxy wars, when outside actors advance their agenda by using local fighters, were especially common during the Cold War, when the United States and the Soviet Union acted as patrons for wars that were in their interest. The United States propped up anticommunist governments, including Indonesia, South Korea, South Vietnam, and Chile, while the Soviet Union did what it could to support Marxist-Leninist regimes throughout the world, including China (initially), North Korea, and North Vietnam. Recognizing that even the most powerful states or richest groups cannot afford to be in constant war with their enemies, these countries choose instead to support dissenters, separatists, and other potential clients of a rival to avoid mutual assured destruction. During the Cold War, proxy conflicts were used to avoid direct opposition between the superpowers.

The goal of this type of conflict is to wear down the enemy, weakening it by encouraging the waste of resources, without expending a tremendous amount of one's own resources or energy. Surrogate conflict can also include the assassination of political leaders or individuals. It often includes direct sabotage. In the early 1980s, for example, the United States "unofficially" provided support, buttressed by a special operations manual of the Central Intelligence Agency (CIA), to Nicaraguan Contra rebels who were fighting the leftist Sandinista government. Similar efforts were taken by the Soviet Union to encourage North Korea to attack South Korea in 1950.

Some turn to this substitute conflict as a way of improving their own image and to place some distance between themselves and the seemingly unsavory battles at hand. It has been argued that a group known as Islamic Jihad, an offshoot of the military wing of Hamas, was used as a proxy to carry out executions on behalf of the government of Iran, which attempted to improve its international image following its isolation during the 1980s.[19] Similar sentiment was expressed after the thirty-four-day war between Israel and Hezbollah, the Iranian-inspired group within Lebanon, in 2006—just as international pressure was focused on the alleged nuclear weapons program within Tehran.[20] In proxy conflict, nationals are involved usually in training and support, employing private armies in a country to put down revolutionary movements, assassinate critics of the regime, and maintain control. Fidel Castro's Cuba was relatively unusual in sending large numbers of soldiers abroad; since many of the fighters were nonwhite, they were welcomed in many places that the Soviets and the East Europeans were not, including Ethiopia, Mozambique, and Angola.

Proxy wars permit the sponsoring agent to focus on "big picture" events and strategy, while others do the "grunt work" on the ground. For example, the early stages of the US-led war in Afghanistan in 2001 were viewed by many as a form of proxy war, using Northern Alliance and other anti-Taliban forces to do the dirty work

while the United States led the air campaign and provided intelligence. The long elusiveness of Osama bin Laden (he was captured and killed in May 2011) was attributed to the use of Afghan, Pakistani, and other ground forces who likely succumbed to bribes from bin Laden's associates to permit him to escape the country. *The Economist* once referred to Afghanistan as "a geographical expression in search of a state,"[21] and the situation has only slightly improved in the years since that statement. In a majority of proxy wars, there are often very real regional conflicts or domestic divisions at the heart, which are greatly amplified by the patronage of outsiders. As is discussed in Figure 11.3, the involvement of so many external forces—many with conflicting agendas—has greatly amplified the nature of the ongoing conflict in Syria.

Faces Behind the Disruption

So who is responsible for acts of violence? As you might imagine, there is great diversity in the types of individuals and groups who believe their use of destructive means is justified. In this section, we discuss some of the major types of groups involved in belligerent activities. The faces behind the disruption can be as diverse as the forms of violence that are employed. For example, even though men make up the majority of individuals who engage in terrorism, women have frequently joined terrorist groups. Some argue that participation in violent groups provides women a rare outlet for gender equality, an argument that is used to explain women's participation in terrorist organizations and revolutions.[22] Women also avoid detection, sometimes making the most of their status as privileged noncombatants. Other explanations include shaming men into action, increasing fear (by making both men and women suspects), and the need for greater numbers of participants, as the numbers of men in detention or under surveillance increases.[23] One question surrounding what appears to be an uptick in the inclusion of women in violent extremism, including suicide terrorism, is whether or not they serve willingly.

In Peru's Shining Path (Sendero Luminoso), large numbers of women participated as equals in the group's apparatus, overcoming the subordinate role and status historically ascribed to them in Peruvian society. And some made it to top positions in the regional command and the National Central Committee, including Abimael Guzmán Reynoso's first wife, Augusta la Torre, who served as the second in command in the organization (Guzmán's second wife, Elena Iparraguirre—also known as Comrade Miriam—also exercised significant influence over the movement, for which she received a life sentence after her third trial in 2006). Women have served as suicide bombers for Boko Haram in Nigeria, and as combatants for the Kurdistan Workers Party (PKK) in Turkey, the Palestinian uprising (INTIFADA), and the Liberation Tigers of Tamil Eelam, along with an increasing number of other movements. It is believed that as many as one-fourth of Russian revolutionaries in 1917 were women.[24] It was a woman who was sent to assassinate India's prime minister, Rajiv Gandhi, in 1991. In 1970 one female Palestinian refugee, Leila Khaled, almost single-handedly hijacked a commercial plane, evacuating all passengers before she blew it up. Even in the famously patriarchal al-Qaeda, the glass ceiling was shattered when a woman dressed as a man sauntered into a meeting of military recruits and launched an explosion that killed five men and wounded at least thirty—thwarting the

Figure 11.3 Syria

For years to come, the word *Syria*—or even just *Aleppo*—will evoke horror in the same ways as Rwanda and Bosnia. The difference is that this time we can't say we didn't know, thanks to a stream of messages from inside the nightmare.

The Syrian civil war started in 2011, as part of the Arab Spring that was sweeping North Africa and the Middle East. But a number of grievances also contributed to the conflict, including the government's repressive response to what started as a peaceful protest.

Within months a rebel army had formed with the intention of overthrowing the government led by Bashar al-Assad, whose father took power in a coup in 1970. The Assad family favored cronies mostly drawn from their own minority Alawite community (a sect affiliated with Shia Islam). Meanwhile, the majority Sunni population, including the Kurds, had been largely excluded from political and economic power. The Assad regime, intensely paranoid about what might happen if it ever lost power, refused any significant reforms. Instead it consistently relied on repression to put down all challenges to the status quo.

It was no different in 2011—nor has it been since. The rebels, with different identities and ideologies, fractured into hundreds of competing groups, some moderate and others, including the radical jihadist Islamic State (IS).

What started out as a civil war quickly descended into a multidimensional proxy war, with external actors picking sides and fighting out their own conflicts on this battlefield. The Obama administration claimed to support moderate rebels, but was cautious about providing them with the lethal assistance they needed to fight Assad, over fears that the weaponry might fall into the hands of jihadists. Meanwhile, Russia, Iran, and the Shiite militia Hezbollah came to the assistance of Assad with air strikes and ground troops.

Fearing that this was part of a larger Shiite conspiracy, the Saudis and Gulf states came in to aid the Sunni rebels. So, Syria became a replay of the Cold War, with the United States and the Russians backing opposite sides. Syria is also a battle for Islam, with Sunnis (Saudis) and Shiites (Iranians) facing each other down. Add Turkey to the mix; given its dislike of Assad, it supported the rebels (as long as they weren't Kurdish, given Turkey's own "Kurdish problem"). And top it off with IS, whom everyone claims to be fighting.

The result is what UN officials have called "a meltdown of humanity." Atrocities have been committed on all sides.[a] Still, the Assad regime is by far the worst offender, outpacing even the Islamic State for war crimes, including torture on an industrial scale, and the use of chemical weapons. As of early 2017 the death toll was estimated at well over 400,000. Nearly half of Syria's population had been forced from their homes, 5 million of them refugees. Those who remain live in a country that remains divided, but now is devastated.

Note: a. Anne Barnard and Somini Sengupta, "Deal Is Reached for Rebels to Leave Last Pockets of Aleppo," *New York Times*, December 13, 2016.

profile used by antiterrorist forces around the world to identify perpetrators.[25] The participation and leadership of women cannot be reduced to ideology or level of restrictions imposed on them. Observers note that some of the women emerging as jihadists throughout Europe are different than their predecessors who worked under the careful supervision of men—they are even a more "feminist type of jihadist," often converts who were turned back from attempts to enter Syria.[26]

Young people have also long been attracted to violence—often drawn to the idea of belonging to a meaningful group that provides direction and identity. We discuss one of the most famous sets of twins—the Htoo brothers from Myanmar—later. But there are others. Shining Path, born in a university setting, appealed especially to students. The most violent stages of China's Cultural Revolution employed the use

of middle and high school–aged "Red Guards" to terrorize those labeled enemies of the CCP and to foment revolutionary fervor throughout the country. In Zimbabwe, both the Zimbabwe African National Union (ZANU) and the Zimbabwe African People's Union (ZAPU) mobilized entire classrooms of children, who left with their teachers to train as guerrillas. The increasing number of children used in suicide attacks—especially girls—has become one of the "defining features" of conflict in the Lake Chad region of Africa, where it is believed that nearly one out of every five suicide bombers is a child.[27] Participants in the Palestinian intifada are believed to be particularly young. Research puts the median age of terrorists in the global south at approximately twenty-two years old, but in some cases, children as young as eight have been recruited to carry out violence. Youth have been active in arson attacks, hand-to-hand combat, sabotage, and suicide missions. Some postulate that their involvement can be explained by the lack of outside commitments that would limit their availability for activities, while others point to youths' propensity for risk-taking, their passion for causes, and their mobility.

Militaries and Militias

In any discussion of the major groups that sponsor violence as a means to achieve goals, we would be remiss if we excluded governments themselves. As sociologist

Figure 11.4   Legality as a Tool of State Terror

Governments possess many means to craft seemingly "legal" ways to impose their will and limit opposition voices. Perceived troublemakers, for example, are often forced into exile: either to remote parts of the country, or outside the state altogether. In China some dissidents have been released from prison, but they are provided a one-way ticket out of the country and often depart without being able to send notice to their families. Other countries place activists under house arrest in remote areas as a way of keeping them out of trouble. In Myanmar, for example, Aung San Suu Kyi spent nearly twenty years in some form of detention, including prolonged periods of house arrest, before she was released in November 2010.

Police brutality is another overt form of state violence. In Egypt, the police are widely detested as the country's worst human rights abusers. But Egyptian police are not unique; state actors in many countries brutalize populations with torture, disappearances, and extrajudicial executions as part of routine public policy. Although official statistics are lacking, it is believed that China annually executes more people than all of the rest of the world combined. As a supposed deterrent, many executions in China occur in public arenas, following sentencing rallies that are broadcast on television. Excluding China, nearly 90 percent of all executions in 2015 occurred in just three countries: Iran, Pakistan, and Saudi Arabia. Iran, which has increased its use of capital punishment even under the relatively moderate Rouhani government, is second only to China. Iran executed 977 people in 2015, most by hanging, including someone arrested as an adolescent for questionable charges related to homosexuality. Globally, the number of executions hit a twenty-five-year high in 2015. But half the world (102 countries) has abolished the death penalty. This includes Turkey, which did so as part of its accession bid to join the European Union. But after a failed coup in 2016, the government was considering reinstatement of the death penalty.

Sources: Amnesty International, "Death Penalty 2015: Facts and Figures," April 6, 2016, www.amnesty .org; "Turkey Coup: Erdogan Backs Return of Death Penalty at Vast Istanbul Rally," BBC News, August 8, 2016, www.bbc.com.

Max Weber highlighted in his classic definition of the "state," one of the greatest powers of governments is their monopoly over the right to use force. This does not mean, of course, that states are the only groups that hold coercive power, nor does it imply that all use of government force is proper or legitimate, but it does accurately imply that governments tend to have the most organized, well-financed, and effective means of making their preferences known. By engaging forces in wartime combat, adopting domestic policies that include executions and punishment, and supporting abductions, assassinations, and forced relocations, it is clear that governments all around the world use violent means to achieve their ends.

As an institution of government, the state military wields tremendous power. Militaries consist of disciplined, organized, and well-funded groups of people with great influence: official armed units are used to implement key directives of governments, often using force. Militaries are found in almost every country of the world. The major exception is Costa Rica, which dissolved its military in the 1950s, even though it still has a small paramilitary force.

Young men under the age of twenty-six nearly exclusively carry out military acts. In World War I, women first donned military uniforms and received military ranking. Yet today in Israel, Eritrea, North Korea, and Norway, both sexes are formally required to enroll in military service, and increasingly women participate in noncompulsory military training and combat as well. Just as it is wrong to assume that all women are mothers, it is also a mistake to think that all mothers are peaceniks and opposed to the use of violence to effect change. African women trained with men and fought alongside them in Zimbabwe's war for liberation. In the mid-1970s approximately one-third of the soldiers fighting for ZANU were female, and some of these women held positions of authority over men. In addition, civilian women provided assistance to the guerrillas as their way of fighting. They cooked for the rebels, and because for a while at least women could better avoid the attention of Rhodesian soldiers, they sometimes disguised their bundles as babies and smuggled supplies to guerrilla bases. Just as women participated in the war effort in various ways, so too did they have different expectations about what the coming change should mean for them. ZANU recognized how important women's support was to the struggle and challenged local norms during the war by making an explicit commitment to women's liberation. However, for various reasons since taking power, the liberation government's position has been described as ambivalent at best. ZANU did push through some significant reforms of benefit to women, but there has been no transformation of gender relations.[28]

Increasingly in modern combat, civilians, especially children, are often the group most victimized by warfare. Although valid statistics are difficult to verify, it is clear that modern wars create far more civilian deaths than military deaths, with a ratio perhaps as high as 75–90 percent.[29] The statistics are even more telling when they are viewed not as raw numbers, but as a trend. Prior to the early 1990s, the ratio of military to civilian casualties was estimated to be eight to one. In the wars of the 1990s, the trend was reversed: for every military fighter who died in combat, eight civilians perished.[30] Some of this can be attributed to the "civilianization" of war, as noncombatants are increasingly targeted for attack or are innocently caught in the crossfire, or suffer because of the lawlessness and impunity that prevail. In Syria, the majority of casualties are male combatants, but the Bashar al-Assad government as

well as rebel groups such as the Islamic State have taken part in the deliberate killing of noncombatants. Nearly 25 percent of all civilians killed by explosive weapons (bombs and shells) were women and children. Indiscriminate weapons have been used in Syria in a targeted manner. In particular, it is the suicide bombing of children at schools and the government's dropping of barrel bombs from helicopters over hospitals that have taken a toll on children.[31]

Another development of modern warfare is the inclusion of large numbers of children as active protagonists of warfare. The conscription and detention of children against their will is viewed by some as one of the "least reported" and "least punished" crimes globally.[32] Although difficult to track, it has been estimated that tens of thousands of children (under the age of eighteen) fight today as soldiers with government and armed opposition groups in over fifty countries. Most child soldiers are between ages fifteen and eighteen; the youngest age recorded by the Coalition to Stop the Use of Child Soldiers is seven. One expert on the topic claims that child soldiers serve in almost 75 percent of the world's conflicts.[33] The presence of children in combat has become a critical problem in Africa and Asia, although youth are used as soldiers, porters, cooks, messengers, checkpoint guards, sexual slaves, and spies throughout the world. Myanmar has the highest numbers of child soldiers in the world, within both governmental armed forces and nongovernmental groups, and the fighters are often under fifteen years of age. Because of their agility and fearlessness, children have also been employed to do much of the more dangerous work in battle zones, including mine-clearing operations. Not surprisingly, poverty and perpetual cycles of conflict are

---

Figure 11.5   The Islamic State

Born of war, feeding off conflict, and aiming to usher in apocalyptic "end times," the Islamic State (IS) has become one of the most violent and visible terrorist groups to develop in recent years. As a jihadist extremist Sunni group known for devastating brutality (including mass killings and public beheadings, the images of which are then splashed over the Internet), IS seized significant amounts of territory in Syria and Iraq in 2014. Its roots may be traced to the war in Iraq, when an al-Qaeda branch in Iraq formed an umbrella organization known as the Islamic State of Iraq and Syria (ISIS). In 2013, its activists joined the rebellion against Bashar al-Assad in Syria and a year later, after successfully overrunning Mosul in northern Iraq, its leaders declared a caliphate (a state governed by *sharia* law that is led by a caliph, or "God's deputy on earth"),[a] and announced the formation of the Islamic State.

With access to substantial wealth, IS has terrorized its perceived enemies—Muslim and non-Muslim alike. This has caused IS to lose much support, even from other committed terrorists, including al-Qaeda leader Ayman al-Zawahiri, who disavowed IS in February of 2014 over its actions in Iraq. Al-Zawahiri warned that such carnage will eventually lose "Muslim hearts and minds."[b] With a highly decentralized set of followers, including individuals who are "inspired" by IS radicalism even without any formal training or ties, coordinated responses against IS have proven difficult. As one observer noted, "Our ignorance of the Islamic State is in some ways understandable: It is a hermit kingdom; few have gone there and returned."[c]

Notes: a. "What Is Islamic State?," BBC News, December 2, 2015.

b. Ibid.

c. Graeme Wood, "What ISIS Really Wants," *The Atlantic,* March 2015, www.theatlantic.com.

viewed as some of the main conditions influencing the increase of child soldiers, although the influence of teachers, family, friends, local politics, and culture all play a role as well.[34] The proliferation of "small arms" (discussed in Chapter 17) has also increased the use of child soldiers, as the ease of modern combat has made strength, size, and experience less important. The Russian AK-47, which flooded markets after World War II, only weighs about 3 kilograms in its modern versions; because it is cheap and mobile, it is something an eight-year-old can maneuver with relative confidence, so nearly anybody can become a "soldier."[35]

Even if they are not formal "soldiers" per se, children have been combatants in some of the world's bloodiest conflicts. In the Palestinian uprising, for example, children have been active agitators against Israeli forces, throwing stones and sabotaging units, and they have paid dearly, often with their lives. Some children are forced to take up arms, but others are given little choice in the face of poverty, discrimination, and the pressure to conscript. Human Rights Watch estimates that in some conflicts, namely, in El Salvador, Ethiopia, and Uganda, as many as 30 percent of child participants have been female. Pregnancy, often the outcome of gang rape by comrade or enemy soldiers, isn't enough to keep young girls out of combat, either. Young girls have been used as suicide bombers in Sri Lanka and Lebanon, and many girls are allocated to soldiers as rewards, as "wives." In Uganda, children have been forced to brutally beat other children to death, their victims lying face down on the ground, with arms and legs restrained.[36]

Young soldiers receive little or no training. In warfare, children are also subjected to severe punishment, sometimes even harsher than what adults would receive. There have also been reports of widespread juvenile disappearance, extrajudicial execution, and torture. Perhaps because they have a less developed sense of right and wrong, children (in some places known as the "lost generation") are said to commit the worst atrocities. Drugs are also used to make children effective killers. Children want approval, and sometimes they find acceptance in the most violent groups. Often, child soldiers are orphans, who together with street children are particularly vulnerable to recruitment and desperately eager to please adults (even if the adult is responsible for their being orphaned). Most have been traumatized themselves, as witnesses to murder of their families, and are sometimes even forced to participate in ritualized killings. The Revolutionary United Front (RUF) in Sierra Leone, for example, trained its child soldiers by ordering them to kill other children or even their own parents or someone they knew so that they wouldn't fear death or try to escape.

In the Sierra Leone civil war, all sides used children as frontline troops, including Liberia. It is estimated that 30 percent of the soldiers in Charles Taylor's National Patriotic Front, which invaded Sierra Leone on Christmas Eve in 1989, were boys under seventeen years old. The RUF has forced children into service, kidnapping them and administering drugs to them—including highly addictive cocaine—against their will. Children have also been targeted as willing suicide agents. During the Iran-Iraq War, thousands of patriotic Iranian children were sent to the front lines, holding the symbolic key to a paradise as martyrs. In Sri Lanka, young Tamil girls (often orphans) were recruited by opposition forces and trained as suicide bombers, known as the "Birds of Freedom."[37]

Child soldiers do not always fight for their own country or ethnic group. In the conflict in the Democratic Republic of Congo, for example, children from Namibia

and Rwanda were brought into the fray. Children have also been recruited into terrorist and separatist groups. Peru's Shining Path is believed to have forcibly recruited several thousand indigenous children. Child soldiers were common in Colombia's nearly fifty-year civil war.

One of the most famous cases of children rebels surrounds the teenage Burmese twins Johnny and Luther Htoo, leaders of the Burmese rebel group "God's Army." Many of the children who fight with this group are orphans of the war in Myanmar. The twins claim mystic powers, including being invulnerable to the personal devastation of landmines and bullets, which are said to "bounce off" the young commanders. They are also said to have invisible soldiers who assist them, and are rumored to have black tongues. Johnny Htoo is said once to have jumped into a stream, after which he was transformed into an old man. He returned to his teenage self after convincing his fellow fighters of his prowess. One of the unique aspects about the group is that these young boys, who became soldiers before they reached the age of ten, have led grown adults into battle. The belief among their followers is that they are not as young as they seem. Rather, in fitting with Karen animist teachings that messiahs will be sent to lead the people through difficult times, they are reincarnations of past revolutionary and legendary heroes. Working in concert with the Vigorous Burmese Student Warriors, God's Army rebels seized hostages throughout Thailand, including once capturing more than 800 patients and staff at a hospital. In the winter of 2001 the twins turned themselves in to police in Thailand, at the age of fourteen.[38]

In Figure 11.6 we present comparative data on militaries in the global south. While we believe this information is a useful starting point, we urge you to consider that countries are notorious for underreporting both the size of their formal military force strength, as well as the amount of budgetary resources committed to the military. One way that governments get around full reporting of their troop strength is by creating paramilitaries and other semimilitary units that are not counted in the official troop total. For example, the PRC, which has undertaken dramatic troop reductions since the mid-1990s, does not include the 1.3 million members of the People's Armed Police (PAP) in its official troop count. After the foundation of the Islamic Republic of Iran in 1979, clerical leaders called for both a standard military to protect the country's borders and maintain internal order, as well as a separate Revolutionary Guard, known as the Pasdaran, to protect the Islamic character of the system. The Revolutionary Guard has fewer troops compared to the regular military, yet is considered the dominant military force and the backbone of major operations. It controls the Basij Resistance force, a volunteer military of approximately 90,000 men and women who, as loyalists to the 1979 revolution, are used to brutally dispel dissent. This ambiguity is one reason why the CIA, in its *World Factbook,* reports the portion of the population available for military service and the portion fit for military service, rather than actual troop numbers. As you can see, despite the fact that China has the world's largest standing army by far, its official military accounts for only a fraction of the labor force, whereas Indonesia and Mexico, both with modest-sized militaries in terms of force strength, show a larger percentage of the overall labor force.

Despite relatively generous expenditures for militaries—when compared to spending for healthcare and education, for example—soldiers in the global south tend to be compensated very poorly. As a result, it is common for groups to turn to extortion at roadblocks, kidnapping, bribery, and other malfeasance to supplement

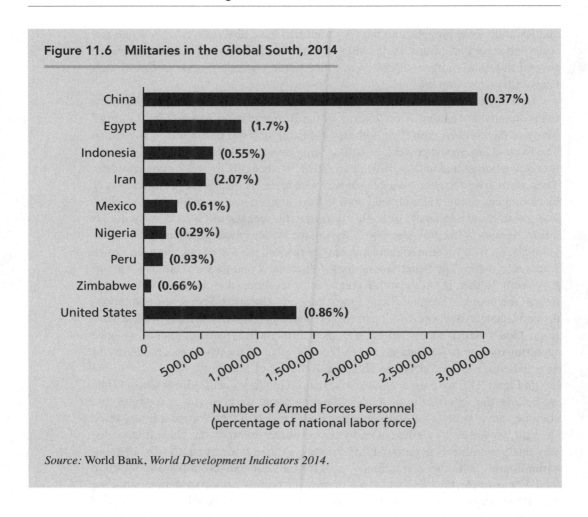

Figure 11.6 Militaries in the Global South, 2014

Source: World Bank, *World Development Indicators 2014.*

their income. Paramilitary police in the restive Indonesian province of Aceh, for example, received 60 cents a day in compensation from the government, which is less than the cost of a pack of cigarettes.[39] This problem has also been identified with the Chinese police force, which is famous for forcibly collecting bribes in the Chinese countryside, a dilemma that other countries face as well.

The declared goal of the modern military is to provide defense and security for a country. Civilian leadership over the military is recognized as a common value in the world today. In this model, the military is simply one of many interest groups lobbying for its own priorities. This norm is known as civilian rule, which has been violated in many countries, and not only in the global south. So-called professional militaries act on the authority of governments and possess restricted powers to challenge civilian political leadership. They develop particularized areas of expertise, such as challenging external enemies, and keep out of areas beyond their purview, such as political infighting. No military is completely professional in this sense, but we can observe varying degrees of professionalism using this metric.

The polar opposite of this civil-military duality—military rule—often begins when elements within the military sense a crisis. The manifestations of this perceived

crisis are varied, but can include societal cleavages, leadership controversies, economic malaise, tensions within the military itself, defeat in war, contagion effects from neighboring countries, external intervention, personality conflicts between the military leadership and political leaders, or simply an easy power grab.[40] In the interest of providing stability, the argument goes, a disciplined, professional military would often be the best candidate to lead an interim transition. Unfortunately, in many situations the perceived "crisis" lasts longer than most civilian leaders originally envisioned and the so-called transition becomes standard operating procedure. Chile, for example, experienced military rule for eighteen years. Military rule is often precipitated by a government overthrow, or a coup d'état, when the governmental leader or part of the leadership is replaced by violence or threat. After a coup, which is usually quick, the military government is often referred to as a junta, or council. Military commanders have then been known to take control of schools, train new soldiers in their own doctrine, and take elaborate measures to silence the masses.

Military coups and military rule have been a common occurrence in the global south. In Iran, the 1921 coup ushered in a "new order," only to be followed by another coup in 1935. Sometimes coups are initially welcomed by the population, such as the Nigerian coup against corruption, fraud, and economic mismanagement in 1983. Many people applauded the military as saviors of the country. Some coups appear to be contagious, following one after the other. Nigeria experienced several military coups in thirty years and has spent much of its independence under military rule. Military coups are not necessarily violent—in fact most are bloodless, although a particularly brutal coup occurred in Chile in 1973, in which at least 2,000 people died. Nearly 300 died in a failed coup in Turkey in 2016 and thousands have been detained, accused of supporting it.

The Ottoman Empire was founded by warriors, and to many this tradition of military dominance rightly continues in the modern Turkish state. Modern Turkey was born of a military coup by the Kemalists in the 1920s, who claimed to be protecting Turkey from Islamic rule (Mustafa Kemal Atatürk was a war hero). Turkey has become famous for military interventionism, often ostensibly in the name of democracy. Ever since, the military has perceived itself as possessing a special role to defend Atatürk's secular republic. Three more coups followed in 1960, 1971, and 1980. In the 1980 coup, a six-man military junta suspended parliament, arrested leaders, and closed the doors on all political parties and independent associations, including unions. The junta also instituted mass arrests and oversaw the drafting of the 1982 constitution, considered to be one of Turkey's most repressive. This power of military regimes to craft democracies that garner favor for themselves, including AMNESTY for their actions after they leave office, is a common occurrence in countries facing activist militaries.[41]

A different type of coup took place in Turkey in February 1997, when the military "encouraged" the resignation of Islamist prime minister Necmettin Erbakan. The prime minister had ruffled many feathers during his tenure, with perceived overtures to Iran, Iraq, and Syria, hosting Islamic shaikhs at his formal residence during the Muslim holy month of Ramadan, and (unsuccessfully) attempting to end the ban on headscarves. After seemingly flagrant Islamic activities in a small town near Ankara marking "Jerusalem night," the military presented Erbakan with a list of measures to limit Islamic expression in Turkey, including the closure of intermediate-level religious

schools, which he eventually signed. One military officer even called the prime minister "a pimp" for undertaking the pilgrimage to Mecca as a guest of Saudi Arabia. When Erbakan urged sanctions against the officer, the military refused.[42]

Even in the absence of outright military rule, there are circumstances when militaries wield a tremendous amount of influence, even in the selection of the prime minister or other executives of government. Such persuasion is often made in threats not to support or protect a leader if he violates the wishes of the military. The term PRAETORIANISM is used to characterize states where civilian authorities face such intimidation. Some more simply call it blackmail. The concept derives from the praetorian guards who protected the Roman emperor. Often they would threaten to withdraw their crucial support if they did not get to choose who would be in power. Similarly, through their threats of vetoes and departure, militaries can shape policy.

Unlike most of its neighbors, Mexico has succeeded in establishing an unwritten deal between civilian and military leaders, as long as the military polices itself for human rights abuses and stays out of politics. However, Mexico had a long tradition of military intervention in politics; much of the nineteenth century was known as the age of caudillos. After the Mexican Revolution, several military figures vied for power. From 1917 through the 1930s, citizen-soldiers ruled, as all of Mexico's presidents during that period had started their careers as officers in the revolutionary army. The military continued to play a very important role in the Institutional Revolutionary Party (PRI) and therefore the government throughout the 1930s. In the early 1940s, President Lázaro Cárdenas began to demilitarize politics by dramatically reducing military expenditures and limiting the military's representation in the party. Since 1943, candidates for president have been automatically disqualified if they have a military background. Over time, the military has largely stayed in the barracks in Mexico, and unlike armed forces elsewhere, the Mexican military has not exploited periods of crisis to expand its influence. Most analysts do not consider the military in Mexico to be an independent political "wild card" in the way that it is in other countries. It is possible that continued instability in Mexico could draw the military into the political arena, but for more than sixty years the state has been largely under the control of civilians.[43]

In many countries of the global south, militaries have a mixed record of achievements and failures. They have been good at providing order and economic growth. Yet they have also racked up a miserable record of human rights protection, especially in circumstances where they rule outright or where they are temporarily installed as an interim government. Some military regimes are characterized as caretaker governments, preoccupied with law and order and less concerned with implementing social changes. Corrective military regimes attempt to create a national identity and promote orderly economic development. Revolutionary military regimes promote the most radical changes of all, highlighting dramatic land reform that is never fully implemented.

Rape has been used as a deliberate military tactic, especially within the strategy of ethnic cleansing, but in other forms of violent warfare as well. It has been common in the wars in Syria, South Sudan, and Colombia, among other countries. Women and girls are frequently victims of gang rape committed by soldiers and militias. The Khomeini regime in Iran set up so-called residential units to suppress female dissidents. The elite Revolutionary Guard used these outposts to continuously

rape women who refused to submit to the regime.[44] Thousands of women in what was for a time known as "the rape capital of the world," the Democratic Republic of Congo—forty-eight every hour in 2006–2007—were raped during the height of that country's long-running war. Some individuals were raped many times and even since the war has died down somewhat, in South Kivu forty women continue to experience sexual violence every day. The United Nations places the blame on government troops, militias, and rebels.[45] In many conflicts around the world, rape has also been used as a form of genocide, as male soldiers and paramilitaries have been ordered to impregnate "enemy" women. Sexual assault has long been part of a purposive strategy, as in Syria, to sever women's ties to the community and to strip them of their dignity and pride. It often leads to the complete ostracism of these women. These trends point to the overall sexualization of war in the modern world, and the development of sexual terrorism.

One example of an entrenched, long-running military government is that of Myanmar, also known as Burma. In the late 1950s the Burmese army gained prestige and importance during the country's struggle for independence. In fact, prior to the beginning of its latest crackdown in the late 1980s, it was the police, not the military, who were the most hated institution in the country. But that changed when the military brutally suppressed popular demonstrations against its rule in 1988. Most estimates claim that 3,000–8,000 people were killed in this assault. Popular disgust with the army increased after it was overwhelmingly defeated by the National League for Democracy in the 1990 elections and refused to step aside. The leader of this political party, Aung San Suu Kyi, spent nearly two decades in detention. Universities, closed for nearly twelve years, reopened in 2000 as a small step toward normalcy.

In many countries, regular military units are declining in numbers, prestige, and the support they receive. Some cannot escape their tarnished reputation; others appear to be bureaucratic beasts lumbering over sick economies. They are being replaced, especially in areas of conflict, by paramilitary units—relatively autonomous armed groups often in charge of security for an individual person, political party, or institution. To avoid the stigma of the appearance of military rule, some governments are turning to civilian militias to handle their security tasks. These can sometimes be virtual death squads, as we have seen in both Rwanda and East Timor. Their funding comes from the government (although often through covert channels) and they usually report directly to military officials. In some cases, including Colombia, paramilitaries comprise off-duty soldiers and police hoping to pocket some extra cash. Paramilitary units are often launched in an attempt by governments to wash their hands of violent acts. In Mexico, anticrime self-defense forces started forming in 2011 in response to the violence unleashed by the cartels and the government's war on drugs. The militias act as vigilantes and are known for arresting people they accuse of working for criminal groups, holding their own court trials, and meting out sentences. In recent years many of them have expanded and become known for increasingly questionable behavior, such as extortion as well as kidnapping and brutalizing police and soldiers and seizing police stations and weapons. President Enrique Peña Nieto has pursued a contradictory policy toward these groups; the government has made efforts to detain those engaged in the worst excesses, but has chosen not to attempt to forcibly dismantle them. The government has attempted to fold them into the police structures, but it hasn't been able to control the militias, or enforce the rules, and thus the militias further

weaken the rule of law in Mexico.[46] Other militias work more closely with the government. In the early 1980s, China created the People's Armed Police, a unit that surged in growth after the crackdown on students in Tiananmen Square in 1989. The PAP, unlike the regular police force in China, is fully armed—it guards government offices, patrols borders, and quells riots and uprisings.

The point is that the power of military units can become extremely dangerous in transitional circumstances, such as after the fall of powerful leaders or a change in power, as rogue groups, still possessing weaponry and the desire for influence, attempt to maintain their power and voice. In Indonesia, a paramilitary group formed from former police cadets who failed the four-year officer course. Some believe that this unit—named Gunung Tidur—was responsible for a fatal series of fires during the May 1998 riots that led to Suharto's downfall.[47] Retired generals, upset at their loss of prestige and patronage, were also blamed for bombing a mosque outside of Jakarta in 1999.[48] Similar episodes have been reported in Tajikistan, Nigeria, and elsewhere.

One case in which the power of militias was highlighted was the chaos following the successful referendum on independence in East Timor in 1999. Violence between rival civilian groups, mostly instigated by the government-backed militias, claimed the lives of thousands and destroyed much of the region. The problem continues in West Timor, where tens of thousands of refugees remained for over a year after the referendum. Militias in West Timor continued to intimidate the refugees to keep them from returning to the independent East Timor (now known as Timor-Leste). As one scholar put it, once the refugees depart, the militias no longer have a reason for existence—they provide job security to a group hungry for employment.[49] In the Molucca Islands, the increased numbers of people fleeing sectarian violence there have exacerbated the refugee crisis, where clashes between Christians and Muslims have claimed thousands of lives.

In addition to traditional government militaries and militia groups, privately employed soldiers play an important role in wars in the global south. Mercenaries are as old as war itself, but in today's world their recruitment, deployment, and action are a multimillion-dollar business. Often, these soldiers-for-hire travel from country to country to earn a financial profit. For example, Serb and Ukrainian soldiers trained fighters in the Democratic Republic of Congo. In fact, foreign mercenaries fueled both sides of the conflict in that country. There and in Angola, over eighty companies were used to funnel soldiers onto the battlefield. The most famous is the now defunct South African–based company Executive Outcomes, which was hired to provide fighters in both Angola and Sierra Leone to guard mines that are the source of "conflict diamonds," precious jewels that are illegally sold on the regular market and used to finance conflict. In South Africa, after a spike in the number of mercenaries being employed from that country, the government passed legislation making it illegal for citizens to fight elsewhere—without prior approval. In fact, immediately after the fall of Baghdad in 2003, when US commanders couldn't spare any troops to provide security for retired army lieutenant-general Jay Garner (who had been named director of reconstruction and humanitarian assistance in Iraq), he hired two men from South Africa who were veterans of that country's apartheid-era Special Air Service. The contract that Garner and his successor, Paul Bremer, signed with them was never completed, as it was belatedly discovered that the men were violating South African law. One of Garner's former bodyguards was later arrested in

Zimbabwe on suspicion of helping to plot a coup in Equatorial Guinea. The man was released but later convicted in South Africa of violating antimercenary legislation.[50] In Colombia, British Petroleum hired a battalion of soldiers to protect its interests, and mercenaries have been hired to protect Firestone's rubber plants as well. Mercenaries have also been active in a separatist conflict that has been fought in Papua New Guinea since the late 1980s. To put down the insurrection, the Papuan government hired soldiers, euphemistically called "military advisers," from the Bahamas-based corporation Sandline.

Governments may possess a monopoly over the right to use force—which states use both to change circumstances and to promote the status quo—but by no means are they the only promoters of violent change. We now turn our attention to some other groups that advocate or promote aggression to achieve their cause.

Terrorists

Who are terrorists? In the mid-1970s, terrorist expert Frederick Hacker argued that terrorists are usually characterized as criminals, crazies, or crusaders, and that sometimes they are characterized as all three.[51] As discussed at the beginning of this chapter, labeling individuals or groups as "terrorists" can be fraught with difficulty and inaccuracies. Why do people turn to tactics that target civilians? Some trace it to feelings of hopelessness, or the belief that there is no other avenue through which people can express their opinions. Terrorism often involves groups who are struggling for resources. In fact, it has been argued that terrorism takes place because modern war, which requires large militaries, advanced weaponry, and the like, has become a luxury tool of rich countries. All in all, terrorism can be a monetarily cheaper alternative to conventional warfare, and yet, due to its ability to foster fear and insecurity, it can be extremely effective in achieving political objectives. Many different types of terrorist groups can be identified. Terrorists may be associated with political revolutionary movements (including the famed "Carlos the Jackal"), national liberation (or separatist) causes (such as the Philippines' Abu Sayyaf and Sri Lanka's Tamil Tigers), or single-issue campaigns (such as the Animal Liberation Front). Such groups are found along all points of the ideological spectrum, but tend to congregate especially on the extreme left (e.g., Peru's Shining Path) and the extreme right (e.g., al-Qaeda).

Terrorist violence is used in many kinds of political activity. Some distinguish forms of terror by categorizing the targets of such activity. Domestic terrorism involves acts that are based in a single country without significant support from outside sources. Actions by the Free Aceh movement in Indonesia would qualify as ethnonationalist domestic terrorism. The Philippines has several Islamist separatist groups who are especially active in the southern regions of the country, including Abu Sayyaf, famous for kidnappings, bombings, and a plot to assassinate then-president Gloria Arroyo in 2008. The 1996 attack on the Japanese embassy in Lima, staged by the Marxist Túpac Amaru Revolutionary Movement, is another example of domestic-centered terrorism.

In contrast, international terrorism includes terror activity that is not limited to one state. An extremely well-coordinated and sophisticated attack in Mumbai in November 2008 left at least 160 people dead, with more than 300 injured. This attack, a siege throughout India's second largest city that lasted three days, was coordinated

by Lashkar-e-Taiba, one of the largest Islamist terrorist organizations in southern Asia, based in Pakistan. The attackers, most of whom were in their early twenties, arrived in Mumbai on inflatable speedboats, armed with Kalashnikovs, hand grenades, and bombs, and proceeded to launch attacks in restaurants, taxis, luxury hotels, a train station, and a Jewish center. The attacks were surprising in both their scope and their preparation: planners used Google Earth to orchestrate their carnage,[52] which was documented in terrifying detail via social-networking sites around the world. One gunman had been instructed by his handler: "Everything is being recorded by the media. Inflict maximum damage. Keep fighting. Don't be taken alive."[53] Only one gunman, Ajmal Kasab, survived, and he was sentenced to death in May 2010.

The deep pockets of international terror networks reach into many different societies as a way of evading detection—transferring funds through the use of promissory notes or other underground methods that require minimal paperwork and are therefore difficult to trace. But it's not all about unmarked Swiss bank accounts. One arrangement is known as *hawala*—which is Hindi for "in trust." This system allows people working in one country to deposit payments (often in currency or gold) at a local office so that a third party can have virtually instantaneous access to the money in another country in a paperless transaction conducted through phone calls and e-mails. Some have described this as the Western Union of the non-Western world.[54] Based in the United Arab Emirates, *hawala* offices are found throughout the Middle East, northern Africa, and Asia. Some banks operating under this system have been accused of funneling profits from customers' fees to terrorist leaders, including Osama bin Laden and other high-ranking members of al-Qaeda, even though the 9/11 Commission confirmed in the latter case that funds were transferred by interbank wire rather than through the *hawala* system.[55] In fact, *hawala* networks have been extremely important in providing financial services and humanitarian aid through nongovernmental organizations (NGOs) in Afghanistan, with sums sometimes reaching as much as $20 million a month.[56]

Another source of creative financing for illicit activities draws on the relationship between drug cartels and terrorist organizations, dating back to the 1970s. Terrorist groups, including the Sunni Taliban regime that formerly ruled Afghanistan, and some extreme Shiite groups in Lebanon, are believed to have financed their operations from the sale of illicit drugs, especially opium.[57] In Peru, Shining Path's numbers (from 4,000 to about 350 members) and activities have declined since the capture of its leaders in 1992 and 2012. But factions are known to offer protection to local peasants and coca growers, particularly in certain remote regions where an estimated 200 tons of cocaine is produced every year. Taxes on coca growers and levies on traffickers' flights out of the region, as well as unauthorized sales of timber and gold mining, have been lucrative sources of revenue for the group, which is now more narco-terrorist gang than political revolutionary movement.[58]

Prior to September 2001, few Americans had heard of al-Qaeda (meaning "The Base"), even though many were familiar with the name of its leader, Saudi fugitive Osama bin Laden. Al-Qaeda, formed in 1988, is a deeply embedded international network of terrorists based in many countries; it supports extremist Sunni Muslim fighters in conflicts around the world, including Chechnya, Tajikistan, Kashmir, and Yemen. But as we have learned since mid-2001, many al-Qaeda operatives live and

work in other countries around the world, with significant bases in Germany, the Philippines, Pakistan, and the United States, among others. Some of the stated goals of this network include the overthrow of nearly all conservative Muslim governments, to be replaced by a more virulent form of Islamic governance, and the expulsion of Western influence from the Muslim world, especially the US presence in Saudi Arabia. Even though al-Qaeda members often mention freedom for the Palestinians in their rhetoric, this seems to always take a backseat to their other concerns. In addition to funding its own terrorist activities, al-Qaeda is believed to be the premier funding source for Islamic extremist activities in the world. In 1996, bin Laden publicly issued his "Declaration of War" against the United States, which he and other members of al-Qaeda view as the chief obstacle to change in Muslim societies. It is important to note that while bin Laden and this group claimed to speak on behalf of Muslims around the world, Muslims have nearly universally denounced al-Qaeda's calls for violence and extremism, before and after September 11.

Terrorist groups combine multiple grievances to craft their own unique expression of rage against the status quo. These groups often present a combination of ideologies and demands and then fit their actions to their strengths and circumstances. For example, Uganda's Lord's Resistance Army (LRA), formed in the 1980s, was for years the most deadly militia in Africa. The group was initially led by then twenty-eight-year-old cult leader Alice Lakwena, and later by her cousin, Joseph Kony, a former Catholic choirboy who is said to be possessed by spirits. First Lakwena (from the mid-1980s) and then Kony (from the late 1980s) promoted the proliferation of gangs, murderers, rapists, and sheer terror, especially in northern Uganda. For nineteen years they fought the Ugandan army, telling young recruits to smear botanical shea butter on their bodies to repel bullets and to sing Christian hymns as they marched straight toward the enemy. They also told recruits that the rocks they threw at soldiers would turn into grenades. After suppression by the Ugandan army, Lakwena fled to Kenya, where she died in 2007. The LRA aimed to re-create the Kingdom of God and establish a state based on the Ten Commandments. In addition to Christian precepts, the group incorporated aspects of both indigenous religions and minor tenets of Islam—Kony announced that Fridays would be a second sabbath, largely as a way to appease his financial sponsors in Khartoum, Sudan. This sponsorship was largely designed to counter Uganda's support of separatists in southern Sudan. Some of the LRA's more unusual tenets, though, including bans on eating the meat of white-feathered chickens and riding bicycles—a primary form of transportation in Uganda—cannot accurately be traced to any of these belief systems. Kony claims that he is instructed by God, and that the LRA is very strict about enforcement: one man was killed for violating the bicycle ban, and LRA soldiers forced the dead man's wife to eat one of his feet or be killed. LRA agents are famous for abducting young teens—as many as 35,000 young girls and boys, according to the United Nations Children's Fund (UNICEF). In 2005 the INTERNATIONAL CRIMINAL COURT (ICC) issued arrest warrants, on charges including twelve counts of crimes against humanity, for Joseph Kony and four LRA associates. These were the first warrants issued by the ICC since its establishment in 2002. As of early 2017 one LRA commander had been brought before the court. Kony remained at large, and the LRA (significantly diminished, with just a few hundred fighters) was operating (and still abducting children) out of the Central African Republic.[59]

Even though terrorism by independent groups is most common, terrorist methods are also advocated by clandestine agents of governments, through government-sponsored or -supported groups designed to intimidate and repress individuals and groups within society. They often use death squads to threaten and eliminate their enemies. Although states risk being ostracized by the international community by engaging in terrorist acts, this is a gamble that some are willing to take. Increasingly, even if groups are not acting on the orders of a government, they are often acting with its support (ideologically and often financially), giving rise to the term *state-sponsored terrorism*.

Because of the passion that groups are able to incite for their causes, attempts to isolate state-sponsored terrorists have been incomplete at best. There is a growing list of known governments that are active in supporting groups beyond their

Figure 11.7   The Israeli-Palestinian Conflict

Perhaps few struggles are more enduring than the ongoing conflict between Arab Palestinians and the Israeli government. This dispute has been the source of five major wars, and has contributed to numerous other regional upheavals, claiming thousands of lives—including children, teenagers, and entire families. The outbreak of conflict, especially following the 1967 Six Day War, has displaced millions of Palestinians, scattering them across multiple states and refugee centers in the region. Terrorist violence has marred all sides in this clash, rife with border disputes, intense religious symbolism, and security concerns. It seems that no one's hands are clean—but each side claims it has been provoked by the other, and both the Israeli government and the Palestinian Authority claim that the injustices of the situation make it difficult for them to control those under their rule. In fact, one of the dangerous turns in the dispute has been the willingness of individuals to take actions into their own hands, sometimes wrapping themselves in nail-studded explosives and taking their own lives—along with the lives of many others—in crowded urban areas. In 2002, Wafa Idris, a volunteer medic with the Palestine Red Crescent Society, was identified as the first female suicide bomber to attack Israel within its borders (she has since been followed by several more). While police attacks and the bulldozing of homes have been commonplace on the Israeli side, suicide bombings have proven to be a weapon of choice for some Palestinians.

Shortly after the death of former Palestinian Authority leader Yasser Arafat, in November 2004, Mahmoud Abbas was elected president of the Palestinian Authority. As the Palestinian Authority increased its level of institutionalization, a surprise parliamentary victory was won by Hamas, the Palestinian Sunni Islamist organization famous for both its comprehensive Palestinian welfare programs, as well as its controversial charter that calls for the destruction of the state of Israel. Following its surprise victory, the United States, the European Union, and Israel imposed an economically crippling response that cut all fund transfers and tax receipts. The controversy only emboldened Hamas and its supporters and made many question the West's hypocritical response to a democratically elected government. Following a World Bank report that documented the devastating effects of these measures, monies were again channeled to the Palestinian people through elaborate means that bypassed the Palestinian Authority. Yet a significant schism between President Abbas (whose base is in the West Bank) and Hamas (who remain in control of the Gaza Strip) has presented an impasse for international negotiations, which once again remain in a deadlock over the fundamental issues of borders, security, settlements, and the status of Jerusalem, the city claimed as a holy city to three major world religions: Christianity, Islam, and Judaism.

shores: the usual suspects include Iran, Cuba, North Korea, and Syria. Cuba, Yemen, and North Korea have been accused of providing safe haven to hunted terrorists. With the insecurity that follows in the wake of terror attacks, it is tempting to divide the world in two, placing countries that cooperate with the US-led global war on terrorism on one side and those that do not on the other. As we discuss in Chapter 19, the BUSH DOCTRINE implicated any country that supports terrorists as being terrorists themselves. Such seeming clarity, though, can be misleading. True, there are some countries that invoke sovereignty—the right to control what happens within one's borders—and argue that they will not cooperate in this war on terror, which they claim is just another attempt by the United States to impose its will on others. Yet there are other countries, including the Philippines and Somalia, that are plagued by weak governments that struggle to control their own territory; therefore their assistance would be impotent at best. As much as President Barack Obama attempted to craft an effective approach to state-sponsored terrorism, including rejecting the image of the global war against it and reaching out to state leaders across the spectrum and the globe, his approach was stalled by debate within his own foreign policy team about the best approach, as well as by the political reality of attempting to change policies that had been so central to his predecessor, George W. Bush. Some have wondered aloud whether much has changed, in terms of outcome. One Bush-era lawyer highlighted that "the change in tone has been important and has helped internationally. But the change in law has been largely cosmetic. And of course there has been no change in outcome."[60]

Iran has long been viewed as a large-scale sponsor of terrorist violence—a charge that leaders in Tehran vehemently deny. The country is suspected of having committed or sponsored assassinations in northern Iraq, attacks against the Kurdish Democratic Party of Iran, and other policies of liquidating the regime's opponents who live outside the country. Iran also stirs the coals with neighboring Iraq by providing safe haven to some of Turkey's PKK operatives. Following the attacks of September 11, the United States argued that it would welcome Iran's support in the war on terror if it withdrew support from perceived terror groups. In fact, the United States needed the support of Iran to help forge ties with the Northern Alliance in Afghanistan. Iran had assisted the Northern Alliance and other anti-Taliban groups through the 1990s, and some viewed their mediation as "essential" to convincing the factions of mujahidin fighters in Afghanistan to work with the United States to topple the Taliban regime.[61] Libya also was long branded an active sponsor of terror. Once behind the wheel of government in 1969, Colonel Muammar Qaddafi sought to launch an Arab-Islamic revolution, for which he trained thousands of foreign terrorists each year in Libyan camps. Among the most famous was Carlos Ramirez Santos, also known as "Carlos the Jackal," who operated on behalf of Libya, Syria, and Iraq until his extradition from Sudan and deportation to France in 1997. By 2003, though, building on the improved relations he experienced after agreeing to turn over the Libyans accused of planting the bomb on Pan Am Flight 103, which killed 207 people, Qaddafi formally declared the existence of his chemical and nuclear weapons programs and invited international inspectors into Libya (although some claim his announcement was in response to the US-led war in Iraq, he had made similar offers, to no avail, beginning in the late 1990s).[62] After the weapons programs were destroyed, the French government followed through on pledges to

help Libya build a peaceful nuclear power program, and in 2006 the United States restored diplomatic relations with Libya, removing it from the list of countries believed to be officially sponsoring terrorism.

Another way to categorize types of terrorism is by focusing on the tools used to provoke fear or cause damage. While nuclear weapons and their delivery tend to be cost-prohibitive and technologically problematic for many countries of the world, bioterrorism is more within their reach. This leads some to refer to biological and chemical weapons as the "poor man's nuclear bomb" and "great equalizer." Biological weapons, including anthrax, the plague, and smallpox, are viewed as an ideal tool for many terrorists today because their effects take days to appear, making an elusive escape more likely. Yet it can be extremely difficult to contain any outbreak resulting from a biological attack, meaning that the perpetrators may themselves be harmed as well. Such weapons remain dangerous because of their availability and potency: small amounts can wreak havoc on large groups of people. They have already been used as weapons of mass destruction—most effectively by Saddam Hussein's forces against the Kurds in Iraq. Iran, victimized by Iraq's use of chemical weapons during the war between these two countries in the 1980s, is also known to be producing (or preparing to produce) biological and chemical weapons.

Chemical weapons, in the form of mustard gas, chlorine, sarin, phosgene, VX, and other agents, are believed to be the easiest-made weapons of mass destruction and are viewed as particularly horrendous because of their invisible and insidious stealth nature.[63] Their ingredients, including pesticides and fertilizers, are readily available. The main obstacle to their effective deployment comes in the difficulty of producing large quantities, as well as a delivery method, because in most cases they must be miniaturized in order to be potently dispensed. As of early 2017, three of the countries included on the US State Department's list of state sponsors of international terrorism (Iran, Syria, and Sudan) are known to possess chemical weapons. After the Assad government in Syria used sarin to kill more than a thousand civilians in a suburb of Damascus in 2013, it was pressured to give up its chemical arsenal. However, the government's use of chemical warfare has not ended; rather, only the type of weapon has changed. There is a great deal of evidence suggesting that Assad has used chlorine gas (which remains legal as a widely available industrial chemical) strategically, to displace civilians from rebel-held areas. Despite its other, mundane uses, chlorine is a terrifying weapon; it is a choking agent that dissolves the lungs and there's no sheltering from it, as there is from other bombs, as it seeps into basements. It is estimated that as of 2016 the government had launched more than 160 chemical weapons attacks killing nearly 1,500 people and injuring approximately 15,000.[64] Another state sponsor of terrorism is the Sudanese government, which is accused of using the blister agent mustard gas on more than thirty occasions in Darfur in 2016, killing more than 250 people.[65] In both Syria and Sudan, many of the casualties have been women and children. The United States and Russia possess the two largest stockpiles of chemical and biological weapons in the world and, despite some progress, have yet to destroy their stockpiles as agreed to in the Chemical Weapons Convention of 1993.[66] In fact, the scourge of these terror agents was introduced by the Western powers, which used them widely in World War I and in the Vietnam War.

Even if conventional nuclear weapons may be out of reach for many states, some believe the world faces an increased threat of nuclear terrorism due to the quantity

of materials relatively unaccounted for—including plutonium and highly enriched uranium—as well as the increased number of nuclear-capable states, discussed in Chapter 17. Even if an individual cannot piece together enough material to build a nuclear bomb, it is believed that a group could still build such a device—widely referred to as a "dirty bomb"—to spread radiological contamination. Widespread destruction can be achieved by wrapping radioactive material (including spent fuel rods) around conventional explosives. Once detonated, in the form of a car bomb, suitcase nuke, or other device, the intense radiation will be far more destructive than the blast itself. As of yet, there are unconfirmed suspicions that Iran received or smuggled nuclear materials out of the former Soviet Union. It is extremely difficult to know if al-Qaeda or other known terror groups have access to such materials, although it is highly plausible.

Revolutionaries

One of China's great revolutionaries, Mao Zedong, once emphasized the violence and uprootedness of revolutions in his famous observation that a revolution "is not a dinner party. . . . A revolution is an insurrection, an act of violence by which one class overthrows another."[67] To elaborate on Mao's prose, a revolution may be defined as a change in regime with the desire to achieve extensive, relatively quick, and often concurrent changes in economic, political, and social structures. Even though many countries claim to hold a revolutionary heritage, if we adopt the conventional definition of revolutions as fundamental transformations in everyday ways of life, they are actually fairly rare events. The classic revolutionary states, in which such dramatic changes were implemented, are China, France, and Russia.[68] Revolutions such as these are unlike other changes of power because their goal is to destroy the existing system, often through the use of charisma and violence. In the Chinese and French Revolutions, for example, people even changed their names and ways of referring to others. Following China's 1949 revolution, it was common for people to refer to each other by the egalitarian moniker "comrade" rather than by surname or title.

Yet there have been many attempts to promote revolutions and revolutionary change beyond the three traditional "grand" revolutions. Many countries in the global south claim a revolutionary heritage, including Iran, Mexico, Turkey, Cuba, Vietnam, and Zimbabwe. Revolutions are often launched from remote regions where governmental groups have less control, and their leaders build their power base through ideological persuasion. Those at the forefront of the revolutionary effort often employ guerrilla tactics, especially the element of surprise, such as when the Zapatistas unexpectedly marched into the city of San Cristobal de las Casas on New Year's Day in 1994. In a nutshell, revolutions are about change.

Revolutions bring new people to power, incorporating groups such as peasants and workers who had otherwise been left out of the process. In this sense, they attempt to "liberate" people—a term that is commonly associated with revolutionary endeavors. Many revolutions are class-based, arising from structural changes that pit one group of people against another. Revolutions can also be born of crises manifested in territorial expansion, economic reorganization, international dislocation, or population expansion. Situations ripe for revolution include those involving widespread misery, oppression, and injustice, combined with either a weak government that is unable to solve the problems facing it or a significant crisis. In these situations,

when "push comes to shove," groups who perceive themselves on the losing end of the bargain concentrate their resources and attempt to overthrow the oppressive system. In revolutionary situations, groups demand some role in decisionmaking, whether facing down military rulers, such as in Mexico, Bolivia, or Cuba; colonial regimes, such as in Vietnam and Algeria; or monarchies, such as in imperial China and Russia. In each of these cases, the entrenched elite was unable (or unwilling) to incorporate the new voices without a fight. Revolutions can also follow the collapse of an empire or regime, as happened with the collapse of the Qing Dynasty in China, the Ottoman Empire in Turkey, and the Qajar Empire in Iran (then known as Persia). A crisis situation unites otherwise disconnected groups to rebel against the status quo and claim power. Successful revolutions often coalesce around a single leader (or small group of leaders) who is able to harness discord into a potent political force.

Sometimes leaders of revolutions are (or become) military leaders as well, including Turkey's Mustafa Kemal Atatürk, Burkina Faso's Thomas Sankara, and Algeria's Houari Boumedienne. Yet not all revolutionary leaders have a military background: Iran's Ayatollah Khomeini was a religious leader, China's Mao Zedong was a librarian, Guinea-Bissau's Amilcar Cabral was a census taker, and most people believe that the Zapatistas' Subcomandante Marcos was once a professor. Revolutionary leaders tend to have charisma and come from the relatively privileged classes—many are leaders of the intelligentsia, among the most educated members of society and accustomed to having their say. Yet the harbingers of revolutionary movements often suffer some sort of major setback, experiencing failed expectations or suffering from an aspiration gap, as discussed earlier in the chapter. Many leaders of revolutions face a tumultuous history in their own countries—difficulties they often rectify with a vengeance against their former suppressers.

For example, Khomeini was exiled to Iraq from 1964 to 1968 for criticizing the Shah and allegedly sparking riots. He was later evicted from the Shia holy city of An Najaf by Saddam Hussein. Khomeini viewed himself as uniquely fit to avenge the problems of the West, especially the humiliations wrought on Muslims in the Middle East. Following his victorious return to Iran in 1979—after mass protests against the Shah's regime had long festered—he quickly acted on these ambitions, transforming the Iranian Revolution into an Islamic Revolution.[69] Mustafa Kemal Atatürk, leader of the 1919 Turkish Revolution, also viewed himself as distinctively able to lead his country down a new path. The difference between their approaches was the role of religion in their revolutions: Khomeini believed that an orthodox version of Islam and a rejection of all things Western were the best corrective to Iran's problems, while Atatürk prescribed an unyielding form of secularism to overcome Turkey's challenges. Both rode the rising wave of nationalism in their respective societies.

Another revolutionary who capitalized on nationalist themes was Ho Chi Minh, leader of the modern revolution in Vietnam, whose name means "Bringer of Light." At the end of World War I, when he was a student in France, Ho approached President Woodrow Wilson with the hope that Wilson's doctrine of self-determination would be applied to Vietnam. Wilson turned Ho away. Ho later founded the Viet Minh (whose name is an acronym for the Vietnam Independence League), but died before his dream of a unified North and South Vietnam could be realized, at tremendous cost. Affectionately known by many Vietnamese as "Uncle Ho," he repelled

French attempts to regain an Asian empire in the 1950s, and later frustrated US attempts to defeat them in the 1960s and 1970s.

Some revolutionary leaders are already incumbent rulers who overthrow their fellow leaders to establish a new governing system. The Turkish Revolution of 1919 is one such example. Some have called it an ELITE REVOLUTION, or a revolution from above—defined by the swift overthrow of the elite by other members of the elite, limited mass participation, and limited violence.[70] Ellen Trimberger argues that the specific characteristics of elite revolutions, especially their restrictions on the involvement of the masses, can lead to situations in which the military may regularly intervene, which certainly holds true for the coup-riddled experience of Turkey.[71] The Peruvian Revolution (by coup), led by General Juan Velasco Alvarado, may also be described as a revolution from above. Despite these examples of elite revolutions, it is important to note that most are made "from below," incorporating the masses or other disenfranchised groups in an overthrow of the power structure. In fact, the Velasco revolution failed in part because it didn't incorporate the participation of other groups, including the people it meant to serve—the peasants.

Women have been active participants in revolutionary struggles and wars: harboring rebels, moving weapons and intelligence through war zones, staffing health organizations, and carrying rifles. Women served key roles in revolutions in Nicaragua, Palestine, South Africa, Zimbabwe, Mexico, and the Philippines. In the Philippine Revolution of 1896–1902, known as the first anticolonial independence movement in Asia, women gained prominence. As one example, Teresa Magbanua was known as the Filipina "Joan of Arc" for her battles against the Spaniards in the late 1800s. In the Mexican Revolution, both Emiliano Zapata's and Pancho Villa's armies included women revolutionaries, called *soldaderas*. They were originally camp followers who fed soldiers and provided services that the government did not. Gertrudis Bocanegra organized an army of women during the Mexican War of Independence in 1810: she died in 1817 after being arrested and tortured. Women often organized their own units, armed themselves, and fought as soldiers equal to the men. In unprecedented numbers, women participated in every aspect of the anti-Somoza effort in Nicaragua; in fact, they made up 30 percent of the Sandinista army and occupied important leadership positions, commanding full battalions. They were mostly young women, and the men with whom they shared units appeared for the most part to accept them. But after the revolution, women were largely ignored, even betrayed, by the Sandinistas.[72] And although there were female soldiers in Namibia, women never rose to officer status. In Namibia and Zimbabwe, female soldiers were often stigmatized after the war for being "mannish" by carrying guns. When Sam Nujoma thanked the Namibian people for their contribution to the country's liberation, he mentioned women specifically but did not recognize them as fighters.

Despite proclamations of great change, revolutions fade away—they are difficult to sustain. Revolutions require resources (personnel, coercion, money), energy (charismatic leaders and committed followers), and a level of ideological zeal and commitment that few societies can maintain for very long, much to the chagrin of both those who led the revolution and those who suffered losses during it. China's Cultural Revolution is the best example of one leader's attempt to literally "continue the revolution" and maintain its legacy.

Terror often plays a large role in revolutions and revolutionary societies. Because revolutions attempt to achieve dramatic changes, there is little room for dissent or discussion. As with much violent conflict, clear sides are chosen by combatants and bystanders alike. Individuals and groups who are viewed to be against the regime are labeled "counterrevolutionaries," a charge that carries great danger, often tantamount to a death sentence. Especially after it is perceived that there has been some setback to revolutionary progress, terror methods, including torture, isolation, and forced labor, are commonly employed as means of holding on to power and keeping the revolution alive.

One of the most problematic legacies of revolutions is the selection of leadership beyond the revolutionary generation. Succession is an issue in many countries of the non-Western world, but especially in those with a revolutionary heritage. Leadership transition in nondemocratic states is rarely orderly. Leaders tend to seek to rule for life, and few mechanisms are put in place to choose their replacements until a crisis precipitates change—which means that leadership turnover happens during times of instability. Plato hypothesized that such circumstances, often deriving from chaotic mass rule, produce authoritarian despots. Deng Xiaoping's death in 1997 passed with barely a hiccup, because Jiang Zemin had been given almost eight years at the helm under Deng's steady hand and continued hold on (informal) power. The formal transfer of power from Jiang Zemin to Hu Jintao in 2002–2003 was similar in some ways, masking the fact that Jiang still controlled the reins, albeit from behind the scenes. Even after the titles of power were conferred to Hu Jintao, the leader of China's so-called fourth generation, Jiang and his protégés continued to exercise power for at least a year afterward. The groundwork for the transition to the fifth generation of CCP leaders (which took place throughout 2012–2013), was set by mid-2010, when Xi Jinping and Li Keqiang had each received promotions to key military and party posts. In Cuba, for years many expressed uncertainty about life after Fidel Castro, an uncertainty that was already apparent even when Castro's less charismatic brother Raul assumed control during an ongoing "temporary" transfer of power after one of Fidel's health crises in July 2006. Since his death in late 2016, in part due to the prolonged transition time since his brother's assumption of power, little has changed. In South Africa, even though there was plenty of worry as Nelson Mandela neared retirement, his protégé, Thabo Mbeki, was able to provide a sense of continuity. However, since then tensions have grown, as Mbeki's second term was cut short due to party infighting. Today, under Mbeki's successor, Jacob Zuma, many find the party of Mandela to be unrecognizable. And in North Korea, in the months surrounding the elevation of one of reclusive leader Kim Jong-Il's sons, Kim Jong-Un, tensions in the region were significantly heightened, especially after North Korea launched artillery attacks against a South Korean island along the disputed maritime border. Some observers believe the actions, part of a larger pattern of North Korean aggression, demonstrated a less than enthusiastic embrace by the Korean military of Kim's designated successor.[73]

Do revolutions often accomplish what their leaders set out to achieve? Since revolutions claim to promote fundamental transformations in power relations, it is important to assess their gains. Few revolutions are total failures, but few accomplish most of their explicit goals, either. In the early years of a revolution, it is common to observe significant attempts at land distribution and social change,

employing at least the rhetoric, if not the reality, of equality. Castro, for example, appeared to be confronting *machismo* with laws requiring men to help with domestic responsibilities, but the laws were rarely enforced. Most revolutions also produce at least some form of leadership change, although one tyrant may simply be replaced by another, or by someone even more despotic.[74] The ruling groups in power after the revolution rarely deliver on the grand pledges they used to mobilize people to join in the first place.

Social stratification is rarely decreased in postrevolutionary societies—rather, the bureaucratic malaise and the expansion of state power that tend to follow revolutionary conflict often increase the gap between rich and poor.[75] Revolutions in the global south have an especially poor record of promoting equality and increased freedom, even if some redistribution of wealth or land reform actually takes place, such as in China and Cuba. In China, Cuba, and Nicaragua, one form of inequality was simply replaced by another, as the former landlords became poor and party leaders became more comfortable. Pledges to promote sexual equality, as well, are often relegated to lower status after the revolution is won, leading many to argue that promises of gender equality are formulated only to secure support of women during the revolutionary fight. In Namibia and Zimbabwe, promises of gender equality were "postponed" in order to appease still-powerful traditional (patriarchal) interests that the vulnerable revolutionary governments needed as allies. In the dangerous attempt to create "new" societies and new cultural foundations, and to do this quickly, huge groups of people often get caught in the crossfire. Although the statistics remain hotly debated, it is estimated that 2–3 million people died during Pol Pot's disastrous communist revolution in Cambodia, and at least 1 million died during the revolutionary fervor in Vietnam. Mao Zedong went to the grave with many deaths on his shoulders: some estimate that as many as 60 million people died in China as a result of his rule.[76]

Due to these broken promises, postrevolutionary societies often face great difficulty dealing with the revolutionary heritage they inherit, and governing groups in these societies tend to be defensive and reactionary. For example, in Iran in 1981, two years after the Islamic Revolution, the government crushed the so-called Marxist mujahidin after they purportedly bombed the Islamic Republic's office in Tehran. The mujahidin had been part of the coalition that overthrew the Shah in the first place, but they quickly fell out of favor with Khomeini and his supporters. The new government executed 6,000 of its members and supporters, and thousands of ordinary people answered the virulent call to attack the "enemies" of Islam. Training camps were established, including one camp in Tehran that was reserved for women trainees only.[77] In Mexico, Cuba, and China, the complex legacy of revolutionary leaders has proved a formidable challenge to the ruling regime that follows it, especially when groups ruling in the name of a revolutionary heritage seem to abandon prior goals and pledges.

To conclude our discussion of revolutions and revolutionary heritage, we compare two revolutions that continue to shape life in the global south. Both the 1979 Iranian Revolution and the 1949 Chinese Revolution were extremely popular with the population. In China, this support was sustained, for the most part, until the crackdown on the students in 1989. In Iran, the "grand coalition" quickly collapsed. Even though it was estimated that approximately one-fifth of the Iranian population

demonstrated against the regime of Mohammad Reza Shah Pahlavi in December 1979, the euphoria ended shortly after it toppled the Shah's regime.[78]

The execution of the 1979 Iranian Revolution was rapid, while the Chinese Revolution was drawn out over twenty-two years of warfare before the PRC was established in 1949. Both revolutions took time to consolidate. In fact, most issues in both societies today emanate from the struggle of trying to be "modern" and relatively integrated without losing the hard-fought gains of the past. Both revolutions replaced imperial eras, even if there was a thirty-eight-year interim period in the case of China. The Iranian Revolution rid society of an unpopular monarch who had already once been deposed, ending 2,500 years of dynastic rule. In China, the Qing Dynasty had collapsed in 1911, but rival groups and factions, including political parties, warlords, and millennial cults, sparred over the country's future throughout most of the transition.

In their attempt to shoot for the moon, revolutionaries sometimes create new problems for themselves and those who follow them. Leaders in both Iran and China, for example, realized that their calls for "revolutionary" families to have many children as a way of prolonging the revolutionary spoils soon created a painful drain on public resources. Mao encouraged population growth throughout the 1960s and early 1970s, yet mandated limits on family size in the late 1970s. In the 1980s, Iran's population jumped from 34 million to more than 50 million. As a result, Iran has introduced one of the world's most comprehensive family-planning programs, making every form of birth control available free of charge and requiring couples to pass a family-planning course before they can legally marry. This initiative prompted the health ministry to send officials door-to-door, with clerics issuing FATWAS to approve intrauterine devices and vasectomies.[79]

Both postrevolutionary societies are now evaluating the modernization of their regimes and the ways that they can continue revolutionary rhetoric while reaching out to other countries. The Iranian Revolution is undergoing an "Islamic Reformation"—defining the proper relationship between Islam and the modern world.[80] Iran leads the Islamic world in this debate, publicly challenging precepts everywhere from the courtroom and editorial pages to the cinemas and blogs. And clerics convicted of taking the debate too far have become celebrities among the ordinary population, especially since the Green Movement of 2009 (discussed in Chapter 9). Ever since the death of Mao Zedong in 1976, Chinese leaders have rethought their revolutionary saga, once even stating that Mao was 80 percent correct and 20 percent wrong in his handling of Chinese affairs. After Deng Xiaoping pushed China to open its doors to the outside world, the Chinese began to question their revolutionary rhetoric more than ever. Few communist cadres had considered rehearsing their memorization of Mao's quotations while sitting at a Starbucks or Kentucky Fried Chicken.

What was accomplished by these two revolutions, grand in scale if not in achievement? In both China and Iran, literacy rates increased dramatically, especially among the youth. Between 1970 and 1990, literacy in Iran topped 90 percent, even as the population doubled.[81] China also achieved dramatic improvements in literacy and healthcare between the 1940s and the 1970s, especially in the countryside. Revolutions in both countries provoked fearful responses from nearby states. Turkey blames the rise of PKK terrorism and separatist claims on the Iranian Revolution, and many of China's Southeast Asian neighbors, led by Indonesia, formed the Association of Southeast Asian Nations (ASEAN) as a way of combating a pos-

sible domino effect of communism throughout the region. Obviously, new cadres of leadership entered the ranks in both countries as a result of their revolutions. As the postrevolutionary generation gives way to the post-postrevolutionary leadership, the combination of pragmatism and revolutionary legacy that is used to justify their rule may become increasingly difficult to maintain.

Conclusions: Whither Violence?

Is the world more violent today than in the past? Those who argue that it is point to the end of the largest military buildup the world has ever seen, the Cold War, and the resulting widespread availability of weapons—to governments, individuals, and organized groups alike. They also find evidence in the renewal of latent issues, such as separatist movements and ethnic violence that were earlier suppressed by authoritarian regimes—as we have witnessed in Yugoslavia, Rwanda, Nigeria, and Indonesia. There are also those who maintain that the world today is no more violent than in the past. They point to current moves toward strengthening regional and international norms against violence, despite the violent nature of governments throughout time and the ongoing determination of violent revolutionaries and terrorists. However the question is answered, it is up to you to weigh the evidence and decide.

As we have shown in this chapter, the use of violence as a means of implementing change is not always ideologically, religiously, or culturally based. Nor is it always the usual suspects (the "criminals, crazies, or crusaders") who are the perpetrators of violence. State-sponsored violence, domestically and internationally, makes up a large proportion of violence in the world today, Western and non-Western alike. Our discussion has also highlighted that it is not only so-called extremists who engage in violent acts. Some groups and individuals feel that it is only through hostility and aggression that they can get the respect, attention, and credence they deserve.

It is tempting when looking at these issues and actors to be reductionist: to claim that the tactics of revolutionaries, terrorists, and government fighters are evil, that actions are always based in fanaticism, or that violence is always irrational. One does not have to condone the use of violence to evaluate such actors on their own terms and attempt to understand why they take the actions they do.

While many see violence as the only way to resolve a situation, it is difficult to make the transition beyond violence. The use of violence is often, although by no means always, self-perpetuating. People are forced to take sides, defining "enemy" groups and dehumanizing neighbors, colleagues, and fellow citizens. Following times of discord and disruption and attempts to move beyond them, there is a great sense that past "scores" need to be settled.

Notes

1. Jon Leyne, "Will Iran's Basij Stay Loyal?," BBC News, August 13, 2009.

2. "Despite the Headlines, Steven Pinker Says the World Is Becoming Less Violent," National Public Radio, *All Things Considered,* July 16, 2016.

3. "The Economics of Violence," *The Economist,* April 14, 2011.

4. Noam Chomsky, *Pirates and Emperors: International Terrorism in the Real World* (New York: Claremont, 1986).

5. For a concise summary of approaches to violence in the literature, see Jack A. Goldstone, ed., *Revolutions: Theoretical, Comparative, and Historical Studies,* 2nd ed. (New York: Harcourt Brace, 1994).

6. "Unrest in DR Congo After TP Mazembe Lose to Inter Milan," BBC News, December 18, 2010.

7. Arend Lijphart, *Democracy in Plural Societies: A Comparative Exploration* (New Haven: Yale University Press, 1977).

8. Charles Euchner, *Extraordinary Politics: How Protest and Dissent Are Changing American Democracy* (Boulder: Westview, 1996).

9. Michael Renner, "How to Abolish War," *The Humanist,* July–August 1999.

10. Daniel C. Diller, ed., *The Middle East,* 8th ed. (Washington, DC: Congressional Quarterly, 1994).

11. Ibid.

12. Yahya Sadowski, "Ethnic Conflict," *Foreign Policy* 111 (Summer 1998).

13. "Aceh's Sharia Court Opens," BBC News, March 4, 2003.

14. Tina Rosenberg, "A Guerrilla War Stoked by a Thirst for Cash," *New York Times,* December 27, 2001.

15. Cited in Gary J. Bass, "What Really Causes Civil War?," *New York Times Magazine,* August 13, 2006.

16. Adrian Edwards, "Global Forced Displacement Hits Record High," UNHCR, June 20, 2016, www.unhcr.org; "Colombia Referendum: Voters Reject FARC Peace Deal," BBC News, October 3, 2016, www.bbc.com; "In Colombia, Turning a Peace Deal into Reality," *New York Times,* December 2, 2016.

17. Toyin Falola, *The History of Nigeria* (Westport: Greenwood, 1999).

18. Eleanor O'Gorman, "Writing Women's Wars: Foucaldian Strategies of Engagement," in *Women, Culture, and International Relations,* ed. Vivienne Jabri and Eleanor O'Gorman (Boulder: Lynne Rienner, 1999).

19. Walter Laqueur, *The New Terrorism: Fanaticism and the Arms of Mass Destruction* (New York: Oxford University Press, 1999).

20. "The Accidental War," *The Economist,* July 22, 2006, p. 13.

21. "A Geographical Expression in Search of a State," *The Economist,* July 8, 2006, pp. 22–24.

22. Amy Caiazza, "Why Gender Matters in Understanding September 11: Women, Militarism, and Violence," Institute for Women's Policy Research, November 2001.

23. Alissa J. Rubin and Aurelien Breeden, "Women's Emergence as Terrorists in France Points to Shift in ISIS Gender Roles," *New York Times,* October 1, 2016.

24. Amy Knight, "Female Terrorists in the Russian Socialist Revolutionary Party," *Russian Review,* no. 38 (1979); Laqueur, *The New Terrorism.*

25. Christopher Dickey, "Women of Al Qaeda," *Newsweek,* December 12, 2005.

26. Rubin and Breeden, "Women's Emergence as Terrorists."

27. United Nations Children's Fund (UNICEF), *Beyond Chibok: Over 1.3 Million Children Uprooted by Boko Haram Violence,* April 2016, www.unicef.org.

28. Sita Ranchod-Nilsson, "'This, Too, Is a Way of Fighting': Rural Women's Participation in Zimbabwe's Liberation War," in *Women and Revolution in Africa, Asia, and the New World,* ed. Mary Ann Tetreault (Columbia: University of South Carolina Press, 1994).

29. Valerie Epps, "Civilian Casualties in Modern Warfare: The Death of the Collateral Damage Rule," *Georgia Journal of International and Comparative Law* 41, no. 2 (2013).

30. Mary Kaldor, *New and Old Wars: Organized Violence in a Global Era* (Stanford: Stanford University Press, 1999).

31. Marisa Taylor, "Study: Quarter of Civilians Killed in Syrian War Are Children, Women," Al Jazeera, September 29, 2015, www.aljazeera.com.

32. "International Court Takes Case of Congo's Child Soldiers," National Public Radio, *Weekend All Things Considered,* October 29, 2006.

33. "Child Soldiers," National Public Radio, *Talk of the Nation,* February 16, 2005. See also P. W. Singer, *Children at War* (New York: Pantheon, 2005).

34. Rachel Brett and Irma Specht, *Young Soldiers: Why They Choose to Fight* (Boulder: Lynne Rienner, 2004), pp. 9–36.

35. Coalition to Stop the Use of Child Soldiers, "Global Report on Child Soldiers 2001," www.child-soldiers.org/news; Juan Forero, "A Child's Vision of War: Boy Guerrillas in Colombia," *New York Times,* December 20, 2000; "Charity Decries Use of Children in War," *CNN World News,* October 31, 1996; "The Weapon That Changed the Face of War," National Public Radio, *Weekend Edition Sunday,* November 26, 2006.

36. "Uganda LRA Rebels 'On Massive Forced Recruitment Drive,'" BBC News, August 12, 2010.

37. Kenneth Walker, "UNICEF Works to Deprogram Children Who Have Been Kidnapped in Sierra Leone and Forced to Commit Murder for the Rebels," National Public Radio, *Morning Edition,* July 6, 2000; Coalition to Stop the Use of Child Soldiers, "Global Report on Child Soldiers 2001.

38. Seth Mydans, "Burmese Rebel Chief More Boy Than Warrior," *New York Times,* April 10, 2000; "Burmese Rebel Twins and Fourteen Followers Surrender in Thailand," Associated Press, January 17, 2001."

39. Rosenberg, "A Guerrilla War Stoked by a Thirst for Cash."

40. Isawa Elaigwu, "Nation-Building and Changing Political Structures," in *UNESCO General History of Africa: Africa Since 1935,* ed. Ali A. Mazrui (London: Heinemann, 1993).

41. Ergun Özbudun, *Contemporary Turkish Politics: Challenges to Democratic Consolidation* (Boulder: Lynne Rienner, 2000).

42. Marvine Howe, *Turkey Today: A Nation Divided over Islam's Revival* (Boulder: Westview, 2000).

43. Miguel Angel Centeno, *Democracy Within Reason: Technocratic Revolution in Mexico* (University Park: Pennsylvania State University Press, 1997).

44. Sorayya Shahri, "Women in Command: A Successful Experience in the National Liberation Army of Iran," in *Frontline Feminisms: Women, War, and Resistance,* ed. Marguerite R. Waller and Jennifer Rycenga (New York: Garland, 2000).

45. Preethi Nallu, "Rape Is Being Used to Terrorise the Population, Says DRC Gynaecologist," *The Guardian* (London), May 22, 2015, www.guardian.com.

46. Vanda Felbab-Brown, "Militias in Mexico: Citizens' Security or Further Conflict Escalation?," *Insight Crime,* December 22, 2015, www.insightcrime.org.

47. John McBeth, "Bombs, the Army, and Suharto," *Far Eastern Economic Review* 164, no. 4 (February 1, 2001).

48. Ibid.

49. "In the Hands of the Militia," *The Economist,* September 16, 2000.

50. "American Use of South African Mercenaries as Bodyguards and Police Trainers in Iraq," National Public Radio, *Morning Edition,* February 15, 2005; "Questions About Mercenary Activities in Africa," National Public Radio, *All Things Considered,* March 17, 2004.

51. Frederick J. Hacker, *Crusaders, Criminals, Crazies: Terror and Terrorism in Our Time* (New York: Norton, 1976).

52. Rahul Bedi, "Mumbai Attacks: Indian Suit Against Google Earth over Image Use by Terrorists," *The Telegraph* (London), December 9, 2008.

53. Vikas Bajaj and Lydia Polgreen, "Suspect Stirs Mumbai Court by Confessing," *New York Times,* July 20, 2009.

54. Mike Crawley, "Somali Banking Under Scrutiny," *Christian Science Monitor,* November 28, 2001.

55. *The 9/11 Commission Report: Final Report on the National Commission on Terrorist Attacks upon the United States* (New York: Norton, 2004), pp. 169–172.

56. Samuel Munzele Maimbo, "The Money Exchange Dealers of Kabul: A Study of the Hawala System in Afghanistan," Working Paper no. 13 (Washington, DC: World Bank, 2003), chap. 3.

57. Laqueur, *The New Terrorism.*

58. Mimi Yagoub, "Peru's Shining Path Is Making a Comeback, Analyst Says," *Insight Crime,* August 25, 2016, www.insightcrime.org; Martin De Angelis, "Peru's Shining Path

Insurgency Reemerges as Security Threat," *Global Risk Insights,* August 17, 2015, www.globalrisksinsights.com.

59. Paul Ronan and Lisa Dugan, "Joseph Kony's LRA Is Still Abducting Children, Even After CAR Votes for Peace," *Newsweek,* March 6, 2016, www.newsweek.com.

60. John B. Bellinger III, a former US lawyer with the National Security Council and State Department, interviewed in Charlie Savage, "Obama Team Is Divided on Anti-Terror Tactics," *New York Times,* March 28, 2010.

61. Ray Takeyh, *Hidden Iran: Paradox and Power in the Islamic Republic* (New York: Holt, 2006), pp. 122–123.

62. Flynt Leverett, "Why Libya Gave Up on the Bomb," *New York Times,* January 23, 2004, p. 23.

63. "A History of Chemical Weapons," National Public Radio, *Talk of the Nation,* May 8, 2006.

64. Jared Malsin, "Assad's Regime Is Still Using Chemical Weapons in Syria," *Time,* September 14, 2016, www.time.com; Kareem Shaheen, "'Almost 1,500 Killed in Chemical Weapons Attacks' in Syria," *The Guardian* (London), March 14, 2016, www.theguardian.com.

65. "Sudan Accused of Chemical Weapons Attacks in Darfur," Al Jazeera, September 29, 2016, www.aljazeera.com.

66. "Global Campaign to Destroy Chemical Weapons Passes 60 Percent Mark," press release, Organization for the Prohibition of Chemical Weapons, July 8, 2010.

67. Mao Zedong, "Report on an Investigation of the Peasant Movement in Hunan: March 1927," in *Selected Readings from the Works of Mao Tsetung* (Peking: Foreign Languages Press, 1971), p. 30.

68. See Goldstone, *Revolutions;* Theda Skocpol, *States and Social Revolution: A Comparative Analysis of France, Russia, and China* (New York: Cambridge University Press, 1979).

69. Elton L. Daniel, *The History of Iran* (Westport: Greenwood, 2001).

70. Ellen Kay Trimberger, "A Theory of Elite Revolutions," *Studies in Comparative International Development* 7 (1972). Trimberger also included the Meiji Restoration of 1868 as an example of this specific type of revolution.

71. Ibid. This point explicitly challenges the theories of Huntington and others who argued against the inclusion of mass mobilization because of its potentially destabilizing outcomes.

72. Margaret Randall, *Sandino's Daughters: Testimonies of Nicaraguan Women in Struggle* (New Brunswick, NJ: Rutgers University Press, 1995).

73. "North Korea Firing: Why Now?," BBC News, November 23, 2010.

74. Jack A. Goldstone, "The Outcomes of Revolutions," in Goldstone, *Revolutions*.

75. Ibid.

76. Stéphane Courtois, Nicolas Werth, Jean-Louis Panné, et al., *The Black Book of Communism: Crimes, Terror, and Repression,* ed. Mark Kramer, trans. Jonathan Murphy (Cambridge: Harvard University Press, 1999). In his study of the Great Leap Forward, Frank Dikötter estimates that this movement alone was responsible for at least 45 million deaths; see Frank Dikötter, *Mao's Great Famine: The History of China's Most Devastating Catastrophe, 1958–1962* (New York: Walker, 2010).

77. Donna M. Schlagheck, *International Terrorism: An Introduction to the Concepts and Actors* (Lexington, MA: Lexington Books, 1988).

78. Dariush Zahedi, *The Iranian Revolution Then and Now: Indicators of Regime Instability* (Boulder: Westview, 2000).

79. Robin Wright, "Iran's New Revolution," *Foreign Affairs,* January–February 2000.

80. Ibid.

81. Ibid.

Chapter 12

Linking
Concepts and Cases

As we have discussed, violent expression can take many forms and derives from many different motivations. In what ways is conflict expressed differently in the countries that we are studying? What are the main sources of discord and how are they expressed? Do you observe any significant differences between the states that were established via revolutionary or liberation wars and those that were not? How do the power and role of the military in each of these states impact the operation of government or the expression of dissenting opinion? What legacies of past conflict can you observe in these states? Based on what you already know about our cases, what type of situation do you expect to find in each of these countries? For example, given what you learned about civil society in Chapter 9, what expectations do you hold for the expression of violence in each of these states?

Case Study: Mexico

It is not unusual today to hear that Mexico is facing its greatest crisis since its revolution due to the violence unleashed by organized crime. The drug trade in Mexico has flourished for some time, but it has grown exponentially in recent decades. Fifty percent of the cocaine entering the United States came through Mexico in 1990 — as of 2013, over 90 percent of it did. Eighty percent of the heroin, methamphetamine, and marijuana brought into the United States comes across the Mexican border. It is widely believed that for decades, various Institutional Revolutionary Party (PRI) governments had worked out an accommodation with the cartels that run this trade. However, over the years, Mexican drug sales to the United States have become more lucrative (estimated to be worth more than $20 billion a year), more competitive, and bloodier.[1]

The situation was out of control and in 2006 President Felipe Calderón declared a war on drugs. In an attempt to decapitate the cartels, he launched a militarized campaign that resulted in a number of high-profile drug seizures, arrests, and extraditions. Calderón eliminated twice as many drug lords as the previous administrations.[2]

However, Calderon's war had the opposite of its intended effect: as one kingpin was removed, intergroup competition soared as his lieutenants fought to succeed him. One consequence of this is the demise of some cartels and their decentralization under three regional crime networks or umbrellas (Sinaloa state in the north, Tamaulipas state in the area around Mexico City, and Tierra Caliente along the Gulf coast).[3]

The stakes were (and are) high because, as Calderón put it, Mexico is next door to the biggest drug addict in the world.[4] As the cartels continue their infighting, they have become increasingly brazen and gruesome in their attacks, assassinating each other and terrorizing ordinary people (including uploading videos of mutilations, beheadings, and the like, to YouTube). During Calderón's presidency violence exploded in Mexico. The homicide rate more than doubled, growing from 9 per 100,000 in 2006 to 22 per 100,000 in 2011.[5] Several Mexican cities had some of the highest murder rates in the world. Between 2006 and 2016, the drug war killed an estimated 100,000 people (many of them innocents caught in the crossfire).[6]

Given the circumstances, more than one analyst has characterized Mexico as a failed state, at risk of rapid and sudden collapse.[7] Although some insist that what Mexico is facing is not a political insurgency, these mafias do mean to influence politics. According to Shannon O'Neil, Mexico's transition to democracy disrupted the long-established understanding between the traffickers and the government that defined the rules of the game in a way that allowed business as usual to go on with limited government interference. The compact was broken; because the government—now democratic—was taking on the cartels, the drug lords decided to undermine the democracy.[8] They have sought to hijack the democratic process, bombing campaign offices, assassinating candidates and government officials, and scaring voters away from the polls.[9]

But the drug trade could not exist as it does without the cooperation of the state. The decentralization of power that came with democratization opened up more channels for misconduct. Local and state officials are coerced or co-opted by the offer "plata o plomo" (silver or lead)—faced with the choice of cash or a bullet. Officials are often too weak to confront criminals or eager to work with them, which leaves criminals free to operate with impunity.[10]

Corruption and impunity on the government's end fuel the conflict. Although there are some who are honest and humane, for years Mexico's police and soldiers have operated with impunity. Complaints are rarely investigated, let alone prosecuted; since 2006 the attorney general's office has reviewed 4,000 complaints of torture and only 15 of them have resulted in convictions.[11] Moreover, Mexico's military are unusually efficient killers, more likely to kill than injure their enemies. In most wars the "kill rate" is four persons injured for every one killed. In Mexico the body count is unheard of: eight killed for every one wounded. In sum, torture, disappearances, and extrajudicial executions—by cartels as well as state actors—grew during Calderón's war on drugs on a scale that is tantamount to crimes against humanity.[12]

President Peña Nieto (of the PRI, the party that long had an "understanding" with the cartels) was elected to office promising to move away from his predecessor's war on drugs. He argued that repairing Mexico's social fabric, which has been torn apart, would be more effective than a military approach in reducing violence.[13] He was able to push through a variety of initiatives aimed at de-escalating the war, but for every advance toward stabilizing the country, there has been a setback. Drug-

related homicides initially declined and the number of complaints against the military dropped sharply between 2011 and 2016.[14] However, in 2016 kidnapping and extortion were way up and the levels of violence were the highest seen since the drug war began.[15] As a result, citizens continue to live in constant danger—and not only because the state is failing to provide security against the cartels and gangs, but also because of crimes of omission or commission by the state.

Given the impunity with which they operate, it would appear that Mexico is still dependent on the army and no less of a mafia state than it was prior to the war on drugs. The cartels are one thing, but there is only so far any Mexican government is likely to go in taking on the security forces. Years ago, in a quid pro quo deal struck in 1946 to promote stability, Mexican officers agreed to stay out of politics as long as the security forces were given near total autonomy and placed beyond scrutiny. As a result, the Mexican military has been unique in its willingness to let civilians rule. Admittedly, this is a less than perfect arrangement, but Mexico is one of the few countries in Latin America that hasn't had a coup in nearly a century. And this is one record that few Mexicans want broken.[16]

Case Study: Peru

Thirty years ago a horrendous civil war was heating up just as Peru was making an attempt at democratization. Just as civilians were resuming power, a leftist insurgency movement, Sendero Luminoso (Shining Path), began its attacks.[17] Sometime earlier, in the impoverished region of Ayacucho, an obscure philosophy professor, Abimael Guzmán Reynoso, had begun to command a following. A personality cult developed around Guzmán; "President Gonzalo," as he was called, considered himself to be the "Fourth Sword of Marxism" (after Marx, Lenin, and Mao). To his followers, this philosopher king was incredibly charismatic. His first supporters were university students and recent graduates—young people from the middle and upper-middle classes seeking social mobility and frustrated by the country's prolonged economic crisis. What became a fanatical guerrilla movement was in many ways more a religion than a political entity; Guzmán's followers were true believers, remarkably devoted to the cause.[18]

Although Shining Path's ideology drew from Marxist philosophy, this was unlike other Latin American revolutions in that Guzmán disdained the Cuban model and rejected Soviet assistance. Rather, Guzmán studied in China and claimed his movement to be orthodox Maoist.[19] Like Mao, Guzmán sought to mobilize the peasantry for a rural revolution. However, the comparison pretty much ends there.[20] According to Guzmán, Peru's social order had to be destroyed to make way for a new one, and this required killing 10 percent of the civilian population. The guerrillas fought a vicious war in the countryside and the cities, killing not only soldiers and government officials, but also development workers and popular community leaders whom Shining Path considered sellouts. The more violence the better, argued the rebels; it was only after purification through bloodshed that Peru would become a Maoist utopia. In this effort, these true believers did their best; it is estimated that in twenty years of terror the government forces (including militias) and the guerrillas killed almost 70,000 Peruvians and that Shining Path was responsible for about 54 percent of the fatalities.[21]

But the military did its part to add to the death toll as well. The newly democratic Peruvian governments adopted similar responses to the insurgency. They declared states of emergency, suspended constitutional guarantees, and to varying degrees turned the war over to the military. Thousands more civilians were killed in the crossfire between Shining Path and the security forces. In its zeal, the military committed gross human rights violations against anyone suspected of being a member of Shining Path. Presidents made a few feeble attempts at controlling the military, but without much success. Most Peruvian leaders equivocated, unable decide whether to fight an Argentine-style dirty war, or to pursue a developmentalist solution, offering massive social assistance and promoting economic development to root out the fundamental causes of the insurgency and win over the population.[22]

On the other hand, President Alberto Fujimori (1990–2000) was very clear on this point. This president favored a no-holds-barred, draconian approach and expanded the military's legal prerogatives to match its actual prerogatives. In return for its loyalty, Fujimori gave the military absolute control over the counterinsurgency program. As a result, in 1992 Peru was identified as having the highest rate of disappearances of any country in the world.[23]

But it was also this free rein that Fujimori credited with his victory over terrorism. In September 1992 not only was Guzmán captured in a hideout above a Lima dance studio, but so were the master computer files for the entire organization. This amounted to a bonanza; police rounded up more than a thousand suspects within a few weeks. Yet even more crucial, the government succeeded in totally destroying Guzmán's mystique. Placed in a cage and dressed in a striped prison uniform, "President Gonzalo" was revealed on television as a meek, paunchy, middle-aged man with thick glasses.[24] Because so much of Shining Path's power was based in the personality cult centered on Guzmán, this dramatic change in persona proved devastating to the movement.

With the war over, Peruvians were left to pick up the pieces. In 2003 a Peruvian TRUTH COMMISSION report found that there were more than 70,000 victims of the war that lasted from 1980 to 2000. According to the report, Shining Path was responsible for the majority of deaths and disappearances, but 37 percent of these crimes were perpetrated by state security forces and paramilitaries.[25] Although the commission called for trials of the members of the armed forces accused of atrocities, only a few officers have been held accountable for their actions during the war (although former president Fujimori was found guilty in 2009 and sentenced to twenty-five years in prison for ordering death squad killings and kidnappings).[26]

The military has enjoyed impunity even since the return to democracy because civilians have been reluctant to assert strong control over the military. In Peru, any encroachment on military autonomy or even mild criticism of the military is taboo—out of fear that it might provoke a coup.[27]

Meanwhile, Shining Path is back. It has reorganized and split into two factions operating in different parts of Peru. They reportedly have less revolutionary zeal than their forebearers and appear to have reinvented themselves as part insurgents and part illicit drug entrepreneurs. Sure, the original group was also involved with coca back in the day, but today this is a major focus of their interest. The rebels provide security for drug gangs, which supply them with money and weapons. Otherwise, relatively little is known about members of the new Shining Path.[28] They have

threatened a gas pipeline that supplies approximately 40 percent of Peru's electricity and is set for expansion. And rebels attacked a military caravan transporting election materials, killing ten people the day before the April 2016 elections.[29]

Although it is no longer considered an existential threat, Shining Path is Peru's largest and most active terrorist group.[30] Democratically elected Peruvian governments have continued the tradition of granting the military the autonomy to fight insurgents as it sees fit. They have intensified counterinsurgency efforts, authorized emergency powers, suspended civil liberties, and granted the armed forces additional authority in the parts of the country where the guerrillas operate. The military is taking Shining Path very seriously, but the few hundred guerrillas are more of a threat to Peru's war on drugs than they are a terrorist threat. Meanwhile, if you ask Peruvians, they will tell you that it is neither drugs nor terrorism that keeps them up at night: it's Peru's crime rates, which are among the highest in Latin America.[31]

Case Study: Nigeria

Since the country's independence in 1960, two government leaders have been assassinated and there have been six successful coups, with many more failed ones. Until 1999 the military had spent more time in power than have civilians, and when civilians have ruled, it has mostly been at the discretion of the armed forces.[32] Even in Nigeria's nearly twenty-year-old democracy, there are concerns that the military considers itself above all other institutions. It may be "above" all other institutions, but it is hardly isolated from the country's myriad social and economic divisions.[33]

Nigeria's various divides have on more than one occasion resulted in open conflicts. When the Ibo, the largest ethnic group indigenous to the southeast, declared their intent to secede and create their own independent country—Biafra—Nigeria descended into a civil war that raged from 1967 to 1970. More than 1 million Ibo died before it was all over—most of them civilians, many of them women and children. Although in the end the military government prevailed, Nigeria had come perilously close to breaking up.[34]

Such a threat remains a possibility and the military would argue that what some might call its outsized role is actually a necessity, given that the country is battling two major insurgencies at the same time. Most Nigerians would agree that the wars, one in the north and one in the southeast, threaten the state. The war in the north poses what most consider the greater menace. In large areas of the country it has posed an existential threat. That challenge is posed by Boko Haram, whose members initially took up arms in several northern cities in 2002 because they were poor, unemployed, and sick of government corruption. They offered political Islam as a solution and seek to transform Nigeria into an Islamic state. Boko Haram, a Hausa expression of disgust with Western education, has decimated education in some areas and tested the capacity of the democratic government. It posed such a security challenge that the 2015 elections had to be delayed so that people could vote. And Boko Haram inspires great fear; it has come to be known for its use of child (often female) suicide bombers on soft targets such as crowded markets.[35] It is estimated that as of late 2016, more than 20,000 people had been killed and 2.6 million internally displaced in clashes between government forces and these militants. Fourteen million people were in dire need of humanitarian aid and tens of thousands of children were at risk of starvation.[36]

The government is allocating enormous amounts of money to the effort, but its performance is abysmal; Amnesty International has accused the military of committing war crimes in its fight against the militant group.[37] Moreover, the government's use of scorched-earth tactics only emboldened these fighters, who most famously kidnapped 278 schoolgirls in 2014, setting off a social media campaign "Bring Back Our Girls." There appears to be no dealing with Boko Haram; when President Goodluck Jonathan proposed an amnesty to end the fighting, Boko Haram ridiculed him for it, saying that it is his government that should beg for amnesty.[38] President Muhammadu Buhari was elected promising to vanquish the militants overnight. With the help of an international coalition, the government had made advances. At one point Buhari even declared a "technical victory," but the insurgents had merely resumed asymmetric warfare and spread into neighboring countries.[39]

Meanwhile, the longer-standing crisis is in the Niger Delta. Located in southeastern Nigeria, the Delta region comprises 70,000 square kilometers of mostly marsh and creeks. Its inhabitants contend that this environment has been ruined by the oil industry and that this has cost them their health and their livelihoods; they have for too long been mistreated as their oil wealth is taken from their states to bankroll the rest of the country. Some of them have taken up arms. Various guerrilla armies, militias, and gangsters are participants in this unconventional war, carrying out kidnappings, pipeline bombings, and piracy. This multidimensional war that has run intermittently as of mid-2016 had reduced Nigeria's oil output by 25 percent, to a twenty-year low.[40]

Given the country's dependence on oil exports, the Niger Delta conflict poses a mortal threat to Nigeria's economy. President Olusegun Obasanjo (a former general) had tried to win this war through major military offensives. However, the military found itself again and again bogged down in the Delta; as it resorted to scorched-earth tactics, innocent residents were caught in the crossfire, with thousands killed and injured. President Umaru Yar'Adua pursued a radically different approach, conceding that many of the militants' demands were justified, and offered them a cease-fire and amnesty. Starting in 2009 he promised to pay fighters who were willing to lay down their weapons ($13 a day) and provide them with job training. He also pledged to spend $1.3 billion to promote economic development. It is estimated that approximately 30,000 fighters (including many senior commanders) took Yar'Adua up on the deal, which did bring a semblance of peace, and oil production returned to preinsurgency levels. There was little progress under President Jonathan, the first Nigerian president to hail from the southeast.[41] Dissatisfied with the way things were going, a new group, the Niger Delta Avengers (NDA), has "returned to the creeks," resumed the war on the oil industry, and is invoking Biafra, calling for a referendum to divide the nation.[42] As of 2016 the NDA wasn't yet wreaking as much havoc on the economy as groups such as the Movement for the Emancipation of the Niger Delta (MEND) had at the height of the insurgency; nor was this war costing as many lives as it did at its peak in 2009 (about 1,000 a year). But it is hurting the economy, which Buhari considers a security issue. With Nigeria in a financial crisis due to falling oil prices, Buhari cut the amnesty program and sent troops to the area in 2016. The president, a former general, has threatened to treat the militants like Boko Haram (a comparison that many in the Delta reject). They have a point: Boko Haram, which pledged allegiance to the Islamic State of Iraq and

Syria (ISIS) in 2015, is actually the world's deadliest terrorist organization. It is so dreadful that they make the Avengers look like comic book heroes.[43]

In the end, there are too few good guys: between the insurgents and Nigeria's murderous military, Nigeria joins a select group of five countries (including Syria, Iraq, Pakistan, and Afghanistan) that account for 80 percent of the world's deaths from terrorism.[44] It might surprise many readers that Nigeria is part of this club because, compared to the others, what's going on in Nigeria gets so little attention.

Case Study: Zimbabwe

Chimurenga is a Shona word that has great salience for all Zimbabweans. It has a number of meanings, but it generally refers to revolution, war, struggle, and resistance. In the First Chimurenga War, in the 1890s, the Shona and Ndebele fought against the loss of their land to white settlers. The result was the Second Chimurenga War and its focal point for Africans also was land—in this case reclamation of what was theirs. This second war is what most people consider to be Zimbabwe's war for liberation, and it was revolutionary in its aims, although not necessarily in its outcome.[45]

Two nationalist movements led the liberation war, the Zimbabwe African People's Union (ZAPU) and the Zimbabwe African National Union (ZANU), an offshoot of ZAPU formed in opposition to it. In 1963 the armed wing of ZANU, the Zimbabwe African National Liberation Army (ZANLA), sent its first group of soldiers to China for guerrilla training. China continued to support ZANU throughout the liberation war, and the Soviet Union provided assistance to ZAPU's armed forces, the Zimbabwe People's Revolutionary Army (ZIPRA). Meanwhile, the West for years largely stood behind the white governments—in effect leaving the Africans little choice but to turn to the communists. This was perfect for white Rhodesians, who joined white South Africans in portraying themselves as the last bulwarks against black communism. Consequently, with the involvement of external actors, Zimbabwe's struggle became for many outsiders a Cold War proxy war.[46]

Justified as a necessary response to the "communist threat," the white government put the country under a state of emergency that would last fifteen years. ZAPU and ZANU were banned and their leaders, including Joshua Nkomo of ZAPU, as well as ZANU's Robert Mugabe and others, were held in detention for nearly a decade. Realizing that the conflict would be protracted, black nationalists knew that they would need a strong base of support and set about mobilizing the masses for it. It was not difficult to raise peasant consciousness—the loss of their land was an issue of great importance for most people. However, as the years dragged on, civilians became increasingly caught in the crossfire. As communities began to tire of the drain of war, conflicts between the guerrillas and their hosts became more common.[47]

All of this was a problem for both ZIPRA and ZANLA, which most analysts today consider more alike than different. While the two groups had their disagreements, both armies were led by nationalists who appealed to Africans as Zimbabweans rather than as Shona- or Ndebele-speakers. Neither liberation army was ethnically homogeneous, but because they tended to recruit from their different areas of operation, they became identified in that way—ZANU as primarily Shona, ZAPU as Ndebele.[48] Despite the rivalry between them, in 1976 the two parties joined forces in an uneasy alliance known as the Patriotic Front (ZANU-PF).[49] With this and other

factors working in their favor, the guerrillas escalated their assault. By 1979 the white government was so weakened that it was forced to negotiate a peace. The Patriotic Front was ready for an end to the carnage as well; although approximately 1,000 whites died defending Rhodesia, it is estimated that some 30,000–80,000 people—mostly black civilians—died in the war for liberation.[50]

However, not long after independence Zimbabwe was back at war; this time the struggle was between the victors. For years there had been tensions between ZANU-PF and ZAPU, but relations became hostile after the 1980 elections, in which ZANU-PF won control of the government. Although each blamed the other for provoking the violence, the four-year civil war that followed clearly had an ethnic dimension. The Fifth Brigade, an entirely ZANU and Shona-speaking elite military unit, was set loose to find dissidents in Matabeleland, a heavily pro-ZAPU region. The countryside was ravaged as the military used scorched-earth tactics. By the time a unity accord was brokered in 1987, between 8,000 and 30,000 more people had been killed, most of them Ndebele civilians.[51] In 1980, Robert Mugabe, a guerrilla fighter and ZANU leader, was elected president in Zimbabwe's first democratic elections.

Since the late 1990s, Zimbabweans have again been braced for conflict. Faced with the strong democratic challenge posed by the Movement for Democratic Change (MDC), the government has resorted to a variety of tactics. The government's Operation Murambatsvina (often translated from Shona as Operation Drive Out Trash) bulldozed the homes and businesses of more than 700,000 people in Harare and other cities. Although the government says it was cracking down on illegal activities and promoting public order, others contend that this mass eviction was ZANU-PF's effort to stave off a possible uprising by dispersing the political opposition, mostly the urban poor.[52] Activists have been attacked, kidnapped, arrested, tortured, and murdered. The biggest strikes since 2007 were met with the worst violence in two decades.[53]

What has the military had to say about all of this? The Zimbabwe National Army was formed in 1980 by integrating the three rival armies (ZANLA, ZIPRA, and the Rhodesian security forces). Although in many ways it remains a revolutionary army, Zimbabwe's military has until recently been considered relatively professional. However, as the government has become increasingly desperate to hold on to power, it has become more politicized. Members of the military hold powerful positions not only in ZANU-PF, but also in the cabinet, parliament, and state agencies. After soldiers rioted in late 2008 over low pay and high inflation, the Mugabe government decided to secure the army's loyalty by giving it the right to plunder. One example is the cash cow known as the Marange diamond fields in eastern Zimbabwe, discovered in 2006. Containing the most extensive deposits in Africa, characterized by one expert as a freak of nature, the Marange fields contained one of the highest concentrations of diamonds in the world. With the blessing of the ruling party, the military moved in, clearing the area by attacking illegal miners, and killing hundreds of them.[54] Despite attempts through the Kimberley Process and other mechanisms to characterize this loot as "blood diamonds" (and prohibit its sale), the Zimbabwean government fought hard and won the right to export millions of carats of these gems on the world market each month—earning the country an estimated $800 million in dividends annually.[55]

Though the military seems sated for now, no one is entirely sure what it will do in the future. Since rumors of a coup plot in 2001, Mugabe has consistently favored officers with the highest-ranking posts within the party. The military is now better

placed to play the role of kingmaker, and it appears that Mugabe has maintained the loyalty of its commanders, at least. However, there must be growing concern among these commanders about the post-Mugabe future. Vice President Emmerson Mnangagwa has the support of many in the military, but there is more than one soldier vying to lead ZANU-PF after Mugabe is gone. Meanwhile, once the old guerrilla's storm troopers, many war veterans have broken with the president, castigating him for the shape the country is in. In response, the president has promised to crush them in another Gukurahundi, a massacre in the 1980s in which the government purge killed more than 20,000 people.[56] Should Mugabe order the elimination of their brethren, the military will find itself making tough choices; coup just might become the most likely of ways in which Mugabe's reign could end.

Case Study: Egypt

It's hard to imagine now, but for many years Egypt was a beacon of tranquility, its society a model of peacefulness and tolerance. Yet this country, which hadn't had a civil war in more than 7,000 years, has turned into a breeding ground of violence. It's a chicken and egg problem: Egypt is widely considered the birthplace of modern jihadism and is the incubator of several terrorist groups.[57] Meanwhile, the authorities have perennially cracked down not only on radical Islamists, but also on all dissent. Like Mubarak, Sisi has no tolerance for criticism. But he's taking it further than Mubarak ever did; for those (of any stripe) who dare to criticize this illiberal government, life is increasingly harsh and brutal.[58] The regime claims that this crackdown is necessary to defend the country, but others argue that it is in fact the government that is the main perpetrator of violence, using the guise of fighting terrorism but only creating more terrorists. And so we must consider the perennial question: Is state violence a necessary response to terrorism? Or is it stoking terror?

Interestingly, many Egyptians welcomed the military back into power in 2013 because they desperately wanted Egypt to avoid becoming another Syria or Iraq.[59] Yet since then, violence and crime disrupt daily life in Egypt at significantly higher levels than they did even under Mubarak. Egypt experienced an average of thirty terrorist acts per month throughout 2014—four times the rate of prior years. By 2015, the average was over a hundred attacks per month.[60] Moreover, Egypt faces multiple, internal threats from different and even competing jihadists. None of them currently pose an existential threat to the government, but its hands are full.[61]

Of the multiple terrorist groups currently operating in Egypt, the most active and capable is the jihadist Sinai Province (SP).[62] This homegrown organization pledged allegiance to the Islamic State (IS) in 2014, declaring its intention to turn the Sinai Peninsula into part of an IS caliphate.[63] The SP, which first emerged after the Egyptian revolution of 2011, is based in the northern Sinai desert, a vast and mostly arid expanse. Largely unpopulated, impoverished, and neglected by the government, the Sinai has for years been a security vacuum, a perfect breeding ground for criminals and extremists.[64]

Despite its relatively small army of 1,000–1,500, Sinai Province has inflicted a large number of casualties. It has made some spectacular raids, killing hundreds of soldiers and police. It has begun to single out soft targets (civilians, particularly Copts, tourists, and foreign workers) and claimed responsibility for the downing of

a Russian passenger jet in 2015. Imitating IS's trademark punishment, the beheading of a Croatian engineer signals that SP has moved away from its prior restraint.[65] And there is growing concern that as attacks by SP and others increase in sophistication, they will target the Suez Canal, vitally important to global commerce.[66]

The Sinai Province is a dangerous, sophisticated terrorist group capable of skillfully planning, coordinating, and executing complex attacks.[67] Yet the Egyptian military, the largest standing military in the Arab world, is known to be more oriented toward fighting interstate warfare rather than asymmetric conflicts. It has struggled against this twenty-first-century threat, resulting in a relentless, brutal, and ineffective counterinsurgency campaign in the Sinai.[68] Rather than addressing the root of the crisis the regime has blamed foreign conspiracies for its problems. But the war at home is against anyone the military government might view as its remaining political opposition—which includes all opponents, both secular and Islamist.[69] For example, on August 14, 2013, in an attack on a Muslim Brotherhood sit-in, Egyptian security forces perpetrated the Rabaa massacre: "one of the world's largest killings of demonstrators in a single day in recent history," with nearly 1,000 casualties.[70]

Is the Sisi government's policy—which includes classifying the Muslim Brotherhood as a terrorist group—actually becoming a self-fulfilling prophecy? Thousands of the group's members (including former president Morsi) have been jailed and a generational schism appears to be deepening. Younger people blame their elders for the Brotherhood's recent failures and threaten to transform the movement into one seeking the violent overthrow of the government.[71] Analysts say that it would be premature to characterize this shift as imminent. Yet by capitalizing on the terrorist threat, President Sisi has moved the story away from democracy to one focused on security.[72] And so far many Egyptians have been willing to let him do so, if it will save them from the fates of their neighbors.

Case Study: Iran

Iran's history of coups, revolution, and violence runs deep. The country's periods of major strife and unrest were each propelled by similar issues: opposition to corrupt, unjust leaders, and resentment against the intrusion of foreign powers. Legacies of these struggles linger today. The debate over Iran's revolutionary legacy and the meaning of its status as a theocracy in the modern world, however, is far from an elite-dominated cleavage. It is a debate central to most public disputes in Iranian society today.

The Iranian military has always been a patron to the powerful. In 1925, after the fall of the Qajar Dynasty, Reza Khan took the historical title for Iranian kings—Shah—adopting the name Reza Shah Pahlavi. With Turkey's Mustafa Kemal Atatürk as his model, the new monarch promoted secularization and limited clerical powers. Pahlavi alienated several groups—especially the religious clergy—in stripping the clerics of land and control of schools, ending polygamy for women, and giving women the right to vote, work, and have abortions. He led from 1925 to 1941, ignoring constitutional limits and using the military to suppress any unrest that threatened to challenge his rule. His son, Mohammad Reza Pahlavi (Shah from 1941 to 1979), continued the reign of absolute power. In the early 1950s there were attempts to challenge the Shah, but with assistance from the United States and Britain he regained full power in a coup d'état against the extremely popular prime minister, Mohammad Mossadeq.

During his tyrannical rule, Mohammad Reza Pahlavi led Iran into an era of growth, with Iran's economy becoming one of the largest in the Middle East by the mid-1970s. But policies that benefited the rich while failing to incorporate unions, intellectuals, and religious leaders led to dashed expectations and increasing perceptions of relative deprivation. In particular, there was a revolution of rising expectations with the higher prices for oil in the 1970s, and then an aspiration gap—as only the Shah and his cronies saw the proceeds. Frustration and aggression simmered and began to hit a breaking point with widespread inflation. Facing increasing calls for reform that would incorporate larger segments of the Iranian population, the Shah buckled down: in 1975 he formed the Resurgence Party (Hizb-i Rastakhiz) from his military connections. Citizens were given the choice to join the party or leave the country. In an attempt to rein in the clerics, the Shah then declared that he was both political leader of the state and spiritual guide of the community, complete with an announcement of the coming of a new civilization that would surpass Sweden in terms of overall human development by the year 2000.[73] The Shah replaced the Muslim calendar with a new royalist calendar, disregarded *sharia* law by raising the minimum age for marriage, and ordered universities not to register women who insisted on wearing the Islamic chador. Each of these moves enraged religious leaders and increased their cries against the moral depravity of the country.

Further, the Shah provoked Sayyed Ruhollah Musavi Khomeini—a cleric whose given name means "Inspired of God"—and his followers when the government published an article ridiculing the cleric in January 1978. Religious demonstrations in the holy city of Qum followed, and the government's violent response left many demonstrators dead, launching a cycle of demonstrations every forty days, concurrent with the ritual in Shia Islam for a religious ceremony to take place for forty days after a death.[74] The continuation of demonstrations, a major movie-theater fire exacerbated by a slow state response, and Khomeini's inflammatory speech commemorating the end of the holy month of Ramadan coincided to lead the country toward revolution. In November 1978 the Shah—who at this time was very ill—placed Iran under military rule. His demise was hastened by his appeal for assistance from the West, and the quick collapse of his own military. Because the system was corrupt to the core, it fell apart easily. What followed was nearly a spontaneous revolution that included many diverse groups from Iranian society. Women wore the veil (declared illegal in 1936) to protest against the Shah and the debauchery of the West. It was an unusual revolution in several ways, being urban in origin, involving relatively little bloodshed, and resulting in the creation of a rightist theocracy that was retrogressive in nature.

One of the biggest surprises of 1979 was the departure of the Pahlavi military after the Shah left for the United States in January. Islamic revolutionaries provided security when airports reopened to allow the exiled Khomeini to return from Paris. Khomeini capitalized on popular discontent—especially among the youth—and successfully urged the military to wholly desert the monarch. The Ayatollah purged monarchists loyal to the Shah by dismissing 12,000 personnel, most of whom were officers, in an attempt to "Islamicize" the military.[75] He then created the Islamic Revolutionary Guard Corps (IRGC), also known as Pasdaran, and later the Basij, a paramilitary resistance force that provided volunteers for the "human wave" attacks during the war with Iraq. Members of the Basij (also known as the "Mobilization of

the Oppressed") remain the regime's chief enforcers, and are known for their brutality. The IRGC was created in 1979 to protect the Islamic character of the system—Khomeini deeply distrusted the loyalty of the conventional military. This group increasingly adopted a key leadership role within Iran, eventually transitioning into a prominent role in the economy, creating what some have termed a praetorian system.[76] Others, highlighting the prominent foreign policy role taken on by the IRGC, state that they are now "effectively the executive arm of the Supreme Leader."[77] They seem to have taken on a more domestic policing role as well, arresting journalists, writers, musicians, and even dual citizens. In this role, they have been explicitly challenged by President Rouhani, who publicly opposed the IRGC by challenging them in a video he posted to his Instagram page—an unprecedented move for an Iranian president.

As a capstone to the revolution, Khomeini activated traditional claims, inspired by seventh-century political philosophy that gave religious leaders divine right of protection, and established their supremacy over both political and spiritual matters. It was the Shah's secularism that had most aggravated Khomeini and his followers, and their revolution called for a new role for Islam in the political state—the establishment of a theocracy. The legitimacy of clerical leaders, while increasingly questioned by some segments of Iranian society today, has been a bedrock of the Islamic Revolution.

Iran's sponsorship of international terrorism is a major source of strained relations with many powers. Iranian support for Hezbollah (Party of God), a radical Shiite Muslim group based in Lebanon and known to be responsible for attacks against the United States (notably the attack on the Marine barracks in Beirut in 1983), is a point of great contention. Hezbollah is known to aspire for a theocratic state along the lines of the Shiite theocracy in Iran, and leaders in the organization maintain close contact with the Iranian Supreme Leader, who serves as a spiritual and political mentor of sorts, as well as the IRGC. Iran also has significant financial and military ties with Hamas (Islamic Resistance Movement). This Sunni Islamist group receives its major funding from Iran, especially since the United States and the European Union cut off funding after Hamas's victory in Palestinian parliamentary elections in 2006. The IRGC is known to have strong involvement in conflicts in Syria, Iraq, Yemen, and Bahrain—exporting weapons, providing military training—and even has a known presence in Latin America (focused on economic and humanitarian projects).[78]

Because of Iran's theocratic rule, enemies of the regime are defined to be enemies of God. One of the Iranian regime's most famous pronouncements of decided enemies was Khomeini's 1989 *fatwa* (religious injunction) against Salman Rushdie, author of the seemingly sacrilegious *Satanic Verses*. This decree provided a sum of over $2 million (plus expenses) for efforts to kill Rushdie. Even though Iranian leaders distanced themselves from the decree in 1998, and attempts on Rushdie's life have failed, attacks on his collaborators have had mixed success; a suicide bomber sent to London accidentally blew himself up in a hotel room, the book's Japanese translator was stabbed to death, and attempts on the lives of the publishers were made as well. Other enemies include political dissidents, such as Shapour Bakhtiar, the last prime minister under the Shah, who was murdered in Paris in August 1991. As many as 200 émigrés are believed to have been abducted, from many countries of the world,[79] and there now seems to be a concentrated effort by some hard-liners within Iran to target dual citizens.[80] Since Iran does not recognize dual citizenship,

those who are arrested are treated as Iranian citizens and are not afforded consular privileges. The case of abducted *Washington Post* reporter Jason Rezaian stands as but one noted example. Violence played an integral role both in the collapse of the Pahlavi Dynasty and in the continuation of the Islamic Republic. As cleavages continue to deepen, and Iran searches for a more active stage in regional and world affairs, the possibilities for political disruption remain.

Case Study: China

Similar to many of the countries we have studied, China has had multiple revolutions rather than a single revolutionary moment. Yet strangely enough, especially for their fervently anti-imperial character, both of China's major revolutions incorporated Western ideas, only later adapting "Chinese characteristics." The first revolution took place in 1912, after the last dynasty of China, the Qing, collapsed. Sun Yat-sen, a Christian medical doctor known as the father of modern China, planned the revolution from Tokyo, Honolulu, Vancouver, and London. Yet the revolution, led by the Nationalist Party (KMT), failed to consolidate, due partly to the focus on establishing a limited republic, and partly to Sun's illness and premature death in 1925, after which China descended into regional chaos. Warlords, individuals who had accrued military and political power over small regions of the country during the unrest that accompanied the collapse of the dynastic period, engaged in violent attempts to regain control over their fiefdoms. Out of this, another Nationalist leader, Chiang Kaishek, rose to the fore. Twice the KMT worked together with the younger, inexperienced, and ill-equipped Chinese Communist Party (CCP), and twice the Nationalists betrayed them, to dire consequences. In the second United Front, as their alliances were called, the KMT and the CCP worked together, some would say in a halfhearted manner, to expel the Japanese, who had invaded the north of China. It was during this conflict—in which the Nationalists gained the reputation as a corrupt band of soldiers who would quickly flee from the advancing Japanese—that the CCP gained the support of many of China's ordinary people. This was especially true in the countryside, which was the main recruiting ground for the fledgling CCP. Even though Mao Zedong was hardly a key member at the first party meetings in Shanghai in 1921, by the late 1920s he had begun to emerge as a revolutionary hero and cultural icon who would impact China, and all of Asia, like no other man. Yet victory over the Nationalists in China's civil war (1945–1949) was not enough. In Mao's attempt to "continue the revolution," he launched the country into a state of virtual civil war during his so-called Cultural Revolution. Even though the main campaigns of the ten-year movement, designed to promote absolute equality and cleanse China of foreign and Confucian influence, were primarily confined to China's major cities, the period is referred to as "the ten dark years," which no Chinese living on the mainland escaped. This decade of unrest—a "planned revolution" of sorts—was rife with purges, public denunciations, propaganda, and ideological fervor.

In the relative calm of the post-Mao period, with economic reform taking precedence over ideological expediency, societal conflict, suppressed by earlier campaigns and a near-complete lack of choice, has begun to resurface. Societal violence has also resurfaced, in ways and numbers not seen since the last years of

the imperial periods. Abduction, robbery, drug smuggling, and sex industries—often involving young girls kidnapped from the countryside—are all on the rise.

In contemporary politics, the role of China's People's Liberation Army (PLA) in governing is difficult to discern, because the institution is so closely intertwined with the CCP. In fact, the PLA, founded in 1927, follows in a long line of military involvement in politics: military commanders established many Chinese dynasties. It is common to hear that the CCP commands the gun, meaning that the PLA is subordinated to the party. Mao argued in 1927 that "all political power grows out of the barrel of a gun," and later that "the party commands the gun, while the gun shall never be or must never be allowed to command the party." Leaders since Mao, though, have attempted to limit party influence over the military, even though Deng Xiaoping, as chair of the Central Military Commission, effectively utilized PLA units to clear Tiananmen Square in 1989. Both Jiang Zemin and Hu Jintao rose to national prominence with weaker ties to the PLA. Yet they successfully courted military clients and were careful to avoid alienating PLA commanders in policy decisions. It is a matter complicated even further by the phenomenon known as "wearing multiple hats"—important political figures hold several posts at the same time. As an example, President Xi Jinping concurrently holds the posts of general secretary, chairman of the Central Military Commission, and president. Yet not every soldier or even military officer is a member of the Chinese Communist Party.

The PLA, in true guerrilla fashion, had won over the "hearts and minds" of the Chinese people during the postimperial struggle, especially in response to the Japanese invasion in the 1930s. As its name suggests, it was the PLA, whose lifeline was the CCP, that broke China's painful cycle of international humiliation at the hands of the imperial powers. Yet to many today, the Chinese military is synonymous with the crackdown on the students in Tiananmen Square, discussed in Chapter 10. For outside observers, it is difficult to understand the profound sense of shock that most Chinese citizens experienced when the army, "their" army, turned so violently against unarmed students in the square in June 1989. Leaders in Beijing had to activate PLA units from north-central China to clear the square, since the original troops, who had trained near Beijing University in the summers, were persuaded by the protesters to avoid firing their weapons.

Espionage is part of the daily business of militaries and governments. China has become a leader in cyber-warfare—part theft of intellectual property and part sophisticated military tactic. Hundreds of thousands of civilian hackers engaged in the so-called China syndrome[81]—breaking into foreign websites, including those of the White House, the US Department of Labor, even the US Office of Personnel Management—compromising, in the latter case, the data of more than 21 million employees.[82] The US Pentagon acknowledges the "steady progress" of the Chinese military in developing online-warfare techniques, in part, perhaps, to make up for an under-developed military, relative to US capabilities.[83] As military intelligence progresses from "cloak-and-dagger to bits-and-bytes," China is moving away from focusing on trade secrets and personal financial data to regional (and possibly international) intelligence needs, backed by a professional bureaucracy that has essentially become a new branch of the Chinese military.[84]

Another type of violence has demanded attention in recent years: attacks against individuals and groups, especially the rash of violent school and workplace attacks.

In one of the school attacks, a villager gruesomely hacked to death seven kindergartners, a teacher, and the teacher's elderly mother. In each of the attacks the assailant was a middle-aged man wielding knives, hammers, or other tools and acting alone.[85] One of China's most well-known bloggers, Han Han, has written that some of these attackers may view their assaults as an effective way to take revenge on a society "that has no way out."[86]

China's PLA is a mighty force that commands the attention of the CCP, whom it is sworn to protect. Targeting both outer space and the deep waters, it is attempting to branch out beyond its long-held strength in numbers to become a diversified fighting force. Beijing's claims to disputed territories within the East China and South China Seas, including the open acknowledgment of the militarization of some of the islands (in direct violation of public statements), raise the likelihood of increased tensions over the control of the military and civilian presence in one of the busiest sets of shipping lanes in the world.[87]

Case Study: Indonesia

Economic protests, sectarian strife, international terrorism, and separatist violence: the Republic of Indonesia has experienced a range of violent expressions in recent decades. Since the late 1990s, Indonesia has faced considerable turmoil, from a major financial crisis to the loss of territory, bloody ethnic and religious conflict, as well as devastating natural disasters. Violence has seeped into many of these challenges.

Indonesia has long struggled with a military that takes matters into its own hands, especially during perceived times of crisis. Prior to the 2000s, military involvement was formally included in the bureaucracy at every level of civil government. Indonesian armed forces have traditionally filled in when there was a vacuum of civilian leadership (including building roads and linking regions to electrical grids), only withdrawing formally from politics in 2004, when their reserved seats in parliament were rescinded.

Riots, led by discontented students and angry middle-class Indonesians, broke out as Suharto clamped down on political expression in the mid-1990s, closing media outlets and political party offices, and later called in the military to quell economic riots in 1998. Suharto's successors failed to learn many valuable lessons about the instability caused by relying on the military to put down civic unrest. President Jokowi is wrestling with growing antiminority sentiment (especially fractured along religious and ethnic lines), known terrorist connections (even if Jakarta has achieved some success fighting terrorism),[88] as well as continued separatist leanings: areas in which the Indonesian military comfortably exerts its influence. Under such pressure, Jokowi, despite his lack of ties to the old military guard, began forging closer ties during his second year in office, leading to a possibly expanding role for the military in politics.[89] Heads definitely turned when Jokowi appointed Wiranto, the former military chief whose record has been tarnished with human rights violations, as the coordinating minister for politics and legal and security affairs.[90]

The fragile religious balance in many regions, held together before by the regime's *pancasila* (literally, "five principles") doctrine, is under strain. Although Muslims in Indonesia are overwhelmingly moderate, Muslim extremism in Indonesia has been on the rise since the late 1990s. Human Rights Watch has documented

a growing trend in violence against religious minorities, even as the Jokowi administration attempts to formally recognize their rights, even expanding beyond the constitutionally protected six main religions.[91] Democratic openings and international events have combined to encourage some "uncivil" groups, which were repressed during the Suharto years, to speak out.

Events suggest that there may be a shift in targets of religious extremism in Indonesia, including the discovery of a significant terrorist training camp in Aceh and headline-grabbing bank robberies that are believed to be sources of financing for extremist training. While foreign tourists were once the primary target, the Indonesian state itself, including police and even the president, is increasingly viewed as the enemy.[92] Yet some Indonesians' roles in regional and even international groups are also raising the specter of a growing challenge. One extremist Islamist group, Jemaah Islamiah (Islamic Organization) (JI), was implicated in the October 2002 attack on a nightclub in a resort area of Bali, which left nearly 200 people dead. This group, known for its desire to establish an Islamic state combining Malaysia, Indonesia, Singapore, and parts of the Philippines, is purported to have links to al-Qaeda, a charge its leaders deny. The Bali attacks killed many foreign tourists and severely curtailed the dominant tourist industry in the area. Jakarta was rocked by twin suicide bombings against luxury hotels frequented by foreigners in July 2009, and again an association with JI was alleged. The target of the 2009 attacks may have been a weekly gathering of Western businesspeople convened by "Mr. Indonesia," James Castle, who has long promoted Indonesia as a wise investment destination. Even if the attacks, which included the Jakarta Marriott (also the site of a car-bomb attack in 2003), weren't against Mr. Castle's group, the Marriott is "an iconic landmark that represents American ownership," in the words of one terrorism expert.[93]

Indonesia's most high-profile terrorist is the JI leader Riduan Isamuddin (known as "Hambali" and described as the Osama bin Laden of Southeast Asia). Apprehended in 2003, and a veteran of the war in Soviet-era Afghanistan, he is accused of helping plan or finance much of JI's activity since 2000, including devastating church and school bombings during Christmas Eve celebrations. He was captured in Thailand in 2003 and held in an undisclosed location before being transferred to Guantanamo. Even though he has sought release since 2010, he remains in US custody as a "high value" detainee and a crucial link between JI and al-Qaeda.[94] Indonesian officials have repeatedly requested that the US continue to hold him, placing him among the so-called "forever prisoners" of Guantanamo.[95]

Separatist violence has also challenged Indonesia in recent years, most visibly surrounding the East Timorese vote for independence. Turnout during the August 1999 poll was outstanding—98.6 percent of those eligible, of whom 78.5 percent rejected integration with Indonesia. Prior to the referendum, violence was a tool used by both sides; pro-integrationists were murdered, as were pro-separatists—often with machetes. After the referendum, violence became rampant, with government-sponsored militias engaged in "political cleansing."[96] The United Nations estimates a total death toll as high as 7,000, with up to 300,000 people displaced during the post-election violence (all of this in a population of 850,000).

Another area ripe with insurgent strife is Western Papua (known until 2007 as West Irian Jaya), on the Indonesian half of the island of Papua New Guinea (this western portion of New Guinea is home to two Indonesian provinces: Papua and Western

Papua). This province provides a classic example of the forced incorporation of a culture that has been sustained because of economic interests (the region has the world's largest copper and gold mines). Although the region was incorporated, as was the rest of Indonesia, by the Dutch, many of the indigenous Papuan people, who are distinct from the dominant Javanese throughout Indonesia, believed they would achieve their independence after the Dutch left, especially after the Dutch agreed to grant them self-rule. The Dutch formally transferred control of Papua to the United Nations, and then to Indonesia, with an agreement that indigenous Papuans would be able to decide, within six years, whether or not to remain part of Indonesia.[97] Indonesian military forces occupied the land in 1963, and the referendum on independence has never been permitted to take place. An autonomy law was promulgated in 2001 that earmarked some relevant government posts for native Papuans and guaranteed that up to 80 percent of the mineral wealth from the region would be returned to it. The murder of a prominent Papuan leader later that year placed the long-term viability of the accord in doubt, and Megawati Sukarnoputri effectively killed the deal when she issued a unilateral decree dividing Papua into three regions in early 2003.[98] Over a decade later, the legality of this partition remains disputed, both in Indonesia and beyond, and independence activists continue to lobby the UN for an independence referendum. This and other flashpoints across Indonesia are likely to continue to challenge political, military, and civil society leaders for years to come.

Now It's Your Turn

What has been the effect of catastrophic violence in the countries that have experienced it? What do you think it takes to become a revolutionary leader? Why are some leaders more successful than others at rallying people to implement change? Do any of our country case studies seem ripe for revolution? How would you compare the various responses of these governments to revolutionaries or perceived insurgents? Why do you think some people believe that violence is the only solution to their dilemmas? What would it take for you to adopt violent means of expression?

Notes

1. Rebecca Gordon, "The Failed War on Drugs in Mexico (and the United States)," *Moyers & Company,* March 27, 2015, http://billmoyers.com.

2. Shannon K. O'Neil, "Mexican-US Relations: What's Next?," *Americas Quarterly* (Council on Foreign Relations) (Spring 2010).

3. "Special Report: Mexico's Cartels Will Continue to Erode in 2016," *Stratfor Analysis,* January 25, 2016.

4. Michele Norris, "Tackling America's Drug Addiction," National Public Radio, *All Things Considered,* June 18, 2010; Enrique Krauze, "The Mexican Evolution," *New York Times,* March 24, 2009.

5. Beatriz Magaloni and Zaira Razu, "Mexico in the Grip of Violence," *Current History,* February 2016.

6. Gordon, "The Failed War on Drugs in Mexico (and the United States)"; Katy Watson, "Marijuana Law Reform: Mexico's President Changes Tack," BBC News, April 22, 2016.

7. Frank James, "Obama Rejects Hillary Clinton's Mexico-Colombia Comparison," National Public Radio, *The Two-Way,* September 9, 2010; Rory Carroll, "Hillary Clinton: Mexican Drug War Is Colombia-Style Insurgency," *The Guardian* (London), September 9, 2010.

8. Shannon O'Neil, "The Real War in Mexico," *Foreign Affairs,* July–August 2008.

9. Randal C. Archibold, "Mexican Leader Pushes Police Overhaul," *New York Times*, October 7, 2010; Marc Lacey, "Mexican Democracy, Even Under Siege," *New York Times*, July 5, 2010.

10. Magaloni and Razu, "Mexico in the Grip of Violence"; John Bailey, *The Politics of Crime in Mexico: Democratic Governance in a Security Trap* (Boulder: Lynne Rienner, 2014).

11. Azam Ahmed and Eric Schmitt, "Mexican Military Runs Up Body Count in Drug War," *New York Times*, May 26, 2016.

12. Elisabeth Malkin, "Report Accuses Mexico of Crimes Against Humanity in Drug War," *New York Times*, June 6, 2016.

13. Magaloni and Razu, "Mexico in the Grip of Violence"; Pamela K. Starr, "Mexico's Problematic Reforms," *Current History*, February 2014.

14. Ahmed and Schmitt, "Mexican Military Runs Up Body Count"; Mary Speck, "The 43 Missing Students Are Not Alone," *World Post*, May 9, 2016; Starr, "Mexico's Problematic Reforms."

15. Magaloni and Razu, "Mexico in the Grip of Violence"; Starr, "Mexico's Problematic Reforms"; Azam Ahmed, "Mexico Asks: What's Next After US Vote?," *New York Times*, November 15, 2016.

16. "Human Rights in Mexico: Untouchable?," *The Economist*, November 3, 2001; Kevin Sullivan and Mary Jordan, "Fox Takes Steps to End Army's Rights Abuses," *Washington Post*, November 11, 2001; Kevin Sullivan, "Memories of Massacre in Mexico," *Washington Post*, February 14, 2002; Ahmed and Schmitt, "Mexican Military Runs Up Body Count."

17. The name "Shining Path" comes from one of Peru's most prominent authors, Jose Carlos Mariategui, who wrote, "Marxist-Leninism will open the shining path to revolution."

18. M. Elaine Mar, "Violence in Peru: Shining Path Women," *Harvard Magazine*, May–June 1996; Cynthia McClintock, *Revolutionary Movements in Latin America* (Washington, DC: US Institute of Peace, 1998).

19. Guzmán broke with China after Mao's death, considering Deng to be a traitor to the revolution. Shining Path preferred its isolation and sought no external support.

20. Carlos Ivan Degregori, "After the Fall of Abimael Guzmán: The Limits of Sendero Luminoso," in *The Peruvian Labyrinth*, ed. Maxwell A. Cameron and Philip Mauceri (University Park: Pennsylvania State University Press, 1997).

21. Peter Flindell Klaren, *Peru: Society and Nationhood in the Andes* (New York: Oxford University Press, 2000); Ramiro Escobar, "Rights-Peru: Reparations Near for Victims of Civil War," Inter-Press Service, May 2, 2006.

22. Klaren, *Peru*.

23. Human Rights Watch, "Peru: Torture and Political Persecution in Peru," December 1997; US Department of State, *Country Reports on Human Rights, 2000* (Washington, DC: US Government Printing Office, 2000); Escobar, "Rights-Peru."

24. Degregori, "After the Fall of Abimael Guzmán"; McClintock, *Revolutionary Movements in Latin America*.

25. William Aviles, "Despite Insurgency: Reducing Military Prerogatives in Colombia and Peru," *Latin American Politics and Society* 51, no. 1 (Spring 2009).

26. "Fujimori Gets Lengthy Jail Term," BBC News, April 7, 2009.

27. Marco Aquino, "Peru Probes Whether Police Killed People to Earn Promotions, Rewards," Reuters, August 1, 2016.

28. Simon Romero, "Cocaine Trade Helps Rebels Reignite War in Peru," *New York Times*, March 17, 2009; "Peru 2016 Crime & Safety Report," Overseas Security Advisory Council, US Department of State, March 14, 2016.

29. Colin Post, "Shining Path Ambush Kills 10 on Eve of Peru's Election," *Peru Reports*, April 12, 2016.

30. "Peru 2016 Crime & Safety Report."

31. Ibid.; Aviles, "Despite Insurgency"; Barnett S. Koven, "The Second Image Sometimes Reversed: Competing Interests in Drug Policy," *E-International Relations*, March 8, 2016.

32. Peter M. Lewis and Pearl T. Robinson, *Stabilizing Nigeria* (New York: Century Foundation, 1998).

33. Toyin Falola, *The History of Nigeria* (Westport: Greenwood, 1999).

34. Ibid.

35. Felix Onuah, "Nigeria Says Has Pushed Boko Haram Out of All but Three Areas," *Reuters*, March 17, 2015.

36. Ibid.; "75,000 Children in Nigeria Could Starve to Death Within Months, Says UN," *Agence France-Presse*, November 15, 2016.

37. "Hope for a New Chapter in US-Nigerian Relations," *Washington Post,* July 23, 2015; James Schneider, "Buhari's Foreign Policy: Closer to Home Than America," *New African,* September 2, 2015; Brandon Kendhammer, "Nigeria's New Democratic Dawn?," *Current History,* May 2015; "Block the Sale of Warplanes to Nigeria," *New York Times,* May 18, 2016.

38. Kendhammer, "Nigeria's New Democratic Dawn?"; Adam Nossiter, "Killings Signal Violent Revival of Nigeria Sect," *New York Times,* October 19, 2010; Remi Adekoya, "Goodluck Jonathan's Report Card for Nigeria? Must Try Harder," *The Guardian* (London), May 7, 2013.

39. Dionne Searcey, "Boko Haram Leader Speaks on YouTube, Deepening Signs of Split," *New York Times,* August 4, 2016.

40. "Nigeria Bomb Toll Rises as Government Admits It Was Warned," *Reuters,* October 2, 2010; Tife Owolabi, "Military Sweep in Nigeria's Delta Risks Fuelling More Dissent," *Reuters,* June 10, 2016; Dionne Searcey, "Nigeria Finds a National Crisis in Every Direction It Turns," *New York Times,* July 17, 2016.

41. Adam Nossiter, "Poverty Could Imperil the Amnesty in Niger Delta," *New York Times,* November 27, 2009; Alex Perry, "In Nigeria, an Ailing President and Peace Process," *Time,* December 21, 2009; Chris Ewokor, "The Niger Delta Avengers: Nigeria's Newest Militants," *BBC Africa,* June 2, 2016.

42. Ewokor, "The Niger Delta Avengers"; Searcey, "Nigeria Finds a National Crisis."

43. Ewokor, "The Niger Delta Avengers"; "Curbing Violence in Nigeria (III): Revisiting the Niger Delta," Africa Report no. 231, International Crisis Group, September 29, 2015; Maggie Fick, "Nigeria: Running on Empty," *Financial Times,* May 30, 2016; Tife Owolabi, "Nigerian Militant Group Says Agrees on Ceasefire, Ready for Dialogue with Government," *Reuters,* August 21, 2016.

44. Kendhammer, "Nigeria's New Democratic Dawn?"; Ewokor, "The Niger Delta Avengers"; "Global Terrorism Index 2015," Institute for Economics and Peace, 2015.

45. D. E. Needham, E. K. Mashingaidze, and Ngwabi Bhebe, *From Iron Age to Independence: A History of Central Africa* (London: Longman, 1985).

46. Ibid.

47. Ngwabi Bhebe and Terence Ranger, "Volume Introduction: Society in Zimbabwe's Liberation War," in *Society in Zimbabwe's Liberation War,* ed. Ngwabi Bhebe and Terence Ranger (Oxford: Currey, 1996).

48. Ibid.

49. From this point on ZANU became known as ZANU-PF—with "PF" indicating "Patriotic Front."

50. Dickson A. Mungazi, *Colonial Policy and Conflict in Zimbabwe* (New York: Crane Russak, 1992).

51. Richard P. Werbner, "In Memory: A Heritage of War in Southwestern Zimbabwe," in Bhebe and Ranger, *Society in Zimbabwe's Liberation War.*

52. "Out in the Cold," *The Economist,* June 11, 2005.

53. Michael Bratton, *Power Politics in Zimbabwe* (Boulder: Lynne Rienner, 2014); MacDonald Dzirutwe, "No 'Arab Spring' in Zimbabwe, Mugabe Warns Protesters," *Reuters,* August 27, 2016.

54. Bratton, *Power Politics in Zimbabwe;* Celia W. Dugger, "Diamond Find Could Aid Zimbabwe, and Mugabe," *New York Times,* June 21, 2010; Celia W. Dugger, "Zimbabwe's Diamond Fields Enrich Ruling Party, Report Says," *New York Times,* June 26, 2009.

55. Dugger, "Diamond Find Could Aid Zimbabwe"; "Zim Targets $800M Annually from Marange Diamonds Chidhakwa," *Channel Zim,* May 4, 2016.

56. Bratton, *Power Politics in Zimbabwe;* Dumisani Muleya, "Mugabe Versus the Military," *Zimbabwe Independent,* June 17, 2016.

57. Tarek Osman, *Egypt on the Brink: From Nasser to Mubarak* (New Haven: Yale University Press, 2010).

58. "Egypt's Brazen Crackdown on Critics," *New York Times,* November 9, 2015; Paul R. Pillar, "Trouble Brewing in Egypt," *Washington Report on Middle East Affairs* 35, no. 4 (June–July 2016), pp. 37–39.

59. Jeremy M. Sharp, "Egypt: Background and US Relations," Congressional Research Service, February 5, 2016.

60. "Egypt's Rising Security Threat," Tahrir Institute for Middle East Policy, November 15, 2015.

61. Barry Rubin, "Revolutionary Salafi Islamists in Egypt: An Analysis and Guide," *Meria Journal* 17, no. 2 (June 1, 2013); "For Egypt, Islamic State One Threat Among Many," *Stratfor Analysis,* July 2015.

62. "CIA Director: US Hasn't Been Able to Curb IS Reach," *New York Times,* June 16, 2016.

63. "Sinai Province: Egypt's ISIS Affiliate," Wilson Center, May 19, 2016.

64. Thomas Chenesseau and Chantal Azzam, "Egypt," *Counter Terrorist Trends and Analysis* 7, no. 1 (January–February 2015).

65. "Sinai Province: Egypt's ISIS Affiliate"; Karen Yourish, Derek Watkins, and Tom Giratikanon, "Where ISIS Has Directed and Inspired Attacks Around the World," *New York Times,* March 22, 2016; "Croatian Hostage 'Killed by IS in Egypt,'" BBC News, August 12, 2015.

66. Sharp, "Egypt."

67. "For Egypt, Islamic State," *Stratfor Analysis.*

68. Sharp, "Egypt."

69. Ibid.

70. Kareem Fahim, "'Systematic' Killings in Egypt Are Tied to Leader, Group Says," *New York Times,* August 11, 2014.

71. Sharp, "Egypt"; "For Egypt, Islamic State," *Stratfor Analysis.*

72. Emad El-Din Shahin, "Egypt's Revolution Turned on Its Head," *Current History,* December 2015.

73. Jerrold D. Green, "Countermobilization in the Iranian Revolution," in *Revolutions: Theoretical, Comparative, and Historical Studies,* 2nd ed., ed. Jack A. Goldstone (New York: Harcourt Brace, 1994).

74. Mark J. Roberts, *Khomeini's Incorporation of the Iranian Military* (Washington, DC: Institute for National Strategic Studies, National Defense University, 1996).

75. Ibid.

76. Elliot Hen-Tov and Nathan Gonzalez, "The Militarization of Post-Khomeini Iran: Praetorianism 2.0," *Washington Quarterly* 34, no. 1 (2011).

77. Kasra Jani, "Iran's Revolutionary Guards Take Lead on Foreign Affairs," BBC News, January 29, 2015.

78. Ibid.

79. Walter Laqueur, *The New Terrorism: Fanaticism and the Arms of Mass Destruction* (New York: Oxford University Press, 1999).

80. Thomas Erdbrink, "Arrest of Homa Hoodfar in Iran Shines Light on Dangers for Dual Citizens," *New York Times,* June 9, 2016.

81. Mara Hvistendahl, "Hackers: The China Syndrome," *Popular Science,* April 23, 2009, www.popsci.com/scitech/article/2009-04/hackers-china-syndrome#.

82. Kristie Lu Stout, "Cyber Warfare: Who Is China Hacking Now?," *CNN News,* September 29, 2016.

83. Siobhan Gorman, August Cole, and Yochi Dreazen, "Computer Spies Breach Fighter-Jet Project," *Wall Street Journal,* April 21, 2009.

84. Stout, "Cyber Warfare."

85. Edward Wong, "Social Tensions Stoke School Attacks, China's Premier Says," *New York Times,* May 15, 2010, p. A5.

86. "Lone Madmen Without Guns," *The Economist,* May 12, 2010.

87. Bill Chappell, "In South China Sea Islands, Anti-Aircraft and Radar Systems Emerge in Full Color," National Public Radio, December 15, 2016.

88. Uri Friedman, "How Indonesia Beat Back Terrorism—for Now," *The Atlantic,* September 25, 2016.

89. Evan A. Laksmana, "Indonesia's Modernizing Military," *Foreign Affairs,* September 3, 2015.

90. Karlis Salnaa and Yudith Ho, "Jokowi Taps Ex-General amid Terrorism Threat, China Tensions," *Bloomberg,* July 27, 2016, www.bloomberg.com.

91. Human Rights Watch, "Indonesia: Events of 2015," in *World Report 2016* (Washington, DC, 2016), www.hrw.org.

92. Aubrey Belford, "Gunmen Storm Indonesian Police Station," *New York Times,* September 22, 2010.

93. Sidney Jones, interviewed by John M. Glionna, "Bombings, Business, and the Future of Indonesia," *Los Angeles Times,* July 19, 2009.

94. "Hunt for Hambali—the Osama of the Far East," *The Telegraph* (London), October 16, 2002; James Vicini, "Guantanamo Prisoner Known as Hambali Seeks Release," Reuters, March 11, 2010.

95. Louisa Loveluck, "High-Profile Guantanamo Prisoner Makes His First Appearance Before a Review Board," *Washington Post,* August 18, 2016, www.washingtonpost.com.

96. Ibid. This is the term Donald Emmerson, an election monitor with the Carter Center and a scholar of Indonesian politics, used to describe the situation.

97. "Indonesian Flashpoints: Papua," BBC News, October 22, 2010.

98. Ann Marie Murphy, "Indonesia and the World," in *Indonesia: The Great Transition,* ed. John Bresnan (New York: Rowman and Littlefield, 2005), p. 277.

Chapter 13

Transitions: Democracy, Dictatorship, and the Messy Middle

Nigerians treat power as a mistress, and something we would not want to share with anybody, not even a friend. —*Kayode Eso, retired Supreme Court justice*[1]

A country without free elections is a country without a voice, without eyes, without arms.
                                                    —*Octavio Paz, writer*[2]

There was a time—not all that long ago—when it appeared we were living in the so-called democratic age. In the mid-1990s, democracy, in its many variations, seemed to become the standard form of government, and freedom was making great strides, even in expected places. Yet for more than a decade now, analysts observe consecutive declines in the measure of global freedom, and the trends appear likely to continue.[3] As a recent Freedom House report contended, democracies are wavering under overlapping tensions, both external and internal, highlighting the tenuous nature of these complex (and often incomplete) processes.[4]

As you read in Chapter 11, violent conflicts and the military's tendency to assume political power pose a variety of problems for many countries. This certainly has an effect on political performance and the prospects for democracy in all of the regions we discuss. Ethnic and religious strife, as well as other divisions, create very real problems for governments—both democratic and nondemocratic—as well as for some countries that seem to fall in between these extremes, what some have termed "the messy middle"—hybrid forms of government that appear to be democratic (or not), yet defy simple regime type.[5] In the most difficult cases, even sovereignty, the state's right to exist, is contested. As in the cases of Israel and Somalia, there are often profound differences over who should be part of a political community or what should be its territorial boundaries. In a democracy, citizens agree that the government can make legitimate claims to their obedience. However, if the military or another powerful group of people does not accept these demands as legitimate, this poses serious problems for the viability of the government. Until such claims are resolved, democracy is imperiled, if not impossible.

What Is Democracy?

But before we can talk about how difficult it is to sustain, we should first ask ourselves, what is democracy? What makes a country democratic? Let us first say that there is wide disagreement over what should be emphasized when defining democracy. There is no single archetype for democracy, no single, unique set of institutions that are characteristic of democracy. In this chapter we will limit ourselves to a discussion of political democracy, as opposed to social or economic conceptions of democracy. As you will soon see, within political democracy there are different kinds of constitutional systems, and democracies vary widely in levels of citizen participation, access to power, checks and balances, governmental responsiveness to popular demands, party strength, and political pluralism. Therefore, in defining democracy we need to be as general as possible to allow for the many systems that are differently democratic.[6]

However, for all its variations, certain minimal criteria must be met for a political system to be considered democratic. Although governments satisfy these criteria to different degrees (and none of them perfectly), three conditions are commonly named as essential to any democracy: the existence of competition, participation, and respect for civil liberties. With the identification of these common denominators we can begin to define democracy. Democracy is one type of political system. As opposed to systems of authoritarianism, in which decisionmaking power is concentrated in the hands of a few and authority is unchallengeable, democracies are based in the decentralization of authority. In democracies citizens take part in making the decisions of government. Put more simply, democracy is a system of governance in which citizens hold their leaders accountable for their public actions. Accountability is ensured through open competition for office. Democracy institutionalizes competition for power through elections that are free and fair and held on a regular basis.[7]

But another important part of competition is inclusiveness, which demands a high level of political participation in the selection of leaders and policies. Where government makes room for people to add their voices, the political process has been opened up to promote effective political participation.[8] In a democracy, citizens should be able to influence public policy. At its core, democratization entails the accommodation of a wide range of opinions. For a country to be considered a democracy, there must be room for a lively and vibrant civil society, with active parties, trade unions, and religious and cultural groups that operate independently of the regime. Of course, it is also expected that people will be free to organize and express themselves without worry of harassment or imprisonment. This is necessary to satisfy the democratic requirements of both participation and competition.

Therefore, participation is expressed as the right of all citizens to take part in the democratic process. "Taking part" can mean any number of things, but it must at the very least include the right to political equality. In democracies there should be very few restrictions on the citizen's right to vote or run for office. No one should be excluded because of gender, ethnicity, religion, class, or sexual orientation. Neither should there be a property or literacy requirement for citizens to participate in the process. The greater the number of people who are denied citizenship and whose opportunities are hurt by such denial, the more unlikely states will be able to achieve a consolidation of democracy, or make it durable. Democratic governments will take pains to be inclusive, to ensure collective as well as individual rights, to ensure that

minority and traditionally oppressed groups have equal representation, and to ensure that the votes of all citizens are weighted equally (one person, one vote).[9]

The term "free" is often used synonymously with the term "democratic." According to the human rights organization Freedom House, the number of countries defined as "free" nearly doubled from 69 in 1989 to 120 in 2000, but fell significantly, to 89, by 2016, continuing the longest downward trend in freedom since Freedom House began the report nearly five decades ago.[10] Less than half the world's population lives in countries ranked as free; in terms of regions, the Middle East is the least free, but Latin America and Africa have witnessed declines as well. The only region that has reported some (modest) progress is the Asia-Pacific, although 42 percent of the population there lives in countries ranked as "not free."[11]

What does "freedom" mean? Countries, or to be more precise, political systems, that are termed "free" generally allow for a high degree of political and civil freedoms, but they do so to varying degrees. Some people offer up the sheer number of elections held in the late twentieth century as evidence that a democratic revolution has taken place. They identify elections as the watershed event marking the democratic transition and treat democracy as an event rather than a process. This is problematic for a variety of reasons. Elections can sometimes result in a setback for democracy, especially if antidemocratic candidates are elected or if divides are deep and elections are perceived as win-or-lose events. This is why democracy must be rooted in a political culture that promotes popular participation, one that tolerates differences and accepts the consensus.[12]

Although there have been significant setbacks over the past few years, it is remarkable that between 1990 and 2005, forty-four of forty-eight countries in sub-Saharan Africa held multiparty elections, compared to only four African countries in 1990.[13] In East Asia in the 1980s, only Japan was considered democratic. Thirty years later, there were five more states in that region holding multiparty elections: Indonesia, Mongolia, Myanmar, South Korea, and Timor-Leste.[14] However, elections alone do not make a democracy. Rather, democracies have electoral and non-electoral dimensions. Be careful not to fall for the FALLACY OF ELECTORALISM, or the tendency to focus on elections while ignoring other political realities. Many countries have gone through the motions of elections, yet power remains in the hands of an oligarchy or the military. Or there are civilian leaders but without broad, unconditional, mass support for democracy or a clear disavowal of authoritarianism.[15] As we will see, individual countries have made significant progress in some areas of political and civil rights, but there are still other crucial reforms that these countries need to address. How rulers come to power is important, but just as important is the strength of democratic institutions and whether they can hold elected leaders accountable for their actions. In determining the success of a democratic transition, it is more important to ask whether the rule of law prevails and whether an independent, impartial judiciary guarantees the protection of political and civil rights, rather than simply relying on the "litmus test" of elections. As of 2015, there were 125 electoral democracies around the world.[16]

Democracies that pass a more comprehensive test are commonly known as LIBERAL DEMOCRACIES. As opposed to the minimal framework of electoral democracies, liberal democracies are based on a deeper institutional structure that offers extensive protections for civil and political rights—individual and group liberties such

as freedom of thought and expression, freedom of the press, and the right to form and join assemblies or organizations, including political parties and interest groups. Where civil rights are protected, people feel that they have the freedom to participate in the political process. Democratizing societies will encourage civil society to flourish, and encourage political parties and interest groups to organize without constraint. Again, there are no perfect democracies. No country completely lives up to all the standards listed here. And what can start as a major political transformation can turn out in a variety of ways.

For example, transitions frequently become sidelined by disputes between democrats over the meaning of freedom, the best constitutional and electoral system, or whether to organize as a unitary or federal state. All democracies, even the most established ones, must continuously work to improve their democratic practices. For example, the economic inequality that exists in the United States (and in every democracy to some degree) has the effect of skewing political power. Despite claims of political equality, the affluent are "more equal than others," because they can use their resources to exert disproportionate influence over policy.[17]

Because of problems with democratic practice, often the line between democratic and nondemocratic regimes is unclear. Several countries are hard to place because they may satisfy some requirements of democracy but not others. Governments that are characterized as "free" or "democratic" commonly experience isolated violations of civil liberties or occasional electoral malpractice. However, they are considered democratic because they meet certain minimal standards (e.g., it must be possible for the ruling party to be voted out of power through a fair electoral process, with basic freedoms continuing into the future). New democracies differ markedly from one another, with varying strengths and weaknesses. Since a "third wave" of democratization began in 1974, more than eighty countries have made significant progress toward democracy. However, contrary to popular belief, there is no end point at which a country can be said to have "attained" democracy. It should be expected that it will take some time for appropriate political systems to be created, and that they will evolve at least partly in response to political failures. Around the world, many in the wave of countries that made a democratic transition have reversed themselves. For example, Mexico had been ranked as "free" for several years, but in 2010 Freedom House dropped its rating to "partly free," largely because of problems associated with its ongoing drug wars—a lowered status that continued through 2016.[18]

Therefore, democratization is something that should be understood as an ongoing, dynamic process instead of a singular achievement. Just as we recognize that some countries may come closer to fitting the democratic ideal than others, we must recognize that a similar continuum exists for their less-than-democratic counterparts. In the end, most governments fall somewhere in between the two poles of democracy and totalitarianism, an extreme form of authoritarianism. Many governments allow for more freedoms than do rigidly totalitarian regimes, but these freedoms are so few that such governments cannot adequately qualify as democracies. As you will see in the next chapter, there is an unusually large array of names for those systems that fall in the "messy middle": somewhere in between. For example, many global south governments, including those of Nigeria or Iran (at the opposite ends of this range), can be viewed as delegative democracies: they are neither liberal democracies nor full-blown dictatorships. Delegative democracies are sometimes

Figure 13.1   Respect for Political and Civil Rights: How Our Cases Rate

Freedom House is a highly respected nongovernmental organization that monitors democratization and human rights worldwide. As part of its work the organization rates every country based on its respect for political rights and civil liberties. Here is how our cases ranked in 2015:

Mexico: Partly Free
Peru: Free

Nigeria: Partly Free
Zimbabwe: Partly Free
Egypt: Not Free
Iran: Not Free
China: Not Free
Indonesia: Partly Free

Source: Freedom House, *Freedom in the World 2016, https://freedomhouse.org.*

called democratic because they have an outward appearance similar to that of their more democratic counterparts. However, delegative democracies are led by elites whose commitment to democracy is contingent and instrumental, not routinized, internalized, and principled.[19] Delegative democracies are a peculiar form of democracy; through competitive elections a majority empowers someone to become the embodiment and interpreter of the nation's interests. No, this doesn't sound very democratic, but as Guillermo O'Donnell contends, delegative democracies can sometimes be more democratic than they are authoritarian. What is important to remember is that even though some governments are doing a better job of promoting certain aspects of democracy than are others, the success is relative and the work is ongoing.[20] A similar concern is raised by the in-between examples, what some have called pseudo-democracies or electoral authoritarian regimes: there are a variety of complex processes involved in governing, and labels can sometimes gloss over achievements (as well as detriments).[21]

Background to the Transition

As mentioned earlier, starting in the 1970s and accelerating through the 1990s, a number of what were sometimes characterized as stunning political changes occurred throughout the world, including the global south. The winding down of the Cold War coincided with a period of what some called a global democratic revolution, as a "third wave" of prodemocracy movements rose up not only in Europe, but also in sub-Saharan Africa, Asia, Latin America, and to a lesser extent the Middle East (the Middle East and North Africa's third wave mostly came later, with the Arab Spring of 2011). Some analysts have characterized the 1970s–1990s as a critical historical moment, "the greatest period of democratic ferment in the history of modern civilization."[22] Much of this commotion grew out of an ABERTURA, or a political opening, associated with a mix of reforms. Countries undertaking such reforms are often described as experiencing a political liberalization. Periods of political liberalization are generally associated with a variety of changes such as greater press freedoms, greater freedom of assembly, and the introduction of legal safeguards for individuals. People living in countries experiencing a political liberalization witness the release of most political prisoners, the return of exiles, and perhaps most important, a growing tolerance of dissent.

At the end of 2016, nearly 40 percent of the world's population was living in countries that could claim to be broadly democratic, with 36 percent living in countries characterized as "not free" (more than half of them living in China alone).[23] However, not all governments that can be described as "broadly democratic" are necessarily headed toward democracy. As O'Donnell has noted, not all processes culminate in the same result. For example, at times over the past decade and a half, China and Iran have been said to have liberalized politically, but this does not mean that they are democratizing or are in the process of a democratic transition. China and Iran do not appear to be on their way toward adopting the kind of political system that the West usually considers democratic. And in both countries, even as gains are made, they can be quickly retracted (as happened with Iran's Green Movement in 2009). On the other hand, what was remarkable about the "third wave" was not only the sheer number of countries that made political reforms, but also the number that began a democratic transition of one kind or another. In understanding how so many countries arrived at this point, it is important to recognize that each country's situation is unique; its citizens are responding to a particular set of historical challenges and socioeconomic problems. Consequently, no single set of determinants can satisfactorily explain the origins and evolution of democratic transitions throughout the world.[24]

As you will recall from Chapter 9, some analysts emphasize the significance of internal factors in understanding change. Their interest is the roles played by domestic actors, whether elites or masses, in the dramatic political events we've been describing. The preceding chapters have demonstrated how people around the world are mobilized by a variety of pressures. Citizens have demanded the opening of political space in which a variety of new relationships can be crafted. Not all of these groups are mobilized by democratic interests, yet whatever their goals, new forms of social mobilization and patterns of state-society relations are emerging in which relationships of power and accountability are redefined. Yet often it has been political elites who have played crucial roles in the political transition. Frustrated over their inability to govern effectively or faced with a crisis of legitimacy, civilian and military leaders have on occasion stood aside to allow for democratic change. Once the transition is under way, elite commitment to democracy (or the lack of such commitment) has often played a large role in its success or failure.

Other analysts emphasize the role played by economic forces in promoting political change. They contend, for example, that the industrialization and economic success of South Korea and Taiwan created in these countries an environment conducive to democratization. There and elsewhere, as the middle class has grown, these citizens have become more politically conscious and vocal in demanding political and civil rights. However, around the world it is more common to find that political change has occurred as people have struggled to cope with devastating economic crises. There are cases from all four regions we study in which the hardship associated with austerity incited popular protests that nearly brought down governments, democratic and nondemocratic. In the immediate post–Cold War period (and since), such demonstrations often persuaded authoritarians to initiate political reform—or at least to effect the appearance of reform.

Although the political liberalization of some countries predated the end of the Cold War, external pressures associated with its demise (such as the withdrawal of superpower support for authoritarians) are recognized as another factor driving re-

Figure 13.2 Is Democracy Universally Desirable?

Operating under the assumption that "all good things go together," starting in the late 1980s, donor countries began pressuring aid recipients to show that they were making political as well as economic reforms. The targets of these reforms frequently criticized such interference with domestic politics, for a variety of reasons. One problem was that developed countries, with their emphasis on political and civil rights over economic and social rights, were arbitrarily assigning certain values as democratic. Advocates of what is called the "Asian values" argument contend that democracy is a Western concept not traditional to most of the world's cultures. Just as cultures that contain a democratic tradition have a better chance of making democracy work, those having little or no experience with democracy face significant disadvantages. These analysts argue that democracy has failed to take root in much of the world because it is not generally accepted there. They contend that it is ethnocentric to assume that democracy is a universal value, because under this definition, democratic values (such as individualism) are unique to the West.[a] Moreover, the West's insistence on respect for democracy, political and civil rights, and environmental concerns is hypocritical, since its own progress in these areas leaves much to be desired. Such an argument is difficult to dispute. Yet democratic principles are hardly unique to the West, just as authoritarian impulse is scarcely restricted to the global south.[b]

Notes: a. Malaysia's Mahathir Mohammad was the strongest spokesperson for this exceptionalist view, which continues to be advocated by some global south leaders. Modern Chinese leaders, for example, continue to argue that universal standards for human rights simply do not exist; rather, developed countries use these standards as a guise for meddling in the internal affairs of other countries. Chinese leaders emphasize that different levels of economic development and political conditions justify varying approaches toward rights and democracy.

b. Amartya Sen, "Democracy as a Universal Value," *Journal of Democracy* 10, no. 3 (July 1999).

form. Yet even now the governments of many countries in the global south continue to be highly extroverted; their survival depends on foreign patronage. As discussed in Chapter 7, since the 1970s, in return for aid, international organizations such as the International Monetary Fund (IMF) have directed developing countries to impose economic reforms on their increasingly disgruntled populations. However, after the Cold War ended, donor countries began to insist that governments throughout the global south initiate political reforms aimed at promoting "good governance"—increasing the accountability and transparency of government.[25] This is the "all good things go together" argument: proponents of neoliberalism tend to assume that economic growth and democratization complement each other and are mutually reinforcing (although there is still disagreement about which comes first).[26] However, the developed countries have never been consistent in their demands for political liberalization; the vigor with which such calls were made varied depending on the target of reform (e.g., for strategic and economic reasons, most Middle Eastern countries were largely exempt from donor attention).

A variety of other external factors have also been used to explain the recent political changes experienced in so much of the world. Some analysts credit the dramatic events of the late twentieth century to a zeitgeist (or "spirit of the times"), unique to the immediate post–Cold War era, because at that moment in history democracy appeared to be breaking out all over the world and democratic ideology had no serious contenders. This zeitgeist is believed by some to have contributed to

a snowballing or demonstration effect as authoritarian governments toppled like dominos.[27] Analysts interested in this facet of change argue that among states closely linked by culture, geography, or some other shared experience, the more successful a transition in any one country in the group, the more likely we are to see similar political change among the other members of that group. This effect has been magnified by the revolution in communications, in particular satellite television, which allows outsiders to watch events literally as they unfold. The intriguing role that this technology plays in political change is only one part of an "international diffusion effect" (what some call the "Twitter effect"), which can change leaders' expectations, affect crowd behavior, and even alter the balance of power almost overnight. Although such effects have mostly been associated with the military coups and the collapse of civilian rule, during the past three decades the information revolution has also worked to support a resurgence of democracy, even if its use is sometimes confined to more secular, affluent, and often bilingual elite, as we observed in the Arab Spring, for example.[28]

After the Transition: Consolidating and Deepening Democracy

One way to understand the resurgence of democracy is to think of it as occurring in phases. Some have taken just the very first (often tentative) step. For example, in late 2016, after twenty-two years of repressive rule, Gambia's dictator (who said he was ready to rule for "a billion years, if God wills it") finally allowed himself to lose elections—but resisted handing over power to the winner until he was able to negotiate his exit, taking a plane full of luxury cars and cash with him.[29] Of the political systems that are democratizing, most have just made the transition from authoritarian rule and begun to establish democratic regimes in the past decade or two. While they vary in terms of the quality of democracy, many countries, including South Africa and Ghana, South Korea and Taiwan, and most of Latin America are well into a second phase of democratization, known as consolidation. When is a democratic transition complete? According to analysts Juan Linz and Alfred Stepan, it is complete when there is sufficient agreement about the political procedures to produce an elected government. It is complete when a government comes to power as the direct result of a free and popular vote, and when this government has the authority to generate new policies. Finally, a democratic transition is complete when we can be sure that the executive, legislative, and judicial power generated by the new democracy is not subservient to other bodies such as the military. Most important perhaps, all politically significant groups agree to abide by the procedural rules of the game. In effect, a democracy has progressed from transition to consolidation when no significant political groups are seriously trying to overthrow the democratic regime or secede from the state.[30] These are the democratic rules and procedures that must be established before one can begin to speak of consolidation.

Even when a transition can be described as complete, there are still many tasks that must be accomplished, conditions that must be established, and culture (attitudes and habits) that must be developed before democracy can be considered durable, or consolidated. How do we know when a democracy has been consolidated? Analysts admit that it is easier to recognize consolidation by its absence. Unconsolidated regimes are fragile, unstable, and plagued by signs of disloyalty.

Figure 13.3   When Islamists Win Elections

Algeria's experience, as well as that of the Palestinians, and Egypt's, have been a lesson for many people seeking change in predominantly Muslim North Africa and the Middle East. Under a variety of pressures for political liberalization, Algeria's authoritarian government allowed democratic elections in 1991. A number of parties organized to participate in these elections, among them the Islamic Salvation Front (FIS), an umbrella party representing many smaller Islamist groups. When the FIS was poised to win a strong majority of seats in a second round of parliamentary elections in 1992, the Algerian government (with the tacit backing of France and the United States) voided the elections, declared the FIS illegal, and set out on a campaign to portray all Islamist contenders for power as a threat to democracy in Algeria and to the West. Supporters of this policy argued that Islamists were totalitarians in disguise, adopting the rhetoric of democracy only to gain power. What happened in Algeria confirmed views of the West as hypocritically supporting democracy only when in its own interests.

In 2006, after the Palestinian movement Hamas won a surprise landslide victory in parliamentary elections, the United States led a group of Western states that immediately set out to isolate and undermine the new democratically elected government (designated by the United States as a terrorist organization because of its attacks on Israel). Similarly, the West was criticized as slow to support Arab Spring uprisings in 2011, including in Egypt, as it feared the Islamist Muslim Brotherhood would move into the vacuum created by President Mubarak's departure. The Brotherhood did move in to that vacuum. Its candidate, Mohammad Morsi, was the first democratically elected president of Egypt and it won more seats in parliament than any other political party. But Egypt's divisions only deepened during its year in power. When the military stepped in to put an end to this experiment in democracy, the Obama administration, which insisted it wasn't taking sides, voiced its deep concern and called for a return to democratic rule. But the United States was also careful not to call it a coup—so as not to imperil US military and economic assistance to Egypt, and Egypt's peace with Israel.[a] The United States has fully resumed its partnership with Egypt, which (under former general Sisi) has resumed its dictatorship.

While such a response may seem reasonable to some, this perceived ambivalence about democracy is problematic—particularly in the Middle East. Whether the United States likes it or not, the Islamist appeal has grown and exists in all Arab countries, and this may be as much due to sympathy for Islamist programs as it is based in resentment of corrupt government and Western hypocrisy.[b]

Notes: a. Dan Roberts, "US in Bind over Egypt After Supporting Morsi but Encouraging Protesters," *The Guardian* (London), July 3, 2013, www.theguardian.com.

b. Emmanuel Sivan, "Illusions of Change," *Journal of Democracy* 11, no. 3 (July 2000); Laith Kubba, "The Awakening of Civil Society," *Journal of Democracy* 11, no. 3 (July 2000).

Beyond this it is hard to define consolidation, because no single indicator other than general stability serves as its marker. We know that the road to consolidation is a long and complicated one. Perhaps the simplest way of telling if consolidation exists is if democracy has become "the only game in town." The majority of people believe that the system is a good one, and that it is the most appropriate way of governing collective life.[31] When this is the case, the regime enjoys broad and deep levels of popular legitimacy.

When a democracy is consolidated, the issue for government is no longer how to avoid democratic breakdown. You know you have a consolidated democracy when, even in the face of extreme economic or political hardship, the overwhelming majority

of people believe that any political change must occur through the democratic system. All political actors have become accustomed to the idea that political conflict will be resolved according to the established rules, and convinced that violations of these rules will be ineffective and costly. In other words, when it is consolidated, democracy becomes a habit; it is routinized and widely accepted. This takes years of practice—some political scientists argue that two generations of uninterrupted democratic rule must pass, allowing the rules of the game to be refined, tested, and strengthened. In Latin America, for example, although several others are consolidating, only Costa Rica is widely considered to be a consolidated democracy.[32]

How do we ensure that democracy lasts that long? Democratic stability is promoted when the rights of the political opposition and minorities are safeguarded. That may sound counterproductive, especially where divisions are deep, but analysts tell us that conflict becomes less intense as it is contained within institutional channels. Most important, over time there is a change in the political culture of elites and masses, as commitment to the democratic framework is no longer simply instrumental but rather a commitment based in principle. As democracies consolidate, we gradually see within them the development of what some analysts call a "civic culture." Although mutual trust between potential opponents, willingness to compromise, and cooperation between political competitors are all identified as key components of civic culture, the particulars of any democratic political culture will vary by country.[33] In general, though, as consolidation proceeds, political elites and the masses gradually internalize democratic values and develop habits of tolerance and moderation. Rights become realities and there is an agreed standard of fairness. Of course, this balanced political culture is only likely to occur where inequalities are relatively low and people can afford not to care too much about politics—and such circumstances do not yet exist in most new democracies. As one analyst put it, "The trick, then, is for democracies to survive long enough—and function well enough—for this process to occur."[34]

In other words, consolidation is another breakthrough of sorts. It is fostered through a combination of institutional, policy, and behavioral changes and is an important achievement for any budding democracy. Yet just because a regime is consolidated does not mean that it is immune to future breakdown. Any number of crises could occur to make a nondemocratic alternative attractive and undo even a consolidated regime. One way of avoiding such breakdown is by recognizing the intimate connection between consolidation and the deepening of democracy. This qualitative shift is sometimes described as a third phase of democratization. Democracies are deepened as they improve, by promoting equality and extending to more citizens the opportunity for participation in political life. By this definition, even older, more established democracies may still become more democratic. All democracies can be improved—that is, made more responsive and representative.[35]

At this stage countries often find themselves in a Catch-22 situation. In what is sometimes called "the democratic dilemma," democracies need to be deepened in order to fully consolidate. However, the deepening of democracy can undermine the prospects of consolidation. Deepening democracy means addressing social and economic inequalities, and this is likely to threaten elite interests and provoke an authoritarian reaction. Consequently, in the short term at least, the most stable democracies are also often the most superficial ones—the ones that forestall neces-

sary changes to minimize the risk of coup. Ironically, because they are defective, "shells of what they could be," these democracies ultimately fail.[36] Incapable or unwilling to deal with the problems of massive inequality, they are vulnerable to "reverse waves" or democratic breakdowns. Such democratic breakdowns should be expected, just as they followed the first and second waves of democratization earlier in the twentieth century. These reverse waves have been traumatic times for human rights and international peace; they gave rise to fascist and communist regimes in the period between World Wars I and II, as well as military dictatorships in the 1960s and 1970s.[37]

Is there any indication that the world is headed in this direction again? Some maintain that the news isn't so bad, in part because things hadn't improved as much as we thought. The number of countries actually embarking on democratic transitions was always overblown. As we will discuss later, there are plenty of examples of "virtual democracies."[38] But nearly two decades into the twenty-first century there were troubling signs that support for democracy in some developing countries was eroding. Since the Great Recession, the number of democracies has stagnated, according to Freedom House, with more than a hundred countries declining in freedom.[39] The expected reverse wave appeared to be hitting all regions, even Latin America, the region furthest along in its transition. For example, a 2014 survey conducted by the highly respected polling organization Latinobarómetro found a continued decline in satisfaction with the level of democratic performance in their country: while 56 percent of citizens support democracy, only 39 percent were satisfied with its performance, with significant concerns about corruption and economic performance.[40] Popular support for democracy continued to be lowest in Paraguay, where a strong authoritarian streak remains: 32 percent of Paraguayans polled stated that in certain circumstances an authoritarian government might be preferable to a democratic one. Paraguay's numbers on this question were significantly higher than those found anywhere else.[41]

While such findings are striking, analysts insist that the lesson to take away from all of this is that democracy is slowing but steadily consolidating. And Latin America's experience is hardly unique. The same questions posed in Asia and Africa elicited similar responses. In its survey of thirteen East Asian countries, Asian Barometer found that the majority polled (outside of China) supported democracy, but that because so many people had little experience with democratic politics and because neither authoritarianism nor democracy were credited with being particularly effective at improving their lives, to some degree many people embraced both authoritarianism and democracy concurrently. This is likely the case elsewhere as well. While just over seven out of ten of those surveyed in nineteen African countries in 2013 said that democracy was always preferable to other forms of government (71 percent), only 46 percent reject all alternative forms of autocratic rule.[42]

Such a relationship hardly provides the best foundation for a successful democracy, but leaders, given the pressures weighing on them, might find it useful. Since the end of the Cold War, leaders in the global south have been faced with donor pressure to democratize (in addition to juggling myriad preexisting and new social, economic, and political crises). These pressures and crises have been managed in a variety of ways. The result, however loosely defined, is a fascinating array of variations on democracy. Catherine Boone identifies the most common manifestations of this crisis management as reform, RECONFIGURATION, and disintegration. In the next section

and continuing into the next chapter we will describe these forms of crisis management as practiced throughout the global south. However, the particulars vary by country, and whether a political system has reformed, reconfigured, or disintegrated can at least in part be explained by the structural differences among states. Individual decisions must also be factored in, as people worldwide make choices and take actions in response to the unique predicaments they face. In other words, just as the extent of the crisis each country faces is a function of the relative weakness of the regime and the strength of the pressures bearing on it, so too is the outcome.[43]

Reform

To review the fundamentals, for a political system to be considered a democracy it must be based in certain principles such as participation, representation, accountability, and respect for human rights. No government has a perfect record in this regard; however, some countries have made more progress in certain areas than in others. Long-standing, well-established democracies exist in India, Costa Rica, Botswana, Mauritius, and a handful of other global south countries. Given the diversity of these countries, it should come as no surprise that no single set of institutions, practices, and values embodies democracy. Similarly, various mixes of these components produce different types of constitutional systems. However, most democracies operate under some variant of the parliamentary system or the presidential system. Although US citizens are most familiar with the presidential system, which is also found in much of Latin America and scattered throughout Africa and Asia, the largest democracy in the world, India, has a parliamentary system, and parliamentary systems are the norm in Europe.

This is significant, since some analysts argue that the choice of constitutional design and electoral system may impact the quality and stability of democracy. There are pros and cons to each constitutional system, and each system involves some trade-offs. Analysts disagree about which is best for developing countries. One group, led by Juan Linz, argues that although the presidential system has worked well for the United States, its record in low-income countries is more problematic. The presidential system tends to concentrate power in the executive branch, perhaps making the president too strong and (where there is little commitment to democratic values or practices) facilitating the abuse of power.[44] In Peru, Zimbabwe, South Korea, and elsewhere, presidential systems have been associated with executive coups (self-coups) and executive strikes against democracy.

This is one of "the perils of presidentialism," based in the tendency for executives in presidential systems to view themselves as having authority independent of the other branches of government. Even when they have won by the slimmest of margins, presidents are more likely than prime ministers to find opposition in the legislative branch irritating and to consider it an interference with their mission. Not all presidential systems suffer from this problem, but where presidentialism exists, whoever is elected president believes he or she has a mandate, or the right to govern as he or she sees fit. Under such circumstances, the executive is constrained only by the "hard facts of existing power relations" and the constitutionally limited term of office.[45]

It might appear that such an approach does not build a strong basis for the development of democratic institutions. Not only does presidentialism adversely af-

fect the quality of democracy, but it is also commonly viewed as a major factor contributing to democratic breakdowns. Part of the reason for this is lack of capacity: while a strong executive is capable of making rapid decisions, it is often less proficient at coping with crises. For example, former Nigerian president Umaru Yar'Adua was so unimpressive and invisible in his first year in office that he was nicknamed "Baba Go-Slow."[46] Still, some presidential regimes (including Nigeria's) have survived extremely difficult challenges. But where there is presidentialism, gridlock (resulting from the mix of a domineering president and a newly assertive legislature) is more likely. And some analysts contend that presidencies tend to be more rigid and are less likely to avail themselves of the creative approaches demanded by most crises.[47]

Fearful that mounting problems will overwhelm a weak or inexperienced government, voters tend to create presidentialist regimes, as they frequently flock to candidates who promise to save the country. Such leaders appear to be strong, courageous, and above partisan interests. This image is very seductive, especially for people who have lived through difficult or uncertain times. Consequently, we should not be shocked by the frequency of presidentialism. It is important to remember that democratic elections are not an end unto themselves. Newly democratizing countries can be expected to continue on in a transition that is not necessarily linear in its progression. There is rarely a simple trajectory from authoritarian to democratic rule; transitions are often longer and more complex. This is in part because the values and beliefs of officials are embedded in a network of inherited power relations and do not change overnight. This helps to explain why elections in newly democratizing countries can be such emotional and high-stakes events. Often the candidates compete for a chance to rule virtually free of all constraints. After the elections, voters are expected to become passive cheerleaders for all of the president's policies.[48]

For these reasons, parliamentary systems are described by Linz as better suited for most countries. According to Linz, parliamentary systems are more stable and more representative than presidential systems. In parliamentary regimes the only democratically legitimate institution is parliament. The executive's authority is completely dependent upon parliamentary confidence. As opposed to presidential systems (in which the executive is usually selected through direct popular elections), in parliamentary systems there is no worry about executives reaching out to appeal to people over the heads of their representatives.[49]

However, Donald Horowitz argues that parliamentary systems can actually end up more polarized and coalitions can end up more unstable than they are in presidential systems, and that this can impede the business of governance. Unlike presidential systems, parliamentary governments risk periodic crises (known as votes of "no confidence") that can result in the ousting of executives and the disruption caused by new elections. On the other hand, Linz argues that what appears to be instability in parliamentary governments can actually be a benefit: since parliamentary systems are more flexible, they are self-correcting. Moreover, Linz contends that fragmentation is not a problem unique to parliamentary systems. Because there are fewer incentives to make coalitions in a presidential system, gridlock is a persistent problem and the legislative and executive branches end up competing against each other rather than working together. Although coalitions and power-sharing are possible under such systems, more often the institutional rivalry associated with

the separation of powers in a presidential system can be extremely destabilizing, especially for unconsolidated democracies.[50]

The tendency of presidential systems toward majoritarianism (in which majorities govern and minorities oppose) makes politics a winner-take-all zero-sum game. Because it creates a sharp divide between the government and the opposition, majoritarianism aggravates divisiveness in countries where it is already a problem. What one wins, the other loses. However, the zero-sum nature of majoritarian politics is also associated with parliamentary systems such as those of Britain, India, Jamaica, and Sri Lanka. In parliaments dominated by a single majority party, this party controls both the executive and legislative branches. Consequently, the prime minister may end up having more effective power than that of the typical president.[51]

Still, not all parliamentary systems are majoritarian. Some forms of parliamentary government tend to be multiparty and to create governments built on what is called a consensus model. As opposed to the sharp divides of majoritarianism, the consensus model found in Turkey and most of continental Europe attempts to share, disperse, and restrain power in a variety of ways. For example, under the consensus model a parliamentary government can promote the creation of broad coalition cabinets and an executive-legislative balance of power. According to Linz, in such parliamentary systems the executive is more accountable before the legislature. This is important, since in deeply divided societies it is crucial that particular groups not be excluded. Government must work to build consensus and give everyone a stake in the system by encouraging coalitions. Yet in presidential systems gridlock is not always the rule and conciliatory practices are not unknown. Actually, some analysts argue that the mode of election (such as single member versus proportional representation) is more important in fostering conciliation and consensus building than whether the constitutional system is parliamentary or presidential.[52]

An additional factor considered in these debates concerns another aspect of rigidity versus flexibility. The proponents of presidential systems argue that the rigidity of fixed presidential terms is an advantage as opposed to the uncertainty and instability that are characteristic of parliamentary politics. However, there are also disadvantages to the inflexibility of presidential systems. Not only is reelection possible only on a fixed term, but it is also very difficult to impeach or remove a president from power before his or her term is over. As a result, the country may be stuck with a "lame duck" government that has lost public confidence and support. Or, because of fixed terms and limits on reelection, experienced and capable leaders must step down at the end of their terms.[53]

Conversely, advocates of parliamentary systems say that such systems are advantaged by their greater flexibility and adaptability. With a vote of "no confidence," in which the majority of members of parliament vote to "censure" the prime minister, the legislative branch can force new elections to be called at any time to turn out an executive who has lost popular support—without regime crisis. And popular, effective executives can be retained indefinitely, whereas a president may be required to retire just as he or she is becoming an adept leader. Moreover, because in presidential systems the executive is both head of government and head of state, there is no constitutional monarch or ceremonial president who serves as a moderating influence on the executive (as there is in parliamentary systems). Although it is increasingly the case in parliamentary systems as

well, presidential systems tend to place a heavy reliance on the personal qualities of a single political leader. Again, Linz argues that this is risky, especially in countries where there is an authoritarian tradition.[54]

In the end, consideration of a country's history and culture is crucial in the selection of a constitutional system, since the issue of "fit" is so important. Lack of synergy between a country and its constitutional system can greatly undermine popular support for democracy. Some countries have switched from one type of constitutional system to another in an effort to get it right: Zimbabwe and Nigeria have replaced parliamentary with presidential systems (Zimbabwe has returned to a parliamentary system, but with the president as head of state and head of government and a prime minister as co–head of government), while many Latin American countries suffering from presidentialist politics have considered adoption of parliamentary forms of government. Still, some analysts argue that the constitutional system matters little, since the differences between the two types of systems are exaggerated—both systems have succumbed to military coup and single-party rule. They add that perhaps other factors, such as political culture or the economy, are more important than institutional choice in promoting durable democracies. The one thing these political scientists seem to agree on is that any system involves some trade-offs.[55]

As you will see in the sections that follow, no matter if it is presidential or parliamentary, democratization must be based on certain bedrock principles: DEMOCRATIC INSTITUTIONALIZATION, political competition, and various forms of horizontal and vertical accountability. Beyond this, there is room for an enormous variety of formal and informal rules and institutions within what we broadly recognize as democracy.[56]

Democratic Institutionalization

Political systems are classified as democratic as long as they have made or are making observable progress toward what is often referred to as democratic institutionalization. In order for democratic systems to be long-lasting and meaningful, democratic institutions must be crafted, nurtured, and developed.[57] When democratic institutions are strong, the processes of government are established and less vulnerable to nondemocratic intrusions (for example, military takeovers). Under such circumstances, citizens and leaders alike can develop reasonable expectations about the rules and procedures of government, which are "above" the whims of individuals or groups. In other words, the rules should be stable and formalized—they should not vary dramatically based on which particular leader is in office. This development of regularized processes is often referred to as institutionalization. Through their various functions, institutions ensure participation, representation, accountability, and respect for human rights.

Democratic institutions are often thought of as the formal, concrete organizations (such as the executive, legislative, and judicial branches of government, as well as political parties and civil society) that are the principal means through which citizens select and monitor democratic government. Yet other democratic institutions are more procedural, such as regularized patterns of interaction that are widely accepted and practiced, like electoral rules, the checks and balances of presidential systems, or the rules governing the transfer of power. Whatever their form, democratic institutions promote (in one way or another) the individual's right to participate in the political life of the community. In their particular capacities, each institution in a democracy serves a critical function.[58]

Political Competition

Political competition is a procedural part of democratic institutionalization. It involves much more than the right to form parties or to take part in elections. For example, in order for parties and candidates to freely compete for political office, they need access to the media, just as citizens need independent sources of information. Individuals and parties seeking power know that positive press and advertising are crucial to any campaign. Media-savvy parties enlist public relations firms to create commercials full of slick images. They hire US spin-doctors to manipulate soundbites so as to put their candidate in the best light. However, they also run extremely negative campaigns, including Internet smear campaigns.

Beyond access to the media, political competition is based in the principle that political parties must be free to organize, present candidates for office, express ideas, and compete in fair elections. Even in democracies, political parties vary enormously in the way in which they select the candidates they put forward; some (such as Nigeria's People's Democratic Party) are the product of insider wheeling and dealing. To help safeguard the process from undue influence of elites, more democracies are developing rules concerning campaign finance, including ceilings on how much money private individuals and groups can contribute to political parties and candidates. Strict enforcement of limits on donations and other aspects of party financing is a necessity. In Mexico, prior to recent reforms, one candidate reportedly spent twenty times the legal campaign limit. This problem has continued, as parties went beyond the limits in the 2006 election.[59]

Campaign finance reform is just one aspect of a number of procedural elements meant to safeguard democracy. Although governments vary widely in terms of these procedural elements (such as when elections are to be held), in democracies the procedures for holding governments accountable are well established and respected. Regular, free, and fair elections are taken for granted in democracies. While elections are often upheld as an indicator of freedom, and they can be an important part of a democracy, in and of themselves they hardly guarantee that a country is democratic. Remember the electoral fallacy: even nondemocratic states may hold elections.

Whether it is the first election or the fiftieth, the orchestration of free and fair elections is a complicated undertaking. This can be quite difficult in a country without reliable transportation and communication facilities, or with an enormous population (India has over 714 million voters). The investment of a great deal of time, money, and effort is necessary long before election day to lay the basis for a legitimate result. Free and fair elections require the creation of an independent electoral commission as well as neutral poll workers and multiple international and domestic observers. Too often electoral commissions (even in transitioning democracies) are nominated and funded by the executive branch. Yet the reputation of such a commission must be beyond reproach as it undertakes the tedious and painstaking work that is critical to the honesty of any vote. In Mexico, a disputed election in 1910 led to the first major social revolution of the twentieth century. Some feared that it might come to this again as citizens poured into Mexico City in 2006 to protest the decision of the country's federal electoral commission in the closest election in Mexican history.

Where no good census exists, just the registration of voters is an enormous task. Sometimes, as in Nigeria, taking a census can be a massive logistical undertaking and a political landmine. Fears that a census will lead to the redrawing of the political map (and redistribution of wealth and power) have resulted in mass

rioting in more than one country. Consequently, Nigeria went fifteen years without a headcount, from 1991 to 2006.[60] In Iran, where the first nationwide census was held in 1956 (before the foundation of the Islamic Republic), leaders launched a fully Web-based census in 2016.[61]

Throughout the global south, political parties are using social networks to publicize electoral malfeasance, and electoral commissions are developing computer programs to organize electoral rolls and prevent fraud. But even these computer programs must be strictly monitored. To protect against fraud and to demonstrate his dedication to democratizing the process, former Mexican president Ernesto Zedillo adopted reforms to ensure that his country's electoral institute was truly nonpartisan. Billions of dollars were spent to compile a reliable list of eligible voters in Mexico. The adoption of national identity cards for the first time afforded millions of women (and others who were less likely to have a driver's license or other form of official identification) the opportunity to vote.[62]

In preparation for the April 2011 elections, Nigeria's voter lists had to be replaced because they included many fictitious names as well as names of deceased individuals. In an effort to help produce a more valid list, the Nigerian government plans to display voters' names on the Internet and is encouraging citizens to text-message the commission with complaints about irregularities.[63]

Figure 13.4 Elections in China

While it should be clear that elections are an extremely important component of democracy, the existence of competitive elections alone is not sufficient evidence of the stirrings of a democratic transition. In the People's Republic of China, for example, truly competitive elections at the local level have taken place since the mid-1980s, although these have been confined to villages and to county-level people's congresses. (A few townships have also experimented with elections, although these moves have been "discouraged" by Beijing.) At the village level, citizens now elect members of "villagers' committees" every three years. These committees are officially nongovernmental organizations, since villages are not a formal level of government. They manage public affairs and social welfare, help maintain public order, and promote economic development, primarily through job creation. Hundreds of millions of Chinese have participated in this grassroots-level exercise, sending 3 million officials to office with some level of popular, albeit limited, mandate.[a] International observers, many under the auspices of the Carter Center, have followed the election campaigns and have consistently noted a level of competition and campaigning previously unknown in China. Political parties other than the Chinese Communist Party (CCP) are not allowed, but candidates are able to run as independents, though the nomination of candidates is tightly controlled.

Observers have noted concerns about voter privacy: People routinely mark their ballots from their seats, rather than using private booths. As this is common practice, people who would attempt to use the more private polling booths might raise suspicion among their fellow villagers. Most analysts believe that these elections have been implemented less to promote democratic sentiment and more to facilitate control over unruly agents in the countryside. Talks about expanding the polls to higher levels of governance (e.g., townships) have stalled. Giving peasants the opportunity to vote out corrupt Communist Party officials is believed by the government to be enough, for now—particularly if it helps citizens view the government as more legitimate.

Note: a. Kerry Brown, *Ballot Box China: Grassroots Democracy in the Final Major One-Party State* (New York: Zed, 2011).

Where citizens have had little or no experience participating in free and fair elections, voter education is a necessity. Beyond ensuring that they have access to the information required to make an informed decision, voters must understand the ballot and be able to indicate their choices. Where a large proportion of the population is illiterate, this requires designing a ballot using symbols or photographs of the candidates as well as the written word. Furthermore, there are a number of practices that democracies use to help ensure that there are no irregularities at the polls or with the count. Voting in most of the world is low-tech; ballots are marked by hand or with fingerprints. Voting using fingerprints helps to cut down on fraud, since the ink stains the skin for a few days and helps deter anyone who might wish to vote twice. Steel ballot boxes with padlocks were used to suggest that the elections could not be stolen and were the fashion in the 1980s in most Latin American countries. For symbolic and practical reasons, transparent ballot boxes are favored in countries as different as Iraq, Zimbabwe, Egypt, and Mexico. As Mexico democratized, it invested in new voting booths. Outfitted with curtains, these booths were a break with the past in that they were designed to accommodate only one person at a time and ensure the privacy of the voter. The impact was enormous: for the first time in their lives, Mexicans could be sure they were voting without someone looking over their shoulders. Similarly, Haiti boasted of its first free and fair election in 1990 with the Creole slogan, "As clean as a knife through a potato."[64]

Beyond efforts to guarantee privacy, local and international election observers must be trained and posted in sufficient numbers to help ensure the fairness of the process. A large part of this involves things like making sure that the process is orderly, that there is no intimidation at the polls, and that no one who is registered to vote is turned away. People often wait for hours to vote in mile-long lines, as turnout for elections is much higher in many countries in the global south than it is in the United States, where it is not unusual for only about 50 percent of registered voters to cast their ballots—even in presidential elections.[65] In addition, the electoral commission must ensure that there are enough ballots at the polls, collect and tabulate the vote accurately (done by hand in most countries), and report the results in a timely manner (as delays tend to draw suspicion and raise tensions).

Taken together, these procedures help to ensure that an authentic democratic transition is under way. For countries experiencing their first democratic elections, or FOUNDING ELECTIONS, these are historic events. They often symbolize a departure from authoritarianism and dramatically demonstrate the power of a mobilized citizenry. In many ways the 2000 presidential vote in Mexico, although the conduct of elections had improved greatly since 1997, symbolized such an event. Virtually everyone agrees that this was the freest and fairest vote ever. The result served as an indicator of the authenticity of Mexico's democratic transition: the governing party allowed itself to lose the elections. It was a surprise for many; the victory by challenger Vicente Fox put an end to over seventy years of uninterrupted one-party rule. There was similar jubilation when democratic elections were held in Nigeria in 1999 after fifteen years of military dictatorship. Likewise, the parliamentary elections in Indonesia in 1999 were celebrated as the freest since 1955, and 2004 was another watershed year when Indonesians directly elected their president for the first time.

While founding elections mark an important watershed event, most analysts agree that it is the second round of elections that is a more vital step toward consolidation, especially if they result in an orderly transfer of power. Many Nigerians

were concerned that their second experience with elections, in 2003, would pose the greatest challenge for their new democracy. To their relief, it went relatively smoothly, compared to their experience a decade earlier, when the presiding dictator, who was unhappy with the result, quickly ended a democratic experiment.

Although there are "dominant-party democracies," such as in Botswana, in which there has never been a transfer of power because one party has always won elections, these countries are also widely regarded as democracies. For as long as the possibility of change through election exists, the system is democratic. Still, for most countries the transfer of power from one party to another is a crucial part of the transition to democracy.

Beyond these procedural elements and general principles, there are a number of other qualities we expect to see in countries making a democratic reform. Some analysts focus on the recruitment of candidates and argue that a democratizing country must allow for the people's representatives to be drawn from an "open" political elite. Candidates for office in democracies are often sensitive to accusations of being part of an "old boys' club" and portray themselves as part of a new "breed" of leaders, capable of making real change. For example, Ahmet Necdet Sezer was the first president in modern Turkish history who was neither an active politician nor a military commander (he was chief justice of the Constitutional Court). Indonesia's Joko "Jokowi" Widodo, elected president in 2014, is the first Indonesian president without connections to the military or political elite (although he had served as mayor and governor, where he brandished his skills). A former furniture maker, he has a penchant for loud rock music, and counts Led Zeppelin and Metallica among his favorite bands. Further removed from the old boys' club is probably Michelle Bachelet, who from 2006 to 2010 served as the first female president of relatively conservative Chile (she was elected again in 2014). Bachelet—a pediatrician, an agnostic single mother with three children by two men (one whom she never married), and the daughter of a general who died in prison under the dictatorship—had never before held elective office.[66] "Outsider" candidates such as Bachelet appeal to voters because they offer the prospect of change; they draw people looking to break the hold of traditional political elites.

Whereas the idea of any elite dominating politics is perhaps antithetical to the democratic ideal, the fact remains that the economically rich have a disproportionate hold on power in both democratic and nondemocratic governments. Yet by "open," it is hoped at least that democratic systems will be more accessible to newcomers, more concerned with the interests of the general public, and more likely to work for the interests of the majority. At the very least, because in democratic systems the political elite can be held accountable to the voters, we can assume that those who are elected will try harder to make good on their promises.

Horizontal Accountability

Horizontal accountability refers to the imperative for various political actors from the different branches of government to work together. The idea is that no branch should overstep its boundaries and seek to dominate the others. In reality, maintaining (or establishing) horizontal accountability is usually about the legislative and judicial branches seeking to limit executive power. This is not quite as true for parliamentary systems, which have a fusion of powers: voters select the legislators (the members of parliament), who then select (or create) the executive (the prime minister). On the other hand, presidential systems are distinguished by a separation of powers in

which each branch of government is independent of the others. Voters in presidential systems directly select the executive as well as the legislators, which can result in divided government (voters have a proclivity to split the ballot) and potential gridlock from power-sharing between the executive and legislative branches.

From the executive point of view, any number of obstacles can interfere with a leader's ability to make good on his or her promises. Ironically, the democratic process itself is likely to be identified as one of those obstacles. For example, former president Fox, although he appeared to have won a clear mandate in 2000, in reality had extremely limited powers; his policy initiatives became mired in gridlock because his party did not have a majority in the Mexican congress. President Enrique Peña Nieto inherited a deadlocked congress but was able in 2012 to make an agreement with the two major opposition parties to stop fighting long enough to push through eighty-five reforms including taking on teachers' unions, breaking up monopolies, and liberalizing the energy sector. The truce, known as the Pact for Mexico, didn't last. By 2014 the grand bargain was over, but it showed Mexico what is possible when adversaries sit down and talk.[67]

The Pact for Mexico was in many ways a political unicorn because what happened in Mexico (for one, glimmering moment) is so rare in presidential systems. In those systems, decentralization produces a separation of powers, allowing for checks and balances on the executive, which can mean gridlock. In Nigeria, Olusegun Obasanjo was constantly at odds with a fractious national assembly. Although his party controlled both houses, the president was known to refer derisively to the young, ambitious lawmakers dominating that body as "children" who were causing him no end of trouble. Deadlock over the budget resulted in policy paralysis; disbursements were put on hold and salaries went unpaid. For their part, the "children," who had campaigned for Obasanjo, soon felt excluded by him. They accused the president of being more authoritarian than democrat, a "my way or the highway" general.[68]

Of course the social and economic crises that the Nigerian and other governments have inherited from their authoritarian predecessors reinforce certain practices and ideas about the proper exercise of political authority. Moreover, dominant political cultures may value decisive leadership over institutional checks and balances. As mentioned earlier, presidentialism is likely to develop where a state of constant crisis has generated a strong sense of urgency. As a parentlike figure, the president (and sometimes the prime minister) tends to become the embodiment of the nation—benevolent guardian and defender of its interests. Because of their stature, presidents may come to see other institutions such as the legislature and courts as nuisances that interfere with the full authority delegated to them.[69]

What we're describing as presidentialism can occur in parliamentary systems as well. For example, Turks voted in a referendum in 2010 for a number of constitutional amendments, including one to allow the parliament more power to appoint judges. Prime Minister Recep Tayyip Erdogan supported the plan as a way to rein in what is seen as a highly politicized judiciary that has consistently overstepped its boundaries, a move that would be helpful for Turkey's accession to the European Union. Critics charge that the changes amount to an effort by the ruling Justice and Development Party (AKP, which controls the legislative and executive branches) to seize control of the judiciary, remove this essential check on government, and secure all power (in effect creating a "civilian dictatorship" with explicit religious undertones).[70] While executives in delegative democracies can often move faster be-

cause of the relative lack of horizontal accountability, it is up to the leader to shoulder the burden of a country's tremendous problems—and should the leader fail, it is perceived as entirely his or her fault.

Vertical Accountability

One of the cardinal rules of democracy is "you can't stay in power by doing nothing." No democracy is likely to be consolidated without high levels of support offered by legitimacy, and no democracy will garner high legitimacy rates without some degree of effective governance. As mentioned earlier, one of the two most commonly understood components of good governance is accountability. But there are two kinds of accountability: horizontal and vertical accountability. By vertical accountability, we refer to a government's relationship with its citizens. The more responsive a government is to popular demands, the more satisfied people will be with the way government works and the more they will support it through hard times. The better the government is at promoting the general welfare, the more that people will trust it, believe the system to be a good one, and remain committed to it.[71] Initiatives associated with vertical accountability include capacity building, establishing the rule of law, reconciling group conflict, and maintaining civilian control over the military.

Capacity building. The ability to strategize, prioritize, and carry out state functions to improve people's lives, or capacity building, is a crucial test for most new democracies. One measure of a government's capacity is its ability to deliver public services. Yet although people commonly cite effectiveness as a highly valued attribute of governments, democracies don't necessarily make for the most efficient of administrations. And decisive action is even more difficult for democracies under economic strain. As discussed in Chapters 6 and 7, undemocratic governments have sometimes proven to be quite capable of delivering not only services, but also economic growth. It could be argued that when it comes to capacity building, democracies are disadvantaged in that, by definition in this type of political system, a variety of actors must be consulted in decisionmaking. Consequently, democracy tends to be a messy and slow business. New democracies certainly face many challenges, and one of the first things their leaders must learn is to restrain expectations. New democracies are often expected not only to stabilize economies and promote economic development, but also to make good on promises of political freedoms and representativeness. They are to be accountable to their citizens, establish order, and promote the rule of law.[72] Beyond that, there are more mundane expectations of new democracies as well. The problem is that often these governments do not inherit usable bureaucracies and therefore lack the administrative capacity to make progress in providing services, implementing policy, and so on. Elected government should at the very least be capable of performing what are commonly regarded as essential functions: collecting taxes, providing a sense of security throughout the country, and enforcing the law, as well as designing and implementing policies responsive to the majority. Some analysts expand the definition of essential functions to include concern with the population's economic and social well-being. This typically includes demands for the supply of public goods (such as the rehabilitation of communications and transportation systems, or the provision of sanitation and electrification). Unless democracy can provide these things, it is unlikely to be viewed favorably for long. But for economic reasons if nothing else, this is out of reach for many governments.[73]

Newly elected governments not only face economic shortfalls, but also often find it extremely difficult to pick up the pieces after years of mismanagement and abuse. It is extremely difficult to increase governmental capacity when the infrastructure has decayed beyond the point of viability. People become bitter where there are long lines for gasoline (especially in countries that are major exporters of oil), or where the electricity and telephone systems are unreliable. Newly elected democratic governments know that they don't have much time to prove themselves. Where citizens have spent years under wasteful authoritarian rule, many expect to see a DEMOCRACY DIVIDEND, a general improvement in quality of life and standard of living in just a few years' time. Yet turning around an economy often takes longer, and although some populations have demonstrated impressive patience, sooner or later they are likely to become frustrated if the benefits of change don't materialize. Under such pressures to perform, communication with the masses is of the utmost importance, and leaders who lose touch with their constituencies soon find themselves out of work. In much of the world, the appeal of populist authoritarians may grow as more people sense that democracy isn't meeting their expectations.[74]

Analysts suggest that democratic transitions are greatly affected by economic factors in a variety of ways. Certainly other factors come into play, but several consecutive years of negative economic growth lessen the chance of survival for a democratic regime (or a nondemocratic regime, for that matter). Poverty and economic inequality are key obstacles to democratization, and many countries that have experienced economic misery have fallen to what is called "the totalitarian temptation" in the search for alternatives. However, poverty does not guarantee failure. Some low-income countries such as Uruguay have completed their transitions and consolidated their democracies despite hardship. The oldest global south democracy (and the world's most populous democracy), India, is often characterized as a puzzle in that it retains democratic governance against all odds—poverty, entrenched caste and religious divisions, and other problems. Certainly such hardship makes these democracies more prone to risk, but a few cases show that it is possible for democracies to survive. To a great extent the ability to survive depends on whom the population blames for the economic problems, and the perceived desirability of political alternatives. Even where democratic government appears to be getting off to a slow start, as long as most people believe that democracy is the best political system for them, it can survive even under difficult economic conditions. If, however, people and their leaders believe democracy is compounding the problem, or that it is incapable of remedying the situation, democratic breakdown is likely.[75]

One of the first initiatives of any new leader (democratic or not) is to attempt to bond with the masses by blaming the country's problems on the previous administration. It is common for candidates to be elected based on their promises to fight corruption—the abuse of power for private gain. Corruption is a problem shared by all forms of government in virtually every country in the world, including the oldest democracies. Indonesian president Susilo Bambang Yudhoyono's government tried to demonstrate this commitment by arresting more than eighty former government officials and ministers. Some of these arrests ended in convictions, including for a member of the president's family. However, from the start of Yudhoyono's second term, his credentials as "Mr. Clean" were questioned. His popularity plummeted (from a 90 percent approval rating in 2009 to 48 percent in 2010), as he was accused of stacking the country's anticorruption commission with yes-men and protecting members of his own entourage.[76]

Such accusations are not uncommon. Nigeria's former president Obasanjo was accused of using his anticorruption zeal in a witch hunt to target his political opponents. When Nuhu Ribadu, his respected anticorruption czar, appeared to be on the verge of accusing powerful state governors of unheard-of levels of grand corruption, Ribadu was demoted, received death threats, and fled into exile. This is a shame, since in 2003 Nigeria was identified by Transparency International, an international watchdog group, as the most corrupt country in the world (Somalia took the title in 2010, and retains it as of late 2016). Nigeria ranked 136th out of 168 countries (the higher the number, the worse the corruption).[77] It is said that Nigeria's national treasury was empty when Obasanjo took office. Switzerland is returning more than $2 billion in funds stolen from Nigeria. Yet this is only the tip of the iceberg; it is estimated that the last dictator alone, Sani Abacha, looted the treasury of up to $5 billion.[78]

Yet fighting corruption by promoting accountability and transparency is crucial if democracies are to progress. In old and new democracies alike, pervasive official misconduct can contribute to democratic breakdown. Bribery, extortion, influence peddling, and other scandals can greatly damage political legitimacy and disillusion people, alienating them from the political process. Clearly, the most stable countries of the world are the least corrupt (and vice versa); five out of the ten most corrupt countries in the world rank among the top ten least-peaceful places as well.[79]

How can corruption be reduced? Most experts recommend a broad strategy based around the idea of increasing transparency, which can be understood in a number of interrelated ways. In one crucial sense, it means openness, particularly in terms of spending and budgetary matters. During Mexico's liberalization, the government began declassifying information and publishing the federal budget in full (something that had traditionally been cloaked in secrecy). A number of countries, including Brazil, have laws requiring budgetary disclosure, but a variety of difficulties prevent citizen oversight, including a lack of complete or specific information or standardization that makes it possible to compare different offices or track expenditures.[80]

Accountability is the goal, but it is not only about punishing wrongdoers; it is also about reducing the incentive to steal. Many countries trying to stem corrupt impulses work to increase the wages of civil servants—although not every country will want to pay their leading executive as much as Singapore's Prime Minister Lee Hsien Loong earns ($2.4 million annually, compared to the US presidential salary of $400,000).[81] Another approach is raising the risks and costs associated with corruption. It means that from top to bottom, from high-ranking officials who treat the state treasury as a private source of wealth, down to police and petty officials who supplement their meager incomes with *una mordida* (a bite) or *bakshish* (a gift), government actors must no longer be allowed to violate the law with impunity, and will be prosecuted if they do. Governments must improve the ability to detect extortion and other abuses so as to better expose, punish, and disgrace those guilty of misconduct. However, the problem in many countries is all-pervasive; too often, graft is understood as the only platform for attaining dreams of wealth and success. Those who are making their way up the ladder find that "fear of the unknown" fuels corruption; they are determined to take their cut before they lose their footing on that ladder.[82] The police are the government actors most likely to demand bribes; daily petty extortions from them and other civil servants hit the poorest the hardest. According to a 2013 Transparency International report, corruption exists everywhere, but it is worse in some places than others. Listed as the worst were Liberia and Sierra

Leone, where more than 75 percent of respondents admitted to paying a bribe in the preceding year. Around the world, the police and judiciary are reportedly the most bribery-prone of public services, although political parties were identified as by far the most corrupt institution. For institutions to be perceived in this way poses a real threat to democracy, since corruption is said to impact the psyche of a nation, breaking trust and creating cynicism. If people don't expect much from elected government, this will limit democracy's life expectancy.[83]

Establishing the rule of law. There are important distinctions between rule of law and rule by law. Rule by law is commonly employed by authoritarian regimes to repress populations—to crack down on "enemies of the state." On the other hand, rule of law is one of the core functions of a high-quality democracy. Though not easy to define, because it comprises several elements (and there is disagreement over what these elements are and how they should be prioritized), at its most basic the rule of law provides the foundation for the enjoyment of political rights and civil liberties. It means that no one is above the law. The government is ruled by law and subject to it. Certainly rule of law can be compromised and there can be gaps or flaws in its operation (in the laws themselves, in the application of the law, in access to the judiciary and a fair process). It is probably best to conceptualize rule of law as existing on a continuum, in that some democracies have made more progress than others in establishing it.[84]

Therefore, there are several different elements that work together in the rule of law. Whether that means making it safe for people to walk around their neighborhoods at night or a policy of zero tolerance for official corruption, strengthening the rule of law is a tremendous challenge for many democratizing regimes. Nearly fifteen years into Mexico's democracy, the number of people who said that they feel unsafe increased, to 73 percent of the population in 2014. That same year, 22.4 million Mexicans (nearly one in five) disclosed that they had been the victims of crime. Yet few Mexicans bother to report crime, perhaps because an estimated 99 percent of crimes in the country go unpunished.[85] Although analysts disagree about whether crime rates have actually risen since the transition to democracy in several Latin American countries, they confirm that the fear of crime has definitely increased. In Argentina and Mexico, fear of crime has become a major election issue and thousands have protested the lack of public security.[86] Around the world, public frustration with democratic governments' inability to impose the rule of law has also led to vigilantism. In some places this amounts to community-based policing, necessary where the government has in effect ceded significant powers to local communities. For example, as violence (and especially kidnappings) continued to rise in Mexico, citizens took matters into their own hands and formed clandestine vigilante groups to fight off drug traffickers and gangs—a development that may make citizens feel safe, but, human rights groups fear, may only worsen the violence.[87]

The rule of law also means that legal systems in democracies should be able to guarantee predictable and impartial treatment from governmental agents, including the police, the military, and judges. This poses a major challenge for many governments, especially where these public servants have long traditions of acting with impunity. In Egypt, under the Mubarak regime, the security forces were given broad powers to arrest people without charge and detain them indefinitely. There and elsewhere, officers see themselves as enforcers for the government, not public servants. They were above the law, rarely punished for abuses.[88] Human rights groups in Nige-

ria and other transitioning democracies report similar problems, with security forces involved in sexual brutality, disappearances, and extrajudicial killings. One way of promoting public security is for democracies to curb the power of ministries of the interior, the agencies whose role it is to police the police, which have often earned the nickname "ministries of fear." People need to be able to trust the police as public servants, and they need to have confidence in the administration of justice.

A strong, efficient, and independent judiciary is another decentralizing institution crucial to the success of both parliamentary and presidential systems. Transitioning democracies must improve performance when it comes to ensuring not only personal security, but also that disputes are settled quickly and fairly. Citizens should not have to fear arbitrary arrest or being left to rot in overcrowded prisons while awaiting charge. A powerful judiciary—professional, depoliticized, and largely free from executive or other partisan interference—can be the greatest protector of a democratic constitution and source of democratic legitimacy. It is the ultimate guarantor of the rule of law.[89] Yet analysts recognize the judicial branch to be one of the democratic institutions that takes the longest to create, and progress is probably most accurately measured by degree. In China, for example, although there have been some reforms, it is still not uncommon for judges to lack even the cursory legal training that lawyers receive; in 2008 a party veteran with no formal legal training was appointed chief justice of the Supreme Court, and a former Court vice president was sentenced to life imprisonment for taking nearly $575,000 in bribes.[90] The Chinese Communist Party still controls the judiciary, directing verdicts and sentences. Torture is widespread and coerced confessions are routine; trials are frequently closed to the public (particularly in politically sensitive cases).[91] These are just a few of the challenges for democracies seeking to impress citizens with a sense of vertical accountability. According to Freedom House, the most significant declines in freedom between 2005 and 2009 were related to rule of law, and challenges implementing the rule of law and freedom of expression continue to be drivers of the global downward trend in democracy experienced through 2016. Too many judicial systems remain weak, unable to act independently and rule impartially. These glaring failures greatly limit the potential for the institutionalization of democratic gains in many countries worldwide.[92] From 2006 to 2016, eighteen countries showed "significant" declines in the rule of law, including Egypt, Venezuela, Kenya, and Hungary, with only three countries showing improvement over the same period (Tunisia, Togo, and Côte d'Ivoire).[93]

Reconciling group conflict. As Robert Dahl notes, at its base the exercise of democracy is the institutionalization of conflict.[94] Unlike autocrats, democratic leaders, because they are accountable to the people, must spend a great deal of their time at least appearing to be responsive to the interests of groups with conflicting interests. States are not independent of ethnicity, class, gender, and other interests, but the legitimacy of democratic governments is partly derived from their ability to appear to be independent of these interests, to modify conflict, and to build consensus. Yet democracy has an inherent paradox: it requires both representativeness and conflict, but not too much of either. Democracy must allow for competition, but only within carefully defined and accepted boundaries. Reconciling group conflict is at the heart of democratic politics, but the ability to do this doesn't happen overnight. New democracies must work to promote understanding and contain conflicts so that cleavages don't tear their countries apart. As mentioned earlier, democracy is institutionalized

competition for power. However, if that competition is too intense, the system can break down entirely. It is therefore crucial that new democracies find mechanisms to mitigate conflict and promote consensus. They must do this in a way that works successfully to pull together all the core principles of democracy: participation, representation, accountability, and respect for human rights.[95]

Cleavages are found in every country in the world. They tend to run along lines of class, ethnicity, religion, region, and party. Ethnicity, because it is wrapped up in issues of identity, is often seen as the most difficult type of cleavage for a democracy to manage. In multinational states, compromise is difficult, and in deeply divided plural societies, ethnicity is often thought to predetermine access to power and resources. What one group wins, another group fears it will lose—and fear of exclusion is not an unreasonable concern, given the experience of many countries. Elections become a desperate struggle between parties, as well as ethnic groups, regions, even religions. The rules matter little, since to lose political power is to lose access to virtually everything that is important. Under these circumstances the potential for polarization is such a real threat that some analysts hold out little hope for democracy where divisions are deep and identity has been politicized.[96]

Democratic governments must therefore attempt to manage or soften this conflict in a variety of ways. As described in more detail in Chapter 11, they can attempt to generate crosscutting cleavages—to find common ground between groups—as well as work to moderate political views and promote tolerance and cooperation. Another way of mediating these pressures is through institutional designs that encourage the decentralization of power. Federal systems of government may be crucial to the survival of democracy where cleavages are deep, since they allow for more autonomy and responsiveness at the local level. They also diminish the winner-take-all character of politics by facilitating greater representation of minorities and other marginalized groups. Conflict may be reduced and interethnic accommodation promoted through other efforts to reconcile historical differences. The protection of minority rights may go a long way toward managing deep divides—for instance, through the recognition of more than one official language, respect for a variety of legal codes, and toleration of parties representing different communities. A number of countries, such as South Africa, have been relatively successful in managing tensions by skillfully crafting democracies that take into account the particular mix of cultures and identities contained within their territory. Some analysts suggest designing coalitions, like Bosnia-Herzegovina's, that allow for a sharing or rotating of power. More commonly such efforts have the goal of ensuring that all people have equal rights to citizenship, and protecting the rights of minorities to retain their own culture, religion, and language. But coalitions are hard to build; South Africans and Bosnians will attest that the divisions in their countries are still very real. Yet ethnic groups that are allowed to share power are much more likely to view a democracy as legitimate.

Unfortunately (and often tragically), in a ploy to win election, some politicians actually encourage "tribalism" and manipulate issues of ethnicity to their own political advantage. It may not be possible to dissipate tribalism by generating crosscutting cleavages (so that the identity and interests of one ethnic or religious group are spread among different classes or regions). In Nigeria, cleavages often coincide, and people are divided by region, ethnicity, and religion.[97] As a result, reconciling group conflict often poses a nearly impossible task for many newly elected governments.

In addition to political cleavages concerning ethnicity and religion, there are also often deep divides over matters concerning women's equality. Although for various reasons some women have also been known to support authoritarians, others have been at the forefront of prodemocracy movements, in part because they expect that democracy's emphasis on human rights will include them and their children. In some cases they have been correct in this belief. As the *abertura* has unfolded, political space has gradually opened to women in several countries. For the first time ever, women were allowed to vote and stand as candidates in Kuwait's 2006 parliamentary elections (although it was not until 2009 that four women won seats).[98]

The lesson here is that simply allowing previously disenfranchised groups the right to participate in elections as candidates and voters is not enough to result in a true *abertura*. Affirmative action to guarantee women's representation in political bodies may be one way of prodding such an opening. Taiwan has an electoral system that reserves 10–25 percent of the seats in legislative bodies for women. Argentina, Afghanistan, and several other countries have adopted quotas as well. Some might argue that quotas are the only way to press toward gender parity in political representation: of the twenty-three countries in which women have attained the critical mass of at least 30 percent of legislative seats, eighteen of them have had quotas. But even when such rules exist (as they do in some form or another in ninety-five countries), they often go unenforced. The proportion of parliamentary seats occupied by women increased by 10 percent between 1997 and 2015. The average proportion of women in parliament worldwide is 22 percent. All regions have to varying degrees moved toward equal representation since 1995, but men still outnumber women by nearly five to one in legislatures around the world.[99] The United Nations Development Fund for Women (UNIFEM) estimates that at the current rate, it will take two generations before the number of women in parliaments worldwide approaches parity.[100]

Rwanda, Bolivia, Andorra, and Cuba are the countries with the largest proportions of women serving in parliament; in terms of regions, the Caribbean takes the lead (followed by developed regions, then Latin America).[101] Rwanda continues to hold the distinction as the country with the highest proportion of women ever recorded by a parliamentary chamber (64 percent in 2015).[102] Reforms in the United Arab Emirates (UAE) and Tunisia have added some women to the political ranks, but in much of the Middle East and Oceania, women's representation remains very low (in Saudi Arabia there are no women in parliament). In general, countries without quota laws are electing women, but more slowly and less steadily.[103]

Yet increasing the formal representation of women doesn't guarantee that the distribution of political resources will change. Moreover, although women are often thought to be less corrupt and more connected to the people, this is not necessarily so. It is clear that women politicians (who often see themselves as needing to conform to succeed) are not usually in a good position to challenge the existing system, which is resistant to change. Even in what appear to be bold political reforms, such "progressive" legislation is mostly a formality that has meant very little change in the lives of women. Liberalizing governments have also been known to extend women's economic rights, such as the right to own property, or the right to equal pay for equal work. But these reforms as well have often disappointed because of a government's failure to implement the new laws or to put resources into programs promoting equality. Democratic and nondemocratic governments commonly include

a ministry or department specifically established to deal with "women's issues." However, it is rare for such offices to hold much power; in most cases they are marginalized and the women heading them are mere tokens in otherwise overwhelmingly male cabinets. Although it could be argued that women's status has generally improved in most regions, progress has come very slowly. Moreover, there continues to be great unevenness in women's experience of gender equality, both between and within countries, based on regional, class, ethnic, and other divides.[104]

As you can see in Figure 13.6, the United Nations Development Programme (UNDP) has developed a composite measure to examine the opportunities that are made available to women in countries around the world. This index, called the Gender Inequality Index (GII), provides a detailed look at the prospects women face in terms of health and educational well-being, as well as economic and political participation and decisionmaking. An examination of the GII rankings for more than a hundred countries shows that overall, the world is doing a better job at narrowing inequalities in healthcare and education than it is regarding economic and political participation. Interestingly, not all countries in the global north are more equal than those in the global south: higher levels of income are not necessarily correlated with expanded opportunities for women. As a 2015 study for the World Economic Forum asserts, no country has eliminated the gender gap, but the Nordic countries have had the most success. In 2015, the United States ranked 8th out of 188 countries (up from 31st in 2009), largely because of the number of women in leading roles in the Obama administration and improvements in closing the wage gap. The United States is now in league with Canada, Ireland, and Singapore. Niger comes in last, with supposedly the largest gender gap in the world.[105]

Sonia Alvarez points out that states are slowest to work on particular types of issues defined as private, outside the "proper" realm of politics. According to UNIFEM, only a fraction of countries (just over 25 percent) specifically criminalize rape in marriage—and even then, the perpetrator is rarely charged.[106] It is only in the past three decades that well-established liberal democracies have begun to deal with sensitive issues of social relations, including spousal rape, sexual harassment, and other forms of violence against women. For example, Turkey did not criminalize marital rape and sexual harassment in the workplace until 2004 and its government recently proposed a law dropping charges against men convicted of sex with underage girls if they marry them (after vociferous protests it dropped the idea).[107] Turkey is by no means unusual; in many democracies (newly established or not) violence against women and girls is pervasive and its perpetrators operate with impunity. In Mexico, where an average of five women are murdered every day, femicide, a distinct crime from homicide (the "murder of women by men motivated by hatred, contempt, pleasure, or a sense of ownership of women") is said to be endemic. A recent reform recognized it as such, making it punishable by forty to seventy years' imprisonment. Yet little has been done to protect women or enhance conviction rates, which are exceedingly low.[108] Therefore, while the *abertura* that comes with a democratic transition offers a range of possibilities perhaps once unheard of, the window of opportunity has only partially opened. Interestingly, sometimes it is the less-than-democratic regimes that can push through policies promoting gender equality. Ironically, in democracies, through a process that is supposed to foster inclusion and consensus building, the promotion of human rights, especially women's rights, may be set aside in the interests of "unity."

Figure 13.5 Shattering Stereotypes

As difficult as it is to achieve gender parity in the legislative branch, progress in electing female executives is even slower. In 2000 there were a total of nine female heads of state or government worldwide. By 2016 there were twenty-two female leaders, constituting roughly 7 percent of all political leaders in the world. Although the global North tends to assume that it is more advanced in this regard, some of the first female heads of government and heads of state in the modern era have come from the global south.

- Sirimavo Bandaranaike of Sri Lanka is considered to be the "dean" of women's leaders. She was the world's first elected female prime minister, serving in that post from 1960 to 1965, 1970 to 1977, and 1994 to 2000.

- Indira Gandhi was prime minister of India from 1966 to 1977 and 1980 to 1984, until she was assassinated. Pratibha Devisingh Patil was the first woman elected as the president of India, serving from 2007 to 2012.

- Benazir Bhutto became Pakistan's elected prime minister in 1988 at the age of thirty-five. The first woman elected to head a modern Islamic country, Bhutto served as prime minister twice and was removed from power twice on corruption charges. In 2007, two weeks before the elections that were likely to return her to power, she was assassinated while leaving a campaign rally. Her widower, Asif Ali Zardari, was elected president in 2008, serving from 2008 to 2013.

- Megawati Sukarnoputri of Indonesia (2001–2004), and Corazon Aquino (1986–1992) and Gloria Macapagal Arroyo (2001–2010) of the Philippines, became the presidents of their countries, replacing men ousted for incompetence and corruption. Megawati, the first daughter of the founding father of Indonesia (Sukarno), lost her bids for reelection in both 2004 and 2009. There were several coup attempts against Aquino and attempts to impeach Arroyo, but both Filipina presidents served out their terms.

- Ellen Johnson-Sirleaf, Africa's first directly elected female leader, took office in 2006 and is currently the president of Liberia. Known as the "Iron Lady" for her resilience in the face of po-

litical persecution, this former World Bank economist is leading the reconstruction of Liberia after a debilitating fourteen-year war.

- Cristina Fernández de Kirchner is Argentina's first elected female president (the second female president to hold the office), having served from 2007 to 2015. Isabel Perón, who was elected vice president, assumed the presidency (1974–1976) after her husband's (Juan Perón's) death. Fernández, often referred to by her initials CFK, is the first democratically elected head of state who replaced a spouse (without his death). She succeeded her husband, Néstor Kirchner, in 2007, and theirs was often characterized as a presidential marriage, as the former president (who died in 2010) openly served as his wife's closest adviser.

- Dilma Roussef, an economist who was also once a young radical who had been imprisoned (and reportedly tortured) by Brazil's military dictatorship, was elected Brazil's first female president in 2010. A protégé of former president Luiz Inácio Lula da Silva (she served as his minister of energy and chief of staff), Roussef expanded upon her predecessor's social welfare policies and was, in 2013, ranked by Forbes as the second most powerful woman in the world (she was listed as the sixteenth most powerful person in the world by Forbes in 2010). She was removed from office after a long-delayed and controversial vote of impeachment in August of 2016.

- Bidya Devi Bhandari is currently serving as the second president of Nepal, and the first woman to serve (since 2015) in this relatively new post (the office was created after Nepal was declared a republic in 2008). Active in politics from a young age, Bhandari also blazed a trail for women by serving as the first female minister of defense of the government of Nepal (from 2009 to 2011).

- The Bahamas, Bangladesh, Belize, Chile, Costa Rica, Dominica, Guyana, Haiti, Jamaica, Kyrgyzstan, Mauritius, Marshall Islands, Namibia, Nicaragua, Rwanda, Trinidad and Tobago, and Turkey are some of the other countries that have elected female presidents or prime ministers.

Figure 13.5 *continues*

Figure 13.5 continued

Certainly some of these women have come to office by making a name for themselves. But in high-income as well as low-income countries, the family name sometimes opens doors for women (and men too) and serves as an important entrée into politics (Hillary Clinton was hardly the first).

Many female presidents and prime ministers have risen to prominence at least partly because they were the widows or daughters of male political leaders (Corazon Aquino, Indira Gandhi, Violeta Chamorro, Megawati Sukarnoputri, and Benazir Bhutto are a few examples).

Civil control over the military. As discussed in Chapter 11, in the face of growing instability, civilian leaders have often sent in the police and even the military to restore order among unruly crowds. Unless they find some other way of building legitimacy, these leaders become heavily dependent on the support of the security forces. However, the military often views itself as the supreme arbiter of the national interest. Its concern over civilian inability to impose calm in the midst of a political or economic crisis has on occasion prompted the military to take matters into its own hands.

A government that must continually look over its shoulder out of fear of an army takeover is in an extremely precarious situation. Many new democracies find themselves coexisting with powerful militaries and must take care not to challenge their prerogatives. Ideally, freely elected democracies would not be constrained or compelled to share power with other actors, including the military. Democratically elected governments should have unquestioned and full authority to generate new policies or carry out their core functions. Therefore, it is crucial that militaries be removed from politics and firmly subordinated to civilian control. MILITARY PROFESSIONALISM, or the military's depoliticization and recognition of civilian supremacy, is absolutely critical to the survival of democracy. The military must view itself as serving the civilian government, not as the definer and guardian of the national interest. This can be achieved: Mexico's military is not considered a threat to civilian control, and it looks like the Turkish and Indonesian militaries are declining in influence as well (although they have by no means been neutralized as political actors).[109]

Unfortunately, few countries experiencing a democratic transition can rest fully assured that the military accepts this subordinate role. Where the transition was preceded by a military regime (or a military-dominated regime), unless it is eliminated by foreign intervention or by revolution, the security forces will still hold a powerful place in government during and after the transition. The military is a crucial part of the government that the new democracy must attempt to manage. Many new regimes have made efforts to establish civilian supremacy, with varying degrees of success. Although ultimately the goal is for military decisionmaking to be subject to civilian control, leaders must consider the military's power in determining when and how far to push reform. As Nigeria began its democratic transition in 1999, analysts agreed on the need to reduce military prerogatives, although they disagreed about whether Olusegun Obasanjo was the man to do it. Wary of other former military leaders who might stage a comeback, Obasanjo purged some army officers associated with the Sani Abacha regime. However, many Nigerians suspect that Obasanjo owed his presidential win to military financiers and doubted he had the will to make

Figure 13.6   Measuring Gender Empowerment, 2014

	Gender Inequality Index Rank	Seats in Parliament Held by Women (percentage of all seats)	Female Labor Force Participation	Female Population with at Least Some Secondary Education (percentage older than 25 years)
China	40	23.6	63.9	58.7
Mexico	74	37.1	45.1	55.7
Peru	82	22.3	68.2	56.3
Indonesia	110	17.1	51.4	39.9
Zimbabwe	112	35.1	83.2	48.7
Nigeria	—	6.6	48.2	—
Iran	114	3.1	16.6	62.2
Egypt	131	2.2	23.7	43.9

Source: United Nations Development Programme (UNDP), *Human Development Report 2015,* tab. 5: "Gender Inequality Index," www.hdr.undp.org/en/composite/GII.

significant reforms in civil-military relations. Under every administration since Nigeria's transition to democracy, soldiers committed massacres without worry of prosecution, in part because the president didn't want to provoke a coup. The military has refrained from intervening in several crises. For example, many worried about a coup when then-president Yar'Adua died in office and when acting president Jonathan upset the rotation, breaking his promise not to run for office. Perhaps this is a sign that Nigeria's democracy is consolidating, since experts warn that if these scenarios had played out ten years earlier, it would have almost certainly led to coup. But it could be argued that the military doesn't have to take center stage because it has so much influence from the wings—and now a friend in the presidency: Muhammadu Buhari, a former general and military dictator, who was elected Nigeria's president in 2015. In Nigeria as in many other democracies, getting (and keeping) the military out of power is a formidable task.[110] In the end, persuading the military to stay out of politics may sometimes necessitate AMNESTY deals that excuse its members from ever facing punishment for their abuses of human rights. This can truly amount to a deal with the devil, as it so often leads to a culture of impunity (among other problems) later on.

Presidents Abdurrahman Wahid and Megawati Sukarnoputri of Indonesia also struggled to gain control over the military, not just the official forces but also the (often more reckless) militia units throughout the country. They are both now gone, but the influence of the military remains. Megawati's successor, Susilo Bambang Yudhoyono, a former army general, ostensibly tried to limit the political role of the armed forces, but they were responsible for widespread abuse (notably in Papua and Aceh) and have yet to be held accountable for past crimes. Some members of the Indonesian special forces division, known as Kopassus, have been convicted of gross human rights abuses, but continue, according to critics, to commit crimes with impunity, even after a

supposed military overhaul.[111] This is not uncommon; during political transitions the military is often in a position to negotiate the terms of its withdrawal so that it retains nondemocratic prerogatives. Ironically, such deals may be a political necessity—to get the military out of the presidential palace—but in the long run they greatly limit the possibilities for consolidation.[112] Consequently, until the possibility of a coup d'état becomes remote, no system can be considered durably democratized.

Conclusions: When the Transition Turns Out to Be the Easy Part

Where democratic experiments have been attempted and failed, it is impossible to identify a singular cause for their failure. The lesson is that we cannot assume there will be a simple, unilinear advance to democracy in the global south, given the heterogeneities and inequalities that exist there. As we've seen in more than one country, democracy can suffer serious setbacks. As we celebrate the countries embarking on their democratic transition, perhaps our interest should be the substance of their institutions, at least as much as their sustainability. And as we have seen with the complex processes required in both the transition and especially in the consolidation of democratic rule, there can be great variety—so much so that we are not always talking about simple democracies or dictatorships, but often, some sort of messy in-between phase (that can itself become consolidated).[113] It is crucial that we find ways to support the deepening of democracy, and avoid undermining it, if we are to improve the chances of its consolidation.

Notes

1. Gilbert da Costa, "Nigerians Wonder: Could a Military Coup Help Us?," *Time*, January 31, 2010.

2. Octavio Paz, "Latin America and Democracy," in *Democracy and Dictatorship in Latin America: A Special Publication Devoted Entirely to the Voice and Opinions of Writers from Latin America*, ed. Octavio Paz, Jorge Edwards, Carlos Franqui, et al. (New York: Foundation for the Independent Study of Social Ideas, 1982), p. 15.

3. Larry Diamond, "Facing Up to the Democratic Recession," in *Democracy in Decline?*, ed. Larry Diamond and Marc F. Plattner (Baltimore: Johns Hopkins University Press, 2015); Arch Puddington and Tyler Roylance, "Anxious Dictators, Wavering Democrats," in *Freedom in the World: 2016* (Washington, DC: Freedom House, 2016).

4. Puddington and Roylance, "Anxious Dictators."

5. Nic Cheeseman, *Democracy in Africa: Successes, Failures, and the Struggle for Political Reform* (New York: Cambridge University Press, 2015).

6. Philippe C. Schmitter and Terry Lynn Karl, "What Democracy Is . . . and Is Not," in *The Global Resurgence of Democracy*, ed. Larry Diamond and Marc F. Plattner (Baltimore: Johns Hopkins University Press, 1993).

7. Puddington and Roylance, "Anxious Dictators."

8. Ibid.; Juan J. Linz and Alfred Stepan, *Problems of Democratic Transition and Consolidation* (Baltimore: Johns Hopkins University Press, 1996); Larry Diamond, Juan J. Linz, and Seymour Martin Lipset, "Introduction: What Makes for Democracy?," in *Politics in Developing Countries: Comparing Experiences with Democracy*, ed. Larry Diamond, Juan J. Linz, and Seymour Martin Lipset (Boulder: Lynne Rienner, 1995).

9. Schmitter and Karl, "What Democracy Is . . . and Is Not."

10. Puddington and Roylance, "Anxious Dictators, Wavering Democrats."

11. Ibid.

12. Adebayo Adedeji, "Popular Participation, Democracy, and Development: Is There a Dialectical Linkage?," in *Nigeria: Renewal from the Roots? The Struggle for Democratic Development,* ed. Adebayo Adedeji, Onigu Otite, Kunle Amuwo, et al. (London: Zed, 1997).

13. Freedom House, *Freedom in the World 2005,* www.freedomhouse.org; Freedom House, *Freedom in the World 2010.*

14. Freedom House, *Freedom in the World 2005;* Freedom House, *Freedom in the World 2010.*

15. Bruce Bueno de Mesquita and Alastair Smith, *The Dictator's Handbook: Why Bad Behavior Is Almost Always Good Politics* (New York: PublicAffairs, 2012); Doh Chull Shin and Jason Wells, "Is Democracy the Only Game in Town?," *Journal of Democracy* 16, no. 2 (April 2005).

16. Larry Diamond, "Introduction: In Search of Consolidation," in *Consolidating Third Wave Democracies,* ed. Larry Diamond, Marc F. Plattner, Yun-han Chu, and Hung-mao Tien (Baltimore: Johns Hopkins University Press, 1997); Diamond, Linz, and Lipset, "Introduction: What Makes for Democracy?"; Schmitter and Karl, "What Democracy Is . . . and Is Not"; Freedom House, *Freedom in the World 2016.*

17. Diamond, Linz, and Lipset, "Introduction: What Makes for Democracy?"

18. Shin and Wells, "Is Democracy the Only Game in Town?"; Gregory D. Schmidt, "Delegative Democracy in Peru? Fujimori's 1995 Landslide and the Prospects for 2000," *Journal of Inter-American Studies and World Affairs* 42, no. 1 (Spring 2000); Jeffrey Herbst, "Understanding Ambiguity During Democratization in Africa," in *Pathways to Democracy: The Political Economy of Democratic Transitions,* ed. James F. Hollifield and Calvin Jillson (New York: Routledge, 2000); Freedom House, *Freedom in the World 2016.*

19. Larry Diamond, "Is the Third Wave Over?," *Journal of Democracy* 7, no. 3 (July 1996); Guillermo O'Donnell, "Delegative Democracy," *Journal of Democracy* 5, no. 1 (January 1994); Larry Diamond and Marc F. Plattner, introduction to Diamond and Plattner, *The Global Resurgence of Democracy.*

20. O'Donnell, "Delegative Democracy." See also Kenneth M. Roberts, *Deepening Democracy? The Modern Left and Social Movements in Chile and Peru* (Stanford: Stanford University Press, 1998); Linz and Stepan, *Problems of Democratic Transition and Consolidation.*

21. See, for example, Larry Diamond, *Developing Democracy: Toward Consolidation* (Baltimore: Johns Hopkins University Press, 1999); Kristian Hoelscher, "Politics and Social Violence in Developing Democracies: Theory and Evidence from Brazil," *Political Geography* 44, no. 1 (2015), pp. 29–39; Richard Joseph, "Africa: The Rebirth of Political Freedom," in Diamond and Plattner, *The Global Resurgence of Democracy;* Steven Levitsky and Lucan A. Way, *Competitive Authoritarianism: Hybrid Regimes After the Cold War* (New York: Cambridge University Press, 2010).

22. Diamond and Plattner, introduction to Diamond and Plattner, *The Global Resurgence of Democracy,* p. ix. See also Linz and Stepan, *Problems of Democratic Transition and Consolidation.*

23. Freedom House, *Freedom in the World 2016,* p. 8.

24. O'Donnell, "Delegative Democracy"; Merilee Grindle, *Challenging the State: Crisis and Innovation in Latin America and Africa* (Cambridge: Cambridge University Press, 1996).

25. Seymour Martin Lipset, *Political Man* (Garden City, NY: Doubleday, 1959); Linz and Stepan, *Problems of Democratic Transition and Consolidation.*

26. According to this view popular with neoliberals, no democracy with a per capita income approaching that of South Korea or Taiwan has ever broken down, while (with some notable exceptions) new democracies in countries with per capita incomes of less than $1,000 have rarely lasted more than a few years.

27. Emmanuel Sivan, "Illusions of Change," *Journal of Democracy* 11, no. 3 (July 2000); Laith Kubba, "The Awakening of Civil Society," *Journal of Democracy* 11, no. 3 (July 2000).

28. "Arab Spring: 10 Unpredicted Outcomes," BBC News, December 13, 2013; Linz and Stepan, *Problems of Democratic Transition and Consolidation.*

29. "Gambia's Yahya Jammeh Ready for 'Billion-Year' Rule," BBC News, December 12, 2011; Kelsey Lilley, "The Gambia Votes: A Rare Victory for Democracy in Africa?," Atlantic Council, December 2, 2016, www.atlanticcouncil.org; Dionne Searcey and Jaime Yaya Barry, "As Gambia's Yahya Jammeh Entered Exile, Plane Stuffed with Riches Followed," *New York Times,* January 23, 2017.

30. Ibid.; Diamond, "Introduction: In Search of Consolidation."

31. Linz and Stepan, *Problems of Democratic Transition and Consolidation;* Diamond, "Introduction: In Search of Consolidation"; Schmitter and Karl, "What Democracy Is . . . and Is Not."

32. Linz and Stepan, *Problems of Democratic Transition and Consolidation;* Diamond, "Introduction: In Search of Consolidation"; "Democracy's Ten-Year Rut," *The Economist,* October 29, 2005.

33. Schmitter and Karl, "What Democracy Is . . . and Is Not."

34. Larry Diamond, "Three Paradoxes of Democracy," in Diamond and Plattner, *The Global Resurgence of Democracy,* p. 104.

35. Diamond and Plattner, introduction to Diamond and Plattner, *The Global Resurgence of Democracy;* Diamond, "Introduction: In Search of Consolidation"; Linz and Stepan, *Problems of Democratic Transition and Consolidation.*

36. Diamond, "Facing Up to the Democratic Recession"; Jorge G. Castañeda, *Utopia Unarmed: The Latin American Left After the Cold War* (New York: Knopf, 1993).

37. Diamond, "Introduction: In Search of Consolidation"; Arturo Valenzuela, "External Actors in the Transitions to Democracy in Latin America," in Hollifield and Jillson, *Pathways to Democracy.*

38. Steven Levitsky and Lucan Way, "The Myth of Democratic Recession," *Journal of Democracy* 26, no. 1 (January 2015).

39. Quoted in Ruchir Sharma, "When Borders Close," *New York Times,* November 12, 2016.

40. Daniel Zovatto, "The State of Democracy in Latin America," Brookings Institution, September 15, 2014, www.brookings.edu/opinions/.

41. "Listen to Me," *The Economist,* November 2, 2013.

42. "Demand for Democracy in Africa Rises, Supply Falls Short," *Afro Barometer,* April 23, 2014.

43. Catherine Boone, "'Empirical Statehood' and Reconfigurations of Political Order," in *The African State at a Critical Juncture,* ed. Leonardo A. Villalon and Phillip A. Huxtable (Boulder: Lynne Rienner, 1998).

44. Juan J. Linz, "The Perils of Presidentialism," in Diamond and Plattner, *The Global Resurgence of Democracy.*

45. Ibid.

46. "Hints of a New Chapter," *The Economist,* November 14, 2009.

47. O'Donnell, "Delegative Democracy"; Grindle, *Challenging the State;* Scott Mainwaring, "Latin America's Imperiled Progress: The Surprising Resilience of Elected Governments," *Journal of Democracy* 10, no. 3 (July 2000).

48. O'Donnell, "Delegative Democracy."

49. Linz, "The Perils of Presidentialism."

50. Donald L. Horowitz, "Comparing Democratic Systems," in Diamond and Plattner, *The Global Resurgence of Democracy.*

51. Ibid.

52. Arend Lijphart, *Patterns of Democracy: Government Forms and Performance in Thirty-Six Countries* (New Haven: Yale University Press, 1999); Linz, "The Perils of Presidentialism"; Horowitz, "Comparing Democratic Systems."

53. Horowitz, "Comparing Democratic Systems."

54. Linz, "The Perils of Presidentialism."

55. Ibid.; Linz and Stepan, *Problems of Democratic Transition and Consolidation.*

56. Linz and Stepan, *Problems of Democratic Transition and Consolidation;* Diamond and Plattner, introduction to Diamond and Plattner, *The Global Resurgence of Democracy;* Diamond, Linz, and Lipset, "Introduction: What Makes for Democracy?"; Horowitz, "Comparing Democratic Systems."

57. Linz and Stepan, *Problems of Democratic Transition and Consolidation.*

58. Ibid.

59. "Fiasco in Tabasco," *The Economist,* October 21, 2000; Joseph L. Klesner, "The July 2006 Presidential and Congressional Elections in Mexico," *Electoral Studies* 26, no. 4 (2007).

60. Dino Mahtani, "Nigeria on Alert as Census Takers Begin Mammoth Task," *Financial Times* (London), March 22, 2006.

61. "Iran's 1st Online National Census Begins," *Tehran Times,* September 25, 2016.

62. Sam Dillon, "Major Party Deal in Mexico to Bring Political Reforms," *New York Times,* July 27, 1996; "The Right to Identity," Council on Foreign Relations, December 11, 2015.

63. "INEC to Display Voter Registration on Internet," *NBF Topics,* December 6, 2010.

64. Philip Rowan, "Democracy's Memorabilia," *Washington Post,* November 30, 2000.

65. Drew Desilver, "U.S. Voter Turnout Trails Most Developed Countries," Pew Research Center, August 2, 2016.

66. Larry Rohter, "Chile Is Ready to Elect a President Like No Other," *New York Times,* January 15, 2006.

67. "Joining Forces: A Motley Political Alliance Scrambles the Presidential Race," *The Economist,* July 8, 2010; Jonathan Tepperman, "How Mexico's President May Have Rescued His Country," *Washington Post,* October 14, 2016.

68. Norimitsu Onishi, "Nigeria's Strongman Is Still Standing," *New York Times,* September 1, 2002.

69. O'Donnell, "Delegative Democracy"; Schmidt, "Delegative Democracy in Peru?"

70. "Q & A: Turkey's Constitutional Referendum," BBC News, September 12, 2010; Marc Champion and Joe Parkinson, "Turks Pass Constitutional Changes," *Wall Street Journal,* September 13, 2010.

71. Rafael Ruiz Harrell, "Building Trust with Mexico," *New York Times,* May 22, 2001; Diamond and Plattner, introduction to Diamond and Plattner, *The Global Resurgence of Democracy;* Adedeji, "Popular Participation, Democracy, and Development."

72. Harrell, "Building Trust with Mexico"; Diamond and Plattner, introduction to Diamond and Plattner, *The Global Resurgence of Democracy;* Adedeji, "Popular Participation, Democracy, and Development."

73. Linz and Stepan, *Problems of Democratic Transition and Consolidation.*

74. Francis Fukuyama, *Political Order and Political Decay: From the Industrial Revolution to the Globalization of Democracy* (New York: Farrar, Straus and Giroux, 2014).

75. Ibid.

76. Patrick Guntensperger, "Yudhoyono Rides Anti-Corruption Wave," *Asia Times,* July 2, 2009; "Students, Workers Protest Yudhoyono, Corruption," Agence France-Press, October 20, 2010.

77. Daniel Howden, "Anti-Corruption Advocate Returns from Exile," *The Independent* (London), June 7, 2010; Transparency International, "Corruption Perception Index 2015," www.transparency.org.

78. "Swiss Poised to Return Nigerian Money," Swiss Broadcasting Corporation, July 30, 2016.

79. Diamond and Plattner, introduction to Diamond and Plattner, *The Global Resurgence of Democracy;* "Paying the Piper," *Foreign Policy* no. 154 (May–June 2006), www.foreignpolicy .com; Transparency International, "Corruption Perception Index 2015."

80. Gisele Craveiro, "Brazil," Global Information Society Watch, 2012.

81. "Why Singapore Has the Cleanest Government Money Can Buy: View," *Bloomberg,* January 24, 2012.

82. Larry Diamond, "The Uncivic Society and the Descent into Praetorianism," in Diamond, Linz, and Lipset, *Politics in Developing Countries;* Olumide Taiwo, "Challenges and Possibilities for Progress in Nigeria," Brookings Institution, June 24, 2010.

83. Transparency International, "Global Corruption Barometer, 2013."

84. Guillermo O'Donnell, "Why the Rule of Law Matters," in *Assessing the Quality of Democracy,* ed. Larry Diamond and Leonardo Morlino (Baltimore: Johns Hopkins University Press, 2005).

85. Patrick Corcoran, "Mexico Crime Survey Reveals Conflicting Trends," *Insight Crime,* October 30, 2014.

86. Matthew Moffett, "Argentina's Crime Wave Becomes Election Issue," *Wall Street Journal,* May 28, 2009.

87. Ioan Grillo, "Mexico's Cartel-Fighting Vigilantes Get Closer to the Texas Border," *PRI,* July 8, 2014.

88. "Ex-Crime Chief Arrested in Mexico," BBC News, November 21, 2008; Kareem Fahim, "Death in Police Encounter Stirs Call for Change in Egypt," *New York Times,* July 18, 2010.

89. Robert I. Rotberg, "Nigeria: Elections and Continuing Challenges," CSR no. 27, Council on Foreign Relations, April 2007; Diamond, Linz, and Lipset, "Introduction: What Makes for Democracy?"

90. "China Vows to Clean Up Judiciary After Conviction of Supreme Court Vice President," *Xinhua,* March 11, 2010.

91. Freedom House, *Freedom in the World 2010.*

92. Mark P. Lagon, "Fraying Rule of Law and Free Expression: The Stakes for Business," Freedom House, April 7, 2016; Arch Puddington, "Erosion of Freedom Intensifies," in Freedom House, *Freedom in the World 2010.*

93. Lagon, "Fraying Rule of Law."

94. Robert Dahl, *Democracy and Its Critics* (New Haven: Yale University Press, 1989).

95. Howard J. Wiarda and Harvey F. Kline, *An Introduction to Latin American Politics and Development* (Boulder: Westview, 2001); Sonia E. Alvarez, *Engendering Democracy in Brazil: Women's Movements in Transition Politics* (Princeton: Princeton University Press, 1990); Diamond, "Three Paradoxes of Democracy."

96. Cheeseman, *Democracy in Africa;* Diamond, "The Uncivic Society."

97. Diamond, Linz, and Lipset, "Introduction: What Makes for Democracy?"; Diamond, "The Uncivic Society."

98. Freedom House, *Freedom in the World 2010.*

99. UN Women, "Power and Decision Making," in United Nations Statistics Division, *The World's Women, 2015,* www.unstats.un.org.

100. Alvarez, *Engendering Democracy in Brazil;* United Nations Development Fund for Women (UNIFEM), *Democratic Governance 2010,* www.unifem.org; United Nations Statistics Division, *The World's Women 2010: Trends and Statistics,* www.unstats.un.org.

101. United Nations Statistics Division, *The World's Women 2015,* p. 121.

102. Ibid., p. 123.

103. United Nations, *The Millennium Development Goals Report 2010,* June 15, 2010, www.un.org; United Nations Statistics Division, *The World's Women 2010: Trends and Statistics.*

104. Abraham Lama, "Women Lawmakers Unite Behind Gender Issues," Inter-Press Service, September 13, 2001; Jane S. Jaquette, "Regional Differences and Contrasting Views," *Journal of Democracy* 12, no. 3 (July 2001).

105. "Global Gender Gap Report 2015," World Economic Forum, 2015; United Nations Development Programme (UNDP), *Human Development Report 2015.*

106. Alvarez, *Engendering Democracy in Brazil;* UN Women, "Facts and Figures: Ending Violence Against Women," February 2016, www.unwomen.org; United Nations, *The World's Women 2015: Trends and Statistics,* p. 160.

107. Pinar Ilkkaracan and Liz Ercevik Amado, "Good Practices in Legislation on Violence Against Women and Problems of Implementation," United Nations Office on Drugs and Crime (UNODC), May 23, 2008; "Turkey Withdraws Child Rape Bill After Street Protests," BBC News, November 22, 2016.

108. Duncan Tucker, "Murdering Mexican Women with Impunity, Al Jazeera, May 13, 2015.

109. Richard H. Kohn, "How Democracies Control the Military," *Journal of Democracy* 8, no. 4 (1997); Richard J. Payne and Jamal R. Nassar, *Politics and Culture in the Developing World* (New York: Pearson, 2012).

110. Gilbert da Costa, "Nigerians Wonder: Could a Military Coup Help Us?"; Richard Joseph, "Economic Transformation and Developmental Governance in Nigeria: The Promise of the Obama Era," Brookings Institution, June 24, 2010, www.brookings.edu.

111. Joe Cochrane, "Killings Raise Doubts on Indonesia Military Overhaul," *New York Times,* April 13, 2013; Charles Fromm, "US Seeks to Resume Indonesian Training," *Asia Times,* March 6, 2010.

112. Linz and Stepan, *Problems of Democratic Transition and Consolidation.*

113. Fukuyama, *Political Order and Political Decay.*

Chapter 14

Authoritarian Backlash: Freedom in Decline?

Mugabe's birthday is like that of Jesus Christ.

> —*State-run newspaper in Zimbabwe on the occasion*
> *of the president's lavish ninety-second birthday party celebrations*[1]

It's a crazy time. Anything could happen. In my opinion, we are facing a tyrannical regime, an old form of dictatorship.

> —*Khaled el-Balshy, Egyptian journalist*[2]

Given the difficulties associated with the democratic transitions described in the preceding chapter, it is important to recognize that transitions can be tough, protracted, and inconclusive. Many countries that began a political liberalization have already returned to authoritarianism, while others hang on precariously, under serious threat. It has long been recognized that the so-called transitions we see in many countries may be more virtual than real. Transitions can be co-opted, controlled, or aborted.[3] Democracies are wavering, or worse, being discarded.[4] As it becomes clearer that the so-called third wave of democratization has passed, are we on the verge of an authoritarian resurgence?

As we will see in this chapter, it is not unusual for authoritarian governments to seek to legitimize their rule through elections. They are not above affecting the appearance of reform and will go to any lengths to hold on to power. They've had experience. In the big picture, there are more types of authoritarian regimes than democracies, and authoritarian leaders have ruled more people (and, as a governing system, authoritarianism has been a dominant governing system longer than democracy).[5] However, with some important exceptions, authoritarians have tended to perform poorly. In Somalia and a handful of other cases, years of authoritarian rule have aggravated various divides to such an extent that the state has disintegrated or collapsed. As we will see, more than a few states today are at risk of imploding or failing.

What Is "Virtual Democracy"?

One could say that there are as many different types of authoritarian systems as there are democracies. They can be right-wing and conservative, seeking to maintain the status quo or even turn back the clock to an idealized time, or they can be left-wing and radical, promoting transformative change. What we see among communal dictatorships, theocracies, and populist dictatorships (to name only a few forms) is that even governments that reject the democratic transition are scrambling to preserve their positions. They are under varying degrees of pressure from donors to at least effect the appearance of reform.

Although these nondemocratic regimes share some important qualities with what we've called "the messy middle's" DELEGATIVE DEMOCRACIES, their leaders are solidly authoritarian. Whereas executives in delegative democracies dominate the other branches of government, the authoritarians described here subvert the entire democratic process. They may not appear quite as repressive as old-style authoritarians. The levels of repression today may not rank equally in terms of severity and magnitude with what occurred during the height of the Cold War. Still, in reconfiguring systems, there are significant restrictions on participation, competition, and civil liberties. They may have elections, but they are patently unfair. In Algeria, for example, when it appeared that the "wrong party" was about to win in 1992, the government canceled the elections. In Côte d'Ivoire, which in 2015 held its first peaceful elections in two decades, one of the incumbent's campaign slogans in 2010 was actually "We win or we win," and this was one promise he made good on, refusing to give up power after more Ivoirians voted for his opponent than for him.[6]

Reconfiguring regimes ban parties at will, and restrict most political organization and competition. Egypt's former president Hosni Mubarak (known as "the last pharaoh") was elected in landslide elections—it helped that the main opposition party had been banned and that his challenger had been just recently released from prison after spending three years there. Reconfiguring regimes are repressive of civil and political freedoms. Like the Mubarak government, they may go to great lengths to appear democratic, but they strenuously avoid any real political reforms, sometimes until it is too late, as Mubarak and some of his neighbors have learned.[7]

Often, governments don't even bother to make it look like an election; they openly interfere with the campaign process and seek to further their political goals by establishing control over television, radio, and newspapers. Authoritarian governments have routinely imprisoned and tortured journalists who are critical of their policies. According to Reporters Without Borders, the Middle East and North Africa continue as the world's most dangerous regions for journalists. Iran and Egypt consistently rank among the Middle East's (and the world's) biggest prison for journalists and Netizens; it is said in Iran that there is "freedom of speech, but not freedom after speech."[8] In much of the world it is not uncommon for journalists and bloggers to be arrested, imprisoned, and tortured, often in the name of "state security." "Preventive measures" including torture and assassination have commonly been used against any who oppose the government, with systematic imprisonment being common. The world has definitely been experiencing a downward trend in press freedom: 2016 had the dubious distinction of shattering the record for number of journalists imprisoned globally—the highest number since the Committee to Protect Journalists began tracking arrests in 1990. The worst offenders are Turkey, China, Egypt, Eritrea, Ethiopia, and Iran.[9]

And the leaders of these countries are frequently quite unabashed about their behavior. They often make EXCEPTIONALIST claims that the rules don't apply to them. President Robert Mugabe, the world's oldest serving head of state, has declared that he will rule Zimbabwe until he is 100 (a statement that he reiterated after his 92nd birthday) and signed into law a constitutional amendment that allows him to choose a successor should he ever decide to retire midterm.[10] Conservatives in Iran say that they want reform, but that it must be in the context of an "Islamic-style" democracy in which conservative clerics still hold political power, befitting of an Islamic, not a liberal, republic. Although these leaders deny the impact international pressure has on them, many are sensitive to their image overseas and few can face down the threat of sanctions. In effect, what many leaders have created is what has come to be known as "donor democracy." In order to keep the flow of aid open, these "democratic authoritarians" must look like they're making respectable progress at "getting politics right." From their point of view, getting politics right may actually mean putting stability first, especially where experiments in democracy have been associated with corruption, inefficiency, instability, and economic chaos. This is the government's point of view in China, which along with Iran is one of a handful of countries that need not much concern themselves with appearances.

Both Iran and China claim to be pursuing their own versions of democracy. In China's case, it is a socialist democracy, "with Chinese characteristics." In Iran's case, at least until its handling of the widespread protests against the disputed election results in 2009, the theocracy could arguably be more outwardly democratic than the governments of many of its neighbors in the Middle East. Leaders of Iran and China insist that their countries are exceptional and will not follow the path of other countries. They continue to buck trends toward democratization, writing off Western democracy as "a great lie" or "bourgeois liberalization" that they hope to keep far from their borders. Chinese leaders have extended their attempts to ward off Western influence by cracking down on this influence in universities, international prep schools, and high schools, where, the regime contends, "hostile" forces attempt to spread their "subversive" ideas.[11]

Yet only a handful of countries have been able to ignore or contain Western pressures for reform. Because of its size and perceived power, China can scorn Western advice on good governance and still rest assured of the continuation of benefits such as most-favored-nation status and membership in the World Trade Organization (WTO). Because there is always someone eager to buy its oil, Iran has so far been similarly well placed to evade Western pressures for democratization (and it has apparently handled pressures for change from within, at least for now).

Until recently, most Middle Eastern governments have not had to bother reconfiguring, because of their oil and because they are relatively pro-Western. Out of fear that democracy might produce governments that are not so compliant (witness the shifts in post-Mubarak Egypt) the West has done little to pressure Saudi Arabia and the other Gulf states to democratize. However complacent the West may have been about its Arab allies, to varying degrees they are corrupt and unpopular—and they are having an increasingly difficult time holding off internal pressures for change.[12] Fewer and fewer dictators can ignore these pressures. Instead, through the use of manipulation and deception, some have become impostors, making what can only be called a pseudotransition. The result is the creation of a virtual democracy

or semidemocracy in which formal democratic political institutions exist to mask the reality of authoritarianism. Again, what they are doing is in effect crisis management. Authoritarians must come up with new survival strategies as the old ones become less viable. Although some, such as Bahrain, Yemen, and Syria, seem to have no problem with it, others find it harder to portray themselves as new democrats and meanwhile fall back on the old strategy of mass repression. Except for a few oil-rich regimes, they can no longer afford to co-opt the opposition with pork barrel items because of an International Monetary Fund (IMF) requirement for economic reform. Instead, they try to create new friends, mobilize old ones, and find new ways to channel and control participation. Often this results in only the most superficial of changes. Of course, each government varies in the degree to which it uses these strategies, reflecting a unique historical context as well as donor response, and this combination of factors explains the variation in results.[13]

Reconfiguration

Perhaps more remarkable than the reforms described in the preceding section is the story of how less-than-democratic leaders have scrambled to hold off pressures for real change by simply appearing to be more democratic. According to Catherine Boone, this scramble can be described as a reconfiguration, which can play out in any number of ways.[14] Reconfigurations are not in themselves necessarily bad things or nonevents. Even the most incremental steps or alterations can accumulate into substantial reform, if not transformative change. Simply the fact that regimes are squirming to renovate or reconfigure is evidence that the pressures upon them offer the potential for more substantive change. Reconfiguring systems may become more democratic or authoritarian. The outcomes will vary because they will be shaped by the choices made by individuals and groups operating under the constraints unique to each country.[15]

Despite the fact that they can come in many different shapes and sizes, there are certain qualities associated with reconfiguring regimes. As we will see, reconfiguring regimes centralize power in the hands of one or a few. They are personally appropriated states, in which the leader becomes interchangeable with the government. With little or no accountability, such governments easily fall prey to the temptations of corruption. To ensure that they retain their position and effect the appearance of legitimacy, they practice what we characterize as "low-intensity democracy." When they can't win elections fairly, they are not above drawing from a bag of tricks—even resorting to various means of repression.[16] Because of their overreliance on the military, reconfiguring regimes often end up as "hard states," which may work to keep them in power in the short term, but ultimately leaves them vulnerable to collapse.

Centralization of Power

Ironically, authoritarians justify their centralization of power as a way to secure their countries from collapse. The leader argues that the country is in crisis, and therefore every institution that might interfere with the effective exercise of power must be controlled. For example, during the Cold War, dictatorships kept judiciaries weak and submissive—so as not to be distracted with questions of constitutionality. However, some courts appear to be taking all this talk about democracy seriously, rendering decisions that proclaim that they cannot be bought or repressed into submission. Yet in

virtual democracies, this is often a thankless task. Although Zimbabwean courts have continually attempted to demonstrate their independence, the president's policy has been to disregard court orders. Judges have been physically harassed and the government has refused to guarantee their security. Vacancies are left unfilled as many independent judges in Zimbabwe have (in one way or another) been forced to resign, but the courts still occasionally act independently; they have dismissed terrorism charges against human rights activists and members of the opposition party because state security forces had abducted and tortured them. However, the security forces retaliated by arresting the magistrate who ordered the release of Roy Bennett (a popular white opposition leader facing terrorism charges).[17] In Iran, the Supreme Leader appoints the head of the judiciary, who appoints senior judges. Frequently trials are closed, confessions are coerced, and the accused are denied access to legal counsel. In the aftermath of the Green Movement in 2009, hundreds were convicted in a televised series of mass show trials, none of which met international standards for justice.[18]

Authoritarians typically demonstrate a similar predilection toward forcing the legislative branch of government into line. For years the parliaments and congresses serving such regimes have in one manner or another become rubber stamps for executive initiatives. There is a dual track of power in Iran and China. In both countries there is a government hierarchy of executive power. But running parallel to most institutions and often trumping the government is the true locus of power in each country. In Iran, the clergy and its institutions are supreme. In China, it is the branches (and "small groups") of the Chinese Communist Party.

Occasionally, however, governments playing at democracy have made the mistake of allowing their hold over the legislature to get away from them. In the 2008 elections in Zimbabwe, Mugabe's party for the first time lost its majority in the parliament. Under increasing pressure after he very nearly lost the presidential elections that year (winning only because the opposition candidate pulled out of the election to boycott in protest of election violence), Mugabe entered into what many saw as a faux power-sharing agreement, creating the post of prime minister for Morgan Tsvangirai. The resulting unity government established in 2009 was largely run by Mugabe, a wily strategist who worked the deal to his benefit at every turn. By the next time round, in 2013, Mugabe moved on without Tsvangirai and the Movement for Democratic Change (MDC), which lost the elections in a landslide.[19] What happens in such cases in reconfiguring regimes is that things change because either the executive has deluded himself into vainly believing that popular support would continue his party's domination at the polls, or he has simply proven unable to control the outcome in the way he could in the past. In Zimbabwe's case, Mugabe has hung on because he outplayed the opposition. As this book goes to press, Mugabe's stated intention of running as his party's candidate in the 2018 election, even though he will be in his mid-nineties, seems at least a possibility.

Personally Appropriated States

As you will recall from the first chapters of this book, most (but not all) global south countries have long histories of authoritarian government that go at least as far back as the colonial period. The result is now a tradition of arbitrary and unchecked power operating in both civilian single-party states and military dictatorships. Whether headed by a civilian or military leader, such governments can best be described as

personalist regimes or "personally appropriated states." By this we mean that there is such a consolidation of power in the hands of one individual that this leader comes to personify the nation. Personality is a big part of being able to pull this off. Personalist leaders tend to be exceptionally charismatic, or at least have a talent for making people believe that they have a near-mystical ability to know what is good for the country. To prove it, such a leader will try to portray himself as a populist, "a man of the people." An example is Mahmoud Ahmadinejad, the fiery nationalist president of Iran (from 2005 to 2013), who won a surprise landslide victory in the 2005 elections. But when he was handed a second term in 2009 (despite allegations of widespread fraud), it led to widespread demonstrations, which were met with a vicious crackdown by security forces.[20]

At least in his first run for the presidency, Ahmadinejad's style worked: a mix of Robin Hood economic populism (promises to fight for the poor and strip power from the rich and privileged) and Islamist hero (accusations that the United States is practicing nuclear apartheid). China's Xi Jinping, shortly after he was named general secretary of the Chinese Communist Party (CCP) in 2012, became known fondly as "Papa Xi," a virtuous husband (his wife was a famous army singer who was a household name long before her husband ever became powerful), friend of peasants, and enemy of the corrupt. His (slightly gilded) life inspired music videos, an entire genre of songs themed to "Big Daddy Xi," and even a popular entrée at a Beijing steamed bun shop.[21] Attempts by political elites to appear to be "regular guys" may be all about winning trust in government (which isn't as crucial for authoritarians as it is in democracies, but it doesn't hurt). It is certainly easier to do when one can manipulate the media with censorship. In fact, by 2016, Chinese state media were told to avoid using the popular nickname for Xi, the strongest leader China has seen since Mao Zedong, out of concerns of a growing personality cult and autocratic perceptions, both at home and abroad.[22]

During the Cold War, many of these leaders literally appointed themselves "president for life." Or, as in the case of the previous rulers of Iraq and Syria, they groomed their sons to succeed them in "hereditary republics." For years, then-president Mubarak was believed to be preparing his son, Gamal, to eventually inherit Egypt's presidency. But Gamal had a reputation as a playboy and no military credentials. The generals said no and Mubarak backed off the idea.[23] Others have so far more successfully constructed a system that guarantees their personal control into perpetuity. As mentioned earlier, President Mugabe's party "won" the two-thirds majority needed for him to change the Zimbabwean constitution, so he can personally install his successor without even calling for elections. These days, it's increasingly looking like that successor might just be his wife.[24]

Corruption

During the Cold War, what sustained such long-standing regimes, besides superpower support, was often a combination of co-optation and repression. Now as then in these PATRIMONIAL regimes, the leader plays the role of the benevolent but stern father. Under the continuation of a very old tradition in much of the world, patron-client relationships are based on reciprocity. The patron allocates resources and in return the client owes the patron his or her political loyalty. Consequently, in China some local governments have been described as mafia states allied with gangs. In

many ways the devastating Sichuan earthquake in 2008 revealed the extent of this problem, as widespread corruption is believed to have fatally compromised construction of schools and other buildings (nicknamed "tofu buildings"), some of which crumbled, killing 70,000, many of them schoolchildren.[25] Even though more than 3 million Zimbabweans were in dire need of food aid, Mugabe hosted one of multiple celebrations of his ninety-second birthday in a drought-stricken region of the country, to the tune of $1 million (with a cake that reportedly weighed more than 200 pounds); local residents scavenged through leftovers from the VIP tables.[26]

Another example of how this patron-client system works is illustrated by the relationship between potentially politically relevant interest groups (such as trade unions or peasant organizations) and the government. Corporatism is most associated with fascism in Nazi Germany, but it has several different meanings. Usually associated with some form of authoritarianism, its conservative advocates claim that it offers an alternative to LIBERAL DEMOCRACY and socialist totalitarianism. In many of the highly personalist regimes in Latin America in the 1960s and 1970s, corporatism took the form of "bureaucratic authoritarianism," in which the military joined with technocrats to promote order and growth. Whatever its variant, corporatism is unique to no single part of the world; it tends to grow wherever there are long traditions of powerful state rule. Corporatism describes the behind-the-scenes relationship between a governing party (or state) and various organized interests or sectors. It is built around a relationship of reciprocity in which the party seeks to control interest groups by recruiting, partially including, or co-opting them. The interest group affiliated with the state gets recognition as an "official" organization, the only one with the right to speak on behalf of a specific group. Although the state defines the powers of these organizations, the organizations do attain some of their objectives, and the state gains a new base of support. While part of the deal is that the interest group must drop at least some of its demands, some groups argue that they are being pragmatic in embracing such relationships, since the only alternative may expose them to massive government repression. Those who place a premium on stability and maintenance of order view corporatism as a benefit; however, under corporatism the masses are left out, and change, if it comes at all, is likely to be slow.[27]

Not only does this kind of co-optation swing elections, but patronage networks also often result in gross governmental excess and a distortion of priorities. In the worst cases, they amount to kleptocracies, in which leaders and their cronies help themselves to the nation's treasury and resources. During Indonesian president Suharto's thirty-two-year reign his family accrued a personal fortune estimated at $15–35 billion. The former president, with great fanfare, was placed under house arrest, but the charges against him were later dropped, ostensibly for health reasons (and reopened briefly in June 2006). His youngest son, Hutomo (Tommy), who held a monopoly on clove processing and controlled many key national industries, was sentenced to eighteen months in prison for a corrupt land deal. He was later sentenced to fifteen years for ordering the murder of a judge who had convicted him on corruption charges. Tommy was freed on "conditional release" after only four years.[28] This was the first time a member of that family had ever been convicted of a crime: Suharto died in 2008, having never fully faced corruption charges due to poor health, and he was buried with full military honors. Few Indonesians were satisfied with the light-handed treatment of the Suharto clan, and it was only in 2015,

when the Indonesian Supreme Court ordered that the family (who remain active in politics) pay back $324 million in state funds, that they have been held accountable in any "significant way" for malfeasance.[29]

Elites also benefit materially when sweetheart deals with multinational corporations create a windfall—and a class of multimillionaires. This appears to already be happening in Afghanistan, where more than $1 trillion in untapped minerals such as gold, copper, iron, and lithium promise to make it one of the most important mining centers in the world. Evidently, the gold rush has already started; in 2009 Afghanistan's minister of mines was convicted of accepting a $30 million bribe in return for awarding China the rights to a copper mine. A United Nations survey found that a majority of Afghans consider public dishonesty to be more of a problem than the war; at least half of the population admitted paying bribes, topping $3.9 billion in 2012 (an increase of 40 percent over 2009).[30] Meanwhile, former president Hamid Karzai's government blocked investigations of his supporters, who have been implicated in a range of scandals, from real estate to drug deals. In fact, graft is so systemic that it is said to provide the Taliban with their primary recruiting tool.[31] Such nepotism and cronyism are hardly a post–Cold War phenomenon. But they have proliferated since the 1990s as political leaders distribute valuable assets and lucrative state contracts to key allies and clients through the privatizations called for by neoliberal reforms. Of course, the extent of corruption varies widely by country. It is important to remember that no government in the world is completely honest. In some countries the corruption can be characterized as the "politics of the belly," in reference to grossly underpaid civil servants who moonlight or take bribes in order to make ends meet. Elsewhere, there may be a long tradition of gift-giving or nepotism, but the government still manages to function. However, in the most predatory states, corruption is so pervasive that the system is rotten. Ultracorrupt states (some of the worst today are said to be Somalia, Sudan, Afghanistan, and North Korea) are often notorious not only for their private use of public resources, but also for their lack of capacity and their incompetence.[32]

Low-Intensity Democracy

Yet despite these failures, reconfiguring regimes are hard to overthrow. Their leaders operate under what Phillip Huxtable calls "the universal law of politics": those in power strive to stay in power.[33] Few authoritarians willingly relinquish the reins of government to anyone but a handpicked successor. Instead of caving in to Western pressures, the "reform" they seek to initiate is entirely on their own terms, with their own timetables, and within the constraints they impose.[34] One common sleight of hand is to rush elections through before the opposition can organize or unify quickly enough to compete against the incumbent. The result is what we call "low-intensity democracy," in which there may be great fanfare about the coming democratic reforms. A new constitution may be created, opposition parties may be legalized, and elections may be held—but the reform process is hijacked. Elections are carefully calculated to produce the victory of the incumbent, who can then resist further change by claiming the popular mandate.[35]

There are a variety of ways of accomplishing this besides garden-variety practices such as stolen or stuffed ballot boxes, or turning away registered voters while allowing unregistered voters to cast their ballots (often more than once). Although many

US voters are alarmed to learn that irregularities have occurred in their own elections, the United States isn't the only place where entire graveyards of the deceased have "voted." Many people around the world vote under the watchful eye of a party functionary. In Indonesia under President Suharto, people were required to vote at work. Their ballots were opened on the spot and tallied on a large board visible to all.[36]

Moreover, the national electoral organizations established by governments are often funded by (and working for) incumbents. International and domestic election observers watch elections to report rule violations and interference with the democratic process, including intimidation and violence at the polls, irregularities in vote counting and tallying, and lack of objectivity at polling stations (i.e., who gets to vote without proper documentation). In one of the worst cases in recent history, in Peru, observers sent by the Organization of American States (OAS) left in protest over the Fujimori government's handling of the 2000 elections. In the first round of voting, for example, the number of ballots cast reportedly exceeded the number of registered voters by 1.4 million. In Peru it is said that the Fujimori government administered the results in a "step-by-step" coup. Concerns were raised again by the OAS in Peru years later when they observed regional and municipal elections in 2016, noting erratic procedures for the disqualification of candidates and expressing concern about the deaths of ten citizens the day before elections.[37] Uganda's 2016 presidential poll was viewed by most observers as "shambolic," with accusations of late arriving election materials (in areas known for their opposition to President Museveni), suppressed turnout, and illegally marked ballots.[38] There and in other countries that are more or less democratic, the collection of ballots can only be described as chaotic, as computer systems have been said to break down for hours or even days, resulting in highly suspicious delays in the count.

Mobilization Through Repression

Not only do reconfiguring regimes interfere with their opponents' ability to campaign for office, but they also run campaigns that are divisive and polarized. In a climate of economic hardship, incumbents can successfully portray democratic politics as a zero-sum game and play up fears, accentuating divisions along ethnic, religious, and other lines to mobilize the public. For years President Mugabe and the Zimbabwe African National Union–Patriotic Front (ZANU-PF) aggravated divisions between urban and rural dwellers to mobilize support. With their hold on power threatened by liberal, prodemocracy movements often centered in the cities, reconfiguring regimes like Mugabe's strike out at their enemies to disperse the opposition (for example, "Operation Drive Out Trash" razed the homes and businesses of 700,000 city dwellers in 2005).[39] Reconfiguring regimes also fall back on their long-established networks of rural support. Despite the fact that they too have been affected by budget cuts, systems of patronage (alliances with local and regional power brokers in the countryside) are often more institutionalized and therefore slower to break apart. Because poverty is often most pronounced in rural areas, the people living there fear losing what little state support they receive. As a result, rural areas are often major bastions of support for governments attempting to reconfigure.[40]

Besides manipulating rural-urban divides, reconfiguring governments may encourage a resurgence of ethnoregional or religious ideologies in order to mobilize populations and divert attention from the government's failures. As a result, ethnic

conflict often worsens under authoritarian rule. Over the years, Mugabe has been accused of cynically manipulating ethnic and racial divides to maintain his power base. Nationalism may also be used to divert attention from the government's failings by identifying scapegoats as the source of the country's problems. For example, leaders may exaggerate the threat by certain out-groups, either foreign or domestic, or hold them responsible for the country's problems. President Mahmoud Ahmadinejad blamed Iran's massive unrest in 2009 on Western provocateurs, attributing the protests to an international conspiracy seeking to promote a soft revolution.[41]

In Zimbabwe, Mugabe originally blamed white farmers for the country's problems. Britain and the opposition Movement for Democratic Change (MDC) were also scapegoated. In speeches, Mugabe corrupted his main challenger's name to "Tsvangison," making it English-sounding to Zimbabweans, and called him a "tea boy," insinuating that Morgan Tsvangirai was a British stooge.[42] For years now, Mugabe has blamed the British government and Western sanctions for most of Zimbabwe's political and economic problems.

In terms of enemies at home, it is not uncommon for women, homosexuals, immigrants, or minorities to be blamed for economic hardship, political instability, or a "decline in values." To legitimate their rule, reconfiguring regimes lash out at all kinds of enemies—real or invented. In an effort to appeal to conservative traditional and religious elements, authoritarian leaders commonly call for a reassertion of identity. According to Human Rights Watch, Egypt's dictatorship, led by Abdel Fattah el-Sisi, is cracking down on gays and lesbians, distracting from the country's multiple problems and inciting moral panic about foreign threats to Egyptian culture. This secular state is also seeking to build legitimacy with its citizenry by appearing "more Islamic than Islamists," partnering with the media to broadcast humiliating public raids and arresting people for vague crimes such as "debauchery" and "insulting public morals," which can result in imprisonments of three to eleven years.[43]

In another example of the use of this strategy to build legitimacy, authoritarians are notorious for manipulating "family values" and reinforcing traditional conceptions of women's proper role. Whereas some women are mobilized by conservative appeals to their "innate" commitment to the family and morality and have even supported military coups against democratic governments, those women who do not or cannot conform to "traditional" roles are designated as traitors. In countries around the world women are stigmatized and even attacked for their inability or unwillingness to stay within the boundaries set for them by the patriarchal order.[44]

Dictatorships worldwide have issued crackdowns for many of the same reasons. Whether it is the imposition of "protective legislation" that denies women access to employment, or reproductive controls that refuse them access to contraception or abortion, what reconfiguring leaders are doing is building political alliances, more specifically partnerships with traditional and conservative elements. For example, in Iran, the Basij, a voluntary militia created after the Islamic Revolution, is known for targeting homosexuals, women, and ethnic and religious minorities. The Basij was responsible for the 2009 shooting death of Neda Agha-Soltan, the young Iranian woman whose murder on a Tehran street was broadcast all over the world, and who has become a martyr of the Green Movement.[45] Although there is no agreement on whether Agha-Soltan was simply in the wrong place at the wrong time or whether it was no coincidence that she was female, we do know that around the world the pol-

itics of exclusion only work to heighten social tensions and violence. As we can see in the worst cases of this, such as Rwanda, scapegoating deepens already-existing divides and renders the prospects for a more authentic democratization at some point in the future all the more difficult.

Hard States

As states weaken and cleavages resurface, the possibility of state collapse grows. Where leaders stubbornly refuse to stand down, the ensuing instability is used as a justification for a more repressive authoritarianism. The late Kim Jong-Il and his son, Kim Jong-Un, who have literally starved North Koreans into submission, are classic examples (the Pyongyang government arguably stands alone as the most repressive in the world today). It could be argued that Robert Mugabe has just been using a lighter touch in Zimbabwe in recent years. When President Mugabe lost the first electoral round in a head-to-head race against his opponent in 2009, he unleashed such an onslaught of violence on opposition supporters (more than 200 were killed and thousands tortured) that their candidate, Morgan Tsvangirai, decided to withdraw before the runoff. Although Tsvangirai would likely have won the elections if they had continued (and been the least bit free and fair), he withdrew to save his supporters, fearing that Mugabe might order another massacre like the one that killed tens of thousands of people in Matabeleland in the 1980s.[46] Governments that commit such atrocities are described as "hard states." In such cases, authoritarianism risks becoming the cause of state collapse. Not to be confused with strong states, hard states such as North Korea, Eritrea, and Myanmar become totally dependent on the military for their survival. In many of these countries the government may have a civilian façade, but the military has an overwhelming influence—it is the only thing propping the government up.

As we have seen in the preceding two chapters, the civil and military spheres in much of the world are not as distinct as they are in consolidated democracies. Howard Wiarda and Harvey Kline argue that such a separation is not traditional in much of Latin America, where an alternation in power between military and civilian rule was for many years the norm. Even today, it is not uncommon for constitutions in Latin America to assign militaries the right, even the obligation, to intervene in the political process under certain circumstances. Similarly, executives are often constitutionally afforded extensive powers to bypass the legislature, and until relatively recently judicial review was not part of the Latin American legal tradition.[47] Consequently, it should be of little surprise that given the upheaval of the 1960s and 1970s, most Latin American countries (including El Salvador, Chile, Brazil, and Argentina) were rapidly becoming hard states. And Latin America was hardly unique.

In China this tendency is called "authoritarian resilience."[48] While some point to the recent significant growth in the number of antigovernment demonstrations in China as a sign that the government will soon collapse or democratize, it is just as likely that these demonstrations will prod the government to make just the reforms necessary to survive. Instead of being a sign of a state's declining power, such modification may actually work to enhance administrative efficiency, further entrenching the government's rule—as we have seen with villagers' committees' elections. Even in the face of mass discontent, such regimes can continue to consolidate power as long as the core leadership can avoid factional struggles and keep the support of the military and police.[49] However, under these and similar circumstances it is not

unheard of for authoritarians to lose this crucial source of support. The security forces step in to fill the political vacuum and to establish order—if nothing else.

While it is common for military leaders to promise a transition to democracy, most coups should be viewed as nothing more than yet another reconfiguration. There are some cases, such as Nigeria, where (at least for a while) it appeared that the promised transition did finally take place. As mentioned in Chapter 13, some people are skeptical about Nigeria, and doubt the military will ever truly turn over power to civilians, because (as in too many cases) such transitions are delayed, incomplete, or temporary. Sometimes military leaders simply reconfigure themselves as civilian candidates for president, hold staged elections, limit the ability of the opposition to compete, and (if all else fails) rig the results. More often, as is feared in Nigeria, the military just continues to govern from the wings. When this is the case, it should fool no one. It amounts to merely another manifestation of virtual democracy.

Disintegration

When the reconfiguration gets out of control, when the government will not budge in the face of overwhelming opposition and when divisions within the military render it unable or unwilling to prevent a breakup, the result is a crisis of governance, or at worst a disintegration. So far, outright disintegration has been the least-frequent outcome associated with this period of crisis management. It is much more common to find countries on the cusp of failure, characterized as "weak" or "failing" states. Yet even those categorized as failed states may not collapse. Most states that fall into these categories are in sub-Saharan Africa, but they can be found in a few other places as well (the states characterized in 2016 as most at risk for failing were Somalia, South Sudan, the Central African Republic [CAR], Sudan, Yemen, and Syria). All told, there were an estimated sixteen countries identified as at a "high" or "very high" risk of social unrest in 2016, including two of our case studies (Nigeria and Zimbabwe). The countries making this list were vulnerable because of a mix of factors: a high degree of income inequality, rising ethnic tensions, and low levels of public trust in institutions (to name just a few). Interestingly it is the "intermediate" regimes—neither consolidated democracies nor hardcore authoritarian regimes—that are believed to be the most susceptible to turmoil.[50]

What differentiates a weak state from a failed state? According to Stuart E. Eizenstat, John Edward Porter, and Jeremy M. Weinstein, the difference isn't so much about poverty per se as it is about lapses in three critical functions of government: the provision of security (and preserving sovereignty over the territory), the provision of basic services, and the protection of civil freedoms. Weak states are deficient in one of these areas, while failed states are not capable of fulfilling any of the three.[51] However, facing internal and external demands for substantive change, weak states (such as Somalia prior to 1991) can quickly erode and collapse, becoming failed states (such as Somalia since 1991). In 2016, analysts listed Somalia along with South Sudan, the CAR, Sudan, Yemen, and Syria as the weakest—in the process of decay and on a long slide toward disintegration.[52]

According to I. William Zartman, disintegration is best conceptualized as a long-term degenerative disease. Countries in decay are in varying stages of decline, but what they have in common is state paralysis: they can no longer perform the func-

tions that make them states. Under such circumstances government retracts and the countryside is left on its own. The state becomes a shell; there is no sovereign authority. Power is up for grabs and warlord politics, or rival power centers, play increasingly larger roles in people's lives. There is a breakdown of law and order, and organized violence becomes generalized. The effect is societal collapse. People retreat into ethnic nationalisms or religious affiliations as a residual source of identity and organization, and no single institution can claim to receive the support of or exercise control over the people living there.[53] Under such circumstances, even the firmness of national borders becomes vulnerable, and the fracturing or breakup of states becomes even more likely. Analysts tell us not to be surprised if such a pattern emerges over the next few years, as previous waves of democratization have been followed by reverse waves of democratic breakdown.[54]

But the degenerative disease that so many states are experiencing does not always prove fatal. A cure or more likely a remission is possible. Some states may survive political turbulence of the kind described, exist on the brink of collapse, and still emerge with new vigor. More analysts are arguing that given the arbitrary boundaries demarcating states, perhaps in some instances fragmentation is not a bad thing. Juan Linz and Alfred Stepan make the interesting point that in order to have a democratic regime, there must first be a viable state.[55] While we must never forget the human tragedy so often associated with disintegration, for some countries disintegration is increasingly being thought of as a necessary first step—before democratization can even be considered. Given the foundation of a more viable state, democratic forces may then regroup and substantive reforms can begin. Although external actors need to be kept in mind for the considerable role they play in shaping outcomes in weak states, what may prove to be more crucial to their recovery is the ability of civil society to rebound. Even a collapsed state can come back from the dead. To some degree, Rwanda is an example of this. The inhabitants of a territory must come together to restore faith in government and to support the successor government. If they can do this, what is left of the state may recover its balance and return to more or less normal functioning. However, if the pieces do not come back together, warlord politics is a likely fate of many weak states. Still, nothing is preordained. Even weak states evolve differently and no outcome is inevitable.[56]

Conclusions: Coping with Reversals and Fragility

Looking back on the dramatic political changes of the past thirty to forty years, most leaders have acceded to internal and external demands for political liberalization not only in a variety of ways, but also to varying degrees, depending on the intensity of the pressures they face. Some leaders have been willing to make the reforms necessary to build the base for a still-fragile democratic system. And while a strong economy is an asset, even democracies in some of the poorest countries, against all odds, have proven to be impressively resilient. Elsewhere leaders have made partial changes, or reconfigured the political system in such a way as to maintain their own power bases. To varying degrees, authoritarians of diverse stripes have effected the appearance of change. During this period of intense reconfiguration and reform that the world is experiencing today, there are some states that appear to be explicitly bucking the liberal democratic trend. In the case of China, for

example, one specialist characterizes efforts by prodemocracy activists as the "lessons of failure."[57] Certainly China is not alone in its ability to hold off change.

Still other political systems have disintegrated (or may yet disintegrate) under the cumulative effect of the pressures already described. Because they are so fragile, some democracies will struggle and eventually fail. Does this sound like the situation in any of our country case studies? A firestorm was created in 2009 when a US Joint Forces Command report listed Mexico along with Pakistan as at risk of rapid and sudden collapse.[58] Since the early 2000s, analysts have compiled the Fragile States Index, using twelve social, economic, and political indicators to analyze how events, people, and movements impact the likelihood of stability or collapse. In this context, Mexico has since been listed only in the "warning" range (at #100), listed as a lower threat than China (#83), Indonesia (#88), and Peru (#98). Zimbabwe ranks at #16 on the 2015 Fragile State Index: as one observer put it, Zimbabwe "got better by doing nothing"—simply by remaining stable without any noticeable gains in human rights, democratic freedom, or economic growth.[59] Nigeria also remains at risk; in both the 2015 and 2016 indices, Nigeria was included in the "high alert" category, ranking #14 and #13, respectively (trending higher in risk).[60] If this already-challenged and rapidly delegitimized democracy continues to find itself unable to deal with factionalized elites and address group grievances and uneven development, it could mean the end of civilian rule—whether through military coup or civil war.[61]

Ironically, given the current climate, it is the reconfiguring regimes (like Zimbabwe, perhaps) that are more likely to survive, at least in the short term. Despite donor talk about the importance of good governance, it is the virtual democracies that are best placed to enforce the economic reforms the donor countries so desire. Perhaps the worst thing for democracy is for developed countries to accept an incumbent's portrayal of political reform as destabilizing and dangerous. Unwilling to budge on neoliberal economic reforms or fearful of political vacuums, too often donors lower the threshold for their political expectations. They back off from demands for reforms such as respect for civil rights, agreeing with authoritarians that perhaps the people "aren't ready yet."

In this time of xenophobia, security concerns, rising nationalism, and fear of Islamism, it is more likely that donors will choose to sit back and accept such rationales. Yet in the case of authoritarians, we know from history that the more repressive a government is, the more likely it will threaten its neighbors, as well as its own people. It is also important not to forget the lessons of Somalia and Afghanistan—states left to fail can pose a world of problems for all of us. Therefore, as Larry Diamond and Marc Plattner observe, it is in our interests to do everything we can to nurture and support fragile democracies.[62] There is nothing inevitable about the triumph or persistence of democracy. Even consolidated democracies can decay if there is a long period of incompetent leadership. In the end, it is important to remember that there are a wide variety of possible outcomes to the transformations under way.

International pressure alone did not create the third wave of democratization, but if international support for it should continue to wane, the viability of already frail democracies will be further diminished. It is therefore crucial that the international community and regional actors assist fledgling democracies in their deepening and consolidation.[63] If the past few years have taught us anything, it is that the flexibility and adaptability of democracies can be severely tested by the resiliency of authoritarians.

Notes

1. Quoted in Hopewell Chin'ono and Norimitsu Onishi, "In Zimbabwe, Mugabe's Birthday Is Rife with Political Jockeying," *New York Times,* February 29, 2016, www.nytimes.com.

2. Leila Fadel, "In Egypt's Broad Crackdown, Prominent Journalists Are Now Facing Trial," National Public Radio, *Morning Edition,* June 2, 2016, www.npr.org.

3. Larry Diamond and Marc F. Plattner, introduction to *The Global Resurgence of Democracy,* ed. Larry Diamond and Marc F. Plattner (Baltimore: Johns Hopkins University Press, 1993).

4. Freedom House, *Freedom in the World 2015,* www.freedomhouse.org; Freedom House, *Freedom in the World 2016,* www.freedomhouse.org.

5. Andrew J. Nathan, "Authoritarian Impermanence," *Journal of Democracy* 20, no. 3 (July 2009), pp. 37–40.

6. Adam Nossiter, "Ensconced in the Presidency: With No Budging in Ivory Coast," *New York Times,* December 26, 2010.

7. Freedom House, *Freedom in the World 2010,* www.freedomhouse.org; "Egypt's Opposition Protests, Challenging Legislative Vote," Associated Press, December 12, 2010.

8. Lionel Beeher, "Q & A: Iran's Waning Human Rights," *New York Times,* August 10, 2006; Reporters Without Borders, "Press Freedom Index 2016," www.rsf.org; Reporters Without Borders, "Press Freedom Index 2010," www.rsf.org.

9. Elana Beiser, "China, Egypt Imprison Record Numbers of Journalists," Committee to Protect Journalists, December 15, 2015; Elana Beiser, "Turkey's Crackdown Propels Number of Journalists in Jail Worldwide to Record High," Committee to Protect Journalists, December 13, 2016.

10. Conor Gaffey, "Zimbabwe's Mugabe Plans to Live to 100 and Won't Retire," *Newsweek,* March 4, 2016, www.newsweek.com; Abraham McLaughlin, "With Party Win, Mugabe's Grip on Zimbabwe Tightens," *Christian Science Monitor,* April 4, 2005; "Mugabe Signs in a Successor Law," BBC News, November 1, 2007.

11. "China Battles Foreign Influence in Education," *The Economist,* November 26, 2016, www.economist.com; Simon Denyer, "China's President Takes Campaign for Ideological Purity into Universities, Schools," *Washington Post,* December 12, 2016, www.washingtonpost.com.

12. Emmanuel Sivan, "Illusions of Change," *Journal of Democracy* 11, no. 3 (July 2000); Laith Kubba, "The Awakening of Civil Society," *Journal of Democracy* 11, no. 3 (July 2000).

13. Merilee Grindle, *Challenging the State: Crisis and Innovation in Latin America and Africa* (Cambridge: Cambridge University Press, 1996); Catherine Boone, "'Empirical Statehood' and Reconfigurations of Political Order," in *The African State at a Critical Juncture,* ed. Leonardo A. Villalon and Phillip A. Huxtable (Boulder: Lynne Rienner, 1998); Larry Diamond, Juan J. Linz, and Seymour Martin Lipset, "Introduction: What Makes for Democracy?," in *Politics in Developing Countries: Comparing Experiences with Democracy,* ed. Larry Diamond, Juan J. Linz, and Seymour Martin Lipset (Boulder: Lynne Rienner, 1995).

14. Boone, "'Empirical Statehood.'"

15. Bruce Bueno de Mesquita and Alastair Smith, *The Dictator's Handbook: Why Bad Behavior Is Almost Always Good Politics* (New York: PublicAffairs, 2012); Grindle, *Challenging the State;* Leonardo A. Villalon, "The African State at the End of the Twentieth Century: Parameters of the Critical Juncture," in Villalon and Huxtable, *The African State at a Critical Juncture.*

16. Bueno de Mesquita and Smith, *The Dictator's Handbook.*

17. Barry Bearak, "Court Ends Terrorism Case Against Zimbabwean Activist," *New York Times,* September 28, 2009; Freedom House, *Freedom in the World 2010.*

18. Freedom House, *Freedom in the World 2010.*

19. "Zimbabwe Election: Mugabe's Zanu-PF 'Wins Majority,'" BBC News, August 2, 2013.

20. Michael Slackman, "Upstart in Iran Election Campaigns as Champion of Poor," *New York Times,* June 23, 2005.

21. Andrew Jacobs and Chris Buckley, "Move Over Mao: Beloved 'Papa Xi' Awes China," *New York Times,* March 7, 2015; Tom Phillips, "'Big Daddy Xi' No More? Chinese President's Nickname Nixed," *The Guardian* (London), May 3, 2016, www.theguardian.com.

22. Phillips, "'Big Daddy Xi' No More?"

23. "Egypt's Opposition Protests, Challenging Legislative Vote," Associated Press; Thanassis Cambanis, "Succession Gives Army a Stiff Test in Egypt," *New York Times,* September 12, 2010.

24. Mugabe's Party Sweeps to Victory," BBC News, April 2, 2005.

25. Andrew J. Nathan, "Present at the Stagnation," *Foreign Affairs,* July–August 2006; Nadja Kostka, "Devastating Earthquake in China Reveals Weak Construction Standards in Sichuan," Transparency International, July 2008, www.transparency.org.

26. Chin'ono and Onishi, "In Zimbabwe, Mugabe's Birthday Is Rife with Political Jockeying"; Ishaan Tharoor, "Zimbabwe's Mugabe Celebrated His 92nd Birthday, While a Starving Nation Got Crumbs," *Washington Post,* March 3, 2016, www.washingtonpost.com.

27. Douglas A. Chalmers, "Corporatism and Comparative Politics," in *New Directions in Comparative Politics,* ed. Howard J. Wiarda (Boulder: Westview, 1985); Roy C. Macridis and Steven R. Burg, *Introduction to Comparative Politics* (New York: HarperCollins, 1991).

28. "Tommy Suharto Freed from Prison," BBC News, October 30, 2006.

29. "Ex-Indonesian Leader Suharto's Family Ordered to Pay Back Millions in Embezzled Funds," *South China Morning Post,* August 11, 2015, www.scmp.com.

30. "Despite Progress, Afghanistan's Total Corruption Cost Increases to $3.9 Billion," United Nations Office on Drugs and Crime (UNODC), February 7, 2013, www.unodc.org.

31. James Risen, "US Identifies Vast Mineral Riches in Afghanistan," *New York Times,* June 13, 2010; UNODC, "Corruption Widespread in Afghanistan, UNODC Survey Says," January 19, 2010, www.unodc.org; Mark Landler, "Envoy Says Corruption Helps Taliban Win Recruits," *New York Times,* July 28, 2010.

32. Christopher Walker and Sanja Tatic, "Corruption's Drag on Democratic States," *Christian Science Monitor,* August 2, 2006; Transparency International, "Corruption Perceptions Index 2015," www.transparency.org.

33. Phillip A. Huxtable, "The African State Toward the Twenty-First Century: Legacies of the Critical Juncture," in *The African State at a Critical Juncture,* ed. Leonardo A. Villalon and Phillip A. Huxtable, 279–294 (Boulder: Lynne Rienner, 1998).

34. Boone, "'Empirical Statehood.'"

35. Grindle, *Challenging the State.*

36. Roger Cohen, "Yes, Democracy Is Imperfect, Even in Those Places That Never Heard of Chads," *New York Times,* November 30, 2000.

37. "Peru: OAS Observation Mission Recommends Deep Electoral Reform," Organization of American States, April 11, 2016, www.oas.org.

38. Richard M. Kavuma, "Ugandan Elections Marred by Shambolic Polls and Claims of Fraud," *The Guardian* (London), February 22, 2016, www.theguardian.com.

39. "Systematic Cleansing in Zimbabwe," *Christian Science Monitor,* June 23, 2005.

40. Boone, "'Empirical Statehood.'"

41. Michael Slackman and Nicholas Kulish, "Iran Continues to Focus on Outside Provocateurs, Now Blaming Germany," *New York Times,* January 27, 2010.

42. "Report: Mugabe Calls Top U.S. Official 'An Idiot,'" Associated Press, July 7, 2009.

43. Graeme Reid, "Dispatches: For Political Gain, Sisi Targets LGBT Community," Human Rights Watch, December 10, 2014.

44. Valentine M. Moghadam, *Globalizing Women* (Baltimore: Johns Hopkins University Press, 2005).

45. Howard J. Wiarda and Harvey F. Kline, *An Introduction to Latin American Politics and Development* (Boulder: Westview, 2001).

46. Freedom House, *Freedom in the World 2010.*

47. Wiarda and Kline, *An Introduction to Latin American Politics and Development.*

48. Andrew J. Nathan, "Authoritarian Resilience," *Journal of Democracy* 14, no. 1 (2003).

49. Nathan, "Present at the Stagnation."

50. Stuart Eizenstat, John Edward Porter, and Jeremy Weinstein, "Rebuilding Weak States," *Foreign Affairs,* January–February 2005.

51. Ibid.

52. Fund for Peace, "Fragile States Index 2016," www.fsi.fundforpeace.org.

53. I. William Zartman, "Introduction: Posing the Problem of State Collapse," in *Collapsed States: The Disintegration and Restoration of Legitimate Authority,* ed. I. William Zartman (Boulder: Lynne Rienner, 1995).

54. Larry Diamond, "Is the Third Wave Over?," *Journal of Democracy* 7, no. 3 (July 1996); Guillermo O'Donnell, "Delegative Democracy," *Journal of Democracy* 5, no. 1 (January 1994); Diamond and Plattner, introduction to Diamond and Plattner, *The Global Resurgence of Democracy.*

55. Juan J. Linz and Alfred Stepan, *Problems of Democratic Transition and Consolidation: Southern Europe, South America, and Post-Communist Europe* (Baltimore: Johns Hopkins University Press, 1996).

56. Monte Palmer, *Comparative Politics: Political Economy, Political Culture, and Political Independence* (Itasca, IL: Peacock, 1997); Zartman, "Introduction: Posing the Problem of State Collapse."

57. Andrew J. Nathan, *China's Transition* (New York: Columbia University Press, 1997).

58. Bernd Debusmann, "Among Top US Fears: A Failed Mexican State," *New York Times,* January 9, 2009.

59. Christine Mungai, "Africa in the Fragile States Index: South Sudan Worst, S. Africa and Senegal on Watch List, Zimbabwe Shines," *Mail and Guardian Africa Newsletter,* June 19, 2015, www.mgafrica.com.

60. Fund for Peace, "Fragile States Index 2016," fsi.fundforpeace.org; Fund for Peace, "Fragile States Index 2015."

61. Ernest Aryeetey, "Can Nigeria Fail?," Brookings Institution, June 24, 2010, www.brookings.edu; "The Failed State Index 2010," www.foreignpolicy.com.

62. Diamond and Plattner, introduction to Diamond and Plattner, *The Global Resurgence of Democracy.*

63. Diamond, Linz, and Lipset, "Introduction: What Makes for Democracy?"; Villalon, "The African State at the End of the Twentieth Century"; Julius E. Nyang'oro and Timothy M. Shaw, "The African State in the Global Economic Context," in Villalon and Huxtable, *The African State at a Critical Juncture.*

Chapter 15

Linking
Concepts and Cases

Great variation exists among our eight case studies in terms of history, economy, and society. In the following pages we will briefly review each country's recent political history, using examples to illustrate some of the concepts discussed in the preceding two chapters. As you read these case studies, look for the major similarities and differences of experience—especially in regard to their REFORM, RECONFIGURATION, or DISINTEGRATION. Keep in mind that because of the dynamic nature of politics, it is likely that some things have changed since this book was published, so further research may be needed to answer some of the questions posed here.

Where, and why, would you locate each case on the continuum from consolidated liberal democracy to authoritarian regime? Why do you think some countries are taking the reformist route while others reconfigure? What are some of the ways in which government leaders attempt to hold on to power? To what extent have the military, the economy, and the existence of pluralism complicated transitions, or consolidation?

In which cases has the population appeared to choose the order provided by authoritarianism over the instability associated with democracy? What are the major supports and constraints for democracy in each country? Where have the constraints become crises, and which are the most prone to disintegration? Which governments are suffering from the worst crises of efficacy? Have they been able to overcome these problems? What are some of the ways countries have attempted to undo decades of corruption? Of those that have made the most progress toward democracy, how have they achieved their success? Conversely, how are the reconfiguring regimes faring now? Which of these countries have made progress toward deepening democracy? In what ways are they accomplishing this?

Case Study: Mexico

Over the past few decades, Mexico has been engaged in one of the world's longest and most dramatic democratic transitions. Until 2000, Mexicans had lived for seventy-one years under a government controlled by the Institutional Revolutionary Party

(PRI). Politics in Mexico was for generations a zero-sum game in which all formal power was centralized under the control of one party. Although this was no democracy, many Mexicans appreciated the relative stability their country enjoyed under the PRI.

Still, since the 1970s, certain factions in the PRI recognized the need for political reform, which occurred in fits and starts. By the mid-1990s it had become clear to many Mexicans that the relative stability provided by one-party rule could not make up for the excesses that came with it. Mexico was experiencing a series of legitimacy crises, most notably associated with an economic collapse in 1994 and a civil war in the south. In addition, Mexicans were rocked by a number of major scandals, pervasive corruption, and a growing lawlessness in the country, much of it linked to Mexico's newly prominent position in the international drug trade. Moreover, Mexico's economic difficulties and growing inequalities were contributing to a situation in which stability could no longer be ensured.

At about the same time that all this was happening, the United States, Mexico, and Canada were moving toward the creation of the North American Free Trade Agreement (NAFTA). Yet its passage was delayed in the US Congress because of a number of concerns, including questions regarding the antidemocratic character of the PRI government. In the end, a combination of internal and external pressures convinced the PRI to move forward with a "silent revolution," or gradual democratization of Mexico.

Despite internal struggles within the PRI over whether such changes would cause the party to lose control of power—or were its best hope for holding on to it—political and economic reform proceeded. The legislative elections of 1997 marked a watershed event, in that for the first time the PRI lost its majority in the Mexican congress. Yet it was President Ernesto Zedillo's dramatic break with the tradition of the *dedazo* (or "the tap of the finger," in which the outgoing president handpicked his successor) that opened up the political space for Mexicans to take part in truly democratic elections.[1] There were some irregularities, but in many ways this election amounted to Mexico's second revolution—after seven decades of uninterrupted rule, the PRI lost and actually allowed itself to be removed from power.

The personality dominating this "electoral revolution" was Vicente Fox of the conservative National Action Party (PAN). Fox campaigned hard in appealing to the average Mexican's dissatisfaction with politics as usual, and he won by a clear margin. Just as surprising as the result of the vote was that the transfer of power was remarkably smooth. However, with a term limit of six years, Fox had precious little time to demonstrate to Mexicans that he could make good on his grand promises. Although the economy did remain relatively stable and the government made some inroads against corruption, Fox's record is widely considered disappointing.[2]

Ironically, part of the reason that President Fox failed to meet the people's high expectations was because Mexico's democracy was working—since 2000 it has become stronger, more accountable, and more transparent. Still, the presidential election of 2006 was extremely divisive. For months up until the election it looked as if Mexicans would choose by a landslide their first leftist president, Andrés Manuel López Obrador, a populist former mayor of Mexico City. However, in the last weeks of the campaign, another career politician, the conservative, Harvard-educated Felipe Calderón, came from behind to win. López Obrador called foul and demanded a recount, claiming that the election had been stolen from him by a conspiracy of government and business elites backing Calderón. It took two months before Mex-

ico's federal electoral tribunal came to the unanimous decision that Calderón was the rightful winner. In this country with a long history of fraudulent elections, López Obrador suspected a continuation of the tradition and refused to accept defeat. Worse, in the months after the painful and protracted election was decided, it appeared that nearly one-third of Mexicans were disillusioned with democracy—and it was not uncommon to hear Mexicans question whether they had a democracy at all.[3]

This lack of legitimacy is very dangerous for any new democracy, and Calderón hardly had a mandate: he won by less than 1 percentage point.[4] The new president's term was plagued by difficulties, but the hallmark of his administration was his declared war on drugs, which most analysts agree only threw fuel on the problem. Some kingpins were put away, only to set off bloody turf wars and succession crises.[5] Meanwhile, as the second PAN administration struggled, the PRI revived and rebranded itself.[6]

Rested and ready, the PRI was building momentum; by 2012 Calderón's term was up, and people were ready for a change. Enrique Peña Nieto, a telegenic young PRI governor of the state of Mexico, won with only 38 percent of the vote and the PRI didn't win the majority in the house it hoped for. Perhaps most notably, in 2013 Mexico's democracy passed a crucial litmus test with a successful alternation in power—ironically, the party that replaced the dictatorship passed the torch to the democratically elected winner: the party that was the dictatorship.

Also auspicious was the new government's recognition that in order to get anything done, cooperation with the opposition was a necessity. The Pact for Mexico, an unprecedented agreement negotiated between the incoming administration and the (usually noncooperative) three main political parties, enabled the government to move forward on a variety of legislative initiatives dealing with the economy, societal rights, justice and security, corruption, and democratic governance.[7]

Why should the opposition cooperate? The PAN hoped to make a comeback as the anti-PRI, showing that it would not be obstructionist and could push forward its own agenda. The PRD, on the other hand, now under more moderate leadership was determined to advance its own goals by not squandering its influence by refusing to negotiate with the president (López Obrador, who again challenged the election result and broke with the PRD to form a new party, was another story). At least for a while, there were good reasons for all three parties to work together, despite years of mutual mistrust. But the tripartisanship fell apart as the president found it increasingly difficult to keep all sides appeased. In the end, the PRD felt betrayed and withdrew from the pact in 2013. And the government never got around to two of the most important issues for Mexicans: corruption and security.[8]

Because of his failures in both areas, Peña Nieto's popularity has tanked to the lowest rating of any president in the past twenty-five years (he and his wife have been caught up in their own corruption scandals). As a result, campaigning got ugly in the 2016 midterm elections, and Mexicans sent the PRI a resounding message with major defeats in local and regional elections and the loss of some key governor seats to the PAN. Outsider, independent candidates were attracting attention, and even López Obrador (who hasn't given up his presidential ambitions) and his relatively new National Regeneration Movement (Morena) Party did well in some states. For the time being at least, the PRI remained the dominant force in politics. But voters made it clear that the PRI wouldn't be able to count on continued control of the presidency the next time up, in 2018.[9]

Case Study: Peru

Whereas most of the rest of Latin America has continued on with a political liberalization dating back to the early 1980s, Peru reversed course—and has since reversed itself again. Although it wasn't a smooth ride, until 1992 Peru was undergoing a democratic transition and was on the same path as many of its neighbors. Not exactly a liberal democracy, most analysts agreed that it had made some progress toward democratic institutionalization. But because it has so consistently swung back and forth between authoritarian and democratic rule, Peru came to be known as an "intermittent democracy."[10]

Based on his experience in a war on drugs, two guerrilla insurrections, and hyperinflation, nearly twenty-five years ago Alberto Fujimori, the democratically elected president of Peru, determined that democratic dialogue was inefficient. Extraordinary circumstances called for extraordinary actions. Frustrated with the limitations placed on him by the checks and balances of Peru's democratic institutions, in 1992 Fujimori assumed for himself the powers of a military dictator. With the assistance of Peru's National Intelligence Service and the military elite, Fujimori concentrated power in his own hands, declared a state of emergency, and dismantled democratic institutions by closing the congress and purging the judiciary. By 1995 he had vanquished his enemies, turned the economy around—and been reelected by a landslide. Although there is room for disagreement as to why Peruvians were willing to surrender their hard-earned but still somewhat restricted democratic liberties to Fujimori, even his enemies admit that the president was able to provide Peruvians with a sense of stability relatively unknown in the Andean region.[11]

While appreciative of the order he provided, by the late 1990s Fujimori was second only to Fidel Castro as the longest-sitting head of state in Latin America. The government had crossed the line from DELEGATIVE DEMOCRACY into authoritarianism and Peru could no longer meet even the minimum qualifications of democracy once Fujimori determined that there was no one else capable of running the country.[12] The president pulled out all the stops and ran what is widely agreed to be the dirtiest campaign and election in the country's history. In the end, large numbers of Peruvians, and most of the world, refused to recognize the result of the 2000 election, in which Fujimori declared himself the winner in his race against civil society leader Alejandro Toledo.[13]

Ultimately it was a corruption scandal that brought Fujimori down. Although mysteries still abound concerning who actually held power in Peru and the military's role in what some call a "clandestine coup," crowds celebrated the president's faxed resignation from Japan in November 2000. (Fujimori later became the first Latin American president found guilty of human rights abuses in a court in his own country. He is serving time for several sentences, including twenty-five years for his role in authorizing death squad killings.)[14]

Since Fujimori's ouster and the return to democracy, Peruvian leaders have been challenged to deal with several problems at once: rebuild democratic institutions, restore the credibility of the judicial system, and establish the rule of law.[15] Peruvians do enjoy more political and civil liberties, the rule of law has been strengthened, Peru's institutions are showing signs of more independence and more accountability, and the country is in better shape economically.[16] Peru continues to have problems with corruption, controlling the military, and restoring Peruvians' faith in

politics. According to one analyst, Peru was like a spouse who had been cheated on: there has been a lot of hurt and mistrust.[17]

It is probably just as well then that Peruvian presidents are prohibited from seeking two consecutive terms, since voters have proven fickle, choosing presidents from the center-right, swinging to the left, and back to the center-right again (during his single term, President Ollanta Humala moved from the far left to the center). This fickleness may be explained by a saying popular during the 2006 elections that compared the two candidates to a choice between "cancer or AIDS."[18] Parties exist, but there is little party loyalty as traditional political parties have become virtually extinct in Peru. Instead, it is more common to find candidate-centered movements closely identified with a single personality or "flash parties," because they are disposable and vanish almost as quickly as they appear.

But many Peruvian voters have proven loyal to personalities, and it is not at all uncommon for once-disgraced politicians to make comebacks. Some fear it, others applaud it, but in some ways even Fujimori is getting a second act. In this case, it is his daughter, Keiko Fujimori, who served as his first lady and at times has vowed to pardon her father if she is elected president (she eventually was pressed to sign a pledge not to pardon him). On the right wing of the spectrum, the younger Fujimori appealed to many fearful of Peru's growing crime rate (a key issue in the election; she has suggested building prisons high in the mountains to punish and isolate criminals). Keiko Fujimori is widely viewed as the toughest on national security and her supporters are nostalgic for her father's iron-fisted record, remembered for vanquishing a terrorist group and hyperinflation. As a result, she was a leading contender in the presidential contests in 2011 and 2016, in 2016 losing by 0.248 percent of the vote in the second round to pro-business former finance minister Pedro Pablo Kuczynski, known as PPK.[19] Fearing a revival of authoritarianism and corruption associated with the elder Fujimori, the third-place leftist candidate at the last minute threw her weight behind center-right Kuczynski—despite the fact that he is identified with the white elite establishment that isn't known for prioritizing the needs of the poor. She was joined by many Peruvians who saw Fujimori as a risk to the democracy. But Fujimori and her party (Popular Force) aren't going away; PPK will have to work with the Fujimoristas, who have reshaped the political landscape, and who hold a majority (73 of 130) of the seats in Peru's parliament, versus the 18 held by Peruvians for Change, PPK's party. This math (and this party rivalry) will pose a challenge to the president's agenda, but the two parties are actually quite alike ideologically and should be able to find room for at least limited cooperation. The 2016 elections mark the first time Peru has had four consecutive democratic transfers of power in more than a hundred years.[20] That feat suggests that democracy has become a habit in Peru and that the country is proving itself not to be an intermittent democracy, after all.

Case Study: Nigeria

As discussed in Chapter 5, Nigeria has come through a nightmare to begin its democratic transition. And in what is surely a case of truth being stranger than fiction, a born-again former military dictator led the way. Until this latest experiment with democracy, in 1999 Nigeria had spent only ten of its nearly forty years of independence under civilian rule. Earlier experiments with democracy failed in the

midst of intense political crises, polarization, incompetence, and a lack of economic development. Nigerians have endured incompetent and corrupt civilian governments; they suffered worse through a civil war and through coup after coup, but the country hit bottom during the five years it spent under the dictatorship of Sani Abacha (1993–1998).

It is difficult to briefly relate just how venal this government was. Those with political power amassed enormous fortunes from the country's oil wealth, to such a degree that Nigerian political culture has been described as "prebendal," or based on the systematic abuse of state office and resources for individual and group gain. This is hardly a fair characterization of the Nigerian people, since most of them received nothing from these transactions. Under both civilian and military rule, the vast majority of Nigerians have been permanent outsiders.[21] For years, those who dared speak out against the government and its abuses were harshly repressed.

Yet in what has been described by many Nigerians as divine intervention, in June 1998 Sani Abacha suddenly dropped dead. And by that time the military had tired of the exercise of government and was willing to give civilians another shot. To create what would become known as the Fourth Republic, Nigerians poured into the voting booths in February 1999. They elected representatives at all levels of government, including the presidency. And although observers cited many electoral abuses, they accepted the results because the irregularities did not appear to be systematic. Olusegun Obasanjo won, the military remained in the wings, and Nigeria began its fourth go at democracy.

Most observers agree that Obasanjo and his People's Democratic Party (PDP) won by a landslide. Yet from the outset there were serious challenges to the president's ability to govern. The country appeared to be fragmenting, and the population was becoming increasingly frustrated with the government's lack of capacity. However, 2003 was hailed as a "judgment year," an important test for democracy in Nigeria in its first civilian-run elections in twenty years. Obasanjo was reelected with 62 percent of the vote.[22]

Still, there was growing public dissatisfaction with the government. Since the military's handover of power to civilian rule in 1999, Freedom House has ranked Nigeria as "partly free." The country's progress on civil and political rights has been mostly stagnant.[23] Between 2000 and 2016, Nigerians' trust in their president fell from 77 to 31 percent, and their satisfaction with democracy fell from 84 to 29 percent. In 2014, two-thirds of Nigerians said that their country is headed in the wrong direction.[24] As of early 2017, Nigeria had managed to survive without a coup and without breaking apart. But the country's democracy, for a variety of reasons, was not consolidating.

What is happening? Nigeria is said to be experiencing a "trapped" transition, a democracy that fails to thrive, or to improve in quality or results. The democratic consolidation has been slow, which is in part due to a variety of factors. These include election crises, but also weakened democratic institutions and a political class who have hijacked the system to promote their own self-interests.[25] For example, there have been several attempts at what some would call manipulating the democratic process. President Obasanjo proposed amending the constitution so that he could have a third term, but in a win for democracy, legislators shot this idea down.[26] The 2007 elections were widely regarded as the least free and fair since 1999, but it

should be noted that something remarkable happened: for the first time in Nigeria's history, one democratically elected leader transferred power to another democratically elected leader. Many marked this rite of passage for the democracy as a sign of its maturing, when President Obasanjo actually retired at the end of his two-term limit and handed over the reins of power to the winner of the elections, Umaru Yar'Adua. But both presidents were from the same party, the People's Democratic Party, and Obasanjo had a lot to do with choosing Yar'Adua as the party's candidate. So, given the circumstances, the outcome was not quite the triumph for democracy that many hoped for: it amounted to one member of the governing party merely handing power over to another. In fact, Nigeria became known as a dominant-party democracy (both houses of parliament and most of the governorships have been PDP).[27]

To his merit, President Yar'Adua recognized that there were problems with the elections that brought him to office and he did initiate a reform of the electoral process. However, about a year before the end of his term the president died while in office, nearly creating a crisis of state. Yar'Adua's vice president and successor, Goodluck Jonathan, a Pentecostal Ijaw from the southeast, was sworn in and at first appeared to abide by the deal for a rotating presidency, promising not to run in the next elections.[28] This was important, since, as far as many people are concerned, Yar'Adua's death meant that northern Muslims hadn't finished their turn at the presidency. However, the system of rotation was the practice but not the law; in the end Jonathan ran as the PDP candidate, violating the unwritten deal regarding a two-term presidential alternation between regions—a deal that is (arguably) responsible for sustaining the longest period of civilian rule since independence. In 2011 tensions were high and the election was ugly; at least 800 people were killed in post-election violence.[29] Many feared that Jonathan's win could bring on a coup, but he managed to serve out his term and even try for another.

Yet despite the advantages of incumbency (access to revenues and patronage networks, influence over the administration of the elections and ballot counting) Jonathan was unable to secure a second term due to the PDP split. Defectors joined with smaller opposition parties to form the All Progressives' Congress coalition, and Muhammadu Buhari, a retired general and former dictator (1983–1985), who had run for president in all four democratic elections since 1999, was finally victorious. The turnout was low, but the process was relatively peaceful and a substantial improvement over 2011. Buhari won 54 percent of the vote, bringing sixteen years of uninterrupted rule by the PDP (self-described as "Africa's largest political party") to an end.[30] With support even outside his traditional base in the north, Buhari, who is known for being tough, promised to vanquish corruption and Boko Haram—and with the savings produced, turn the economy around. Those might be hard promises to keep, since early on in his administration, there were already signs of trouble between him and the national assembly, where his own party, the All Progressives Congress (APC), was in the majority but where the PDP held a strong minority of seats.[31] Regardless of how that plays out, it is important to step back and recognize that in 2015 Nigeria marked a major milestone in its democratic transition. Until that year no democratically elected Nigerian president had ever before handed power over to another democratically elected leader—from another party. This amounted to a significant achievement for Nigeria's democracy, as one sitting president—and one party—actually stepped aside for another to take power.

Case Study: Zimbabwe

Since the overthrow of white minority rule in 1979, Robert Mugabe and his party, the Zimbabwe African National Union–Patriotic Front (ZANU-PF), have effectively dominated the country's politics. It should be pointed out that when he was first elected, this hero of the war for liberation inherited from colonial Rhodesia a highly centralized state and powerful security force. Over time, the president has established a state and security force that is just as centralized and powerful as the one he once fought. For years now he has claimed that the country is democratic, yet he has made a determined effort to undermine Zimbabwe's democratic institutions since the mid-1980s. He does have some popular support, especially in rural areas. Through alternating policies of co-optation and repression, Mugabe has so far been largely successful at controlling his opponents.[32]

Until about a decade ago, Mugabe could count on the full cooperation of the legislature in this effort, since party loyalists held virtually all the seats in the House of Assembly. However, by the late 1990s, internal and external pressures forced the president to undertake a reconfiguration. Not wanting to be seen by the world as a dictator, Mugabe very much needed the prestige of legitimacy, and believed he could obtain this with the pretense of democracy. However, at about this time a new opposition group, the Movement for Democratic Change (MDC), was rapidly gaining popularity in the cities. Meanwhile, the economy was in shambles and Mugabe, desperate for foreign aid, knew that the parliamentary elections due to be held in 2000 had to at least appear to be democratic.[33]

Recognizing these realities, Mugabe met these expectations partway. He did not outlaw opposition parties, but did not intervene in preelection violence aimed against them. In the elections that followed, irregularities were attributed to all sides, but human rights organizations report that ZANU-PF supporters were particularly violent—beating, gang-raping, and killing opposition candidates and their supporters. If the right to campaign is as important as the right to vote, then clearly these elections were marred from the start. Yet here again is evidence of a reconfiguration: Mugabe permitted the opposition a partial success. Perhaps it was just part of the democratic façade erected to assuage donors, but for the first time in two decades, ZANU-PF actually lost its two-thirds majority.[34]

Since then, the Mugabe government has become more adept at crushing any checks on its authority. The government threatened to ban the MDC (the only opposition party of any significance), and party leader Morgan Tsvangirai was tried for treason, a crime punishable by death (he was acquitted). In 2005 the then eighty-one-year-old Mugabe crowed that he would remain in power as president until the age of 100, and events since then suggest that he is intent on keeping his word. For the 2008 presidential elections, whether due to mounting internal and external pressures or to Mugabe deluding himself that he could actually win, the government continued to reconfigure. However, when it appeared that for the first time in three decades Mugabe would actually lose power—he came in second place to Tsvangirai in the first round of the vote—the president and his party reverted to old tactics. The lead-up to the runoff elections was so bloody that Tsvangirai pulled out to save his supporters, and Mugabe, in a one-man race, celebrated victory with 85 percent of the vote.[35]

After months of pressure from Zimbabwe's neighbors, the country's three main parties—ZANU-PF, the MDC-T (the main branch of the MDC, led by Tsvangirai),

and the MDC-M (a smaller faction of the MDC, led by Arthur Mutambara)—agreed in February 2009 to form a unity government. Despite grave reservations, Tsvangirai entered into the pact, as he put it, "to change the fronts on which we wage the struggle."[36] However, it was clear before long that Mugabe held the reins (leaving Tsvangirai with responsibility but no power).[37] "Power-sharing" proved to be a rocky road, as it became increasingly clear that the MDC was being played. As a result, the MDC's energies dissipated; outmaneuvered, it became even more divided and drained of resources. The presidential and parliamentary elections in 2013 amounted to a devastating loss for the MDC. It put an end to the power-sharing charade and left Mugabe and ZANU-PF back solidly in charge, where it remained as of early 2017.[38]

But there are growing signs of trouble from within the ruling party. In fact, some analysts believe that Mugabe may have stayed in power even longer than he prefers, because he thinks that he's the only person who can win elections and hold the party together. Or, it may be that the top brass would prefer that Mugabe step down, but fear that the party would collapse into warring factions without him.[39]

They may both be right. An unusually public divide appears to have riven ZANU-PF's politburo, its supreme decisionmaking body. The schism is based in regional and clan rivalries as well as ego and good old power politics—but not ideology. There are few reformers left in the mix now. A few years ago the various camps came to blows and moderate Joyce Mujuru, a veteran liberation fighter (also known as "Comrade Spillblood"), was purged. That left other ambitious, hard-line contenders such as Emmerson Mnangagwa, known as "the Crocodile" and head of the faction known as Team Lacoste, to vie against Mugabe's wife, Grace, who leads another faction, Generation 40.[40] There are others positioning themselves for power as well. But Mnangagwa is supported by war veterans, who had been Mugabe's staunchest defenders for decades, though they have broken with the president, blaming him for corruption and the economic crisis. The veterans have gone further, threatening war if Mnangagwa is not Mugabe's successor. For his part, Mugabe, who appears to favor his wife's Generation 40, has characterized these veterans as dissidents and promised a crackdown of genocidal proportions if they don't stop agitating.[41]

Meanwhile, Comrade Spillblood, Mujuru, has joined the opposition and launched a new party. At this point, should she throw her hat in the ring for the presidency, she'd be up against Mugabe, who has vowed to run again in 2018.[42] Still, however one defines "dignified exit," a transition could happen at any time. The president appears frail; he has been seen sleeping at public events and at one of them repeated an entire speech he had just read.[43] The current constitution is unclear about how to select a successor if the president dies or becomes incapacitated—although the notoriously avaricious Grace Mugabe has declared that her husband will continue to rule from the grave.[44] If the party were to turn on itself and split, it could open up a number of new possibilities—and likely mean a great deal of instability for all inside and outside its confines. Is the end of an era coming? Sooner or later, the world's oldest head of state will be out of the picture, but his death won't necessarily mean real change for Zimbabwe. ZANU-PF will still be left with a choice: either to retrench into a hard-line dictatorship or to put up a candidate who can actually win votes.

Case Study: Egypt

Is Egypt destined to live under dictatorship? There appear to be just enough people (inside it and out) who prefer it that way. Perhaps this is because compared to many other Arab dictators, Hosni Mubarak ran a "soft" dictatorship: he ruled under a state of emergency and heavy policing. He was an autocrat, like his predecessors Nasser and Sadat, and all three were military men who ruled with the support of a small elite, through patronage.[45] He used some of the trappings of democracy to maintain his hold on government. But Mubarak, who assumed power in 1981, was "like the guest at a party who refused to leave."[46] Thirty years on, Mubarak insisted that he had to stay, as he was the only alternative to chaos.[47]

But Mubarak's "win" of a fifth term in 2005, followed by rumors that if Mubarak ever did step down, his playboy son was the heir apparent, breathed new life into the opposition. In late 2010, the protests toppled Tunisia's dictator and the Arab Spring began to sweep the region. Given a deteriorating economic situation and a lack of economic prospects, Egyptians (especially the young) were ripe for revolution. Those under age forty (nearly 75 percent of the population) had only ever lived under two presidents.[48] Moreover, the social contract had fractured. There had long been an understanding between the government and citizens that those who kept their heads down, who "walk by the wall," could avoid trouble from the security forces. Yet Facebook was disseminating graphic evidence showing that no one was safe in Egypt anymore.[49]

All of these feelings were amplified by social media, which helped mobilize and organize an uprising. Young men and women of all political stripes, including some who usually avoided politics, convened in Cairo's Tahrir Square on January 25, 2011. They came initially to demand police reform. But before long protesters were calling for Mubarak's resignation and were joined by tens of thousands more (including Muslim Brotherhood members) in what would become Egypt's largest demonstrations in fifty years.[50] (As discussed in Chapter 10, the Muslim Brotherhood is an Islamist political movement trusted as competent and moral by many Egyptians due to a record for social welfare and religious instruction that no other group in Egypt can match. Since the early twentieth century with the slogan "Islam is the solution," it has resisted secularism in favor of a religious revival.)[51] For a brief, awe-inspiring eighteen days, reformists and revolutionaries, secular and religious people from across the political spectrum, came together in a coordinated fashion to demand political freedoms and economic justice. The protests spread across the country, despite repeated police crackdowns that resulted in the deaths of approximately 850 (mostly young) people. In the face of government violence, with few exceptions, the protesters maintained a nonviolent stance and refused to back down.[52]

Faced with a standoff, the military, the most powerful and admired political institution in the country, was finally persuaded that Mubarak had to go. But the military had only sacrificed Mubarak to protect their own interests. It is part of what is known as the Deep State, the core of military, security, political, and business interests that has run the country behind the scenes since 1952.[53] So, what happened after Tahrir was a quiet coup; Mubarak was moved aside, which allowed the military to openly take control of the transition—and in time, the country. But first the Muslim Brotherhood, the only group that had the money and organization to run a nationwide campaign, (briefly) prevailed in relatively free and fair elections in which it won control of parliament and its presidential candidate, Mohammad Morsi, won with 51 percent of the vote.[54]

Yet it was only a matter of time before the Tahrir protesters turned on each other. Although the Brotherhood had long claimed to defend individual rights and a civil state, many were skeptical of its democratic credentials. Morsi was blamed for adopting a winner-take-all swagger and displaying (what his critics called) the Brotherhood's true authoritarian streak. Morsi and his supporters argued that his government was only wresting control of the political transition from foreign enemies and the Deep State. In the end, the military found it impossible to tolerate such assertiveness from a civilian president and accomplished what it probably had in mind all along: a reconquest. It was assisted by hundreds of thousands of young Egyptian demonstrators who went back out in the streets to protest that the revolution had been hijacked. On July 3, 2013, Tahrir's secularists, liberals, and nationalists finally united—to applaud the overthrow of Egypt's first democratically elected government, after just one year in power.[55]

Fatigued, many Egyptians welcomed the military's return to power, which was followed by elections in 2014 that brought to power a little-known retired general, Abdel Fattah el-Sisi. This new president could be confident of the support, not only of all state institutions and economic elites, but also of many Egyptians who feel that he saved them from Islamists. There are still some who criticize the government, but the opposition is weak. It is as if Tahrir never happened.[56] All the preexisting problems remain unresolved. But Tahrir shows that the world doesn't always evolve slowly; sometimes it has a capacity for surprise and makes staggering leaps. In this case, Egyptians made the leap in that they conquered their fear and learned that they can topple a government.[57] This revolution, this change in outlook, can't be reversed and has set the terms for what will come—even if for Egypt great change in terms of meaningful citizenship and dignity has proven out of reach, at least for now.

Case Study: Iran

Iran is a country gripped by competing visions of its revolutionary legacies and future goals, which greatly impacts the scripts upon which its transitions are written. It has undergone cyclical changes, especially in its relationship with the Western world. The 1979 revolution, which overthrew Shah Mohammad Reza Pahlavi, sought to overturn the attempts at "Westernization" and establish an indigenous Islamic Republic under the leadership of Supreme Leader Ayatollah Ruhollah Khomeini. Former president Ali Akbar Hashemi Rafsanjani is often credited with maneuvering Iran through a murky decade of economic struggles and international isolation, and concurrently launching the country in an *abertura*-type direction. This helped promote a reform movement embodying limited pluralism that gained prominence during Mohammad Khatami's presidency from 1997 to 2005. Khatami campaigned on a reformist platform calling for relaxed social and cultural norms, mild openness to Western culture, and the inclusion of women in governance. Yet this movement activated a powerful conservative reaction, from both leaders and citizens. This prepared the foundation for the populist presidency of Mahmoud Ahmadinejad that followed (2005–2013). While, early on, the president was welcomed for his humble beginnings, he is now viewed as one of the most divisive presidents of Iran, having left the country isolated and in economic malaise.[58] Especially in his second term, Ahmadinejad flaunted his disregard for rules and procedures, tallying

a record 4,943 notifications from parliament for failing to implement various laws.[59] Ahmadinejad's tumultuous presidency was followed by the centrist-moderate Hassan Rouhani in 2013. Rouhani, a cleric, former nuclear negotiator, and academic, is viewed as the leader of the so-called Coalition of Hope, which includes reformists, centrists, and pragmatic conservatives who support the nuclear agreement with the P5+1 (the permanent five members of the UN SECURITY COUNCIL plus Germany) as well as Iran's easing of tensions with the West. This coalition though, even if currently in favor (especially after resounding parliamentary victories in 2016), enjoys less support outside urban Tehran. Rouhani, who was victorious in 2013 with over 50 percent of the vote (greater than all five of his harder-line conservative opponents combined), faces a delicate balancing act within the Islamic Republic's complex web of political and religious institutions. Having completed a doctorate from a Scottish university in the 1990s (his PhD thesis examined the flexibility of *sharia* law in the Iranian context), he is a leader accustomed to straddling multiple viewpoints, from which he has developed a reputation as a pragmatist.

Power in the Islamic Republic has long been concentrated in a single leader or small group of leaders who remain unaccountable to democratic procedures (the elected president, for example, is "head of government," but the more powerful position is "chief of state," held by the Supreme Leader). Elections in Iran are competitive, participatory, and raucous, yet they are not reflective of the true power dynamic within the country. Candidates are first vetted by the Council of Guardians, set up in 1979 to interpret legislation and ensure its conformity with the sacred law of Islam. This twelve-person group, whose members are appointed to power (six by the Supreme Leader), approves all legislation before it becomes law. Additionally, the council determines whether or not candidates are eligible to serve in public office, before they withstand the public votes. In the 2016 parliamentary elections, the council approved its lowest rate of candidates ever (6,229 out of 12,123), a rate attributable to an increase both in the number of candidates as well as in the amount of scrutiny afforded them. All new members of parliament (as opposed to incumbents) are also now required to hold an advanced degree (at least at the master's level), a law passed in response to the steady decline in the number of clerics in parliament.[60]

Iran has virtually no horizontal accountability across institutions. The Supreme Leader, for example, is answerable only to the religious jurisprudence of the Assembly of Experts, an eighty-eight-member body that is elected every eight years (and selects the Supreme Leader). Both the president and elected members of parliament are subordinate to the Supreme Leader. Major organizations, including public security, military, and broadcasting units, are not accountable to the executive or legislature. Within the judicial system, there is not even an attempt to feign autonomy. Judges are held to both political and religious qualifications. Religious judgments (*fatwas*) cannot be repealed by civil courts. The Supreme Leader's veto reigns supreme. For example, Iran's Supreme National Security Council voted in favor of improved relations with the United States in 2000, but Ali Sayyid Khamenei vetoed the motion.[61]

The disputed 2009 elections (Iran's tenth presidential ballot) signaled a defining blow to the already weak façade of any meaningful form of democracy in Iran, illustrating yet again that elections (alone) do not constitute a democracy. The widespread electoral fraud revealed the hollow nature of reform at the top in Iran. The concerns around the election, and especially the violence that followed its conclusion, demon-

strated that Iran is certainly experiencing a virtual democracy, as discussed in Chapter 14. Matters shifted significantly during the 2013 presidential elections when, bowing to surging voter turnout, polling stations stayed open for five hours longer than originally planned, and Rouhani pulled out a surprising—and resounding—victory.

Reformists have been, and will likely continue to be, frustrated by the clerical leadership that blocks many of the changes they desire. We must be careful, though, not to assume that all clerical and other "religious" leaders and activists hold the same view. Many so-called deeply religious individuals within the Islamic Republic are fundamentally opposed to the actions of the Council of Guardians or the Supreme Leader. Iranian clergy have, at various times, served as both supporters and opponents of social and political movements in Iran, with a long tradition of clerical involvement in popular freedom movements.[62] It seems increasingly obvious that the voices who consider such core questions as the importance of nationalism, the scope of individual and social freedoms, and the role of religion and politics are not going to disappear. Indeed, it is accurate to claim that they have been on the Iranian political agenda for over a century.[63] These competing forces are likely to continue to battle it out as Iran forges its way through the twenty-first century.

Case Study: China

Until 2013 or 2014, one could confidently state that life for ordinary citizens in China is freer than it has ever been since the commencement of the People's Republic. Yet under the leadership of Xi Jinping (who will likely lead both the Chinese Communist Party [CCP] and the state from 2012 to 2022), freedoms have been retracting. The so-called Imperial President has launched coordinated campaigns to limit the (already severely restricted) liberties gained in the 1990s and 2000s. Arrests, surveillance, and harassment are becoming commonplace for perceived troublemakers; lawyers, journalists, and labor activists have been arrested without cause. In 2015, authorities brazenly arrested a group of well-known feminists on March 8, International Women's Day. As one observer put it, "any rights activist can be a target at any time."[64] To the extent that China is consolidating the regime, it is consolidating authoritarianism.

Yet the Chinese political system is less random, and more institutionalized, than it has ever been. This is mostly due to changes introduced by Deng Xiaoping in the 1980s. As a victim of Mao Zedong's ideological and personal purges, Deng set out to depersonalize Chinese politics and place the country again onto the path of "normalcy." Some of the biggest developments are happening at the local levels, including elections for local committees and congresses. The biggest hindrance to true political liberalization (on a national scale) is the dominance of the CCP, and especially the lack of separation between party and government in almost all public affairs. Political stagnation stands in stark contrast to the dynamism of the Chinese economy, which has captured the attention of many since the 2000s began. As a PBS documentary once asked, "China's economy has evolved, but has its government?"[65] The answers are complex.

Chinese elite politics has been dominated by strong personalities. People commonly refer to generations of leaders: Mao Zedong led the first generation, Deng Xiaoping the second, Jiang Zemin the third, Hu Jintao the fourth, and now Xi Jinping at the helm of the fifth. Leaders are handpicked years in advance to help avoid

ugly power struggles that could endanger the party's sense of legitimacy among the population—in 2017, the CCP Party Congress will begin selections for the next round of leadership changes slated for 2022 (although there are rumors that Xi will delay appointing a successor).

Government and party leaders vigorously emphasize the "unity of the Chinese nation" and the dangers of instability and chaos if this unity is challenged. Yet this harmony is not as prevalent as leaders would like their people to believe: China is an extremely decentralized country with a surprisingly weak central government that has a difficult time enforcing its mandate at the local levels. Until recently, the central government had difficulty even collecting tax monies from its provinces. Central leaders today battle the seemingly rampant corruption that challenges not only the façade of harmony but the precarious legitimacy of the regime as well. It is no surprise, therefore, that Xi Jinping has made the anticorruption campaign one of his signature achievements in office (to, so far, mixed results).

A natural disaster in the spring of 2008 revealed to many outside of China both the deep roots of corruption throughout the country as well as the devastating human toll from it. This earthquake, which occurred months before Beijing hosted the 2008 Summer Olympic Games, killed at least 68,000 people (rendering nearly 5 million additional people homeless), including many children who were attending school in shoddily constructed buildings at the time of the tremor. Immediately after the earthquake, allegations of corruption began, made clearer by the fact that school buildings, even many that had been recently constructed, had collapsed in a heap of dust while nearby buildings were left standing, unscathed. Many of these buildings consisted of what locals called "tofu buildings," which resemble jiggling blocks of the soft bean curd that serves as a staple in many East and Southeast Asian diets. The Chinese construction sector, in general, operates under a cloud of deep suspicion. The Supreme People's Procuratorate, the major prosecuting agency of the central government, announced that bribery in urban construction cases accounted for nearly 40 percent of all the business bribery it dealt with during the first six months of 2009, with three-fourths of the bribes being marked "major or serious" cases involving more than $7,000.[66] The Chinese construction boom was ripe for hasty deals that went unregulated and largely, in the absence of a calamity, unnoticed.

Many challenge any sense of meaningful participation in China because of what is lacking: elections at the provincial and national levels, competitive political parties that promote the articulation of varied interests, and a separation of powers between governmental and party institutions. Yet others argue that, underneath the surface, Chinese citizens are developing ways of influencing decisionmaking, building what Kevin O'Brien and Lianjiang Li have termed "rights consciousness"—the promotion of a sense of efficacy and involvement in local and even national affairs.[67] Importantly, this behavior is most prominent in the Chinese countryside, where the bulk of the population remains today. The type of protest culture that O'Brien and Li document may not change national policy priorities, but it has potential to grow into an ingrained sense of power among the population in the face of unjust leaders.

Change is clearly the name of the China game—one scholar even referred to the state's current iteration as "China 2.0" to distinguish it from earlier monolithic versions of the People's Republic.[68] Calls for reform emanate from leaders and citizens alike, although the meaning of "reform" is certainly in the eye of the beholder.

The type of regime this is likely to produce will depend upon the complex narratives yet to be written in the world's most populous state.

Case Study: Indonesia

The politics of transition in Indonesia began with a bang: following the resignation of President Suharto in May 1998, the country embarked on an uncertain path of reform. The post-Suharto leadership inherited a series of grave problems, headlined by a great sense of betrayal, corruption, and hopelessness that followed the economic collapse of 1997. The degree of challenge was so high that *The Economist* stated that, following Suharto's fall, "the very integrity of the country seemed in doubt."[69] A key turning point in this effort to jump-start political progress was the 1999 parliamentary election, characterized by Freedom House as "reasonably free although not entirely fair." The rainbow of parties able to compete during this election was a vivid departure from the past, when Suharto's political machine, Golkar, dominated. Out of this election, a ruling coalition formed, led by a presidential team made up of leaders from two competing parties. Yet the least of the problems faced within transitional Indonesia was differing party loyalties. They needed to clean out a political system infested with corruption, tame a military accustomed to wielding considerable influence, and manage an economic recovery often made worse by international demands. Significantly, in 2004, Susilo Bambang Yudhoyono (SBY), a former army general who had served as minister of security, was elected in Indonesia's first direct election for president (prior executives were elected by the legislature, which was composed of a combination of elected and appointed officials). This election, along with the 2005 peace deal between Jakarta and rebels in Aceh province, motivated Freedom House to upgrade Indonesia's 2006 rating to "free" status, a rating it lost in 2014 due to a decline in civil liberties—especially legislation restricting the activities of nongovernmental organizations (NGOs).

Indonesia has had a series of significant presidential elections: 1999 was the first election after the fall of the authoritarian system. The year 2004 was important because it was the first direct election of the chief executive. Turnout (almost 80 percent) was impressive, and the polls were conducted without violence.[70] Tallying the vote is a hugely complex operation in Indonesia, as the state has more than 175 million registered voters spread across 17,000 islands. Five candidates ran, with former president Megawati Sukarnoputri facing SBY in a runoff. SBY won comfortably with 60 percent of the vote. SBY, who in addition to his former military service is also a lifelong music enthusiast with three romantic pop albums to his credit, won reelection to a second five-year term in 2009. *Time* magazine contended that the elections in 2009 "silenced skeptics who doubted whether Indonesia—with its diversity of islands, religions and ethnicities" was fit for democracy.[71] The election of Joko "Jokowi" Widodo in 2014 was another pivotal election, as Jokowi became the first elected president without significant ties to the political or military elite. Campaigning as the "people's president," the former mayor of a city the size of Cleveland (who has a well-known taste for heavy metal music), he raised the hopes of ordinary Indonesians. As a tradesman with significant small business experience, he is comfortable with the bread-and-butter issues such as healthcare, education, and traffic. Although he was initially dismissed by many outside observers as Megawati's puppet (a *Wall Street Journal*

headline blared, "Mega's message to Jokowi: I'm the boss!"), he is holding his own.[72] As president, the tasks of governing are formidable, including some significant challenges within his own party, the Indonesian Democratic Party–Struggle (PDI-P), founded (and still led) by Megawati. As we have discussed in Chapter 12, civil liberties are in decline. Hopes that such issues would dissipate under Jokowi were dashed throughout 2015, and appeared to be trending worse.[73]

Most acknowledge Indonesia as a consolidated democracy, although the quality of its democracy can be challenged, especially the personalist rivalries that dominate its complex political party system.[74] Analysts express concern primarily around religious expression and the lack of formidable protections to other minorities, including sexual minorities. Women and girls continue to face a harsh climate throughout the country, with more than 300 discriminatory local regulations, including "virginity tests" and regulations that permit employees within the defense ministry to take on a second wife if their first spouse was "unable to bear children."[75]

Despite struggles, including a Kafkaesque bureaucracy, Indonesia is making small strides against corruption. It used to rank as one of the most corrupt countries in the world (in 2009, Transparency International ranked Indonesia 111th out of 180 countries surveyed for its Corruption Perceptions Index), but in 2015 it ranked 88th out of 168. Within its annual report, Transparency International lauded Indonesia's progress (improving to 88th from 107th in 2014), but noted that it is "still plagued by a high degree of corruption," especially challenged by bribery and continued weak rule of law.[76] Corruption colors many aspects of daily life in Indonesia, from renewing a driver's license to banking. Citizens especially distrust the police and the judiciary—dubbed the "court mafia" by many citizens.[77] The military is still viewed with disdain, and former abuses have yet to be rectified. To date, no senior military leaders have ever been convicted for their abuses of power during the Suharto era or since, although, in a significant turn of events during the Jokowi presidency, officials are opening the books and openly discussing matters related to the deadly anticommunist massacre that took place after the 1965 coup that unseated Sukarno (in which an estimated 500,000 people were killed).[78]

National identity as an "Indonesian" remains a relatively new concept for most people, who are distinct from other Indonesians in terms of language, culture, history, and religion. The cautious words of a government spokeswoman during the debate over East Timor in 1999 remain in the hearts of many across the archipelago: "Indonesia is an abstract concept, based on the former Netherlands East Indies. If we start allowing different parts to break away, it will be dismembered before we know where we are."[79] As discussed in Chapters 13 and 14, the consolidation of democracy can be more difficult and complex than the genesis of democratic change, and struggles surrounding identity and inclusion mar this lengthy process. Due to the arbitrary enforcement of defamation laws, widespread self-censorship in the media, and an overall "climate of fear" surrounding the discussion of powerful forces within the country, Human Rights Watch argues that Indonesian democracy remains on "shaky ground."[80]

The citizens of Indonesia have struggled through a tremendously difficult path following the collapse of the authoritarian system. Despite some downward trends, changes in political structures and attitudes give rise to cautious optimism for the future of the world's fourth most populous state. It remains to be seen how Indonesia's "people's president" manages the complex dynamics before him.

Now It's Your Turn

After considering the problems of democratization described in this chapter, how do you think democracy can be made more sustainable? In your view, what are the most important factors in determining the overall success or failure of a democracy? Given what you know of these cases, do you find the Western model of democracy's divisiveness appropriate here? Could this model be applicable for much of the global south? What would you think are the challenges of having a democratic system during a crisis situation? What would be its benefits? Do you think it likely that political liberalization alone can address the needs of countries experiencing great economic and political instability? Are there any circumstances in which you believe disintegration might be a better outcome? Why?

Notes

1. Daniel C. Levy and Kathleen Bruhn, "Mexico: Sustained Civilian Rule Without Democracy," in *Politics in Developing Countries: Comparing Experiences with Democracy,* ed. Larry Diamond, Juan J. Linz, and Seymour Martin Lipset (Boulder: Lynne Rienner, 1995).

2. John Rice, "Mexico's Fox Admits Efforts Have Fallen Short," Associated Press, September 4, 2003.

3. Jorge G. Castañeda, "A Way to Peace in Mexico," *New York Times,* September 6, 2006.

4. Enrique Krauze, "Furthering Democracy in Mexico," *Foreign Affairs,* January–February 2006.

5. "Rising Violence, Fading Hopes," *The Economist,* July 10, 2010.

6. Luis Rubio and Jeffrey Davidow, "Mexico's Disputed Election," *Foreign Affairs,* September–October 2006; Marla Dickerson, "A Free Market Man for Mexico," *Los Angeles Times,* July 16, 2006; Elisabeth Malkin, "In Mexican Vote, Nostalgia for Past Corruption," *New York Times,* July 6, 2009.

7. Pamela K. Starr, "Mexico's Problematic Reforms," *Current History,* February 2014.

8. Ibid.

9. Patrick J. McDonnell and Cecilia Sanchez, "Major Election Losses Could Threaten Ruling Party's Grip on Mexican Presidency," *Los Angeles Times,* June 7, 2016.

10. "Peru's Presidential Election: The Known Against the Unknown," *The Economist,* June 3, 2006.

11. "Deconstructing Democracy: Peru Under Alberto Fujimori," Washington Office on Latin America, February 2000.

12. Ibid.

13. Cynthia McClintock and Abraham Lowenthal, foreword to *The Peruvian Labyrinth: Polity, Society, Economy,* ed. Maxwell A. Cameron and Philip Mauceri (University Park: Pennsylvania State University Press, 1997).

14. Simon Romero, "Peru's Ex-President Convicted of Rights Abuses," *New York Times,* April 7, 2009.

15. Gonzalo Ruiz Tovar, "Toledo's Biggest Achievement Was Survival as Peru's Leader," Deutsche Presse-Agentur, July 27, 2006.

16. Ibid.

17. "A Murky Democratic Dawn in Post-Fujimori Peru," *The Economist,* April 7, 2001; David Gonzalez, "New Chance for Peru's Chief to Take Reins," *New York Times,* January 13, 2002; "Peru's New Government: Teething Troubles," *The Economist,* December 8, 2001; Steven Levitsky and Cynthia Sanborn, "A Hard Choice in Peru," *New York Times,* May 9, 2001; Ernesto García Calderón, "Peru's Decade of Living Dangerously," *Journal of Democracy* 12, no. 2 (April 2001).

18. Simon Romero, "Leading Again, Peru's President Still Unpopular," *New York Times,* August 27, 2010.

19. "Peru Politics: Presidential Field Widens," *The Economist,* November 11, 2010; Dan Collyns, "Why Peru's Traditional Political Parties Are Losing Ground," BBC News, October 27, 2010.

20. Andrea Zarate and Nicholas Casey, "Pedro Kuczynski Holds Thin Lead over Keiko Fujimori in Peru Presidential Election," *New York Times,* June 6, 2016; Colin Post, "Shining Path Ambush Kills 10 on Eve of Peru's Election," *Peru Reports,* April 12, 2016.

21. Larry Diamond, "The Uncivic Society and the Descent into Praetorianism," in Diamond, Linz, and Lipset, *Politics in Developing Countries.*

22. Craig Timberg, "Hope Tempered by Skepticism as Nigeria Faces Historic Vote," *Washington Post,* November 13, 2006.

23. Freedom House, *Freedom in the World 2016.*

24. Craig Timberg, "Support for Democracy Seen Falling in Africa," *Washington Post,* May 25, 2006; Jacob Poushter, "6 Facts About Public Opinion in Nigeria Before Election Day," Pew Research Center, March 24, 2015; Jay Loschky, "Ahead of Poll, Few Nigerians Trust in Elections," Gallup, January 13, 2015.

25. J. Shola Omatola, "Trapped in Transition? Nigeria's First Democratic Decade and Beyond," *Taiwan Journal of Democracy* 9, no. 2 (2015); Peter M. Lewis, "Nigeria: Cycles of Crisis, Sources of Resilience," in *Coping with Crisis in African States,* ed. Peter M. Lewis and John W. Harbeson (Boulder: Lynne Rienner, 2016).

26. "Nigerian Vice-President Vows to Pursue Presidential Quest," BBC News, November 13, 2006.

27. Omatola, "Trapped in Transition?"

28. Olumide Taiwo, "Challenges and Possibilities for Progress in Nigeria," Brookings Institution, June 24, 2010; Richard Joseph and Alexandra Gillies, "Nigeria's Season of Uncertainty," *Current History,* May 2010; Gilbert da Costa, "Is Goodluck Jonathan the Answer to Nigeria's Woes?," *Time,* February 13, 2010, www.time.com.

29. Kathleen Caulderwood, "Nigeria Election 2015: Struggling Economy Poses Problems for Jonathan or Buhari," *International Business Times,* March 26, 2015; John Campbell, "Good Luck, Jonathan: The Problem with Democracy in Nigeria," *Foreign Affairs,* January 27, 2015.

30. Brandon Kendhammer, "Nigeria's New Democratic Dawn?," *Current History,* May 2015.

31. Campbell, "Good Luck, Jonathan"; Kendhammer, "Nigeria's New Democratic Dawn?"

32. Michael Bratton, *Power Politics in Zimbabwe* (Boulder: Lynne Rienner, 2014).

33. Robert I. Rotberg, "Africa's Mess, Mugabe's Mayhem," *Foreign Affairs,* September–October 2000.

34. "Zimbabwe at the Abyss," *The Economist,* June 29, 2000.

35. Celia W. Dugger and Barry Bearak, "Mugabe Sworn to Sixth Term After Victory in One-Candidate Runoff," *New York Times,* June 20, 2008.

36. Celia W. Dugger, "Opposition Party to Join Zimbabwe's Government," *New York Times,* January 31, 2009.

37. "Zimbabwe: Power-Sharing for Bankrupt Beginners," *Africa Confidential* 50, no. 3 (February 6, 2009); Celia W. Dugger, "Rift Endangers Power-Sharing Deal in Zimbabwe," *New York Times,* October 10, 2010.

38. "Crime and Amnesty," *Africa Confidential* 50, no. 10 (May 15, 2009); Celia W. Dugger, "Fears Growing of an Iron Grip over Zimbabwe," *New York Times,* December 26, 2010; "Zimbabwe: Stranded in Stasis," International Crisis Group, February 26, 2016.

39. "Still Adored," *The Economist,* December 19, 2009.

40. Mabasa Sasa, "No Imminent Elections," *New African* 493 (March 2010).

41. "Mugabe Calls War Vets Dissidents, Threatens Another Gukurahundi," *New Zimbabwe,* September 6, 2016; Stephen Chan, "Looking Beyond Mugabe," *New York Times,* October 26, 2015.

42. "Veterans Condemn Robert Mugabe in Surprise Backlash," *The Guardian* (London), July 21, 2016.

43. Hopewell Chin'ono and Norimitsu Onishi, "In Zimbabwe, Mugabe's Birthday Is Rife with Political Jockeying," *New York Times,* February 29, 2016.

44. "Zimbabwe: Stranded in Stasis"; "Letter from Africa: Zimbabwe's Flag Fury," BBC News, June 1, 2016.

45. Thanassis Cambanis, *Once Upon a Revolution: An Egyptian Story* (New York: Simon and Schuster, 2015).

46. Ashraf Khalil, *Liberation Square: Inside the Egyptian Revolution and the Rebirth of a Nation* (New York: St. Martin's, 2011).

47. Cambanis, *Once Upon a Revolution.*

48. Scott Anderson, "Fractured Lands: How the Arab World Came Apart," *New York Times,* August 14, 2016.

49. Cambanis, *Once Upon a Revolution.*

50. Khalil, *Liberation Square.*

51. Cambanis, *Once Upon a Revolution.*

52. Khalil, *Liberation Square;* Cambanis, *Once Upon a Revolution;* "Tahrir Square's Place in History," BBC News, November 22, 2011.

53. Cambanis, *Once Upon a Revolution;* Emad El-Din Shahin, "Egypt's Revolution Turned on Its Head," *Current History,* December 2015.

54. Cambanis, *Once Upon a Revolution.*

55. Ibid.

56. Jeremy M. Sharp, "Egypt: Background and US Relations," Congressional Research Service, July 24, 2015; Hanan Badr, "Public Sphere, New Media, and Political Culture in Post-Revolutionary Egypt," *OIS Media Culture in Transformation: Political Communication, Social Networking, and Transition in Egypt* 4 (2016), www.perspectivia.net; Alaa Al Aswany, "Sisi's Choices: Good and Bad," *New York Times,* June 15, 2014.

57. Cambanis, *Once Upon a Revolution;* Aswany, "Sisi's Choices: Good and Bad."

58. Scott Peterson, "After 8 Defiant Years, Ahmadinejad Leaves Iran Isolated and Cash-Strapped," *Christian Science Monitor,* August 2, 2013.

59. Ibid.

60. Emma Borden and Suzanne Maloney, "Iran's Guardians' Council Has Approved a Record-Low Percentage of Candidates: What Will That Mean for the Upcoming Vote?," Brookings Institution, February 24, 2016, www.brookings.edu.

61. Scott Peterson, "Iran Opens Door—a Little—to US," *Christian Science Monitor,* February 25, 2000.

62. Mehrangiz Kar, "Reformist Islam Versus Radical Islam in Iran," Working Paper no. 4 (Washington, DC: Brookings Project on US Relations with the Islamic World, November 2010), p. 1.

63. Ali Gheissari and Vali Nasr, *Democracy in Iran: History and the Quest for Liberty* (New York: Oxford University Press, 2006), pp. 147–148.

64. "Why China Arrested, Then Released, Five Feminists," *The Economist,* April 27, 2015, www.economist.com.

65. "China's Government Has Evolved, but Has Its Government?," *PBS Newshour,* December 10, 2010.

66. "40 Percent of All Business Bribes in Construction Sector: SPP," *Xinhua,* September 3, 2009.

67. Kevin J. O'Brien and Lianjiang Li, *Rightful Resistance in Rural China* (New York: Cambridge University Press, 2006).

68. Maria Yue Zhang and Bruce W. Stening, *China 2.0: The Transformation of an Emerging Superpower—and the New Opportunities* (Singapore: Wiley, 2010).

69. "Indonesia's Future: A Golden Opportunity," *The Economist,* September 10, 2009.

70. Nelly van Doorn-Harder and R. Michael Feener, "Indonesia," in *Muslim Cultures Today,* ed. Kathryn M. Coughlin (Westport, CT: Greenwood Press, 2006), p. 86.

71. Hannah Beech, "Indonesia Elections: A Win for Democracy," *Time,* July 8, 2009.

72. Anita Rachman and Ben Otto, "Mega's Message to Jokowi: I'm the Boss," *Wall Street Journal,* April 11, 2015.

73. Kikue Hamayosu and Ronnie Nataatmadja, "Indonesia in 2015: The People's President's Rocky Road and Hazy Outlooks in Democratic Consolidation," *Asian Survey* 56, no. 1 (2006).

74. Kikue Hamayotsu, "Indonesia in 2014: The Year of Electing the 'People's President,'" *Asian Survey* 55, no. 1 (2015).

75. Human Rights Watch, "Indonesia: Events of 2015," www.hrw.org.

76. Transparency International, "Global Perceptions Index 2015."

77. "Indonesia Fights Corruption with People Power," BBC News, November 6, 2009.

78. "Indonesia Discusses Massacres That Killed 500,000," BBC News, April 18, 2016; "SBY's Feet of Clay," *The Economist,* October 21, 2010.

79. "Indonesia: Fraying at the Edges," *The Economist,* August 21, 1999, p. 33.

80. Christen Broecker, "Indonesia's Democracy Still on Shaky Ground," Human Rights Watch, May 19, 2010.

PART FOUR

The International System

We live in a global economic, political, and cultural world, in which no country is an island completely isolated from the influence of other regions. The geographical lines that divide governments are in many ways less important today than they were at the beginning of the twentieth century. This development has profound effects on the issues that face us all, as well as on the institutions through which we handle these issues. In the chapters that follow, we examine some of the issues that are decidedly multinational if not global in scope, and discuss some of the institutions, both regional and global, that have developed in response.

Chapter 16

Sovereignty and the Role of International Organizations

We the peoples of the United Nations, determined to save succeeding generations from the scourge of war . . . and to reaffirm faith in fundamental human rights, in the dignity and worth of the human person, in the equal rights of men and women and of nations large and small, and to establish conditions under which justice and respect for the obligations arising from treaties and other sources of international law can be maintained, and to promote social progress and better standards of life in larger freedom . . . have resolved to combine our efforts to accomplish these aims.
　　　　　　　　　　　　　　　　　　　　—*Charter of the United Nations*

Among many developments in past decades, few parallel that of the increased interconnectedness of the world's states and of issues that affect citizens of the globe. We begin this chapter with a discussion of the role of states, acting not alone but rather in regional and global organizations, with special attention to the United Nations. What are some of the issues that these organizations have tackled? Have they achieved much success? Next we discuss groups that have organized independently of governments, by highlighting the development of nongovernmental organizations (NGOs) in the world today. We conclude with discussion of some of the major global challenges facing our world, and discuss the capacity of NGOs at the regional and international level to resolve these issues.

　　The rise of groups outside of the traditional nation-state in part has led to a rethinking of the idea of national sovereignty, commonly understood as government's autonomy or independence to act, especially within its own borders. The legitimate authority over any given territory, usually viewed as the entitlement of the state, includes the right to self-defense and the determination of its own destiny. The principle of sovereignty implies a degree of nonintervention in one's affairs. Yet some have argued that state sovereignty may be limited when countries are unable (or unwilling) to protect their citizens from crimes against humanity, which include ethnic cleansing, mass rape, and genocide (or the systematic decimation of people). This approach, known as the RESPONSIBILITY TO PROTECT (R2P), promotes awareness of the

403

state's need to shield its citizens from harm. It also calls on the international community to support the UN and other organizations in establishing an early warning capacity to help prevent such atrocities in the first place. How can the international community respond to mass executions within other countries, or the systematic rape and torture of vulnerable groups? How should other countries respond? These are not new questions in international relations. Rather, they are reminders that the questions surrounding our past inaction in the face of mass violence, especially the Holocaust, have not all been answered, and that the controversy over how and when to intervene in others' affairs still haunts our world.

Despite the euphoric claims of globalism and our interconnected twenty-first-century world, systematic torture and the murder of specifically targeted groups of people continue to take place today, and we continue to struggle with how to respond. Does sovereignty mean that government leaders can violate the human rights of individuals and groups within their borders? As we discuss here, some now argue that humanitarian needs in countries or regions permit (or even require) the response of other countries, including a military response. Yet a central tension remains: Do problems that cross national borders demand an international response? What if the problem is confined within a single state? Are other countries justified to take action, in the name of promoting human rights? How should this response be coordinated, implemented, and monitored? This approach poses many other questions: What degree of suffering warrants a response from others? Under what conditions is international action justified? Who has the legitimacy to carry out such actions? How are the objectives of intervention determined? Is unilateral action, undertaken by a single state or group, justified as long as it is in the name of humanitarian needs? Does a multilateral approach, involving the coordinated effort of multiple governments, necessarily make an action more legitimate? The answers to these questions have the capacity to dramatically change the way in which nation-states and the governments that lead them view themselves and their roles.

To this point in the book, much of our discussion has centered on the role of state actors. Yet recognizing the principle of interdependence, supranational organizations that go beyond single nation-states have taken a more active role in international affairs. Some of this action is taken by groups of governments who willingly forgo some degree of their independent sovereignty in order to accomplish particular goals. Other action is taken by nongovernmental actors who organize not around their governmental identity, but rather around a particular cause or interest. Both types of organizations are increasingly prominent on the world stage.

International Governmental Organizations

International governmental organizations (IGOs) comprise official representatives of states who gather to discuss responses to issues and conflicts that affect the world community. We have already discussed two prominent IGOs, the International Monetary Fund (IMF) and the World Bank, which were both established at the 1944 Bretton Woods conference. In this section we discuss the role of IGOs and other multilateral institutions in resolving global issues. We focus on both regional and global IGOs as a tool of fostering cooperation among governments. One important feature of IGOs is that their memberships comprise official governmental represen-

tatives, and their goals are to calibrate the policies of like-minded states as well as to solve contentious issues that arise between conflicting state policies and goals. These goals are different from those of the other major type of organizations discussed in this chapter, the nongovernmental organizations.

Each of these organization types poses different challenges for the global south. Often, less powerful countries are excluded from decisionmaking structures within these organizations, either explicitly or implicitly. This contradiction of universal membership is most stark with respect to the United Nations, in which each state is guaranteed a relatively equal voice in some chambers, most notably the GENERAL ASSEMBLY, but not others, including the much more powerful Security Council. The lack of transparency—clear, publicly available decisionmaking processes—challenges both the participation of many states and groups as well as the perception that actions taken by these organizations are positive. Many of these organizations are undergoing reform to fix these drawbacks, but formidable obstacles remain.

Regional Organizations

Over the past several decades there has been a proliferation of regional economic blocs, free trade areas, CUSTOMS UNIONS, and COMMON MARKETS. Since the late 1970s the impetus for this growth has come both from the desire to form regional trade organizations as well as in defensive response to globalization. Regionalism is a framework of cooperation, with an indefinite duration, intended to include multiple issues, most often economic or security-related in nature.[1] The latter part of this explanation captures the transition that has touched many organizations in the global south; quite a few began with an initial focus on economics and trade within a defined (although not absolute) geographical space, and are now adopting other complementary agendas as well.[2]

A few observations on regional alliances focus our attention on some of the unexpected aspects of these organizations. Sometimes, former enemies (or countries with continuing hostilities) seek alliances as a way to formally move beyond their conflict. In Latin America, for example, Peru is a member of many regional organizations to which countries it has had past disputes with also belong, including Ecuador and Bolivia. The Association of Southeast Asian Nations (ASEAN) began largely in response to the regional perception of the growing communist threat in Southeast Asia. ASEAN's predecessor, the Southeast Asia Treaty Organization (SEATO), was distinctly strategic in focus. Member states within this organization continue to hold competing views on a variety of issues, including economic growth, the environment, and threats to security.

Another regional organization that originally brought together states in the larger interest of promoting stability and a common defense is the Southern African Development Community (SADC). The SADC was established in 1980 to provide political and economic protection against the apartheid regime in South Africa (which itself joined the SADC after its independence in 1994).[3] From the start, members recognized the gains to be had through consultation and cooperation. The SADC has been praised for its realistic priorities for regional planning.[4] Leaders have promoted small-scale irrigation over grandiose dams, as well as the use of appropriate technology, including attempts to combat widespread deforestation by developing more fuel-efficient stoves and alternative energy sources for cooking pots. As we

find in other regional organizations, members have benefited from functionalist arrangements on technical matters, including efforts to sustain tropical forests, curtail the illegal trade in ivory and diamonds, promote the repatriation of refugees, and manage the distribution of limited natural resources, including through oil and natural gas pipelines. The fifteen SADC member states have expressed an interest in closer economic integration, including the promotion of a free trade area, a customs union, and a common market—work that has been plagued by nontariff barriers, poor transportation infrastructure, and inadequate energy supplies.[5]

Increased interaction and contact can have many unintended consequences. Just as regional organizations developed to promote greater economic integration or cooperation in security matters, less formalized interaction has helped to promote regional solidarity through personal and cultural exchanges. For example, South American member states of Mercosur, also known as the Common Market of the South, exchange mayors, provincial governors, and students, and Spanish is now obligatory in Brazilian schools as a way to promote regional cohesion.[6] An agreement signed with the Andean Community of Nations in December 2004 furthered such integration. Mercosur formed in the absence of developed linkages among states, and, even though trade among its members was approximately $108 billion in 2015 (three times what it was in 2000), it constitutes only approximately a 5 percent share of total members' trade. The bloc is also struggling with the possible suspension of Venezuela (a member since 2012) for its human rights abuses and lack of democracy.[7]

Two other prominent regional actors, ASEAN and the Organization of American States (OAS), had their genesis during the Cold War, forming as alliances to combat the rise of communist governments. Both organizations have moved beyond this ideological focus in the post–Cold War era, with ASEAN welcoming its former nemesis, China, on a consultative basis. Current member states of ASEAN, formed in 1967, are Brunei, Cambodia, Indonesia, Laos, Malaysia, Myanmar, the Philippines, Singapore, Thailand, and Vietnam, with consultative status held by the "dialogue partners": Australia, Canada, China, the European Union (EU), India, Japan, New Zealand, the Republic of Korea, Russia, and the United States. The China-ASEAN Free Trade Area was established in January 2010 to further increase regional integration, prompting some fears about international competition among Indonesian farmers.

With the commencement of the ASEAN Regional Forum (ARF) in 1994, the non-economic aspect of the organization has again been highlighted. This component of ASEAN was developed in order to promote peace and security in the Asia-Pacific region. Greater participation by China will be needed in order to bring more power to the association, and, in recent years, conflicting maritime claims have dominated much of the forum's discussion. Now with twenty-seven members, the ARF has become a high-profile forum for discussing security issues across the region. With an emphasis on consensus, the emphasis within the ARF is much more on dialogue than decisionmaking.

The OAS, the preeminent organization for the Western Hemisphere, began with an agreement among member states in 1948, and the organization was launched three years later. All thirty-five countries in the region are official members, although the current government of Cuba has been denied its attendance rights since 1962, largely at the demand of the United States. US dominance of the OAS during the Cold War

meant that the organization focused on isolating Marxist governments and fighting against leftist rebels. Since the end of the Cold War, the emphasis has shifted greatly. The priorities of the OAS today are to preserve and strengthen democracy through the promotion of social justice, human rights, and good governance, and to provide solutions to the debt crises many member states face. It often sends observer delegations to watch elections in member states—as it did, for the first time in the United States, in 2016.[8]

Despite the presence of many regional economic organizations in Latin America, the OAS has also helped promote microenterprise and telecommunications trade, while shining attention on abuses of labor rights and the need to promote SUSTAINABLE DEVELOPMENT throughout the region. The OAS has been a major diplomatic player and peacemaker in the region as well. It also was a leading regional voice in challenging Alberto Fujimori's hijacking of Peru's presidential elections in 2000, and suspended Honduras from the organization after a constitutional crisis in 2009, when, for the first time in the organization's history, the OAS invoked the part of its charter that calls for the suspension of a member for an "interruption of democratic order."[9] This focus on democracy was not as prominent, though, as OAS states lifted the ban (in place since 1962) on Cuba's membership in June 2009 (an invitation that Havana promptly rejected). President Raul Castro reiterated Cuba's lack of interest in joining the organization, even after the thawing of relations with the United States, in mid-2016.[10]

In Africa, the premier regional organization is the African Union (AU), which succeeded the Organization of African Unity (OAU) in 2002. Few mourned the loss of OAU, scorned by many as the "dictators' club" for its failures to protect citizens against tyrannical leaders.[11] AU architects hope that it will one day operate along the lines of the European Union, with a pan-African parliament (launched in 2004), a central bank (with plans for a common currency by 2023), and an AU-wide court of justice. With the same members and many of the same problems as its precursor organization, the African Union has a stronger charter (but not yet larger funds) to promote integration between the fifty-four African member states (covering the whole continent and several island states, with the exception of Morocco, which has applied to return to the organization it quit in 1984).

The African Union's mission is to promote peace and prosperity in a united continent. Reflecting on past weaknesses of the AU and similar multilateral institutions, by design the African Union is attempting to limit the gross abuse of power in the name of state sovereignty. The OAU operated under the principal of noninterference, meaning that member states should stay out of each other's business, which resulted in the failure to act to stop atrocities. Taking this criticism into account, the AU shifted to a policy of indifference. The organization established its right to intervene against genocide or gross human rights abuses in any member states. Peacekeeping forces under AU command have served in several countries, including Somalia, Burundi, and Sudan. In 2016 the AU was considering sending a regional force to intervene in the conflict in South Sudan, although the South Sudanese government opposed it. The organization is planning a new rapid response standby force, but like its predecessor the AU has struggled to fund its operations.[12] This has hamstrung the effectiveness of its forces, which creates resentment and mistrust among civilians who are frustrated by its lack of capacity.

Based in the belief that one can't have peace without prosperity, the other major focus of the AU is the improvement of living standards for citizens across the continent. In this light, the New Partnership for Africa's Development (NEPAD), an ambitious recovery and antipoverty program that ties good governance (which involves transparency, accountability, and similar reforms) to increasing aid and investment from high-income countries (HICs). Through voluntary, independent "peer reviews" of performance, African governments encourage each other to follow a program of agreed standards aimed at remedying institutional deficiencies and promoting sustainable development. For example, some members (such as Mali) have been suspended over coups, and are only readmitted once constitutional rule is resumed. It's a work in progress, and one that will take time, resources, and determination to implement.

Other IGOs bring together states across multiple geographic regions in order to highlight a common identity or cause. One of the largest IGOs in the world today is the Organization of the Islamic Conference (OIC), which encompasses fifty-seven states across four continents and includes nearly one-third of the members of the United Nations—from Albania and Nigeria to Guyana and Indonesia. (Despite the presence of approximately 175 million Muslims in India, its membership has been blocked by Pakistan.) The goals of the OIC, founded in 1969 after an arson attack against Al-Aqsa Mosque in Jerusalem, are to promote cooperation among members, safeguard Islamic holy sites, and eliminate racial discrimination and colonialism. Trying to coordinate such a diverse group of states, even though unified by religious identity, has proven quite difficult, and while the OIC has carved out an important role as a facilitator of discussion among states, it has also lacked the teeth to implement decisions made within its chambers. In part because of its broad reach, the organization has suffered some famous disputes among members, and has been unable to unite even on some key proposals, including following up on promises for aid in the aftermath of natural disasters and implementing a coordinated economic policy toward the state of Israel.

How can membership in a multilateral organization, with either a regional or a global scope, change conduct within a country? Turkey's decades-long attempt to join the European Union provides a possible test case. Turkish leaders submitted their formal application for full membership in 1987, but the EU did not accept Turkey as a candidate until December 1999. Formal accession negotiations did not begin until 2005, and it is unlikely that Turkey will be able to complete the full accession process before 2020. This is due to a number of problems, including its continued sparring over the divided status of Cyprus and Turkey's human rights abuses. In an effort to acquire EU membership, Turkey's parliament has enacted some reforms that could have favorable outcomes for the respect of human rights: military judges have been removed from civilian courts, longer prison terms have been established for those guilty of torture, and it banned the use of capital punishment during peacetime. However, many within Turkey are growing weary of the demands for change coming from the European Union, and believe that the republic will likely be permanently excluded from EU membership because of the Union's status as a "Christian club," as elaborated by former EU Commission president Jacques Delors. Opinion polls within Turkey show that support for EU membership is waning. Turkey may provide a good study of both how some domestic

decisions are influenced by the desire to acquire membership in broader associations, as well as the difficulties in expansion and absorption of new members from the perspective of multilateral organizations.

The United Nations

Among the myriad international organizations that exist in the twenty-first century, the United Nations, founded in the immediate aftermath of World War II, stands alone as the most universally recognized. Its goal, as stated in the UN Charter, is intricately tied to the period from which it grew: to "save succeeding generations from the scourge of war." Its predecessor, the League of Nations, a product of World War I, was unsuccessful in reaching this goal, as World War II broke out within two decades of its establishment. While the causes of the League's failures are still hotly debated, many have identified one of its key weaknesses as the granting of equal voice to every member state. This, some argue, failed to accurately reflect differences in power and influence. Today's United Nations comprises 193 member states, following the admission of South Sudan in 2011, and its organizational structure gives greater influence to some countries than others—an issue we will return to later. The main headquarters of the UN are in New York City, with principal offices in Geneva (headquarters of offices for human rights and disarmament), Vienna (headquarters of offices for drug-abuse monitoring, criminal justice, peaceful uses of outer space, and trade law), and Nairobi (headquarters of offices on human settlements and environmental programs). Through its committees, agencies, assemblies, and related organizations, the United Nations gathers leaders to debate and define policy goals, set standards, and monitor compliance with internationally agreed programs in pursuit of its overarching goal—to promote the peaceful resolution of conflict throughout the world.

The UN Charter, signed in 1945, outlines the principles of COLLECTIVE SECURITY, state SOVEREIGNTY, and the equal rights of SELF-DETERMINATION of all peoples. Collective security embodies the concept that states can impede an aggressor state by binding together in a cooperative framework. The goal of such action is to prevent conflict, but if conflict does occur, aggression is met with a united force of collaborators. It is a tactic that combines the pooled resources and power of united countries, seemingly indicative of "world opinion," with the threat to use force if security and peace are threatened.

During the Cold War, collective security took a backseat to the old power politics the UN was designed to replace; the one collective security action was that taken in Korea from 1950 to 1953, made possible only because the Soviet Union boycotted the Security Council to protest the exclusion of the People's Republic of China from the United Nations. The force was commanded by a US general whose orders came from Washington rather than the United Nations per se. The operation of collective security was more evident in action taken following Iraq's invasion of Kuwait in 1990, when the powerful, veto-wielding, permanent members of the Council all acquiesced in agreement to combat the invasion.

Again, though, this action must be viewed only as a limited example of collective security, especially given the commanding role of the United States during the war. The doctrine of self-determination, although incompletely applied, has been an important force for non-Western peoples within the United Nations. In a nutshell, the concept embodies the belief that all peoples of the world have the right

to rule themselves, rather than being ruled by external, colonial powers. The processes of decolonization, spearheaded by African and Asian representatives to the UN, led to the peaceful independence of many states, especially in the 1950s and 1960s. However, as discussed in Chapter 4, the remnants of colonialism, including the vestiges of imperial governments, continued well into the twentieth century.

Chapter XI of the UN Charter establishes a pivotal role for member states regarding "non-self-governing territories." Members of the United Nations have a responsibility to assist in the establishment of self-government where it does not yet exist. The independence of Namibia in 1990 is one of the most unusual cases of UN-supervised decolonization. Formerly known as South West Africa, the territory was placed under the responsibility of the United Nations, rather than being given status as a member state, in 1950, after South Africa refused to administer the territory as it previously had under the League of Nations system. More recently, this aspect of the Charter has enabled the United Nations to assist in the development of newly self-governing states, such as East Timor (now known as Timor-Leste), which achieved its independence from Indonesia in 2002. Currently, fewer than twenty non-self-governing territories remain under the tutelage of a United Nations member state, with the United Kingdom and the United States as the dominant administering authorities.

One of the most important General Assembly resolutions passed in the United Nations is the 1948 Universal Declaration of Human Rights (UDHR). The development and acceptance of this document have helped to promote a wide-ranging body of human rights law, including treaties that recognize economic, social, cultural, political, and civil rights. Articles 1 and 2 of the Universal Declaration state that "all human beings are born equal in dignity and rights" and are entitled to rights "without distinction of any kind such as race, color, sex, language, religion, political or other opinion, national or social origin, property, birth or other status." Through its committee structure, fact-finding missions, international conferences, and advocacy, the UN attempts to promote these ideals in all of its work.

Organization of the United Nations. The main structures within the United Nations include the General Assembly, the Security Council, the Economic and Social Council (ECOSOC), and the International Court of Justice (ICJ), the principal judicial organ. The General Assembly, in which each member state is represented, makes recommendations in the form of nonbinding resolutions. Some committees of the UN write reports analyzing the implementation of standards and solutions, or propose new organizations to monitor situations. The main aim of the UN is to promote consensus, and this work is achieved through the laborious and detailed processes of drafting resolutions that have the support of a plurality of state representatives. Although all nonbudgetary resolutions in the General Assembly are nonbinding, they highlight steps that governments should take to resolve conflict and promote peace and prosperity, and elements of resolutions are often incorporated into the national laws of the supporting countries. The General Assembly is the most procedurally democratic arm of the United Nations, since each state gets one vote, irrespective of size, power, or prestige. From the speeches and debates within the General Assembly, we can ascertain a great deal about the voice of world opinion.

One of the most visible agencies of the UN is the Security Council, which can initiate binding action, including final approval of the General Assembly's choice of

Secretary-General, the chief administrative officer of the United Nations. Additionally, the Security Council recommends states for membership to the General Assembly. The Secretary-General, referred to by some as the "punchbag in chief,"[13] is appointed by the General Assembly on the recommendation of the Security Council for a five-year, renewable term. Since 1946, half of the Secretaries-General have come from countries in the global south: U Thant, of Burma, who served from 1961 to 1971; Javier Pérez de Cuéllar, of Peru, from 1982 to 1991; Boutros Boutros-Ghali, of Egypt, from 1992 to 1996; and Kofi Annan, of Ghana, who led the organization from 1997 to 2006. Ban Ki-moon, a former South Korean minister of foreign affairs and trade, served as the eighth Secretary-General of the United Nations, from 2007 until the end of 2016, the second man from Asia to hold this post. He was replaced by António Guterres, of Portugal, on January 1, 2017. A former prime minister of Portugal (1995–2002) and president of the Socialist International (1999–2005), he was elevated to the post of Secretary-General largely due to his experience as the UN High Commissioner for Refugees (UNHCR) from 2005 to 2015. During his tenure at the UNHCR, Guterres expanded the emergency response of the organization and led the agency, one of the world's largest humanitarian organizations, during the worst human displacement crisis since World War II, as we discuss in Chapter 17. His candidacy marked the first time that Secretary-General candidates had to present their platform in public hearings at the UN General Assembly—where he emerged as a surprising choice, in part because many believed it was time for a woman to be the world's top diplomat. In the end, though, with surprisingly quick agreement by the major members of the UN Security Council, and welcomed transparency in the early nomination process, he was elected in a rare show of unity.[14]

As the name implies, the Security Council is designed to deal with threats to peace and security. It convenes a meeting at the call of any member state that feels threatened or violated, and it often summons representatives of conflicting sides to present their case to the chamber. Representatives on the Security Council are often required to make very rapid decisions that carry great weight. In circumstances determined to constitute "threats to the peace, breaches of the peace, or acts of aggression," as defined by CHAPTER VII of the UN Charter, the Security Council can order binding action, including economic sanctions or the use of armed force. In the post–Cold War era, the Security Council has been more activist, especially in terms of peacekeeping and humanitarian issues.

There are two sets of countries that sit in the Security Council. Reflective of their strength, the five post–World War II powers—the United States, the Soviet Union, the United Kingdom, France, and China—were given permanent, veto-power seats in the Security Council.[15] These countries are known as the permanent five members (P5). This privileged position was given to the powerful countries of the mid-1940s to recognize their importance at the time of the UN's birth, a lesson taken from the experiment with the League of Nations. Granting these countries a veto over substantive (not procedural) matters bestows on them a tremendous amount of power; a single no-vote by any of these five countries will halt any action taken by the Security Council. Members' use of their veto power has fluctuated across time, with vetoes being used much more frequently to block action during the Cold War than since the 1990s. The most frequent invoker of the veto has been Russia (formerly the Soviet Union), with 134 vetoes from 1946 through 2016. The United States ranks

second in its use of vetoes, registering eighty-three since 1946. China has used vetoes the least, tallying only eleven since 1946.[16] Yet even if the veto is rarely used today, the threat of its action can certainly change policy proposals and influence the topics that are brought to the Security Council for discussion. It is a powerful tool that the vast majority of member states do not have, nor are they likely to have in the future.

The second group within the Security Council consists of ten other states, elected by the General Assembly on a temporary, two-year rotating basis, without veto power. Some voices, within both the Western and the non-Western world, argue that this structure is outdated and needs to be modified, both to more accurately reflect the balance of power in today's world, and to be more representative of non-Western countries. As *The Economist* put it nearly a decade ago, "An increasingly unrepresentative, anachronistic Security Council speaks with diminishing authority."[17] Western countries dominate its membership. Most glaringly, no Muslim-majority country has a lasting seat within this powerful chamber—Turkey and Indonesia are consistently raised as the most likely claimants of the so-called Muslim seat on the Security Council. Former Secretary-General Kofi Annan, among others, frequently called for increasing the size of the Security Council to give it more diversity and a stronger voice for developing nations. According to the proposals, an enlarged Security Council could include a permanent seat from each region of the developing world, including, for example, permanent (nonveto) positions for Africa, Asia, and Latin America to be rotated among states in these regions. Currently, there is a regional focus to the election of nonpermanent members; five are elected from Africa and Asia combined, one from Eastern Europe, two from Latin America, and two from Western Europe and other areas. Another proposal for a larger Security Council could include permanent states irrespective of regions. Brazil, Germany, and Japan are the states most often cited, because of their realized or potential economic strength, although former US president Barack Obama expressed his support for India's permanent representation on the Security Council during his visit to India in November 2010 (much to the surprise of many). Germany and Japan also argue that they contribute more financially to the UN than Russia, China, Great Britain, and France, making them deserving of a more permanent voice in the UN's chamber of power. The challenge is crafting a Council that is "large enough to be representative, but small enough to do business."[18]

Any change in the makeup of the Security Council will require an amendment to the UN Charter (which has happened only twice since 1945), and is likely to take a long time. Gaining the approval of the current P5 is only the first step, to be followed by approval and ratification by two-thirds of all UN member states. In addition to P5 concerns, opposition to Security Council enlargement also comes from less powerful states that are not currently represented in the Security Council, but that fear the power such a change could give to their adversaries. Pakistan, for example, opposes any proposal that might give India a role. Iran favors an increase in geographic representation, but wants to limit the exercise of veto power. Argentina, Bangladesh, Malaysia, and Egypt oppose any new members to the Security Council—often because they do not favor particular candidates for this new membership. The number of competing reform proposals, and the fierceness of both support and opposition for these plans, demonstrate the power of the Security Council as well as widespread distrust of a group that increasingly operates behind closed doors. At best, today's Security

Council represents the world power structure as it was in 1945, heavily favoring the victors of World War II in an institution designed to give equal voice to all states. At worst, it is an enduring legacy of big-power politics that operates without systematic input from the majority of people whom it is designed to serve.

Both supporters and critics commonly discuss the need for UN reform. Within the UN system, advocates point to the need to modify structures and operating procedures to accommodate the increased membership, mandate, and visibility of the services the organization provides. In just over seventy years, membership mushroomed from 50 original member states to 193, with very few fundamental changes in between. Trying to create a unified, efficient, and streamlined approach to the wide variety of crises (political, humanitarian, environmental, and others) to which the United Nations responds, proves difficult, as each situation has unique needs and vulnerabilities. The committee charged with reviewing UN operations—convened by the Secretary-General himself—has concluded that UN programs and responses are often "fragmented and weak," lacking the capacity to enforce plans and proposed solutions.[19] More to the point, a former assistant secretary-general for field support, who left office only after he published a scathing op-ed of failures of the organization, which he firmly believes in and wants to succeed, argued that the UN is "a Remington typewriter in a smartphone world."[20]

After a series of high-profile blunders, including an "oil for food" scandal that reached all the way to former Secretary-General Kofi Annan, all agree that stricter financial management within the organization is necessary. The problems associated with being a consensus-driven body can also impede the work of the organization, as was seen in the Geneva-based Human Rights Commission, which was replaced by a smaller Human Rights Council in 2006. The new council includes a process for reviewing the human rights situation in all countries that are members of the General Assembly, and selects its members through a simple-majority vote of all Assembly members rather than by approving regional slates as in the past. These changes were designed to help minimize the presence of human rights violators on the council, and counter their ability to avoid criticism by gaining a seat. The new council also meets throughout the year—rather than the six-week session of the old Human Rights Commission—as a way to respond to crises and highlight the continuous importance of human rights protection.

Another area of controversy within the United Nations surrounds its expanding mandate to take action in countries in the name of humanitarian relief or responsibility to protect. One of the fundamental questions plaguing UN strategies is the hot topic of intervention: When and how should a global body respond to crises in another state's affairs? Since the end of the Cold War, the United Nations has increased its activism, first in military opposition to the Iraqi invasion of Kuwait, and later with involvement in internal conflicts in the former Yugoslavia, Somalia, Cambodia, El Salvador, the Democratic Republic of Congo, and East Timor, among others. The fundamental right to sovereignty of all states—the almost sacred principle upon which the United Nations is based—is enshrined in the UN Charter. State leaders who resist UN action in their countries predictably invoke this principle, which helps explain why there has been no UN response to humanitarian crises in Tibet (due to China's objection) or Chechnya (over Russia's opposition). It has also plagued the crafting of any coordinated response to the devastating crisis in Syria.

As a large, global body consisting of representatives from almost every country of the world, what can the United Nations realistically accomplish, in addition to providing a forum for discussion and diplomatic solutions to problems? The primary modes of influence available to UN actors include censure, economic sanctions, and intervention, either with or without military backing. These actions are permissible under Chapter VII of the UN Charter, which authorizes the Security Council to take enforcement measures to either maintain or restore international peace and security. During the Cold War, Chapter VII provisions were invoked twice: to impose economic sanctions on the white minority regime in southern Rhodesia in 1965, and to impose an arms embargo against the South African apartheid regime in 1977. The latter set of sanctions is now viewed as the most comprehensive package implemented under Chapter VII provisions. They were lifted with the end of apartheid in 1994.

Sanctions imposed under Chapter VII authority have been a more common tool in the post–Cold War era. They have been invoked against Iran, Iraq, the former Yugoslavia, Libya, Haiti, Côte d'Ivoire, Liberia, Rwanda, Somalia, Angola, Sudan, and Sierra Leone, with consideration of sanctions in many other cases. Sanctions can be either mandatory (all member states face risk of punishment if they do not comply) or voluntary. Their imposition is nearly always controversial, because they risk harming ordinary citizens more than powerful leaders. In their favoritism of one group over another, they can prolong and deepen existing conflict. In Bosnia, for example, economic sanctions tied the hands of the Bosnian Muslims while the Bosnian Serbs were being rearmed by Serbia. Sanctions can also worsen already difficult situations faced by civilian populations. In part due to the widespread recognition of the human toll of sanctions against Iraq from August 1990 to March 2003, the Security Council approaches sanctions and their utility with great caution. Since the mid-1990s the United Nations has applied more selective or targeted sanctions, banning financial transactions, travel, or arms trade in an attempt to bring countries in line with the desires of the international community.

Peacekeeping operations. The term "United Nations" often conjures an image of the so-called peacekeepers—the people who wear the famous "blue hats." Yet the processes of "keeping the peace" in areas marred by conflict have fundamentally changed. As the plan was originally designed in the late 1940s, soldiers participating in PEACEKEEPING OPERATIONS (PKOs) were supposed to keep warring parties separated, provide monitors between former combatants, or guarantee a cease-fire, as they did in the first UN peacekeeping mission, designed to observe the Arab-Israeli truce in 1948. (Peacekeeping is a much more elaborate process than peacemaking, which is viewed as bringing the warring parties to agreement. Ideally, but not always, peacekeeping forces pick up where the peacemakers leave off.) Peacekeeping troops can fight only if attacked, and they can remain only as long as all warring parties agree to their presence.

Before we discuss their tasks, let's clarify who the peacekeepers are. The UN Department of Peacekeeping Operations coordinates the work of approximately 100,000 uniformed personnel globally, serving in sixteen operations on four continents as of mid-2016.[21] After an increase in troops under former president Obama, the United States is followed by Pakistan and Bangladesh as the next largest troop contributors.[22] PKO forces are also often drawn from regional groups, in the attempt

to avoid aggravating conflict by inviting "outsiders" into local conflicts. Some have proposed increasing the contingency of so-called regional cops, which are funded internationally but sanctioned by the United Nations to enforce Security Council mandates. They could provide the legitimacy of the international community but place the onus on self-interested, local agents.

The United Nations has supported seventy-one peacekeeping operations since 1948, with prominent PKO missions responding in Haiti, Sudan, the Democratic Republic of Congo, East Timor, and Cyprus. Peacekeepers have also been involved in the coordination of administrations in Kosovo (where they operate parallel to the North Atlantic Treaty Organization [NATO], which handles military matters). Responsibilities placed on the individuals who don the blue helmets of the United Nations, a color explicitly chosen because it is not worn in combat, are likely to increase in the future.

Yet peacekeeping has become a dangerous business, especially in immediate postconflict situations, when the presence of peacekeepers is largely unwelcome. For example, following the 1999 election in East Timor, a UN-sponsored relief office in West Timor was stormed by angry crowds, and the bodies of three UN workers (from the United States, Croatia, and Ethiopia) were burned in the streets. The United Nations and international diplomats expressed disappointment in the outcome of the trials for these deaths, as the accused were tried for "mob violence resulting in death" rather than manslaughter. This was particularly disturbing after the defendants openly admitted complicity in the aid workers' deaths, expressing national pride rather than remorse.[23] In the Central African Republic in 2014, forces including soldiers from France, the Democratic Republic of Congo, and the Republic of Congo were alleged to have engaged in a "persistent pattern" of rape and abuse— against precisely the people they were sent to protect, including children. Even after a UN official sent a report on child sexual abuse to the UN Human Rights Council and the United Nations Children's Fund (UNICEF), neither took action.[24]

In addition to the danger, peacekeepers often have a limited mandate. In 1995, Dutch peacekeepers stood helplessly by in Srebrenica, Bosnia, as Serbs murdered thousands of Muslim men and boys. And the mostly Belgian UN force pulled out of Rwanda at the start of the genocide in 1994, after a number of their own were killed. The same mistake was repeated in Mali in early 2013, when 10,000 soldiers and police officers were sent to respond to a terrorist outbreak without sufficient training. PKO missions are limited by financial constraints as well. Many states demonstrate a tremendous lack of commitment, especially financial, refusing to pay even when they vote to authorize a mission. The United States shoulders much of the blame in this regard: even though it has long been the single largest financial contributor to the UN, it has also, since the 1990s, refused to pay a significant portion of its PKO dues, pressing for reforms instead.[25] The trend has shifted, but is likely to fluctuate with a change in presidential administration: timely payment of dues to international organizations was an emphasis of President Obama, but President Trump and his supporters have expressed much less support for the UN or its missions. Many within the UN express concern that the United States and the UN could return to the tense relations experienced under the George W. Bush administration, when the US ambassador to the UN, John R. Bolton, famously quipped that the organization would only be effective if it lost its top ten floors (where the senior leaders have their offices).[26]

Another common problem is that the presence of peacekeepers can give citizens a false sense of security, while the forces lack the real power to intervene (or they bring new problems with them). As a devastating outbreak of cholera ravaged crisis-weary Haiti in mid-2010, serious allegations—initially rebuffed by the UN—charged Nepali PKO forces as responsible for the disease. There was an active outbreak of cholera in Nepal at the time, and the allegations state that forces did not adequately separate their waste, allowing it to infect canals and water sources. It took the UN until 2016 to admit that its operations may have played a role in the initial outbreak of the cholera epidemic in Haiti—which eventually killed at least 10,000 and sickened hundreds of thousands more, yet UN leaders contend that their legal responsibilities are limited.[27] An even darker side of PKOs is emerging, as troops have been implicated in charges of sexual exploitation, human trafficking, and abuse. UN officials call the sexual violence in Congo the worst in the world.[28] PKOs are impotent at best, complicit at worst: "Despite more than 10 years of experience (in Congo) and billions of dollars, the peacekeeping force still seems to be failing at its most elemental task: protecting civilians."[29] Unfortunately, the debacle involving the impotence of UN forces in Congo (during which women in their eighties were repeatedly gang-raped while peacekeepers were deployed nearby) seems to reflect a pattern of neglect throughout Africa as well. One observer has called Congo "the U.N.'s crowning failure" and "the African equivalent of Afghanistan" because of the conflict's violence and complexity.[30]

These challenges within peacekeeping operations are related to UN interventions more generally. The UN and related agencies need better staffing and processes in order to collect information and respond to, even potentially prevent, outbursts of violence that require international action. Following the crisis in Rwanda in 1994, former Secretary-General Annan (who was at the time of the genocide the head of the UN's peacekeeping office) repeatedly argued for the need for better intelligence-gathering. While increased intelligence capacity might be necessary, many view this assertion by Annan (which Bill Clinton supported) to be a halfhearted attempt to excuse the explicit decision not to take action in Rwanda even after evidence of the coming genocide was made available to the Secretary-General. If peacekeeping missions need anything, critics argue, it is better equipment, common training for interoperability, and updated maps: UN troops got into trouble when they became lost in Sierra Leone's countryside and their radios did not work.

One comprehensive strategy, suggested by Francis Deng, the Secretary-General's special adviser for the prevention of genocide, comprises three phases: monitoring developments to draw early attention to an impending crisis; interceding in time to avert the crisis through diplomatic initiatives; and mobilizing international action when necessary. Ideally, problems should be addressed and solved within domestic frameworks, with international involvement only after the failure of internal efforts. In some cases, where the consequences of delay are grave, the international community may need to act earlier. But crisis-induced reactions are often more symbolic than effective in addressing the causes of conflict, as we've learned from Somalia and elsewhere. External intervention is a major intrusion. Though some will welcome it because of the promise of tangible benefits, we should expect peacekeepers to encounter resistance on grounds of national sovereignty or pride, so the justification for intervention must be reliably persuasive, if not beyond reproach. Deng says

that the difference between success and failure is the degree of spontaneous acceptance or rejection by the local population.[31]

Another struggle in responding to crises is the lack of a streamlined process that allows for quick and efficient action. Currently, only after the Security Council has authorized an intervention, and only after the host country has agreed to that intervention, can the Secretary-General and General Assembly then begin assembling a collection of troops from countries that volunteer them. The requirement for host-country authorization is at least partly to blame for Sudan's long-standing refusal to allow African Union troops to be replaced by UN peacekeeping forces, even though hybrid forces were also proposed for consideration.

Many have highlighted the need for a trained army ready for emergency intervention. One proposal calls for a rapid reaction force that would be composed of up to 15,000 personnel, including military, police, medics, and conflict transformation specialists, and could be ready to deploy within forty-eight hours of Security Council authorization. Standby units have long been discussed within the United Nations, but their actualization has taken on greater urgency following the Rwandan genocide and the continuing crisis in Darfur.[32] While concerns surround the creation, maintenance, and potential misuse of such a force, recent intervention failures may be enough to overcome past objections.

Additionally, as mentioned, there is a growing sense among many that some issues, particularly the most egregious violations of human rights, require humanitarian intervention by the world community. The United Nations has been one of the most active organizations in coordinating the implementation of, and transition beyond, humanitarian response teams. No longer is the United Nations a neutral arbiter along buffer zones. The defining point it faces now is a clearer, more universal acceptance of its new role, particularly in response to emerging needs.

The need for a coordinated international intervention arises, according to one point of view, because powerful nations do not have direct interests at stake, and are therefore unwilling to get involved. There is often a delay, during which time rebel forces may try to "finish the job" before "outsiders" arrive. Humanitarian intervention, especially, requires distinguishing between the "good guys" and the "bad guys," and it is not always clear which side is the most deserving of support. Sometimes intervention can strengthen the weaker side, giving it little incentive to compromise and prolonging the conflict that troops were sent to end. As we have seen in many cases, noble intentions can lead to disastrous consequences, especially if they are not backed up with sufficient international determination, including military force, finances, and the willingness to stay until the problem, sometimes intractable, is solved.

Most of the problems with PKOs are exacerbated by the fact that we ask peacekeepers today to do much more than their original mandate—they are called on to clear landmines, monitor elections, seize weapons, enforce international law, contain violence, protect civilians, supervise postwar reconstruction, and arrest war criminals.[33] Peacekeepers have been placed in charge of disarmament operations as well, a mix of policing and military operations that is untenable at best. Where is the line between keeping the peace and quelling unrest? Increasingly, peacekeepers are forced to walk this dangerous line. The accumulation of tasks by PKO forces has been challenged by both the financiers of the missions, and more importantly by the recipients of the action, who often have little if any say in operations in their own country. The other

view is that humanitarian interventions smack of imperial control because of the particularistic politics that are involved in each case. "Humanitarian" may sound well and good, but these interventions are also designed to achieve political objectives.[34] Such actions for the international community are taken in uncharted territory, and often have unintended effects. As we have seen, peacekeeping and humanitarian intervention can clearly make a bad situation worse.

Some interventions have exacerbated or prolonged crises, since they diffuse the specific interests that foreign powers, such as France or the United States, seek to project or protect. While participants ostensibly need to be impartial, the longer multinational forces stay, the greater the danger of loss of impartiality and therefore effectiveness in carrying out their mandate. Mission mandates need to be clear and achievable: an imprecise mandate is a recipe for confusion and a worsening of the crisis. Often the immediate purpose of humanitarian interventions is to deliver relief. But to have a lasting impact, such missions must move beyond Band-Aids to promote more substantive change, which can be a massive undertaking.

Lasting peacekeeping also includes state reconstruction, a focus that was ignored in Rwanda after efforts failed so miserably in Somalia. In a sense, peacekeepers are asked to engage in a complex process of engineering, including the preventive work that could be done by other agencies within the UN. Societies torn apart by strife need a comprehensive approach that pays more attention to the conditions that led to the crisis in the first place. Also, peacekeeping efforts especially need to encourage the rebuilding of civil society, which, as discussed in Chapter 9, emerges rather than being created. The processes of peacekeeping need to provide protections for minority groups and individuals, as well as reassure people that it is acceptable to express opinions without fear of reprisal. The rule of law, or the impartial and universal application of legal norms, must gradually prevail. A lesson we have learned from mistakes in past operations is that we cannot rush to elections: nascent parties need time to consolidate, form platforms, and present them to voters. In addition, there is a huge need to defuse armed movements, which is a controversial undertaking and difficult to implement. When major portions of the society feel unsafe, they are unlikely to surrender their sometimes only means of defense to outside intruders in the name of "making the peace." Otherwise it will be easy for disenchanted groups to reject election results, with or without violent means, and voters will have little choice but to vote on the basis of ethnic or religious identity. Elections held under the wrong conditions can be a real setback for democratization.[35]

The United Nations and social development. In recent years the crisis-response aspect of the United Nations has received much of the limelight. The world community, however conflicted, has strongly voiced its conviction that governments (and agents acting in the name of governments) may be held accountable for actions within their own borders. The UN and its agencies have also been at the forefront of attempts to promote international law and universal principles. Since its inception in 1945, a key aspect of the United Nations has been its promotion of peace through programs designed to enhance the well-being and development of the world's population. One aspect of social development it has attempted to tackle is child neglect and abuse. Many children are forced to forgo daytime educational opportunities to make money on city streets, shining shoes, washing cars, or collecting recyclables.

Educational programs under the auspices of the United Nations Children's Fund allow these street children to receive an education in the evenings. As discussed in Chapters 5 and 9, child labor is a huge (and complex) problem in the global south.

The Convention on the Rights of the Child (CRC), adopted in 1989, is perhaps the most broadly signed convention in the world (the only two UN member states that haven't ratified it are Somalia and the United States). Establishing the standards that all civilized countries should attempt to meet in caring for their children, the CRC is comprehensive in scope, promoting four core principles: nondiscrimination; devotion to the best interests of the child; the right to life, survival, and development; and respect for the views of the child.

Among other things it calls for the protection of children from abuse and abandonment, as well as the provision of basic needs, including prenatal healthcare. The CRC urges governments to abolish prejudicial treatment of children, including treatment before they are born. Although the convention does not directly address the issue of abortion, it can be read to challenge the use of prenatal sex selection, a practice in which parents choose to abort female fetuses and carry male fetuses to full term, which is especially evident in China and India. In China, where traditional preferences and low-tech means have been accelerated by its "one child" population policy and cheap, accessible ultrasounds, preferential sex selection (before and after pregnancy) has distorted the gender ratio in the country.

The United Nations has also been a pivotal IGO in promoting the rights of women. As one example, in the 1940s, women's rights were viewed as something separate from the universal human rights of all people. Largely due to efforts of the UN and related agencies, this status changed by the 1990s to completely incorporate, in theory at least, women's rights within the notion of universally applicable human rights.[36] One of the most important documents attempting to institutionalize these ideas is the 1979 Convention on the Elimination of All Forms of Discrimination Against Women (CEDAW).

The convention, which has the force of international law, has been ratified by 186 of the member states of the United Nations and is considered to be the most wide-ranging attempt to eliminate discriminatory acts against women. Many refer to it as the "International Bill of Rights of Women," in that it establishes minimum standards for combating prejudice based on gender. It is also the only human rights treaty that affirms the reproductive rights of women. The convention recognizes that socially defined gender roles require provisions against discrimination and abuse that go beyond equal treatment of men and women. CEDAW asserts the inhumanity of torture and cruel and degrading treatment, and stresses that intimate violence is no less severe than violence committed by the state. It also focuses on the need to combat military sexual slavery, workplace abuse, and violence in the family. CEDAW condemns the use of rape as a tool to humiliate women and their communities. Of the countries on which we focus, seven have ratified the document: China (1980), Mexico (1981), Peru (1982), Indonesia (1984), Nigeria (1985), Turkey (1985), and Zimbabwe (1991). The United States joins Iran, Sudan, Somalia, Nauru, Palau, and Tonga in not yet having ratified the treaty, and is the only industrialized country in the world to hold this dubious honor. This document served as the springboard for the commencement of global conferences on women, held in Mexico City (1975), Copenhagen (1980), Nairobi (1985), and Beijing (1995).

Each of these events, and meetings held to monitor the implementation of proposals from each conference, sparked a related increase in the number of women-related NGOs and networks of organizations designed to investigate and resolve issues, including marriage and reproductive rights, healthcare and educational inequities, and physical, sexual, and psychological abuse, in times of both peace and conflict, faced by women.[37] In fact, at each UN-sponsored world conference on women, a meeting in conjunction with NGO representatives was held as a way to complement the work of the conference and increase networking opportunities made available to all participants.

Activists in each country have used the force of CEDAW to accomplish varying aims. Many signatory states have altered their constitutions and national laws in order to enter into compliance with the treaty. In Nepal, CEDAW has empowered women to push for stiffer penalties for rape, as well as legislation that, for the first time, codifies women's right to inherit property. In Botswana, CEDAW was used to challenge citizenship laws under which children of a woman married to a foreigner were not considered citizens of the state (even though children of a man married to a foreigner were granted all the rights of citizenship). In Afghanistan, legislation to eliminate violence against women was based on CEDAW components, notably making rape a crime for the first time in the country's history as well as nullifying forced marriages and early marriages without consent of the female partner.[38]

In 1994 a special rapporteur on violence against women was appointed. This has enabled more direct investigation and advocacy on behalf of the rights enshrined in CEDAW. For example, the rapporteur conducts field visits to countries that have ratified CEDAW to investigate claims of breaches of the human rights of women and girls, acting as an advocate and working to ensure proper punishment. Additionally, since an optional protocol took effect in December 2000, women may bypass their national governments and complain directly to the United Nations. The most prominent case to use this optional protocol, which has been ratified by seventy-eight countries, is the inquiry into the murders of nearly 300 women in Ciudad Juárez, Mexico (whose deaths still remain a mystery).

The United Nations and justice: tribunals, truth commissions, and courts. The United Nations and other IGOs have been integral in dealing with violent legacies of states in transition and international crimes against humanity. This work demonstrates the enabling role that international organizations can play in assisting countries during transitional periods. There are two primary types of institutions designed with this type of mandate: war crimes tribunals and truth commissions.

Criminal tribunals are established nationally (and sometimes internationally), often following the breakup of a regime or the end of a war or other act of aggression. Two of the most famous such tribunals were the Nuremberg and Tokyo trials following World War II. Yet these initial tribunals, though international in name, were largely controlled by the victorious Allied powers to prosecute aggressors from the defeated Axis states.[39] War tribunals are based on the Geneva Conventions, and attempt to locate and prosecute "persons responsible for serious violations of international humanitarian law." Ad hoc international criminal tribunals have been established to investigate the war in the former Yugoslavia (operating since 1991) and the genocide in Rwanda (operating since 1997).

In March 2003 the United Nations established an international criminal tribunal to prosecute former Khmer Rouge leaders in Cambodia. Justice has been particularly slow-going in the investigations of the more than 1.7 million deaths during the 1975–1979 Khmer Rouge period. In fact, it wasn't until mid-2010 that the first senior member of the Khmer Rouge regime was sentenced (Kang Guek Eav, also known as "Duch"). He was the only one of five defendants to acknowledge guilt, admitting to overseeing the torture and killing of more than 14,000 people. Duch, who was sixty-seven years old at the time of his sentencing, will likely serve only nineteen years of his thirty-five-year sentence, even though he was convicted of both war crimes and crimes against humanity, because the tribunal took into account time already served. As many of the likely defendants enter their twilight years (and some of the most brutal Khmer Rouge leaders have already died), many fear the time for achieving any sort of justice is running out.

Tribunals are quite concrete—their goal is to investigate claims of human rights violations and atrocities, to hold trials, and to punish responsible individuals. A major part of the investigation of such tribunals includes the perusal of murder sites and purported mass graves in which aggressors attempted to conceal the evidence of their crimes. One of the difficulties faced by the International Criminal Tribunal for Rwanda (ICTR), based in Arusha, Tanzania, was the sheer number of accomplices and perpetrators of the crimes—tens and possibly hundreds of thousands—which is "beyond the capacity of any justice system to arraign and judge," in the view of one analyst.[40]

The tribunal has been criticized for being slow and expensive; its total cost over two decades of operation was over $2 billion. By its close in late 2015, the Rwandan tribunal had indicted ninety-three individuals and sentenced two-thirds of them. This ad hoc tribunal, created as a temporary body to rule on atrocities committed during the 1994 genocide in Rwanda, rendered the first genocide convictions under international law, including one against Jean Kambanda, the prime minister at the time of the carnage. Another important precedent set by the ICTR is that it was the first to convict for rape as a war crime. However, another criticism of the tribunal is that it did not include much attention to abuses committed by the Tutsi forces nor did it provide compensation for the victims or survivors.[41]

For these tribunals to be established, governments must grant their approval, and often the logistics of a tribunal need to be approved by the affected national legislatures. While this can provide a lengthy hindrance to the commencement of tribunals, an opening is usually found after a change of regime or the death of an authoritarian leader. For example, Indonesia repeatedly rejected calls to establish a tribunal for East Timor that would investigate the human rights abuses that occurred in the territory during the 1975–1999 Indonesian occupation. Former president Abdurrahman Wahid once stated that even if former general Wiranto, who is widely blamed for either ordering or failing to stop the militia violence, were convicted, he would be pardoned in the interest of maintaining national harmony. (Years later, President Jokowi appointed Wiranto as a security minister, in a move decried by many.)[42] In response to widespread pressure to bring the responsible parties to justice, Indonesia established an ad hoc human rights tribunal, which has been largely dismissed as a meaningless façade. The United Nations established a Serious Crimes Investigation Unit to hear trials concerning alleged crimes against humanity in Dili, the capital of Timor-Leste,

but Jakarta has virtually blocked action in this regard by refusing to extradite the accused. Although the investigatory unit has already processed more than eighty cases, it is unable to prosecute Indonesian military figures. Finally, in 2002, the Commission for Reception, Truth, and Reconciliation in East Timor was founded, and within three years it had produced a lengthy report detailing abuses, but it too has been under pressure to promote reconciliation rather than justice.

The initiative to establish the International Criminal Court (ICC) began in 1948 to address a need to replace ad hoc, conflict-specific tribunals with a permanent war crimes tribunal. The ICC, which entered into force July 1, 2002, does not replace national courts, but rather serves as a court of last resort when they are unwilling or unable to handle cases. The idea of such a court was tabled by superpower politics during the Cold War, but was resurrected in the early 1990s. In 1998, 160 states signed an agreement to create this permanent court (with the conspicuous exception of the United States, which has expressed concern that politically motivated cases will be brought against it). The ICC, which deals only with crimes committed after its establishment, is located in The Hague, with the International Court of Justice. (The ICJ is empowered to hear cases waged between governments, while the ICC allows individuals and groups to prosecute individuals for genocide, war crimes, and crimes against humanity. Additionally, the ICJ is a civil court, while the ICC prosecutes criminal cases.)

At the ICC a panel of eighteen judges hears cases—with the maximum allowable penalty of life imprisonment. The ICC is designed to put on trial not only the most notorious abusers of human rights. So far, nearly all of those indicted are African. This fact has won the body scorn from many African heads of state, who accuse it of neocolonial bias. Some, including Burundi, South Africa, and Gambia, have registered their intention to withdraw from the body and others are likely to follow, given the support for the idea of a mass withdrawal at the African Union. Supporters of the Court point out that the chief prosecutor, Fatou Bensouda, is from Gambia and that the ICC is conducting investigations and may bring forward cases from Colombia, Afghanistan, and the UK in Iraq. But it will take a conviction of a leader from outside Africa to win over skeptics.[43]

Somewhat similar to international tribunals, truth commissions are designed to air grievances about past wrongs committed by individuals or groups as a way to prevent future crimes against humanity, to restore a semblance of "normalcy" after periods of unrest, and to promote a human rights culture. Yet truth commissions are different from war crimes tribunals in a few very important ways. Trials are designed to punish, and may deprive individuals of life, liberty, or property. Truth commissions vary in their aims; they often seek to promote individual and structural healing, piece together past reality, and establish a historical memory so that it can never be denied. Because they are separate from courts of law, truth commissions do not usually have the right of subpoena; they are less bound by concerns of due process and may admit hearsay and other forms of evidence that would be unacceptable in a war crimes tribunal.[44]

The most widely known truth commission is the Truth and Reconciliation Commission of South Africa. However, other truth commissions (some dating back to the 1970s) have been established in Haiti, Guatemala, Uganda, Bolivia, Argentina, Zimbabwe, Uruguay, Chile, Nigeria, and the Philippines. Not all truth commissions are the same, and few follow the model established in South Africa, which granted

widespread amnesty to participants in exchange for their role in the investigation. Some of these commissions, such as the ones in Guatemala and El Salvador, are established under UN auspices, while others are domestic initiatives alone. Some, but not most, allow amnesties. A few truth commissions are established for the primary purpose of honoring those hurt by abuse and promoting closure, while others gather information and pass it on to courts for prosecution.

Truth commissions are generally established after a civil war, or after an authoritarian government steps aside, as part of a democratic transition. Timor-Leste fits this description. Its truth commission, known as the Commission for Truth and Friendship, makes creative use of local customs. Those who are accused of the most serious crimes will be brought before courts, but because there are too many people to handle, the approximately 10,000 East Timorese who participated in lesser crimes with Indonesian-backed militias will come before the truth commission. Many of these people are hiding out in West Timor, afraid they might be lynched if they return home. For those who want to come home, the truth commission will bring them before local village councils. If they admit their crimes and apologize, they will be sentenced to community service. According to local custom, they will then be safe from acts of revenge.

Some critics of truth commissions characterize them as "some-of-the-truth commissions" or "Kleenex commissions" that do more harm than good. Many people resist the idea of granting amnesties to individuals who admit to committing atrocities, in return for their cooperation with the commission. The trade-off is viewed as necessary in order to allow a more complete airing of misdeeds, including public testimony that often allows victims (or their families) to confront the perpetrators of the crime. Several truth commissions have televised their proceedings. They vary over whether they provide the names of those who come forward. Despite their differences, the goal of truth commissions is to make sure that the acts of injustice cannot be ignored, even if, in the end, the commissions breach justice by "letting some people off the hook."[45] For a variety of reasons, truth commissions often face powerful resistance and need money, a broad mandate, and high-level backing if they are to succeed. South Africa's Archbishop Desmond Tutu, in his justification for amnesties in the South African trials of apartheid leaders, argued that criminal justice can be sacrificed if it leads to a greater sense of social justice.

* * *

As you can see, the tasks before the United Nations are enormous, and some may say nearly impossible to achieve. Many around the world, including leaders within the organization itself, are increasingly questioning the relevance of the United Nations, especially as powers beyond the formerly dominant United States and European states assert their role, making compromise more difficult. Many question whether the most well-known IGO is "at the center of global responses" to the big problems facing the world as it moves toward "mini-lateral cooperation" of smaller coalitions of big countries instead; as one analyst put it, the UN is no longer "the only game in town."[46] Organizations such as the Group of 20 (G-20), with more manageable memberships and less pomp, may actually provide more latitude for discussion and negotiation among world leaders.

As one historian (who also serves as an informal adviser for former Secretary-General Ban) stated, "The U.N. is not the sun of the international solar system; everything doesn't revolve around it. But it is the final reference point on most issues, which have to come to the U.N. for legitimacy."[47]

It should be clear that international governmental organizations have played a pivotal role in the world community, sometimes fostering cooperation among governments, and other times taking action against governments that are perceived to be violating universal norms of conduct. All organizations have their limitations, and generally IGOs are constrained by the fact that they are established by governments to act in the interest of governments. This means that they are beholden to the interests and concerns of powerful elite groups, and that political agendas, as we have seen, tend to predominate over the humanitarian interests that they profess to promote. And despite the talk of inclusion and equal voting privileges for small states as well as big states, weaker governments of the global south can get caught in big-power agendas that limit their voice and ability to take action. In the end, while states participating in IGOs give up some degree of sovereignty in order to work in concert with others, that power can be snatched back when considered necessary. We now turn to another type of collaborative organization—groups of people who organize outside state authority to promote particular agendas in the global community.

International Nongovernmental Organizations

In Chapter 5 we discussed the influence of some NGOs, namely, multinational corporations. International NGOs are private, transnational associations of individuals or groups that organize around a shared interest or understanding, and have strong ties to civil society, which we introduced in Chapter 10. NGOs are extremely diverse, in their size, organizational structure, and range of interests. Their numbers exploded in the 1980s, to the point that many countries have thousands, if not tens of thousands, of NGOs or affiliates. Even though scarce resources for programming and advocacy present formidable obstacles to groups in the global south, NGOs have a strong presence. They include universities, civic organizations, churches, and other religious institutions.

You are probably aware of many such organizations, even if you do not identify them as NGOs per se: Habitat for Humanity, the International Federation of Red Cross and Red Crescent Societies, the International Planned Parenthood Federation, Greenpeace, Oxfam, War Child, Amnesty International, Catholic Relief Services, Lutheran World Relief, Bread for the World, Save the Children, and Goodwill Industries International are just some of the most widely recognized. These organizations are powerful in that they help countries incorporate ideas into national (and international) policies and programs. They are also vital in shaping and conveying public opinion to large gatherings of policymakers. They may be national or international in scope. NGOs are often able to open previously closed discussions or bring attention to taboo topics, including violence against women and child labor. NGOs rarely work alone. Rather, they work together with other organizations and with governments in order to promote their causes, often by hosting international meetings in conjunction with other associational conferences, such as those of the United Nations, a presence that has increased dramatically since the early 1970s.

What can NGOs accomplish that national governments cannot? NGOs such as Amnesty International have been especially critical in exposing human rights abuses and educating citizens about their rights, with less of the government interference that mars the work of peacekeeping missions. NGOs work in dangerous circumstances and under many rules, and they are often subject to retaliation. Often, these organizations voice impatience with the slow action of government-based organizations. Nongovernmental organizations are less beholden to bureaucratic and electoral interests, and they have power that IGOs such as the UN, which is bound to act only on the expressed interests of its members through the Security Council, do not. Even though they are made up of individuals and interest groups, their target audience is most often the governments of countries or world opinion. Many of the issues that we have discussed throughout this book have NGOs associated with them.

One of the best-known associations of NGOs dedicated to the promotion of human rights is Amnesty International. Its success, in part, is due to a wide-reaching network of local (often university-based), national, and international offices. One of the key areas that Amnesty International focuses on is advocacy for individual political prisoners and prisoners of conscience—people who suffer persecution for their beliefs. Amnesty International has been particularly effective in targeting governments to reveal violations of universal standards of human rights. Additionally, its members coordinate campaigns for the release of political prisoners throughout the world, and spearhead an international campaign against the use of capital punishment. One of this organization's greatest strengths is its work in raising the awareness of particular issues by publicly turning the spotlight on countries that abuse human rights.

Another NGO that campaigns for humanitarian issues and also works "on the ground" is the International Federation of Red Cross and Red Crescent Societies (IFRC), part of the larger International Red Cross and Red Crescent Movement, which also includes the International Committee of the Red Cross (ICRC) and the more than 180 national Red Cross and Red Crescent Societies around the world. This is a highly acclaimed and almost universally accepted set of organizations that works largely independently of governments so that it can remain impartial in handling humanitarian crises during times of both peace and war. Because the IFRC is not tied to any official government, or even to the United Nations, it can accomplish tasks or change its mandate without needing to muster the will of the international community or the consensus of multiple nation-states. Unlike the campaigning organizations discussed earlier, the IFRC attempts not to change opinion, but rather to take action, promoting the most universal perspective of humanity—protection and humane treatment of all individuals, even combatants wearing enemy uniforms.

The International Red Cross and Red Crescent Movement's record of humanitarian interventions is quite impressive. The complexities facing refugees, particularly related to legally defined "genuine refugees" versus "DISPLACED PERSONS," serve as a case in point. The ICRC has successfully procured legal exemptions to allow its representatives to come to the aid of displaced persons in conflict-ridden areas, where other international organizations, notably those affiliated with the UN, lack jurisdiction to respond.[48] It has also been quite active in repatriating prisoners of war, including 10,000 Iraqi prisoners held in Iran.

The ICRC, based in Geneva, Switzerland, has been absolutely pivotal in promoting global cultural values, especially related to times of war. In fact, as an NGO

it was a key player in the drafting and signing of the first Geneva Convention in 1864, also known as the "Red Cross Convention," which when combined with follow-up conventions provides the universally acknowledged rules of warfare. The ICRC stressed that states need to protect the worth and dignity of individuals "even when this is most difficult and costly for states."[49] It has also been instrumental in advocating the need for quality medical care, even during times of strife, and especially for the protection of medical-care providers who identify themselves in war-torn areas with the recognizable symbol of either the red cross or the red crescent.

Yet not all NGOs attempt to maintain the neutrality of the International Red Cross and Red Crescent Movement. Two NGOs that attempt to promote advocacy within particular substantive topics—medicine and journalism—irrespective of geopolitical borders, are the Paris-based associations Doctors Without Borders (Médecins sans Frontières [MSF]) and Reporters Without Borders (Reporteurs sans Frontières [RSF]). MSF was founded in 1971—in the aftermath of the Biafran War in Nigeria—to publicly challenge the neutrality of the IFRC. The organization unites medical professionals around the world in order to provide medical training and emergency assistance, especially in areas of conflict. In 1999, MSF won the Nobel Peace Prize for its humanitarian work with victims of wars, famine, and other disasters. MSF has also been very active in refugee issues, particularly in camps and temporary settlements. MSF is famous for its fierce independence, but it does not attempt to appear neutral in the face of conflict.

The goal of Reporters Without Borders, founded in 1985, is to publicize threats to the free flow of information in an increasing number of forums, especially by highlighting the arrest and torture of journalists who suffer because of their profession. It publishes an annual report of press freedoms in countries around the world, highlighting the arrests, kidnappings, imprisonment, torture, and murder of journalists. Not surprisingly, many reporters suffer these fates when they investigate and attempt to report on corruption, abuse of power, or drug trafficking, especially if they highlight the complicity of politicians. More than half the member states of the United Nations impose limits on freedom of the press, and, as discussed in Chapter 13, RSF and similar organizations call out the worst violators.

A new direction in press freedom that RSF and other NGOs are pressing is the free flow of information on the Internet. Increasingly, many non-Western countries are imposing restrictions on communication via this channel, by installing filters that block access to websites, forcing computer users to register, or sharply limiting access for all citizens. RSF publishes annual lists of "Enemies of the Internet," which detail access restrictions as well as punitive efforts taken against individuals who use this medium to express their views.

Other NGOs promote environmental causes. The better-known environmental NGOs include the Nature Conservancy, Greenpeace, and the World Wildlife Fund. These are huge, multinational organizations with very large budgets to accomplish advocacy, education, and mobilization around environmental issues. These NGOs, even more than others, have linked arms with similar-minded organizations in networks to accomplish great feats. Greenpeace, for example, states that one of its primary goals is to stop the "chemicalization" of the planet, especially by ending the threat of nuclear weapons and nuclear power as well as other forms of "dirty" technology, and to limit ozone depletion caused by the production and use of greenhouse

gases. It has also been highly critical of genetically modified organisms and crops. Yet Greenpeace is also linked with other human rights and environmental organizations that promote responsive government and biodiversity.

Churches and religious institutions are other examples of NGOs that have crossed over into multiple issue areas in order to promote human welfare. The Catholic Church, for example, is a widely recognized NGO with a high degree of activism in the global south, directly and through its many institutions. One of these is Caritas, which attempts to promote Christian ideals of social justice and charity by working with and for impoverished peoples. Like many NGOs, Caritas is part of an international-level umbrella organization, but most of its work is increasingly being conducted at the regional, even the state, level. Another religiously affiliated NGO is the International Association for Religious Freedom (IARF), which, having been established in 1900, predates many other NGOs. The goal of the IARF, which is one of many NGOs affiliated with the United Nations, is to promote the universal right of freedom of religion. The IARF includes peoples of many faiths, including Buddhists, Hindus, Humanists, Sikhs, Universalists, Christians, and indigenous peoples, in its advocacy and operation. The IARF has linked arms with many other initiatives and NGO networks, participating, for example, in the Jubilee Debt Campaign effort to increase debt relief for the most impoverished nations.

NGOs have become increasingly prominent within state networks of global power and influence in recent decades. They serve a particularly prominent role within the United Nations, where they increasingly work in a consultative capacity.[50] Although NGOs are currently confined to ECOSOC committees, without any formal access to the General Assembly and its committees, there is much pressure to change this. Within the United Nations, NGOs cannot vote, because they do not represent a state, but they are welcomed as participants in most UN debates because of their grassroots experience and data, which states may not be able or may not have the desire to gather. As interest groups, they actively lobby delegates and provide connections between grassroots citizenry and international diplomatic channels that otherwise do not exist. Additionally, NGOs work with UN agencies in the field, taking on massive grassroots tasks that the overburdened and overly bureaucratized UN agencies would be less able to accomplish. For example, over 500 NGOs work with the United Nations High Commissioner for Refugees to intervene in crisis situations where refugees are involved.[51]

* * *

We have discussed a wide array of organizations, both national and international in scope, with differing levels of expertise and involvement. Increasingly, many question whether these organizations are necessary, or even relevant. To be sure, they have both strengths and weaknesses. Perhaps, though, the increasing push from many countries, especially those within the global south, to join and become active members in these organizations, is a sign of some level of vitality. Taking the United Nations, for example, nearly every state that is eligible for membership has sought a seat in this world body—the only countries that lack membership are the Vatican (which holds observer status) and several "microstates" with extremely small populations.[52] Including more voices makes things messier, but perhaps more inclusive as well.

The struggle to balance representation, efficiency, and productivity takes on more urgency as the global community faces ever more complex challenges to life in the twenty-first century. It is to those issues that we now turn.

Notes

1. This perspective is based largely on the views on "new regionalism" expressed by Sheila Page in her book *Regionalism Among Developing Countries* (New York: St. Martin's, 2000), pp. 5–6.

2. Michael Hirsh, "Calling All Regio-Cops: Peacekeeping's Hybrid Future," *Foreign Affairs,* November–December 2000.

3. Page, *Regionalism Among Developing Countries.*

4. Carol B. Thompson, "Beyond the Nation-State? Democracy in Regional Economic Context," in *Democracy and Socialism in Africa,* ed. Robin Cohen and Harry Goulbourne (Boulder: Westview, 1991).

5. Trade Law Centre for Southern Africa, "SADC's Free Trade Area Slow to Pick Up," January 12, 2010, www.tralac.org.

6. Page, *Regionalism Among Developing Countries.*

7. Danielle Renwick, "Mercosur: South America's Fractious Trade Bloc," Council on Foreign Relations, October 5, 2016.

8. Brian Naylor, "Another Election Day First: OAS Will Observe U.S. Voting," National Public Radio, September 13, 2016.

9. Mary Beth Sheridan, "For U.S. and OAS, New Challenges to Latin American Democracy," *Washington Post,* July 6, 2009.

10. "Cuba Will Never Rejoin OAS over Venezuela Row, Says Castro," BBC News, June 5, 2016.

11. Paul Reynolds, "African Union Replaces Dictators' Club," BBC News, July 8, 2002.

12. "Profile: African Union," BBC News, February 5, 2016.

13. Rob Watson, "What Makes a Good UN Secretary General?," BBC News, October 2, 2006.

14. Julian Borger, "António Guterres to Be Next UN Secretary General," *The Guardian* (London), October 5, 2016.

15. Because much of the world did not recognize the Communist Party's leadership of the People's Republic of China (PRC) on the mainland, the "China seat" was occupied by the Nationalist Party, which operated from Taiwan after its loss to the CCP in 1949. The Taiwanese government of the Republic of China occupied this position until 1971, when the PRC first joined the United Nations.

16. Data compiled from "Security Council—Veto List," Dag Hammarskjöld Library, http://research.un.org/en/docs/sc/quick (data through December 5, 2016); and http://globalpolicy.org/security-council/tables-and-charts-on-the-security-council-0-82/use-of-the-veto.html. The total number of vetoes cast by the current representative of the China seat in the UN, the People's Republic of China, is only five, with their first veto being cast in 1972. Representatives from the Republic of China on Taiwan registered the other veto credited to the Chinese delegation. Also, it is important to note that Russia and China both vetoed five Security Council resolutions (each related to the Syrian crisis) between 2011 and 2016.

17. "Thinking the UNthinkable," *The Economist,* November 13, 2010.

18. Ibid.

19. "Panel to Recommend Simplified UN," BBC News, November 8, 2006.

20. Anthony Banbury, "I Love the U.N., but It Is Failing," *New York Times,* March 18, 2016, p. SR5.

21. United Nations Department of Peacekeeping Operations, "Fact Sheet: United Nations Peacekeeping," August 31, 2016, www.un.org.

22. Center on International Cooperation, *Annual Review of Global Peace Operations, 2010* (Boulder: Lynne Rienner, 2010), p. 3.

23. Irwan Firdaus, "Three E. Timorese Sentenced in Deaths of Aid Workers," Associated Press, May 5, 2001.

24. Banbury, "I Love the U.N.," p. SR5; Kambiz Foorohar, "The UN Peacekeepers Rape Scandal Gets Worse," *Bloomberg,* June 16, 2016.

25. US officials claim that Washington has paid in full, although United Nations officials contest that; see "U.N. Official: U.S. Is $1.2 Billion in Arrears at U.N.," Reuters, October 14, 2010. Part of the challenge is found in "contested arrears"—monies that Washington disagrees it owes to the organization. Another reason why figures may be contradictory at times is that the peacekeeping budget is often left out of the full UN budget, since missions are approved and financed on a case-by-case basis.

26. Somini Sengupta and Rick Gladstone, "Donald Trump and the U.N.: Signs of Clashing Views on Many Issues," *New York Times,* November 19, 2016, www.nytimes.com.

27. Jonathan M. Katz, "U.N. Admits Role in Cholera Epidemic in Haiti," *New York Times,* August 17, 2016.

28. Jeffrey Gettleman, "Frenzy of Rape in Congo Reveals U.N. Weakness," *New York Times,* October 3, 2010.

29. Ibid.

30. Ibid.

31. Francis Mading Deng, "State Collapse: The Humanitarian Challenge to the UN," in *Collapsed States: The Disintegration and Restoration of Legitimate Authority,* ed. I. William Zartman (Boulder: Lynne Rienner, 1995).

32. Olivia Ward, "United Nations 'Army' Proposed," *Toronto Star,* June 15, 2006.

33. Mary Kaldor, "Humanitarian Intervention: A Forum," *The Nation,* May 8, 2000. In this piece, Kaldor argues that "a genuine humanitarian intervention is much more like policing than warfighting or traditional peacekeeping." See also Kaldor's book *New and Old Wars: Organized Violence in a Global Era* (Stanford: Stanford University Press, 1999).

34. These two opposing views are expressed by Mahmood Mamdani in "Humanitarian Intervention: A Forum," *The Nation,* May 8, 2000.

35. Ibrahim A. Gambari, "The Role of Foreign Intervention in African Reconstruction," in Zartman, *Collapsed States.*

36. Karen A. Mingst and Margaret P. Karns, *The United Nations in the 21st Century,* 3rd ed. (Boulder: Westview, 2007).

37. Nitza Berkovitch, "The Emergence and Transformation of the International Women's Movement," in *Constructing World Culture: International Nongovernmental Organizations Since 1875,* ed. John Boli and George M. Thomas (Stanford: Stanford University Press, 1999).

38. Waxhma Frogh, "CEDAW Ratification Would Be a Triumph for Afghan Women," *The Hill,* November 17, 2010. Frogh, an Afghani activist, provided testimony before the US Senate Judiciary subcommittee hearing on CEDAW ratification, stating, "The U.S. failure to ratify CEDAW is of huge international significance."

39. Richard J. Goldstone, "Bringing War Criminals to Justice During an Ongoing War," in *Hard Choices: Moral Dilemmas in Humanitarian Intervention,* ed. Jonathan Moore, 195–210 (Lanham: Rowman and Littefield, 1998).

40. Martin, "Hard Choices After Genocide," p. 159.

41. Alastair Leithead, "Rwanda Genocide: International Criminal Tribunal Closes," BBC News, December 14, 2015.

42. "Jokowi Urged to Reverse Wiranto's Appointment," *Jakarta Post,* July 28, 2016, www.thejakartapost.com.

43. Karen Allen, "Is This the End for the International Criminal Court?," BBC News, October 24, 2016.

44. Robert I. Rotberg and Dennis Thompson, eds., *Truth v. Justice: The Morality of Truth Commissions* (Princeton: Princeton University Press, 2000).

45. This is a dominant perspective expressed by many, although not all, of the contributors to the Rotberg and Thompson collection on truth commissions: Rotberg and Thompson, *Truth v. Justice;* and Priscilla B. Hayner, *Unspeakable Truths: Confronting State Terror and Atrocity* (New York: Routledge, 2001).

46. Interview with Stewart M. Patrick, "Crisis of Relevance at the UN," Council on Foreign Relations, September 20, 2010.

47. Colum Lynch, "U.N. Struggles to Prove Its Relevance," *Washington Post,* September 19, 2010.

48. "When Is a Refugee Not a Refugee?," *The Economist,* March 3, 2001.

49. Martha Finnemore, "Rules of War and Wars of Rules: The International Red Cross and the Restraint of State Violence," in Boli and Thomas, *Constructing World Culture,* p. 150.

50. On the role of NGOs in the United Nations, see Mingst and Karns, *The United Nations in the Post–Cold War Era* (Boulder: Westview, 1995), p. 77.

51. "When Is a Refugee Not a Refugee?," *The Economist.*

52. Courtney B. Smith, *Politics and Process at the United Nations: The Global Dance* (Boulder: Lynne Rienner, 2006), p. 278.

Chapter 17

Confronting Global Challenges

We see the damage occurring now. We're trying to beat back the sea.
—*Foreign Minister Tona A. deBrum of the Marshall Islands,*
highlighting the immediacy of his country's climate crisis[1]

The future of the continent (of Africa) is on the line.
—*World Bank president Jim Yong Kim, at the*
height of the Ebola outbreak of 2014[2]

As we have discussed throughout this book, state borders have less salience, or meaning, than ever. Thanks to the revolution in information communication technologies, information flows more rapidly (and in most cases, more freely) than ever before. Boundaries are permeable, challenges spread across borders quickly, and many challenges today take on a cross-national, even global, dimension. The question becomes, then, what are the best methods to approach these far-reaching issues? First, we take a brief look at some of the key global issues of our world today. Because of the scope and breadth of these issues, many believe that real solutions to these problems can be found only in a multilateral response, meaning the conduct of activities by three or more states.

Many of these global challenges illustrate examples of the so-called free-rider problem, which shows that individuals (or groups) can benefit from attempts to solve a problem without contributing to its cause. Similarly, people can attempt to skirt limits or constraints without being caught. This provides individuals and groups little incentive to put forth the effort or the resources to solve problems, which is the main reason why many contend that these issues need larger, global responses in order to successfully combat further decay. Exacerbating this free-rider problem is the long-term view on change: we may not see the lasting effects of changes made today for many years to come. This delay in results often limits people's sense of urgency for taking action now, and underscores the need for global organizations and specialized institutions that can reach large audiences to take leadership.

Environmental Degradation: Science and Global Politics

Since at least the 1980s, scientists have been clamoring for aggressive policies to curtail the impact of human behavior on the natural environment. Many view the environment as the clearest example of the interconnectivity of this planet's residents. Pollution, whether in the form of air, water, land, or otherwise, does not stop at border control. Fish swim in shared waters, moving between the sovereign areas of particular states and the universal seas. Air damaged in one region often worsens as it travels to another. Most scientists agree that modern environmental problems are initiated and worsened by human activity. As one analyst put it, "no other narrative envelopes all of humanity in quite the same way, forcing answers about the ethics of food, of oil, of technology, of economic security, of democratic republics and command capitalism, of colonialism and indigenous peoples, of who in the world is rich and who in the world is poor."[3]

Many are familiar with the problem of global warming brought on by industrial emissions that trap heat close to Earth's atmosphere and contribute to higher average temperatures across the planet. These phenomena are not natural—they are consequences of human consumption patterns. Although the actual degree increase is debated (and based on future models), there is widespread agreement that the average global temperature is increasing.[4] The greatest greenhouse gas–emitting nations include China, the United States, India, and Brazil. As industrialization and urbanization continue, emissions will also continue to rise. China's demand for energy is producing a surge in emissions, as the International Energy Agency has projected "that China's emissions of energy-related greenhouse gases will grow more than the rest of the world's combined increase by 2020."[5]

International conferences to discuss sources of the problems and potential solutions have been held since the mid-1980s. After meetings in Montreal in 1987, governments committed to reducing all substances, but especially human-made materials, that deplete the world's ozone layer. At the Rio de Janeiro meetings in 1992, greater cooperation was forged between developed and less developed states, promoting "common but differentiated" responsibilities for the environment. The expressed goal is to foster all countries' right to development while chipping away at a growing problem at the same time. The spirit of Rio was widely adopted as a workable solution to environmental issues, and, with the adoption of the Framework Convention on Climate Change, the United Nations formally recognized, for the first time, the explicit dangers of climate change.

Further negotiations led to a comprehensive first set of actions that were approved at the Kyoto conference in 1997. Signatories agreed to reductions in greenhouse gas emissions, differentiated by their economic status. The lion's share of responsibility was placed on developed countries, from which the largest portion of harmful emissions originates. The Kyoto Protocol to the United Nations Framework Convention on Climate Change called on thirty of the most developed countries to cut combined emissions of greenhouse gases by an average of 5 percent below their 1990 levels by 2012 (less developed countries will be required to reduce emissions during the second "commitment period," at a later date). The allowance of different emission rates, based on level of development, ultimately led to Kyoto's undoing, especially with China, India, and Brazil exempt from targets (one of the main reasons why the United States failed to ratify it). Some have argued that Kyoto's emphasis

on defensive reductions, rather than proactive developments of alternatives, was the crux of the challenge.[6] Negotiations limped along, with particularly challenging talks in Copenhagen in 2009 widely viewed as disastrous.[7] When the Kyoto protocols expired in 2012, the prospects of a meaningful global agreement on curbing greenhouse gas emissions looked dim.

It was in this context that the world's leaders again gathered in an attempt to strike a most challenging balance: how to get countries to work together to help mitigate future challenges without permitting significant shirking of responsibility. In the case of responses to climate change, the challenge was even starker because the countries with the most greenhouse gas emissions are often spared the effects, while those at most risk of harm due to climate change are the least complicit in it. Oxfam estimates that the poorest half of the global population, many of whom are in the most vulnerable geographic locations prone to changes in sea level, are responsible for approximately 10 percent of total global emissions.[8] Some have captured this dynamic by contrasting the free-riders (countries that are top emitters yet mostly immune to the impact) and the "forced riders" (countries that have low emission rates yet are extremely vulnerable to rising sea levels and other impacts of climate change).[9]

After nearly two weeks of intense formal negotiations, in December 2015 world leaders established a legally binding and universal agreement on climate change—a dramatic achievement more than two decades in the making. Even though many believe that the stated goal—that of keeping global warming below 2 degrees Celsius—is far less than what is actually needed, supporters hailed this agreement, set to enter into force in 2020, as the "turning point in the climate crisis."[10] The hope is that the promises of these cuts, agreed to by more than 150 countries, are just the beginning of the change, and that there will eventually be agreement that will come closer to decreasing the rate of warming to 1.5 degrees Celsius. Participants all knew that Paris was "never imagined as a silver bullet . . . but rather (an agreement) to stave off the most devastating effects of climate change."[11] Even as the reality that the Trump administration may attempt to withdraw US support for the Paris Agreement (a move that more than 360 US companies explicitly asked Trump to reconsider), leading diplomats said that "they expected the pact to be followed with or without the United States."[12] Others argued that even though the United States was a "central broker" of the Paris deal, other countries, including China, were emerging as the new climate diplomats, highlighting the role of China's reductions (from 2012 to 2015) in helping level off planet-warming emissions for three years running.[13]

Population centers in the global south, already strained by limited resources and increasing urbanization, will face greater pressures in the coming decades as today's world population of just over 7 billion people (in 2016) swells to more than 9.7 billion by 2050, with nearly all of that increase projected to be in developing countries.[14] Additionally, the world is host to weather-related natural disasters that tend to defy efforts of prevention, including extreme bouts of heat or cold, as well as severe events such as hurricanes and tsunamis. The disastrous tsunami that was triggered by an earthquake off the west coast of Indonesia on December 26, 2004, claimed the lives of nearly 280,000 people and destroyed the livelihoods of 3 million. In the summer of 2010, Pakistan faced its worst flooding in eighty years, with most estimates reporting 20 million people affected (and a death toll ranging from 1,300 to 1,600). Recovery from the 2010 earthquake in Haiti, which claimed nearly 230,000

lives, was made more difficult by flooding and landslides that many attribute to population concentration, deforestation, and climate change.

Other environmental issues place clearer culpability on human behavior, with clearly uneven impacts being felt in developing versus developed countries. The divide between cause and impact—the "people most at risk from climate change live in countries that have contributed the least to the atmospheric buildup"—runs counter to the notion that "we're all in this together" and points to another way of viewing an extremely unequal world.[15] Deforestation, caused in part by increased agriculture and changing food patterns among humans, is believed to account for up to 20 percent of all greenhouse gas emissions. The availability of safe drinking water dominates environmental agendas in many regions of the developing world. Access to safe, clean water is a political issue in many regions of the world, even though most estimate that it only costs about $25 to provide an individual in the developing world with safe, clean water for the rest of his or her life.[16] With over 260 rivers either crossing or marking international political boundaries, the potential for conflict over this necessary natural resource is ripe—in fact, nearly 80 percent of all violent disputes over water resources around the world have occurred in the Middle East.[17]

The Food and Agriculture Organization (FAO) of the United Nations estimates that only about 20 percent of agricultural land in developing countries is irrigated; more land will be needed to sustain an increase in food production. Additionally, water control could be used as a form of ecoterrorism if, for example, one government attempts to block the water supply from a river or other source from traveling to another region. Turkey, for example, controls the waters of the Tigris and Euphrates, on which both Syria and Iraq are dependent. Dams being built in southwestern China are draining water tables and worsening droughts not only in China but also in Thailand and Myanmar, leading to calls for water reform.

Migrants: Record Numbers, Compounded Challenges

One of the greatest crises facing the world community is the widespread displacement of the world's people. In the aftermath of the Arab Spring, the ongoing war in Syria, and continued struggles in Iraq, Afghanistan, Yemen, Somalia, and elsewhere, immigration became the focus of both domestic and international policies around the world. Since its establishment in 1951, the United Nations High Commission for Refugees (UNHCR), which twice received the Nobel Peace Prize (1954 and 1981), has been the main international agency to assist people in these processes. One of the major responsibilities of the UNHCR is to find "durable solutions" for the world's refugees. This includes searching out possibilities for repatriation, through voluntary return to their homeland, integration into another country via the granting of asylum, or resettlement in a third country. Unfortunately, the complex tasks facing this agency, and others related to the handling of refugees, are increasing manifold.

As this book goes to press, migration figures have shattered records multiple years in a row, with nearly 1 percent of the world's population being displaced from their homes—with the highest percentage coming from the Middle East (where nearly one in twenty persons were displaced from their homes in 2015).[18] This upward trend, which began in 2011, seems unlikely to reverse itself anytime soon. In 2015, the United Nations High Commissioner for Refugees reported that there were

65.3 million displaced persons in the world, meaning that, on average, twenty-four people flee each minute—which is more than four times the rate of exodus just ten years earlier.[19] One of the most alarming trends is the increase in refugees under the age of eighteen: the UNHCR reports that 51 percent of the refugee population in 2015 were children, a rate that had more than quadrupled since 2013.[20]

According to the UNHCR, the key source countries of human displacement include Syria, Afghanistan, Somalia, South Sudan, Sudan, the Democratic Republic of Congo, the Central African Republic, Myanmar, Eritrea, and Colombia. Where do migrants go? Many assume that displaced persons are exclusively crowding the borders of the developed states. Statistics, however, tell a very different story. Turkey has become a gatekeeper of sorts in recent years for migrants traveling from the global south to Europe. The other major refugee-hosting countries in 2015 were Pakistan, Lebanon, Iran, Ethiopia, Jordan, Kenya, and Uganda.[21] In a very short time frame, Syria went from being one of the major host states of migrants (second only to Pakistan as a host state for refugees in 2008) to the major source state of migration since 2011.[22]

Sometimes an image serves as an indelible symbol of the vast problem. Such was the tragic photograph of a Turkish police officer gently carrying the lifeless body of a three-year-old Syrian boy of Kurdish background, who died, along with his five-year-old brother and mother, attempting to cross the Mediterranean and travel to the Greek Island of Kos, in September of 2015. At least twelve people died in this singular journey alone, which cost families thousands of dollars to attempt. Throughout 2016, a year in which migrant deaths spiked to record levels, there were multiple mass incidents—3,700 migrants died in one week alone, and the Italian navy and coast guard rescued more than 6,000 migrants in a single day.[23]

The dangers of migration have always been steep, but they are, in this area of unprecedented displacement, increasing. People seeking passage find human smugglers to facilitate their journey. This is a lucrative, sometimes comprehensive business that thrives on the risks some people will take in the hope of a better life. Observers contend that human smuggling is now "big business . . . being done on an almost industrial scale."[24] Smugglers take advantage of the absence of government controls, have little incentive to invest in seaworthy vessels, and go to great lengths to avoid detection. The result is that inflatable rafts overloaded with thousands of people venture out onto the high seas. After a controversial deal was signed between the European Union (EU) and Turkey, ostensibly aimed at decreasing the flow of migrants across the Mediterranean, even more perilous routes were selected, leading to greater deaths even as fewer individuals attempted passage.[25] The deal—roundly condemned by human rights and migrant groups alike—created a "refugee buffer zone" between Syria and Europe, with Turkey taking in migrants attempting transit to Europe in exchange for billions of dollars and visa-free travel to Europe for its citizens. Migrants landing in Greece were to be sent back across the Mediterranean to Turkey, where they were to be processed for resettlement in EU states. The agreement was meant to break the business model of human smugglers, but it encouraged more dangerous routes of passage and excluded all refugees except Syrians.[26]

While the European migrant crisis received the lion's share of media and popular attention, with the EU under immense pressure to maintain open borders under strain, let us not forget the other regions of the world that are attempting to deal with an influx of battered peoples seeking refuge. After Thailand cracked down on smuggling

rings transporting migrants to Malaysia, smugglers fled, leaving boats filled with migrants lurching at sea. Malaysia, Thailand, and Indonesia all turned away boats filled with desperate people, even if Malaysia and Indonesia eventually agreed—under great pressure—to temporarily accept them. Most migrants were Rohingya migrants fleeing Malaysia, as well as economic migrants from Bangladesh.[27]

For the most part, conflict within each one of these regions is confined to single countries; they are wars within, rather than between, nation-states. The internal nature of these conflicts, over which states can claim sovereignty, makes a response by the outside community more difficult, because aggressors (and their supporters) may frame it as an unwelcome invasion into internal matters. World leaders struggle to cope with these changes and with these forms of violence. In the case of international refugees, it is illegal under international law to force "genuine" refugees to return to the country from which they fled, even though the United States and other countries have done so. But how should international organizations respond?

Much attention within the United States has been focused on migration from Latin America, especially Mexico. Since the mid-1980s, a disastrous earthquake and a long economic crisis have pushed larger numbers of Mexicans north in search of work. This out-migration serves as an important source of income for these countries, as wages are sent home in the form of remittances. In addition, where there is high unemployment with few prospects, out-migration functions as a safety valve, releasing pressure on already overburdened governments. Even where unemployment is relatively low, as long as the wage differentials are as high as ten to one (as they are on average between the United States and Mexico), people will continue to leave their countries.

On the other hand, the slow economic recovery in the United States and stronger border enforcement are said to explain why more people returned to Mexico than entered the United States between 2009 and 2014, amounting to a net loss of 140,000 migrants.[28] Interestingly, this increased out-migration comes at a time when the United States and other developed countries have attempted to build the walls higher and to militarize the borders to cut down on illegal migration—the "Great Wall of Mexico," part of a series of several barriers strategically placed along the southwest border of the United States, to curb illegal immigration. A major part of Donald Trump's campaign rhetoric in 2016 surrounded his insistence that the United States would "build a wall" around the US-Mexican border, and that the Mexicans would "pay for it." Whether he meant this metaphorically or not, it seems that such barriers tend only to exacerbate the situation.[29] Other countries have tried it; the Spanish government erected a 10-foot-high fence around Melilla, a contested territory off the coast of northern Africa that has become a major crossing point for migrants, in order to keep out people attempting transit from Morocco or sub-Saharan African countries. However, these actions have only forced people to find ever more difficult and dangerous routes.

Terminological debates about "types" of refugees capture the emerging problem: while a technical definition exists, based in the 1951 UN Convention Relating to the Status of Refugees, many feel it is far too narrow and that it fails to provide an accurate picture of modern migration. This difficulty is only compounded by the complex reasons that people flee: some, although they are believed to be a minority, seek better economic opportunities. Of course, it is often difficult to untangle individuals'

motivations, and economic rationales can be as much about "pure survival" as they are political. Others fear political persecution and violence. In fact, many flee violence for a safe but poverty-filled future. The reasons people pack up may be diverse, but their situation as displaced people tends to be uniformly dangerous. Many trade one set of insecurities for another when they seek asylum in countries experiencing conflict. The Convention Relating to the Status of Refugees confines the status of "refugee" to "a person who, owing to a well-founded fear of being persecuted for reasons of race, religion, nationality, or membership of a particular social group or political opinion is outside the country of his nationality and unable, or, owing to such fear, is unwilling to avail himself of the protection of that country."

Refugee camps are not the "safe havens" that many might expect. Officially, displaced people are the responsibility of their home governments, which in many cases are the source of their persecution in the first place. Examples of violence are widespread, including assault, gang rape, sexual mutilation, and torture, perpetuated by organized crime, military police forces, antigovernment activists, local residents, humanitarian workers, peacekeepers, and even the refugee community itself.[30] This violence is a frightening expression of part of the underbelly of globalization. Afghan refugees in Iran have been attacked and killed by mobs. Indonesian militias routinely raided refugee camps in West Timor, stoning, beating, and sometimes killing displaced citizens from the east. Burmese refugees in Thailand were attacked when Burmese military representatives crossed the border and destroyed their camp, killing some, injuring scores, and leaving many without any shelter in an already perilous situation.

Children, who make up nearly half the world's refugee population, are forced to educate themselves, or put up with woefully inadequate makeshift schools.[31] They end up finding other ways to spend their time, including adopting various survival tactics such as the illicit distribution of drugs, weapons, and sexual favors. Refugees and displaced persons are common targets for exploitation and harassment by soldiers, militia members, and even refugee camp officials. Not only do these uprooted people need assistance in the short term, including food, shelter, clothing, and protection, but they face daunting long-term needs as well. Refugees cannot remain as such forever; the vast majority desire repatriation in their home country, or asylum in a country of choice that would allow them to start their lives relatively anew.

In other areas, internal refugees are holed up in internment camps, ostensibly for their own safety, but in reality to prevent them from aiding the opposition groups that purportedly threaten government or other powerful forces. Whole families have been murdered while they slept in such camps. Refugees are being "warehoused," or confined to camps or segregated settlements for five years or more, often while being denied basic rights enshrined in the Convention Relating to the Status of Refugees. Refugees in a protracted situation without any lasting end in sight have the right to employment, freedom of movement, and education, although these privileges, including basic noninterference in personal affairs, are rarely afforded them.[32] Entire generations have grown up as refugees—the average stay in refugee camps is now more than twelve years, as ad hoc creations to help people in crisis become new settlements. One observer highlighted the "purgatory of camp life," as provisions for shelter (usually tents but sometimes thatch with unbaked bricks) provide woefully inadequate protection against weather, looting, and harassment.[33]

People already facing tremendous dislocation and vulnerabilities get lost in the shuffle as attention moves beyond their prolonged plight.

Contrary to popular belief, it is other developing countries that serve as the host countries for refugees. The ratio of refugee population to total population in less developed states, especially Iran, Pakistan, Kenya, and Guinea, is much higher than the ratio in the developed countries, including Germany, the United States, and Canada. Combined, the six wealthiest countries (which make up more than half of the world's economy) host 8.8 percent of the world's refugees. In 2016, Jordan, Turkey, Pakistan, South Africa, and the Palestinian territories hosted more than 50 percent of the world's refugees and asylum seekers.[34] Economic struggles and high unemployment rates have motivated Western and non-Western governments to reject new arrivals, confine refugees to camps and prisons, and even deport them.

Another dark side of migration can be found in human trafficking. One of the fastest-growing criminal enterprises and a multibillion-dollar industry, trafficking in humans is second only to the illicit smuggling of drugs. Human trafficking touches nearly every country in the world today, with Asia (East and Southeast) and sub-Saharan Africa being the primary sources for trafficked individuals. Research has shown a strong correlation between the affluence of the destination and the share of persons trafficked there from other countries.[35] The forms of exploited labor in which these individuals engage are varied—including domestic work, mail-order brides, illicit adoptions in rich countries, and street-begging to finance third parties, as well as commercial sex enterprises. Although both males and females are subject to this particular form of forced labor, it is estimated that the majority are female, and up to 33 percent are minors—with the ratio being two girls for every one boy trafficked for sex each year.[36]

Children are viewed as a desirable commodity in this abhorrent industry fueled by misconceptions. Popular myths that children are free of AIDS and that sex with a virgin can cure disease have greatly contributed to the growth of this form of child labor in nearly every corner of the world. The chaos that follows large-scale disasters provides opportunities for this illicit trade to flourish; after Haiti's January 2010 earthquake (the worst in the region in 200 years), it is believed that over 1.2 million children were directly affected. It is estimated that prior to the disaster, 2,500 children were trafficked each year from Haiti across the border into the Dominican Republic to work as domestic labor, in begging cartels, and in the pornography and sex industry. With children lost or separated from their families (or families so desperate that they abandon their children), many are rightly concerned about an escalation in child trafficking following the earthquake.[37]

Disease and Public Health

In Chapter 7 we discussed the connection between health and poverty. The deprivation of citizens in the global south, sometimes due to economic malaise, violence, and war, has in many cases led to the complete failure of public health systems. The UN has long drawn an explicit link between financial well-being and health. Consistently, the leading causes of death around the world include heart disease, respiratory infections, AIDS, diarrhea, tuberculosis, and malaria.

Health crises demonstrate the world's deepening interdependence in at least two very stark ways: first, diseases cross increasingly porous borders without consider-

ation of economic, political, or other status; and second, they require the coordinated response of multiple actors, including state and nonstate alike. One vivid example of the health vulnerabilities that have been deepened by globalization is the potential for another flu pandemic that, even if it does not reach the mortality levels of the 1918 "Spanish influenza" outbreak (which claimed 40–50 million lives worldwide), could still lead to an estimated 2–7 million deaths and significantly disrupt life in every country of the world.

One of the first tests of recently developed global plans to respond to a disease pandemic was the outbreak of what later became known as severe acute respiratory syndrome (SARS), in 2003. This mystery illness, which presented as a flulike condition, was first discovered in Vietnam, and within two weeks of the initial diagnosis following the death of a Toronto man, the World Health Organization (WHO) issued a global alert. The outbreak had actually begun two months earlier in one of China's southern provinces, and the epicenter of the disease was one of Hong Kong's major hotels where a Chinese doctor who had treated some of the earlier cases fell ill. Because of the port city's status as a major transit point in Asia, and the rapidity with which cases spread from Asia to North America, the response by the WHO and governments was swift—regulating air travel, monitoring healthcare workers, and quarantining anyone believed to be a carrier of the virus. Despite frightening pictures of people with ventilated masks covering their mouths in major cities across multiple continents, efforts to control transmission of the syndrome were successful. DNA analysis quickly uncovered the genetic code of the disease, its spread was halted, and, even though it claimed approximately 750 lives globally, there were no confirmed cases of the disease by late 2004.

Yet diseases mutate. Similar to other deadly strains of viruses, another viral culprit, known alternatively as "avian influenza" or more simply "bird flu," began in China. Bird flu is one of sixteen known subtypes of the influenza virus. This particular strain was directly transmitted from birds to humans in Hong Kong in 1997, and the disease spread throughout Asia. In just two years, human infections multiplied, hitting Vietnam, Cambodia, Thailand, Indonesia, Turkey, Azerbaijan, Egypt, and Djibouti, with outbreaks among poultry populations in many other states. Concerns about this particular virus, scientifically known as H5N1 for the combination of two specific proteins appearing on its surface, surround its reach within the poultry population (it had already caused the largest poultry outbreak on record, devastating many local economies) and its ability to mutate and become more virulent. Indeed, H5N1 is feared as a strain with pandemic potential because of its possible mutations and adaptation into a virus that is contagious among humans and for which humans would lack natural immunity. Even if this variant of the flu does not mutate to become easily transmissible between humans, the WHO and other health agencies view an impending flu pandemic of some type as very likely, and "once a fully contagious virus emerges, its global spread is considered inevitable."[38] The H1N1 (also known as "swine flu") pandemic in 2009 reignited this debate, even if, in the end, that particular strain did not become the crisis many feared. This outbreak is believed to have started in Mexico and the United States, and quickly spread worldwide.

The most recent outbreak of the Ebola virus in 2014 was a painful lesson in the needs for disease surveillance, clearer communication, better understanding of cultural practices (especially burial practices), and the need for coordinated responses.

The disease spiraled out of control—raging especially in Guinea, Liberia, and Sierra Leone—not because of accumulated flaws in the global health system, but because of the absence of "a system at all," according to one observer.[39] This latest outbreak—which hit the healthcare worker and first-responder communities especially hard—revealed the gaps between the aspirations of global health officials and the realities of controlling infectious diseases.[40] One official described the response as "using a pea shooter against a raging elephant."[41] More than 10,000 lives were lost, 3,000 US military personnel were sent to West Africa, and terrible flaws in emergency response were revealed. Will we be better prepared the next time?

Then there is Zika, the mosquito-borne virus that is linked to an outbreak of babies with under-developed brains. Even though the disease was first detected in Africa in the late 1940s, there is no known cure. As the WHO forecasted Zika's likely spread across nearly all of the Americas, the capacity of regional and global response systems to rapidly changing health epidemics was tested. But, by the end of 2016, the international public health emergency was declared over, with the UN and affiliated agencies calling for sustained efforts to continue to address the disease. Nevertheless, there was serious discussion about delaying or relocating the Rio Olympic Games, despite WHO assurances of safety (some delegations from wealthier countries, including South Korea, sported specially made suits enhanced with natural mosquito repellant).

Yet such resources as eucalyptus-infused athletic suits are available only to the very few. Many view the struggle over medicines and vaccines to be part of the classic struggle between haves and have-nots. Similar to many of the issues that we have examined in this book, there are few simple solutions. Although many efforts have been undertaken at the global level, most have not yet been effectively implemented on the ground. For example, a global program launched in 1988 to completely eradicate polio through a wide-reaching vaccination plan cosponsored by the WHO has been stalled by lack of medical professionals in needed areas, lack of political will to implement national programs, and even rumors. The disease has decreased more than 99 percent since 1988, with seventy-four known cases in 2015 (the disease is confined to Nigeria, Pakistan, and Afghanistan).[42] Yet any case is problematic, because of its opportunity to reignite an outbreak.

Despite this, Jeffrey Sachs, who serves as special adviser to the United Nations on the implementation of the Millennium Development Goals, contends that it would only require residents of the richer regions of the world to donate the cost of one cup of Starbucks coffee per year to eradicate this gigantic killer.[43] As with so many challenges, polio knows no human-made borders, and because infection does not always lead to paralysis, there may be many more cases lying dormant than policymakers and activists realize.

One example of how the global healthcare crisis is disproportionately affecting low-income countries (LICs) is the HIV/AIDS pandemic. The world has been living with AIDS for over thirty-five years—highlighting the sobering reality that its spread, especially in the global south, continues. The United Nations has created an agency devoted entirely to the problem, and even the Security Council has labeled HIV/AIDS a threat to international peace and security. Progress has been made, though, as the numbers of new HIV infections and deaths from AIDS are falling globally, down significantly since the peak of the epidemic in 1999.[44] The emphasis in AIDS eradication, one of the targets included within the Sustainable Development Goals, is the

commitment to end the AIDS epidemic by 2030. In order to accomplish this critical task, significant gains must be made in access to medicines. Much controversy has surrounded AIDS medications regarding their availability and cost and the development of generic alternatives. Yet some doctors suggest that we need to worry less about the cost of the drugs and more about the shortage of condoms (for males and females alike). Even this most basic means of prevention is out of reach of the poorest who need it, despite the large sums of money that governments, international agencies, and nongovernmental organizations (NGOs) are spending.[45]

Perhaps more governments need to follow the examples of Uganda and Thailand, and break taboos by instituting aggressive public education campaigns. Uganda was one of the most open countries in terms of HIV acknowledgment in the 1980s, when even in the United States and many European countries, leaders were slow to discuss the epidemic, or falsely believed it was a disease that affected only gay men. In South Africa, which continues to experience one of the most severe epidemics of AIDS, although new infections there are starting to slow, former president Nelson Mandela surprised many with his candor when, in an attempt to help stimulate more accurate public discussion about the disease, he announced that his son had died of AIDS.

Others, such as Botswana, which has consistently ranked as among the countries with the highest rates of HIV infection, test all patients entering clinics or hospitals. However, we should not underestimate how difficult this can be, since many political and religious leaders often object to the explicit language that is necessary to inform people about how the disease is transmitted, or how widespread it has become. In many countries, conservatives block the distribution of female condoms or vaginal microbicides (which a woman can use with or without her partner's cooperation or knowledge), which they believe contribute to promiscuous behavior. Adding to the tragedy is the fact that very often women are already infected before they become aware of their HIV status. AIDS has now become the leading cause of death and disease among reproductive-age women worldwide, and in sub-Saharan Africa, more than half of those living with HIV/AIDS are women.[46]

Screening for HIV infection is physically and financially inaccessible for many people worldwide. Yet testing is crucial. There are programs that provide pregnant women with a short course of anti-AIDS medicines, such as AZT, a failed cancer drug that can delay the onset of AIDS. With testing and counseling, because mother-to-child transmission of HIV can be virtually eliminated through the use of such drugs, safe delivery practices, and the safe use of breast milk substitutes, pregnant women can play a huge role in containing the spread of HIV.[47] However, as important as such programs are, they are limited in their effectiveness. If state leaders and nongovernmental organizations are indeed committed to providing treatment to all who need it, a commitment that is questionable at best, another pitfall emerges: How will governments of the developing world provide for those so-called medical pensioners whose life is prolonged, albeit by the regular delivery of drugs and support facilities? In most cases, a basic health infrastructure must be built where none exists. Expensive laboratory work must be done on a continual basis to monitor this complicated regimen of drugs. Otherwise, it is feared that drug-resistant strains will develop, as they have for malaria and tuberculosis.

Still, we need to remember that the anti-AIDS drugs now available offer treatment, not a cure. And they do nothing to prevent transmission of the disease. Pre-

vention and education remain critical in this process, despite their expense. But the failure to treat the disease will lead to even higher costs that we cannot even begin to tabulate. The first step to treatment and prevention is awareness of one's HIV status, which is why some of the most successful programs have promoted simple, confidential testing—both to encourage quick treatment and also to decrease the likelihood of infecting others. Prevention efforts are targeting some surprising enablers of the disease. The United Nations has identified soldiers as major carriers of HIV and, alarmingly, discussed the role of international peacekeepers in continuing the spread of this deadly virus. Since 1981, when the disease was first recognized within the medical community, more UN peacekeeping troops have died of AIDS (or will soon die) than have been killed in combat.[48]

Clearly, none of these issues can be understood in isolation. Health is a multifaceted aspect of daily living, directly impacted by socioeconomic status, opportunities for education and employment, and interconnected social and political realities, among other factors. And it's not just the headline-grabbing ailments that cause suffering and premature death around the world—tens of thousands of people in the LICs die each day of complications from childbirth, diarrhea, asthma, and other conditions that are closely connected to the lack of basic healthcare resources. Yet there can be apathy among citizens of the developed world about health problems such as diarrhea, even though more than 525,000 children (under the age of five) die of the dehydration caused by this ailment every year—this accounts for 9 percent of all deaths among children globally.[49] This is entirely preventable, and does not require complex deals between global drug companies or fistfuls of pills, just oral rehydration therapy and basic sanitation. Even though high-profile rock stars aren't likely to devote a world tour to building more toilets around the world, the construction of basic latrine systems could go a long way toward curbing unnecessary deaths. One study found that more than 2.5 billion people live without access to toilets, and 780 million lack access to fresh, safe drinking water.[50]

How important is the lack of basic healthcare around the world? Some have argued, at least in the case of the HIV pandemic, that it was only after scientists emphasized the security and political implications of the continued spread of the disease—rather than "simply" a humanitarian catastrophe—that many political leaders took notice.[51] Jeffrey Sachs has argued that AIDS and malaria in Africa may be larger obstacles to economic growth than debt, which is already crippling.[52]

Weapons Proliferation

The proliferation of weapons is an issue of increasing concern in the post–Cold War era, in which larger numbers of states are deciding to invest resources to acquire conventional weapons as well as nuclear and other weapons of mass destruction (WMDs). Without doubt, conventional weapons—weapons that lack chemical, biological, or nuclear components—are dangerous, but their impact is limited. The advent of the nuclear age in the 1940s changed all this, as the destruction of the entire planet became a possibility. While from the 1950s to the 1980s a limited number of large and powerful states pursued nuclear weapons, the tide seems to be changing, and some have claimed we are currently living in a "second nuclear age."[53] While Western militaries dominated the world for the past 200 years, we now face a dis-

tinct shift in the balance of power as non-Western states, particularly throughout Asia, acquire weapons to challenge Western dominance. Especially concerning are the WMDs, an umbrella category describing weapons that incorporate nuclear, biological, chemical, and radiological agents that can, as their label suggests, bring harm to large groups of people in one blow. One of the gravest dangers of WMDs is the difficulty of their detection; a sufficiently lethal dose of agents could be loaded into a container and shipped, largely undetectable, anywhere around the world. Unfortunately, multibillion-dollar efforts by the United States to provide antimissile defensive systems only exacerbate the desire and urgency to build weapons that can evade such error-prone mechanisms. There is much uncertainty about WMDs. Yet what is certain is that the atmosphere is a much different one than of DETERRENCE based on the "mutual assured destruction" that marked the nuclear race during the Cold War. Now, individuals and groups can wreak havoc on a population without endangering themselves and with a much broader blanket of anonymity.

Many believed that the end of the Cold War in the late 1980s would lead to a safer, less militarized world. This has not been the case. Especially within the emerging economies, the acquisition of advanced weaponry, with which come attention and inclusion in the world's "elite nuclear club," has significantly increased since the mid-1990s. In 1998 alone, India detonated five atomic bombs, followed by Pakistan's own tests; North Korea fired a multistage rocket over Japan; and Iran, India, and Pakistan each tested intermediate-range ballistic missiles. China has deployed short-range missiles aimed at Taiwan and fortified its longer-range missile system. Throughout Asia and the Middle East—Israel, Syria, Iraq, Iran, Pakistan, India, China, and North Korea—the military focus is shifting "from infantry to disruptive technologies" based on chemical, biological, and nuclear weapons capable of delivery by ballistic missiles.[54] Two states in particular—North Korea and Iran—have tested the limits of the Nuclear Non-Proliferation Treaty (NPT), which has been in force since 1970, and is viewed as one of the most widely subscribed arms control treaties in history.

The NPT has been formally supported by 190 member states of the United Nations. Its weaknesses and contradictions, though, were highlighted by the tit-for-tat nuclear tests by India and Pakistan in 1998, two of the states that have neither signed nor ratified the NPT, and by the openly secret "basement bomb" arsenal possessed by Israel, which remains an unofficial nuclear weapons state. Even before North Korea became the first country to withdraw from the NPT in 2003 (it is notable that South Africa is the only NPT signatory to formally dismantle its nuclear weapons program, which it completed in 1994), many countries have challenged the relevance of the NPT, which restricts the legal possession of nuclear weapons to states that tested nuclear weapons prior to 1967, when discussions that led to the NPT began. Increasingly, it appears that "nonproliferation" is becoming a quaint term with little punch behind it. Mohammed El Baradei, former director-general of the International Atomic Energy Agency (IAEA) and 2005 recipient of the Nobel Peace Prize, captured the hypocrisy poignantly, characterizing the original nuclear weapons states (United States, Great Britain, France, Russia, and China), in their failure to comply with their own promises to ultimately eliminate their own stockpiles, as an offensive group who continue "to dangle a cigarette from their mouth and tell everyone else not to smoke."[55]

The need for energy is at least the official justification for the recently overt uranium enrichment within Iran, a nuclear program that has its roots in US assistance

to the administration of Reza Shah Pahlavi in the 1950s. Although Iranian politicians continuously assert Iran's right as a signatory of the NPT to enrich uranium for domestic energy consumption, many within Iran and beyond have raised eyebrows at these intentions. Iran became a "nuclear capable" state in the spring of 2006, when then-president Ahmadinejad personally announced that Iranian scientists had enriched small quantities of uranium. As a result, Iran faced crushing sanctions from the United States, European Union, and the United Nations. After months of negotiating, in early 2016, a controversial, landmark agreement between the so-called P5+1 (permanent five members of the UN Security Council plus Germany) and Iran brokered a way out of the sanctions, in exchange for the dismantling of Iran's weapons-grade enrichment and the acceptance of regular inspections by the International Atomic Energy Agency. Tehran also agreed to a UN arms embargo (for up to five years, unless the IAEA determines that an earlier lifting is permissible), as well as a ban on the import of ballistic missiles (for up to eight years).[56] Iran gained the right to produce nuclear energy; the United States achieved assurances that Tehran's nuclear weapons program would be halted (Washington contends that prior to the agreement, Tehran had stockpiled enough enriched uranium and centrifuges to create between eight and ten bombs).[57] To the skeptics, however, Iran gained everything upfront (having most of its previously frozen assets unlocked, sanctions lifted, and trade resumed), without significant guarantees of compliance (expressing concern about the waiting period between announced inspections and access). Such is the challenge of dealing with near-nuclear-capable states, as we will see later.

The other major nuclear challenge hails from a much more isolated regime in North Korea. A landmark attempt to end the active nuclear weapons program in North Korea was signed with the United States in 1994 (known as the Agreed Framework), under which the United States would provide power reactors and oil in exchange for the supervised conclusion of this weapons program. In 2002, former president Kim Jong-Il confirmed the suspicions of many by restarting the country's main nuclear reactor at Yongbyon and forcing two UN inspectors to leave the country. Since 2002, tensions have continued to rise as North Korean leaders assert their "right" to nuclear development and warn in their weighty "doomsday" talk of impending nuclear war brought on by the enemies of the North Korean regime. Six-party talks hosted by China (also including representatives from South Korea, Japan, Russia, and the United States) since 2003 have, at times, decreased immediate tensions in the region, although they have produced little of substance to date. These talks were expanded to include Germany in autumn of 2009. More than once, a potential trade of nonaggression promises from the United States for an end to North Korea's pursuit of nuclear weapons technology has been floated, to no avail. Others, including Japan and South Korea, have provided energy supplies—including electricity and technology for various reactors—in the hope of stalling the regime's march toward nuclear weapons. Despite these efforts, the noose around the North Korean economy and society tightened following two sets of UN sanctions imposed after missile tests in July 2006 and an underground nuclear test in October that same year, both of which were backed by North Korea's lone ally, China. Allegations of illicit deals, including the sale of SCUD missiles to Yemen and heroin to Australia, have helped marginalize Kim and his regime even further, which many believe explains some of the motivation for his continued agitation.

Tensions were heightened once again throughout 2010: North Korea sank a South Korean warship (killing forty-six soldiers), and then unveiled a previously unknown uranium enrichment facility—with 2,000 centrifuges—to a visiting Stanford scientist. North Korea then attacked a South Korean island just 13 kilometers from the North Korean coast, which killed two South Korean soldiers and two South Korean civilians. It is always difficult to discern the motivation behind such acts, but most analysts believe the moves were connected to the unveiling of Kim's heir, Kim Jong-Un (who took power after his father's death in late 2011). As with all of the other issues covered in this chapter, actions in one state have domino effects in others—the immediate fallout from North Korea's provocative nuclear tests included loud calls within Japan and South Korea to seek greater deterrence themselves, which could potentially lead to a renewed arms race in northern Asia. Kim Jong-Un has continued testing the resolve of the international community with North Korea's weapons programs and has significantly increased tensions with a series of five weapons tests (through late 2016). What is known is that North Korea possesses nuclear weapons: what is not known is whether they are plutonium (with a finite stockpile) or uranium (which, with the proper technology, can be enriched indefinitely). To date, Pyongyang also appears unable to miniaturize the weapon such that it can be placed on the tip of a missile. Having restarted (and invigorated) the testing program again in 2015, this thorny regional and (increasingly global) challenge is unlikely to be resolved in the short-term future.

Increasingly, the world has the capability to wage an arms race unlimited by the globe; it is taking place in space, through the placement of satellites, radar systems, and arms above Earth's atmosphere. The United States was the only delegation within the Conference on Disarmament to oppose the establishment of a committee on the prevention of an arms race in space. Currently, most weapons systems employed in outer space are for defensive purposes. The increasing presence of these weapons, though, threatens to challenge the integrity of past arms control agreements. As the United States and Russia are joined by China in the race to explore outer space, these challenges are likely to increase. China is the third country to have placed one of its citizens in space, and the country is working to build a space station, conduct a lunar landing by 2025, and send probes to Mars and Venus.

Another type of weapon that greatly impacts ordinary people, especially the rural poor of LICs, is landmines. They have been used on a large scale since World War I, and the problems surrounding them are many, including their long life span after war or conflict ceases. Masterfully hidden during conflict, they remain concealed today by overgrown foliage, tending to victimize innocent civilians who are unsuspecting of their presence (most researchers estimate that 80 percent of landmine casualties are civilians). The people most likely to encounter mines are the economically poor, especially peasant farmers and their children. Complicating matters even more, many of the mines are washed out of the ground and deposited elsewhere, often on previously cleared land. Additionally, a mine can cost as little as $3 to make, and over $1,000 to clear. There are millions of active mines scattered in over seventy countries on every continent, although Africa is the most heavily mined continent on Earth. People have been killed or injured by landmines in every country in southern Africa, with the exception of Lesotho and Mauritius. It is believed that Somalia, Ethiopia, Eritrea, and Sudan each have 500,000 landmines, with 250,000 in

Rwanda. It is currently estimated that there is one mine for every fifty-two people in the world.[58] Landmines have exacted a huge human toll in many war-scarred countries, especially Angola, Afghanistan, Cambodia, Mozambique, and Vietnam. In addition to the physical toll they take when they explode, their presence also denies people the use of land that could be vital to their subsistence.

If there is one topic that demonstrates the interconnectedness between NGOs, international governmental organizations (IGOs), and national governments in recent years, it is the International Campaign to Ban Landmines (ICBL), an international effort including over a thousand organizations based in sixty countries. The coalition was awarded the 1997 Nobel Peace Prize for its efforts. In March 1999 the most quickly promulgated arms treaty in history, known as the Ottawa Treaty, entered into force, banning antipersonnel landmines. This treaty, in the works since 1971, was finally adopted in 1997 in a novel process: it abandoned formal UN channels and explicitly incorporated voices from NGOs. As a result of the "back doors" that were used to move the process along, many refer to the Ottawa Treaty as a "breakaway treaty." The final process took only a little over a year to conclude.[59] Even though a larger area was cleared of landmines in 2005 than ever before, casualties from mines (mostly civilian children) rose to more than 7,000, an 11 percent increase over previous years.[60] Even with 151 countries committed to the treaty, at least three governments still actively employ landmines in their battles—Burma, Nepal, and Russia—and important players such as China, Russia, Israel, and the United States remain outside of its requirements.

The International Committee of the Red Cross (ICRC), in cooperation with countries such as Canada (which spearheaded the effort), South Africa, Belgium, and Norway, as well as multiple IGOs and NGOs, worked on this treaty, which has been ratified by 112 governments around the world. Former mine producers that have signed the Ottawa Treaty include Brazil, Canada, Chile, Nicaragua, Peru, South Africa, Thailand, Uganda, and the United Kingdom. The remaining mine producers that oppose the treaty include China, Cuba, Iran, Iraq, Russia, Serbia, Singapore, the United States, and Vietnam. The treaty prohibits the use, stockpiling, production, and transfer of antipersonnel landmines. In addition, the campaign has established an international fund, administered by the United Nations, to promote and finance victim assistance programs, and promotes awareness programs, all in the effort to eradicate the mines worldwide.

As if the problem with major weapons systems weren't enough, the presence of small, portable weapons—such as machine guns, assault rifles, and hand grenades—is on the rise. Indeed, these are the weapons—rather than nuclear bombs—that are responsible for most of the injuries and deaths in today's world. Small-arms proliferation seems to be out of control and free trade and open borders have only expanded it. It is estimated that over $10 billion worth of automatic rifles, machine guns, mortars, and other light arms are sold each year. It may not sound like a lot in terms of money, but this trade is extremely deadly. Some analysts estimate that the Rwandan genocide was carried out with less than $25 million in imported arms, with much of the killing done with a huge cache of machetes imported from China, whose military is known for exporting small weapons throughout Africa.[61] Technical improvements in the manufacturing of weapons, which make them lighter and easier to conceal, exacerbate the problem. This trade in small arms is illegal, and difficult

to track or control. No one, not individual countries, not the UN, keeps good records on the small-arms trade. And there's no international movement for this issue like there is for landmines. However, recognizing that the black market in these weapons assists drug cartels, urban gangs, and guerrillas, the Organization of American States (OAS) has attempted to curb the trade. The OAS began a program of registering guns to help track where they ended up, establishing uniform procedures among its members.[62] At the global level, the United Nations hosted a conference on the illicit trade in small arms in July 2001. It was a controversial meeting, as the agenda only included the illegal trade of arms, so that the big dealers, including the United States, Russia, and China, wouldn't lose a huge export industry.

Yet larger forces were at play and, after seven long years of negotiation, in late 2013, the UN Arms Trade Treaty (ATT) was signed by 115 states, including the United States (the only "no" votes in the General Assembly were cast by Iran, North Korea, and Syria). This treaty, which entered into force in December 2014 (without US ratification) is designed to regulate the international transfer of conventional arms. As with all UN resolutions, this treaty first affirms the sovereign right of all states to determine weapons laws within their own country; the ATT is meant to decrease the illicit trade among illegal arms dealers. In fact, the ATT had the support not only of many transitioning states in the global south, but also that of some of the world's largest arms exporters who wanted to continue to guard the credibility of the legal arms trade.[63]

Some regional attempts to contain the arms trade have been promoted by the OAS, the African Union, and the European Union. A major global initiative targeted to change the behavior of arms-providing states is Costa Rican president Óscar Arias's International Code of Conduct on Arms Transfers. Arias, who crafted a Central American peace plan barring outside aid to guerrillas in El Salvador and Nicaragua in the 1980s, brought together sixteen other Nobel laureates with international nongovernmental organizations to present this initiative to the United Nations. The plan calls for developed countries to refuse to sell arms to countries that violate basic human rights or are involved in armed aggression or terrorism. If such a plan were to be implemented, it could dramatically change the global weapons landscape. For example, the United States routinely ships weapons to countries whose militaries are known to be abusive, including Colombia, Turkey, Indonesia, Saudi Arabia, and Egypt. Such trade would be barred under the proposed code. It also calls for all countries to report their weapons sales and purchases to the United Nations, under the current system of voluntary compliance. Arias points out that if 10 percent of the world's military spending, approximately $1 trillion annually, were spent on human development, preventable disease and hunger could be ended, and education and sanitation could be made universal. In 2008, 147 member states of the United Nations voted to move forward with work on the treaty, with only the United States and Zimbabwe voting against it.

Conclusions: The Future of Global Capacity for Response

What are the advantages of responses by global or regional actors? Multilateral responses can give less powerful countries a stronger voice because they can find strength in numbers. In the United Nations, for example, two-thirds of all member states are developing countries. Although there are limits to what individual countries can achieve,

as we have seen, the sheer number of developing countries represented in the UN provides a channel for diplomatic influence that they cannot find elsewhere. Multilateral efforts can also compel action when individual states either will not or cannot comply, due largely to financial constraints. Multilateralism can also promote an internationally acceptable setting in which nations can more freely negotiate in an atmosphere of compromise and diplomacy, which would be more difficult to achieve with individual states.

Yet an "international community" seems to exist more in symbol than reality. Contrary to the exasperated claims of some, we do not have a world government, nor are we close to achieving one. The coordinated response of major powers is about as close as we have come to a singular community in action, and this response has been limited. Much of the world, especially the powerful countries, continues to frame matters in terms of major powers and large countries, as has been evidenced in more than one of the issues discussed in this chapter.

What differences exist between regional and global responses? Because of the limited scope and number of actors, it may be easier to build consensus for action within a regional context, although this is not always the case. For global responses, consensus (or at least verification of the absence of opposition) takes more time to craft. For some regions, assembling an intervening force would be difficult, because of historical or contemporary problems that make no one trustworthy. The larger organizations bring more economies of scale and more people to the table, but they are also more bureaucratically cumbersome—a common criticism of the United Nations— and it is easier in the larger global organizations to leave out voices of the disenfranchised and less powerful. Or, even if the opportunity to speak and participate is present, many of the non-Western countries feel they still have no teeth in these institutions. Regional organizations and specialized NGOs overcome some of these problems of size, but they can also lack influence and might. Yet even international organizations such as the United Nations do not have compelling force; more powerful countries can bypass the UN if they feel their sovereignty would be impeded. The clearest recent example of such diversion was the action of the North Atlantic Treaty Organization (NATO) in Kosovo taken on behalf of the Albanian Serbs: the US-led coalition bypassed the Security Council because China and Russia would have vetoed the measure as an unwanted and unwarranted intrusion of state sovereignty, though the UN did later take on a role, providing a Security Council resolution and sanctioning a peacekeeping force.

Yet an overarching concern for the global south, in the face of much multilateral activity, is the responsiveness of such forces to the needs and concerns of the less powerful. Organizations, large and small, make decisions affecting individuals who have little or no impact on the process. The need to include disparate, less powerful voices is especially magnified at higher levels. While the problems inherent in this enterprise have been brought to our attention through street demonstrations against the World Bank and the International Monetary Fund, the same is true with the United Nations and nongovernmental organizations that take action in the name of the people. How to make such organizations more representative and more accountable will remain a huge task for the future. If these institutions are perceived to be overtly partisan, they will lose their legitimacy and ability to act. Multilateral institutions are favored because they seemingly prevent (or at least limit) the im-

pulse for self-interest or self-delusion. But they are problematic because, in the search for consensus, they can sit idly by while massacres, such as those in Darfur, take place. Faced with changing conceptions of sovereignty and global action, many speak of a forthcoming "borderless world." Yet from the global south it appears that some borders are as sturdy as ever—if not stronger.

Notes

1. Quoted in Coral Davenport, "The Marshall Islands Are Disappearing," *New York Times*, December 2, 2015.

2. Quoted in Lena Sun, Brady Dennis, Lenny Bernstein, and Joel Achenbach, "Out of Control: How the World's Health Organizations Failed to Stop the Ebola Disaster," *Washington Post*, October 4, 2014, www.washingtonpost.com.

3. Robinson Meyer, "Is Hope Possible After the Paris Agreement?," *The Atlantic*, December 12, 2015, www.theatlantic.com.

4. Justin Gillis, "Short Answers to Hard Questions About Climate Change," *New York Times*, November 28, 2015.

5. Keith Bradsher, "China Fears Warming Effects of a Rising Consumer Class," *New York Times*, July 5, 2010, p. B5.

6. Damian Kahya, "Global Warming Talks Just Hot Air?," BBC News, December 3, 2010.

7. Mark Lynas, "How Do I Know China Wrecked the Copenhagen Deal? I Was in the Room," *The Guardian* (London), December 22, 2009, www.guardian.co.uk.

8. Deborah Hardoon, Sophia Ayele, and Ricardo Fuentes-Nieva, "An Economy for the 1%," briefing paper, January 18, 2016, www.oxfam.org.

9. Justin Worland, "How Climate Change Unfairly Burdens Poorer Countries," *Time*, February 5, 2016, www.time.com.

10. Meyer, "Is Hope Possible After the Paris Agreement?"

11. Keith Bradsher, "The Paris Agreement on Climate Change Is Official, Now What?," *New York Times*, November 3, 2016.

12. Coral Davenport, "At U.N. Meeting, Diplomats Worry Trump Could Cripple Climate Pact," *New York Times*, November 15, 2016.

13. Ibid.

14. United Nations, "World Population Prospects: The 2015 Revision," www.un.org/esa/population.

15. Andrew C. Revkin, "The Climate Divide: Rich Nations Find It Easier to Adapt," *New York Times*, April 2, 2007. See also "Developing Countries and Global Warming: A Bad Climate for Development," *The Economist*, September 17, 2009.

16. "Owners of Ethos Trying to Provide Clean Drinking Water to People in the Third World Who Lack It," National Public Radio, *Day to Day*, January 18, 2005.

17. Integrated Regional Information Networks (United Nations), "Water Is Running Out: How Inevitable Are International Conflicts?," *World Press Review*, October 23, 2006.

18. Phillip Connor, "Nearly 1 in 100 Worldwide Are Now Displaced from Their Homes," *Fact Tank*, August 3, 2016, www.pewresearch.org.

19. United Nations High Commissioner for Refugees (UNHCR), *Global Trends: Forced Displacement in 2015*, June 20, 2016, p. 2, www.unhcr.org.

20. Ibid., p. 3; UNHCR, "Worldwide Displacement Hits All-Time High as War and Persecution Increase," June 18, 2015, www.unhcr.org.

21. UNHCR, *Global Trends*, p. 15.

22. UNHCR, *2008 Global Trends: Refugees, Asylum-Seekers, Returnees, Internally Displaced, and Stateless Persons*, June 16, 2009, p. 8.

23. Nick Cumming-Bruce, "'The Worst We Have Ever Seen': Fewer Migrants, More Death," *New York Times*, October 25, 2016; Laura Smith-Spark, "Mediterranean Migrant Deaths Reach Record Level in 2016," *CNN News*, October 26, 2016, www.cnn.com.

24. Cumming-Bruce, "'The Worst We Have Ever Seen.'"

25. Ibid.

26. Merrit Kennedy, "Turkey and the EU Strike Controversial Migration Deal in Brussels," National Public Radio, March 18, 2016.

27. Joe Cochrane, "Lives Still in Limbo, One Year After Southeast Asia Migrant Crisis," *New York Times,* June 18, 2016.

28. Ana Gonzalez-Barrera, "More Mexicans Leaving Than Coming to the U.S.," Pew Research Center, November 19, 2015.

29. Stephen Collinson and Jeremy Diamond, "Mexican President Disputes Trump over Border Wall Payment Discussion," *CNN News,* September 1, 2016.

30. Office of the United Nations High Commissioner for Refugees, *The State of the World's Refugees 2006: Human Displacement in the New Millennium* (New York: Oxford University Press, 2006), pp. 65–66.

31. "UNICEF Reports 28 Million Children Homeless Globally Due to Conflict," *Deutsche Welle,* July 9, 2016, www.dw.com.

32. Merrill Smith, "Warehousing Refugees: A Denial of Rights, a Waste of Humanity," in *World Refugee Survey 2004* (Washington, DC: US Committee for Refugees and Immigrants).

33. Elizabeth Cullen Dunn, "The Failure of Refugee Camps," *Boston Review,* September 28, 2015, www.bostonreview.net.

34. "Six Richest Countries Host Less Than 9% of Refugees," Oxfam International, July 18, 2016, www.oxfam.com.

35. United Nations Office on Drugs and Crime (UNODC), "Global Report on Trafficking in Persons, 2014," www.unodc.org.

36. Ibid.

37. M. P. Nunan, "Haiti Protects Its Border Against Post-Earthquake Child Trafficking," United Nations Children's Fund (UNICEF), October 15, 2010.

38. "Ten Things You Need to Know About Pandemic Influenza," World Health Organization (WHO), October 14, 2005.

39. Olsa Khazan, "How to Prevent the Next Ebola," *The Atlantic,* March 18, 2015, www.theatlantic.com.

40. Lena Sun, Brady Dennis, Lenny Bernstein, and Joel Achenbach, "Out of Control: How the World's Health Organizations Failed to Stop the Ebola Disaster," *Washington Post,* October 4, 2014, www.washingtonpost.com.

41. Ibid.

42. WHO, "Fact Sheet: Poliomyelitis," April 2016, www.who.int.

43. "Groups Take Aim at Tuberculosis," National Public Radio, *Morning Edition,* March 8, 2006.

44. "HIV Epidemic 'Halted,' Says UN," BBC News, November 23, 2010.

45. "Unhappy Anniversary," *The Economist,* June 3, 2006, p. 24.

46. "AIDS 'Key Cause of Female Death,'" BBC News, March 3, 2010.

47. "Preventing Mother-to-Child Transmission of HIV," *Avert,* November 6, 2006, www.avert.org.

48. Nancy van Itallie, "Health," in *A Global Agenda: Issues Before the Fifty-Fourth General Assembly of the United Nations,* ed. John Tessitore and Susan Woolfson (Lanham: Rowman and Littlefield, 1999). Van Itallie states that this revelation led to the first health-related resolution in the Security Council, sponsored by Richard Holbrooke, for "voluntary and confidential testing and counseling" of UN peacekeepers.

49. "Diarrhoea Remains a Leading Killer of Young Children, Despite the Availability of a Simple Treatment Solution," UNICEF, November 2016.

50. Linda Poon, "Diarrhea 101: Time to Talk About Something We Don't Usually Talk About," National Public Radio, November 18, 2016.

51. Geoffrey Cowley, "The Life of a Virus Hunter," *Newsweek,* May 15, 2006, p. 63.

52. Bill Saporito, "The Jeff Sachs Contradiction: Celebrity Economist," *Time,* March 14, 2005, p. 49.

53. James R. Holmes, "US Strategy in the Second Nuclear Age," *The Diplomat,* March 6, 2014; Paul Bracken, "The Second Nuclear Age," *Foreign Affairs,* January–February 2000.

See also Paul Bracken, *Fire in the East: The Rise of Asian Military Power and the Second Nuclear Age* (New York: HarperCollins, 1999).

54. Bracken, "The Second Nuclear Age."

55. Quoted in the presentation speech for the 2005 Nobel Peace Prize delivered by Ole Danbolt Mjøs, chairman of the Norwegian Nobel Committee, December 10, 2005, http://nobelprize.org.

56. "Iran Nuclear Deal: Key Details," BBC News, January 16, 2016.

57. Ibid.

58. UNICEF, "The Legacy of Landmines," in *The State of the World's Children 1996,* www.unicef.org. See also www.oneworld.org/guides/landmines.info.html.

59. For a detailed account of the ICBL treaty, see Maxwell A. Cameron, Robert J. Lawson, and Brian W. Tomlin, eds., *To Walk Without Fear: The Global Movement to Ban Landmines* (New York: Oxford University Press, 1998).

60. "Record Area Cleared of Landmines," BBC News, September 13, 2006.

61. "Controlling Deadly Trade," *Christian Science Monitor,* June 26, 1998; Stephen D. Goose and Frank Smyth, "Arming Genocide in Rwanda: The High Cost of Small Arms Transfers," *Foreign Affairs,* September–October 1994.

62. "Controlling Deadly Trade," *Christian Science Monitor.*

63. Rachel Stohl, "Tell the Truth About the Arms Treaty," *New York Times,* April 11, 2013.

Chapter 18

Linking
Concepts and Cases

We have discussed a wide range of issues and concerns in the preceding few chapters. To illustrate these ideas further, it may be useful to consider the following questions as you study the cases. What different postures toward the international community do you observe the leaders of these countries taking? What are the perceived trade-offs between isolation and integration? Do you observe any differences between how leaders may want to be seen and how they are actually perceived? What do countries seek from international or regional cooperation? What regional or global issue stands as a priority for each of these countries? In which countries has the international community tried to alter behavior through the threat of punitive action? Why have some attempts been more successful than others?

Case Study: Mexico

When he was elected in 2000, President Vicente Fox hoped that part of the "democracy premium" gained from the political transition would allow for significant changes in Mexico's relations with the rest of the world. It could be argued that since becoming a democracy Mexico has been more innovative and successful in its foreign policy than in any other area. Presidents Fox, Calderón, and Peña Nieto have all adopted unusually ambitious and activist foreign policy agendas. This marks a break with the past. With a few notable exceptions, for decades the Institutional Revolutionary Party (PRI) took an isolationist approach to the world. Under the Estrada Doctrine (named after a foreign minister), the PRI chose a policy of nonintervention in the affairs of other countries. It rarely condemned other governments or spoke up against human rights abuses. PRI governments were careful to uphold the principle of sovereignty so as to keep others from discussing Mexico's own record.[1]

Since making its democratic transition, Mexico has the credibility to play a larger role on the world stage, especially through activities within the United Nations. Mexico was a founding member of the UN, but over the years Mexican governments have considered the UN to be dominated by developed countries and been distrustful of it. For more than twenty years, they chose not to compete in Security Council elections

for rotating membership. That all changed after the democracy's founding elections. In 2001 Mexico won a nonpermanent seat within the Security Council. Since then, Mexico has become a supporter of UN reform, but instead of adding more permanent seats, it supports expanding the Security Council to twenty-six long-term members mostly from Africa, Asia, the Americas, and the Caribbean.[2] In another break with past policy, Mexicans participated in peacekeeping operations (PKOs) in Western Sahara, Haiti, and Lebanon. And despite some outcry that it breaks with the country's long tradition of noninterference in the affairs of others, Peña Nieto, in coordination with the UN, is planning to establish a training camp to form Mexican international peacekeepers. Previously, Mexicans had participated in peacekeeping operations only in El Salvador after the war there, as highway patrol officers.[3]

Perhaps an even bigger test of the president's determination to depart from the principle of nonintervention was Mexico's willingness to criticize others for their human rights abuses. Such a proactive stance would amount to one of the biggest foreign policy changes undertaken by the new government. It would not be easy (nonintervention is named as a central principle in the Mexican constitution), but it appears that the shift has occurred. For example, under the PRI, Mexico was one of the few Latin American countries that consistently refused to join the United States in denouncing Cuba. However, under the leadership of Fox (of the conservative National Action Party [PAN]) Mexico voted at the UN to criticize Cuba's human rights record, following which Mexico's relationship with Cuba sank to its lowest point in many years. After a series of incidents and accusations, both countries withdrew their ambassadors.[4] Since then, Mexico and Cuba's relations have been repaired, and under PRI leadership relations are described as cordial. The two countries have signed accords for cooperation in fighting human trafficking, and plan to increase trade and investment.[5]

As mentioned, part of Mexico's reluctance to take a more active role in the world was motivated by a desire to deflect outside criticism of its own authoritarian record. After the founding elections marking its transition to democracy, Fox argued that Mexico was ready to become a "proactive defender of human rights" abroad.[6] Mexico proudly became the 100th country to ratify the convention creating the International Criminal Court. However, instead of standing in judgment, the democracy has found itself in the uncomfortable position of being judged. Cases have been brought to the ICC and other international tribunals, accusing the Mexican military of torture (the Court has not responded to the petition).[7] In 2015 and 2016 the United Nations and the Inter-American Commission on Human Rights criticized Mexico for enforced disappearances, executions, and torture, and for sweeping it under the carpet. The Mexican government rejected the criticism, denying that the problem was as bad as reported. However, the UN special envoy established to study torture in Mexico maintained that it was time for Mexico to show itself to be a serious democracy.[8]

Another matter that has hurt Mexico's image on the international stage is migration—as a transit and destination country. Historically, Central Americans have sought refuge in Mexico, or traveled through the country to reach the United States. Over the past few years, and after a surge of refugees (most notably unaccompanied minors) from Honduras, Guatemala, and El Salvador in 2014, the United States and Mexico cooperated in a crackdown to stop them before they reached the United States. They rationalize the policy as necessary to disincentivize the trip, arguing that to grant

these kids asylum would just encourage more to make the dangerous journey.[9] Together the United States and Mexico have forcibly returned more than 800,000 refugees to the countries they were fleeing, 40,000 of them children. Experts on the region maintain that this poses a very real risk; unknown numbers have been terrorized. No one knows how many have been raped or killed because of this deportation policy. Because Mexico refuses to serve as a safe haven, and because it is violating international law by returning people before they can be screened or get a hearing (less than 1 percent of children apprehended by Mexican authorities are granted refugee status or other protections), it has been on the hot seat at international forums.[10]

Although Mexico has been outspoken on a variety of matters, one global issue on which it has become a leader is climate change. In part this is because Calderón (who is a former energy secretary) has taken a personal interest in the matter. Hosting an environmental conference in Cancún in 2010, he called on high- and low-income countries (particularly the United States and China) to stop blaming each other for the problem of global warming and to accept shared responsibility for it. The Mexican president has proposed a "third way" for countries like Mexico: commit to reductions in greenhouse gases in return for technology transfers and aid from the big polluters. Calderón has also called for the creation of a "green fund" to aid poorer countries in reducing their emissions and adapting to climate change. Mexico was one of the first low-income countries to publish a full inventory of its greenhouse gas emissions (the world's fifteenth largest economy, it is one of the world's top ten emitters).[11] Its performance has fallen a bit in recent years, dropping from a score of "very good" to "moderate" on the Climate Change Performance Index, which rates countries on their greenhouse emissions and policy. In 2016 Mexico ranked twenty-eighth out of sixty-one countries (having fallen from eleventh in 2010). But it remained far ahead of the United States, which was ranked thirty-fourth in 2016.[12] Peña Nieto and the PRI have continued to keep the issue on the agenda. In 2015, Mexico promised to cut greenhouse gas emissions by 22 percent by 2030 by shifting to heavier reliance on renewable resources. In doing so, it became the first developing nation to formally pledge to cut global-warming pollution. He continued this pledge in 2016, joining the leaders of the United States and Canada in announcing a joint goal of generating 50 percent of North America's electricity from zero-carbon sources by 2025.[13] In sum, Mexico has been out in front, taking leadership and serving as a role model on the issue of climate change. Mexico has significantly shifted its role on the international stage and stepped up to shape the world's agenda.

Case Study: Peru

Peru has long had ties with the United States and other countries, but the Andean state's primary international interest has been its relationship with its neighbors. In that relationship, Peru has wavered and often appeared irresolute. On the one hand, it has asserted its desire for regional cooperation. The country took an early interest in promoting inter-American solidarity at the 1826 Panama Conference. At the Lima Conference of 1847–1848, Peru joined Bolivia, Chile, Colombia, and Ecuador in calling for a defensive alliance and eventual confederation. On the other hand, despite being a longtime member of the Organization of American States (OAS) and the Andean Community of Nations (CAN), Peru has had an on-and-off relationship

with its neighbors. It has welcomed the economic cooperation that comes with integration, but has never pursued it fully. It is only an associated member of the Common Market of the South (Mercosur); as such it receives some preferential treatment but does not have full voting rights or complete access to the markets of full members. Peruvian governments have sometimes expressed their interest in joining Mercosur as a full member and establishing a common foreign policy among CAN members. At other times, Peru has threatened to quit such integration efforts altogether. However, under President Kuczynski, Peru will likely continue with free trade, pursuing newer, outward-looking initiatives, such as the Trans-Pacific Partnership and the Pacific Alliance, to create even larger trade zones.[14]

Such capriciousness toward its neighbors may be explained by a history of difficult relations in the region. As much as it recognizes the need for cooperation, Peru has just as consistently asserted its desire for independence and determination to pursue what it views as its national interest. As a result, Peru has often found itself in competition with its neighbors—all of which are seeking commercial advantage. The IRREDENTIST conflicts that have divided the region are based in Spain's failure to mark clear boundaries between its administrative units during colonialism. Consequently, Peru has had long-standing border disputes with Chile and Ecuador. Relations with Chile have been tense since the 1879 War of the Pacific, in which Peru lost large tracts of land to its neighbor. A peace deal was signed, but for decades Peru challenged Chile's control over a maritime boundary that gave it rights over a rich fishing area. In 2014 the International Court of Justice ended up ordering Chile to turn over a large part of its claim on the Pacific Ocean to Peru, but a smaller area than Peru had hoped for. Still, both governments accepted the ruling, have said they will abide by it, and are expected to develop closer ties.[15]

Peru and Ecuador have fought a series of brief wars for the past six decades over a 60-mile stretch of Amazonian territory that was never well demarcated. Peru's dispute with Ecuador over the Cenepa River Basin (known as the "Alsace-Lorraine of the Andes") dates back to the early nineteenth century and is centered on questions of territory, water, and mineral rights. For Ecuador, the Cenepa provided the country with badly needed access through the Amazon to distant markets and the Atlantic. But Peruvian presidents treated control of the Cenepa as a matter of national pride. Following a brief conflict in 1995 that resulted in an indecisive outcome, mediators from Brazil, Argentina, the United States, and Chile were able to set the matter to rest in 1998, ending one of the longest disputes in the region.[16]

Although relations have improved in recent years, Peru's conflicts with Chile and Ecuador have proven to be highly politicized, emotionally charged issues that have periodically disrupted inter-American relations. For example, the Peruvian government and press have often accused Chile of being imperialist, acting arrogantly toward Peru, viewing itself as "successful" and "modern," and putting down Peru as "backwards," "uncivilized," and "poor."[17] Peru's relations with Venezuela and Bolivia (in particular, the personal animosity between then-presidents Alan García, Hugo Chávez, and Evo Morales, respectively) could best be described as a cold war. On more than one occasion, García accused Chávez of interference in Peruvian domestic politics and even of fomenting unrest by supporting violent protests by various antigovernment groups.[18] Relations have improved since and although it is unlikely that Peru would come to blows with these two countries, the name-calling

has at times been fierce—in part because their ideological differences are stark (the Venezuelan leadership is leftist and highly critical of the United States, whereas Peruvian presidents—even left-leaning Humala—have embraced the United States and neoliberalism). For example, at a meeting of the Organization of American States, president-elect Kuczynski called for Latin America's leaders to pressure Venezuela on its human rights record. He also called on Venezuela's president to respect the opposition's victory in congressional elections. Kuczynski drew attention to the brutal economic crisis in Venezuela and offered economic assistance in the event of a political transition. Venezuelan president Maduro did not respond directly to his Peruvian counterpart, but in the past such criticism has been dismissed as part of a right-wing plot to destabilize his government.[19]

This kind of give-and-take is a common pattern in Peru's conflicts with Chile and Ecuador (as well as with Venezuela and Bolivia): each side blames the other for behaving aggressively. Meanwhile, analysts have accused all the governments involved of making their border disputes into nationalist issues to divert public attention away from domestic problems. Some say that a spy scandal in which a Peruvian intelligence official was charged with selling military secrets to Chile is an example of this.[20]

Although the war of words is not over, a least for now it appears that most of Peru's border disputes with its neighbors have been put to rest. However, regional rivalries were not helped by the Fujimori government's huge military budgets, or its purchase of fighter jets. Some analysts believe that such actions pushed the region perilously close to an arms race—and a dangerous and unnecessary waste of precious funds, given the fact that the parties involved are democracies that pose no serious security threat to each other. For the past several years, though, flush with cash from the higher prices they've received for their exports, several countries in the region, including Peru, have increased their spending on weapons. Peru has called out other countries for this, but it too is shopping for its military, which is relatively small. Peru in particular is looking to keep up with its coastal competition and build up a more modern, robust naval presence. It is also building up its antinarcotics force with spending on observation satellites for mapping as well as hovercraft and other specialized equipment necessary for operations in the remote Amazon regions under coca cultivation.[21]

For all its thorny relations with its neighbors, Peru is also known for its statesmanship. As a small to medium-sized power, Peru has been impressively active in a variety of capacities. It was a founding member of the United Nations and has had a continuous presence in twenty peacekeeping missions over the years, including a major deployment and ongoing mission to Haiti, as part of an international effort aimed at establishing stability in the region's poorest country.[22] Its diplomatic corps has long enjoyed a reputation of being first-rate. Peruvian career diplomat Javier Pérez de Cuéllar served two terms as UN Secretary-General, from 1982 to 1992. Peru was also instrumental in the crafting of peace accords that ended long-standing wars in more than one Central American state. It played a leadership role in the negotiation of several multilateral conventions, including the Law of the Sea conferences. Backed by several nongovernmental organizations (NGOs), Peru has successfully negotiated debt-for-nature swaps with the United States to fund conservation work in its western Amazonian rainforests. As Peru continues consolidating its democracy, look for similar accomplishments, and for Peru to return as a

voice for the non-Western world at the UN, in the Non-Aligned Movement (NAM), and in other international arenas.[23]

Case Study: Nigeria

Nigeria is known as the giant of Africa. It is Africa's largest democracy and the continent's second largest economy. Nigeria is also a regional power—and some believe it to have the potential to be a superpower. However, during the last years of the Abacha dictatorship, Nigeria had become an international pariah of sorts, isolated for its role as a hub in the transshipment of illegal narcotics and slapped with a variety of minor sanctions for its human rights abuses. That status has changed dramatically since Nigeria's latest attempt at democracy in 1999, as the country has resumed its traditional place in international politics. A founding member of the Organization of African Unity (OAU) and one of the first countries to hold the chairmanship of the OAU's successor, the African Union (AU), Nigeria has taken an interest in a variety of issues that do not directly affect the country, such as Western Sahara and Darfur. These efforts have won it the title "Africa's leader" and for many years Nigeria was viewed as the voice for the region at international forums. Nigeria has assumed leadership roles in a number of international governmental organizations (IGOs), including the Organization of Petroleum Exporting Countries (OPEC) and the Commonwealth. Since independence the country has been a major contributor of troops to more than twenty-five UN peacekeeping missions—in the Democratic Republic of Congo, Lebanon, Iran, and Iraq, among other countries.[24] If Africa ever attains a permanent seat on the Security Council, there is a good chance that two old rivals, South Africa and Nigeria, would campaign hard for it.

Because it is such a giant, what happens in Nigeria affects much of the rest of the continent. Democratic consolidation in Nigeria would contribute positively to the political liberalization throughout the region. On the other hand, a return to authoritarianism and continued fragmentation in Nigeria would undoubtedly contribute to state decay and disintegration in neighboring countries. Thus the relationship goes both ways. Nigerian leaders have taken the position that their country cannot achieve its economic goals if West Africa is unstable. Consequently, Nigeria has imposed what some call a "Pax Nigeriana." It has played the role of regional power broker in the Economic Community of West African States (ECOWAS), and has claimed West Africa, where Nigeria has its greatest security concerns, as its sphere of influence. Willing to violate the OAU's principle of noninterference in the internal affairs of others, Nigeria has viewed itself as an arbiter of both civil and interstate disputes—to the point that some characterize it as being hegemonic.[25] When it went into Liberia in 1990 it was the first African country ever to intervene in the affairs of a neighbor not threatening war. After years of sending troops to intervene in the civil war in Liberia, it went on to Sierra Leone, where Nigeria led the 1998 intervention by the ECOWAS Cease-Fire Monitoring Group (ECOMOG), a multilateral armed force. Ironically, Nigerian dictator Sani Abacha sent 15,000 soldiers to reinstall a democratically elected government in Sierra Leone. Although some questioned Nigeria's motives, it should be noted that in the late 1990s Nigeria spent more on international peacekeeping operations in Africa than did the United States, Britain, or France. Since the mid-2000s, security challenges at home have affected its role, but Nigeria

is one of the largest contributors of personnel and it is said to have participated in nearly every UN peacekeeping mission. Nigeria has been willing to do what the "world's leaders" have shied away from.[26]

Darfur is the perfect example of this. For years a skeletal crew of 7,000 ill-equipped (and often unpaid) African Union peacekeepers (mostly Nigerian and Rwandan) served mostly as a token international presence, often unable to do much more than bear witness to the atrocities committed against civilians. Nigeria intervened in Guinea-Bissau and elsewhere to quash military takeovers. And the country has played a leading diplomatic role in Africa, attempting to broker peace talks in Côte d'Ivoire, Sudan, and Zimbabwe. In 2006, it was Nigeria that helped to convince Liberian warlord Charles Taylor to step down from power by offering him refuge. It was also Nigeria that turned Taylor over to an international tribunal, to be tried for crimes against humanity. Under Olusegun Obasanjo, Nigeria gave South Africa some stiff competition for the title of Africa's ambassador to the world.[27]

Obasanjo clearly enjoyed basking in his glory as Africa's chief diplomat, and Nigerians are sometimes said to have an exaggerated view of the importance of their country on the world stage. That role has diminished significantly since Obasanjo's retirement, given Umaru Yar'Adua's long illness and the distractions regarding Goodluck Jonathan's right to replace him as president. For example, although Nigeria was elected to serve as a nonpermanent member on the UN Security Council in 2013, the Yar'Adua and Jonathan governments were not able to make much of the opportunities to lead. Many of its West African neighbors are experiencing political crises, but in a departure from past practice, Nigeria has held back from its traditional inclinations. It did not overturn the 2009 coup in Niger or intervene to stabilize Guinea or Guinea-Bissau (and this has greatly diminished the ability of ECOWAS to respond to events). In Côte d'Ivoire, President Jonathan urged Laurent Gbagbo, the intransigent incumbent who refused to step down after losing elections, to recognize the outcome of the elections and threatened to use force if he did not step down.[28]

It was a hard pill to swallow when Nigerians, having become accustomed to the limelight as leaders of Africa, learned that one of their countrymen had attempted to take down a US airliner in 2009 on Christmas Day (the so-called underwear bomber). Nigerians were stung by their country's inclusion on terrorist watch lists and many felt that their country had no place on a roll-call that included Yemen and Iran.[29] Perhaps the most significant indicator of changing fortunes for Nigeria, though, is that instead of heading up interventions around the world, Nigeria had to look inward. Tellingly, neither president has asked for help in the Niger Delta. President Jonathan resisted, but his successor, President Buhari, has been more willing to ask for international assistance in quelling the so far intractable conflict against Boko Haram in the northeast. Buhari has been more willing to cooperate with his neighbors to establish information-sharing and build trust, after decades of mistrust. Long-standing, low-simmering border conflicts between the neighbors leave them sensitive about allowing foreign troops on their soil. Yet regional cooperation has proven key to gains against Boko Haram because for years Boko Haram has exploited the porous borders between these countries. As of 2016 this coalition of African Union forces included Nigeria, Chad, Benin, Cameroon, and Niger, supported by mercenaries from South Africa and Russia, as well as the United States, Britain, and France, which are providing satellite intelligence and air support. It is due to their more concerted efforts that they have been able to make headway against

Boko Haram.[30] If the United States or another power were to actively intervene in this war (even at the government's request), it would mark a huge shift in Nigeria's view of itself—and its role on the world stage.

Case Study: Zimbabwe

Because it is a relatively small, landlocked country, most people might expect Zimbabwe to be relatively uninvolved in foreign affairs and very inward-looking. However, Zimbabwe has long had a special place on the international stage and the Zimbabwean government has been unusually vocal at international forums. A leader of the frontline states bordering South Africa, Zimbabwe was key in the anti-apartheid movement (and suffered for it). Similarly, Zimbabwe has long pursued a policy of active nonalignment and was punished by the United States when it refused to vote alongside the superpower at the UN. On the other hand, for being willing to stand up to the leader of the Western world, Zimbabwe's President Robert Mugabe won the admiration of many non-Western people.

However, for years now, many analysts have been concerned that Mugabe is taking the country down with him—just when it appears that Zimbabwe may need the world most. Meanwhile, for most of the past decade the Zimbabwean economy has continued to spiral downward, and Mugabe has lashed out at all who are critical of him. Much of this criticism from the West has come since 2000, when Zimbabwe began a controversial land reform. Led by Britain, the United States and other Western countries criticized the government's handling of redistribution of land and the growing deterioration in human rights of all sorts.

Mugabe's response to such concerns has been to strike out in defiance. He has especially singled out Zimbabwe's former colonizer, Britain, for his anger. Arguing that because it was the British whose policy created the problem, Mugabe maintained that it was Britain that had an obligation to pay for the land redistribution and reform. In response, Britain pointed out that over two and a half decades, it and the United States had paid millions of dollars for land reform (the Zimbabwean government maintains it needed billions). The donors eventually suspended the aid because the land being transferred wasn't going to the poor, but to Mugabe's cronies.[31]

As a result, between 2000 and 2008, relations between Zimbabwe and Britain were at their lowest point since independence. Mugabe accused Britain of sponsoring his opposition, the Movement for Democratic Change (MDC), and seeking to govern the country "by remote control."[32] To signal its disapproval of the way Mugabe has been running the country, Britain (and the West) sought to isolate Zimbabwe and force change through the imposition of a range of punitive measures. These included targeted sanctions and a travel ban on Mugabe and his political elites. In response to reforms such as the (at best halfhearted) establishment of a government of national unity in 2009 and the adoption (at least) of a progressive constitution in 2013, as well as peaceful but flawed elections in 2013, European Union (EU) members responded by easing up on the sanctions and gradually normalizing relations. In November 2014, the EU took a significant step in reengaging Zimbabwe by providing direct financial assistance. Western development aid and loans to Zimbabwe are gradually resuming, but the major investment that Zimbabwe really needs won't come until donors see more movement in the way of political reforms.[33]

China takes a very different approach. Through its "Look East" policy starting in 2003, Zimbabwe found a new sponsor (with its policy of noninterference, one that is far less likely to lecture on human rights or democracy) and a mutually beneficial relationship that actually stretches back to the days of the liberation struggle. Zimbabwe needed an alternative source of aid, credit, and foreign investment; China was seeking to expand its political influence and its markets. The two supported each other at the UN; Zimbabwe lined up behind the One China policy and China protected Zimbabwe by vetoing sanctions in the Security Council. And for several years there, Chinese industries were hungry for Zimbabwe's mineral products.[34] Despite China's recent slowdown, it is Zimbabwe's most important economic partner, with bilateral trade worth more than $1 billion annually. This partnership is important to both countries, and there are signs that China is beginning to position itself for a post-Mugabe Zimbabwe.[35]

Like China, African governments have called for quiet diplomacy, "constructive engagement," and a less heavy-handed approach from the international community. This is also in part due to sentimental reasons; for many Africans, Mugabe will always be lionized as a liberation hero.[36] This is especially true in southern Africa, and it largely explains the patience the Southern African Development Community (SADC) has displayed for the Zimbabwean president. Its neighbors have a track record of mediating disputes (they negotiated the power-sharing agreement in 2008 that helped to reduce the election violence that year). They certainly have an interest in a peaceful transition in Zimbabwe, as it is their economies that are most bound up together and it is they who will receive the largest numbers of refugees should things turn violent. This is especially true of South Africa, although South African president Jacob Zuma has been distracted by internal challenges and has been somewhat less protective of Mugabe than his predecessors from the African National Congress (ANC).[37] Given their long and close relationship, South Africa has more potential to mediate a peaceful transition than any other country. But it can't be surprising that South African leaders have chosen to proceed carefully. With the exception of Mugabe, no single actor can do much to influence the succession. But a well-coordinated, multilateral strategy aimed at contingency planning can help reduce the negative consequences for all.[38] It appears that the West has come to accept the Africans' argument. In return for even the smallest gestures by the Mugabe government, it is now betting on change through constructive engagement and Zimbabwe's reengagement with the world.

Case Study: Egypt

Not that long ago, Egypt was a real leader in the Middle East, a model for others, and a force to be reckoned with in the world. Under Gamal Abdul Nasser in the 1950s and 1960s, during what some have characterized as a period of national grandeur, Egypt basked in the limelight. Attractive to others for its compelling combination of hard and soft power, many saw this country as the natural leader of the Arab and Islamic world.[39] Not only was Nasser recognized as a principal in the nonaligned movement and Pan-Arabism, but Cairo was home to the Arab League. From many Egyptians' perspective, this is only rightfully so; as mother to the world, this country has a strong belief in its own exceptionalism—and it is by far the most populous country in the Arab world, with a quarter of the world's Arab population.[40]

But Egypt's devastating losses in wars to Israel in the 1960s and 1970s, especially the 1967 war with the loss of the Sinai, were a tremendous blow. Most Egyptians continued to scorn Israel, but the offer of return of territory and the rebuilding of its military with huge amounts of US aid—in return for peace with Israel—proved hard to resist. Still, this bargain (the Camp David peace accords of 1979) contributed to Egypt's fall from grace, at home and throughout the Middle East. Ostracized by its Arab allies, the once-proud nation was widely regarded as a yes-man to the United States.[41]

Yet in the West, Egypt has been praised for its willingness to make peace, and has long been recognized for its contributions to international peacekeeping and diplomacy. Boutros Boutros-Ghali, an Egyptian diplomat, served as UN Secretary-General from 1992 to 1996 and was the first African and the first Arab to hold the post.[42] Egypt has long been a major contributor to UN peacekeeping efforts. Another Egyptian, Mohamed El Baradei, won the Nobel Peace Prize in 2005 for his work as the director-general of the International Atomic Energy Agency. For many years, Egypt took the lead in nonproliferation efforts in the Middle East.[43]

But Egypt is best known for its active involvement in attempts to broker a peace between Israel and the Palestinians. This was possible because of its unique relationship with Israel. Mubarak made with his Israeli counterparts what is often called a "cold peace": the two governments worked hard at never letting on how relatively well they worked together.[44] After Mubarak's ouster and during President Morsi's short time in office, relations with Israel cooled significantly, as Morsi was viewed as supporting Hamas, widely considered to be the Muslim Brotherhood in Palestine. It came as a surprise to many when President Morsi persuaded its ally Hamas to enter into a cease-fire with Israel. Since Morsi's overthrow in 2013 the relationship has normalized due to Israel's relief at seeing the end of Islamist control of its closest (and only) ally in the region. Actually, it has been Egypt's relationship with the Palestinians that has taken a turn since then. President Sisi has a very different relationship with the Palestinian organization Hamas. Hamas is banned in Egypt, accused of interfering in Egyptian affairs by supporting the Muslim Brotherhood and Sinai Province, both of which the government has declared terrorist groups. For its part, Hamas distrusts the Sisi government as well, as Egypt has blown up tunnels in the Sinai that are a lifeline to Gaza's economy.[45] The Sisi government is siding with Israel to crush Hamas (and indirectly get at the Muslim Brotherhood)—despite the fact that most Egyptians sympathize with the Palestinians. So, although the relationship with Israel has its challenges, the two share a common adversary in Hamas and an interest in border security.[46] As a result, Egypt can no longer portray itself as an objective third party or true mediator in the conflict.[47] This is just another example of how Egypt's role in the world has changed, as it had for decades been considered central to the Israeli-Palestinian dialogue.

Another way that things have changed is that instead of Egypt taking a leading role in the region, other powers in the region have been taking a leading role in Egypt.[48] As discussed in Chapter 19, Egypt's relationship with the United States is not what it used to be either, and although a relationship still continues (Egypt is the second largest recipient of US aid), the United States has less influence over Egypt now. Egypt has diversified its donor pool. Not only has it expanded ties with Russia, France, and China, but it could also be said to be under the protection of Saudi

Arabia and its Gulf allies. With the exception of Qatar, which backed the Muslim Brotherhood and its first president, these are like-minded Arab governments that view Islamism as an existential threat.[49] The Gulf states have embraced the Sisi regime, not only because they feared the rise of Islamism with the Morsi government or more of the chaos in the neighborhood that would come with another collapsed state: just as threatening to them is the possibility that a successful democracy in Egypt might inspire further demands for democratization in their countries.[50] In fact, analysts estimate that the Gulf states spent billions to overturn Morsi and bring Sisi to power.[51] Although the funds slowed to a trickle ($12 billion) in 2016 due to lower oil prices, they continue to support the renewal of "apolitical Islam" in Egypt. For a while there they were providing huge amounts of annual economic assistance ($30–$60 billion) in grants and loans to keep Egypt afloat and prevent economic failure—without any pressure over the treatment of political prisoners or civil rights.[52] Clearly, the Sisi administration is glad to have this kind of help, with few strings attached. Tensions between Egypt and Saudi Arabia have risen recently over Syria. Egypt, which was aligned, rhetorically at least, with the Saudis in supporting the Syrian rebels, has made a realignment. Egypt is increasingly supporting Assad, who is backed by Iran, the Saudis' nemesis. Sisi's tilt to Assad is based in part in their shared interest in fighting militant Islamist insurgents. But Egypt's shift is more likely due to its preoccupation with crushing the Muslim Brotherhood, its desire to reclaim some relevance, and to show its independence by moving closer to Russia, with whom it has voted at the UN on Syria. At any rate, Egypt's attempt to assert itself means drama for its relationship with its Saudi benefactor. But it is unlikely to mean a breakup. Neither can afford to walk away from the other.[53]

Case Study: Iran

Iran, similar to many countries of the global south, is struggling to find its way in the international community. Since the mid-twentieth century it has vacillated between the US-led, post–World War II alliance system, isolation after the 1979 revolution, and a gradual and conflicted opening of arms to the international community. Former president Mohammad Khatami softened Iran's image abroad, including in the West, even making overtures to the United States, known since Khomeini's rise in 1979 as the "Great Satan." While President Khatami's successor, Mahmoud Ahmadinejad, openly embraced confrontation, especially with Israel and much of the Western world, the president who succeeded Ahmadinejad, Hassan Rouhani, is attempting to rectify many of the imbalances that were created by Iran's estrangement within the region and the world. His shift in approach is not welcomed by all, including many within the leadership, highlighting a "fierce power struggle . . . between those who want to open up Iran and reconcile with the rest of the world, and Khamenei and his supporters who have been frozen in the revolutionary era of 1979."[54] As Iran transforms from pariah state to regional power,[55] many are ill at ease.

Iran has long been a regional contender for the top spot in the Middle East. The collapse of the Soviet Union increased Iran's regional importance, by allowing the restoration of ties between the Caucasus and Central Asia. These newly independent states, concerned about their survival, found an economic and security patron in Tehran. Hezbollah—armed and trained by Iran—waged a short yet successful war

against Israel in 2006, in a conflict viewed by many as a proxy showing of Tehran's growing assertiveness. The reorganization of Iraq after the fall of Saddam Hussein, during which the formerly suppressed Shiite majority gained prominence, achieved "what Iran's revolution had failed to do"—namely, pose a serious challenge to Sunni Arab domination in the Middle East.[56] Tehran's continued support for the Syrian government, and growing role in Syria's civil war (including the deployment of Islamic Revolutionary Guard members), present a force projection and clear claim for recognition as a key regional player.

Since the birth of the Islamic Republic in 1979, one of the most important issues facing Iran was its animosity toward Iraq, a tension that erupted in a devastating war from 1980 to 1988. This conflict ended more out of exhaustion than anything—Iran grudgingly accepted UN Security Council Resolution 598, which called for the cessation of hostilities and the exchange of prisoners of war—and Ayatollah Ruhollah Khomeini compared signing the resolution to "drinking poison."[57] Many believed that once the secular Sunni leader Saddam Hussein was out of the picture, closer ties between Iran and Iraq (dominated by religious Shiite Muslims) could form.[58] Reality could not be further from the case. While Ahmadinejad hoped to unite Shiites and Sunnis in a grand anti-US alliance, promoting a brand of populism that Prince Hassan of Jordan has labeled "an alternative to civil society in the Middle East,"[59] the schisms between the two groups have only hardened. Conflicts born of the Arab Spring have solidified the sectarian divide, as Shiite Muslims become increasingly marginalized in Sunni-government states, and Sunni extremists denounce Shiites as heretics. Iran's support of Syria's Bashar al-Assad (an Alawite within the Shia tradition), is a major part of this dynamic.

In the crowded regional environment of the Middle East, Iran's reemergence marks Saudi Arabia's decline, with the potential to dramatically reshape power dynamics in the region and beyond. The escalation of tension between these two regional rivals, sparked by Saudi Arabia's execution of an outspoken Shiite cleric in early 2016, threatens to destabilize the region further by escalating both sides' involvement in regional proxy wars, especially in Syria and Yemen. After the execution of Shiite Shaikh Nimr (a Shiite leader who had called for free elections and the overthrow of the Saudi royal family), protesters in Tehran ransacked the Saudi embassy. While President Rouhani tried to temper Iran's response, Khamanei admonished, "God's hand of retaliation will grip the neck of Saudi politicians."[60] These two regional giants harbor a significant lack of trust, with Saudi concerns about Iranian expansionism and support for regional militias, and Iranian concerns about Saudi attempts to isolate Iran even further and limit Shiite influence throughout the region.

Iran's controversial uranium enrichment program, pursued in secret (and in violation of the Nuclear Non-Proliferation Treaty) for eighteen years before being disclosed by a dissident group in 2002, has focused global opposition against the regime. The international response to Iran's uranium enrichment program has been challenged by the concern raised by some, including Russia and China, who long maintained that economic sanctions against the regime would cause too much pain for the civilian population (and harm their own business deals with the regime as well). Security Council sanctions, which necessitate the lack of disapproval from all UN permanent members, have been watered down in order to avoid a veto, and other multilateral sanctions (implemented by the United States, the European Union, South

Korea, and Japan) remain limited. Sanctions were increased in 2012, as Tehran continued to insist on its sovereign right to enrich uranium and produce fuel. Negotiations on a joint comprehensive action plan between Iran and the P5+1 (the five permanent members of the UN Security Council plus Germany) led to a final agreement, signed in July of 2015, in which members agreed to lift most sanctions against Iran in exchange for limits on its nuclear programs. After verification by the International Atomic Energy Agency (IAEA) that Tehran had indeed dismantled core parts of its nuclear program (and shipped 98 percent of its nuclear fuel out of the country), weapons-related sanctions against the Islamic Republic were lifted in January 2016, with concomitant agreements to unfreeze approximately $100 billion in assets, mostly from past oil sales.[61] This controversial agreement, which supporters tout as the best way to ensure that Iran's nuclear program will be exclusively peaceful, was met with concern and even scorn in many circles, including throughout the Middle East, as a possible boost to Iran's cash flow and power.

Iran was a charter member of the United Nations, and it has a rocky history of ties with the organization. Its leaders strongly condemned UN failings during and after the war with Iraq in the 1980s. In 1987, moderate president Ali Khatami portrayed the UN as "a paper factory for issuing worthless, ineffective orders."[62] The populist Ahmadinejad used his face time at the UN to sharpen his country's anti-US credentials with vitriolic speeches that often sent delegations outside General Assembly chambers in protest.[63] President Rouhani, in contrast, avoided anti-American denunciations in his General Assembly addresses.[64] In claiming to speak for the Muslim world, Tehran has long supported the proposal that an Islamic country be made a permanent member of the Security Council during future reforms. Iranian leaders continue to raise their profile with the United Nations, including being elected to the UN Commission on the Status of Women in mid-2010, even as Iran faces nearly annual censures within the General Assembly on its human rights record, including "pervasive gender inequality and violence against women."[65]

The Islamic Republic of Iran has the potential to exert great influence—regionally and internationally. It is increasing its connections with Russia and Turkey, and extending more connections to Brazil, Gambia, Uganda, and China. Domestic debates on the pros and cons of greater incorporation into the world community, regional reconfiguration and insecurities, and continued international tensions surrounding Tehran's policies will frame what direction this influence will take.

Case Study: China

China views itself as a global player, especially since its economic transformation and role after the Great Recession. Indeed, many analysts, Chinese and non-Chinese alike, are of the mind that China is the most likely country to become a superpower in the twenty-first century. At the very least, Beijing is charting an alternative to a world dominated by the hegemonic United States, increasingly gaining credence as a responsible stakeholder in global affairs.

Regionally, Chinese leaders have the dubious honor of being viewed as the one true ally of the unpredictable regime in North Korea. Beijing was a major convener of the six-party talks (which include China, the United States, North Korea, South Korea, Russia, and Japan) that were designed to manage Pyongyang's nuclear

weapons program. China's attempts to stabilize the North Korean situation are largely out of self-interest—estimates vary, but it is believed that during particularly difficult times, such as the winter months, as many as 500 North Korean refugees cross the border into northeastern China each week. Beijing has also been a leading advocate of closer ties between North and South Korea, widely referred to as the "Sunshine" policy. Ironically, China has much security to lose if North and South Korea reunify—a united Korean peninsula could reopen major power surges for influence, and could invite a strong US presence on China's northeastern border. Even though China officially laments the presence of more than 29,000 US troops in Korea, their withdrawal could have a potentially destabilizing effect. The People's Republic of China (PRC) has also attempted to play the mediator role in the ongoing dispute (the fires of which it helps fan) between India and Pakistan. China (allied with Pakistan) views itself as an important balancing force to India, which is allied with the United States. Beijing perceives India to be its greatest threat, which helps explain the assistance the country has provided to Pakistani leaders in the development of long-range missiles that could carry nuclear weapons.

China's military might catches the world's attention and its recent achievements in outer space continue that pattern. Beijing forces used a medium-range ballistic missile to shoot down an aging weather satellite in 2007, and China launched a robotic lunar orbiter in 2007 and again in 2010. The Japanese government recently issued an explicit warning about China's military growth, adjusting Tokyo's long-term regional defense policy in response to Beijing's increasing military spending, military modernization campaigns, and increased naval assertiveness—including the "reclamation" of new islands in the shallow waters of the East China and South China Seas, an area of overlapping territorial claims surrounded by rich natural resources, especially oil and natural gas.[66]

Beijing is also becoming an increasingly important player in the Middle East. Part of this is driven by trade and energy. Chinese trade with the Middle East nearly doubled between 2005 and 2010 (China remains Iran's largest trading partner in 2016); bilateral trade between them totaled $52 billion in 2014.[67] In early January 2016 (two weeks after the historic nuclear accord with Iran was implemented), Xi Jinping traveled to Tehran, marking the first visit by a PRC official to the Islamic Republic in fourteen years. Xi was also the first leader from the negotiating group to travel to Iran, eager to tap into the recently available post-sanctions market.[68]

With its increasing economic might, China has become the arms supplier of choice to many non-Western countries, especially those that are otherwise barred from being able to purchase these items—including Sudan. Among its most exported items are guns (especially AK-47s), leg-irons, anti-riot equipment, and armored vehicles. Beijing is also becoming a ranking weapons exporter, with foreign sales nearly doubling between 2011 and 2015. Even though the PRC still ranks third (behind the United States and Russia) in this regard, it is developing a formidable domestic industry that is fueling a conventional arms race throughout the region: China's primary export market for weapons includes Pakistan, Bangladesh, and Myanmar.[69]

In the United Nations, Chinese delegates tend to view themselves as the self-proclaimed leaders of the developing countries, in large part because of the power they hold with their veto option in the Security Council. PRC diplomats use this veto infrequently, but strategically, often to lash out at Taiwan's supporters. For example, in

February 2000, China vetoed a resolution to extend the peacekeeping operation in Macedonia, because Macedonia had recently recognized Taiwan as an independent country. China has taken similar action against Guatemala, often voting against any measure the state sponsors, because Guatemala has lobbied other UN members for the admission of Taiwan to the UN. While from its soapbox China often preaches the importance of sovereignty, this claim is never meant to include the territory of Taiwan, for which the principle of Chinese territorial integrity is deemed much more important. China is not likely to budge on the contested issue of Taiwan's relationship with the United Nations anytime soon. These acts have impelled others to bend to China's will—South Africa, for example, switched its diplomatic recognition from Taiwan to China in 1997, in part because it hoped the move would garner China's support for a new permanent seat on the Security Council. Some have accused China of using its UN permanent-member power irresponsibly, especially as Beijing helped stall UN action in Sudan's troubled Darfur region.[70] From Beijing's point of view, China was speaking up for Sudan's sovereign right to control what happens within its borders. Chinese diplomats made similar arguments when asked to defend their numerous vetoes against UN Security Council action in Syria, especially between 2011 and 2016.[71]

China has had a very vocal role in the ongoing debate over UN reform in general, but especially in debates over possible reform of the Security Council. Beijing supports enlargement of the Security Council (and surprisingly endorsed Germany and Brazil as two potential newcomers), while closely guarding its own spot as the lone "Asian seat" within the chamber (not wanting to see either Japan or India emerge as regional rivals).[72] In debates over the future of the United Nations, Beijing's voice is well placed to carry much weight.

Once the problem child on environmental issues, China has quickly emerged as the "world's new leader in climate diplomacy," especially in light of concerns that the United States will adopt a less participatory approach under the Trump administration.[73] Many give credit to China's ability to curtail emissions from 2013 to 2016 for helping level off global emissions, and China's support of the Paris climate agreement was critical for the agreement's eventual success.[74]

As China continues to promote its political, economic, cultural, and military ties with other developing countries, including the use of its so-called soft power to market its own "brand" of affairs, its reach and influence are very likely to increase.

Case Study: Indonesia

In the not too distant past, Indonesia was a pivotal regional actor, with aspirations toward becoming the leader of countries that refused to line up with either the United States or the Soviet Union. In this latter goal it was a catalyst in efforts to organize non-Western countries during the Cold War. Throughout the 1990s and early 2000s the instability of the Indonesian state, rocked by economic, political, ethnic, and natural crises, aroused concern among its neighbors in the region and within the global community alike. Former president Susilo Bambang Yudhoyono (SBY) worked to launch a more engaged path, regionally and globally, promoting the image of a country with "1,000 friends and zero enemies."[75] President Joko "Jokowi" Widodo arrived in office with no foreign policy experience (you may remember that he was a furniture salesman and former governor of Jakarta). In his first year in office, he delegated

foreign policy appearances (including at the United Nations General Assembly), to his vice president, and his presence at the Paris climate meetings "did not make a difference"—prompting calls for him to "step up his game in foreign policy."[76]

Throughout the Cold War, Indonesia was a proud "holdout" during the superpower-dominated contest, occupying a position that became known as "rowing between two reefs." Indicative of this approach, which is different from neutrality, Indonesia was a founding member of the Non-Aligned Movement, an organization of developing countries that formed in 1961 in opposition to the bipolarity of the Cold War. The NAM grew out of a joint conference of African and Asian leaders in 1955, known as the Bandung Conference, named for the Indonesian city in which it was held. In the face of rising superpower tensions, and the division of many countries into blocs that supported either one side or the other, leaders of many former colonial countries gathered to convey their assessment of world affairs. Since the 1960s the NAM has provided a forum to discuss decolonization, debt relief, total nuclear disarmament, and UN Security Council reform. The organization has also sent fact-finding and relief missions to conflict zones, including Somalia and Bosnia-Herzegovina. All the while, members of the organization claimed independence from the "East-West ideological conflict," concentrating instead on North-South economic cleavages. Yet even though Indonesian leaders publicly proclaimed "an active and independent foreign policy," the 1965 anticommunist coup won it the favor and support of many of the Western powers—especially the United States. Although the NAM is less independent than it claims to be, it remains a valuable forum for many non-Western countries. In the 2009 summit, for example, which was held in Egypt, members again called on the United Nations to be more truly representative of the smaller countries of the world community.

Ideological and ethnic tensions exist between Indonesia and its giant neighbor to the northwest, China. For almost four decades, this animosity was dominantly ideological in nature, as Indonesia was the focal point of anticommunist struggle in the region. Much of the impetus for forming the Association of Southeast Asian Nations (ASEAN) in the late 1960s was to fortify an anticommunist alliance among states in the region. This focus gradually subsided, though, and China now holds "dialogue status" within the organization. Indonesia views its neighbor's increasingly active role in ASEAN in zero-sum terms: as Beijing becomes more influential, Jakarta's level of influence is likely to wane. Disputes over territory and access to shipping and fishing lanes in the South China Sea have also animated much of ASEAN's work in recent years, and China, as the primary power seeking land reclamation (i.e., building islands by dredging reefs), has become the target of much criticism, including from Jakarta. Although Indonesia has traditionally placed itself as a neutral arbiter within ASEAN, between China on one hand and Vietnam and the Philippines on the other, as China increases its talk of "overlapping claims" on the waters close to the (undisputed) Natuna Islands, Jakarta's ire increases.[77] Indonesia plays a significant role within ASEAN, and some observers draw a clear connection between the "overall strength of ASEAN" and the "willingness of Indonesia to play that role of diplomatic broker."[78]

Indonesia's treatment of its sizable ethnic Chinese population has also been a focal point of tensions between the two countries. In the riots of 1998 and thereafter, ethnic Chinese communities throughout Indonesia—especially Chinese women—

have been targeted in mob attacks, mass rape, and discrimination. Ethnic Chinese business communities in Indonesia have been scapegoated as well, especially as Indonesian families watch their disposable incomes plummet. As the environment for religious and ethnic minorities continues to weaken within Indonesia, attacks against ethnic Chinese are likely to increase.

Multilateral institutions, especially the United Nations and the International Monetary Fund (IMF), have played a key although not always positive role in Indonesia since 1997. You may remember the discussion of conditionality from Chapter 6. IMF demands for the financial bailout package in 1998, after the collapse of the Indonesian currency, led to wide-scale looting and riots across the country. As the Great Recession unfolded in 2008, SBY stated bluntly that his country "will not follow the IMF's formula in coping with the global financial crisis. . . . We still need to learn from that experience (of a decade ago)."[79] Amongst many Indonesians, a sense of "seething bitterness" remains from the austerity requirements of 1998 and 1999, and even though the IMF recognizes that emerging economies like Indonesia deserve a greater voice, many within Indonesia question the degree to which such institutions serve the interests of Indonesians.[80]

Indonesia's relations with the UN in recent years have mostly surrounded the independence of East Timor in 1999 and the violence that ensued. Regionally, Australia was a main player in urging Indonesian president B. J. Habibie to call for the East Timor referendum, and the Commonwealth also provided a large number of peacekeeping troops in the aftermath of the vote. Despite the passage of time and the achievement of sovereignty within the country now known as Timor-Leste, the dust has yet to settle. Members of the international community demanded that Indonesia establish a war crimes tribunal for the East Timor violence, but this was rebuffed by Jakarta. As a result, Indonesia organized a reception, truth, and reconciliation commission in East Timor that was designed to be weak—its final report, released in January 2005, chalked up the atrocities within East Timor to the behavior of "rogue elements" within the military. For its part, the United Nations did establish a serious crimes investigation unit, but it too has been largely impotent. Many shake their head at the realization that Suharto, widely believed to be responsible for two times as many deaths as Saddam Hussein and Slobodan Milosevic combined, has been able to escape any and all wheels of justice.[81] Attempts by Papuan self-determination activists, who seek UN support in calling for an internationally supervised vote on self-determination by the people living in Western Papua (formerly known as Irian Jaya), are likely to continue to be met with fierce resistance by Jakarta, especially since, at least through 2016, Australia and New Zealand continue to back Jakarta's claim of sovereignty over the Papuans. For all of his populist rhetoric and lack of connections to the prior regime, even Jokowi rebuffs claims that human rights abuses in Papua demand international action, stating that domestic responses are sufficient.[82]

Indonesia has started to become a major player in Southeast Asian affairs, and its continued outreach to Australia and China, as well as its leadership in ASEAN, seem calculated to ensure Indonesia's presence throughout Asia for decades to come. As the world's fourth most populous state, ringed by some of the globe's busiest fishing lanes, Indonesia possesses global influence. Yet as *The Economist* pointed out, domestic challenges could derail its future ambitions: "a failure to prosper at home would turn the spotlight away from Indonesia's desire to solve global problems, and

towards its capacity to generate them."[83] With a strong economy, and an increased sense of self-confidence, Indonesians seem well on their way toward charting an increased voice within Southeast Asia, and potentially beyond.

Now It's Your Turn

What significant events or issues would you add to this discussion that have become prominent since this book was published? Have any of the concerns covered in this chapter been significantly resolved—or have any situations dramatically worsened? What role do you believe truth commissions serve in promoting peace and justice? If you were the leader of a country torn apart by conflict, how would you best prescribe picking up the pieces and moving on? In your mind, have any recent events warranted an international tribunal or the commissioning of a peacekeeping operation? Are there any countries that seem to be impacted by regional or global matters more than they are able to influence affairs themselves? How differently would you look at some of the IGOs and NGOs studied in this chapter if you were a resident or a leader in one of these countries of the global south? Some people argue that, in general, the richer the country and the more its economy is geared toward trade, the more active and complex its foreign policy. The corollary would then be that the poorer the country, the more focused its leaders tend to be on domestic issues. Do you find this to be the case with the countries studied here? Why or why not?

Notes

1. "Breaking Foreign Policy Taboos," *The Economist,* August 24, 2000.

2. "Mexico Calls for Expansion, Reform of U.N. Security Council," *Fox News Latino,* December 29, 2014.

3. "Peña Nieto Harshly Criticized for Mexican UN Peacekeepers," *Telesur,* September 29, 2015.

4. Ginger Thompson, "Mexico and Peru Withdraw Ambassadors from Cuba," *New York Times,* May 3, 2004.

5. "The Presidents of Mexico and Cuba Announce New Accords and Closer Ties," Associated Press, November 6, 2015.

6. "Fox Announces 'More Dynamic' International Role for Mexico," EFE News Service, January 6, 2001.

7. Ginger Thompson, "Mexico's Self-Image Problem," *New York Times,* April 25, 2016.

8. Azam Ahmed, "Few Expect Mexico's Government to Suffer at Polls, Despite Outrage over Abductions," *New York Times,* April 25, 2016; "Mexico: UN Experts Welcome Inter-American Commission on Human Rights Report on Disappeared, Executed, and Tortured Students," UN Human Rights Office of the High Commissioner, September 9, 2015.

9. Jens Manuel Krogstad, "U.S. Border Apprehensions of Families and Unaccompanied Children Jump Dramatically," Pew Research Center, May 4, 2016.

10. Nicholas Kristof, "We're Helping Deport Kids to Die," *New York Times,* July 16, 2016.

11. Peter Vanham, "Top 10 Things to Know About the Mexican Economy," World Economic Forum, May 5, 2015; Johannes Friedrich, Mengpin Ge, and Thomas Damassa, "Infographic: What Do Your Country's Emissions Look Like?," World Resources Institute, June 23, 2015.

12. Jan Burck, Franziska Marten, and Christoph Bals, "The Climate Change Performance Index Results 2016," *Germanwatch,* December 2015.

13 Ioan Grillo, "Climate Change Is Making Mexico City Unbreathable," *Salon,* June 6, 2015; Ian Austen and Coral Davenport, "Climate Change High on Agenda as Obama and Trudeau Meet for Summit," *New York Times,* June 27, 2016.

14. Matthew Taylor, "The Significance of Peru's June 5 Election," Council on Foreign Relations, May 12, 2016.

15. Gideon Long, "Chile-Peru: Moving on from the Past," BBC News, January 28, 2014.

16. Monica Herz and João Pontes Nogueir, *Ecuador vs. Peru: Peacemaking Amid Rivalry* (Boulder: Lynne Rienner, 2002); Gabriel Marcella and Richard Downes, *Introduction to Security Cooperation in the Western Hemisphere: Resolving the Ecuador-Peru Conflict*, ed. Gabriel Marcella and Richard Downes (Boulder: Lynne Rienner, 1999).

17. G. Van Der Ree, "Chile's (Inter)National Identities: Framing the Relations with Bolivia and Peru," *Bulletin of Latin American Research* 29, no. 2 (2010).

18. Lucien Chauvin, "Peru Sees Shadowy Hand of Chávez, Everywhere," *Christian Science Monitor*, April 3, 2008.

19. Ryan Dube, "Peru's Incoming President Pressures Venezuela on Human Rights, Economic Crisis," *Wall Street Journal*, June 13, 2016.

20. Ronald Bruce St. John, *The Foreign Policy of Peru* (Boulder: Lynne Rienner, 1992).

21. "Peru Slates 'Needless' Arms Spending in Latin America," United Press International, May 19, 2010; "The Rising Tide of Peruvian Defense Spending," *Avascent*, February 6, 2014.

22. Wilder Alejandro Sanchez, "Peacekeeping Contributor Profile: Peru," Council on Hemispheric Affairs, October 2013.

23. St. John, *The Foreign Policy of Peru*.

24. Matthew Schroeder, "US Security Assistance and Africa: Challenges of Weapons Sales and Military Aid," in *Security, Reconstruction, and Reconciliation: When Wars End*, ed. Muna Ndulo (New York: University College London Press, 2007).

25. Okon Akiba, *Nigerian Foreign Policy Towards Africa: Continuity and Change* (New York: Peter Lang, 1998).

26. Jean Herskovits, "Nigeria's Rigged Democracy," *Foreign Affairs*, July–August 2007; Leonard H. Robinson Jr., "Clinton Visit Raises Hopes for Nigeria," *Chicago Sun-Times*, August 27, 2000; Adesoji Adeniyi, "Peacekeeping Contributor Profile: Nigeria," Providing for Peacekeeping, 2016.

27. Herskovits, "Nigeria's Rigged Democracy."

28. "Nigeria Urges UN to Authorise Force in Côte d'Ivoire," *Mail and Guardian* (London), January 24, 2011.

29. Richard Joseph and Alexandra Gillies, "Nigeria's Season of Uncertainty," *Current History*, May 2010; John Campbell, "Examining the US-Nigerian Relationship in a Time of Transition," US Senate Committee on Foreign Affairs, Subcommittee on African Affairs, February 23, 2010.

30. Tolu Ogunlesi, "Terror's Nameless Victims in Nigeria," *New York Times*, December 2, 2015; Alex Thurston, "Managing Expectations Could Be Toughest Challenge for Nigeria's Buhari," *World Politics Review*, September 24, 2015; Eric Schmitt and Dionne Searcey, "US Plans to Put Advisers on Front Lines of Nigeria's War on Boko Haram," *New York Times*, February 25, 2016.

31. "Top of His Head," *The Economist*, November 13, 1997; "Q&A: Mugabe's Zimbabwe," BBC News, December 19, 2003.

32. Andrew Meldrum, "Africa Needs More Courage, Says Mugabe," *The Guardian* (London), February 21, 2006.

33. Chido Munyati, "Why US Reengagement Is Critical to Zimbabwe's Debt Arrears Clearance Strategy," *Foreign Policy Journal*, March 4, 2016; "EU Relations with Zimbabwe," European External Action Service, n.d.

34. Andrew Meldrum and Jonathan Watts, "China Gives Zimbabwe Economic Lifeline," *The Guardian* (London), June 16, 2006.

35. Norimitsu Onishi, "'No One Is Safe': Zimbabwe Threatens to Take Foes Farms," *New York Times*, August 28, 2016; Samuel Ramani, "Is China Ready for a Post-Mugabe Zimbabwe?," *The Diplomat*, August 13, 2016.

36. Christina Lamb, "Mugabe: Why Africa Applauds Him," *New Statesman*, August 7, 2006.

37. "Africa to Press for End to Zimbabwe Sanctions," *New York Times*, September 7, 2009.

38. George F. Ward, "Political Instability in Zimbabwe," Council on Foreign Relations, March 2015.

39. Afaf Lutfi al-Sayyid Marsot, *A History of Egypt: From the Arab Conquest to the Present* (Cambridge: Cambridge University Press, 2007).

40. Thanassis Cambanis, *Once Upon a Revolution: An Egyptian Story* (New York: Simon and Schuster, 2015).

41. Marsot, *A History of Egypt*.

42. Robert D. McFadden, "Boutros Boutros-Ghali, Former U.N. Secretary General, Dies at 93," *New York Times,* February 16, 2016.

43. Patricia M. Lewis, "A Middle East Free of Nuclear Weapons: Possible, Probable, or Pipe-Dream?," *International Affairs* 89, no. 2 (March 2013).

44. Marsot, *A History of Egypt*.

45. Ali Jarbawi, "Sisi and the Palestinians," *New York Times,* June 1, 2014; Zachary Laub, "Interview: Washington's Egypt Dilemma," Council on Foreign Relations, June 23, 2015, www.cfr.org.

46. Isabel Kershner, "Egyptian Minister Visits Israel in Push for Peace with Palestinians," *New York Times,* July 10, 2016.

47. "No Longer a True Mediator," *The Economist,* July 25, 2014.

48. Caroline Barnett, "Egypt in the Region," *Rocky Harbors: Taking Stock of the Middle East in 2015,* Center for Strategic and International Studies, 2015.

49. Jeremy M. Sharp, "Egypt: Background and US Relations," Congressional Research Service, July 24, 2015.

50. Laub, "Interview: Washington's Egypt Dilemma."

51. Cambanis, *Once Upon a Revolution*.

52. Karen E. Young, "Declining Gulf States' Financial Support Adds to Egypt's Currency Woes," Arab Gulf States Institute in Washington, March 15. 2016; Elissa Miller, "Five Years On: Egypt's International Relations," Atlantic Council, January 25, 2016; Scott Anderson, "Fractured Lands: How the Arab World Came Apart," *New York Times,* August 14, 2016.

53. Nour Youssef and Diaa Hadid, "'We Don't Owe Anyone': Egypt Jousts with Its Chief Benefactor, Saudi Arabia," *New York Times,* November 1, 2016; Anne Barnard, "Egypt and Turkey Soften Positions on Syria, Benefiting Assad," *New York Times,* December 2, 2016; Steven A. Cook, "Egypt's Nightmare," Council on Foreign Relations, November–December 2016.

54. Muhammad Sahimi, "Iran's Incredible Shrinking Ayatollah," *National Interest,* May 8, 2016, www.nationalinterest.org.

55. Samia Nakhoul, "Iran Moves from Pariah State to Regional Power," Reuters, January 17, 2016.

56. Vali Nasr, *The Shia Revival: How Conflicts Within Islam Will Shape the Future* (New York: Norton, 2006), pp. 241–250.

57. "Economic Squeeze Made Iran Accept Peace," United Press International, July 19, 1995.

58. "Iraq: What Iran and Syria Want," BBC News, November 13, 2006.

59. John Simpson, "Iran's Growing Regional Influence," BBC News, September 20, 2006.

60. Ben Hubbard, "Saudi Arabia Cuts Ties with Iran Amid Fallout from Cleric's Execution," *New York Times,* January 3, 2016.

61. David E. Sanger, "Iran Complies with Nuclear Deal; Sanctions Are Lifted," *New York Times,* January 16, 2016.

62. Elaine Sciolino, "Iranian President Paints a Picture of Peace and Moderation," *New York Times,* September 22, 1998, p. A12.

63. "Walkout at U.N. as Ahmadinejad Speaks," *CNN News,* September 23, 2011, www.cnn.com.

64. Rick Gladstone, "Iranian's U.N. Speech Appears to Favor Engagement," *New York Times,* September 27, 2015.

65. Louis Charbonneau, "U.N. Committee Slams Iran over Human Rights Record," Reuters, November 18, 2010.

66. "Japan Defence Review Warns of China's Military Might," BBC News, December 17, 2010.

67. Golnar Motevalli, "China, Iran Agree to Expand Trade to $600 Billion in a Decade," *Bloomberg,* January 23, 2016.

68. Ibid.

69. Jethro Mullen, "China's Weapons Sales to Other Countries Are Soaring," *CNN News,* February 22, 2016; Megha Rajagopalan, "China's Weapons Exports Surge over Past Five Years: Report," Reuters, February 21, 2016.

70. "Responsible China?," *Washington Post,* September 6, 2006, p. A14.

71. Fred Pleitgen, Richard Roth, and Angela Dewan, "Syria War: Russia, China Vote Against Aleppo Ceasefire," *CNN News,* December 5, 2016.

72. J. Mohan Malik, "Security Council Reform: China Signals Its Veto," *World Policy Journal* (Spring 2005), pp. 20–21.

73. Coral Davenport, "At U.N. Meeting, Diplomats Worry Trump Could Cripple Climate Pact," *New York Times,* November 15, 2016.

74. Ibid.

75. "Indonesia's Place in the Global Jungle," *The Economist,* March 31, 2010.

76. Heru Prama Yuda, "US-ASEAN Summit: Key Points for President Jokowi," *Jakarta Post,* February 9, 2016, www.thejarkartapost.com.

77. Eveline Danubrata, "Amid South China Sea Uncertainty, Indonesia Stages a Show of Force," Reuters, October 6, 2016.

78. Ibid.

79. Marwaan Macan-Markar, "Indonesia: Saying No, Thank You to IMF Loans," Inter-Press Service, November 26, 2008.

80. Peter Alford, "Fifteen Years After Humiliation, Indonesia Turns the Tables on the IMF," *The Australian,* July 11, 2012, www.theaustraliancom.au.

81. Slobodan Lekic, "Suharto Avoids International Tribunal," Associated Press, March 28, 2006.

82. "West Papua Liberation Movement Lobbies at the UN," *Radio New Zealand,* December 9, 2016, www.radionz.co.nz.

83. "Indonesia's Place in the Global Jungle," *The Economist,* March 31, 2010.

Chapter 19

Global South Perspectives on the United States

We really want the U.S., naturally. It has a huge role, a huge weight.
— *Salaheddine Mezouar, foreign minister of Morocco, at the annual
United Nations summit on climate change and global warming*[1]

America's unipolar moment has passed.
— The Economist *on United Nations reform*[2]

The Lone Superpower: The Limits of Strength

Leaders are noticed. As the leading military and political power in the world, the United States possesses both great influence and great responsibility. In responding to and solving global problems, the United States plays a critical role, but certainly not always a benign one. Many American students are surprised to hear that the United States is viewed with both respect and contempt beyond its borders. Some have a difficult time seeing that actions of the United States are viewed as threatening to many, because Americans tend to believe that their actions are taken in the name of some larger, more noble cause. Yet it is important to remember that others take actions, some of which we deem irresponsible or even reprehensible, with seemingly good motivations as well.

In the early decades of the twenty-first century, the United States stands as the world's strongest country, the world's lone superpower. Yet many are openly questioning the durability of this status. Whether or not it is technically accurate by definition, many view the United States as an empire—willing and able to exert influence beyond its borders. Sometimes this happens in the pursuit of a worthy goal. Other times, US actions have been less noble. One particularly controversial example may help illustrate this dilemma. Since the early 1950s, US presidents have intermittently considered some form of missile defense as a way to protect the United States and some of its allies from attack, including, by the 1980s, investigation of the feasibility of a space-based system of deterrence. Yet this pursuit, which requires the United States to break hard-won arms accords, is viewed by

other states as a unilateral expansion of already dominant US capability, since it would neutralize others' ability to respond defensively to a US attack. Initiatives to extend the military arms race into outer space, including space-based lasers and interceptors, add to this perception.

Another example can be found in US trade laws. The US embargo against Cuba, in place since 1962, was the most enduring trade limitation in modern history, despite the fact that it has very little support beyond Washington. Every year since 1991, the General Assembly of the United Nations has overwhelmingly passed a nonbinding resolution condemning the embargo, with two and sometimes three countries siding with the United States on the issue. The US perspective has been that the United States will trade with Cuba after it shows signs of political reform. As an editorial in *Newsweek* argued, "The embargo is the perfect example used by anti-Americans everywhere to expose the hypocrisy of a superpower that punishes a small island while cozying to dictators elsewhere."[3] Even as President Obama signed an executive order lifting many of the trade limits on Cuba (as part of the normalization of US-Cuba ties that began in 2014), restrictions remain in place (and there is a real possibility that President Trump may roll back many of Obama's executive actions). In 2016, the United States abstained from the UN vote condemning the embargo (Israel joined as the only other abstention), to great applause from the world body.[4] Yet, as the US embargo can only be rescinded by Congress, and both President Trump and many leading Republicans staunchly oppose such steps, Obama's actions may have been a temporary reprieve.

The United States has also staked out the position that countries should not do business with known terrorists, a contention voiced more strongly after the events of September 11, 2001. The perspective beyond US borders, though, is that the United States does not have the authority to tell other countries with whom they should be conducting business. US sanctions against Iran, meant to strengthen Security Council sanctions in 2010, received mixed responses around the world (and many of these sanctions remained in place after the lifting of UN sanctions in January 2016). India's secretary of foreign affairs stated that "unilateral sanctions recently imposed by individual countries [could] have a direct and adverse impact on Indian companies, and, more importantly, on our energy security."[5] China and Russia expressed similar concerns, primarily in response to business interests. These actions invite claims from countries that the United States is invoking extraterritoriality, or the attempt to impose one's rules and laws outside of one's own sovereign territory.

The criticism expands well beyond US trade interests. The US treatment of detainees at the Guantanamo Bay naval base has evoked similar calls. This prison camp, built on contested US territory in Cuba, began detaining alleged terrorists in 2002, riling human rights activists around the world and propelling many of those held into legal limbo—the names and nationalities of the detainees were not released until 2006, after a Freedom of Information Act request was filed by media outlets. Nearly five years after the camp opened, after the US Supreme Court branded the detention unconstitutional, the George W. Bush administration reversed its previous decision that, because of the unique characteristics of the US war on terrorism, these individuals were ineligible for protection under the Geneva Conventions. When pictures surfaced documenting overt abuse of prisoners at the hands of US soldiers at Abu Ghraib prison in Baghdad, and gruesome accounts of the killing

of twenty-four Iraqi civilians in Haditha in retaliation for a roadside bomb that killed one Marine, many wondered aloud whether these scandals were representative of a larger US approach, rather than isolated incidents. Obama's record on Guantanamo was not much better. Despite the executive order (issued on his second day in office) to shut down the detention camp within one year, he left office in 2017 with seventy-six prisoners in legal limbo: unable to be returned home and barred (by Congress) from being taken to the United States for trial. As a candidate, Donald Trump vowed to expand the facility, stating, "we're gonna load it up," possibly even detaining American citizens accused of terrorism (even though such a move would violate current US law).[6] To many outside of the United States, these pledges sound like forms of vigilante justice.

Some perceive the United States as a government that abides by laws only when it is useful, while attempting to force others to follow US laws and policies, even in foreign countries. In this sense, many countries of the world believe that the United States holds an exceptionalist view of its place in the world. The examples are plentiful. The United States condemned the Iraqi invasion of Kuwait in 1990, yet the same US leaders had ordered the invasion of Panama in 1989 in order to capture President Manuel Noriega and try him for criminal drug operations in the United States. The United States long produced the most greenhouse emissions of any other country in the world (surpassed by China in 2006), yet US presidents have sought exceptions from international environmental treaties designed to combat these ills. The lack of US support for the International Criminal Court (ICC), discussed in Chapter 16, including the demand that US military personnel be exempt from its jurisdiction, is yet another case in point. Even though the United States had won an agreement on amendments to protect Americans from frivolous suits, Washington suspended military assistance to thirty-five countries for failing to immunize Americans from prosecution by the ICC.[7] US leaders rejected international protocols on germ warfare and demanded amendments to an accord on the illegal sale of small arms. Even if these policies do not convey a growing sense of isolationism, as some claim, there has been a clear increase in US unilateralism—even prior to the globally unpopular Iraq War.

There are still other examples. President Bill Clinton, facing pressure from the Pentagon, refused to sign the Ottawa Treaty in 1997, which outlaws landmines, because an exception for the Korean peninsula was not granted. In 1999 the US Senate rejected the Nuclear Test Ban Treaty because—even though US leaders have made clear that they would like the rest of the world to halt weapons development—they don't want to have their own hands tied. On the grounds that outsiders would be able to call for inspections in an imperfect system, President George W. Bush also discarded the biological weapons draft protocol from 1972 (which 143 countries, including the United States, had ratified), and opposed international efforts to limit the trade in small arms. At the same time that pressure was building on Iran, which as a signatory to the Nuclear Non-Proliferation Treaty (NPT) was not permitted to develop nuclear energy programs, the United States crafted a sweetheart deal to provide nuclear technology to India, which is not party to the NPT and therefore, per international agreements, cannot legitimately receive this technology. It is more difficult to lead by example if one keeps breaking the rules, and others are bound to challenge this power. The hypocrisy of US actions becomes glaring in the eyes of

some, as a Chinese diplomat shared: "When you tell us that we support a dictatorship in Sudan to have access to its oil, what I want to say is, 'And how is that different from your support of a medieval monarchy in Saudi Arabia?'"[8]

The United States also faces criticism for failing to provide support to international movements promoting the same rights and privileges that Americans espouse the world over, including women's rights and the rights of persons with disabilities. In 2012, the US Senate failed (by six votes) to ratify the Convention on the Rights of Persons with Disabilities, which has been in effect since 2008, even though it was modeled after the Americans with Disabilities Act and enjoyed largely bipartisan support.[9] Also, as discussed in Chapter 16, the United States is the only industrialized country not to have ratified the Convention on the Elimination of All Forms of Discrimination Against Women (CEDAW). Ratification of the convention, which the US delegation helped draft in 1979, has been caught up in domestic politics and concern by some critics that UN committee members would have authority over private decisions and US laws (which they would not, due to the principle of sovereignty). The US Senate Foreign Relations Committee even supported ratification of the convention in 2002, but the full measure, which is vehemently opposed by the pro-life lobby, was never introduced to the full Senate for a vote. This has not only harmed the credibility of the United States in some circles, but it has been used by others to deny women's rights in other countries as well. As one Afghani activist testified before the US Senate Judiciary Committee, "Even in Afghanistan . . . conservative elements use this [US failure to ratify] to attack women's rights defenders. They say that if the United States believes in women's rights as a universal right, why haven't they signed on to CEDAW?"[10]

Additionally, the United States often withholds support for international organizations that conduct work seen as being in opposition to the policy goals of some interest groups in the country—even if the action is perfectly legal in other societies of the world. One clear example of this is the US condemnation of organizations that provide family-planning or abortion services. US presidents Ronald Reagan, George H. W. Bush, and George W. Bush each denied funding to any agency that views abortion as a policy option, describing themselves as taking a moral stance on such "right to life" issues. Meanwhile, the same leaders sided with businesses to oppose international efforts to eliminate child labor. The United States refuses to sign treaties prohibiting the use of child soldiers, and, until the US Supreme Court ruled the practice unconstitutional in 2005, remained one of the few countries in the world that executed juveniles. To many, the contradiction is glaring.

As the world's leading power, the United States faces a paradox: it is often expected to respond, even when its leaders and citizens do not want to. In part this is due to a history of involvement (sometimes welcomed, sometimes not), and in part this is due to the role of being perceived as the leading voice on core issues. A paradox of power is that the lack of response—as we have seen in the muted engagement with many of the Arab Spring transitions, for example—can sometimes speak more loudly than coordinated engagement. In this view, Obama's attempts to decrease the US footprint in the Middle East after 2012 can be perceived as problematic as Bush's unilateral moves after September 11. As one observer put it, the "notion of neutrality, for a country as powerful as the United States, is illusory."[11]

Shifting from Anti-Americanism to "Post-Americanism"?

Following the events of September 11, 2001, it became common to discuss the ways the world had permanently changed. While it certainly is true that few Americans will view themselves or their personal safety in the same way for a very long time, many voices in the global south argued that it wasn't the world, but rather the United States and its self-image that have been changed by those tragic events. Although both the method and the magnitude of the actions on that day shocked many, much of the world has lived for a long time in fear of violence and terrorism.

The drop in sentiment toward the US government came hard and fast. In the weeks following September 11, the Bush administration crafted a wide-reaching coalition of support, uniting many countries of the world, Western and non-Western alike, against terrorism. Indeed, few countries explicitly condemned the US- and British-led strikes on Afghanistan, which began approximately one month after the attacks on the United States. Yet after the war was launched, some expressed apprehension over the emergence of the Bush Doctrine, which divided the world neatly in two: linking any country that "supports" terrorists to be on the same playing field as terrorists themselves.[12] While it may be temptingly simple to view the world in such stark terms, reality is rarely that clean-cut, as is evident in the case studies presented in this volume. In their efforts to support the US coalition in the war in Afghanistan, many countries, especially Pakistan, Turkey, and Indonesia, invited intense opposition among their own populations.

The tone was ratcheted up another notch when preemptive action—acting on the threat of an attack—became a principal component of Bush's foreign policy. President Bush then labeled Iran, Iraq, and North Korea as part of an "Axis of Evil" in his 2002 State of the Union address. This call provoked angry responses not only from these countries, but from others as well, including US allies in Europe and countries that supported the US war on terrorism.[13] It was perceived particularly offensively within Iran, the country that had, just weeks before Bush's speech before both houses of the US Congress, been so integral in helping the United States topple the Taliban in Afghanistan (by mediating between the United States and the Northern Alliance).[14]

Such actions have contributed to much of the animosity, mistrust, and ill will the United States encounters worldwide. Sometimes this hostility is manifested in condemnations of US actions, or the exclusion of the United States from international bodies. In 2001, for example, the United States for the first time failed to be reelected to a seat on the UN Human Rights Commission (which former first lady Eleanor Roosevelt helped create in the late 1940s). Shortly thereafter, the United States lost its seat on the UN's International Narcotics Control Board—the primary drug enforcement commission in the United Nations system. Some interpreted the Narcotics Board vote to be an expression of dissension against US drug control policies. After these actions, both of which resulted from secret ballots, some countries' leaders expressed a sense of justice. It is important to emphasize that it was not only countries from the global south that voted the United States out of these seats: negative votes included US allies in the Western, developed world. On the Human Rights Commission, country representatives expressed dissension related to US votes on issues discussed throughout this book.

The vocal criticisms of the United States became deafening after the US-led invasion of Iraq in 2003. The war had been justified in large part by US vice president Dick Cheney's so-called 1 percent doctrine—if there were even a 1 percent chance of terrorists acquiring weapons of mass destruction, the United States would be justified to act preemptively. This didn't sit well with the world, even with many US allies. Assisted by the so-called coalition of the willing, which included only a fraction of the world's states that had supported the 1990 invasion, this action was explicitly taken without UN approval because of the lack of support from even US allies within the Security Council's veto-wielding countries (notably France). Bush and the leading voices within his administration became wildly unpopular around the world, and the former president was accused of doing more harm to America's image and its global relations than any other US president in recent history.[15]

What—if anything—changed during President Obama's tenure? Facing intense criticism about a lackluster foreign policy approach that seemed to be accomplishing little, then–secretary of state Hillary Clinton proposed a "new moment" in US foreign policy, highlighting the essential nature of US leadership at the same time that she envisioned new and different ways of leadership.[16] Early on, President Obama sketched out a very ambitious foreign policy agenda, including eliminating nuclear weapons and elevating the concern about climate change to a top priority. When the dust on his two-term presidency settles, though, there are significant foreign policy aims that were never accomplished, including the closing of Guantanamo Bay, as well as a successful conclusion to the war in Afghanistan (the official war ended in 2014, but the country remains mired in conflict in which the US remains heavily involved).

Shortly after Barack Obama's election, pollsters spoke of a perceived "Obama effect," or a boost in pro-American sentiment, during his administration. It is true that there were noticeable gains in positive public opinion toward the United States, as measured by the annual polling by the Pew Global Attitudes Project. President Obama received more popular ratings in countries around the world than he does in the United States, and views of the United States, which "improved markedly" after Obama's inauguration in 2009, remained much more positive than they were during the George W. Bush years.[17] President Obama was awarded the Nobel Peace Prize in 2009 (even though he had not even been in office nine months)—in a decision that was not only an admitted surprise to him, but viewed as a mistake, even to many of the president's supporters. The secretary of the Nobel Peace Prize committee even later viewed the decision with regret.[18] But in many ways, this decision captured the outsized hope that many projected onto the new face of the world's lone superpower.

These hopes were at least partially dashed as, despite his messianic campaign rhetoric, Obama governed from a largely realist stance, crafting the so-called surge of American troop deployment in Iraq, averting any impactful support for Syrian rebels against President Bashar al-Assad, and approving a massive operation of drones around the world. The drone program—which the Obama administration did not even publicly acknowledge until 2013—invited significant moral, legal, and even strategic questioning, especially as its application stretched from Pakistan, Afghanistan, Yemen, and Libya into Somalia and elsewhere, with widespread civilian casualties and questionable intelligence gains.[19] Even the signing of the 2015 Paris Agreement on Climate Change, viewed by some as the "trophy" of Obama's second term as president, was seen as "too little" from around the world community,

and "too much" from within the United States.[20] Opinion polls suggest the lack of clear consensus about the trajectory of US power during the Obama years, even if it is Americans, more so than citizens in other countries around the world, who perceive the power of their country to be in decline.[21]

Was there any sort of Obama Doctrine, along the lines of the doctrines of so many other presidents? This has been an issue of great debate. Clearly, President Obama was much less comfortable with intervention than former presidents, and attempted to forge multilateral responses to the degree possible. Analysts can disagree on the degree to which this has been successful, but it was an enduring theme of Obama's policy responses. Asked once to define his approach, the president stated that the United States "remains the most powerful, wealthiest nation on Earth, but we're only one nation, and . . . problems that we confront, whether it's drug cartels, climate change, terrorism, you name it, can't be solved just by one country."[22] President Obama moved far away from the "democracy promotion" and interventionist agenda of his predecessor, to the praise—and disdain—of many. Human rights seemed to fall by the wayside, especially when the United States failed to characterize the Egyptian military's overthrow of democratically elected President Morsi as a coup in 2013. Even after Human Rights Watch called it the "worst mass killing in modern Egyptian history," the president (and Congress) continued to provide substantial military aid to Cairo, despite the legal obligation to suspend such aid in the event of a coup.[23] Some derisively framed the Obama Doctrine—especially after the formal withdrawal of US forces in Iraq—as "American retreat."[24]

As this book goes to press, the Donald Trump administration is in its early stages, and many around the world are expressing concern about the talk of isolationism that animated much of the 2016 US presidential election. As candidate Trump promised to end US support for the Paris Agreement on Climate Change, the executive director of the Sierra Club stated that "Donald Trump has the unflattering distinction of being the only head of state in the entire world to reject the scientific consensus that mankind is driving climate change."[25] In this particular area, world leaders express a surprising amount of unity in stating that the agreement will go forward—with or without the United States.[26]

It is too early to know how President Trump's foreign policies will vary from candidate Trump's statements, and we all know that rhetoric during a campaign (especially one as divisive as the 2016 US presidential election) can vary quite a bit from policy implemented in office. But much of the world—especially the global south—has expressed some level of concern about what will happen if President Trump carries out many of his stated goals captured in his proposed foreign policy emphasis on "America First." Trump has stated that he will "no longer surrender this country or its people to the false song of globalism."[27] To some around the global south, the possibility that the United States will take a strongly isolationist turn is unwelcome at best, and dangerous at worst. Candidate Trump often lambasted current US foreign policy for promoting "raw deals" in our relations with other countries, allies and foes alike. His comments on climate change (referring to it as a "hoax"), insistence that he will "build a wall" to limit illegal migration from Mexico (and that the Mexican government will pay for it), as well as his calls to restart the use of waterboarding (and "much worse") for interrogation of extremists, set off alarm bells for many.[28]

Twenty years ago, journalist Fareed Zakaria claimed that we were moving into a "post-American world." It was his contention that for the first time in living memory, the charge was not being led by the United States, and that the world was experiencing "tectonic power shifts" as new powers arose.[29] While the United States maintains its dominance in the areas of military and politics, power is shifting in other dimensions, including industrial, financial, social, and cultural power. Pundits commenting on the strengths of the United States point to its status as a flexible society, open to competing views and welcoming of other peoples and cultures.[30] Various crises facing the United States and the global community—how to respond to migration, climate change, extremism, and more—seem to be pushing some to turn inward, in the direction of less rather than more engagement. Some believe focusing on "America First" will allow the United States to take care of its own, unencumbered by messy commitments and diversions on the world stage. They contend that the United States should be "out of the world order business" and that it is high time to behave like a "normal" rather than an "abnormally unselfish" nation that sometimes works to the benefit of others more than itself.[31]

Supporters of this view believe that the "comforting story" of the United States as the sole superpower is an "outdated myth," and that only with its relative decline can we begin to create something akin to a truly international order, rather than one reliant on the leadership of a single country.[32] Yet others decry the decline of US leadership, believing that this path makes the United States (and other countries) more vulnerable to problems, even if they take time to fester. As this book goes to press, it is not yet clear whether President Trump will follow through on his campaign pledges to conduct mass deportations, curtail Muslim immigration or even travel to the United States, ratchet up the war on terror, increase tariffs on imports from targeted countries, or withdraw from long-standing alliances. The new president promises a whirlwind of change. America is divided between those who are excited by that prospect—and those who are frightened by it.

Meanwhile, the world, including the global south, is watching this unfold and keenly interested in whether this most unorthodox of leaders will usher in the transformation he has promised. In the coming months and years we are likely to hear a cacophony of voices from outside the United States reacting to America's own democratically elected regime change. We encourage you to hear these voices and approach each of these perspectives critically—to try to understand the sources of the views expressed. One does not need to agree with an opinion in order to try to understand it, and most perceptions are based on a combination of facts and fears. It is not un-American to attempt to see the world through others' eyes. In fact, such an exercise is likely to increase a commitment to the ideals upon which the United States was founded and must continue to foster.

Notes

1. Quoted in Coral Davenport, "At U.N. Meeting, Diplomats Worry Trump Could Cripple Climate Pact," *New York Times,* November 15, 2016.

2. "Thinking the UNthinkable," *The Economist,* November 13, 2010.

3. Moises Naim, "The Havana Obsession: Why All Eyes Are on a Bankrupt Island," *Newsweek,* June 12, 2009.

4. Somini Sengupta and Rick Gladstone, "U.S. Abstains in U.N. Vote Condemning Cuba Embargo," *New York Times,* October 26, 2016.

Figure 19.1   Could the Next Superpower Come from the Global South?

As history has shown us, a single country cannot remain the preeminent power forever. Empires based in Greece, Rome, Turkey, and China once ruled large regions of the world, seemingly unchallenged. Increasingly it looks as though the next major power could come from the global south. Many point to the People's Republic of China as the rising superpower for the twenty-first century.

To many, China's outsized role in world affairs is not surprising. China's self-perception and role started to shift in 2008, and gained momentum as it came through the Great Recession relatively unscathed. If China is successful in its reemergence as a global superpower, it would be the first nation in history to have gone into decline after a period of greatness, only to recover its former glory.[a]

India, with its impressive economic growth, diplomatic influence, and dominant regional presence, is also making a play. It appears to be emerging from its nonalignment to become a "swing state" in the global balance of power—

developing strong partnerships throughout Asia and the Middle East, and with Western powers as well. Prior to its recession and political turmoil in 2015 and 2016, Brazil was included in this club as well. Even Jacques Martin, who has strongly argued that China will dominate the next century, makes room for other players, stating, "If the twentieth-century world was shaped by the developed countries, then that of the twenty-first century is likely to be molded by the developing countries, especially the largest ones."[b] "Superpower" or not, it seems clear that power in the twenty-first-century world is becoming dispersed, rather than concentrated in one country, region, or worldview.

Notes: a. Geoffrey Murray, *China: The Next Superpower—Dilemmas in Change and Continuity* (New York: St. Martin's, 1998).

b. Jacques Martin, *When China Rules the World: The End of the Western World and the Birth of a New Global Order* (New York: Penguin, 2009), p. 428.

5. Quoted in Kim Ghattas, "US Gets Serious on Iran Sanctions," BBC News, August 3, 2010.

6. Connie Bruck, "Why Obama Has Failed to Close Guantánamo," *New Yorker,* August 1, 2016; David Welna, "Trump Has Vowed to Fill Guantanamo with 'Some Bad Dudes'—but Who?," National Public Radio, *All Things Considered,* November 14, 2016.

7. Karl E. Meyer, "America Unlimited: The Radical Sources of the Bush Doctrine," *World Policy Journal* (Spring 2004), p. 5; "The International Criminal Court: For Us or Against Us?," *The Economist,* November 22, 2003, p. 27.

8. Quoted in Fareed Zakaria, *The Post-American World* (New York: Norton, 2008), p. 35.

9. Brian Montopoli, "U.N. Treaty on Disabilities Falls Short in Senate," *CBS News,* December 4, 2012.

10. Quoted in Waxhma Frogh, "CEDAW Ratification Would Be a Triumph for Afghan Women," *The Hill,* November 17, 2010. (Afghanistan ratified CEDAW in 2003 and Qatar became the most recent state to ratify in 2009.)

11. Shadi Hamid, "Islamism, the Arab Spring, and the Failure of America's Do-Nothing Policy in the Middle East," *The Atlantic,* October 9, 2015.

12. It has not been unusual for US presidents and other powerful members of their administrations to announce paradigms for US foreign policy. In the 1820s, James Monroe argued (in what later became known as the Monroe Doctrine) that the United States should limit European expansion into the Western Hemisphere, straining relations with Europe, and announced the United States as the "protector" of the Americas. The Truman Doctrine was used throughout the Cold War to contain totalitarian, namely, communist regimes. In the 1980s, Ronald Reagan challenged the legitimacy of nondemocratic, especially communist regimes and proclaimed both the right and the responsibility of the United States to provide assistance to movements that challenge them. The Powell Doctrine (named for former chairman of the Joint

Chiefs of Staff and former secretary of state Colin Powell) stated that US troops should enter battle only with decisive force and clear objectives (it was actually an idea promoted by Secretary of Defense Casper Weinberger). We discussed the Clinton Doctrine in Chapter 17, namely, the justification of the right to intervene in another state's sovereign affairs when there are gross violations of human rights.

13. "China Berates Bush for 'Axis of Evil,'" *Reuters World Report,* January 31, 2002; Jefferson Morley, "'Axis of Evil' Worries Friends and Foes Alike," *Washington Post,* February 1, 2002; Thomas E. Ricks, "European Security Leaders Alarmed by Bush's Stance: US Officials in Munich Stress Urgency of Anti-Terror Initiative," *Washington Post,* February 3, 2002; Thomas L. Friedman, "Crazier Than Thou," *New York Times,* February 13, 2002.

14. See Ray Takeyh, *Hidden Iran: Paradox and Power in the Islamic Republic* (New York: Times Books/Holt, 2006), esp. pp. 117–130.

15. Molly Moore and Peter Finn, "Around the Globe, Relief over U.S. Vote," *Washington Post,* November 10, 2006, p. A6.

16. Cited in Glen Kessler, "Clinton Declares 'New Moment' in U.S. Foreign Policy in Speech," *Washington Post,* September 9, 2010.

17. Richard Wike and Jacob Poushter, "As Obama Years Draw to Close, President and U.S. Seen Favorably in Europe and Asia," Pew Global Attitudes Project, June 29, 2016; "Obama More Popular Abroad Than at Home, Global Image of U.S. Continues to Benefit," Pew Global Attitudes Project, June 17, 2010.

18. "Nobel Secretary Regrets Obama Peace Prize," BBC News, September 17, 2015.

19. James Downie, "Obama's Drone War Is a Shameful Part of His Legacy," *Washington Post,* May 5, 2016; "Global Opposition to U.S. Surveillance and Drones but Limited Harm to America's Image," Pew Global Attitudes Project, July 14, 2014; Wike and Poushter, "As Obama Years Draw to Close."

20. Jonathan Rauch, "What Obama Got Right," *The Atlantic,* December 2016.

21. Wike and Poushter, "As Obama Years Draw to Close."

22. Stephen F. Hayes, "Thoughts on an 'Obama Doctrine,'" *Weekly Standard,* December 10, 2009.

23. Hamid, "Islamism, the Arab Spring, and the Failure."

24. Frederick W. Kagan and Kimberly Kagan, "Retreating with Our Heads Held High," *Weekly Standard,* October 21, 2011, www.weeklystandard.com.

25. Michael Brune, executive director of the Sierra Club, quoted in Robinson Meyer, "What President Trump Will Mean for Earth's Climate," *The Atlantic,* November 9, 2016, www.theatlantic.com.

26. Davenport, "At U.N. Meeting, Diplomats Worry."

27. "The New Nationalism," *The Economist,* November 19, 2016.

28. Max Boot, "Trump's 'America First' Is the Twilight of American Exceptionalism," *Foreign Policy,* November 22, 2016.

29. Fareed Zakaria, "Why Do They Hate Us? The Politics of Rage," *Newsweek,* October 15, 2001.

30. See Zakaria, *The Post-American World,* esp. chap. 15; James Fallows, *Postcards from Tomorrow Square* (New York: Vintage, 2008), esp. chap. 7.

31. Robert Kagan, "Trump Marks the End of America as World's 'Indispensable Nation,'" *Financial Times,* November 19, 2016.

32. Zachary Karabell, "The Upside of a 'De-Americanized' World," *The Atlantic,* October 17, 2013.

Chapter 20

Linking
Concepts and Cases

In the preceding chapter we discussed how countries throughout the global south have attempted to deal with the United States as a superpower. We focused on how the Obama administration had the potential to change global south views of the United States. Has Obama been able to significantly alter US relations with the global south generally, but in particular with our cases? Would you characterize the foreign policy of the Obama administration (compared to that of his predecessors) as one of "change"—or continuity? What is the likely future trajectory for bilateral ties with these countries, especially under the Trump administration? Which issues are more or less likely to be important in the next five to ten years?

Case Study: Mexico

"Poor Mexico. Poor United States. So far from God. So near to each other."[1] This expresses the ambivalence many Mexicans have about living next door to the United States, known throughout Latin America as "the colossus of the North." This sense only grew during the 2016 presidential elections in the United States, as many Mexicans were alarmed by Republican nominee Donald Trump's characterization of Mexicans and his statements in regard to immigration and trade. As you may recall, building a wall (and making Mexico pay for it) was a hallmark of the Trump campaign. Former president Fox punched back, saying that Trump epitomized the ugly American, the gringo hated around the world.[2] He joined many Mexicans who were worried about what a Trump presidency could mean for Mexico and US-Mexican relations. Certainly this kind of talk has stirred Mexican nationalism. But Mexico having a love-hate relationship with the United States is nothing new. As one analyst put it, this proximity means that Mexico and the United States are prisoners of each other's problems.[3]

The Mexico-US relationship is one of interdependence, yet it is not and has never been one of equal dependence. Since the North American Free Trade Agreement (NAFTA) was instituted in 1994, cross-border trade between Mexico and the world's largest economy has boomed. From 1990 to 2015, US imports of Mexican goods rose by 882 percent and US exports to Mexico rose by more than 730 percent

in that same period.[4] Mexico depends on its neighbor to buy 80 percent of its exports, and the United States invests more there than any other country. Two-way trade between the two amounted to a whopping $531 billion in 2015.[5] But grievances in the United States around the loss of manufacturing jobs as corporations relocate to Mexico and pay workers a fifth of what they would be paid in America are what got President Trump elected. And he has promised to rewrite or scrap NAFTA, regardless of the fact that Mexico is the second biggest consumer of US exports and, according to the US Commerce Department, over 1 million US jobs depended on sales to Mexican consumers as of 2014.[6]

Although during the Obama years the US-Mexico relationship was relatively harmonious, for Mexico engaging the United States often means discussing problems that have been festering for years. In the past, too often the United States treated Mexico as a source of its problems and never considered how it might be contributing to troubles in Mexico. As at least one Mexican president has pointed out, Mexico has the misfortune of living next door to the world's biggest drug addict. Americans, who compose 5 percent of the world's population, constitute 30 percent of the world demand for illegal drugs—and spend an estimated $100 million a year on them.[7] From Mexico's perspective, it helped that President Obama admitted that the United States shared in the responsibility for the drug violence in Mexico. It is also in the interests of the United States to strengthen law enforcement in the country that supplies its habit. For example, the Obama administration also strengthened efforts at demand reduction (i.e., drug education and treatment programs) in the United States. It also expanded the George W. Bush–era military assistance provided through the Mérida Initiative, which allocated more than $2.5 billion between 2008 and 2015 to help in Mexico's drug war.[8] However, some have criticized the United States for continuing to work closely with the Mexican military and provide it with aid despite its human rights record. A law known as the Leahy amendment bars the United States from providing training or equipment to foreign troops who commit gross human rights violations.[9] From Mexico's standpoint, the disbursement of these funds has come too slowly and the United States has not made enough progress on curtailing the shipment of weapons (particularly the semiautomatic assault rifles used in drug violence) from the United States to Mexico. According to the US Department of Justice, approximately 70 percent of the guns used by Mexican traffickers originate in the United States.[10]

Another tie that binds the United States and Mexico is migration. As of 2014, Mexicans composed about half of the estimated 11 million unauthorized immigrants living in the United States. In recent years the number of people entering the United States illegally has fallen, and more Mexicans have been returning to Mexico than migrating to the United States.[11] Yet President Trump conveyed the views of many on the northern side of the border when he attributed the loss of jobs and rising crime rates to illegal immigration. Mexican presidents are concerned as well, about the increasing dangers faced by Mexicans seeking work in the United States. They have long sought to make it easier for Mexicans living illegally in the United States to obtain temporary legal work and to extend to them protections that they do not currently enjoy.[12] Nearly two decades later, this issue has not been resolved.

In effect, for citizens of Mexico and the United States, the immigration problem remains extremely divisive. Many Mexicans expected that Obama's presidency

would usher in the long-awaited immigration reform. Without support in Congress, that proved an impossibility. Obama did take executive actions to protect people brought to the United States illegally as children and grant a reprieve to parents of people who are American citizens or lawful permanent residents, but he also deported record numbers of people living in the United States illegally—so many so that he became known as "the deporter-in-chief."[13] It is hard to predict whether President Trump will take as hard a line on Mexico as he did in the campaign, but he was elected promising to roll back Obama's policies and mass deportations.

If President Trump makes good on his pledges to renegotiate NAFTA, deport migrants, and tax remittances to build a wall between the United States and Mexico, Mexico will go into severe economic shock, which will have political reverberations in Mexico—and the United States.[14] First of all, it is important for Americans to understand that although there is little Mexico can do to pressure the United States, it is very much in the interests of the United States for democracy to work in Mexico. However, improving the security situation of its neighbor will mean dealing with a number of facets of their relationship simultaneously. It will be impossible to make progress in curtailing drug violence without also dealing with trade and immigration.[15] This complicates the task, and agreement between these two democratic states is likely to become more difficult than it has been in the past, because a democratic Mexico means that the Mexican president is also constrained by his own constituency.[16] It is important to remember that Mexico's president cannot appear to be a "yes man" to the United States. From Mexico's perspective, the United States must accept and understand this.

Case Study: Peru

In many ways Peru is a pivotal country for the United States. However, the Peru-US relationship has had its ups and downs, and at times that relationship has been strained. Since the mid-nineteenth-century guano boom, the United States has had significant economic interests in Peru. The United States and Peru are strong allies and work cooperatively in a variety of areas, most notably counternarcotics. They also are trading partners; the United States is one of Peru's top customers (along with China); they have been bound together by the US-Peru Trade Promotion Agreement, as well as several multilateral agreements, which until recently included the Trans-Pacific Partnership.[17] Clearly, Peru's government, which is very supportive of free trade, is concerned about what will happen to its relations with a United States led by Donald Trump.

During the Cold War, Peru was viewed by the United States as a highly sensitive security zone. Since then, the country has been of particular importance to the United States as the Andes have become a major battlefield in the US war on drugs. For decades US forces have worked closely with local police in crop eradication and drug interdiction in Peru, Bolivia, and Ecuador. The war on drugs has been the centerpiece of US policy in the region and Peru has been a major recipient of US military assistance. Some economic aid was set aside for crop substitution and "alternative development," with the view that drug eradication was a development issue. However, the US "Andean strategy" aimed to cut off the cocaine trade at its source of supply using a military approach. For several years, it appeared that this strategy was working, as coca cultivation in Peru plummeted in the late 1990s.

Convinced that counternarcotics operations in the region could not continue without Alberto Fujimori's support, the United States overlooked the growing authoritarianism of his government. Humanitarian and drug-fighting assistance continued as the democracy eroded because the United States feared that the instability associated with the drug war in Colombia could spread to Peru. Although US military assistance was appropriated only to fight the drug war, some of this money was diverted by Peru for use in its war against the Shining Path (Sendero Luminoso) guerrillas, under the argument that the terrorists were playing a central part in the drug trade. Consequently, the United States became an important ally for the Peruvian government in its civil war.

It is interesting that even though they're not always recognized as such, drug cartels are criminal terrorist groups. And the war on terrorism and the war on drugs are a lot alike. In neither case is the United States likely ever to win a final victory, but the consequences of not dealing with these problems could be even worse than waging a war without end.[18] And in the Andes, there have long been connections between narcotrafficking and terrorism. At this point no one is saying that there is much of a chance of an attack on the United States from the region, and Peru's cartels are relatively peaceful, compared to Mexico's. There isn't anywhere near the kind of bloodletting that we've seen in Mexico, in part because the government hasn't gone after kingpins or adopted a Calderón-style war on drugs. In fact, the past two Peruvian presidents pardoned hundreds of drug traffickers. But between the drug business, illegal gold-mining, human trafficking, and the trade in other illicit goods, including timber and antiquities, there is a great deal of money to be made (most estimate $5 billion–$7 billion a year).[19] It can't help but fuel corruption.

Remember *plata o plomo* from Mexico? In Peru, because *plata* (silver) always works, *plomo* (lead) isn't needed. But that could change, things could escalate, and the combination of guerrillas and drug lords has the makings of plenty of instability.[20] Although most analysts discount the threat a newly reconstituted Shining Path poses for Peru, recent attacks suggest that Shining Path is regrouping (mostly with money from drug trafficking) and acting more like a cartel than a guerrilla movement. As of 2015, the United States was spending approximately $50 million a year on counternarcotics in Peru.[21] But Peru is no longer winning its war on drugs. In what some have described as the "balloon effect," as one drug producer gets squeezed, production shifts to another part of the region. It works like this: in the late 1990s, at the same time that there was a significant dip in coca production in Peru, there was a proportional increase in production in Colombia. Since then, eradication efforts have been more successful in Colombia—and thus coca production in Peru recovered and continued to rise. The two countries go back and forth, trading the title of world's top coca producer.[22] Although Peru reduced its coca crop in 2015, it was still producing record amounts of the stuff, worth more than $1 billion a year for Peru's cartels. No one knows exactly how much of the country has it under production, nor how much is cultivated, although it is estimated that 325 tons of cocaine is produced each year in Peru.[23]

We shouldn't be surprised by such inconsistencies, given that Peru's leaders are caught between two constituencies, the United States and their own citizens. The relatively leftist President Ollanta Humala (2011–2016) was concerned that forced eradication, which is highly controversial in Peru, would aggravate social unrest in

the regions where coca is produced. Coca farmers have violently resisted eradication efforts precisely in the remote areas of the country where Shining Path has held on. From the perspective of many Peruvians, who remember the bloody civil war not too long ago, this is a concern. When trying to understand why foreign leaders adopt seemingly erratic policies it is important to keep in mind that domestic considerations are paramount for democratically elected governments, which are accountable to their people. Particularly when it comes to counternarcotics policy in Peru, the United States needs to remember that it's not dealing with a dictatorship, rethink its strategy, and adopt a more flexible approach.[24]

Case Study: Nigeria

Despite its enormous significance and potential, US presidents have generally shown little interest in Nigeria, or in Africa for that matter. Bill Clinton was the first US president to visit Nigeria since Jimmy Carter's trip in 1977, and Barack Obama never visited as president. And Trump rarely mentioned Africa, let alone Nigeria, in the campaign. Yet Nigeria is too big to ignore. Only South Africa rivals it as a regional superpower. Described as Africa's equivalent to Brazil, India, or Indonesia, Nigeria is vital to US interests for several reasons. It was until recently the largest oil exporter in Africa (as of mid-2016 it was second only to Angola), and the fourth largest foreign supplier of oil to the United States, exporting 1.6–2 million barrels a day.[25] In addition, with a population of approximately 174 million, it is not only the region's most populous country, but also the largest market in sub-Saharan Africa, full of tremendous trade opportunities. One in six Africans is Nigerian. And present-day Nigeria is part of the region that was home to the ancestors of most African Americans. Although Nigeria has historically been more closely tied to Britain (its former colonizer), Nigerian-US ties have grown closer as the United States seeks strategic partners in Africa.

However, until recently the US approach to Nigeria was described as paradoxical, alternating between close diplomacy and benign neglect.[26] The Nigeria-US relationship hit its lowest point after it became clear that the results of the presidential elections of 1993 would never be respected. However, despite claims by the United States about its concern for the democratic process, in the mid-1990s it was Nigeria's role in the international drug trade that provoked the most serious US response. Not a major producer of narcotics, Nigeria has become a leading hub in the transshipment of drugs from Latin America and Asia to the United States and Europe. In the 1990s, Nigerian "swallowers," or human couriers, were believed to be responsible for nearly 40 percent of the heroin entering the United States. In response, the United States placed sanctions on Sani Abacha's government—which in turn basically thumbed its nose at the world. Since 1999, however, Nigerian governments have cooperated with international efforts to curb the flow of drugs, and although the country is still a hub for their transit, it has been removed from the US government's list of major drug trafficking countries.[27]

Although the United States was not willing to call for a boycott of Nigerian oil or to press for democratic change as hard as some would have liked, US relations with Nigeria during the Abacha years were probably worse than with any other regional power, except for Iran. However, all that changed with the democratic transition in Nigeria in 1999. Nigeria has been brought back into the fold. Since

its return to democracy, economic ties between Nigeria and the United States have grown. Not only did the United States support the debt relief described in Chapter 9, but US companies such as Chevron and Exxon-Mobil are two of Nigeria's largest investors. US-Nigerian trade has grown steadily over the past decade, and total (two-way trade) was valued at $18 billion in 2013. Nigerian goods such as cocoa and cotton have duty-free access to US markets until 2025 under an extension of the African Growth and Opportunity Act (AGOA)—although the vast majority of what Nigeria sells in the United States under AGOA is oil and natural gas.[28] For many years the United States needed to diversify its oil dependence away from the Middle East, and its relationship with Nigeria and other African oil and gas producers grew. In 2010, for example, 40 percent of Nigeria's oil exports went to the United States. However, from 2010 to 2014, growing US oil production meant significantly reduced dependence on foreign oil, including US imports from Nigeria. By 2015 things had changed dramatically; the United States, which was once Nigeria's single largest oil buyer, was now producing most of the oil it consumed; only about 24 percent of the petroleum consumed by the United States was from foreign sources, the lowest amount since 1970. But that was beginning to turn around in 2016 as the oil glut (and sharp decline in oil prices) dampened the enthusiasm of US domestic producers. As a result, foreign imports began to rise again. In 2016, Nigeria's petroleum sales to the United States hit a three-year high, and Nigeria was desperate for the turnaround.[29]

Although Nigeria is less important to the United States than it used to be when it comes to oil, something that makes the US-Nigeria relationship more important than ever is security cooperation. Nigeria is West Africa's unrivaled military power. The United States wants a moderate ally in the region and recognizes that Nigeria is a regional powerhouse essential to any international effort to stabilize not only West Africa, but also the continent. Since the debacle in Somalia in 1993, the slogan "African solutions for African problems" has been popular in the West.[30] There are certain problems in Africa that the United States cannot ignore, and one convenient compromise is to promote Nigeria's role as a regional peacekeeper, since it is cheaper to train and equip Nigerian troops than it is to send US forces.

The United States is not only increasing its arms sales and military training in Nigeria, but also seeking to establish informal bases through which it could quickly deploy US troops and equipment to Africa. Nigeria is a member of the US-sponsored Trans-Sahara Counterterrorism Partnership, through which the United States provides assistance to African governments and in return seeks cooperation in the global war on terror. This program has been criticized by some who predict that it will be used by unpopular regimes against political opponents they choose to characterize as terrorists. Although energy security is clearly a critical US interest, and US military planners talked openly of a scenario of intervening in Nigeria to ensure the security of that country's oil fields, as of 2016 this had not come to pass. Instead, President Obama was a supporter of the amnesty deal described in Chapter 12.[31]

Despite its economic interests, it has been not the oil conflict in the southeast but the war in Nigeria's north that has captured US attention. Presidents Jonathan and Buhari have repeatedly asked the United States to send not only military advisers but also combat soldiers, perhaps special-forces troops to fight militant jihadists in Africa. The United States has trained and equipped Nigerian soldiers. It provided

$80 million in support of this cause in 2014. It also assists with surveillance of the group from Cameroon, where about 250 US service members are deployed. The United States also maintains a drone base in Chad. But closer cooperation between Nigeria and the United States has been limited. US officials were hesitant to share intelligence with Nigerian forces due to fears that the military had been infiltrated by Boko Haram. In addition, the United States had very real concerns about abuses committed by Nigerian security forces, as discussed in Chapter 12. The United States blocked the sale of US-made helicopters to Nigeria in 2014 due to these concerns, and for a while bypassed Nigeria to work directly with neighboring Cameroon, Chad, and Niger. This infuriated the Jonathan government, which accused the United States of hampering the war against Boko Haram. Relations between the United States and Nigeria cooled perceptibly but have repaired somewhat under President Buhari, due to his high-profile attempts to root out corruption in the ranks and cooperate with the multinational force.[32] But due to the military's continued poor human rights record, Obama chose not to lift the arms embargo. This is a message that the US president sent his counterpart in Nigeria: Nigeria needs to do better. Nigeria is important to the United States for a variety of reasons. Whether the next administration recognizes it, what happens in Nigeria does affect US interests—and it is one country that Americans are likely to hear much more of in future years.

Case Study: Zimbabwe

It could be argued that the United States has been on the wrong side of history in much of southern Africa. During the Cold War the United States at various times directly and indirectly supported white governments in the region, for economic as well as strategic reasons. US paranoia that Africans were procommunist became a self-fulfilling prophecy, as black nationalists had nowhere but the Soviet Union and China to turn. This did not make for an auspicious start to relations between the United States and the new government of Zimbabwe. Although the United States welcomed Zimbabwe's independence in 1980 with a significant aid package, relations between the two countries cooled quickly. This difficult relationship fell to its lowest point in the mid-1980s and again at the turn of the twenty-first century. At times the Zimbabwe-US relationship has been marked by outright hostility.[33]

At independence, Zimbabwe was eager to assert itself in international forums. As an aspiring leader of the third world in the Non-Aligned Movement (NAM) and as one of the "frontline states" opposed to the racist government in South Africa, Zimbabwe was determined to shape its own policy. The government had taken an outspoken stance in criticizing US policy, especially US policy toward apartheid South Africa. Over time, the rhetoric became more hostile, as the Mugabe government accused the United States of sponsoring terrorism, and of "international bullyism," for supporting apartheid-backed rebels in Angola, Mozambique, and elsewhere. When Zimbabwe indicated that it would vote its own conscience at the United Nations on issues important to the United States, the United States slashed foreign aid to Zimbabwe in the 1980s. In response, Mugabe demonstrated a character trait that defines him even today. Ever defiant, he is notoriously resistant to Western pressure. Swearing that Zimbabwe would be no one's puppet, Mugabe famously proclaimed that Zimbabwe "would rather be poor, eat grass, and be sovereign."[34]

Although relations gradually improved and aid resumed in the years that followed, by 2001 the relationship was again at a low point. In response to then–US secretary of state Colin Powell's condemnation of Mugabe's "totalitarian methods," Mugabe told the United States to leave Zimbabwe alone and mind its own business. In response, the US Senate passed the Zimbabwe Democracy and Economic Recovery Act of 2001. Instead of general trade sanctions, which have been criticized as hurting the poor, these were targeted, personal sanctions. Much like the European Union (EU), the United States imposed an arms embargo, as well as travel and economic sanctions against Mugabe, his family, his associates, and other senior government officials. These sanctions have been renewed every year since.[35]

President Obama's approach to Zimbabwe was a continuation of the George W. Bush policy of isolation, and Mugabe continued to view the United States with hostility. Over the years the Mugabe government has described its efforts as a continuation of the liberation struggle and reminded the world that Zimbabwe is nobody's colony. According to Mugabe, not only is the United States to blame for the suffering of millions of Zimbabweans, but it is also promoting regime change. Although the Obama administration was originally unenthusiastic about the idea of a unity government when it was established in 2009, Prime Minister Morgan Tsvangirai was greeted warmly at the White House. Obama listened to Tsvangirai's plea to normalize relations, but Obama's position was that as long as Mugabe held the reins of power, the United States would not change its policy. The United States has provided significant assistance, approximately $130 million annually mostly for health programs and other development assistance, and mostly through civil society groups. US law required that in order for the United States to support financial assistance to Zimbabwe (such as the clearance of debt arrears or the opportunity to benefit from market access to the United States), the US president must certify that several conditions have been met, including the restoration of the rule of law in Zimbabwe, land reform, and a freer environment for holding elections. That did not happen under the government of national unity (which ended in 2013), nor since.[36]

Still, more than fifteen years of targeted sanctions had little impact. Because of the strained relations, the United States has little influence in Zimbabwe. As unpalatable as it may be, many of Mugabe's strongest critics now believe that the world should begin to normalize relations with the regime. Perhaps it is time to plan ahead to prepare for the eventual transition of power. The United States could begin a dialogue with Zimbabweans across the political spectrum about areas of possible cooperation such as trade and food assistance. The aim should be to minimize the potential for a succession crisis and resulting civil unrest by laying the groundwork for a better relationship with the post-Mugabe government.[37]

For his part, the ninety-something Mugabe reminds us that he's not going anywhere anytime soon. He came out early against Hillary Clinton's candidacy, characterizing her as a warmonger likely to continue Obama's sanctions and support the opposition. On the other hand, the Zimbabwean president enthusiastically celebrated the election of Donald Trump, whom he describes as a fellow populist who has shaken up the establishment and been unfairly attacked by the media. Mugabe has gone so far as to call for a restoration of relations with the United States. It remains to be seen whether this will happen, as Trump did not mention Zimbabwe (or outline his Africa policy) during the campaign. Given Trump's stated disinclination to

push human rights and the fact that the United States has relatively few economic interests there, under his administration the United States may direct little of its attentions to Zimbabwe—which would suit Mugabe just as well.[38]

On the other hand, it could be argued that the world only has to put up with Mugabe for a few more years, and in the meantime it should cultivate moderates both within and outside the Zimbabwe African National Union (ZANU). Sure, Trump may mean to break with the long-standing US policy that would prefer to see the opposition come together to push ZANU out of power, but the party will likely survive Mugabe, so it is important for the United States to find people it can work with.[39]

Case Study: Egypt

For decades, Egypt was the closest Arab ally of the United States. The two are still important to each other, but the relationship (which was always transactional) has altered in recent years. The fundamentals haven't changed, but it isn't what it once was. Some say that the United States has less influence over the Egyptian state than at any time in the past four decades.[40] Each can be accused of having a wandering eye: Egypt is looking for new partners to make up for what it isn't getting from the United States, and the United States is more interested in the war in Syria, Iran's nuclear program, and the continuing Palestinian-Israeli conflict. The two have grown apart and clearly each would say that the other has not lived up to expectations. They remain united only by a common, core interest. But there's no getting around that things aren't right between the United States and Egypt. The Trump presidency could very well mean a turning point in the relationship and a bigger change in policy than we have seen in some time.

Historically, due to its geography and diplomacy, Egypt has been crucial to US national security interests. It is home to the Suez Canal and since 1979, when Egypt became the first Arab state to sign a peace deal with its former foe, the United States has rewarded Egypt, making it the second largest recipient of American aid (a total of more than $76 billion since 1948, ranging from $1 to $2 billion a year).[41] Their close partnership is also a strategic benefit to the United States, as it allows the United States to project power in the region. In sum, it has for decades been a foundation of US policy in the Middle East.

This relationship continued and expanded to include cooperation in the war on terror. However, recognizing that US support for dictatorships might actually be fueling terrorism, President George W. Bush briefly pressed Egypt for democratic reforms. After some resistance, Mubarak did allow for freer, though still limited, elections in 2005. But when the Muslim Brotherhood won nearly 20 percent of the seats, the United States backed off and Mubarak rolled back the reforms.[42]

Out of fear of the alternative, US presidents, Democrat and Republican alike, have put stability above democracy and stood steadfastly by President Mubarak. They were (and are again) willing to put democracy on the back burner and overlook human rights abuses—in return for Egypt's cooperation on Israel and terrorism.[43] Thus the relationship between the United States and Egypt could be described as a marriage of convenience; neither was exactly happy with the way things were, but neither was willing to risk a breakup.

For years, the United States largely left Mubarak to his own devices, to hound anyone who dared to criticize the regime.[44] President Obama is remembered in Egypt

for his Cairo speech, early in his first term, in which he called for a new beginning between the West and the Muslim world. But his administration did not break much with his precedessors' policy. It tried to nudge its ally with gentle public admonishments, but Obama was surprised by the events of 2011 and slow to warm to the Tahrir uprising.[45] During that heady time, the US president's policy to Egypt was most often described as cautious. But as Mubarak set his police loose on mostly non-violent crowds, the Obama administration balked and broke with that decades-long US policy that banked on authoritarians to provide stability. Fearful of the greater conflagration to come if Mubarak insisted on staying, the United States publicly called for an orderly transition of power.[46]

Moreover, the Obama administration chose to stand by the stated commitment of the United States to democracy, accepting the result of the freest and fairest elections in Egyptian history and reversing the past US policy of hostility to the Muslim Brotherhood. This was a policy based in pragmatism; the United States was seeking to engage in a working relationship with the democratically elected government, one that was promising to international commitments, including the peace treaty with Israel. And Morsi reciprocated, proving instrumental in mediating a cease-fire between Hamas and Israel in 2012.[47]

Yet about a year later, when President Morsi was removed from office in a coup in 2013, the Obama administration took a pragmatic approach once more. It condemned the military's removal of a democratically elected government but chose not to call it a coup, because to do so would have meant (under US law) an immediate cutoff of aid to Egypt—and a likely end to Egypt's peace deal with Israel.[48] After the military resumed power, the Obama administration declared that the US-Egypt relationship could not return to "business as usual," but in effect it has. Obama froze some military aid and kept Sisi at a distance, but for the most part the relationship went unchanged.[49]

What threat to national security could justify the resumption of aid to a dictatorship that overthrew a democratically elected government? The Islamic State of Iraq and Syria (ISIS)—and its presence in the Sinai. The counterterrorist imperative has ushered in a strengthening of the strategic relationship. And yes, this confirms US hypocrisy in the eyes of many, who find the continuity in policy between the Bush and Obama administrations striking. There were some differences of nuance, but for all the talk about how different the two presidents would be, for both, national security, broadly defined, trumped everything else.[50]

All the indicators suggest that President Trump will likely continue this tradition. In his campaign he promised to take the fight to the terrorists but to pursue an otherwise isolationist policy. Trump has made it clear that he has no interest in lecturing others on human rights abuses. He has no problem with working with autocrats and much prefers the stability they offer to the alternative. Trump has described Sisi as "a fantastic guy" and Sisi was the first foreign leader to congratulate Trump on his victory. Early in his term, Trump appeared to value the US military relationship with Egypt and continued access through the Suez Canal. Trump and Sisi have bonded over their shared determination to fight terrorism. The US president has promised his Egyptian counterpart support in his war against Sinai Province. And Trump may go further, adding the Muslim Brotherhood to the US list of Foreign Terrorist Organizations, which would have political ramifications throughout the region. Although some members have committed violent acts, the Brotherhood has foresworn violence. It influences a variety of political parties, including moderates, in several countries.[51]

Such a designation would impede the US ability to pursue dialogue in the region. Although President Trump is likely to talk less about human rights and democracy than his predecessors, it is important to keep in mind that people in the Middle East and the rest of the world, much of which is as polarized as the United States, pay attention to the disconnect between the stated ideals and actions of the United States.

Case Study: Iran

With the more recent history of strained ties between Iranian leaders and the United States (the BBC once called the relationship "one of the most antagonistic in the world"),[52] it may be tempting to discount their significant relations prior to the Islamic Revolution. Such an omission would be a mistake, though. In fact, the coziness of the Shah with Western leaders after World War II is indeed the source of much of the mistrust that has permeated the relationship since. Many Iranians viewed the West, especially the United States, as double-talking supporters of a corrupt and antidemocratic regime. Iran long considered the United States its archenemy, and fierce animosity reigned on both sides, especially after 1979, when hostages were held at the US embassy in Tehran for 444 days (the embassy today serves as a militia training center and museum of the "den of spies").[53] Yet increasingly, neither side can ignore the other. Iran's access to oil in the Persian Gulf solidifies its status as a central player in Middle Eastern affairs. Even though US influence in the region may wane in the future, US support of Israel, which Iran and some other Muslim states find very troubling, will continue to color whatever type of relationship unfolds between Tehran and Washington. Anti-Americanism played a major part in the revolution that established the Islamic Republic: one analyst states that Ayatollah Ruhollah Khomeini pursued two goals in the 1979 revolution: the establishment of a theocracy, and the "declaration of independence" from US and British control.[54]

Since 1980 the United States has lacked diplomatic ties with Iran; Pakistan represents Iranian interests in Washington, and Switzerland represents US interests in Tehran. Other Western powers, however, have normalized their political relations with Tehran (in 1999, the United Kingdom, the last European Union country without a diplomatic emissary to Iran, exchanged ambassadors with Tehran).[55] Within the Islamic Republic, the weekly jeers of "death to America" continue. Former president Mahmoud Ahmadinejad thrived on attacking Washington, D.C., and Supreme Leader Sayyid Ali Khamenei often references the "global arrogance" of the United States.[56] While current president Rouhani has attempted to shift this tone, he has encountered resistance, especially among the leadership. The challenges in this bilateral nonrelationship are marked as much by domestic politics on each side as they are by significant policy and ideological differences between them.

The September 11 attacks and the wars in Iraq and Afghanistan seemed, at first, to shift the calculus in US-Iranian ties, with some encouraging normalization.[57] The bipartisan (US) Iraq Study Group explicitly recommended working with Iran to stabilize the situation in Iraq,[58] to little result. Today, some conservatives within Iran promote a conspiracy theory (emblazoned in murals on the walls of the former US embassy) that September 11 was engineered by the United States and Israel to help justify invading the Middle East.[59]

Almost all commercial transactions between the United States and Iran were banned from 1995 until 2016, under a 1995 executive order that was reinforced with

the 1996 Iran-Libya Sanctions Act. This US law imposes penalties on foreign firms that invest in either Iran or Libya, which both stand accused by the US government of supporting terrorism. As tensions over Iran's uranium enrichment programs increased, these limitations became even more wide-ranging. It is not only the clerics in Tehran who are bothered by these actions: India, Russia, and European governments including Germany and France have expressed their displeasure at this perceived US meddling in their financial affairs. As sanctions were eased after the implementation of the joint action plan, there was still some reticence on the part of banks and businesses to do business with Iran, both due to concern of US retaliation, challenges with the Iranian banking system, as well as Iran's support of Syrian leader Bashar al-Assad.[60]

While the nuclear-related sanctions were lifted after 2016, sanctions focused on the country's support of terrorism, human rights abuses, and ballistic missile program all remain, and the United States opened up far less than the EU, in terms of trade and business with Iran.[61] The United States remains at odds with Iran on many issues. For example, just as the nuclear accord was being rolled out, Iran held ten US sailors for more than twenty-four hours after their US Navy patrol boats veered into Iranian waters in the Persian Gulf.[62] Iran was officially designated by the US State Department as a state sponsor of terrorism in 1984, and, for multiple years running, the US ranks the Islamic Republic as the "foremost state sponsor of terrorism," even as ISIS ranked as the greatest global threat.[63] The United States alleges Iranian complicity in the bombing of US Marine headquarters in Beirut (1983), and in the 1996 Khobar (Saudi Arabia) bombing of US military barracks, which killed nineteen members of the US Air Force. Iran has also been implicated through its ties to the Shiite group Hezbollah, even though Tehran insists they are not substantial, and the US contends that the Islamic Republic is involved in multiple activities designed to destabilize the region.

Iran's concerns with the United States are as deep-rooted as the counterperspective. Iran views the United States as the source of most of its problems—there is much remaining anti-American sentiment tied to the Central Intelligence Agency–engineered coup that toppled the popular government of Prime Minister Mohammad Mossadeq in 1953, as well as to US support for the unpopular regime of Shah Mohammad Reza Pahlavi. After the Islamic Revolution of 1979, hundreds of millions of dollars' worth of military equipment, which the former Shah had ordered and paid for, was embargoed, and the financing was impounded. The decision to permit the ailing Shah to enter the United States was viewed by many ordinary Iranians as part of a larger, Western, anti-Iranian conspiracy to again restore a dynasty. Iranian animosity only increased after President Ronald Reagan's decision to support Saddam Hussein during the 1980–1988 Iran-Iraq War, and continued while the United States attempted to maintain its influence in the region, which often necessitated hostile acts toward Iran. For example, in July 1988 a missile fired from a US vessel shot down an Iranian plane flying to Dubai, and 250 Iranians were killed. Iranian leaders were also upset that the international community seemed to take little action against its neighbor, Iraq, which had killed tens of thousands of Iranians with chemical weapons. Iran alleged that German chemical firms were assisting Iraq with its production of weapons of mass destruction.[64] Iranian leaders believed they were snubbed at the conclusion of the Gulf War, as they were excluded from postwar discussions, even though they tacitly assisted the effort to oust Saddam Hussein from

Kuwait. Iranians also believe that the US-led sanctions unduly and unfairly hindered the development of the Iranian economy, which had already been battered during the eight-year Iran-Iraq War. Iranian leaders feel that they are adrift in a hostile international environment that has been made so largely by efforts of the United States.

What is the outlook for the future? Iranian leaders will continue to be consumed with the balance of how to accommodate Western power without losing their Islamic identity. The divided nature of the Iranian political system complicates negotiations with foreign powers; as one exasperated diplomat once observed, "progress made in talks with one part of Iran's government is often undermined by statements from another."[65] Potential rapprochement with the United States will not be entered into lightly—from either side. Discussions within the US foreign policy establishment about possible normalization of relations were met with solid resistance within the Bush administration. Under President Obama, the nuclear deal between Iran and the P5+1 (formally known as the Joint Comprehensive Plan of Action [JCPOA]) was a significant achievement on many levels, especially linking Iran economically with Europe (and to the United States, to a lesser extent) as well as some gains in international legitimacy. As a candidate, Donald Trump often stated that he would "tear up" the nuclear accord with Iran, and he is likely to find significant Republican support to do so.[66] President Trump has repeatedly claimed that the deal is not tough enough and that the United States should walk away from the agreement. While Iran has already reaped the financial benefits of the JCPOA (through the lifting of sanctions), the benefits outside the Islamic Republic (Iran's lack of a nuclear weapons program) are only realized if the deal holds. It is clear that the first months if not years of the Trump administration's foreign policy in the Middle East will likely be animated by the decision on whether or not to continue with the JCPOA as is, revise it, or completely start from scratch.

While the United States and Iran have improved relations, they have not achieved political reconciliation, and small steps forward may be reversed in the coming years. Despite many shared interests (especially opposition to al-Qaeda and Islamic State, as well as regional stability in the Middle East), they have numerous (and sizable) conflicting interests; tension and competition remain. Normalization now seems but a distant possibility—especially during the Trump administration—at the same time that the search for a workable relationship between Tehran and Washington seems ever more important.

Case Study: China

The United States opened a formal diplomatic relationship with the People's Republic of China during the 1970s, under the leadership of staunchly anticommunist president Richard M. Nixon. Previously the United States had supported the rival of the Chinese Communist Party, the Nationalist Party, which had been exiled to Taiwan after its defeat in 1949. Nixon's rationale for rapprochement with China, for which he faced much criticism, was that one could view the world in terms of a "strategic triangle" encompassing the United States, China, and the Soviet Union. Opening formal ties with China would exploit hostilities between the two communist giants and ultimately, it was hoped, limit the influence of communism throughout the world. After the 1970s the US relationship with China, like the relationship between most Western powers and China, became centered on its commercial

strengths, especially the vast market that it provided for Western goods and services. This financial focus continues, although its importance may wane as China exerts its growing strength in other arenas.

After the initial honeymoon period, China-US relations have had cycles of highs and lows, from Tiananmen Square (1989), to Bill Clinton's successful China tour (1998), to the bombing of the Chinese embassy in Belgrade (1999), to the collision of a Chinese jet with a US Navy surveillance plane (2001), which killed the Chinese pilot and resulted in China detaining the US crew for nineteen days. In the wake of the Great Recession, as China finds new, more confident footing as a country rich with financing for countries in need, it is clear that Sino-US relations are entering a new era. The relationship that began in the 1970s as a Cold War compromise is clearly now facing tensions as China's power and influence rise.

Many within the Chinese foreign policy establishment have framed US behavior as arrogant, self-interested, and imposing—the behavior of a hegemon. Beijing continues to find fault with US policy in much of the world, and is especially critical of Washington's defense agreement with Japan, strategic ambiguity toward Taiwan, and its overall ability to exert greater amounts of power (both hard and soft) around the world. Chinese citizens now identify the United States as the main threat to the country, greater than economic instability or terrorism. Pew data report that in 2016, 45 percent of Chinese saw US power as a threat, up from 39 percent in 2013. More than half of respondents said they believe the United States is trying to prevent China from becoming an "equal power" and 77 percent said they believe that their way of life needs to be protected from foreign influence, up 13 percent since 2002.[67]

China's status as a tremendous trading partner is the focal point of many of its bilateral ties, and its relations with the United States are not much different. But how long trade can continue to gloss over important differences between the two, and perhaps more important, how a financial showdown may repair itself, remain to be seen. China was only recently (late 2016) unseated (by Japan) as the largest creditor of the United States, holding the largest supply of US Treasury securities.[68] US appeals for currency revaluation have dissipated now that the United States (and other major economies) look to Beijing with concern that it carefully manage its economic rebalancing so as not to set off a domino effect of instability.

The question that is likely to arouse the most suspicion and ire, especially during the Trump years, is the status of Taiwan. Let's be clear: from Beijing's point of view, this is a nonstarter: Taiwan is a renegade province that has been illegitimately separated from the Chinese Mainland, and all Chinese on both sides of the Taiwan Straits need to work toward the eventual reunification. Beijing has long suspected—decades before Donald Trump controversially received a congratulatory call from Taiwanese leader Tsai Ing-Wen—that the United States is determined to limit the development of their country and influence. This belief is based on US efforts to arm Taiwan, and other perceived challenges to Chinese sovereignty, including meeting with Tibetan leaders in the halls of the White House. The "deep freeze" that sets in each time China protests US arms sales to Taiwan (a staple since the 1980s), including in 2010 when US defense secretary Robert Gates was refused his request to stop in Beijing during his travels in Asia, may be paltry compared to a Chinese response to deeper overtures toward Taiwan.[69] When, even before he was inaugurated, Donald Trump stated that he was not sure the United States should feel bound by the "One China" understanding, heads turned all around Beijing. Bilateral ties under the

Trump administration got off to a rocky start—even during the 2016 presidential campaign—as Trump insisted on branding China a "currency manipulator," repeating the falsehood that the Chinese yuan remained undervalued (therefore harming US competitiveness in China), and by threatening to impose high tariffs on Chinese goods "on day one" of his administration.[70]

Longtime China-watcher Kenneth Lieberthal, of the Brookings Institution, has highlighted the dissipating levels of trust between US and Chinese leaders in recent years.[71] The list of major global issues that cause strife among leaders in both countries includes trade, North Korea, Iran, and the environment—hefty issues to be sure. Yet despite all of the friction, there is no doubt that Beijing's ties with the United States are the most important piece of its foreign policy.

Some claim that a "G-2" assemblage of Washington and Beijing is forming as the two great powers of the early twenty-first century seek common strategic interests, perhaps at the expense of their own allies. Others, including President Trump, suggest that it is time for the United States to "de-friend" China, or at the very least recognize that the US relationship with the world's emerging superpower is not all that unique compared to China's relationship with key allies of the United States, including the European Union and Japan.[72] Somewhere between these two extremes, Washington and Beijing will craft a working relationship that is likely to shape the outcome of many pressing global issues over the next decades.

Case Study: Indonesia

Indonesia's ties with the Western world have long been strained. Some of this derives from Indonesia's experience with the Dutch and its prolonged fight for acceptance as an independent state. As a founder of the Non-Aligned Movement in the 1960s, Indonesia positioned itself to be largely independent of the West, and indeed sometimes in opposition to it. The latter part of the Sukarno era was very anti-Western and specifically anti-American. After the 1965 anticommunist coup, in a period of US history that remains under scrutiny, the United States cultivated a close relationship with Suharto's Indonesia, viewing it as a regional stronghold against communism. Yet Western powers maintained a cozy relationship with Suharto at great cost, ignoring human rights atrocities and propping up a military regime, all in the name of regional stability. Since Suharto, the inconsistencies of the Indonesia-US relationship have become more visible and have been exacerbated by instability throughout the archipelago. In its war on terrorism, the United States views Indonesia as a critical strategic ally, the "voice of moderation in the Muslim world," as one US State Department official put it.[73] This badge, though, is uncomfortable for many ordinary Indonesians.

The events of September 11, 2001, put Indonesian leaders in a very tight spot, especially with US leaders. Political newcomer Megawati Sukarnoputri stepped into office in the summer of 2001 with more than a handful of domestic challenges, and her job became even more difficult after the commencement of the US-led wars in Afghanistan and Iraq. As the leader of the state with the world's largest Muslim population, her support of Washington rankled some Indonesian citizens. Many viewed her initially unqualified support of US efforts to be blasphemous against the Islamic people. As the war on terrorism waged further, this perception grew stronger. In 2004 a respected Indonesian survey institute found that 55 percent of Indonesian citizens believed that the United States was at war with Muslim countries, rather than with terrorists who

happen to be Muslim.[74] When George W. Bush made a six-hour stop in Indonesia in 2006, for example, some demonstrators chanted, "We hope Bush dies."[75]

In part because of his childhood connections to Indonesia, many expected President Barack Obama to extend a closer US relationship to this major Southeast Asian state. (Obama lived outside of Jakarta for four years as a young boy, attending both Catholic and public schools; one of the elementary schools he attended erected a statue of him on its grounds.) After having twice postponed his first official state visit, he returned to Jakarta in November 2010 to both cheering and jeering crowds, praising Indonesia as a model of pluralism and democracy. In a deeply personal speech in Jakarta, Obama stated (in both English and Indonesian), "Indonesia is part of me."[76] Yet he faced skepticism from many. As Pew Research Center studies report, since 2000, Indonesians' views of the United States have fluctuated quite a bit, with favorable views of the United States bouncing from 61 percent in 2002 to 15 percent in 2003 (shortly after the US-led invasion of Iraq), 37 percent in 2008, and 63 percent in 2009.[77] Perhaps expectations were too high, but at the end of the Obama presidency, Indonesians framed the bilateral relationship as "disappointingly lukewarm," stating the reality that "Indonesia remains off Washington's geostrategic map."[78] One thing is for certain: Indonesian-US ties are changing under President Trump. Even if he moderates some of his fiery anti-Muslim rhetoric, ordinary Indonesians (and leaders alike) express concern that his protectionist economic priorities may cut into Indonesian exports, that his emphases on limiting support to crucial allies in the region (especially Japan) may ignite a regional arms race, and, in general, that shifting American priorities in Asia will be accompanied by harmful instability.[79] Some hope that, especially as Jokowi charts a more assertive maritime role for Indonesia, including explicit challenges to China's view that there are "overlapping claims" to waters close to Indonesia's Natuna Islands, perhaps President Trump may help Jakarta develop more maritime capabilities as a way to balance China.[80]

China fares prominently in the strategic calculations of leaders in both Washington and Jakarta. The United States served as a buffer for Indonesia during the early decades of the Chinese communist revolution. For many years, the United States has framed its alliance with Jakarta in part to help counterbalance the influence of Beijing. This multipronged approach, and the power it gives to Jakarta, are not lost on Indonesia's (or China's) leaders. While former President Susilo Bambang Yudhoyono (SBY) has promoted an amicable relationship with the United States (he participated in military training in the United States in the 1970s and 1980s), his administration has also sought favorable relations with China and Russia, in part to avoid US supervision and influence. Memories of US embargoes on weapons and military training, in place from 1991 until 2005, remain vivid (the United States lifted the embargo and prior restrictions on military training to demonstrate an open hand to Indonesian citizens, especially as Washington watched its perception in the Muslim world plummet). In recent years, under both SBY and Jokowi, Indonesia has sought to diversify its ties, turning first to Russia, and more recently to China, to help limit its dependence on a single state. Jakarta's leaders realize Indonesia's key geopolitical position, and recognize that there may be some benefits to being caught in the middle of two powers, especially as they seek investment (and assurances from both).[81]

Indonesia's relations with the Western world, dominated by its ties with the United States, are most definitely changing from the days when Jakarta orchestrated the global movement to chart an independent path. Because of the US president's

connections to the country, many believed Washington and Jakarta would develop a special alliance under Obama's watch. The path that these changes portend, however, remains to be seen. As it is increasingly seen to be a country caught between the United States (which emphasizes Jakarta's credentials as the world's third largest democracy and as a model of democracy in an Islamic country) and China (which emphasizes its economic ties with the world's fourth most populous state), it seems Indonesia has come full circle. In the 1950s it was caught between the superpowers of the United States and the Soviet Union. Today it again finds itself straddling two large powers with conflicting worldviews.

Now It's Your Turn

How do recent events complement or challenge the material presented in the case studies? If you had to brief a US government delegation on the perceptions of a particular bilateral relationship between the United States and the global south, what issues and perspectives would you highlight? Do you believe that many Americans understand or can agree with some of the concerns expressed by peoples in the countries we have studied? Why or why not? How would you explain the animosity expressed in some corners of the world toward the United States? What do you think are the sources of the love-hate relationship between the Western and non-Western worlds? If you had to outline a policy plan for future US relations with one of the countries studied here, what would it entail? How would this proposal be different if you were to chart it from the perspective of a country in the so-called global south?

Notes

1. Arlos Fuentes, *The Crystal Frontier* (New York: Farrar, Straus and Giroux, 1997), p. 266.

2. Kirk Semple, "Mexico Prepares to Counter 'the Trump Emergency,'" *New York Times,* May 22, 2016; Eli Watkins, "Ex-Mexican President Vicente Fox Knocks Trump, Sanders," *CNN Politics,* May 10, 2016.

3. Roderic Ai Camp, *Politics in Mexico: The Decline of Authoritarianism* (New York: Oxford University Press, 1999); Andrew Selee and Peter H. Smith, "Challenges of Partnership," in *Mexico and the United States: The Politics of Partnership,* ed. Peter H. Smith and Andrew Selee (Boulder: Lynne Rienner, 2013).

4. Fred Imbert, "Clinton vs. Trump: What Mexicans Think About the US Election," *CNBC News,* June 15, 2016.

5. Azam Ahmed, Kirk Semple, and Paulina Villegas, "Mexico Braces for the Fallout of a Trump Presidency," *New York Times,* November 9, 2016.

6. Office of the United States Trade Representative, "Mexico," 2016; US Department of State, "US Relations with Mexico," July 12, 2016.

7. Matt Femer, "Americans Spent About a Trillion Dollars on Illegal Drugs in the Last Decade," *Huffington Post,* March 13, 2014; Mario Berlanga, "A Victimless Crime?," *New York Times,* September 27, 2016.

8. Clare Ribando Seelke and Kristin Finklea, "U.S.-Mexican Security Cooperation: The Mérida Initiative and Beyond," Congressional Research Service, February 22, 2016.

9. Azam Ahmed and Eric Schmitt, "Mexican Military Runs Up Body Count in Drug War," *New York Times,* May 26, 2016.

10. Marc Lacey and Ginger Thompson, "As Clinton Visits Mexico, Strains Show in Relations," *New York Times,* March 25, 2009; US Government Accountability Office, "Firearms Trafficking: U.S. Efforts to Combat Firearms Trafficking to Mexico Have Improved, but Some Collaboration Challenges Remain," January 11, 2016.

11. Michael Hoefer, Nancy Rytina, and Bryan C. Baker, "Estimates of the Unauthorized Immigrant Population Residing in the US, January 2009," Population Estimates, US Department of Homeland Security, January 2010, www.dhs.gov; Semple and Villegas, "Mexico Braces for the Fallout of a Trump Presidency."

12. Hoefer, Rytina, and Baker, "Estimates of the Unauthorized Immigrant Population."

13. Steven Nelson, "Dreamers' Nightmare: DACA Dies If Obama Immigration Action Goes Down," *US News,* January 19, 2016; "Barack Obama: Deporter-in-Chief," *The Economist,* February 8, 2014.

14. Elisabeth Malkin, "Trump's Policies Add Urgency to Efforts to Revive Mexico's Oil Trade," *New York Times,* November 28, 2016.

15. Shannon K. O'Neil, "The Real War in Mexico," *Foreign Affairs,* July–August 2009.

16. Gary Martin, "It's Not All Smiles as Leaders Meet," *San Antonio Express-News,* November 10, 2006.

17. Maureen Taft-Morales, "Peru in Brief: Political and Economic Conditions and Relations with the United States," Congressional Research Service, June 7, 2013.

18. Cited in Dennis Jett, "Remember the Drug War?," *Washington Post,* January 13, 2002.

19. Robert Muggah and Jeremy McDermott, "A Massive Drug Trade, and No Violence," *The Atlantic,* April 24, 2013.

20. Ibid.

21. "Cocaine Is Winning the Drug War in Peru," Associated Press, October 14, 2015; Taft-Morales, "Peru in Brief."

22. "The Balloon Effect," *New York Times,* June 14, 2010; Nick Miroff, "Colombia Is Again the World's Top Coca Producer," *Washington Post,* November 10, 2015, www.washingtonpost.com.

23. Barnett S. Koven, "The Second Image Sometimes Reversed: Competing Interests in Drug Policy," *E-International Relations,* March 8, 2016; "Peru 2016 Crime & Safety Report," Overseas Security Advisory Council, US Department of State, March 14, 2016; Taft-Morales, "Peru in Brief"; Muggah and McDermott, "A Massive Drug Trade, and No Violence."

24. Koven, "The Second Image Sometimes Reversed"; Taft-Morales, "Peru in Brief."

25. Omoh Gabriel, "Oil Exports on Course Despite Militants' Attacks," *The Vanguard,* June 22, 2016; Chibuike Oguh, "U.S. Oil Imports from Nigeria Hit Three-Year High," *Financial Nigeria,* March 24, 2016, www.financialnigeria.com/u-s-oil-imports-from-nigeria-hit-three-year-high-news-474.html.

26. Stephen Wright, *Nigeria: Struggle for Stability and Status* (Boulder: Westview, 1998).

27. US Department of State, "Country Report: Nigeria," 2015, www.state.gov.

28. Office of the US Trade Representative, "Nigeria," May 1, 2014.

29. US Energy Information Administration, "Frequently Asked Questions," March 8, 2016, www.eia.gov/tools/faqs/faq.cfm?id=32&t=6.

30. William D. Hartung and Frida Berrigan, "Militarization of US Policy, 2000–2005," *Synthesis/Regeneration* 39 (Winter 2006), www.greens.org

31. Ibid.; Jean Herskovitz, "Nigeria's Rigged Democracy," *Foreign Affairs,* July–August 2007; Conn Hallinan, "Africa: No Butter, but Lots of Guns," Institute for Policy Studies, July 10, 2010; "Nigeria Oil Rebels Say Mulling Obama's Truce Appeal," Reuters, May 4, 2008.

32. Neanda Salvaterra and Drew Hindshaw, "Nigerian President Goodluck Jonathan Wants US Troops to Fight Boko Haram," *Wall Street Journal,* February 13, 2015; Helene Cooper and Dionne Searcey, "After Years of Distrust, U.S. Military Reconciles with Nigeria to Fight Boko Haram," *New York Times,* May 15, 2016.

33. Bernard Gwertzman, "Aid to Zimbabwe Suspended by U.S.," *New York Times,* July 10, 1986; Gregory Elich, "The Battle over Zimbabwe's Future," *Global Research,* April 13, 2007, www.globalresearch.ca.

34. Quoted in Mike Nizza, "Mugabe Loses Honorary Degree from U Mass," *New York Times,* June 13, 2008.

35. "Gloomy Days in Zimbabwe," *Chicago Tribune,* August 4, 2001; "US Sanctions Against Zimbabwe to Stay in Place," *VOA News,* May 29, 2015.

36. George F. Ward, "Political Instability in Zimbabwe," Council on Foreign Relations, March 2015.

37. Ibid.

38. Lynsey Chutel, "With Donald Trump in the White House, Robert Mugabe Wants to Restore Ties with the U.S.," *Huffington Post,* November 16, 2016.

39. Stephen Chan, "Looking Beyond Mugabe," *New York Times,* October 26, 2015; Chido Munyati, "Why US Reengagement Is Critical to Zimbabwe's Debt Arrears Clearance Strategy," *Foreign Policy Journal,* March 4, 2016.

40. Scott Anderson, "Fractured Lands: How the Arab World Came Apart," *New York Times,* August 14, 2016.

41. Ibid.; Liam Stack, "A Gloomy Egypt Sees Its International Influence Wither Away," *New York Times,* August 2, 2016.

42. Ashraf Khalil, *Liberation Square: Inside the Egyptian Revolution and the Rebirth of a Nation* (New York: St. Martin's, 2011); Barbara Ann Reiffer-Flanagan, "Democratic Dreams Neglected in the Land of the Pharaohs: US Democracy Assistance in Egypt," *Human Rights Review* 15, no. 4 (December 2014).

43. Ann R. Pierce, "US 'Partnership' with the Egyptian Muslim Brotherhood and Its Effect on Civil Society and Human Rights," *Global Society* 51 (2014).

44. Khalil, *Liberation Square.*

45. "Egypt's Brazen Crackdown on Critics," *New York Times,* November 9, 2015; Orla Guerin, "Trump Era Heralds Warming of US-Egypt Ties," BBC News, February 7, 2017.

46. David E. Sanger, "As Mubarak Digs In, U.S. Policy in Egypt Is Complicated," *New York Times,* February 5, 2011; Khalil, *Liberation Square.*

47. Augustus Richard Norton, "The Return of Egypt's Deep State," *Current History,* December 2013.

48. Rieffer-Flanagan, "Democratic Dreams Neglected."

49. Ibid.; Michael Wahid Hanna, "Getting over Egypt: Time to Rethink Relations," *Foreign Affairs,* November–December 2015; Declan Walsh, "Talk of a Terror Listing by US Alarms Some Allies in Arab World," *New York Times,* February 21, 2017.

50. Elissa Miller, "Five Years On: Egypt's International Relations," Atlantic Council, January 25, 2016; Peter Baker, "Obama Removes Weapons Freeze Against Egypt," *New York Times,* March 21, 2013.

51. Cristiano Lima, "Trump Praises Egypt's al-Sisi: 'He's a Fantastic Guy,'" *Politico,* September 22, 2016; Stack, "A Gloomy Egypt Sees Its International Influence Wither Away"; Peter Baker, "White House Weighs Terrorist Designation for Muslim Brotherhood," *New York Times,* February 7, 2017.

52. "Iraq: What Iran and Syria Want," BBC News, November 13, 2006.

53. Thomas Erdbrink, "Former American Embassy in Iran Attracts Pride and Dust," *New York Times,* October 31, 2013.

54. John Simpson, "Iran's Growing Regional Influence," BBC News, September 20, 2006.

55. UK-Iranian relations were downgraded by Iran after new sanctions were implemented in November 2011, related to Iran's nuclear program. After the UK embassy compound in Tehran was stormed by hundreds of Iranian students, the UK closed its embassy in Tehran and ordered the Iranian embassy in London also closed, and British interests in Iran were maintained by the Swedish embassy in Tehran while Iranian interests in the UK were maintained by the Omani embassy in London. Both countries announced they would restore diplomatic relations after progress in nuclear talks, and the embassies were reopened in August 2015. See "British Embassy in Tehran Reopens Four Years After Closure," BBC News, August 23, 2015.

56. Karim Sadjadpour, "The Sources of Soviet Iranian Conduct," *Foreign Policy,* November 2010.

57. Ray Takeyh, *Hidden Iran: Paradox and Power in the Islamic Republic* (New York: Times Books, 2006), pp. 117–118.

58. James A. Baker III and Lee H. Hamilton, *The Iraq Study Group Report* (New York: Random, 2006), pp. 50–53. The group begins this section (which also discusses Syria) by stating, "Dealing with Iran and Syria is controversial. Nevertheless, it is our view that in diplomacy, a nation can and should engage its adversaries and enemies to try to resolve conflicts and differences. . . . Accordingly, the Support Group should actively engage Iran and Syria in its diplomatic dialogue, *without preconditions*" (p. 50, emphasis added).

59. William Brangham, "Photos: Eerie Remnants of the Former U.S. Embassy, 35 Years After Iran Hostage Crisis," *PBS Newshour,* March 2, 2015.

60. Matthew Lee, "Kerry: US Open to Further Clarifying Iran Sanctions Relief," Associated Press, June 15, 2016.

61. Merrit Kennedy, "Implementation Day Arrives: Sanctions on Iran Are Lifted," National Public Radio, January 16, 2016.

62. Helene Cooper and David E. Sanger, "Iran Seizes U.S. Sailors Amid Claims of Spying," *New York Times,* January 13, 2016, p. A1.

63. Ryan Browne, "State Department Report Finds Iran Is Top State Sponsor of Terror," *CNN News,* June 2, 2016.

64. Hooman Peimani, *Iran and the United States: The Rise of the West Asian Regional Grouping* (Westport: Praeger, 1999).

65. Bill Hess, "Will Saudi Arabia and Iran Ever Get Along?," Brookings Middle East Politics and Policy Blog, April 20, 2016.

66. Eric B. Lorber, "President Trump and the Iran Nuclear Deal," *Foreign Policy,* November 16, 2016, www.foreignpolicy.com; J. Matthew McInnis, "Why Trump Might Not Need to Rip Up the Iran Nuclear Deal," *Fortune,* November 21, 2016, www.fortune.com.

67. "What Most Chinese Fear: The U.S.," *Wall Street Journal, China RealTime Report,* October 5, 2016.

68. Min Zeng, "Japan Dethrones China as Top U.S. Foreign Creditor," *Wall Street Journal,* December 15, 2016.

69. David A. Graham, "So, Why Can't You Call Taiwan?," *The Atlantic,* December 2, 2016; Evan Osnos, "The Real Risk Behind Trump's Taiwan Call," *The New Yorker,* December 3, 2016; Michael Wines, "Behind Gusts of a Military Chill: A More Forceful China," *New York Times,* June 9, 2010, p. A8.

70. Ari Shapiro, "Trump's Plan for China Tariffs Could Lead to 'Collateral Damage' on Both Sides," National Public Radio, December 7, 2016.

71. "The Outlook for China," roundtable convened at the Brookings Institution, Washington, DC, March 18, 2010, p. 29.

72. Elizabeth Economy and Adam Segal, "Time to Defriend China," *Foreign Policy,* May 24, 2010.

73. "Indonesia-Military Assistance," Office of the Spokesman, US Department of State, January 4, 2006.

74. "Iraq a Key Point of Difference During Visit," *Jakarta Post,* November 20, 2006.

75. "Indonesians Protest US President's Visit," National Public Radio, *Morning Edition,* November 20, 2006.

76. Quoted in Norimitsu Onishi, "In Jakarta Speech, Some Hear Cairo Redux," *New York Times,* November 10, 2010.

77. Richard Wike, "Indonesia: The Obama Effect," Pew Research Center, March 17, 2010.

78. Meidyatama Suryodiningrat, "News Analysis: Jokowi, Obama Put Smile on Second-Rate Relationship," *Jakarta Post,* October 26, 2015, www.thejakartapost.com.

79. Jon Emont, "Indonesia Savored Its Ties to Obama, Now It Prepares to Say Goodbye," *Washington Post,* December 6, 2016.

80. Stanley Weiss, "It's Time for the U.S. Pivot to Indonesia," *Huffington Post,* September 23, 2016, www.huffingtonpost.com.

81. Aaron Walayat, "Stuck in the Middle with You: Indonesia in US-China Relations," *US-China Perception Monitor,* April 11, 2016, www.uscnpm.org.

PART FIVE
Conclusion

Chapter 21

Looking Forward: Contested Images of Power

You must be the change you want to see in the world.
—*Mahatma Gandhi, Indian political and spiritual leader (1869–1948)*

So where do we go from here? Our world in the early twenty-first century is rife with potential conflicts as well as potential new alignments. Interactions between the governments, societies, cultures, and economies of the world may very well chart whether this future follows a path of peace and prosperity or stagnation and decline. If there is one lesson that we have highlighted throughout this book, though, it is that it will take an increased recognition of all of the world's peoples in order to craft any meaningful, lasting solutions to the current challenges we face, and to those that we do not yet envision.

In recent years, there has been a good deal of conversation about the ways in which the world has changed since the end of the superpower Cold War conflict, the events of September 11, 2001, and the Arab Spring transitions a decade later. With some distance now from each of these periods, we have the chance to discern lessons learned and opportunities missed. In the wake of the September 11 attacks, for example, then–UN Secretary-General Kofi Annan said that one of the lessons of that day that had not received much attention was that we can't ignore inhumane conditions in the rest of the world. The economic and social problems of others have a direct impact on US national security (and world security). Annan is joined by many others who argue that terrorism isn't the only scourge threatening world security. According to former Costa Rican president and Nobel laureate Óscar Arias, "terrorism is one of many challenges to humanity, but the basic threats to world peace are poverty, inequality, illiteracy, disease, and environmental degradation."[1] These words seem more prescient now than ever.

Some contend that we are living through the end of an open world order, and that "deglobalization," a decades-long trend that was launched by the 2008 global recession, is hitting its stride.[2] Trade is more restricted, migrants are more encumbered. Identities, especially national and ethnic identities, seem more hardened, especially

as part of the wave of populism that is sweeping many parts of the globe—North and South alike. Many of the economic challenges in the global south—income disparity, for example—are increasingly recognized as scourges within developed countries as well, as gaps in income, education, and opportunity become more pronounced.

We've picked up some lessons from the past few decades of experience trying to cope with, and improve, when possible, disparities in the human condition. Challenges are rarely (if ever) isolated events: we need a truly multipronged strategy for curbing the appeal of violence and extremism. Sickness, for example, is closely related to political instability; countries with high infant mortality rates are more likely to fall into civil wars. The absence of political voice or economic opportunity serves as an "incubator" for terrorists. The lack of access to safe drinking water leads militaries to battle. Poverty worsens as economic stagnation deepens and assistance falters. We now have overwhelming data that point to long-term positive outcomes of educating girls, including decreasing infant mortality, improving health outcomes throughout society, raising economic standards within society, and decreasing the appeal of violence.

As we contemplate policy responses to the range of threats in the world today, it seems that we need to move beyond the spread of nuclear weapons and the threat of terrorism, to the root causes of conflict. These are not necessarily new ideas. Many argue that we need to do whatever we can to reduce the number of fragile states around the world, since the combination of long-term grievances, masses of refugees, horribly uneven development, lack of human rights, and security challenges is known to produce human misery and political conflict. Former US defense secretary Robert Gates has argued that "dealing with such fractured or failing states is, in many ways, the main security challenge of our time."[3] Yet we lack a coherent strategy.

What is to be done? The question can be raised in terms of foreign aid, which could be a much more effective instrument for change than it has been. Used in the proper way, foreign aid can be one of the best weapons against violence. For example, George W. Bush supported debt relief and provided aid through programs such as the President's Emergency Plan for AIDS Relief (PEPFAR), viewed by some to be one of the major foreign policy achievements of his administration, which continued under Barack Obama.[4] But this assistance, which makes antiretroviral therapy accessible to more than 2 million Africans, has been extremely limited, and continued funding will likely be flat at best, despite President Obama's stated support as well as widespread recognition of the program's success. A *Wall Street Journal* op-ed jointly penned by Madeleine Albright and Colin Powell, two former US secretaries of state, highlights the fundamental connection between richer and poorer countries and the imperative to maintain our awareness of interdependence: "Our country's economic health and security are inextricably linked to the prosperity and security of the rest of the world . . . (even in the midst of an economic crisis) pulling back from global engagement is not an option."[5] As the United States ushers in the Trump presidency, hinged on the promise of promoting "America First" policies, perhaps some level of disengagement will be considered more seriously than it has in a long time. If this is the case, the United States is not alone: protectionist policies propped up by populist leaders are prominent in many regions of the world. Regional associations, such as the European Union, trade deals, and alliances—some of which have persisted since the end of World War II, are weakening and facing calls for their dissolution.

The other major tool for influence is the military. With the Marshall Plan, the United States once recognized how poverty bred instability and that promoting the development of other countries was a national security issue for the United States. However, during the Cold War, US foreign aid was used to promote stability by propping up dictators—Washington's assistance to Indonesia's Suharto fits this mold precisely. The United States needs to remember the important role that aid can play in promoting stability, but this time it must not use it just to bribe authoritarians into helping in the war on terror. There is a high price for such a policy: the United States it is still paying for cozying up to the Iranian Shah for all those years. US policies in Pakistan and Afghanistan and elsewhere—if seen to be promoting security over human rights—risk similar blowback.

Joseph Nye's concept of "soft power," or the ability to influence others by attracting them to one's values, ideals, and norms, is increasingly tendered as a way to understand a country's (or organization's) appeal and leverage. Nye has argued, "When Washington discounts the importance of its attractiveness abroad, it pays a steep price."[6] In a sense, soft power is about public diplomacy. It is something that, as of late, others have been aggressively promoting as well, especially the Chinese throughout the developing world, with investment and engagement across Africa, the Middle East, and increasingly in South America.[7] Few have claimed that soft power is a zero-sum game, but China's offering up of an alternative to US policies is quite attractive to some countries that are frustrated with perceived US meddling and infringement. And a recent report contended that "the US has reserves of soft power that it has underused in recent years."[8] But soft power is different than the traditional military and economic policy levers, which are wielded by states to demonstrate (and increase) their influence. While governments can manage and promote soft power, much of its appeal actually comes from citizens—from the observed interactions between leaders and led, and from the projection of a sense of civic duty, commitment, and often, philanthropy. This is why awareness—call it global literacy, if you will—is so important, especially the appreciation of difference and the ability to comprehend that others may not see the world from a singular perspective.

For many people around the world, including some of its closest allies in the West, the United States lost the moral high ground with its unilateral actions during the 2000s. This was most clear when the United States and Great Britain, with clear disapproval from a majority of their colleagues—friend and foe alike—within the United Nations, waged war against Saddam Hussein and his purported weapons of mass destruction—which have never been found. As Richard Haass, president of the Council on Foreign Relations, said about this decision, "the full consequences . . . cannot yet be measured."[9] As much as many believed President Obama would bring a completely new approach and, by connection, new perceptions of the United States, significant changes have yet to be realized. As the United States works its way out of the global recession, it again faces accusations of exceptionalist behavior. As we discussed in Chapter 19, whether it is accurate or not, many around the world view the United States in retreat, leading to rearmament in the face of insecurity. Military spending is spiking in many regions of the world, including East Asia (up 75 percent since the prior decade), Eastern Europe (up 90 percent), and Saudi Arabia (up 97 percent).[10]

As this book goes to press, the war in Syria rages forward, with no solutions in sight. The world faces an unprecedented refugee crisis that is inviting a nationalist

(and indeed xenophobic) backlash. Iran rises and North Korea rattles. Climate change threatens coastal communities the world over, yet major countries, the United States included, continue to entertain "debates" about its existence. Borders seem more resilient than ever, and popular sentiment leans much more toward nationalism and much less toward internationalism. What balance of values and policies will follow? From where will the next major challenges to peace, security, and freedom emerge?

Notes

1. Quoted in Mike William, "Slow-Burning Problems Could Singe US," *Montreal Gazette,* February 14, 2002, p. A19.
2. Ruchir Sharma, "When Borders Close," *New York Times,* November 13, 2016, p. SR7.
3. Robert M. Gates, "Helping Others Defend Themselves: The Future of U.S. Security Assistance," *Foreign Affairs,* May–June 2010.
4. Neil Patel, "Emergency to Efficiency," *Harvard Political Review,* December 5, 2010.
5. Madeleine K. Albright and Colin L. Powell, "Don't Forget About Foreign Aid," *Wall Street Journal,* May 5, 2009.
6. Joseph S. Nye Jr., "The Decline of America's Soft Power: Why Washington Should Worry," *Foreign Affairs,* May–June 2004, p. 17.
7. Joshua Kurlantzick, *Charm Offensive: How China's Soft Power Is Transforming the World* (New Haven: Yale University Press, 2007).
8. Carola McGiffert, ed., *Chinese Soft Power and Its Implications for the United States* (Washington, DC: Center for Strategic and International Studies, 2009), p. 126.
9. Quoted in "Viewpoints: The World Since 9/11," BBC News, September 8, 2006.
10. Sharma, "When Borders Close."

Acronyms

AGOA	African Growth and Opportunity Act
AIIB	Asian Infrastructure Investment Bank
AKP	Justice and Development Party (Turkey)
ANC	African National Congress
APC	All Progressives Congress (Nigeria)
ARF	ASEAN Regional Forum
ASEAN	Association of Southeast Asian Nations
ASG	Abu Sayyaf Group (Philippines)
ATT	Arms Trade Treaty
AU	African Union
BRICET	Brazil, Russia, India, China, Eastern Europe, Turkey
BRICM	Brazil, Russia, India, China, Mexico
BRICs	Brazil, Russia, India, China
BRICS	Brazil, Russia, India, China, South Africa
CAN	Andean Community of Nations
CCP	Chinese Communist Party
CCT	conditional cash transfer
CEDAW	Convention on the Elimination of All Forms of Discrimination Against Women
CIA	Central Intelligence Agency (United States)
CRC	Convention on the Rights of the Child
DRC	Democratic Republic of Congo
ECOMOG	ECOWAS Cease-Fire Monitoring Group
ECOSOC	Economic and Social Council (UN)
ECOWAS	Economic Community of West African States
EPZ	export processing zone
EU	European Union
FAO	Food and Agriculture Organization (UN)
FARC	Revolutionary Armed Forces of Colombia
FDI	foreign direct investment
FIS	Islamic Salvation Front (Algeria)
G8	Group of Eight

G-20	Group of 20
GATT	General Agreement on Tariffs and Trade
GDI	Gender-Related Development Index
GDP	gross domestic product
GII	Gender Inequality Index
GNI	gross national income
GNP	gross national product
HDI	Human Development Index
HIC	high-income country
HIPC	highly indebted poor country
IAEA	International Atomic Energy Agency
IARF	International Association for Religious Freedom
IBRD	International Bank for Reconstruction and Development (World Bank)
ICBL	International Campaign to Ban Landmines
ICC	International Criminal Court
ICJ	International Court of Justice (UN)
ICRC	International Committee of the Red Cross
ICTR	International Criminal Tribunal for Rwanda
IFI	international financial institution
IFRC	International Federation of Red Cross and Red Crescent Societies
IGO	international governmental organization
ILO	International Labour Organization
IMF	International Monetary Fund
IPCC	Intergovernmental Panel on Climate Change
IPE	international political economy
IRGC	Islamic Revolutionary Guard Corps (Iran)
IS	Islamic State
ISI	import substitution industrialization
ISIS	Islamic State of Iraq and Syria
ITU	International Telecommunication Union
JCPOA	Joint Comprehensive Plan of Action
JEI	Jamaat-e-Islami (Pakistan)
JI	Jemaah Islamiah
KMT	Nationalist Party (Kuomintang) (China)
LDC	less developed country
LGBT	lesbian, gay, bisexual, transgender
LIC	low-income country
LLDC	least–less developed country
LMICs	low- and lower-middle-income countries
LRA	Lord's Resistance Army (Uganda)
MDC	Movement for Democratic Change (Zimbabwe)
MDGs	Millennium Development Goals
MDRI	Multilateral Debt Relief Initiative
MEND	Movement for the Emancipation of the Niger Delta (Nigeria)
Mercosur	Common Market of the South (also known as Mercosul)
MNC	multinational corporation

MNLF	Moro National Liberation Front (Malaysia)
MOSOP	Movement for the Survival of the Ogoni People (Nigeria)
MSF	Médecins sans Frontières (Doctors Without Borders)
NAFTA	North American Free Trade Agreement
NAM	Non-Aligned Movement
NATO	North Atlantic Treaty Organization
NDA	Niger Delta Avengers (Nigeria)
NEPAD	New Partnership for Africa's Development
NGO	nongovernmental organization
NIC	newly industrializing country
NIDL	new international division of labor
NIEO	new international economic order
NIMBY	"not in my backyard"
NPT	Nuclear Non-Proliferation Treaty
OAS	Organization of American States
OAU	Organization of African Unity
OECD	Organization for Economic Cooperation and Development
OIC	Organization of the Islamic Conference
OPEC	Organization of Petroleum Exporting Countries
P5	permanent five members of the UN Security Council
P5+1	permanent five members of the UN Security Council plus Germany
PAN	National Action Party (Mexico)
PAP	People's Armed Police (China)
PDI-P	Indonesian Democratic Party–Struggle
PDP	People's Democratic Party (Nigeria)
PEPFAR	President's Emergency Plan for AIDS Relief
PKI	Communist Party of Indonesia
PKK	Kurdistan Workers Party (Turkey)
PKO	peacekeeping operation
PLA	People's Liberation Army (China)
PPK	Pedro Pablo Kuczynski
PPP	purchasing power parity
PQLI	Physical Quality of Life Index
PRC	People's Republic of China
PRD	Party of Democratic Revolution (Mexico)
PRI	Institutional Revolutionary Party (Mexico)
R2P	responsibility to protect
RSF	Reporters sans Frontières (Reporters Without Borders)
RUF	Revolutionary United Front (Sierra Leone)
SADC	Southern African Development Community
SAP	structural adjustment program
SARS	severe acute respiratory syndrome
SBY	Susilo Bambang Yudhoyono (Indonesia)
SDGs	Sustainable Development Goals
SEATO	Southeast Asia Treaty Organization
SOE	state-owned enterprise

SP	Sinai Province (Egypt)
TINA	"there is no alternative"
UAE	United Arab Emirates
UDHR	Universal Declaration of Human Rights
UDI	Unilateral Declaration of Independence (Rhodesia)
UNAIDS	Joint United Nations Programme on HIV/AIDS
UNCTAD	United Nations Conference on Trade and Development
UNDP	United Nations Development Programme
UNEP	United Nations Environment Programme
UNHCR	United Nations High Commission(er) for Refugees
UNICEF	United Nations Children's Fund
UNIFEM	United Nations Development Fund for Women
VPN	virtual private network
WHO	World Health Organization
WID	women in development
WMD	weapon of mass destruction
WTO	World Trade Organization
ZANLA	Zimbabwe African National Liberation Army
ZANU	Zimbabwe African National Union
ZANU-PF	Zimbabwe African National Union–Patriotic Front
ZAPU	Zimbabwe African People's Union
ZIPRA	Zimbabwe People's Revolutionary Army

Glossary

abertura A Portuguese term borrowed from the Brazilian experience, describing a political opening that may or may not lead to democratization. *See* **political liberalization**.

absolute poverty The term used by the United Nations to describe dire material hardship, a standard of living beneath human dignity. It is a crushing poverty in which people lack access to the basic necessities of life such as food, clean water, shelter, and healthcare.

accountability A characteristic of democracy existing when government is held responsible for its actions. Governments that are promoting accountability seek to control corruption not only by reducing the incentive to steal, but also by raising the costs and risks of official misconduct and demonstrating to the population that no one can violate the law with impunity.

acephalous society A "headless society" or "stateless society" in which there is no full-time executive; rather, groups of people are governed by committee or consensus.

amnesty A pardon granted by governments to individual and often groups of offenders as a gesture of reconciliation, often during a transition or change of regime.

aspiration gap Disparity between what is desired or hoped for and what can be attained. This concept helps us understand the consequences of unmet expectations.

austerity plan Another name for structural adjustment, denoting the hardship associated with implementing such measures. *See* **structural adjustment program**.

authoritarianism A nondemocratic political system in which the ruler depends on coercion rather than popular legitimacy to remain in power. Such systems are characterized by their abuse of human rights. Power is concentrated in the executive branch of government, and executives act with little if any interference from legislatures or judiciaries.

"Axis of Evil" The phrase included in President George W. Bush's 2002 State of the Union address to label Iran, Iraq, and North Korea as threats to world peace due to their attempts to obtain nuclear, chemical, or biological weapons and their alleged support of terrorism.

bottom-up approach An approach to change or development in which policies or projects are initiated and directed from the grassroots or masses.

bourgeoisie Originally from the French word *bourg* for "market town," this became a prominent term of analysis in Marxist socialism, separating the working class (known as the proletariat) from the landowning merchant classes and capitalist entrepreneurs (known as the bourgeoisie). In the Marxist framework, it is the bourgeoisie who will be eliminated by class struggle to produce a classless, communist society. *See also* **proletariat**.

BRICs Brazil, Russia, India, and China; a grouping used to refer to the world's fast-growing emerging economies that are also taking a greater role in political forums. Other countries are sometimes added to the grouping (such as South Africa, South Korea, and Mexico), contributing to an alphabet soup of acronyms.

Bush Doctrine President George W. Bush's foreign policy approach following the terrorist attacks of September 11, 2001. He conceptually divided the world community into two categories—those who support terrorists versus those who fight terrorists. The doctrine may be summed up in his statement that "either you are with us, or you are with the terrorists." In many parts of the world, this simplification was rejected as self-serving and unreflective of the complexities of the twenty-first century.

cadre party A type of political party dominated by personality-driven cliques and factional groupings that depends on local notables to choose and groom candidates. Cadre parties are recognized for their limited recruitment and are often found in states with limited voting rights. The term *cadre* has also been used to refer to the most dedicated members of a political party.

case study A detailed examination of a particular phenomenon or institution (in this context, a state). A method that seeks to find and demonstrate causal connections by tracing them through a series of cases, which are then compared.

caudillo A political strongman, often a member of the military.

Chapter VII The section of the UN Charter that permits the Security Council to "order binding action, including economic sanctions and the use of armed force." It sets enforcement mechanisms to prevent or deter threats to international peace. So-called Chapter VII authority has been used often since the end of the Cold War to justify intervention in conflict or unstable circumstances.

civil society Generally refers to voluntary social interactions between individuals that are independent of the government. Civil society organizations are commonly recognized as intermediaries between the government and the family. As a concept,

civil society (also known as public space) includes nongovernmental organizations, social movements, and professional associations.

class (social) A number of people or things grouped together. A group of people who are linked together because of certain things held in common, such as occupation, social status, or economic background.

cleavage A socially supported division between groups in society who are significant enough to have forms of expression. Cleavages are often based on ethnicity, socioeconomic factors, or gender. Scholars have highlighted two dominant patterns of such divisions. Coinciding cleavages are clear and distinct, in which multiple competing viewpoints or points of division line up in clearly divided categories, presenting a situation that is more ripe for conflict. Crosscutting cleavages are mixed between and among various groups, producing an outcome in which cleavages are dispersed throughout society; therefore, those seeking support from the population must appeal to a wider variety of groups.

Cold War The period of intense US-Soviet rivalry that ran from World War II until the dissolution of the Soviet Union in 1991. Although this antagonism was played out in many different ways across every part of the world, it is known as being "cold" because, fearing nuclear catastrophe, the two parties never engaged in direct military confrontations.

collective security The principle that aggression against one state is taken as an aggression against all. Agreement to collectively resist aggression against another is a founding idea of the United Nations. Collective security arrangements are pursued by states in the hope of deterring threatening action.

common market Allows for the free circulation of goods, services, and capital between member states.

comparative advantage Liberal principle that holds that efficiency is maximized through specialization in production.

comparative studies This approach seeks to comprehend the complexity of human experience by adopting an eclectic, multidisciplinary approach. It utilizes the comparative method to produce generalizations that describe, identify, and explain trends—and even predict human behavior. This approach identifies relationships and interactions between actors, as well as patterns of behavior, by making comparisons (of two or more countries or of one country over time) to find similarities and differences in experience.

comprador The indigenous elite who dominate the economies and politics of many non-Western countries. They often enter into sweetheart deals with foreign interests—at great cost to the local majority.

conditional cash transfer (CCT) Government programs that make cash assistance to poor families conditional on a receiver's actions and are often related to child welfare (e.g., assistance of $35 a month to parents who take their children to a doc-

tor for medical checkups or who enroll them in school). Such programs, if well designed and implemented, serve as a long-term investment in human capital and development. CCTs exist in a variety of forms in more than thirty countries.

consolidation Said to exist when democracy has put down deep roots and is durable—when democracy "is the only game in town." Democracies become consolidated by becoming more inclusive, by respecting human rights, and by guaranteeing equal representation to minorities and other marginalized groups. Stability, citizen loyalty, and a widespread belief that the system is good are all signs of consolidation.

convergence Said to be attained when less developed countries "catch up" with developed countries.

corporatism Terminology describing relations between groups and political authority; government restricts the development and operation of independent organizations. In corporatist systems, society is divided by functions (such as unions, professional associations, etc.), and government attempts to coordinate society by balancing groups that must negotiate with government for legal or economic benefits.

corruption Official misconduct or the abuse of power for private gain. A problem in both developed and less developed countries that has contributed to the breakdown of both military and civilian governments as populations call for accountability and transparency.

cross-national analysis A study comparing two or more countries in order to make larger generalizations.

cultural relativism The view that worldwide there is no commonly held morality. Rather, human rights and other ethical issues vary depending on the group, and consequently the promotion of any set of moral codes as somehow universal is misplaced and imperialistic.

Cultural Revolution Formally called the Great Proletarian Cultural Revolution, a chaotic period in modern Chinese history, officially from 1966 to 1969, when Chairman Mao Zedong directed the Red Guards to attack officials to prevent the spread of capitalism and materialism. Many individuals (especially businesspeople and intellectuals) were sent to the Chinese countryside to "learn from the peasants," while others were sent to "reeducation" camps to have their problems rectified. Most analysts today argue that the chaos of the Cultural Revolution did not truly end until Mao's death in 1976.

customs union A form of economic integration in which states agree to promote trade among members by eliminating tariffs and nontariff barriers, and to cooperate to protect their producers by setting a common tariff against nonmember states.

delegative democracy A political system that has an outward appearance of being democratic, and is more democratic than authoritarian. However, such systems are

led by elites whose commitment to democracy is said to have limits. In delegative democracies, the executive claims to personify the nation's interests and therefore has the exclusive right to interpret them.

democracy (political) "Government by the people," existing in several variations and operating through different kinds of constitutional systems. A type of government or political system that is based on a decentralization of power and built on the principle of popular sovereignty: in democracies people choose their representatives, who compete for political office through free and fair elections held on a regular basis. Consequently, citizen participation and respect for civil liberties are integral to democracy, as citizens must have the freedom to hold political leaders accountable for their actions.

democracy dividend Popular expectation that after years of abuse, the transition to democracy will bring an economic expansion, an end to corruption, and an improved quality of life. There is usually much goodwill created by a democratic transition; however, this honeymoon is often short-lived and the resulting disillusionment is dangerous for fragile new democracies.

democratic institutionalization The process of crafting, nurturing, and developing democratic institutions to ensure participation, representation, accountability, respect for human rights, and so on. Institutionalization refers to the development of regularized processes; as democratic institutionalization occurs, "the rules of the game" become stabilized and formalized.

democratic transition A phase of political liberalization in which a political system is democratizing (opportunities for political participation and competition are expanded, free and fair elections are scheduled, and so on). Not every political liberalization results in a democratic transition, and not all democratic transitions result in democracy—they can turn out many different ways.

deterrence Defense policy in which a country attempts to prevent attack by threatening credible retaliation. The logic of deterrence is that an initiating action will cause mutual suicide. The greatest deterrents are considered to be nuclear weapons— the mere possession of nuclear weapons is believed sufficient to deter an enemy, because unless a country's entire nuclear arsenal could be wiped out by a first strike, the destruction caused by the inevitable retaliation would be too great a price to pay.

development There is little agreement on how best to describe development. The UN defines political development as "the achievement of a stable democracy that promotes the economic well-being of its citizens in an equitable, humane, and environmentally concerned manner." Some identify it as a process associated with increasing humans' choices and opportunities. Development is now widely recognized as promoting material and nonmaterial forms of well-being; it is associated with improved living standards, although it rests on political participation and human security and is concerned with the distribution of and access to resources. Often confused with "growth," development should be understood as both a process and an end.

devotee party Type of political party that is dominated by a charismatic leader.

disintegration When political reconfiguration spirals out of control. Divides are aggravated by internal and external demands for change, the military's unwillingness or inability to prevent a breakup, and the state's inability to meet demands for change. Weak states are said to "implode"—to decay and collapse from within.

displaced persons People who are forced to flee their homes but who have not crossed internationally recognized borders. The numbers of internally displaced people are often higher than official counts of refugees, and are considered to be more reflective of the magnitude of human suffering.

divide and conquer A common means of colonial conquest in which a usurping power sets two parties against each other, aggravates tensions to the point that the parties bleed each other dry, and then moves into the vacuum. Also known as divide and rule.

due process The expectation that certain procedures must always be followed in making policy; guarantees of fair legal procedures designed to protect the rights and liberties of individuals.

economic liberalization Neoliberal economic reforms that dismantle government controls and promote opening up economies to foreign trade and investment. Also known as market reforms.

efficacy An attitude about one's competence to effect change; a perception of ability or the sense that one's participation can make a difference. A sense of efficacy is an important factor in the decision to be engaged in public affairs—people with a strong sense of efficacy are more likely to be active in civic life than those who believe their actions would be worthless. The antonym of efficacy in this sense would be *alienation*.

elite revolution Special type of revolution that is rapid and swift, with minimal participation by those outside of the initiating core and with limited violence. Also known as revolution from above.

elites Those who hold more power than others, whether cultural, political, economic, social, or otherwise. According to elite theory, elites are always outnumbered by those ostensibly holding less power, often referred to as the masses. Elites possess certain advantages, of wealth, privilege, education, training, status, political power, and the like.

empire The largest, most complex form of state organization, distinguished from a chiefdom by the size of the territories and the populations it controls. Empires are usually vast and impose a centralized government or single sovereign over a collection of different communities or nations. Empires often dominate regional and international trade; known for their large militaries, they frequently amass great riches through conquest and demands for tribute.

essential functions The most basic duties expected of elected governments, such as collecting taxes, enforcing laws, designing policies, and being responsive to the majority.

exceptionalist A belief or behavior that demonstrates the view that one's group is different from the norm, and therefore above the rules by which others are supposed to abide. An exceptionalist view of a group or event emphasizes the singular, unique qualities of whatever is being examined—making it seem that any particular circumstance is difficult to compare to another.

export processing zone (EPZ) A special trade area established by less developed countries to attract foreign investment. In the hope of creating jobs, obtaining technology transfers, and other benefits, EPZs offer low or no taxes and guarantee cheap, docile labor and minimal government regulation or interference with regard to health or environmental codes or the repatriation of profits.

extraterritoriality Imposing one's rules and laws outside of one's own sovereign territory. Extraterritoriality was invoked during the colonial period; now, many developing countries view the United States as attempting to return to this state of affairs by insisting that foreign countries abide by US laws or policies.

fallacy of electoralism The mistake of focusing on elections as "proof" of democracy and ignoring other political realities.

fatwa A religious judgment issued by Muslim clerics.

formal sector The "above-ground" part of the economy (as opposed to the informal sector), calculated into gross domestic product.

founding elections The first elections marking a democratic transition, symbolizing a departure from authoritarianism.

Four Tigers Hong Kong, Singapore, South Korea, and Taiwan—distinguished by their record of strong growth rates and their shared reliance on state capitalism.

General Agreement on Tariffs and Trade (GATT) International economic organization formed to help liberalize and manage global trade after World War II. Established to promote the rules of conduct for free trade (such as lowering tariff rates and discouraging protectionist policies) and to provide a forum for the resolution of trade disputes. GATT was eventually overwhelmed by the growth in the volume of world trade and was replaced with the World Trade Organization (WTO) in 1995.

globalization Describes the world's increasing interconnectedness, particularly in regard to communications, economies, and cultures, and associated with faster and greater international flows of trade, investment, and finance as well as migration, cultural diffusion, and communication—more specifically, a process describing the spread of capitalism and "modernization" worldwide. Alternatively viewed as a positive force that promotes development and brings the world closer together, or as a

negative phenomenon contributing to worsening under-development and the homogenization of the world's cultures.

grassroots-based approach An approach that is designed, implemented, and controlled by local communities. Often lauded for being not only more democratic in principle but also more effective in operation. *See* **bottom-up approach**.

greenhouse effect An increasingly substantiated theory that Earth is experiencing a gradual rise in temperatures and that this is due to human activity. This global warming is associated with buildup of greenhouse gases (most notably carbon dioxide), which are released by the burning of fossil fuels. As these waste gases collect in the upper atmosphere, the sun's heat becomes trapped, warming the planet (much like glass traps heat in a greenhouse). Although scientists continue to disagree about the rate of warming, most highly respected climatologists expect that if trends continue, the greenhouse effect will contribute to massive alterations in climate, which will contribute to a variety of consequences, some of them near cataclysmic.

Group of 20 (G-20) Founded in 1999, the G-20 is a forum that brings together finance ministers and central bank governors from the leading industrialized and emerging market economies in a regular dialogue to discuss a range of key issues in regard to the global economy. Together the partners constitute 90 percent of the world's gross national product, 80 percent of world trade, and two-thirds of the world's population.

growth A summation of economic performance referring to an increase in the volume of trade or economic output of a country, measured by gross domestic product (GDP), gross national income (GNI), or gross national product (GNP). Growth is usually a key indicator of a healthy economy, measured against the previous performance of each national economy, not a single worldwide standard (e.g., a 10 percent growth rate in a small economy, albeit impressive, actually indicates a smaller amount of absolute economic activity than a single-digit growth rate in a larger economy).

guerrilla From the Spanish, literally "little war." Guerrillas are loosely organized, nonuniformed combatants, often small in number. Guerrilla tactics are mobile and swift, incorporating the element of surprise with sabotage, hit and run, and ambush, all in violation of conventional laws of warfare.

hegemon A strong, controlling force that attempts to impose its preferences on others. Used in discussions of international affairs to describe the dominance of a specific country. If the nineteenth century was the period of British hegemony, the post–Cold War era is one of US hegemony, with the United States being the sole remaining superpower.

highly indebted poor country (HIPC) A country falling into this category is eligible for a program of debt relief if it makes the required neoliberal economic reforms.

human security Defined as the absence of structural violence, which is understood as widespread poverty and other forms of economic, social, and environmental

degradation. Human security is a new but increasingly recognized understanding of security that goes far beyond issues of armaments and territorial security. It addresses individual and collective perceptions of present and potential threats to physical and psychological well-being.

identity The collective aspect or characteristics by which a person or group is known. Humans have multiple identities that they choose to emphasize, depending on context. Common identities uniting people in action include race, class, gender, and region.

ideology The belief systems of individuals and groups; a linked set of ideas that describe the world, help people understand their role within society, and arouse them to take action, whether to change or preserve the existing situation.

import substitution industrialization A development strategy especially popular in the mid-twentieth century that seeks to diversify economies and lessen the dependence of less developed countries (LDCs) on foreign imports of manufactured goods. It encourages industrialization headquartered within LDCs by subsidizing and protecting local producers from foreign competition.

informal sector Also known as the informal economy, the informal sector is a shadow economy comprising semilegal or illegal activities that are unreported, unregulated, and untaxed—and therefore not included in the calculation of a country's gross domestic product. Because it is so often the case that their opportunities in the formal economy are limited, women compose a large number of informal-sector workers.

integration A process that increases the quantity and quality of interconnectedness between countries through small or large steps; promotes cooperation between countries based on common security or economic concerns. For example, the European Union began in the 1950s (as the European Economic Community) as an agreement on coal and steel and over the years has moved increasingly toward the creation of a single market—the world's largest.

interdependence A political and economic relationship based on mutual vulnerability between two countries, each of which is sensitive to what happens in the other. The term implies that even developed countries are bound to less developed countries by interdependence, as opposed to those who characterize the relationship as one of dependence—largely the dependence of less developed countries on developed countries.

International Criminal Court (ICC) The world's first permanent international criminal court, the ICC was established by the Rome Statute in 1998 and entered into force in 2002. More than a hundred states have ratified the Rome Statute in recognition of the Court's authority. The Court resides in The Hague, where this independent entity serves as a mechanism for trying individuals accused of committing the world's most serious crimes: war crimes, crimes against humanity, and genocide.

international economic system The network of world trade, which is based on the remains of what was known as the Bretton Woods system. Formed in the post–World War II period, this international economic system has been dominated by developed countries under US leadership. Bretton Woods gave lip service to liberal economic policies such as open economies and free trade. However, even its most ardent advocates routinely practiced protectionist policies that have hamstrung the development of less developed countries. Consequently, critics of this system argue that it is structured to benefit the already rich, to the detriment of the poor.

international financial institution (IFI) An organization that governs fiscal matters within and between states. Most IFIs (such as the International Monetary Fund and the World Bank) promote the neoliberal agenda and are run by developed countries—with very little input from the less developed countries over which they have tremendous influence.

international governmental organization (IGO) An organization with two or more member states that may serve as a forum for discussion to promote cooperation on either regional or functional (issue-oriented) matters. The largest IGO is the United Nations; however, IGOs can be very limited in scope and membership as well.

International Monetary Fund (IMF) Central to the world financial system, this international organization is dedicated to promoting market economics. Established soon after the 1944 Bretton Woods conference, the IMF is a global lending agency originally created to aid in the postwar recovery of Europe and Japan. Rich countries continue to dominate the IMF, which operates under a weighted voting system based on the amount of money members donate to the organization. The IMF is charged with several responsibilities, including stabilization of exchange rates and promotion of fiscal conservatism. One of its most important roles is to assist with balance of payments problems, and in this capacity it serves as an international credit bureau—for countries. Just as is the case with individuals, countries are assigned credit ratings. If the IMF blackballs a country, it will have a very difficult time obtaining credit—from the IMF or from any international financial institution, for that matter. On the other hand, in order to remain in good stead with the IMF, countries must accept conditionality, or demonstrate their willingness to submit to neoliberal economic reforms such as those promoted through extended-credit facilities.

international political economy The study of the relationship between politics and economics at the international and transnational levels; examines how international politics affects the world's economies and how economics affects international political relationships. Advocates of this approach contend that an understanding of international political economy is necessary since economic factors shape most areas of political life. International political economy focuses on issues such as world markets, global financial institutions, and multinational corporations.

intifada From the Arabic, meaning "shivering" or "shaking off." The term was first applied to the Palestinian uprising against Israeli occupation from 1987 to 1993, in protest of killings near a Palestinian settlement. Another intifada began in the fall of 2000.

irredentist war A form of violent interstate conflict stemming from a nation's efforts to redraw political boundaries to include territory considered its homeland or to unite with its people living on the other side of a border.

jihad From the Arabic, signifying "struggle." Although it has recently been taken to narrowly mean a "holy war," its more accurate meaning encompasses the internal struggle that faithful Muslims undergo in their attempts to contend with the challenges facing them. Jihad also encompasses the requirements for a permissible and legitimate war, similar to other faith traditions' teachings on justifiable combat.

legitimacy The popular perception on the part of large numbers of people that the government, its leaders, and its policies are valid, right, just, and worthy of support. A legitimate regime is not necessarily the same as a legal regime, nor does it mean that a regime is democratic. A political regime is legitimate when it is accepted by the majority of its citizens as right and proper enough to be obeyed in most instances. Legitimacy can be achieved through all sorts of means, including propaganda, clientelism, and coercion.

legitimate trade The trade of raw materials in Africa, which Europeans began to pursue more ardently to serve the needs of industry. For a variety of reasons, by the early nineteenth century the "legitimate trade" had displaced the "illegitimate trade" (the term abolitionists had used for the slave trade) along the African coast.

liberal democracy A political system that has undertaken (and continues to undertake) comprehensive political reform in which democratic institutions are routinized and internalized and civil and political rights are protected—so much so that democracy is said to be "consolidated."

liberation theology A movement that started within the Catholic Church in Latin America and has spread to other Christian churches and regions of the world; an action-oriented ideology that promotes social justice through local activism. Liberation theology teaches that the cause of poverty is capitalism, and that the Church should lead a revolution to establish governing systems that will redistribute wealth, end all forms of imperialism, and promote democracy. It was especially popular throughout the 1980s, but has faced opposition because of its use of Marxist revolutionary ideals.

mandatory system The system for administering the territories taken from Germany and its allies after World War I, under Article 22 of the Charter of the League of Nations. The League appointed states such as Britain, France, and South Africa to help prepare the mandates for their eventual independence, yet in many cases the mandatory system was considered no more than "a fig leaf for colonialism." Later, when the mandates became trust territories administered by the United Nations, the mandatory powers were held somewhat more accountable for their actions.

maquiladora A subsidiary of a multinational corporation that assembles imported parts and exports manufactured goods; originally the assembly plants that have proliferated along the US-Mexican border since the implementation of the North American Free

Trade Agreement (NAFTA). However, the term is now sometimes used to describe such enterprises wherever they exist in the non-Western world.

mass party A type of political party that attempts to be as inclusionary as possible, often attempting to incorporate less politically engaged individuals and groups into the political process. Mass parties are marked by a formal nationwide structure, and are used to mobilize large groups of voters.

masses Relative to the elites, the masses are those who lack power and influence and who always outnumber the elites; the vast majority of the population in a country tend to be lumped into the category of the "masses" or the "common people."

mercantilism A precapitalist stage of development marked by accumulation of capital and accomplished through trade and plunder on a worldwide scale. This aggressive economic policy was the guiding force behind the conquest of many areas; it provided the capital base for Europe's industrialization. In its more contemporary form, mercantilism describes the situation when a power seeks commercial expansion to achieve a surplus in its balance of trade.

military professionalism Critical to the survival of democracies, this term refers to the military's depoliticization. Where it exists, coups d'état are unthinkable, as the military recognizes the supremacy of civilian rule and views itself as serving civilian government.

Millennium Development Goals (MDGs) A global action plan to end poverty by 2015. The plan comprises eight goals such as halving the percentage of people who go hungry, promoting universal primary education, and reducing the loss of biodiversity. Agreed upon in 2000 by 189 countries at the United Nations Millennium Summit, the plan provides a blueprint for ending poverty and a pledge to galvanize the world into achieving it.

mother country Another name for a colonizing country; its use denotes the exclusive ties that bound the colonies to the mother country much like an umbilical cord. Also refers to the parental role the colonizers portrayed themselves as playing in the non-Western world.

Multilateral Debt Relief Initiative (MDRI) An enhancement of the highly indebted poor countries (HIPC) initiative, the MDRI cancels the eligible debt of the poorest countries that have "graduated" or completed their HIPC requirements. Under this program, monies saved from the cancellation of this debt are to be used to meet the Millennium Development Goals.

multinational corporation (MNC) A business enterprise headquartered in one country (usually a developed country) with activities abroad stemming from direct foreign investment located in several countries. As MNCs conglomerate and form near-monopolies, international trade is increasingly dominated by a handful of cor-

porations. Enormously powerful because they are so flexible, they can readily move capital, goods, and technology to fit market conditions.

multinational state A political unit of organization that includes two or more ethnic or national groups. Largely due to colonialism's arbitrary boundaries, a nation may or may not reside within the political boundary of a state, thereby producing a multinational state.

nationalism A set of political beliefs that center around the shared sense of characteristics attributable to a group of people known to each other as a nation. Nationalism has been used to promote the interests and needs of a particular group of people, and has been a particularly strong rallying force, both uniting and dividing groups.

nation-state A term that combines the ideals of two concepts. A nation is considered to be a group of people who recognize a similarity among themselves because of common culture, language, or history. Nations often but do not always coincide with political boundaries of states, thereby producing multinational states. A state is considered to be a political entity with legal jurisdiction and physical control—an internationally recognized government.

neocolonialism A term used to describe the condition from which many non-Western states today suffer, as they continue to be indirectly controlled by their former colonizers or other developed countries; said to exist because less developed countries operate under so many of the constraints of colonialism that they are considered independent only in name.

neoliberalism The contemporary version of procapitalist liberal economic strategy, which holds that all benefit from an open economy and free trade, or the unencumbered movement of goods and services between states. It is the dominant view held by the governments of developed countries and most international financial institutions, such as the World Bank and the International Monetary Fund. Neoliberals fervently believe that globalization is a positive force and that the current international economic system based on free competition can work for all if countries will just embrace it. Most "third world" countries then must adopt the proper reforms, promote openness, and prepare for a period of austerity to get their economic houses in order.

new international division of labor (NIDL) Whereas the "old" international division of labor described the relationship between developed and less developed countries, with the former as producers of manufactured goods and the latter as producers of raw materials, the "new" division points to a shift in the product cycle, with an increasing number of less developed countries moving into manufacturing while developed countries become dominated by the service sector.

new international economic order (NIEO) A comprehensive attempt by less developed countries to reform the international economic system. Debated in the 1960s and 1970s at the United Nations Conference on Trade and Development (UNCTAD)

and other forums, the Group of 77 called for a series of changes (from increased foreign aid, to a code of conduct for multinational corporations, to elaborate efforts to stabilize the price of exports from less developed countries) aimed at "leveling the playing field" of opportunities for development. Although some of the proposals continue to be discussed today, only marginal changes have come of the NIEO so far.

newly industrializing country (NIC) Also known as a new industrial economy or an emergent economy. NICs are countries such as China, Mexico, South Korea, and Taiwan that in the past few decades have shifted from agrarian to increasingly industrial economies, due largely to strong state intervention and investment by multinational corporations. The high productivity of the cheap labor force in these countries has enabled the NICs to compete aggressively in the international market with developed countries, effectively driving their textile and other sectors out of business. *See* **Four Tigers**.

Non-Aligned Movement (NAM) Formed in 1961 in opposition to the polarizing tendencies of the Cold War, the NAM is an alliance of over a hundred countries that shunned military alliances and coalitions with other states—especially the dominant powers during the Cold War, during which time the NAM advocated the neutrality of its members. Prime Minister Jawaharlal Nehru of India, President Josip Broz Tito of Yugoslavia, and President Gamal Abdul Nasser of Egypt founded the movement as a vehicle for non-aligned countries to come together to solve mutual problems without benefit of military alliance. A summit is held every three years.

nongovernmental organization (NGO) A private association of voluntary membership that works together to accomplish set goals. The numbers of NGOs in the world exploded throughout the 1980s, and continue to swell. General examples of NGOs include universities, churches, and civic and professional associations. Increasingly at the global level, the "on the ground" competency of NGOs is being recognized in policy- and decisionmaking. One of the foremost examples of the partnership between NGOs and international organizations was the Ottawa Treaty process, which was born of the efforts of the International Campaign to Ban Landmines.

nonintervention Not interfering in the internal affairs of other countries; associated with sovereignty, nonintervention is an international principle traditionally thought to promote international stability.

parliamentary system A democratic constitutional system in which citizens select members of parliament, and executive authority is dependent on parliamentary confidence. Variously characterized as flexible and unstable, gridlock is much less likely in a parliamentary than in a presidential system. Since the majority party in parliament selects the executive, the prime minister can usually be confident that his or her initiatives will be warmly received by the legislature. In a parliamentary system, new elections are called by the prime minister, and can be called at any time (within a certain time frame). As opposed to presidential systems, effective executives can be kept in power indefinitely. However, the system is self-correcting for executive abuse, since the legislative branch can censure and rid itself of an errant executive

with much more ease than the painstaking process of impeachment necessary in a presidential system.

party system Referencing the collection of political parties in a given state or region—analysts often distinguish between single-party systems and multiparty systems, based on the number of active and viable parties in the regime. For example, a one-party-dominant system is one in which there are political alternatives but in which a single party exercises a near-monopoly on power, either due to the lack of alternatives or because of the overwhelming support of citizens. A multiparty system is one in which there are two or more major contenders for power.

patrimonialism A form of governance that exists when the ruler treats the state as his or her own personal property. Appointments to government office are assigned on the basis of loyalty to the ruler, who plays the role of a benevolent but stern parent, often through a mixture of co-optation and repression.

patron-client relationship A method of co-optation based on a relationship of reciprocity in which the powerful patron (a leader, party, agency, or government) allocates resources to his or her clients (the people) with the expectation that the clients will pledge to the patron their political loyalty.

peacekeeping operation (PKO) A noncombat military operation mandated by the UN Security Council and sent into conflict areas in an attempt to promote a peaceful transition. PKOs consist of outside forces acting on the consent of all major belligerent parties. Their tasks range from keeping apart hostile parties to helping them work together peacefully. PKOs have monitored cease-fires, created buffer zones, and helped to create and sustain nascent political institutions. PKO forces are often distinguished by their famous "blue helmets."

personalist regime Also known as a personally appropriated state—an authoritarian style of government. This regime exists when a single, highly charismatic individual, who represents him- or herself as the personification of the nation, holds unchecked power. It may exist under civilian or military rule, when the leader seeks to guarantee his or her personal control in perpetuity, as "president for life" or through a hereditary republic.

political culture The context out of which political action is taken, recognizing the importance of systems of values and beliefs. While few people would deny that culture impacts people's views on politics and government, it has been difficult to articulate the precise connections between these variables and political outcomes. In 1959, Gabriel Almond and Sidney Verba identified three root (or "civic") cultures in the countries they studied: participant, subject, and parochial.

political liberalization A process of political reform based on the extension of civil and political rights, and the promotion of a more open political system. Signs that a system is liberalizing politically include a variety of changes, such as an increasing tolerance of dissent and the release of political prisoners. Although they are

often associated with democratization, not all political liberalizations will result in democracy. Also known as an *abertura*.

political spectrum Conceptual map used to compare and contrast political ideologies. Along a horizontal line, ideologies are listed according to their views on change, the role of government in economic matters, and the relationship between religious institutions and their place in politics. The modern convention of the "left-right" political spectrum derives from legislative arrangements in the National Assembly of France, when those who supported the monarch and the Catholic Church sat on the right of the monarch, and those who favored democracy and revolution sat on the left.

populist An agenda, political party, campaign, or image designed to appeal to the "common people" rather than to the minority elite, rallying them around a shared sense of belonging and promising many things. The term was originally used to describe political movements in Europe at the end of the nineteenth century that appealed to the rural poor. The term is now used to describe mass political movements, or party platforms that purport to represent sentiment akin to the collective voice of ordinary people on social and economic issues.

praetorianism Military supremacy in politics; a type of increased involvement by soldiers in politics when military officers threaten or use force to influence political decisions and outcomes. The term derives from the praetorian guards of the Roman Empire, who were established as a unit to protect the emperor but who abused their power to overthrow and select the emperor themselves.

presidential system A type of democratic constitutional system in which citizens directly select both their legislators and their executive. Because the executive and legislative branches are elected separately, it is not uncommon for one party to hold the presidency and another to dominate the legislature. As a result, gridlock is much more likely in a presidential than in a parliamentary system. Although there are checks and balances between the various branches of government, the executive is relatively independent of the legislature, and power tends to concentrate in the executive. The rigidity of a fixed presidential term means that it is harder to remove an errant executive from power, and effective executives are constitutionally prohibited from serving beyond the prescribed term.

proletariat The socioeconomic group (or class) identified in Marxist socialism, defined by their relationship to the means of production. The proletarians are the workers who will unite together in revolutionary zeal to overcome the more powerful and entrenched bourgeoisie. Karl Marx argued that most workers own nothing but their labor (unlike artisans, who may own their machinery or tools). The proletariat is commonly called the working class.

proxy war A type of warfare undertaken by the superpowers during the Cold War. In an attempt to avoid the massive casualties associated with mutual assured destruction, the superpowers took sides in conflicts around the world, choosing intermediaries and supplying and arming them to play out the East-West rivalry with less risk of escalation to nuclear war.

reconfiguration A form of crisis management in which governments take very small steps or effect the appearance of reform while maintaining significant restrictions on civil liberties, political participation, and competition. Analysts maintain that reconfiguration is not necessarily antidemocratic in nature—even incremental steps may add up to more substantive reforms, which may in turn contribute to democratization.

reform (political) *See* **political liberalization**.

relative deprivation A comparative statement that reveals the sense that individuals or groups are not doing as well as other groups.

relative poverty Denotes a trend in terms of the gap between rich and poor countries. While some countries have made progress in eliminating absolute poverty, rising incomes during the economic boom of the 1990s have actually contributed to widening inequality overall. Consequently, while absolute poverty is said to have declined, for many less developed countries relative poverty has increased.

rescue package An assortment of loans, credits, and other forms of aid offered by the International Monetary Fund and other international financial institutions to countries suffering from massive economic dislocation (such as much of Asia during the "Asian flu" of the late 1990s). Aimed at stabilizing these economies, such packages are offered, however, only to countries willing to accept certain conditions, such as a neoliberal series of economic reforms.

resource mobilization A conceptual approach to collective behavior and social movements that emphasizes the resources necessary for success, taking into account both the material and the nonmaterial needs of participants in collective action.

responsibility to protect (R2P) An evolving international norm establishing the right of humanitarian intervention. In response to then–UN Secretary-General Kofi Annan's 2000 call to establish a global consensus on when such interventions should occur, UN member states adopted R2P as a key principle of international affairs at the 2005 World Summit. The principle emphasizes the responsibilities of sovereignty, which include protecting their populations from coordinated acts of violence, especially war crimes, crimes against humanity, and genocide. Under R2P, if a government is unable or unwilling to guard the safety of its citizens, the international community has a responsibility to help or intervene, using diplomatic channels and even military force as a last resort.

revolution Meaning "to turn around," a revolution is the attempt (often sudden) to promote fundamental change in political and social institutions of society, often accompanied by violence and economic and cultural upheaval.

revolution of rising expectations The recognition that improvement (often in the economy, but also in life choices and options) is often not as great as predicted or promised. Leaders often deliver inflated promises to their people, and rapid change can often increase hopes and desires for the future. The concept of

"rising expectations" is used to distinguish from the "revolution of falling expectations," in which people anticipate a bad future and the future turns out to be even worse than expected.

rule of law A situation in which the power of individuals is limited by a supreme set of rules that prevent arbitrary and unfair actions by governmental officials. A reliance on written rules to govern and operate, rather than on the vice and virtue of rulers.

secession The act of withdrawing or breaking away from some organized entity such as a nation, as when Bangladesh seceded from Pakistan in 1971.

secularism The separation of civil or educational institutions from ecclesiastical control; the act of de-emphasizing spiritual or religious perspectives in political, cultural, or social life.

self-determination The right of a people who share cultural ties and live in a given territory to choose their own political institutions and government. A central international political concept of the twentieth century associated with nationalism and anticolonial movements.

sharia Sometimes known as *shariat,* from the Arabic, meaning "way" or "road." *Sharia* is Muslim religious (or canonical) law based on rules for moral conduct developed over the first few centuries after the death of the prophet Mohammed. *Sharia* governs both the individual and social lives of believers, and provides followers with a basis for judging actions as good or evil. Despite debates over the degree of observance and the role of authorities for enforcement, most agree that a common understanding of *sharia* unites most Muslims around the world.

social movement Human beings with a common purpose engaged in discussion and action designed to bring about change. Social movements are responses to a perceived state of affairs and often identify specific groups in society as the source of the problem to be rectified. Often, collective actions stimulate a countermovement in response.

sovereignty Freedom from foreign control; a principle widely accepted in international law that speaks to a state's right to do as it wishes in its own territory; a doctrine that holds that states are the principal actors in international relations and the state is subject to no higher political authority. Also refers to widespread international acceptance of a particular country's control of territory.

state An organized political entity that occupies a specific territory, has a permanent population, is controlled by a government, and is regarded as sovereign. Currently there are approximately 190 recognized states worldwide. *See* **nation-state**.

state capitalism An economic system that mixes capitalism with government planning; private enterprise accounts for most of the country's economic activity, but the

government intervenes on the side of business with subsidies and other supports aimed at promoting domestic producers' competitiveness on the world market.

state society A centralized form of political organization; an outgrowth of the sedentarization of human populations, the intensification of agricultural production, and population booms. State societies are distinguished by increasing social stratification as classes emerge and power is centralized in the hands of full-time political leaders. This broad category includes many different forms of political organization, from simple, small states to immense empires.

stateless nation A group of people (with a shared identity based on language, ethnicity, religion, or common heritage) who consider themselves to have no country to call their own; people without citizenship in any state.

stateless society A smaller, decentralized grouping of the type in which the earliest humans lived. It is relatively democratic in that power is shared and there are no full-time political leaders. Also known as **acephalous society**.

state-owned enterprise (SOE) A business that is owned and operated wholly or partially by the government. In many countries, SOEs have been concentrated in sectors thought vital to the national economy. They were built from nationalized properties, as an attempt to reclaim a country's resources from foreign domination or to promote import substitution industrialization. Throughout much of the world, SOEs have been large employers. However, they have been criticized as notoriously inefficient drains on state budgets. Also known as state-owned industry.

state-sponsored terrorism (or state terror) Violent methods used by government forces or vigilante groups acting with at least the tacit approval of state officials to intimidate and coerce people, often the state's own citizens.

structural adjustment program (SAP) The neoliberal prescription offered by international financial institutions to indebted countries. As a condition for international assistance (*see* **rescue package**), countries must commit to an SAP, usually a three- to five-year program that includes a variety of reforms associated with economic liberalization (e.g., privatization, devaluation of currency, cutting social spending, raising taxes, welcoming foreign investment, etc.).

structuralism A school of thought that includes a range of opinion from radical to reformist. Structuralists share the view that the current international economic system works to the benefit of the already rich and that globalization is inherently disadvantageous to poor countries. Structuralists are highly critical of neoliberal programs, which they see as dooming much of the world to underdevelopment.

sustainable development An approach that considers the long-term impact on the environment and resources of current development strategies.

sweatshop A place of labor, usually a factory. The term is used derisively to describe a business establishment profiting from inhumane working conditions.

terrorism The use of violence or the threat of violence and intimidation to achieve aims and spread a message. Terrorists aim for symbolic targets to manipulate adversaries and to achieve political, religious, or ideological objectives.

theocracy From the Greek, meaning "government of God"—a system of rule based on religion and dominated by clergy. Rules are often inspired by some form of holy book.

top-down approach As opposed to a bottom-up approach, top-down policies are ostensibly aimed at benefiting the majority and are initiated by elites.

totalitarianism A full-blown dictatorship, marked by the severity and magnitude of the state's interference in the lives of its citizens. In totalitarian systems the state, guided by an overarching ideology, attempts to exercise absolute control over virtually every aspect of citizens' lives. Power is concentrated in the hands of the leader or party and dissent is not tolerated. There is no right of political competition or participation, leaders are not accountable for their actions, and the state violates civil and human rights with impunity. Classic examples of totalitarian states include fascist regimes such as Nazi Germany, as well as Communist Party–dominated states such as Joseph Stalin's Russia and Mao Zedong's China.

transparency A policy promoted to reduce corruption; exists when the government is open about its spending and budgetary matters, and people are encouraged to report misconduct.

truth commission An official mechanism launched usually during periods of political transition to investigate wrongs of the recent past, especially human rights abuses. Truth commissions represent attempts to deal with the past by promoting the public acknowledgment of wrongdoing, sometimes as an alternative to criminal prosecution. There are multiple models of truth commissions, which vary in the scope of crimes examined, mandate and investigation, and the types of justice employed. Most truth commissions are established to achieve an accurate historical description of what took place, to promote reconciliation, and to help promote more durable democracies by creating a culture of human rights. Truth commissions are viewed by many as but one part of the complex healing process after periods of trauma, but much disagreement about their long-term impact remains.

United Nations Preceded by the League of Nations, the UN was founded in 1945 as an international governmental organization that now includes almost all of the world's states. It provides a forum at which complaints are heard and conflicts are discussed and sometimes resolved. The UN is also involved in promoting human development through the work of its specialized agencies, which promote standards for world heath, education, and the environment in addition to commonly accepted terms for trade and commerce.

United Nations General Assembly An organ of the United Nations in which each member state is represented; it is primarily a deliberative organization centered around debate and discussion. Some matters, including those on peace and security and the admission of new members, require a two-thirds majority; others are adopted by a simple majority. Decisions of the General Assembly have no legally binding force on governments, but they represent the weight of world opinion.

United Nations Secretary-General The chief administrative officer of the United Nations. The Secretary-General is nominated by the Security Council and elected by a two-thirds majority in the General Assembly for a five-year renewable term. In addition to presiding over the United Nations, the Secretary-General has become increasingly more visible in mediating and responding to global issues outside UN organizations. Ban Ki-moon of the Republic of Korea served from 2007 to 2016. His successor is António Guterres of Portugal.

United Nations Security Council The most powerful organ within the UN system. Its representatives include five permanent members (the P5), which have veto power, and rotating members that do not have veto power. The ten nonpermanent members are elected to two-year terms by the General Assembly. Under the UN Charter, the Security Council possesses as its primary responsibility the maintenance of international peace and security. The Council works to achieve this through many means: mediation, cease-fire directives, and the use of peacekeeping forces, to name a few.

Universal Declaration of Human Rights (UDHR) The most comprehensive international statement on human rights. With over thirty articles pertaining to a wide array of political, civil, economic, social, and cultural rights, the UDHR was put forward in 1948 as a general resolution of the United Nations.

universalism The view that conceptions of human rights and morality do not depend on whether a group or culture recognizes them as such; rather, these principles are universal. Universalists argue that human rights are timeless, global in relevance and scope; there is a common morality that applies across cultures, and human rights are an entitlement all people share—no matter who they are or where they live.

vanguard party Literally the "leading" party—Vladimir Lenin's term for the Communist Party, supposed to take a front role in the overthrow of capitalism and transition to communism. Lenin prescribed that a single, elite, highly disciplined party would be necessary to lead the revolution of the proletarians, or the workers. Lenin's idea of a vanguard party has been used by Marxist socialist states such as China and North Korea to argue against the creation of competing political parties, producing a monopoly of control with which other socialists disagree.

weapons of the weak Forms of confrontation that often go unnoticed because they tend to be concealed, disguised, or subtle—employed by the ostensibly powerless, including women, minorities, and peasants. Commonly used tactics include rumor, deception, hoarding, and suicide.

World Bank Also known as the International Bank for Reconstruction and Development (IBRD), the World Bank was formed as part of the Bretton Woods system in 1944, along with its counterpart organization the International Monetary Fund (IMF). Like the IMF, the World Bank is controlled by developed countries, as voting power is based on a country's financial contribution to the Bank. Its responsibilities are wide-ranging; although it was originally created to fund the reconstruction of postwar Europe and to promote a stable international economic system, it now focuses its efforts on long-term loans and projects in the non-Western world and more recently in Eastern Europe and the former Soviet republics.

World Trade Organization (WTO) Founded in 1995, the WTO is an institution designed to promote free trade and mediate trade disputes; an updated and expanded product of the General Agreement on Tariffs and Trade (GATT), which focused on manufactured goods. Compared to GATT, the WTO has much more extensive monitoring and enforcement powers, although some less developed countries fear that this international governmental organization is working primarily for the benefit of developed countries.

zero-sum game A situation in which there can be only one winner and one loser. One actor's gain is another's loss (as opposed to non-zero-sum game, in which all can be winners or all can be losers).

Selected Bibliography

Aarts, Paul, and Francesco Cavatorta, eds. *Civil Society in Syria and Iran: Activism in Authoritarian Contexts*. Boulder: Lynne Rienner, 2012.

Acemoglu, Daron, and James Robinson. *Why Nations Fail: The Origins of Power, Prosperity, and Poverty*. New York: Crown, 2013.

Afolayan, Funso. "Nigeria: A Political Entity and a Society." In *Dilemmas of Democracy in Nigeria,* edited by Paul A. Beckett and Crawford Young, 45–62. Rochester, NY: University of Rochester Press, 1997.

Ai Camp, Roderic. *Politics in Mexico: The Decline of Authoritarianism*. New York: Oxford University Press, 1999.

Almond, Gabriel A., and Sidney Verba, eds. *Civic Culture: Political Attitudes and Democracy in Five Nations*. Princeton: Princeton University Press, 1963.

Alvarez, Sonia E. *Engendering Democracy in Brazil: Women's Movements in Transition Politics*. Princeton: Princeton University Press, 1990.

Annan, Kofi. *We the Peoples: The Role of the United Nations in the Twenty-First Century*. Report issued to the UN General Assembly, Spring 2000.

Axworthy, Michael. *Revolutionary Iran: A History of the Islamic Republic*. New York: Oxford University Press, 2013.

Bailey, John. *The Politics of Crime in Mexico: Democratic Governance in a Security Trap*. Boulder: Lynne Rienner, 2014.

Bakewell, Peter. *A History of Latin America*. Malden, MA: Blackwell, 1997.

Barber, Benjamin R. *Jihad vs. McWorld*. New York: Times Books, 1995.

Berkovitch, Nitza. "The Emergence and Transformation of the International Women's Movement." In *Constructing World Culture: International Nongovernmental Organizations Since 1875,* edited by John Boli and George M. Thomas, 116–121. Stanford: Stanford University Press, 1999.

Bethell, Leslie, ed. *Ideas and Ideologies in Twentieth-Century Latin America*. Cambridge: Cambridge University Press, 1996.

Bhebe, Ngwabi, and Terence Ranger. "Volume Introduction: Society in Zimbabwe's Liberation War." In *Society in Zimbabwe's Liberation War,* edited by Ngwabi Bhebe and Terence Ranger, 6–34. Oxford: Currey, 1996.

Blumi, Isa. *Foundations of Modernity: Human Agency and the Imperial State*. New York: Routledge, 2012.

Boahen, A. Adu. "Africa and the Colonial Challenge." In *UNESCO General History of Africa: Africa Under Colonial Domination, 1800–1935,* edited by A. Adu Boahen, 1–18. London: Heinemann, 1985.

———."Colonialism in Africa: Its Impact and Significance." In *UNESCO General History of Africa: Africa Under Colonial Domination, 1880–1935,* edited by A. Adu Boahen, 782–809. London: Heinemann, 1985.

Bogle, Emory C. *The Modern Middle East: From Imperialism to Freedom, 1800–1958.* Upper Saddle River, NJ: Prentice Hall, 1996.

Boli, John, and George M. Thomas, eds. *Constructing World Culture: International Nongovernmental Organizations Since 1875.* Stanford: Stanford University Press, 1999.

Boltvinik, Julio, and Araceli Damián. "Irrelevance of the MDGs and a Real Solution to Poverty: Universal Citizen's Income." In *Poverty and the Millennium Development Goals: A Critical Look Forward,* edited by Alberto Cimadamore, Gabriele Koehler, and Thomas Pogge, 173–202. London: Zed, 2016.

Boone, Catherine. "'Empirical Statehood' and Reconfigurations of Political Order." In *The African State at a Critical Juncture,* edited by Leonardo A. Villalon and Phillip A. Huxtable, 129–142. Boulder: Lynne Rienner, 1998.

Bottaro, Jean. *Nationalism and Independence in India.* New York: Cambridge University Press, 2016.

Bourne, Richard. *Catastrophe: What Went Wrong in Zimbabwe?* London: Zed, 2011.

Bracken, Paul. *Fire in the East: The Rise of Asian Military Power and the Second Nuclear Age.* New York: HarperCollins, 1999.

Bratton, Michael. *Power Politics in Zimbabwe.* Boulder: Lynne Rienner, 2014.

Bresnan, John, ed. *Indonesia: The Great Transition.* New York: Rowman and Littlefield, 2005.

Brewer, Douglas J., and Emily Teeter. *Egypt and the Egyptians.* Cambridge: Cambridge University Press, 2007.

Brumberg, Daniel, and Farhi Farideh. *Power and Change in Iran: Politics of Contention and Conciliation.* Bloomington: Indiana University Press, 2016.

Bueno de Mesquita, Bruce, and Alastair Smith. *The Dictator's Handbook: Why Bad Behavior Is Almost Always Good Politics.* New York: PublicAffairs, 2012.

Burbank, Jane, and Frederick Cooper. *Empires in World History: Power and the Politics of Difference.* Princeton: Princeton University Press, 2010.

Burkholder, Mark A., and Lyman L. Johnson. *Colonial Latin America.* New York: Oxford University Press, 1998.

Cambanis, Thanassis. *Once Upon a Revolution: An Egyptian Story.* New York: Simon and Schuster, 2015.

Carmody, Pádraig. *Globalization in Africa: Recolonization or Renaissance?* Boulder: Lynne Rienner, 2010.

Castañeda, Jorge G. *Utopia Unarmed: The Latin American Left After the Cold War.* New York: Knopf, 1993.

Centeno, Miguel Angel. *Democracy Within Reason: Technocratic Revolution in Mexico.* University Park: Pennsylvania State University Press, 1997.

Chalmers, Douglas A. "Corporatism and Comparative Politics." In *New Directions in Comparative Politics,* edited by Howard J. Wiarda, 56–79. Boulder: Westview, 1985.

Chalmers, Douglas A., Maria do Carmo Campello de Souza, and Atilio A. Borón. *The Right and Democracy in Latin America.* New York: Praeger, 1992.

Chazan, Naomi, Peter Lewis, and Robert Mortimer. *Politics and Society in Contemporary Africa.* Boulder: Lynne Rienner, 1999.

Cheeseman, Nic. *Democracy in Africa: Successes, Failures, and the Struggle for Political Reform.* New York: Cambridge University Press, 2015.

Chomsky, Noam. *On Anarchism.* New York: New Press, 2013.

———. *Pirates and Emperors: International Terrorism in the Real World.* New York: Claremont, 1986.

Cimadamore, Alberto D., Gabriele Koehler, and Thomas Pogge. "Poverty and the Millennium Development Goals: A Critical Look Forward." In *Poverty and the Millennium Development Goals: A Critical Look Forward,* edited by Alberto Cimadamore, Gabriele Koehler, and Thomas Pogge, 173–202. London: Zed, 2016.

Collis, Maurice. *Cortés and Montezuma*. New York: New Directions, 1999.

Cortright, David, and George Lopez. *The Sanctions Decade: Assessing UN Strategies in the 1990s*. Boulder: Lynne Rienner, 2000.

Coughlin, Kathryn M., ed. *Muslim Cultures Today: A Reference Guide*. Westport: Greenwood, 2006.

Courtois, Stéphane, Nicolas Werth, Jean-Louis Panné, et al. *The Black Book of Communism: Crimes, Terror, and Repression*, edited by Mark Kramer, translated by Jonathan Murphy. Cambridge: Harvard University Press, 1999.

Crenshaw, Martha, ed. *Terrorism in Context*. University Park: Pennsylvania State University Press, 1995.

Cribb, Robert, and Colin Brown. *Modern Indonesia: A History Since 1945*. New York: Longman, 1995.

Crowder, Michael. *The Story of Nigeria*. London: Faber and Faber, 1978.

Dahl, Robert. *Democracy and Its Critics*. New Haven: Yale University Press, 1989.

Daniel, Elton L. *The History of Iran*. Westport: Greenwood, 2001.

Danopoulos, Constantine P., and Cynthia Watson, eds. *The Political Role of the Military: An International Handbook*. Westport: Greenwood, 1996.

de Waal, Victor. *The Politics of Reconciliation: Zimbabwe's First Decade*. Trenton, NJ: Africa World, 1990.

Degregori, Carlos Ivan. "After the Fall of Abimael Guzmán: The Limits of Sendero Luminoso." In *The Peruvian Labyrinth*, edited by Maxwell A. Cameron and Philip Mauceri, 179–191. University Park: Pennsylvania State University Press, 1997.

Diamond, Jared. *Guns, Germs, and Steel: The Fate of Human Societies*. New York: Norton, 1997.

———. "Introduction: In Search of Consolidation." In *Consolidating Third Wave Democracies*, edited by Larry Diamond, Marc F. Plattner, Yun-han Chu, and Hung-mao Tien, xv–xlix. Baltimore: Johns Hopkins University Press, 1997.

———. "Introduction: What Makes for Democracy?" In *Politics in Developing Countries: Comparing Experiences with Democracy*, edited by Larry Diamond, Juan J. Linz, and Seymour Martin Lipset, 1–66. Boulder: Lynne Rienner, 1995.

———. "Three Paradoxes of Democracy." In *The Global Resurgence of Democracy*, edited by Larry Diamond and Marc F. Plattner, 95–107. Baltimore: Johns Hopkins University Press, 1993.

———. "The Uncivic Society and the Descent into Praetorianism." In *Politics in Developing Countries: Comparing Experiences with Democracy*, edited by Larry Diamond, Juan J. Linz, and Seymour Martin Lipset, 417–492. Boulder: Lynne Rienner, 1995.

Dikötter, Frank. *Mao's Great Famine: The History of China's Most Devastating Catastrophe, 1958–1962*. New York: Walker, 2010.

Dimitrijevic, Vojin. "Human Rights and Peace." In *Human Rights: New Dimensions and Challenges*, edited by Janusz Symonides, 47–70. Brookfield, VT: Ashgate, 1998.

Duverger, Maurice. *Political Parties: Their Organization and Activity in the Modern State*. New York: Wiley, 1963.

Easterly, William. *The White Man's Burden: Why the West's Efforts to Aid the Rest Have Done So Much Ill and So Little Good*. New York: Penguin, 2007.

Eatwell, Roger. *Fascism: A History*. New York: Penguin, 1997.

Ebrey, Patricia Buckley. *The Cambridge Illustrated History of China*. New York: Cambridge University Press, 2010.

Economy, Elizabeth C., and Michael Levi. *By All Means Necessary: How China's Resource Quest Is Changing the World*. New York: Oxford University Press, 2014.

Ehteshami, Anoushiravan. *After Khomeini: The Iranian Second Republic*. New York: Routledge, 1995.

Elaigwu, J. Isawa. "Nation-Building and Changing Political Structures." In *UNESCO General History of Africa: Africa Since 1935*, edited by Ali A. Mazrui, 435–467. London: Heinemann, 1993.

Emmerson, Donald K. *Indonesia Beyond Suharto: Policy, Economy, Society, Transition*. Armonk, NY: Sharpe, 1999.

———. "Voting and Violence: Indonesia and East Timor in 1999." In *Indonesia Beyond Suharto,* edited by Donald K. Emmerson, 354–357. Armonk, NY: Sharpe, 1999.

Esty, Daniel C. "Environmental Protection During the Transition to a Market Economy." In *Economies in Transition: Comparing Asia and Eastern Europe,* edited by Wing Thye Woo, Stephen Parker, and Jeffrey Sachs, 357–385. Cambridge: Massachusetts Institute of Technology Press, 1997.

Euchner, Charles. *Extraordinary Politics: How Protest and Dissent Are Changing American Democracy*. Boulder: Westview, 1996.

Evans, Tony. *Human Rights in the Global Political Economy: Critical Processes*. Boulder: Lynne Rienner, 2010.

Fallows, James. *Postcards from Tomorrow Square*. New York: Vintage, 2008.

Falola, Toyin. *The History of Nigeria*. Westport: Greenwood, 1999.

Falola, Toyin, and Robin Law, eds. *Warfare and Diplomacy in Precolonial Nigeria*. Madison: University of Wisconsin–Madison Press, 1992.

Farmer, Edward L., Gavin R. G. Hambly, Byron K. Marshall, et al. *Comparative History of Civilizations in Asia*. Reading, MA: Addison-Wesley, 1977.

Ferguson, Niall. *Dead Aid: Why Aid Is Not Working and How There Is a Better Way for Africa*. Vancouver: Douglas and McIntyre, 2010.

Finnemore, Martha. "Rules of War and Wars of Rules: The International Red Cross and the Restraint of State Violence." In *Constructing World Culture: International Nongovernmental Organizations Since 1875,* edited by John Boli and George M. Thomas, 149–168. Stanford: Stanford University Press, 1999.

Frank, Andre Gunder. *Capitalism and Underdevelopment in Latin America*. New York: Monthly Review, 1967.

Freeman, Charles. *Egypt, Greece, and Rome: Civilizations of the Ancient Mediterranean*. Oxford: Oxford University Press, 2004.

Friedman, Thomas L. *The Lexus and the Olive Tree*. New York: Farrar, Straus and Giroux, 1999.

Fukuyama, Francis. *Political Order and Political Decay: From the Industrial Revolution to the Globalization of Democracy*. New York: Farrar, Straus and Giroux, 2014.

Fyle, Magbaily. *Introduction to the History of African Civilization*. Lanham: University Press of America, 1999.

Galeano, Eduardo. *Open Veins of Latin America*. New York: Monthly Review, 1973.

Gamer, Robert E. *Understanding Contemporary China*. Boulder: Lynne Rienner, 1999.

Gamson, William A. "The Social Psychology of Collective Action." In *Frontiers in Social Movement Theory,* edited by Aldon D. Morris and Carol McClurg Mueller, 53–76. New Haven: Yale University Press, 1992.

Garner, Roberta. *Contemporary Movements and Ideologies*. New York: McGraw-Hill, 1996.

George, Susan. *The Debt Boomerang: How Third World Debt Harms Us All*. Boulder: Westview, 1992.

Gheissari, Ali, and Vali Nasr. *Democracy in Iran: History and the Quest for Liberty*. New York: Oxford University Press, 2006.

Ghonim, Wael. *Revolution 2.0: The Power of the People Is Greater Than the People in Power*. New York: Houghton, Mifflin, Harcourt, 2012.

Gilley, Bruce. *China's Democratic Future: How It Will Happen and Where It Will Lead*. New York: Columbia University Press, 2004.

Goldschmidt, Arthur, Jr. *Modern Egypt: The Formation of a Nation-State*. Boulder: Westview, 2004.

Goldstein, Joshua S. *International Relations*. 4th ed. New York: Longman, 2001.

Goldstone, Jack A. "The Outcome of Revolutions." In *Revolutions: Theoretical, Comparative, and Historical Studies,* 2nd ed., edited by Jack A. Goldstone, 194–195. New York: Harcourt Brace, 1994.

———. "Revolutions in World History." In *Revolutions: Theoretical, Comparative, and Historical Studies,* 2nd ed., edited by Jack A. Goldstone, 315–318. New York: Harcourt Brace, 1994.

Goldstone, Richard. "Bringing War Criminals to Justice During an Ongoing War." In *Hard Choices: Moral Dilemmas in Humanitarian Intervention,* edited by Jonathan Moore, 195–210. Lanham: Rowman and Littlefield, 1998.

Gould, Benina Berger. "Ritual as Resistance: Tibetan Women and Nonviolence." In *Frontline Feminisms: Women, War, and Resistance,* edited by Marguerite R. Waller and Jennifer Rycenga, 213–234. New York: Garland, 2000.

Graham, Richard. *Independence in Latin America.* New York: McGraw-Hill, 1994.

Green, Jerrold D. "Countermobilization in the Iranian Revolution." In *Revolutions: Theoretical, Comparative, and Historical Studies,* 2nd ed., edited by Jack A. Goldstone, 136–146. New York: Harcourt Brace, 1994.

Grindle, Merilee. *Challenging the State: Crisis and Innovation in Latin America and Africa.* Cambridge: Cambridge University Press, 1996.

Gurtov, Mel. *Superpower on Crusade: The Bush Doctrine and US Foreign Policy.* Boulder: Lynne Rienner, 2006.

Hacker, Frederick J. *Crusaders, Criminals, Crazies: Terror and Terrorism in Our Time.* New York: Norton, 1976.

Han Han. *This Generation: Dispatches from China's Most Popular Literary Star (and Race Car Driver).* Edited and translated by Allan H. Barr. New York: Simon and Schuster, 2012.

Hanlon, Joseph, Jeannette Manjengwa, and Teresa Smart. *Zimbabwe Takes Back Its Land.* Boulder: Lynne Rienner, 2012.

Hemming, John. *The Conquest of the Incas.* Boston: Houghton Mifflin Harcourt, 2003.

Herz, Monica, and João Pontes Nogueir. *Ecuador vs. Peru: Peacemaking Amid Rivalry.* Boulder: Lynne Rienner, 2002.

Heywood, Andrew. *Political Ideas and Concepts: An Introduction.* New York: St. Martin's, 1994.

Hirschman, Albert O. *Exit, Voice, and Loyalty: Responses to Decline in Firms, Organizations, and States.* Cambridge: Harvard University Press, 1970.

Hochschild, Adam. *King Leopold's Ghost.* Boston: Houghton Mifflin, 1998.

Hollifield, James F., and Calvin Jillson, eds. *Pathways to Democracy: The Political Economy of Democratic Transitions.* New York: Routledge, 2000.

Horowitz, Donald L. "Comparing Democratic Systems." In *The Global Resurgence of Democracy,* edited by Larry Diamond and Marc F. Plattner, 127–133. Baltimore: Johns Hopkins University Press, 1993.

Huntington, Samuel P. "Democracy's Third Wave." In *The Global Resurgence of Democracy,* edited by Larry Diamond and Marc F. Plattner, 3–25. Baltimore: Johns Hopkins University Press, 1993.

Huxtable, Phillip A. "The African State Toward the Twenty-First Century: Legacies of the Critical Juncture." In *The African State at a Critical Juncture,* edited by Leonardo A. Villalon and Phillip A. Huxtable, 279–294. Boulder: Lynne Rienner, 1998.

Ignatieff, Michael. *Human Rights as Politics and Idolatry.* Princeton: Princeton University Press, 2001.

Jaquette, Jane, ed. *The Women's Movement in Latin America: Participation and Democracy.* Boulder: Westview, 1994.

Jayawardena, Kumari. *Feminism and Nationalism in the Third World.* London: Zed, 1986.

Johnson, Paul. *The Civilization of Ancient Egypt.* New York: HarperCollins, 1999.

Joseph, Richard, and Alexandra Gillies, eds. *Smart Aid for African Development.* Boulder: Lynne Rienner, 2009.

Judt, Tony, and Denis Lacorne, eds. *With Us or Against Us: Studies in Global Anti-Americanism.* New York: Palgrave Macmillan, 2005.

July, Robert W. *A History of the African People.* Prospect Heights, IL: Waveland, 1992.

Kaldor, Mary. *New and Old Wars: Organized Violence in a Global Era*. Stanford: Stanford University Press, 1999.

Keen, Benjamin, and Keith Haynes. *A History of Latin America*. Boston: Houghton Mifflin, 2000.

Keightley, David N. *The Origins of Chinese Civilization*. Berkeley: University of California Press, 1983.

Kemp, Geoffrey. *Forever Enemies? American Policy and the Islamic Republic of Iran*. Washington, DC: Carnegie Endowment, 1994.

Kesselman, Mark, Joel Krieger, and William A. Joseph. *Introduction to Comparative Politics: Political Challenges and Changing Agendas*. Boston: Houghton Mifflin, 2000.

Khalil, Ashraf. *Liberation Square: Inside the Egyptian Revolution and the Rebirth of a Nation*. New York: St. Martin's, 2011.

Kinsbruner, Jay. *Independence in Spanish America: Civil Wars, Revolutions, and Underdevelopment*. Albuquerque: University of New Mexico Press, 2000.

Klaren, Peter Flindell. *Peru: Society and Nationhood in the Andes*. New York: Oxford University Press, 2000.

Kohut, Andrew, and Bruce Stokes. *America Against the World: How We Are Different and Why We Are Disliked*. New York: Times Books, 2006.

Kurlantzick, Joshua. *Charm Offensive: How China's Soft Power Is Transforming the World*. New Haven: Yale University Press, 2007.

Kurniawan, Eka. *Man Tiger*. Translated by Labodalih Sembiring. New York: Verso, 2015.

Laqueur, Walter. *The New Terrorism: Fanaticism and the Arms of Mass Destruction*. New York: Oxford University Press, 1999.

Levitsky, Steven, and Lucan Way. "The Myth of Democratic Recession." In *Democracy in Decline?*, edited by Larry Diamond and Marc F. Plattner, 58–76. Baltimore: Johns Hopkins University Press, 2015.

Levy, Daniel C., and Kathleen Bruhn. "Mexico: Sustained Civilian Rule Without Democracy." In *Politics in Developing Countries: Comparing Experiences with Democracy*, edited by Larry Diamond, Juan J. Linz, and Seymour Martin Lipset, 171–217. Boulder: Lynne Rienner, 1995.

Lewis, Bernard. *The Middle East: A Brief History of the Last 2,000 Years*. New York: Scribner, 1997.

Lewis, Peter M. "Nigeria: Cycles of Crisis, Sources of Resilience." In *Coping with Crisis in African States*, edited by Peter M. Lewis and John W. Harbeson, 147–170. Boulder: Lynne Rienner, 2016.

Lijphart, Arend. *Democracy in Plural Societies: A Comparative Exploration*. New Haven: Yale University Press, 1977.

———. *Patterns of Democracy: Government Forms and Performance in Thirty-Six Countries*. New Haven: Yale University Press, 1999.

Linz, Juan J., and Alfred Stepan. "The Perils of Presidentialism." In *The Global Resurgence of Democracy*, edited by Larry Diamond and Marc F. Plattner, 108–126. Baltimore: Johns Hopkins University Press, 1993.

———. *Problems of Democratic Transition and Consolidation*. Baltimore: Johns Hopkins University Press, 1996.

Lipset, Seymour Martin. *Political Man*. Garden City, NY: Doubleday, 1959.

Lloyd, Alan B. *Ancient Egypt: State and Society*. New York: Oxford University Press, 2014.

Lynch, Marc. *The New Arab Wars: Uprisings and Anarchy in the Middle East*. New York: PublicAffairs, 2016.

Mackey, Sandra. *The Iranians: Persia, Islam, and the Soul of a Nation*. New York: Penguin, 1996.

MacKinnon, Rebecca. *Consent of the Networked: The Worldwide Struggle for Internet Freedom*. New York: Basic, 2012.

Mamdani, Mahmood. *Citizen and Subject: Contemporary Africa and the Legacy of Late Colonialism*. Princeton: Princeton University Press, 1996.

Mao Zedong. "Report on an Investigation of the Peasant Movement in Hunan: March 1927."
In *Selected Readings from the Works of Mao Tsetung,* 23–59. Foreign Languages Press,
1971.

Marsot, Afaf Lutfi al-Sayyid. *A History of Egypt: From the Arab Conquest to the Present.*
Cambridge: Cambridge University Press, 2007.

Martin, Jacques. *When China Rules the World: The End of the Western World and the Birth
of a New Global Order.* New York: Penguin, 2009.

Mazrui, Ali A., ed. *UNESCO General History of Africa: Africa Since 1935.* London: Heinemann, 1993.

McClintock, Cynthia. *Revolutionary Movements in Latin America.* Washington, DC: US
Institute of Peace, 1998.

Meyer, Milton W. *Asia: A Concise History.* Lanham: Rowman and Littlefield, 1997.

Minelli, Laura Laurencich. *The Inca World.* Norman: University of Oklahoma Press, 2000.

Moaveni, Azadeh. *Honeymoon in Tehran: Two Years of Love and Danger in Iran.* New York:
Random, 2009.

Moghadam, Valentine M. *Globalizing Women.* Baltimore: Johns Hopkins University Press,
2005.

———. *Gender and National Identity: Women and Politics in Muslim Societies.* London: Zed,
1994.

Moin, Bager. *Khomeini: Life of the Ayatollah.* New York: St. Martin's, 2000.

Monga, Célestin. *The Anthropology of Anger: Civil Society and Democracy in Africa.* Translated by Linda L. Fleck and Célestin Monga. Boulder: Lynne Rienner, 1996.

Morris, Stephen D. *Political Corruption in Mexico: The Impact of Democratization.* Boulder:
Lynne Rienner, 2009.

Murphy, Ann Marie. "Indonesia and Globalization." In *East Asia and Globalization,* edited
by Samuel S. Kim, 209–232. New York: Rowman and Littlefield, 2000.

Murray, Geoffrey. *China: The Next Superpower—Dilemmas in Change and Continuity.* New
York: St. Martin's, 1998.

Nasr, Vali. *The Shia Revival: How Conflicts Within Islam Will Shape the Future.* New York:
Norton, 2006.

Nelson, Sarah Milledge. *Ancient Queens: Archaeological Explorations.* Walnut Creek, CA:
AltaMira Press, 2003.

*The 9/11 Commission Report: Final Report on the National Commission on Terrorist Attacks
upon the United States.* New York: Norton, 2004.

Nyang'oro, Julius E., and Timothy M. Shaw. "The African State in the Global Economic
Context." In *The African State at a Critical Juncture: Between Disintegration and Re-
configuration,* edited by Julius E. Nyang'oro and Timothy M. Shaw, 27–44. Boulder:
Lynne Rienner, 1998.

Nye, Joseph, Jr. *Soft Power: The Means to Success in World Politics.* New York: Public
Affairs, 2004.

O'Brien, Kevin J., and Lianjiang Li. *Rightful Resistance in Rural China.* New York: Cambridge University Press, 2006.

O'Gorman, Eleanor. "Writing Women's Wars: Foucaldian Strategies of Engagement." In
Women, Culture, and International Relations, edited by Vivienne Jabri and Eleanor
O'Gorman, 91–116. Boulder: Lynne Rienner, 1999.

Oliver, Roland. *The African Experience.* Boulder: Westview, 1999.

Osman, Tarek. *Egypt on the Brink: From Nasser to Mubarak.* New Haven: Yale University
Press, 2010.

Osnos, Evan. *Age of Ambition: Chasing Fortune, Truth, and Faith in the New China.* New
York: Farrar, Straus and Giroux, 2014.

Page, Sheila. *Regionalism Among Developing Countries.* New York: St. Martin's, 2000.

Patil, Vrushali. *Negotiating Decolonization in the United Nations.* New York: Routledge,
2008.

Payne, Leigh A. *Uncivil Movements: The Armed Right Wing and Democracy in Latin America*. Baltimore: Johns Hopkins University Press, 2000.

Payne, Richard J., and Jamal R. Nassar. *Politics and Culture in the Developing World*. New York: Pearson, 2012.

Paz, Octavio. "Latin America and Democracy." In *Democracy and Dictatorship in Latin America: A Special Publication Devoted Entirely to the Voice and Opinions of Writers from Latin America,* edited by Octavio Paz, Jorge Edwards, Carlos Franqui, et al., 5–17. New York: Foundation for the Independent Study of Social Ideas, 1982.

Peimani, Hooman. *Iran and the United States: The Rise of the West Asian Regional Grouping*. Westport: Praeger, 1999.

Pempel, T. J. "The Developmental Regime in a Changing World Economy." In *The Developmental State,* edited by Meredith Woo-Cumings, 137–181. Ithaca: Cornell University Press, 2001.

Phimister, Ian. *An Economic and Social History of Zimbabwe, 1890–1948*. London: Longman, 1988.

Pisani, Elizabeth. *Indonesia, Etc.: Exploring the Improbable Nation*. New York: Norton, 2015.

Pomfret, John. *The Beautiful Country and the Middle Kingdom: America and China, 1776 to the Present*. New York: Holt, 2016.

Pye, Lucian W. *China: An Introduction*. 3rd ed. Boston: Little, Brown, 1984.

Radelet, Stephen. *The Great Surge: The Ascent of the Developing World*. New York: Simon and Schuster, 2015.

Ranger, Terence. *Peasant Consciousness and Guerrilla War in Zimbabwe*. London: Currey, 1985.

Roberts, Kenneth M. *Deepening Democracy? The Modern Left and Social Movements in Chile and Peru*. Stanford: Stanford University Press, 1998.

Sachs, Jeffrey. *The End of Poverty: Economic Possibilities for Our Time*. New York: Penguin, 2006.

Said, Edward W. *Reflections on Exile*. Cambridge: Harvard University Press, 2001.

Schelander, Björn, and Kirsten Brown. *Exploring Indonesia: Past and Present*. Honolulu: Center for Southeast Asian Studies, 2000.

Schell, Orville. "Letter from China." *New Yorker,* July 1994. Reprinted in *The China Reader: The Reform Era,* edited by Orville Schell and David Shambaugh, 246–256. New York: Vintage, 1999.

Schmitter, Philippe C., and Terry Lynn Karl. "What Democracy Is . . . and Is Not." In *The Global Resurgence of Democracy,* edited by Larry Diamond and Marc F. Plattner, 39–52. Baltimore: Johns Hopkins University Press, 1993.

Schneider, Thomas. *Ancient Egypt in 10 Questions and Answers*. Ithaca: Cornell University Press, 2013.

Schroeder, Matthew. "US Security Assistance and Africa: Challenges of Weapons Sales and Military Aid." In *Security, Reconstruction, and Reconciliation: When Wars End,* edited by Muna Ndulo, 284–306. New York: University College London Press, 2007.

Selee, Andrew, and Peter H. Smith. "Challenges of Partnership." In *Mexico and the United States: The Politics of Partnership,* edited by Peter H. Smith and Andrew Selee, 1–12. Boulder: Lynne Rienner, 2013.

Shahri, Sorayya. "Women in Command: A Successful Experience in the National Liberation Army of Iran." In *Frontline Feminisms: Women, War, and Resistance,* edited by Marguerite R. Waller and Jennifer Rycenga, 185–192. New York: Garland, 2000.

Shawcross, William. *Deliver Us from Evil*. New York: Simon and Schuster, 2000.

Siapno, Jacqueline. "Gender, Nationalism, and the Ambiguity of Female Agency in Aceh, Indonesia, and East Timor." In *Frontline Feminisms: Women, War, and Resistance,* edited by Marguerite R. Waller and Jennifer Rycenga, 275–296. New York: Garland, 2000.

Singer, P. W. *Children at War*. New York: Pantheon, 2005.

Skidmore, Thomas E., and Peter H. Smith. *Modern Latin America*. New York: Oxford University Press, 1992.

Skocpol, Theda. *States and Social Revolution: A Comparative Analysis of France, Russia, and China*. New York: Cambridge University Press, 1979.

Smith, Courtney B. *Politics and Process at the United Nations: The Global Dance*. Boulder: Lynne Rienner, 2006.

Smith, Mike. *Boko Haram: Inside Nigeria's Unholy War*. New York: Tauris, 2016.

Stiglitz, Joseph. E. *Globalization and Its Discontents*. New York: Norton, 2007.

Stoez, David, Charles Guzzetta, and Mark Lusk. *International Development*. Boston: Allyn and Bacon, 1999.

Sweig, Julia E. *Friendly Fire: Losing Friends and Making Enemies in the Anti-American Century*. New York: PublicAffairs, 2006.

Takeyh, Ray. *Hidden Iran: Paradox and Power in the Islamic Republic*. New York: Time Books, 2006.

Tarrow, Sidney. *Power in Movement: Social Movements and Contentious Politics*. New York: Cambridge University Press, 1998.

Teichman, Judith A. *The Politics of Inclusive Development: Policy, State Capacity, and Coalition Building*. New York: Palgrave Macmillan, 2016.

Thompson, Carol B. "Beyond the Nation-State? Democracy in Regional Economic Context." In *Democracy and Socialism in Africa,* edited by Robin Cohen and Harry Goulbourne, 216–227. Boulder: Westview, 1991.

Tilly, Charles. "Reflections on the History of European Statemaking." In *The Formation of National States in Western Europe,* edited by Charles Tilly, 3–83. Princeton: Princeton University Press, 1975.

Valenzuela, Arturo. "External Actors in the Transitions to Democracy in Latin America." In *Pathways to Democracy: The Political Economy of Democratic Transitions,* edited by James F. Hollifield and Calvin Jillson, 116–129. New York: Routledge, 2000.

Varshney, Ashutosh, ed. *Collective Violence in Indonesia*. Boulder: Lynne Rienner, 2009.

Verba, Sidney. "Comparative Political Culture." In *Political Culture and Political Development,* edited by Sidney Verba and Lucian Pye, 512–560. Princeton: Princeton University Press, 1965.

Verba, Sidney, Victor H. Nie, and Jae-on Kim. *Participation and Political Equality: A Seven-Nation Comparison*. New York: Cambridge University Press, 1978.

Villalon, Leonardo A. "The African State at the End of the Twentieth Century: Parameters of the Critical Juncture." In *The African State at a Critical Juncture,* edited by Leonardo A. Villalon and Phillip A. Huxtable, 3–26. Boulder: Lynne Rienner, 1998.

Walter, Andrew, and Xiaoke Zhang. "Debating East Asian Capitalism: Issues and Themes." In *East Asian Capitalism: Diversity, Continuity, and Change,* edited by Andrew Walter and Xiaoke Zhang, 3–28. New York: Oxford University Press, 2012.

Waters, Matthew W. *Ancient Persia: A Concise History of the Achaemenid Empire, 550–330 B.C.E.* New York: Cambridge University Press, 2014.

Werbner, Richard P. "In Memory: A Heritage of War in Southwestern Zimbabwe." In *Society in Zimbabwe's Liberation War,* edited by Ngwabi Bhebe and Terence Ranger, 192–205. Oxford: Currey, 1996.

West, Guida, and Rhoda Lois Blumberg, eds. *Women and Social Protest*. New York: Oxford University Press, 1990.

Wiarda, Howard J., and Harvey F. Kline. *An Introduction to Latin American Politics and Development*. Boulder: Westview, 2001.

Wills, A. J. *An Introduction to the History of Central Africa: Zambia, Malawi, and Zimbabwe*. New York: Oxford University Press, 1985.

Wilson, Frank L. *Concepts and Issues in Comparative Politics: An Introduction to Comparative Analysis*. Upper Saddle River, NJ: Prentice Hall, 1996.

Woo, Wing Thye, Stephen Parker, and Jeffrey Sachs, eds. *Economies in Transition: Comparing Asia and Eastern Europe*. Cambridge: Massachusetts Institute of Technology Press, 1997.

Wright, David C. *The History of China*. Westport: Greenwood, 2001.

Wright, Stephen. *Nigeria: Struggle for Stability and Status*. Boulder: Westview, 1998.

Xi Jinping. *The Governance of China*. Beijing: Foreign Languages Press, 2014.

Yu Kien-hong, Peter. *The Party and the Army in China: Figuring Out Their Relationship Once and for All*. Working Paper no. 7. Singapore: East Asian Institute, 1998.

Zahedi, Dariush. *The Iranian Revolution Then and Now: Indicators of Regime Instability*. Boulder: Westview, 2000.

Zakaria, Fareed, *The Post-American World*. New York: Norton, 2008.

Zartman, I. William. "Introduction: Posing the Problem of State Collapse." In *Collapsed States: The Disintegration and Restoration of Legitimate Authority*, edited by I. William Zartman, 1–14. Boulder: Lynne Rienner, 1995.

Zhang, Maria Yue, and Bruce W. Stening. *China 2.0: The Transformation of an Emerging Superpower—and the New Opportunities*. Singapore: Wiley, 2010.

Index

About the Book

In this now classic text, December Green and Laura Luehrmann show how history, economics, and politics converge to create the realities of life in the global south.

The authors offer an innovative blend of theory and empirical material as they introduce the politics of what was once called the "third world." They consistently link theoretical concepts to a set of eight contemporary case studies: China, Egypt, Indonesia, Iran, Mexico, Nigeria, Peru, and Zimbabwe.

Features of the fourth edition, revised and updated from cover to cover, include

- An entirely new case study, Egypt.
- Analysis of the status of regime transitions around the world.
- A "report card" on the Millennium Development Goals.
- Attention to the UN Global Goals for Sustainable Development and the New Development Bank.
- More discussion of contentious politics, social mobilization, and everyday forms of resistance.
- New material on such continuing challenges as migration, human trafficking, weapons proliferation, pandemic diseases, and the impact of climate change.

The result is a text that has been successfully designed to challenge students' preconceptions, arouse their curiosity, and foster critical thinking.

December Green and **Laura Luehrmann** are professors of political science in the School of Public and International Affairs at Wright State University.

the 1990s, is in transition, with a new president and a decidedly different approach to global politics and international affairs.

Even though much has changed since the publication of the first edition, there are some controversies that have not only endured but also deepened. Take the debate surrounding globalization, for example. As this book goes to press, many of the most vexing issues facing citizens and leaders around the world (economic stagnation, immigration, environmental degradation, and gender inequalities among them) are rooted in the unfulfilled promises of positive changes that were, it was hoped, to accompany the so-called shrinking of the world.

* * *

We received much assistance throughout the duration of this project, and we owe gratitude to many. Special thanks to Dean Kristin Sobolik of the College of Liberal Arts at Wright State University for her support. Our colleagues in the Department of Political Science (now part of the School of Public and International Affairs) have been particularly helpful in the formulation and completion of this book. We give special thanks to Joanne Ballmann and Renée Harber for their assistance and moral support. We are grateful to those who provided critical feedback, research assistance, and help with preparing figures throughout the text, especially Rahimullah Akrami, Alysa Birdsall, and Nickii Webb.

We've said it before, and it remains as true today as it was then: we both want to convey our profound debt to our students, whose questions have motivated much of the shape of this book. Their insights, curiosities, and frustrations helped clarify what we believed we needed to include in an introductory text, and they continue to inspire us to always ask better questions and to try to capture an ever-changing world in terms that are meaningful.

We are also grateful to all the wonderful people at Lynne Rienner Publishers, but particularly to Lynne Rienner, for understanding the need for this book and for going above and beyond, using her experience and expertise to refine it. Her support in carrying the book to a fourth edition is greatly appreciated. Special thanks to Steve Barr and Shena Redmond, our directors of production, and to our excellent copyeditor, Jason Cook. Their diligence has helped us present a clearer, more accurate book.

—December Green
Laura Luehrmann

Preface

Looking back on it, the two of us are sometimes stunned by the changes both in the world and in this textbook since the first edition was published in 2003. We wrote that original book in the ashes of September 11, 2001, when we were all coming to grips with one of the most audacious terrorist attacks ever, and the United States was in the dawn of a new era of global engagement and leadership. HIV/AIDS was ravaging much of the world, and widespread awareness of greenhouse gas emissions and the vast extent of human-made climate change was just emerging. In the first edition, there was no discussion of social media. Yet we contended then, as we do even more strongly now, that the voices of people beyond the developed world—in what can be called the developing world, third world, majority world, or global south (controversies we address in Chapter 1)—need to be heard. We also argued then (and now) that attention must be paid to the so-called ordinary people, the less visible yet increasingly consequential individuals (often organized in groups) who rally to either preserve or change the status quo. Whether it is an aggrieved fruit seller in Tunisia, a poet in Iran, or a labor activist in China, often the people who may spark the greatest degree of change within their societies are those who normally never make headlines.

Look at the changes we have witnessed in the past few years: the United States has reestablished ties with Cuba (severed since 1961), Iran is emerging from a decade of UN sanctions levied against it to curtail its nuclear program, and North Korea is being led by a young and increasingly unpredictable heir who is as isolated as was his grandfather. Hopes for a democratic windfall from the so-called Arab Spring of 2011 have been dashed, and China's reemergence, although wobbly at times, is challenging much of the security framework of East Asia. We are living in an era of polarization, where compromise seems elusive and, even in liberal democracies, violence mars some of the most profoundly important discussions of our time. Authoritarianism, seemingly in retreat in the early 1990s, appears to be ascendant, as strong leaders combine the powerful forces of nationalism with technology, sometimes under their direct control. The role of the United States, the undisputed superpower since

Figures

Contents

To our colleague, friend, and mentor
Charlie Funderburk

Thanks for your guidance, encouragement,
and especially for your friendship.

We miss you, but your inspiration and spirit remain.

Published in the United States of America in 2017 by
Lynne Rienner Publishers, Inc.
1800 30th Street, Boulder, Colorado 80301
www.rienner.com

and in the United Kingdom by
Lynne Rienner Publishers, Inc.
3 Henrietta Street, Covent Garden, London WC2E 8LU

Library of Congress Cataloging-in-Publication Data
Names: Green, December, author. | Luehrmann, Laura, 1969– author.
Title: Comparative politics of the global South : linking concepts and cases /
  December Green and Laura Luehrmann.
Other titles: Comparative politics of the "Third World"
Description: Fourth edition. | Boulder, Colorado : Lynne Rienner Publishers, Inc., 2017. |
  Revised edition of: Comparative politics of the "Third World," 3rd ed.
  2011. | Includes bibliographical references and index.
Identifiers: LCCN 2016059509 | ISBN 9781626376502 (pbk. : alk. paper)
Subjects: LCSH: Developing countries—Politics and government—Case studies.
  | Developing countries—Economic policy—Case studies.
Classification: LCC JF60 .G74 2017 | DDC 320.309172/4—dc23
LC record available at https://lccn.loc.gov/2016059509

British Cataloguing in Publication Data
A Cataloguing in Publication record for this book
is available from the British Library.

Printed and bound in the United States of America

 The paper used in this publication meets the requirements
of the American National Standard for Permanence of
Paper for Printed Library Materials Z39.48-1992.

5 4 3 2 1

FOURTH EDITION

COMPARATIVE POLITICS OF THE GLOBAL SOUTH

LINKING CONCEPTS & CASES

DECEMBER GREEN
LAURA LUEHRMANN

LYNNE
RIENNER
PUBLISHERS

BOULDER
LONDON

COMPARATIVE POLITICS
OF THE GLOBAL SOUTH